The Zohar

by

Rav Shimon bar Yochai

From The Book of Avraham

with

The Sulam Commentary

by

Rav Yehuda Ashlag

The First Ever Unabridged
English Translation with Commentary

Published by
The Kabbalah Centre International Inc.
Dean Rav S. P. Berg Shlita

Edited and Compiled by
Rabbi Michael Berg

Published by
The Kabbalah Centre International Inc.

155 E. 48th St., New York, NY 10017
1062 S. Robertson Blvd., Los Angeles, CA 90035

Director Rav Berg

First Printing 2001
Revised Edition 2008

Printed in USA

ISBN: 1-57189-163-3

May my family allow the joy of the tree of life into their lives.

May my soul mate and I be blessed with righteous children,
who bring light of peace to the world.

And may there be unity in Israel.

Amen.

Daniel Ben Aharon Hacohen

APPLYING THE POWER OF THE ZOHAR

The Zohar is a book of great mystical power and wisdom. It is Universally recognized as the definitive work on the Kabbalah – and it is also so Much more.

The Zohar is a wellspring of spiritual energy, a fountainhead of metaphysical power that not only reveals and explains, but literally brings blessing, protection, and well-being into the lives of all those who read or peruse its sacred texts. All that is required is worthy desire, the certainty of a trusting heart, and an open and receptive mind. Unlike other books, including the great spiritual texts of other traditions, The Zohar is written in a kind of code, through which metaphors, parables, and cryptic language at first conceal but ultimately reveal the forces of creation.

As electrical current is concealed in wire and cable before disclosing itself as an illuminated light bulb, the spiritual Light of the Creator is wrapped in allegory and symbolism throughout the Aramaic text of the Zohar. And while many books contain information and knowledge, the Zohar both expresses and embodies spiritual Light. The very letters on its pages have the power to bring spiritual wisdom and positive energy into every area of our lives.

As we visually scan the Aramaic texts and study the accompanying insights that appear in English, spiritual power is summoned from above – and worlds tremble as Light is sent forth in response.

It's primary purpose is not only to help us acquire wisdom, but to draw Light from the Upper Worlds and to bring sanctification into our lives. Indeed, the book itself is the most powerful of all tools for cleansing the soul and connecting to the Light of the Creator. As you open these pages, therefore, do not make understanding in the conventional sense your primary goal.

Although you may not have a knowledge of Aramaic, look first at the Aramaic text before reading the English. Do not be discouraged by difficulties with comprehension. Instead, open your heart to the spiritual transformation the Zohar is offering you.

Ultimately, the Zohar is an instrument for refining the individual soul – for removing darkness from the earth – and for bringing well being and blessing to our fellow man.

Its purpose is not only to make us intellectually wise, but to make us spiritually pure.

Torah

Also known as the Five Books of Moses, the Torah is considered to be the physical body of learning, whereas the Zohar is the internal soul. The literal stories of the Torah conceal countless hidden secrets.` The Zohar is the Light that illuminates all of the Torah's sublime mysteries.

Beresheet	Genesis
Shemot	Exodus
Vayikra	Leviticus
Bemidbar	Numbers
Devarim	Deuteronomy

Prophets

Amos	Amos
Chagai	Haggai
Chavakuk	Habakkuk
Hoshea	Hosea
Malachi	Malachi
Melachim	Kings
Michah	Micah
Nachum	Nahum
Ovadyah	Obadiah
Shmuel	Samuel
Shoftim	Judges
Tzefanyah	Zephaniah
Yechezkel	Ezekiel
Yehoshua	Joshua
Yeshayah	Isaiah
Yirmeyah	Jeremiah
Yoel	Joel
Yonah	Jonah
Zecharyah	Zechariah

Writings

Daniel	Daniel
Divrei Hayamim	Chronicles
Eicha	Lamentations
Ester	Esther
Ezra	Ezra
Nechemiah	Nehemiah
Iyov	Job
Kohelet	Ecclesiastes
Mishlei	Proverbs
Rut	Ruth
Sir Hashirim	Songs of Songs
Tehilim	Psalms

The Ten Sfirot – Emanations

To conceal the blinding *Light* of the Upper World, and thus create a tiny point into which our universe would be born, ten *curtains* were fabricated. These ten *curtains* are called Ten Sfirot. Each successive Sfirah further reduces the emanation of *Light*, gradually dimming its brilliance to a level almost devoid of *Light* – our physical world known as *Malchut*. The only remnant of Light remaining in this darkened universe is a *pilot light* which sustains our existence. This Light is the life force of a human being and the force that gives birth to stars, sustains suns and sets everything from swirling galaxies to busy ant hills in motion. Moreover, the Ten Sfirot act like a prism, refracting the Light into many *colors* giving rise to the diversity of life and matter in our world.

The Ten Sfirot are as follows:

Keter	Crown
Chochmah	Wisdom
Binah	Understanding
Da'at	Knowledge
Zeir Anpin	Small Face, (includes the next six Sfirot):
Chesed	Mercy (Chassadim - plural)
Gvurah	Judgment (Gvurot - Plural)
Tiferet	Splendor
Netzach	Victory (Eternity)
Hod	Glory
Yesod	Foundation
Malchut	Kingdom

The Partzufim - Spiritual forms

One complete structure of the Ten Sfirot creates a *Partzuf* or Spiritual Form. Together, these forces are the building blocks of all reality. As water and sand combine to create cement, the Ten Sfirot combine to produce a Spiritual Form *[Partzuf]*. Each of the Spiritual Forms below are therefore composed of one set of Ten Sfirot.

These Spiritual Forms are called:

Atik	Ancient
Atik Yomin	Ancient of Days
Atika Kadisha	Holy Ancient
Atik of Atikin	Anceint of Ancients
Aba	Father
Arich Anpin	Long Face
Ima	Mother
Nukva	Female
Tevunah	Intelligence
Yisrael Saba	Israel Grandfather
Zachar	Male

These names are not meant to be understood literally. Each represents a unique spiritual force and building block, producing a substructure and foundation for all the worlds make up reality.

The Five Worlds

All of the above Spiritual Forms *[Partzufim]* create one spiritual world. There are Five Worlds in total that compose all reality, therefore, five sets of the above Spiritual Forms are required.

Our physical world corresponds to the world of: Asiyah – Action

Adam Kadmon	Primordial Man
Atzilut	Emanation
Briyah	Creation
Yetzirah	Formation
Asiyah	Action

The Five Levels of the soul

Nefesh	First, Lowest level of Soul
Ruach	Second level of Soul
Neshamah	Third level of Soul
Chayah	Fourth level of Soul
Yechidah	Highest, fifth level of Soul

Names of God

As a single ray of white sunlight contains the seven colors of the spectrum, the one Light of the Creator embodies many diverse spiritual forces. These different forces are called *Names of God.* Each Name denotes a specific attribute and spiritual power. The Hebrew letters that compose these Names are the interface by which these varied Forces act upon our physical world. The most common Name of God is the Tetragrammaton (the four letters, *Yud Hei Vav Hei* יהוה.) Because of the enormous power that the Tetragrammaton transmits, we do not utter it aloud. When speaking of the Tetragrammaton, we use the term *Hashem* which means, *The Name.*

Adonai, El, Elohim, Hashem, Shadai, Eheyeh, Tzevaot, Yud Hei Vav Hei

People

Er	The son of Noach
Rabbi Elazar	The son of Rabbi Shimon bar Yochai
Rabbi Shimon bar Yochai	Author of the Zohar
Shem, Cham, Yefet	Noach's children
Shet	Seth
Ya'akov	Jacob
Yishai	Jesse (King David's father)
Yitzchak	Isaac
Yosef	Joseph
Yitro	Jethro
Yehuda	Judah

Angels

Angels are distinct energy components, part of a vast communication network running through the upper worlds. Each unique Angel is responsible for transmitting various forces of influence into our physical universe.

Adriel, Ahinael, Dumah (name of Angel in charge of the dead), Gabriel, Kadshiel, Kedumiel, Metatron, Michael, Rachmiel,

Raphael, Tahariel, Uriel

Nations

Nations actually represent the inner attributes and character traits of our individual self. The nation of Amalek refers to the doubt and uncertainty that dwells within us when we face hardship and obstacles. Moab represents the dual nature of man. Nefilim refers to the sparks of Light that we have defiled through our impure actions, and to the negative forces that lurk within the human soul as a result of our own wrongful deeds.

Amalek, Moab, Nefilim

General

Aba	Father Refers to the male principle and positive force in our universe. Correlates to the proton in an atom.
Arvit	The Evening prayer
Chayot	Animals
Chupah	Canopy (wedding ceremony)
Et	The
Avadon	Hell
Gehenom	Hell
Sheol	Hell The place a soul goes for purification upon leaving this world.
Ima	Mother The female principle and minus force in our universe. Correlates to the electron in an atom.
Kiddush	Blessing over the wine
Klipah	Shell (negativity)
Klipot	Shells (Plural)
Kriat Sh'ma	The Reading of the Sh'ma
Mashiach	Messiah
Minchah	The Afternoon prayer
Mishnah	Study
Mochin	Brain, Spiritual levels of Light
Moed	A designated time or holiday
Negev	The south of Israel
Nukva	Female
Partzuf	Face
Shacharit	The Morning prayer
Shamayim	Heavens (sky)
Shechinah	The Divine presence, The female aspect of the Creator
Tefilin	Phylacteries
The Dinur river	The river of fire
Tzadik	Righteous person
Zion	Another name for Jerusalem
Yisrael	The land of Israel The nation of Israel or an individual Israelite
Zohar	Splendor

The Hebrew vowels

Chirik אִ, Cholam אוֹ אֹ, Kamatz אָ, Patach אַ, Segol אֶ, Sh'va אְ, Shuruk אוּ אֻ, Tzere אֵ.

The Twelve Tribes

Asher, Dan, Ephraim, Gad, Issachar, Judah, Levi, Menasheh, Naphtali, Reuben, Shimon, Zebulun

Jewish Holidays

Rosh Hashanah	The Jewish New Year
Yom Kippur	Day of Atonement
Sukkot	Holiday of the Booths
Shmini Atzeret	The day of Convocation
Simchat Torah	Holiday on which we dance with the Torah
Pesach	Passover
Shavout	Holiday of the Weeks

כרך ט

פרשת בא, בשלח

Vol. IX

Bo, Beshalach

A Prayer from The Ari

To be recited before the study of the Zohar

Ruler of the universe, and Master of all masters, The Father of mercy and forgiveness, we thank You, our God and the God of our fathers, by bowing down and kneeling, that You brought us closer to Your Torah and Your holy work, and You enable us to take part in the secrets of Your holy Torah. How worthy are we that You grant us with such big favor, that is the reason we plead before You, that You will forgive and acquit all our sins, and that they should not bring separation between You and us.

And may it be your will before You, our God and the God of our fathers, that You will awaken and prepare our hearts to love and revere You, and may You listen to our utterances, and open our closed heart to the hidden studies of Your Torah, and may our study be pleasant before Your Place of Honor, as the aroma of sweet incense, and may You emanate to us Light from the source of our soul to all of our being. And, may the sparks of your holy servants, through which you revealed Your wisdom to the world, shine.

May their merit and the merit of their fathers, and the merit of their Torah, and holiness, support us so we shall not stumble through our study. And by their merit enlighten our eyes in our learning as it stated by King David, The Sweet Singer of Israel: “Open my eyes, so that I will see wonders from Your Torah” (Tehilim 119:18). Because from His mouth God gives wisdom and understanding.

“May the utterances of my mouth and the thoughts of my heart find favor before You, God, my Strength and my Redeemer” (Tehilim 19:15).

Bo

Names of the articles

		Page No.
1.	"If there an angel over him, an interpreter"	3
2.	"Now there was a day…and the Adversary came also among them"	6
3.	The crocodiles	22
4.	"For Hashem will pass through...on the lintel, and on the two side posts"	37
5.	"And it came to pass, that at midnight"	46
6.	"All things have I seen in the days of my vanity"	67
7.	"And he smelled the smell of his garments"	73
8.	"A lamb, according to the house of their fathers"	79
9.	Leaven and leavened dough	82
10.	Matzah of Judgment	84
11.	Relating the praise of the exodus from Egypt	90
12.	The Pascal sacrifice	94
13.	"Sanctify to Me all the firstborn"	99
14.	"For you saw no manner of form"	107
15.	The Tefilin	116

1. "If there an angel over him, an interpreter"

A Synopsis

Rabbi Yehuda tells us that people who study Torah and observe its commandments have an Advocate stand up for them before God rather than an Accuser, for just as there are accusers in the world below, there are adversaries above as well. Rabbi Chiya wonders why if someone keeps the commandments it is necessary to have an angel intercede for him. Rabbi Yehuda answers that it is true that God sees everything, but He gave permission to the Other Side to accuse people in this world.

1. וַיֹּאמֶר יְיָ אֶל מֹשֶׁה בֹּא אֶל פַּרְעֹה כִּי אֲנִי הִכְבַּדְתִּי אֶת לִבּוֹ וְגוֹ'. רִבִּי יְהוּדָה פָּתַח וְאָמַר, אַשְׁרֵי הָעָם יוֹדְעֵי תְרוּעָה יְיָ' בְּאוֹר פָּנֶיךָ יְהַלֵּכוּן. כַּמָּה אִצְטְרִיכוּ בְּנֵי נָשָׁא, לְמֵהַךְ בְּאָרְחֵי דְּקוּדְשָׁא בְּרִיךְ הוּא, וּלְמִטַּר פִּקּוּדֵי אוֹרַיְיתָא, בְּגִין דְּיִזְכּוּן בָּהּ לְעָלְמָא דְּאָתֵי, וּלְשֵׁזָבָא לוֹן מִכָּל קִטְרוּגִין דִּלְעֵילָּא וְתַתָּא. בְּגִין, דְּהָא כְּמָה דְּאִשְׁתְּכָחוּ מְקַטְרְגִין בְּעָלְמָא לְתַתָּא, הָכִי נָמֵי אִשְׁתְּכָחוּ מְקַטְרְגִין לְעֵילָּא דְּקַיְימֵי עֲלַיְיהוּ דִּבְנֵי נָשָׁא.

1. "And Hashem said to Moses, 'Go in to Pharaoh, for I have hardened his heart...'" (Shemot 10:1). Rabbi Yehuda opened the discussion, saying: "Happy is the people that know the joyful note; they shall walk, Hashem, in the light of Your countenance" (Tehilim 89:16). How much should people walk in the ways of the Holy One, blessed be He, and observe the commandments of the Torah in order to merit the World to Come, and that they mey be delivered from all Accusers above and below. For as there are Accusers in the world below, so there are Adversaries above whose functions is to ACCUSE people.

2. אִינּוּן דְּעַבְדִין פִּקּוּדֵי אוֹרַיְיתָא, וְאַזְלֵי בְּאוֹרַח מֵישָׁר, בִּדְחֲלָא דְּמָארֵיהוֹן, כַּמָּה אִינּוּן סַנֵּיגוֹרִין דְּקַיְימִין עֲלַיְיהוּ לְעֵילָּא, כְּמָה דְּאַתְּ אָמַר אִם יֵשׁ עָלָיו מַלְאָךְ מֵלִיץ אֶחָד מִנִּי אָלֶף וְגוֹ'. וּכְתִיב וַיְחֻנֶּנּוּ וַיֹּאמֶר פְּדָעֵהוּ מֵרֶדֶת שַׁחַת מָצָאתִי כֹפֶר. בְּגִין כַּךְ, זַכָּאָה אִיהוּ מַאן דְּנָטִיר פִּקּוּדֵי אוֹרַיְיתָא.

2. Those who observe the commandments of the Torah and walk the right path in fear of their Master, good Advocates are situated above them, as is written: "If there be an angel over him, an interpreter, one among a thousand...then He is gracious to him, and says, 'Deliver him from going down to the pit: I have found a ransom'" (Iyov 33:23). Therefore, fortunate is he who observes the commandments of the Torah.

3. אָמַר לֵיהּ רִבִּי חִיָּיא, אִי הָכִי, אֲמַאי אִצְטְרִיךְ הָכָא מַלְאָךְ דְּלֶיהֱוֵי סַנֵּיגוֹרָא עָלֵיהּ דְּבַר נָשׁ וְהָא כְּתִיב כִּי יְיָ׳ יִהְיֶה בְּכִסְלֶךָ וְשָׁמַר רַגְלְךָ מִלָּכֶד, וּכְתִיב יְיָ׳ יִשְׁמָרְךָ מִכָּל רָע. דְּהָא חָמֵי קוּדְשָׁא בְּרִיךְ הוּא, כָּל מַה דְּבַר נָשׁ עָבֵיד בְּעָלְמָא, הֵן טָב הֵן בִּישׁ. וְכֵן הוּא אוֹמֵר, אִם יִסָּתֵר אִישׁ בַּמִּסְתָּרִים וַאֲנִי לֹא אֶרְאֶנּוּ נְאֻם יְיָ׳.

3. Rabbi Chiya said to him: If so, why is it necessary to have an angel to intercede for the person, seeing it is written: "For Hashem will be your confidence and will keep your foot from being caught" (Mishlei 3:26). "Hashem will guard you from all evil" (Tehilim 121:7). For the Holy One, blessed be He, sees everything that a man does in the world, both good and evil. And so He says, "'Can any hide himself in secret places that I shall not see him?' Says Hashem" (Yirmeyah 23:24). IF THIS IS SO, WHY DO WE NEED AN ANGEL TO INTERCEDE OR ACCUSE?

4. אָמַר לֵיהּ רִבִּי יְהוּדָה, כֹּלָּא הָכִי הוּא וַדַּאי. אֲבָל הָא כְּתִיב, וְגַע אֶל עַצְמוֹ וְאֶל בְּשָׂרוֹ. וּכְתִיב, וַתְּסִיתֵנִי בוֹ לְבַלְּעוֹ חִנָּם. לְאַחֲזָאָה דְּהָא רְשׁוּ אִתְמְסַר לְסִטְרָא אַחֲרָא לְקַטְרְגָא, עַל מִלִּין דְּעָלְמָא, וּלְאִתְמַסְּרָא בִּידוֹי. וְכָל אִלֵּין אָרְחִין טְמִירִין קָמֵי קוּדְשָׁא בְּרִיךְ הוּא, וְלֵית אַנְתְּ כְּדַאי לְמֵהַךְ אֲבַתְרַיְיהוּ, בְּגִין דְּאִינּוּן נִמּוּסִין דְּקוּדְשָׁא בְּרִיךְ הוּא, וּבְנֵי נָשָׁא לָאו אִינּוּן רַשָּׁאִין לְדַקְדְּקָא אֲבַתְרַיְיהוּ, בַּר אִינּוּן זַכָּאֵי קְשׁוֹט דְּיַדְעִין רָזֵי אוֹרַיְיתָא, וְאָזְלִין בְּאָרְחָא דְּחָכְמְתָא לְמִנְדַּע אִינּוּן מִלִּין סְתִימִין דְּאוֹרַיְיתָא.

4. Rabbi Yehuda said: Certainly it is so THAT THE HOLY ONE, BLESSED BE HE, SEES EVERYTHING. But it is written: "And touch his bone and his flesh" (Iyov 2:5), and "although you did move me against him to destroy him without cause" (Ibid. 3). This shows that permission was granted to the Other Side to accuse in worldly matters, and they should be given into his hands. All these things are to stay concealed before the Holy One, blessed be He, and you have no right to follow them TO INVESTIGATE THEM, because they are the statutes of the Holy One, blessed be He. Humans are not permitted to be particular about them except for those truly Righteous who know the secrets of the Torah and go in the way of wisdom to know these hidden things in the Torah. THIS IS THE MEANING OF: "HAPPY IS THE PEOPLE THAT KNOW THE JOYFUL NOTE (LIT. 'TRUAH')" (TEHILIM 89:16), THAT IS, THEY KNOW THE WAYS OF BLESSED HASHEM, AND THAT HE BRINGS EVIL AND GOOD THROUGH MESSENGERS, ALTHOUGH HE CAN DO IT HIMSELF. SO IN THE PASSAGE: "GO IN TO PHARAOH," THE HOLY ONE, BLESSED BE HE, WANTED PHARAOH TO LET THE CHILDREN OF YISRAEL GO, EVEN THOUGH HE WAS ABLE TO TAKE THEM OUT AGAINST HIS WILL.

2. “Now there was a day...and the Adversary came also among them”

A Synopsis

Rabbi Elazar begins by talking about Rosh Hashanah (the Jewish New Year), Judgment Day. He says there are messengers who are appointed by God to watch over the actions of people, and at Judgment Day these messengers accuse those whose actions were improper. When Yisrael sin, they weaken God, but when they perform good actions they give might and power to Him. Rabbi Elazar speaks about “The Adversary also came among them,” and recounts the conversation between God and Satan wherein God distracts Satan from his accusation of Yisrael, by asking him if he has considered His servant Job. Satan always requests justice from God. We read that Job was judged as he had judged Yisrael, since he had been one of Pharaoh’s advisors. The Satan was given permission to afflict Job’s bones and flesh, but not to kill him. We are told that God does not want to destroy the whole world on the word of the Accuser, since the Accuser’s desire is always to destroy. The discussion turns to “The End of all Flesh” which is the Satan, and “the end of days” that is in Holiness. On Rosh Hashanah those who come before God with repentance deserve to be written on the side of Life; those who come with evil actions are written on the Other Side, which is Death. We are told then of the balance, where the world is half Life and half Death, and the actions of one Righteous man or one wicked person can tip the balance so that all the world is written to Life or Death. A person should not be set apart by himself because he can be noticed and accused from above. Job, who was set apart, and who was tested severely, did not even then join the Other Side. He should, however, have given a part of his sacrifice to the Other Side because then the Other Side would have removed himself from the Temple. The conclusion of this section is that God judged Job, giving him first good and then bad and then good again; thus it is proper for a person to know good and bad, and to return himself to good.

5. רִבִּי אֶלְעָזָר פָּתַח, וַיְהִי הַיּוֹם וַיָּבֹאוּ בְּנֵי הָאֱלֹהִים לְהִתְיַצֵּב עַל יְיָ׳ וַיָּבֹא גַם הַשָּׂטָן בְּתוֹכָם. וַיְהִי הַיּוֹם: דָּא רֹאשׁ הַשָּׁנָה, דְּקוּדְשָׁא בְּרִיךְ הוּא קָאֵים לְמֵידָן עָלְמָא. כְּגַוְונָא דָּא, וַיְהִי הַיּוֹם וַיָּבֹא שָׁמָּה. הַהוּא יוֹמָא יוֹם טוֹב דְּרֹאשׁ הַשָּׁנָה הֲוָה.

5. Rabbi Elazar opened the discussion, saying: “Now there was a day when the sons of Elohim came to present themselves before Hashem, and the

Adversary came also among them" (Iyov 1:6). "Now there was a day," refers to Rosh Hashanah, the day that the Holy One, blessed be He, rises to judge the world. Similarly, "And it happened one day, that he came there" (II Melachim 4:11). That day was the holy day of Rosh Hashanah.

6. וַיָּבֹאוּ בְּנֵי הָאֱלֹהִים, אִלֵּין רַבְרְבִין מְמָנָן שְׁלִיחָן בְּעָלְמָא, לְאַשְׁגְּחָא בְּעוֹבָדִין דִּבְנֵי נָשָׁא. לְהִתְיַצֵּב עַל ה׳: כְּמָה דְּאַתְּ אָמֵר, וְכָל צְבָא הַשָּׁמַיִם עוֹמְדִים עָלָיו מִימִינוֹ וּמִשְּׂמֹאלוֹ. אֲבָל לְהִתְיַצֵּב עַל ה׳ בְּהַאי קְרָא אַשְׁכַּחְנָא רְחִימוּתָא דְּקוּדְשָׁא בְּרִיךְ הוּא עֲלַיְיהוּ דְּיִשְׂרָאֵל. בְּגִין, דְּהָנֵי שְׁלִיחָן, דְּאִינּוּן מְמָנָן לְאַשְׁגָּחָא עַל עוֹבָדִין דִּבְנֵי נָשָׁא, אַזְלִין וְשָׁאטִין וְנַטְלִין אִינּוּן עוֹבָדִין כֻּלְּהוּ, וּבְיוֹמָא דְּקָאֵי דִּינָא לְמֵיקַם, לְמֵידַן עָלְמָא, אִתְעָבֵידוּ קַטֵיגוֹרִין לְמֵיקַם עֲלַיְיהוּ דִּבְנֵי נָשָׁא. וְתָא חֲזֵי, מִכָּל עַמִּין דְּעָלְמָא, לָא קַיְימִין לְאַשְׁגָּחָא בְּעוֹבָדֵיהוֹן, בַּר בְּיִשְׂרָאֵל בִּלְחוֹדַיְיהוּ, בְּגִין דְּאִלֵּין בְּנִין לְקוּדְשָׁא בְּרִיךְ הוּא.

6. "And the sons of Elohim came." These are the appointed ministers whose mission in the world is to observe the actions of people. "To present themselves before Hashem," as is written: "And all the hosts of heaven standing by Him on His right hand and on His left" (I Melachim 22:19). But in the passage: "To present themselves before Hashem," I have found the love of the Holy One, blessed be He, toward Yisrael. These messengers who are appointed to observe the actions of people wander around IN THE WORLD and take all these actions, and on the day that Judgment rises to judge the world, they became accuser so they are DEMOUNCING against people. Come and behold: of all the nations in the world, THE MINISTERS stand to watch over the activities of Yisrael only, because they are the children of the Holy One, blessed be He.

7. וְכַד לָא אִשְׁתְּכָחוּ עוֹבָדִין דְּיִשְׂרָאֵל כַּדְקָא יָאוֹת, כִּבְיָכוֹ״ל אִינּוּן מְמָנָן שְׁלִיחָן, כַּד בָּעָאן לְקַיְּימָא עַל אִינּוּן עוֹבָדִין דְּיִשְׂרָאֵל, עַל ה׳ וַדַּאי קַיְימִין, דְּהָא כַּד יִשְׂרָאֵל עַבְדִין עוֹבָדִין דְּלָא כַּשְׁרָן, כִּבְיָכוֹ״ל מַתִּישִׁין חֵילָא דְּקוּדְשָׁא בְּרִיךְ הוּא. וְכַד עַבְדִין עוֹבָדִין דְּכַשְׁרָן, יַהֲבִין תּוּקְפָּא וְחֵילָא לְקוּדְשָׁא בְּרִיךְ הוּא. וְעַל דָּא כְּתִיב, תְּנוּ עֹז לֵאלֹהִים. בְּמָה. בְּעוֹבָדִין דְּכַשְׁרָן. וְעַל דָּא, בְּהַהוּא יוֹמָא, כֻּלְּהוּ רַבְרְבָן מְמָנָן

אִתְכְּנָשׁוּ עַל ה׳. עַל ה׳ וַדַּאי, דְּהָא כֵּיוָן דְּעַל יִשְׂרָאֵל אִתְכְּנָשׁוּ, עָלֵיהּ אִתְכְּנָשׁוּ.

7. When the actions of the children of Yisrael were found to be improper, the appointed messengers stand against these actions of Yisrael, and stand by Hashem. For when the children of Yisrael perform actions that are not good, they weaken, so to speak, the strength of the Holy One, blessed be He. When they perform good actions, they give might and power to the Holy One, blessed be He. Of this, it is written: "Give strength to Elohim" (Tehilim 68:35). How IS STRENGTH GIVEN? By good actions. Therefore, all the appointed ministers gathered by (lit. 'upon') Hashem on that day. 'Upon' Hashem most certainly, for they gathered TO BRING ACCUSATIONS upon Yisrael, WHICH AMOUNTS TO having gathered against Hashem TO WEAKEN HIS STRENGTH, SO TO SPEAK.

8. וַיָּבֹא גַּם הַשָּׂטָן בְּתוֹכָם, גַּם, לְאַסְגָּאָה עֲלַיְיהוּ, דְּכֻלְּהוּ אַתְיָין לְמֶהֱוֵי קַטֵיגוֹרִין עֲלַיְיהוּ דְּיִשְׂרָאֵל, וְדָא אִתּוֹסָף עֲלַיְיהוּ, בְּגִין דְּאִיהוּ דַּילְטוֹרָא רַבְרְבָא מִכֻּלְּהוּ, קַטֵיגוֹרָא מִכֻּלְּהוּ, כֵּיוָן דְּחָמָא קוּדְשָׁא בְּרִיךְ הוּא, דְּכֻלְּהוּ אַתְיָין לְקַטְרְגָא. מִיָּד וַיֹּאמֶר יְיָ׳ אֶל הַשָּׂטָן מֵאַיִן תָּבֹא. וְכִי לֹא הֲוָה יָדַע קוּדְשָׁא בְּרִיךְ הוּא, מֵאָן הֲוָה אָתֵי. אֶלָּא לְאַיְיתָאָה עוֹבָדָא לִרְעוּתֵיהּ.

8. "The Adversary also came among them." The word "also" adds to THE CHILDREN OF ELOHIM, because they all came to accuse Yisrael, and THE ADVERSARY also joined them because he was the greatest slanderer of them all. As soon as the Holy One, blessed be He, saw that they all came to accuse, immediately, "And Hashem said to the Adversary, 'From where do you come?'" (Iyov 1:7), SINCE HE WAS THE GREATEST OF THEM ALL. HE ASKS: Did not the Holy One, blessed be He, know where he came from SO THAT HE HAD TO ASK HIM? HE ANSWERS: Rather only to allow the matter to the wishes of the Satan, MEANING THAT WITH THESE WORDS HE GAVE HIM AN OPENING TO ACCUSE AS HE WISHES.

9. וַיֹּאמֶר יְיָ׳ אֶל הַשָּׂטָן וְגוֹ׳ וַיַּעַן הַשָּׂטָן אֶת יְיָ׳ וַיֹּאמַר מִשּׁוּט בָּאָרֶץ. מִכָּאן אוֹלִיפְנָא, דְּיִשּׁוּבָא דְּאַרְעָא אִתְמְסָר לְסִטְרִין אַחֲרָנִין, בַּר אַרְעָא

דְּיִשְׂרָאֵל בִּלְחוֹדָהָא. כֵּיוָן דְּאָמַר מִשּׁוּט בָּאָרֶץ, אַשְׁגַּח קוּדְשָׁא בְּרִיךְ הוּא, דְּבָעֵי לְמֶהֱוֵי דַּלְטוֹרָא עֲלַיְיהוּ דְּיִשְׂרָאֵל. מִיָּד, וַיֹּאמֶר יְיָ אֶל הַשָּׂטָן הֲשַׂמְתָּ לִבְּךָ עַל עַבְדִּי אִיּוֹב כִּי אֵין כָּמוֹהוּ בָּאָרֶץ.

9. "And Hashem said to the Adversary… Then the Adversary answered Hashem and said, 'From going to and fro in the earth'" (Iyov 1:7). From here I learned that the settling of the earth is given over to Others Side, NAMELY THE SEVENTY NATIONS, except for the Land of Yisrael exclusively, WHICH IS SECURED IN HOLINESS FOR THE CHILDREN OF YISRAEL. THEREFORE, since he said, "From going to and fro in the earth," THE WORD "EARTH" IS UNSPECIFIED AND MEANS THE LAND OF YISRAEL. The Holy One, blessed be He, saw that the Satan wanted to slander Yisrael AND NOT JOB OR OTHERS WHO WERE CONSIDERED OF THE NATIONS WHO INHABIT THE OTHER LANDS. Immediately, "Hashem said to the Adversary, 'Have you considered my servant Job, that there is none like him on earth…'" (Ibid. 8).

10. חָמָא שַׁעֲתָא לְמֵיהַב לֵיהּ חוּלָקָא, בְּמָה דְּיִתְעֲסַק, וְיִתְפְּרַשׁ מִנַּיְיהוּ דְּיִשְׂרָאֵל, וְהָא אוּקְמוּהָ, לְרַעְיָא דְּבָעָא לְמֶעְבַּר עָאנֵיהּ בְּחַד נַהֲרָא וְכוּ', מִיַּד אִתְעֲסַק בֵּיהּ הַהוּא שָׂטָן, וְלֹא קִטְרֵג עֲלַיְיהוּ דְּיִשְׂרָאֵל.

10. He saw THAT NOW WAS the opportune time to give THE SATAN a portion with which to be occupied, so he would be kept afar from Yisrael. They explained this to be similar to a shepherd who wanted to get his sheep across a river WHEN A WOLF CAME TO ATTACK THE SHEEP. WHAT DOES AN EXPERIENCED SHEPHERD DO? HE TAKES A BIG HE-GOAT AND GIVES IT TO THE WOLF, SAYING: LET HIM FIGHT WITH THE HE-GOAT UNTIL I LET MY SHEEP CROSS OVER THE RIVER AND THEN I WILL RETURN AND TAKE THIS ONE ALSO. THE HOLY ONE, BLESSED BE HE, DID LIKEWISE. HE GAVE JOB TO THE ADVERSARY TO BE OCCUPIED WITH SO HE WOULD NOT ACCUSE YISRAEL. Immediately, the Satan busied himself with him and did not accuse Yisrael.

11. וַיַּעַן הַשָּׂטָן אֶת יְיָ וַיֹּאמַר הַחִנָּם יָרֵא אִיּוֹב אֱלֹהִים. לָאו תָּוְהָא לְעַבְדָּא דְּמָארֵיהּ עָבֵיד לֵיהּ כָּל רְעוּתֵיהּ, דִּיהֵא דָּחִיל לֵיהּ, אַעְדֵּי אַשְׁגָּחוּתָךְ מִנֵּיהּ, וְתֶחֱמֵי אִי דָּחִיל לָךְ וְאִם לָאו.

2. "Now there was a day...and the Adversary came also among them"

11. "And the Adversary answered Hashem and said, 'Is it for naught that Job fears Elohim?'" (Ibid. 9). It is not surprising that a servant, whose master does his desire, fears him. Remove Your supervision from him and You will see if he still fears You or not.

12. ת״ח, בְּשַׁעֲתָא דְעָאקוּ, כַּד אִתְיְיהִב חוּלָקָא חֲדָא לְהַאי סְטָר לְאִתְעַסְקָא בֵּיהּ, אִתְפְּרִישׁ לְבָתַר מִכֹּלָּא. כְּגַוְונָא דָא שָׂעִיר בְּר״ח. שָׂעִיר בְּיוֹמָא דְכִפּוּרֵי. בְּגִין דְּאִתְעַסַּק בֵּיהּ, וְשָׁבִיק לְהוּ לְיִשְׂרָאֵל בְּמַלְכֵיהוֹן, וְהָכָא, מָטָא זִמְנָא לְמֵיטַל חוּלָקָא דָא, מִכָּל זַרְעָא דְאַבְרָהָם, בְּסִטְרָא אַחֲרָא. כְּמָה דְאַתְּ אָמֵר, הִנֵּה יָלְדָה מִלְכָּה גַּם הִיא וְגוֹ׳ אֶת עוּץ בְּכוֹרוֹ וְגוֹ׳.

12. Come and behold: During a time of duress, when a portion is given to this Side with which to occupy itself, it goes away by following it entirely. Similarly, a he-goat is sacrificed on the first day of the month and on Yom Kippur (Day of Atonement). THIS IS THE SECRET MEANING OF GIVING A PORTION TO THE OTHER SIDE, WHICH IS GIVEN TO IT in order that it shall be occupied, and so leave Yisrael in their kingdom. The time had arrived to take this portion from the whole seed of Abraham FOR the Other Side, as was written: "Behold Milkah, she also has born...Utz his firstborn..." (Beresheet 22:21). JOB WAS IN THE LAND OF UTZ, MEANING THAT HE WAS OF THE FAMILY OF ABRAHAM.

13. ות״ח, בְּשַׁעֲתָא דְאָמַר מִשּׁוּט בָּאָרֶץ, בָּעָא מִינֵּיהּ, לְמֶעְבַּד דִּינָא בְּיִשְׂרָאֵל, דְּהָא דִּינָא הֲוָה לֵיהּ עַל אַבְרָהָם, לְמִתְבַּע מְקוּדְשָׁא בְּרִיךְ הוּא. בְּגִין, דְּלָא אִתְעֲבֵיד דִּינָא בְּיִצְחָק, כַּד אִתְקְרִיב ע״ג מַדְבְּחָא, דְּהָא לָא הֲוָה לֵיהּ לְאַחְלְפָא קָרְבְּנָא דְאַזְמִין עַל מַדְבְּחָא, בְּאֳחֲרָא, כְּמָה דְאַתְּ אָמַר, לֹא יַחֲלִיפֶנּוּ. וְהָכָא קָאֵים יִצְחָק עַל גַּבֵּי מַדְבְּחָא, וְלָא אִשְׁתְּלִים מִנֵּיהּ קָרְבְּנָא, וְלָא אִתְעֲבֵיד בֵּיהּ דִּינָא, וּבָעָא דָא מֵעִם קוּדְשָׁא בְּרִיךְ הוּא, כְּמָה דְבָעָא דִינֵיהּ דְּיוֹסֵף לְכַמָּה דָרִין. וְכָל מַה דְבָעָא, בְּאוֹרַח דִּינָא בָּעָא.

13. Come and behold: When THE ADVERSARY said, "From going to and fro in the earth," he requested Hashem to execute Judgment on the children of

Yisrael. THE UNSPECIFIED WORD "EARTH" REFERS TO THE LAND OF YISRAEL, because he had an accusation against Abraham and he claimed it from the Holy One, blessed be He. AND THAT WAS because justice was not performed against Isaac when he was offered on the altar, and he should not have exchanged the offering that he prepared on the altar for another, NAMELY THE RAM, as it is written: "And he should not exchange it" (Vayikra 27:10). Isaac was already on the altar. He was not consummated to be a sacrifice, yet no punishment was carried against him. He requested this from the Holy One, blessed be He, as he requested Justice for the selling of Joseph for many generations. Anything that THE SATAN requests, HE REQUESTS by means of Judgment.

14. וּמֵהַהוּא זִמְנָא דְּאִשְׁתְּזִיב יִצְחָק, וְאִתְחַלַּף קָרְבָּנֵיהּ, זַמִּין לֵיהּ קוּדְשָׁא בְּרִיךְ הוּא, לְהַהוּא מְקַטְרְגָא, הַאי לְחוּלָקֵיהּ, כְּמָה דְּאַתְּ אָמֵר הִנֵּה יָלְדָה מִלְכָּה גַּם הִיא וְגוֹ׳ אֶת עוּץ בְּכוֹרוֹ. וְהָכָא, מָטָא לְמֵיטַל חוּלָקֵיהּ עָלֵיהּ, מִכָּל זַרְעֵיהּ דְּאַבְרָהָם, וְלָא יִקְרַב בְּסִטְרָא אַחֲרָא.

14. After Isaac was saved and his offering exchanged, the Holy One, blessed be He, prepared this FOR the Accuser, NAMELY JOB, for his portion. AS IT IS WRITTEN: "Behold Milkah, she also has born...Utz his firstborn..." NAMELY JOB, WHO DWELT IN THE LAND OF UTZ. THIS WAS SAID IMMEDIATELY AFTER THE BINDING OF ISAAC. Here, AT THE BIRTH OF UTZ, THE SATAN arrived to take for his portion from all the seed of Abraham, so he would not approach TO DAMAGE another side, NAMELY THE CHILDREN OF YISRAEL.

15. וְכֹלָּא בְּדִינָא אָתָא. כְּמָה דְּאִיהוּ דָּן, הָכִי אִתְּדָן. בְּגִין דְּאִיּוֹב מִקְּרִיבֵי עֵיטָא דְּפַרְעֹה הֲוָה, וְכַד קָם פַּרְעֹה עָלַיְיהוּ דְּיִשְׂרָאֵל, בָּעָא לְקַטְלָא לוֹן. אָמַר לֵיהּ לָא, אֶלָּא טוֹל מָמוֹנֵהוֹן וּשְׁלוֹט עַל גּוּפֵיהוֹן, בְּפוּלְחָנָא קַשְׁיָא, וְלָא תִּקְטוֹל לוֹן. אָמַר לֵיהּ קוּדְשָׁא בְּרִיךְ הוּא, חַיֶּיךָ, בְּהַהוּא דִּינָא מַמָּשׁ, תְּהֵא דָּאִין, מַה כְּתִיב, אוּלָם שְׁלַח נָא יָדְךָ וְגַע אֶל עַצְמוֹ וְאֶל בְּשָׂרוֹ וְגוֹ׳. בְּמָה דְּאִיהוּ דָּן, הָכִי אִתְּדָן. ואע״ג דִּבְכָל שְׁאַר הֲוָה דָּחִיל לְקוּדְשָׁא בְּרִיךְ הוּא.

15. Everything is according to Justice. Just as JOB judged, so was he judged. Job was one of Pharaoh’s advisers. When Pharaoh arose against Yisrael and wanted to kill them, JOB said to him: ‘No, just take their money and rule over their bodies with hard labor, but do not kill them’. The Holy One, blessed be He, said to him: ‘I swear on your life that you shall be judged with the same punishment THAT YOU PRONOUNCED AGAINST THE CHILDREN OF YISRAEL. It is written: “But put forth your hand now, and touch his bone and his flesh...” (Iyov 2:5). He HIMSELF was judged as he judged YISRAEL. Even though he feared the presence of the Holy One, blessed be He, in all other things, AS IS WRITTEN ABOUT HIM: “AND HE FEARED ELOHIM,” HE WAS NOT SPARED FROM JUDGMENT.

16. ת״ח, מַה כְּתִיב, אַךְ אֶת נַפְשׁוֹ שְׁמוֹר. וְאִתְיְהִיב לֵיהּ רְשׁוּ, לְמִשְׁלַט עַל בִּשְׂרָא, בְּגִין רָזָא דִּכְתִּיב, קֵץ כָּל בָּשָׂר בָּא לְפָנַי וְאוּקְמוּהָ, בָּא לְפָנַי וַדַּאי, וְדָא אִיהוּ קֵץ כָּל בָּשָׂר, וְלֹא רוּחָא. וְאִיתְּמַר, דְּאִיהוּ קֵץ דְּאָתֵי מִסִּטְרָא דְּחֹשֶׁךְ, כְּמָה דְּאַתְּ אָמֵר, קֵץ שָׂם לַחֹשֶׁךְ וּלְכָל תַּכְלִית הוּא חוֹקֵר. וּלְכָל בִּשְׂרָא, בְּגִין דְּאִית קֵץ אַחֲרָא, וְאִקְרֵי קֵץ הַיָּמִין, וְדָא אִיהוּ קֵץ אַחֲרָא, מִסִּטְרָא דִּשְׂמָאלָא, דְּאִיהוּ חֹשֶׁךְ. וע״ד אִתְיְיהִיב לֵיהּ רְשׁוּ בְּעַצְמוֹ וּבְשָׂרוֹ.

16. Come and behold: it is written, “Only spare his soul” (Ibid. 6). He was given permission to rule over his flesh. For this is the secret of the verse: “The End of all Flesh has come before Me” (Beresheet 6:13). And it was explained, “Has come before Me,” assuredly MEANS THAT THE END OF ALL FLESH, WHICH IS THE SATAN THE DESTROYER, “HAS COME BEFORE ME” TO RECEIVE PERMISSION. This is WHAT IS CALLED ‘the End of all Flesh’ and not CALLED ‘THE END OF ALL spirit’. They explained that it is the end that comes from the side of darkness, NAMELY FROM THE ASPECT OF THE JUDGMENTS OF THE MALE, as written: “He put an end to darkness, and searches out all perfection” (Iyov 28:3). “ALL PERFECTION” RESEMBLES “all flesh,” for there is another end which is the “end of days (also: ‘right’)” (Daniel 12:13), WHICH IS IN HOLINESS. This one HERE is a different end from the left side, which is dark. Therefore, he received permission to afflict his bone and flesh.

17. וַתְּסִיתֵנִי בוֹ לְבַלְּעוֹ. אִי הָכִי, לָאו בְּדִינָא הֲוָה, אֶלָּא בְּמֵימַר הַהוּא מְקַטְרְגָא, דְּאָסִית לֵיהּ, וְאַסְטֵי לֵיהּ. אֶלָּא, כֹּלָּא בְּדִינָא הֲוָה, וְהָכִי אָמַר

לוֹ אֱלִיהוּא, כִּי פֹעַל אָדָם יְשַׁלֶּם לוֹ וּכְאֹרַח אִישׁ יַמְצִיאֶנּוּ. וְהָכִי הֲוָה כְּמָה דְּאִתְּמַר, כְּמָה דְּאִיהוּ גָּזַר, הָכִי אִתְגְּזַר עָלֵיהּ.

17. "Although you did move Me against him, to destroy him without cause" (Iyov 2:3). HE ASKS: If so, then was he punished unlawfully, only because of the talk of the Accuser who provoked Him and turned Him. HE ANSWERS: Rather, everything was only done according to Justice, and Elihu did say to him: "For the work of a man shall He pay back to him, and according to his ways will He cause to befall every man" (Iyov 34:11). As we said, as he decreed against the children of Yisrael by Pharaoh, such was decreed against him.

18. וְהַאי דְּאָמַר וַתְּסִיתֵנִי בוֹ לְבַלְּעוֹ חִנָּם, וַתְּסִיתֵנִי לְבַלְּעוֹ לָא כְּתִיב, אֶלָּא וַתְּסִיתֵנִי בוֹ, בֵּיהּ קַיְּימָא בְּדַעְתֵּיהּ, דְּאִיהוּ חָשִׁיב דְּהָא תְּסִיתֵנִי, כְּמָה דְּאָמַר וְעַל עֲצַת רְשָׁעִים הוֹפָעְתָּ. כְּגַוְונָא דָּא, וַיְפַתּוּהוּ בְּפִיהֶם וּבִלְשׁוֹנָם יְכַזְּבוּ לוֹ. וַיְפַתּוּהוּ וַיְכַזְּבוּ לוֹ. לָא כְּתִיב, אֶלָּא וַיְפַתּוּהוּ בְּפִיהֶם. בְּפִיהֶם קַיְּימָא מִלָּה דָּא דְּהָא אִתְפַּתָּה.

18. Yet He said, "Although you did move Me against him, to destroy him without cause." THE EXPLANATION IS THAT it is not written: 'Although you did move Me to destroy him', rather it says, "Although you did move Me against (or: in) him," which means in his mind. For he thinks that "you did move Me," as JOB said, "And shine upon the counsel of the wicked" (Iyov 10:3). Similarly, "Nevertheless they did flatter Him with their mouths, and they lied to Him with their tongues" (Tehilim 78:36), WHICH IS ALSO DIFFICULT, FOR IS IT POSSIBLE TO ENTICE THE HOLY ONE, BLESSED BE HE? It is not written: 'They did flatter Him with, and they lied to Him," but rather, "They did flatter him with their mouths." Only by their mouths it was so, that He was enticed, MEANING THAT THEY THOUGHT SO, BUT IN TRUTH IT WAS NOT SO.

19. א"ר אַבָּא, כֹּלָּא הוּא שַׁפִּיר, אֲבָל הָכִי אוֹלִיפְנָא, דִּתְנָן, סָלִיק וְאַסְטִין. וְכִי אִיהוּ יָכִיל לְאַסְטָנָא. אִין. דְּהָא אִיהוּ מֶלֶךְ זָקֵן וּכְסִיל, דִּכְתִיב טוֹב יֶלֶד מִסְכֵּן וְחָכָם מִמֶּלֶךְ זָקֵן וּכְסִיל. וע"ד, יָכִיל לְאַסְטָנָא לְבַר נָשׁ. מַאי טַעֲמָא. בְּגִין דְּאִיהוּ מְהֵימָן עַל עוֹבָדוֹי דִּבְנֵי נָשָׁא.

2. "Now there was a day...and the Adversary came also among them"

19. Rabbi Aba said: This is all well, but so have I learned. We learned, "He goes up and accuses." HE ASKS: Can he accuse BEFORE THE HOLY ONE, BLESSED BE HE, WHO KNOWS EVERYTHING? HE ANSWERS: Yes, because he is an old foolish king, as written: "Better is a poor and wise child than an old and foolish king" (Kohelet 4:13). SINCE HE IS A KING OVER PEOPLE, he can therefore accuse man. What is the reason? Because he is trusted over the actions of people. SINCE HE REIGNS OVER THEM, HE IS TRUSTED OVER THEIR ACTIONS.

20. ת״ח, הַאי בְּדִינָא דְּיָחִיד, אֲבָל בְּדִינָא דְּעָלְמָא, כְּתִיב, וַיֵּרֶד יְיָ׳ לִרְאוֹת. אֵרֲדָה נָּא וְאֶרְאֶה. דְּלָא אִתְיְיהִיב מְהֵימָנוּתָא אֶלָּא בִּידֵיהּ בִּלְחוּדוֹי, דְּהָא לָא בָּעָא לְאוֹבָדָא עָלְמָא, עַל מֵימָר דְּהַהוּא מְקַטְרְגָא, דְּתִיאוּבְתֵּיהּ אִיהוּ תָּדִיר לְשֵׁיצָאָה. מְנָלָן דִּכְתִּיב, קֵץ שָׂם לַחֹשֶׁךְ וּלְכָל תַּכְלִית הוּא חוֹקֵר. לְשֵׁיצָאָה כֹּלָּא, הוּא חוֹקֵר. וְדָא אִיהוּ קֵץ כָּל בָּשָׂר בָּא לְפָנַי, וַדַּאי בְּגִין לְשֵׁיצָאָה.

20. Come and behold: THIS IS SO ONLY with judging an individual, but concerning the judging of the world, it is written: "And Hashem descended to see" (Beresheet 11:5), "I will go down and see" (Beresheet 18:21). He was not trusted, rather it was in the hands OF THE HOLY ONE, BLESSED BE HE, alone because He did not want to destroy the world according to the word of the Accuser, whose desire is always to destroy. How do we know that? Because it is written: "He put an end to darkness, and searches out all perfection" (Iyov 28:3), MEANING that he searches to destroy everything. And this is the meaning of: "The End of all Flesh has come before Me" (Beresheet 6:13). THE ADVERSARY, WHO IS CALLED "THE END OF ALL FLESH," has certainly come to destroy.

21. ות״ח, וַיְהִי הַיּוֹם וַיָּבוֹאוּ בְּנֵי הָאֱלֹהִים לְהִתְיַצֵּב עַל יְיָ׳. כְּמָה דְּאִתְּמַר. וְהַהוּא יוֹמָא, קַיְימִין תְּרֵין סִטְרִין, לְקַבְּלָא בְּנֵי עָלְמָא. כָּל אִינּוּן דְּאַתְיָין קָמֵי קוּדְשָׁא בְּרִיךְ הוּא בִּתְיוּבְתָּא וּבְעוֹבָדִין טָבִין, אִינּוּן זַכְיָין לְמֶהֱוֵי כְּתִיבִין לְגַבֵּיהּ דְּהַהוּא סִטְרָא דְּאִיהוּ חַיִּים, וְאַפִּיק תּוֹצְאוֹת חַיִּים. וּמַאן דְּאִיהוּ מִסִּטְרֵיהּ, אַכְתִּיב לְחַיִּים. וְכָל אִינּוּן דְּאַתְיָין בְּעוֹבָדִין בִּישִׁין, אִינּוּן כְּתִיבִין לְהַהוּא סִטְרָא אַחֲרָא דְּאִיהוּ מוֹתָא, וְאִקְרֵי מָוֶת, וּבֵיהּ שַׁרְיָא מוֹתָא.

21. Come and behold: "Now there was a day when the sons of Elohim came to present themselves before Hashem" (Iyov 1:6), as explained THAT IT WAS ON ROSH HASHANAH. For on that day, two sides are before the world. All those who come before the Holy One, blessed be He, with repentance and good deeds, merit to be written on that side which is Life, which brings out the effects of life. And whoever is from its side is recorded for Life. All those who come with evil actions are written on the Other Side, which is Death. It is called 'death', and in it death dwells, TO KILL PEOPLE.

22. וּבְהַהוּא יוֹמָא, קַיְימִין אִלֵּין תְּרֵין סִטְרִין: חַיִּים, וּמָוֶת. אִית מַאן דְּאַכְתִּיב לְסִטְרָא דְּחַיִּים. וְאִית מַאן דְּאַכְתִּיב לְסִטְרָא דְּמָוֶת. וּלְזִמְנִין דְּעָלְמָא שַׁרְיָא בְּאֶמְצָעִיתָא, אִי קַיְּימָא חַד זַכָּאָה בְּעָלְמָא, דְּאַכְרַע עָלַיְיהוּ, כֻּלְּהוּ קַיְימִין וְאַכְתִּיבוּ לְחַיִּים. וְאִי חַד חַיָּיבָא אַכְרַע עָלְמָא, כֻּלְּהוּ אַכְתִּיבוּ לְמִיתָה.

22. On that day these two sides exist, Life and Death. Some are written to the side of Life, and some are written to the side of Death. Sometimes the world is in the middle, MEANING HALF DESERVING AND HALF GUILTY. If there is one righteous man to tip the balance in the world, they all stand and are written to Life, but if one wicked person ever balances the world, they are all written to Death.

23. וְהַהוּא זִמְנָא, עָלְמָא הֲוָה קַיָּים בְּאֶמְצָעִיתָא, וְהַהוּא מְקַטְרְגָא בָּעָא לְאַסְטָאָה. מִיָּד מַה כְּתִיב, הֲשַׂמְתָּ לִבְּךָ עַל עַבְדִּי אִיּוֹב כִּי אֵין כָּמוֹהוּ בָּאָרֶץ וְגוֹ'. כֵּיוָן דְּאִשְׁתְּמוֹדַע אִיהוּ בִּלְחוֹדוֹי, מִיַּד אַתְקִיף בֵּיהּ מְקַטְרְגָא. וְע"ד תָּנֵינָן, דְּלָא אִצְטְרִיךְ לֵיהּ לְבַר נָשׁ לְאִתְפָּרְשָׁא מִכְּלָלָא דְּסַגִּיאִין, בְּגִין דְּלָא יִתְרְשִׁים אִיהוּ בִּלְחוֹדוֹי, וְלָא יְקַטְרְגוּן עָלֵיהּ לְעֵילָּא.

23. The time that the world was in the middle, MEANING HALF GUILTY AND HALF MERITORIOUS, the Prosecutor wanted to accuse AND TO TIP THE WORLD TO THE SCALE OF GUILT. Immediately, it is written, "Have you considered my servant Job, that there is none like him on earth..." (Iyov 1:8). As soon as he was set apart, the Accuser immediately attacked him. Therefore, we learn that a person should not remove himself from the community so that he will not be noted apart, and he will not be accused from above.

24. דִּכְתִּיב בַּשּׁוּנַמִּית, וַתֹּאמֶר בְּתוֹךְ עַמִּי אָנֹכִי יוֹשָׁבֶת. לָא בְּעֵינָא לְאַפָּקָא גַּרְמָי מִכְּלָלָא דְּסַגִּיאִין, בְּתוֹךְ עַמִּי יָתִיבְנָא, עַד יוֹמָא דָּא, וּבְתוֹךְ עַמִּי, בִּכְלָלָא חֲדָא אִשְׁתְּמוֹדַע לְעֵילָּא. וְהָכָא אִיּוֹב, כֵּיוָן דְּאִשְׁתְּמוֹדַע לְעֵילָּא וְאִתְרְשִׁים, מִיַּד אַתְקִיף בֵּיהּ מְקַטְרְגָא, וְאָמַר הֲחִנָּם יָרֵא אִיּוֹב אֱלֹהִים, כָּל מַה דְּדָחִיל לָךְ וְאִתְתָּקַף, לָאו לְמַגָּנָא עָבֵיד, הֲלֹא אַתָּה שַׂכְתָּ בַעֲדוֹ וּבְעַד וְגוֹ׳. אֲבָל טוֹל כָּל הַאי טָבָא דְּאַנְתְּ עָבֵד לֵיהּ, וּמִיָּד אִם לֹא עַל פָּנֶיךָ יְבָרְכֶךָּ. יִשְׁבּוֹק לָךְ, וְיִתְדַּבַּק בְּסִטְרָא אַחֲרָא, דְּהָא הַשְׁתָּא בְּפָתוֹרָךְ אִיהוּ אָכִיל, סָלִיק פָּתוֹרָךְ מִנֵּיהּ, וְנֶחֱזֵי מִמָּאן אִיהוּ, וּבְאָן סִטְרָא יִתְדַּבַּק.

24. It is written by the Shunamit woman: "And she said, 'I dwell among my own people,'" (II Melachim 4:13) MEANING she does not want to be set apart from the public. I dwell among my people to this day, and I will be known among my people as one whole above. Since Job was known above and was distinguished, the Accuser immediately attacked him and said, "Does Job fear Elohim for naught?" The reason he fears You and has fortified himself WITH GOOD DEEDS is not for naught; "Have You not made a hedge about him…" (Iyov 1:10). However, take away from him all this good that You did for him, and You will immediately see if "he will curse You to Your face" (Ibid. 11). He will leave You and cleave to the Other Side. For he eats at Your table at present; remove Your table from him and we will see whose he is, and to which side he will cleave.

25. מִיָּד, וַיֹּאמֶר יְיָ אֶל הַשָּׂטָן הִנֵּה כָל אֲשֶׁר לוֹ בְּיָדֶךָ. לְאַחֲזָאָה, דִּדְחִילוּ דְּאִיּוֹב לְגַבֵּיהּ דְּקוּדְשָׁא בְּרִיךְ הוּא, הוּא לְנַטְרָא עוּתְרֵיהּ. וּמֵהָכָא אוֹלִיפְנָא, דְּכָל אִינּוּן דְּדַחֲלִין לֵיהּ לְקוּדְשָׁא בְּרִיךְ הוּא, עַל עוּתְרַיְיהוּ, אוֹ עַל בְּנַיְיהוּ, לָאו אִיהוּ דְּחִילוּ כַּדְקָא יֵאוֹת. וְעַל דָּא קִטְרֵג הַהוּא מְקַטְרְגָא וְאָמַר, הֲחִנָּם יָרֵא אִיּוֹב אֱלֹהִים הֲלֹא אַתָּה שַׂכְתָּ בַעֲדוֹ וְגוֹ׳ מַעֲשֵׂה יָדָיו בֵּרַכְתָּ. וְעַל דָּא אִיהוּ דָּחִיל לָךְ וְאִתְיְיהִיב לֵיהּ רְשׁוּ לְקַטְרְגָא בֵּיהּ, וּלְאַחֲזָאָה, דְּלָא פָּלַח אִיּוֹב לְקוּדְשָׁא בְּרִיךְ הוּא בִּרְחִימוּ.

25. Immediately "And Hashem said to the Adversary, 'Behold, all that he has is in your power,'" (Ibid. 12) to show that the fear of Job for the Holy One, blessed be He, was to guard his wealth. From here, we learn that all those who fear the Holy One, blessed be He, because of their wealth or their children, do not have proper fear. Therefore, the Accuser accused and said, "Is it for naught that Job fears Elohim. Behold you have made a hedge about him...You have blessed the works of his hands." Therefore, he fears You. Then he was granted permission to persecute him and show that Job did not serve Hashem out of love.

26. דְּכֵיוָן דְּאִתְנַסֵּי, נָפַק מֵאוֹרְחָא, וְלָא קָאֵים בְּקִיּוּמֵיהּ, מַה כְּתִיב, בְּכָל זֹאת לֹא חָטָא אִיּוֹב בִּשְׂפָתָיו. לֹא חָטָא בִּשְׂפָתָיו אֲבָל בִּרְעוּתֵיהּ חָטָא, וּלְבָתַר חָטָא בְּכֹלָּא.

26. As soon as he was tested, he left the path and did not retain his integrity. It is written: "In all this, Job did not sin with his lips" (Iyov 2:10), but he did sin in his will. Afterwards, he sinned in everything; AS IT IS WRITTEN THAT HE SAID, "THE EARTH IS GIVEN INTO THE HAND OF WICKED..." (IYOV 9:24) AND SIMILARLY, RABA SAID, "JOB ABUSED IN TORRENTS..." LOOK THERE.

27. וְאִי תֵּימָא דְּלָא אִתְנַסֵּי בַּר נָשׁ, הָא כְּתִיב ה׳ צַדִּיק יִבְחָן וְגוֹ׳. וּבְגִין כַּךְ אִתְנַסֵּי אִיּוֹב. ואע״ג דְּלָא קָאֵים בְּקִיּוּמֵיהּ כַּדְקָא יֵאוֹת, לָא נָפַק מִתְּחוֹת רְשׁוּתָא דְּמָרֵיהּ לְאִתְדַּבְּקָא בְּסִטְרָא אַחֲרָא.

27. One may question why no person was tested EXCEPT JOB? Indeed, it is written: "Hashem tries the righteous..." (Tehilim 11:5). Therefore, Job was ALSO tried. Even though he did not retain his strength as he should have, he did not leave the domain of his Master to join the Other Side.

28. וְכַמָּה הֲוָה הַהוּא נִסּוּתָא דִּילֵיהּ. תְּרֵיסַר יַרְחֵי, שׁוּלְטָנוּתָא דְּהַהוּא סִטְרָא אַחֲרָא. כְּמָה דְּתָנֵינָן, דִּינָא דְּחַיָּיבַיָּא בַּגֵּיהִנָּם י״ב יַרְחֵי, וּבְגִין דְּלָא אִתְדַּבַּק בְּסִטְרָא אַחֲרָא כְּתִיב, וַיְיָ׳ בֵּרַךְ אֶת אַחֲרִית אִיּוֹב מֵרֵאשִׁיתוֹ.

28. HE ASKS: How long was his test? HE ANSWERS: The duration of the dominion of the Other Side is twelve months. As we learned, the punishment of the wicked in Gehenom lasts twelve months. Since he did not join the Other Side, it is written: "So Hashem blessed the latter end of Job more than his beginning" (Iyov 42:12).

29. ר׳ שִׁמְעוֹן אָמַר, הַאי דְּאִיּוֹב, לָאו נִסּוּתָא אִיהוּ דְּקוּדְשָׁא בְּרִיךְ הוּא, כְּנִסּוּתָא דִּשְׁאַר צַדִּיקַיָּא, דְּהָא לָא כְּתִיב וְהָאֱלֹהִים נִסָּה אֶת אִיּוֹב, כְּמָה דִּכְתִּיב וְהָאֱלֹהִים נִסָּה אֶת אַבְרָהָם. דְּאַבְרָהָם, אִיהוּ בִּידֵיהּ אַקְרִיב לִבְרֵיהּ יְחִידָאי דִּילֵיהּ לְגַבֵּי קב״ה, וְאִיּוֹב לָא יָהִיב כְּלוּם, וְלָא מָסַר לֵיהּ לְקוּדְשָׁא בְּרִיךְ הוּא כְּלוּם.

29. Rabbi Shimon said: Job's was not a test from the Holy One, blessed be He, like the test of the other Righteous men, because it is not written: 'And the Elohim tested Job', as in: "Elohim did test Abraham" (Beresheet 22:1). Abraham offered his only son to the Holy One, blessed be He, with his own hand. But Job gave nothing, and did not give anything to the Holy One, blessed be He.

30. וְלָא אִתְּמַר לֵיהּ, דְּהָא גַּלֵּי קָמֵיהּ, דְּלָא יָכִיל לְקַיְּימָא בֵּיהּ, אֲבָל אִתְמְסָר בִּידָא דִּמְקַטְרְגָא. וּבְדִינָא דְּקוּדְשָׁא בְּרִיךְ הוּא אִתְעֲבֵיד, וְקוּדְשָׁא בְּרִיךְ הוּא אִתְּעַר דִּינָא דָּא, לְהַהוּא מְקַטְרְגָא לְגַבֵּיהּ, הה״ד הֲשַׂמְתָּ לִבְּךָ עַל עַבְדִּי אִיּוֹב וְגוֹ׳.

30. He was not told about the test AS ABRAHAM WAS, because it was revealed before Him that he would not be able to withstand it properly. It was instead given over to the Accuser. And it was done through the Judgment of the Holy One, blessed be He, BECAUSE HE BROUGHT THE HEAVY LABOR ON THE CHILDREN OF YISRAEL IN EGYPT. The Holy One, blessed be He, aroused this Judgment by the Accuser, as written: "Have you considered my servant Job?" (Iyov 1:8)

31. פָּתַח וְאָמַר, וַיְהִי מִקֵּץ יָמִים וַיָּבֵא קַיִן מִפְּרִי הָאֲדָמָה. מִקֵּץ יָמִים, וְלָא מִקֵּץ יָמִין. אִיהוּ דָּחָה לְקֵץ יָמִין, וְאִתְקְרִיב לְקֵץ יָמִים. וְהָא

אוֹקִימְנָא, וְאַתָּה לֵךְ לְקֵץ. וְאָמַר דָּנִיאֵל, לְאָן קֵץ, לְקֵץ הַיָּמִין, אוֹ לְקֵץ הַיָּמִים. עַד דא״ל לְקֵץ הַיָּמִין. וע״ד דָּוִד דָּחִיל וְאָמַר, הוֹדִיעֵנִי יְיָ׳ קִצִּי וּמִדַּת יָמַי מַה הִיא, אוֹ לְקֵץ הַיָּמִים אוֹ לְקֵץ הַיָּמִין. וְהָכָא מַה כְּתִיב וַיְהִי מִקֵּץ יָמִים, וְלֹא מִקֵּץ יָמִין, ובג״כ לָא אִתְקַבַּל קָרְבָּנֵיהּ, דְּהָא מִסִּטְרָא אַחֲרָא הֲוָה.

31. He opened the discussion, saying: "And in process of time it came to pass (lit. 'at the end of days'; Heb. *yamim*) that Cain brought of the fruit of the ground" (Beresheet 4:3). It is written "the end of *yamim*" and not 'the end of right (Heb. *yamin*). "THE END OF DAYS" IS THE OTHER SIDE AND THE END OF RIGHT IS HOLINESS, since he rejected 'the end of right' but came near 'the end of days'. And we explained, THAT IT IS WRITTEN: "But go you your way till the end be" (Daniel 12:13), and Daniel said, "To which end" – if to "the end of right" or to "the end of days"? The HOLY ONE, BLESSED BE HE, said to him, "to the end of right," WHICH IS IN HOLINESS. This is what David feared and said, "Hashem, make me know my end, and the measure of my days, what it is" (Tehilim 39:4), MEANING either "the end of days" or "the end of right." And here is it written: "at the end of days," WHICH PERTAINS TO THE OTHER SIDE and not 'the end of right', WHICH IS IN HOLINESS. Therefore his offering was not accepted, because it was from the Other Side.

32 ת״ח, מַה כְּתִיב וְהֶבֶל הֵבִיא גַּם הוּא. מַאי גַּם הוּא. לְאַסְגָּאָה דָּא בְּדָא, קָרְבָּנֵיהּ לְקוּדְשָׁא בְּרִיךְ הוּא הֲוָה כֹּלָּא, וְעִקָּרָא דְּקָרְבְּנָא לקב״ה, וְיָהַב חוּלָקָא לְסִטְרָא אַחֲרָא, כד״א וּמֵחֶלְבֵיהֶן. וְקַיִן, עִקָּרָא עָבֵד מִקֵּץ יָמִים, רָזָא דְּסִטְרָא אַחֲרָא, וְיָהִיב חוּלָקָא לְקוּדְשָׁא בְּרִיךְ הוּא, וְעַל דָּא לָא אִתְקַבַּל.

32. Come and behold: "And Abel, he also brought..." (Beresheet 4:4). HE ASKS: What is the meaning of "also"? HE ANSWERS: "Also" is to add one to the other, MEANING THAT HE ALSO BROUGHT SOME TO THE OTHER SIDE, LIKE CAIN. However, his offering was entirely to the Holy One, blessed be He, NAMELY, the main part of the offering was to the Holy One, blessed be He. But he gave a portion to the Other Side, as written: "and of the fat parts thereof" (Ibid.)–WHICH MEANS THAT THE MAIN PART OF THE OFFERING, NAMELY THE FAT PARTS, WAS OFFERED TO HASHEM, AND

HE GAVE THE INFERIOR PART TO THE OTHER SIDE. But Cain made the main part of the offering for the end of days, which is the secret of the Other Side, and only gave a portion to the Holy One, blessed be He. Therefore, it was not accepted.

33. בְּאִיּוֹב מַה כְּתִיב, וְהָלְכוּ בָנָיו וְעָשׂוּ מִשְׁתֶּה וְגוֹ׳, וְשָׁלְחוּ וְקָרְאוּ לִשְׁלֹשֶׁת אַחְיוֹתֵיהֶם לֶאֱכֹל וְלִשְׁתּוֹת עִמָּהֶם וַיְהִי כִּי הִקִּיפוּ יְמֵי הַמִּשְׁתֶּה וְגוֹ׳, וּבְמִשְׁתְּיָא בְּכָל יוֹמָא מְקַטְרְגָא שְׁכִיחַ, וְלָא יָכִיל לֵיהּ. מְנָא לָן. דִּכְתִּיב, הֲלֹא אַתָּה שַׂכְתָּ בַעֲדוֹ וּבְעַד בֵּיתוֹ וּבְעַד כָּל אֲשֶׁר לוֹ מִסָּבִיב וּלְעוֹלָם לָא יָהִיב חוּלָקָא כְּלָל לְגַבֵּיהּ, דְּהָא כְּתִיב וְהֶעֱלָה עוֹלוֹת מִסְפַּר כּוּלָּם. עוֹלָה סַלְקָא לְעֵילָּא, וְלָא יָהִיב חוּלָקָא לְסִטְרָא אַחֲרָא. דְּאִלְמָלֵא יָהַב לֵיהּ חוּלָקָא, לָא יָכִיל לֵיהּ לְבָתַר, וְכָל מַה דְּנָטַל מִדִּילֵיהּ נָטַל.

33. Of Job it is written: "And his sons used to go and feast...and they used to call for their three sisters to eat and drink with them. And when the days of feasting were gone about..." (Iyov 1:4-5). At the feast, the Accuser was present every day, but he could not overcome him. How do we know? Because it is written, "Have You not made a hedge about him, and about his house..." (Ibid. 10). But he never gave a part TO THE OTHER SIDE, because it is written: "And offered burnt offerings according to the number of them all" (Ibid. 5). The burnt offering rises high up and does not give a part to the Other Side. Had he given him a part, THE ADVERSARY would not have been able to overcome him afterwards; and everything that the Satan took from him was his BECAUSE HE DID NOT GIVE THE SATAN A PART OF HIS OFFERINGS.

34. וְאִי תֵּימָא אֲמַאי אַבְאִישׁ לֵיהּ קוּדְשָׁא בְּרִיךְ הוּא. אֶלָּא. דְּאִלְמָלֵא יָהַב לֵיהּ חוּלָקָא, יִפְנֵי אָרְחָא וְיִסְתְּלַק מֵעַל מַקְדְּשָׁא, וְסִטְרָא דִּקְדוּשָּׁה אִסְתְּלִיק לְעֵילָּא. וְאִיהוּ לָא עָבֵד כֵּן, וע״ד קוּדְשָׁא בְּרִיךְ הוּא תָּבַע בְּדִינָא.

34. One may ask why the Holy One, blessed be He, did harm to him, BECAUSE HE DID NOT GIVE A PORTION TO THE SATAN. HE ANSWERS: Had he given a part TO THE OTHER SIDE, it would have cleared the way OF

HOLINESS, BECAUSE THE OTHER SIDE would have gone from the Temple. Then, the Holy Side would have ascended high up. Because he did not do so, the Holy One, blessed be He, demanded justice from him.

35. תָּ"ח, כְּמָה דְּאִיהוּ אִתְפְּרַשׁ, וְלָא אַכְלִיל טוֹב וָרָע, אִיהוּ דָּן לֵיהּ בְּהַהוּא גַּוְונָא, יָהִיב לֵיהּ טוֹב, וּלְבָתַר רָע, וּלְבָתַר אֲהַדְרֵיהּ לְטוֹב. דְּהָכִי אִתְחָזֵי לב"נ, לְמִנְדַּע טוֹב, וּלְמִנְדַּע רַע, וּלְאַהְדְּרָא גַּרְמֵיהּ לְטוֹב, וְדָא אִיהוּ רָזָא דִּמְהֵימָנוּתָא. ת"ח, אִיּוֹב מֵעַבְדֵי פַּרְעֹה הֲוָה, וְדָא הוּא דִּכְתִּיב בֵּיהּ, הַיָּרֵא אֶת דְּבַר יְיָ' מֵעַבְדֵי פַּרְעֹה.

35. Come and behold: In the same way that he separated and did not combine good and evil – IN THAT HE DID NOT GIVE A PART TO THE OTHER SIDE SO AS TO PURIFY HOLINESS, AS MENTIONED EARLIER – He judged him, first giving him good and afterwards bad; then, He again established him in goodness. This is proper for a person, to know good and know evil, and to return himself to good. This is the secret of the Faith, WHICH IS THE NUKVA. Come and behold: Job was one of the servants of Pharaoh, as indicated by the verse: "He that feared the word of Hashem among the servants of Pharaoh" (Shemot 9:20).

3. The crocodiles

A Synopsis

Rabbi Shimon speaks about "Behold, I am against you, Pharaoh, king of Egypt, the great crocodile that couches in the midst of his streams." He explains that God brought Moses into the innermost rooms to see the secret of the great crocodile, from where many levels evolve and descend. As Moses was afraid, God had to wage war with the crocodile Himself. Rabbi Shimon turns to, "And Elohim created the great crocodiles (Heb. *taninim*) and every living soul that crawls the waters swarmed forth according to their kinds." He says that the crocodiles are the Levyatan and his spouse. God killed the female, leaving only the male – otherwise the world could not have survived. "The streams" in the scripture are the nine rivers that he lies in, corresponding to the nine Sfirot. The crocodile comes into the river Keter whose waters are serene and quiet, which strengthens the river. Rabbi Shimon describes the rise and flow of the rivers, the emergence of the ten rivers including Keter, and the nine crocodiles, one in each river. There is a long description of the implications of the correspondence between the ten crocodiles and the ten acts of creation in Beresheet. The grasses beside the rivers are explained to be the light that sprouts from the sowing of the confined hidden light. Rabbi Shimon says that "And Elohim said, 'Let there be luminaries in the firmaments of the heavens'" refers to the Piercing Serpent that tempted Eve. Since this serpent is on dry land it always triumphs when it battles the crocodile that is in the water.

36. אָמַר רִבִּי שִׁמְעוֹן, הַשְׁתָּא אִית לְגַלָּאָה רָזִין, דְּאִינּוּן מִתְדַּבְּקִין לְעֵילָּא וְתַתָּא, מַה כְּתִיב בֹּא אֶל פַּרְעֹה, לֵךְ אֶל פַּרְעֹה מִבָּעֵי לֵיהּ, מַאי בֹּא. אֶלָּא, דְּעָיֵיל לֵיהּ קוּדְשָׁא בְּרִיךְ הוּא, אִדָּרִין בָּתַר אִדָּרִין, לְגַבֵּי תַּנִּינָא חֲדָא עִלָּאָה תַּקִּיפָא, דְּכַמָּה דַּרְגִּין מִשְׁתַּלְשְׁלִין מִנֵּיהּ. וּמַאן אִיהוּ. רָזָא דְּהַתַּנִּין הַגָּדוֹל.

36. Rabbi Shimon said: Now it is proper to reveal secrets that are attached above and below. It is written: "Come to Pharaoh," but it should have said 'Go to Pharaoh'. What is the meaning of "Come"? HE ANSWERS: He brought MOSES in to the innermost rooms, to a very powerful crocodile, from which many levels evolve and come down. And what was it? It was the secret of the great serpent.

37. וּמֹשֶׁה דָּחִיל מִנֵּיהּ, וְלָא קָרִיב אֶלָּא לְגַבֵּי אִינּוּן יְאוֹרִין, וְאִינּוּן דַּרְגִּין דִּילֵיהּ, אֲבָל לְגַבֵּיהּ דָּחִיל וְלָא קָרִיב, בְּגִין דְּחָמָא לֵיהּ מִשְׁתָּרֵשׁ בְּשָׁרָשִׁין עִלָּאִין.

37. Moses was afraid and approached only the rivers that were at his grade. But he feared THE SERPENT itself, and did not approach because he saw that it was rooted in high sources.

38. כֵּיוָן דְּחָמָא קוּדְשָׁא בְּרִיךְ הוּא דְּדָחִיל מֹשֶׁה, וּשְׁלִיחָן מְמָנָן אַחֲרָנִין לְעֵילָּא, לָא יַכְלִין לְקָרְבָא לְגַבֵּיהּ. אֲמַר קוּדְשָׁא בְּרִיךְ הוּא, הִנְנִי עָלֶיךָ פַּרְעֹה מֶלֶךְ מִצְרַיִם הַתַּנִּים הַגָּדוֹל הָרוֹבֵץ בְּתוֹךְ יְאוֹרָיו. וְקוּדְשָׁא בְּרִיךְ הוּא אִצְטְרִיךְ לְאַגָּחָא בֵּיהּ קְרָבָא, וְלֹא אַחֲרָא. כְּמָה דְּאַתְּ אָמַר, אֲנִי ה׳, וְאוּקְמוּהָ רָזָא דְּחָכְמְתָא דְּהַתַּנִּים הַגָּדוֹל הָרוֹבֵץ בְּתוֹךְ יְאוֹרָיו לְאִינּוּן מָארֵי מִדִּין, דְּיַדְעִין בְּרָזִין דְּמָארֵיהוֹן.

38. When the Holy One, blessed be He, saw that Moses was afraid and that other appointed messengers above could not approach him, the Holy One, blessed be He, said: "Behold, I am against you, Pharaoh, king of Egypt, the great crocodile that couches in the midst of his streams" (Yechezkel 29:3). The Holy One, blessed be He, had to wage war with him and no other. He said, "I am Hashem." WE INTERPRET THIS TO MEAN I AND NOT A MESSENGER. They explained the secret of the wisdom of, "the great crocodile that couches in the midst of his streams," to those scholars of jurisprudence, who recognize the secret of their Master.

39. פָּתַח ר״ש וְאָמַר, וַיִּבְרָא אֱלֹהִים אֶת הַתַּנִּינִם הַגְּדוֹלִים וְאֵת כָּל נֶפֶשׁ הַחַיָּה הָרוֹמֶשֶׂת אֲשֶׁר שָׁרְצוּ הַמַּיִם לְמִינֵיהֶם. הַאי קְרָא אוּקְמוּהָ לֵיהּ. אֲבָל וַיִּבְרָא אֱלֹהִים אֶת הַתַּנִּינִים הוּא רָזָא דָּא לִוְיָתָן וּבַת זוּגוֹ. תַּנִּינִם חָסֵר כְּתִיב, בְּגִין דְּקָטַל לְנוּקְבָא, וְסַלְּקָא קוּדְשָׁא בְּרִיךְ הוּא לְצַדִּיקַיָּא. וְאוּקְמוּהָ.

39. Rabbi Shimon opened the discussion, saying: "And Elohim created the great crocodiles (Heb. *taninim*), and every living creature that moves, which the waters brought forth abundantly after their kind" (Beresheet 1:21). This passage was explained. Yet "And Elohim created the crocodiles," is a secret. It is the Leviathan and his spouse. "*Taninim*" is spelled without the *Yud* because the Holy One, blessed be He, killed the female and brought her up for the Righteous, as it was explained. THEREFORE, ONLY THE ONE GREAT CROCODILE (*TANIN*) REMAINED. AND KNOW THAT THE LEVIATHAN IS A KOSHER FISH, AS OUR SAGES SAY.

40. הַתַּנִּים הַגָּדוֹל, תֵּשַׁע יְאוֹרִין אִינּוּן, דְּאִיהוּ רָבִיץ בֵּינַיְיהוּ, וְחַד יְאוֹרָא אִיהוּ, דְּמֵימָיו שְׁכִיכִין, וּבִרְכָאן דְּמֵימִין דְּגִנְתָּא, נַפְלִין בֵּיהּ תְּלַת זִמְנִין בְּשַׁתָּא. וְכַד תְּרֵין זִמְנִין, מִתְבָּרֵךְ הַהוּא יְאוֹרָא וְלֹא כ"כ, וְכַד חַד לָאו הָכִי.

40. The great crocodile IS THE MALE LEVIATHAN THAT REMAINED ALIVE. IT IS SAID ABOUT HIM, "THAT COUCHES IN THE MIDST OF HIS STREAMS." There are nine rivers that he lies in, CORRESPONDING TO NINE SFIROT: CHOCHMAH, BINAH, DA'AT, CHESED, GVURAH, TIFERET, NETZACH, HOD AND YESOD. And there is one river whose waters are quiet. THIS IS KETER. The blessings of the waters of the Garden, WHICH IS MALCHUT OF ATZILUT, pour into it three times a year. THIS IS THE SECRET OF THE THREE COLUMNS – RIGHT, LEFT AND CENTRAL, OF WHICH IT IS SAID, "THREE TIMES A YEAR SHALL ALL YOUR MALES APPEAR" (DEVARIM 16:16). If they pour in twice, MEANING ONLY TWO COLUMNS, RIGHT AND LEFT, the river is blessed, but not as much BECAUSE THE CENTRAL COLUMN IS MISSING. If only one pours in, MEANING EITHER ONLY THE RIGHT OR ONLY THE LEFT, it is not BLESSED BY IT. THE NINE RIVERS, THE LOWER NINE SFIROT, RECEIVE FROM THE RIVER, WHICH IS KETER.

41. וְהַאי תַּנִּינָא, עָאל בְּהַהוּא יְאוֹרָא, אִתְתָּקִיף וְאָזִיל וְשָׁאט עָאל גּוֹ יַמָּא, וּבָלַע נוּנִין לְכַמָּה זִינִין, וְשָׁלִיט, וְתָב לְהַהוּא יְאוֹרָא. אִלֵּין תִּשְׁעָה יְאוֹרִין אַזְלִין וְסַלְּקִין וְסַחֲרָנֵיהּ כַּמָּה אִלֵּין וַעֲשָׂבִין לְזִנַיְיהוּ, יְאוֹרָא קַדְמָאָה.

41. This crocodile comes into that river, WHICH IS KETER OF THE RIVERS, becomes strengthened by it, continues to swim and enters into the sea, WHICH IS MALCHUT OF ATZILUT, where it swallows many kinds of fish and rules. THESE ARE LEVELS IN THE SEA THAT ARE INFERIOR TO HIM;

HE SWALLOWS THEM AND THEY BECOME PERFECTED IN HIM. He returns to that QUIET river, and these nine rivers continue to rise TO HIM, MEANING TO RECEIVE THEIR SUSTENANCE, BECAUSE THEY RECEIVE THEIR SUSTENANCE FROM THE QUIET RIVER, WHICH IS THEIR KETER. There are various kinds of trees and vegetation around THE RIVER. It is the first river AMONG THE RIVERS, NAMELY KETER.

42. נָפְקָא מִסִּטְרָא שְׂמָאלָא, בְּחַד צִנּוֹרָא דְּנָגִיד וְנָפִיק, תְּלַת טִפִּין, וְכָל טִפָּה וְטִפָּה אִתְפְּרַשׁ לִתְלַת טִפִּין, וְכָל טִפָּה וְטִפָּה אִתְעָבֵיד מִנֵּיהּ יְאוֹרָא חַד, וְאִלֵּין אִינּוּן תִּשְׁעָה יְאוֹרִין, דְּמִתְתָּקְפִין וְאַזְלִין וְשָׁטָאן וְסָחֲרָן בְּכָל אִינּוּן רְקִיעִין.

42. AND NOW HE EXPLAINS THE SYSTEM OF THE EMERGENCE OF THE TEN RIVERS. Three drops emerge from the left side, from one conduit that is drawn and emerges, THAT IS, YESOD OF ZEIR ANPIN. THEY ARE FROM THE THREE COLUMNS – RIGHT, LEFT, AND CENTRAL–INCLUDED IN THE LEFT COLUMN. Every drop spreads into three drops AND THEY BECOME NINE DROPS. One river is formed from each separate drop. These are the nine rivers that grow strong and continue to flow and encircle all the firmaments.

43. מִמַּה דְּאִשְׁתְּאַר מֵאִינּוּן טִפִּין כַּד סַיְימִין לְמֵיפַק, אִשְׁתְּאַר טִפָּה חֲדָא, דְּנָפְקָא בִּשְׁכִיכוּ, נָפַל בֵּינַיְיהוּ, וְאִתְעָבֵיד מִנֵּיהּ יְאוֹרָא חֲדָא. הַאי יְאוֹרָא אִיהוּ, הַהוּא דְּאַמָרָן דְּאַזְלָא בִּשְׁכִיכוּ.

43. After these drops finish coming out, of those that remain, NAMELY ALL THE ASPECTS OF KETER AND CHOCHMAH THAT ARE ABOVE BINAH THAT ARE NOT DRAWN THROUGH THE THREE COLUMNS, THERE remains one drop. It emerges silently and falls AMONG THE RIVERS. And from it, one river is formed. This is the river that we said flows silently, NAMELY THE QUIET RIVER MENTIONED ABOVE.

44. הַאי יְאוֹרָא, כַּד הַהוּא נָהָר דְּנָגִיד וְנָפִיק, אַפִּיק טִפִּין אַחֲרָנִין דְּבִרְכָּאן, מִסִּטְרָא דִּימִינָא, מַה דְּאִשְׁתְּאַר מֵאִינּוּן טִפִּין, אִשְׁתְּאַר טִפָּה חֲדָא בִּשְׁכִיכוּ מֵאִינּוּן בִּרְכָּאן, וְנָפַל בְּהַהוּא יְאוֹרָא דְּאִיהוּ שָׁכִיךְ. וְהַאי

אִיהוּ יְאוֹרָא דְּעָדִיף מִכֻּלְּהוּ.

44. The stream that comes out and flows, YESOD IN ZEIR ANPIN, pours out other drops of blessings from the right side, THAT IS, WHEN IT BESTOWS UPON MALCHUT FROM THE THREE COLUMNS THAT ARE INCLUDED IN THE RIGHT COLUMN. FROM WHATEVER WAS LEFT OF THESE DROPS AND DID NOT EMERGE WITH THEM AT THE TIME, NAMELY THOSE SFIROT ABOVE BINAH THAT ARE NOT DRAWN WITH THE THREE COLUMNS AS MENTIONED, there remains one drop from these blessings that EMERGES SILENTLY AND falls into that quiet river. THUS THE QUIET RIVER ALSO HAS THE ILLUMINATION OF THE RIGHT. This is the best river.

45. כַּד נָפְקִין וּמִתְפָּרְשָׁן אִינּוּן אַרְבַּע נַהֲרִין דְּנָפְקִין מִגִּנְתָּא דְּעֵדֶן, הַהוּא דְּאִקְרֵי פִּישׁוֹן, נָפִיל בְּהַהוּא יְאוֹרָא וְאִתְכְּלִיל בֵּיהּ. וע״ד מַלְכוּת בָּבֶל, אִתְכְּלִיל בְּהַאי. וּפִישׁוֹן אִיהוּ מַלְכוּת בָּבֶל. מִיְאוֹרָא דָּא אִתְזָנוּ וְאִתְמַלְיָין כָּל אִינּוּן יְאוֹרִין אַחֲרָנִין.

45. When these four rivers that emerge from the Garden of Eden separate, that river called Pishon falls into the QUIET river and merges with it. Therefore, the Kingdom of Babylon is associated with this RIVER, for Pishon is the Kingdom of Babylon. BECAUSE PISHON IS THE FIRST STREAM OF THE FOUR RIVERS AND BABYLON IS THE FIRST OF THE FOUR EMPIRES, OF WHICH IT IS SAID: "YOU ARE THE HEAD OF GOLD" (DANIEL 2:38), AND THEREFORE PISHON IS BABYLON. From this QUIET river, all the other rivers are sustained and filled.

46. בְּכָל יְאוֹרָא וִיאוֹרָא, אַזְלָא וְשָׁאט חַד תַּנִּינָא, וְאִינּוּן תֵּשַׁע. וְכָל חַד וְחַד נָקִיב נוּקְבָא בְּרֵישֵׁיהּ, כד״א, שִׁבַּרְתָּ רָאשֵׁי תַנִּינִים וְגוֹ׳. וַאֲפִילּוּ הַאי הַתַּנִּין הַגָּדוֹל הָכִי הוּא, בְּגִין דְּכֻלְּהוּ נַפְחִין רוּחִין לְגַבֵּי עֵילָּא וְלֹא לְתַתָּא.

46. In each river, one crocodile swims. Thus there are nine crocodiles. Each has a hole punctured in his head, as is written: "You broke the heads of the sea monsters in the water" (Tehilim 74:13). And even this great sea monster is so, because they all blow air upwards and not downwards.

47. כְּתִיב בְּרֵאשִׁית בָּרָא אֱלֹהִים. וּכְתִיב וַיִּבְרָא אֱלֹהִים אֶת הַתַּנִּינִים הַגְּדוֹלִים, בְּכָל עוֹבָדָא דְּאִינּוּן עֶשֶׂר אֲמִירָן, קַיְימִין לָקֳבְלַיְיהוּ אִינּוּן עֶשֶׂר יְאוֹרִין. וְחַד תַּנִּינָא מִתְרַפְרְפָא בְּרוּחָא, לָקֳבֵל כָּל חַד וְחַד.

47. It is written: "In the beginning Elohim created" (Beresheet 1:1), and also: "And Elohim created the great crocodiles" (Ibid. 21). IN BOTH CASES IT IS WRITTEN, "CREATED." THIS TEACH US that for every action of the ten sayings IN THE WORKS OF CREATION, there are ten rivers, and one crocodile blows wind against each of them. THIS MEANS THAT ONE CROCODILE FOR EACH OF THE TEN RIVERS BLOWS WIND AGAINST THE ACT CORRESPONDING TO HIM OF THE TEN SAYINGS OF CREATION.

48. וְעַל דָּא, חַד לְשַׁבְעִין שְׁנִין מִזְדַּעְזָע עָלְמָא, בְּגִין דְּהַאי הַתַּנִּין הַגָּדוֹל כַּד הוּא סָלִיק סְנַפִּירוֹי וְאִזְדַּעְזַע, כְּדֵין כֻּלְּהוּ מִזְדַּעְזְעָן בְּאִינּוּן יְאוֹרִין, וְכָל עָלְמָא מִזְדַּעְזְעָא, וְאַרְעָא מִתְחַלְחֲלָת, וְכֻלְּהוּ כְּלִילָן בְּהַאי תַּנִּין הַגָּדוֹל.

48. Therefore, the world shakes once in seventy years, since everything in the river shakes WHEN this great crocodile raises his fins and shakes. The whole world shudders and the earth trembles, for they are all included in this great crocodile.

49. וְהָאָרֶץ הָיְתָה תוֹהוּ וְגוֹ', אָמַר רִבִּי שִׁמְעוֹן, עוֹבָדָא דִּבְרֵאשִׁית, חַבְרַיָּא לָעָאן בֵּיהּ, וְיַדְעִין בֵּיהּ, אֲבָל זְעִירִין אִינּוּן, דְּיַדְעִין לְרַמְזָא עוֹבָדָא דִּבְרֵאשִׁית, בְּרָזָא דְּתַנִּין הַגָּדוֹל. וע"ד תָּנֵינָן, דְּכָל עָלְמָא לָא מִשְׁתַּלְשְׁלָא אֶלָּא עַל סְנַפִּירוֹי דְּדָא.

49. "And the earth was without form" (Ibid. 2). Rabbi Shimon said: The friends are familiar and are occupied with the works of Creation. But few know the works of Creation as alluding to the great crocodile. We learned that the whole world evolves AND COMES from the fin OF THE GREAT CROCODILE. THEREFORE, WE MUST UNDERSTAND HOW HE IS ALLUDED TO THROUGHTOUT THE WORKS OF CREATION.

50. ת"ח וְהָאָרֶץ הָיְתָה תֹהוּ וָבֹהוּ וְגוֹ', תָּנֵינָן הָיְתָה, וְאוֹקִימְנָא. בְּגִין

דִּבְהַאי יְאוֹרָא קַדְמָאָה דְּקָאמְרָן, כַּד הַאי הַתַּנִּין הַגָּדוֹל עָאל בֵּיהּ, כְּדֵין אִתְמַלְיָיא, וְשָׁאטֵי וְדָעִיךְ נִיצוֹצִין דְּאִתְלְקָטוּ בְּאִינּוּן עָלְמִין דְּאִתְחֲרָבוּ בְּקַדְמֵיתָא.

50. Come and behold: IT IS WRITTEN, "And the earth was without form and void..." We learned that it "was" EARLIER; NAMELY, IT WAS FORMLESS BEFORE THE CORRECTION BEGAN, and it has been explained. When the great crocodile enters that first river, NAMELY THE QUIET RIVER, it becomes full. It swims and extinguishes the sparks that were gathered in from the worlds that were destroyed earlier.

51. אִינּוּן תַּנִּינִין אַחֲרָנִין דְּקָאמְרָן, הֲווֹ וְלָא הֲווֹ, אֲמַאי. בְּגִין דְּאִתְחֲלָשׁ חֵילַיְיהוּ דְּלָא יְשַׁשְׁטְשׁוּן עָלְמָא, בַּר לְשַׁבְעִין שְׁנִין, חַד זִמְנָא, וְאִינּוּן אִתְתְּקָפוּ בְּחֵילָא דְּהַהוּא תַּנִּין הַגָּדוֹל, וְהַאי אִיהוּ בִּלְחוֹדוֹי לְאִתַּתְקְפָא. וְאִלְמָלֵא נוּקְבֵיהּ קַיְּימַת לְגַבֵּיהּ, לָא יָכִיל עָלְמָא לְמִסְבַּל לוֹן.

51. Those other crocodiles that we mentioned were and were not, FOR THEIR ILLUMINATION WAS NOT REVEALED IN THEM, SO IT IS AS THOUGH THEY DID NOT EXIST. THIS IS SO, because their strength was weakened so they would not destroy the world, except once every seventy years, when they grow strong with the power of that great crocodile, which alone grows strong. If his female had been alive with him, the world would not have survived them.

52. עַד לָא קָטַל קב"ה לְנוּקְבָא, הָאָרֶץ הָיְתָה תֹהוּ. תֹהוּ הָיְתָה. וּלְבָתַר דְּקָטַל לָהּ, הֲוָה בֹּהוּ, שָׁרָאת לְאִתְקַיְּימָא. וְחֹשֶׁךְ עַל. עַד לָא הֲוַת נְהִירָא עוֹבָדָא דְּעָבֵד.

52. Until the Holy One, blessed be He, killed the female OF THE LEVIATHAN, the earth was without form. It was formless and THE EARTH was void after He slew her, WHICH MEANS THE EARTH started to be sustained: "And darkness was ON THE FACE OF THE DEEP" (Beresheet 1:2). It still had not illuminated DUE TO THE ACTION THAT HE PERFORMED.

53. מֶה עָבֵיד קוּדְשָׁא בְּרִיךְ הוּא, מָחַץ רֵישֵׁיהּ דִּדְכוּרָא לְעֵילָּא, וְאִתְכַּפְיָא, בְּגִין דְּהָא תְּהוֹמָא לְתַתָּא, לָא הֲוָה נָהִיר. מ"ט לָא הֲוָה נָהִיר, בְּגִין דְּהַאי הַתַּנִּין הַגָּדוֹל, הֲוָה נָשִׁיב רוּחָא עַל תְּהוֹמָא, וְאַחְשִׁיךְ לֵיהּ, וְלָא מְרַפְרְפָא לְתַתָּא.

53. What did the Holy One, blessed be He, do? He crushed the head of the male OF THE GREAT CROCODILES. AND THE CROCODILE was subdued because the deep below did not illuminate. HE ASKS: What is the reason that it did not illuminate? HE ANSWERS: Because this great crocodile blew wind over the deep, darkened it, and it did not hover below.

54. וְעָבַר רוּחָא אַחֲרָא דִּלְעֵילָּא, וְנָשַׁב וּבָטַשׁ בְּהַהוּא רוּחָא, וְשָׁכִיךְ לֵיהּ, הֲדָא הוּא דִּכְתִּיב וְרוּחַ אֱלֹהִים מְרַחֶפֶת עַל פְּנֵי הַמָּיִם. וְהַיְינוּ דְּתָנֵינָן, דְּקוּדְשָׁא בְּרִיךְ הוּא בָּטַשׁ רוּחָא בְּרוּחָא, וּבָרָא עָלְמָא.

54. Then another wind from above crossed, blew and struck that wind and placated it, FOR IT NEUTRALIZED IT. That is what is written: "And a wind from Elohim moved over the surface of the water" (Beresheet 1:2). So we learned that the Holy One, blessed be He, struck one wind with another and created the world.

55. וַיֹּאמֶר אֱלֹהִים יְהִי אוֹר וַיְהִי אוֹר, נָהִיר נְהִירוּ דִּלְעֵילָּא, וּבָטַשׁ עַל גַּבֵּי רוּחָא דְּנָשִׁיב, וְאִסְתַּלָּק מֵעַל תְּהוֹמָא, וְלָא חָפָא לֵיהּ. כֵּיוָן דִּתְהוֹמָא אִתְנְהִיר, וְאִיהוּ אִסְתַּלָּק, כְּדֵין הֲוָה נְהִירוּ.

55. "And Elohim said, 'Let there be light.' And there was light" (Ibid. 3), because the Supernal Light illuminated and struck on the blowing wind and it was removed from over the deep and did not cover it. As soon as the deep was lit up and the wind left, it became light, AS IS WRITTEN: "AND THERE WAS LIGHT."

56. דָּא נָהִיר עַל רֵישֵׁיהּ, וּמַיָּא הֲווֹ נַפְקֵי מִגּוֹ אֲפוּתֵיהּ, וְרוּחָא נָשִׁיב לְעֵילָּא. וְנָהִיר מִנְּהִירוּ דָּא, עַד דַּהֲוָה נָחִית נְהוֹרֵיהּ, מְנַצְנְצָא לְשַׁבְעִין וּתְרֵין נְהוֹרִין דְּשִׁמְשָׁא, כֵּיוָן דְּאִינּוּן נְהוֹרִין אִתְרְשִׁימוּ בְּגוֹ שִׁמְשָׁא לְתַתָּא, הֲווֹ חַיָּיבַיָּא דְּעָלְמָא יַדְעִין בְּהוּ, וַהֲווֹ פַּלְחִין לְשִׁמְשָׁא. כֵּיוָן

דְּאִסְתַּכַּל קוּדְשָׁא בְּרִיךְ הוּא בְּאִינּוּן חַיָּיבַיָּא, סָלִיק נְהוֹרֵיהּ וְגָנִיז לֵיהּ אֲמַאי גָּנִיז לֵיהּ. בְּגִין דְּהַהוּא תַּנִּין, הֲוָה סָלִיק וְנָחִית, וּבָטַשׁ בְּאִינּוּן יְאוֹרִין, עַד דְּגָנַז לֵיהּ וְלָא אִתְגַּלְיָא.

56. This light shone over the head OF THE GREAT CROCODILE. Water flowed from its nostrils TO SUSTAIN THE OTHER LEVELS, and wind blew up. AND HE EXPLAINS WHY THE WATER FLOWED OUT, AND WIND BLEW ABOVE, SAYING THAT THIS IS BECAUSE BEFOREHAND, this COMPLETE luminary illuminated until the light descended FROM BINAH and sparkled to the 72 lights of the Sun, WHICH IS ZEIR ANPIN. Since these lights were impressed in the sun below, wicked people in the world knew of them and worshipped the sun, MEANING THEY WORSHIPPED TO DRAW THE LIGHT FROM ABOVE DOWNWARDS. When the Holy One, blessed be He, observed that these wicked WANTED TO DRAW THE LIGHT FROM ABOVE DOWNWARDS, He raised the Light and concealed it. Why did He conceal it BECAUSE OF THE ACTIONS OF THE WICKED? For this crocodile was ascending and descending, AND ALSO DREW THE LIGHT FROM ABOVE DOWNWARDS BECAUSE OF THE ACTIONS OF THE WICKED, and struck these rivers, until He hid the Light and it was no longer visible.

57 וְזָרַע לֵיהּ זְרוּעָא בְּחַד צַדִּיק, דְּאִיהוּ גַּנָּנָא דְּגִנְתָּא, וּזְרוּעָא דְּזָרַע בְּגִנְתָּא, בִּגְנִיזוּ בִּטְמִירוּ דְּהַאי אוֹר אִיהוּ.

57. And He sowed that seed through one Righteous, WHICH IS YESOD OF ZEIR ANPIN, who is the Gardener of the Garden. The seed sown in the Garden, WHICH IS MALCHUT, is the storing and concealing of this Light – MEANING THAT CONCEALMENT DOES NOT CONNOTE ABSENCE, BUT RATHER THE OPPOSITE. IT IS THE ASPECT OF THE SEED PLANTED FOR THE UPCOMING BLESSING, AS THE CONCEALMENT ITSELF WILL BECOME LIGHT AGAIN, LIKE A PLANT THAT COMES FORTH FROM A SEED.

58. כַּד הַאי הַתַּנִּין הַגָּדוֹל, חָמֵי דְּצָמַח בְּגִנְתָּא זְרוּעָא דְּאוֹר דָּא, כְּדֵין אִתְּעַר לְסִטְרָא אָחֳרָא, לְהַהוּא נָהָר דְּאִקְרֵי גִּיחוֹן. וְאִתְפְּלָגוּ מֵימוֹי דְּהַאי גִּיחוֹן, חַד שְׁבִילָא דִּילֵיהּ, אִיהוּ אָזִיל גּוֹ הַהוּא זְרוּעָא דְּאַצְמְחָא גּוֹ גִּנְתָּא, וְאַנְהִיר בֵּיהּ בְּרִבּוּ דִּזְרוּעָא דָּא, וְאִקְרֵי גִּיחוֹן.

58. When this great crocodile saw that the seed of this Light grew in the garden, WHICH IS MALCHUT, he awakened to provide for the second side, the SECOND river OF THE FOUR RIVERS called Gichon. And then the waters of the River Gichon were divided BY one path OF THE CROCODILE, FOR THE REASON THAT WILL BE EXPLAINED FURTHER AHEAD. THE CROCODILE goes to the seed that has sprouted AND HAS BECOME LIGHT in the Garden, WHICH IS MALCHUT, AND RECEIVES IT and illuminates upon THE RIVER with THE LIGHT OF the greatness of this seed, and it is called 'Gichon'.

59. וּמִגּוֹ הַהוּא רְבוּ דִּזְרוּעָא דָּא, אִסְתְּלַק לִרְבוּ דִּשְׁלֹמֹה מַלְכָּא, כַּד אִסְתְּלַק לְמַלְכוּ, דִּכְתִּיב וְהוֹרַדְתֶּם אוֹתוֹ אֶל גִּיחוֹן, וּכְתִיב וּמָשַׁח אוֹתוֹ שָׁם. שָׁם, וְלֹא בַּאֲתַר אַחֲרָא, בְּגִין דַּהֲוָה יָדַע דָּוִד מַלְכָּא דָּא, וּמֵימוֹי אַחֲרָנִין אִסְתְּלָקוּ לְמַלְכוּ אַחֲרָא, וְדָא אִיהוּ מַלְכָּא דְּאִיהוּ תַּקִּיפָא.

59. And from that greatness of this seed, King Solomon rose to greatness when he rose to kingship, as written: "And bring him down to Gichon…anoint him there" (I Melachim 1:33-34). Bring him "there" and not to a different place, because King David knew that other waters rise to a different kingdom, and THIS MALCHUT FROM GICHON is a stronger kingdom.

60. וְהַאי הַתַּנִּין הַגָּדוֹל, אִתְּעַר לֵיהּ, וְאִסְתַּלָּק סְנַפִּירוֹי דְּהַאי תַּנִּין, בְּהַהוּא נָהָר, לְאִתַּתְקְפָא בֵּיהּ. וְכָל אִינּוּן שְׁאַר יְאוֹרִין כֻּלְּהוּ, סַלְּקִין וְנַחְתִּין בְּתֻקְפָּא דְּהַאי הַתַּנִּין הַגָּדוֹל, וְתָאַב וְעָאל לְהַהוּא יְאוֹרָא שְׁכִיכָא, וְאִשְׁתְּכַךְ בֵּיהּ.

60. This great crocodile became aroused toward it, THE RIVER GICHON, TO SUSTAIN IT. The fins of this crocodile, WHICH ARE HIS MALCHUT, were elevated in that river, GICHON, and grew stronger in it. And all the other rivers ascended and descended by means of the great crocodile. AFTER SHINING ON THE RIVER GICHON, he again entered that quiet river and became quiet in it.

61. וּכְדֵין, כַּד הַהוּא אוֹר אִתְגְּנִיז לְעִיוּלָא לֵיהּ הַהוּא גִּנְּתָא דְּקָאמְרָן, כְּדֵין נָפַק חֹשֶׁךְ קַדְמָאָה, וּבָטַשׁ עַל רֵישֵׁיהּ, בְּהַהוּא נוּקְבָּא דְּאִתְמַתְּחָא

בֵּיהּ, וְאִתְפָּרַשׁ חַד חוּטָא, בֵּין הַהוּא נְהִירוּ דְּאוֹר דָּא דְּאִתְגְּנִיז, וּבֵין הַהוּא חֲשׁוֹכָא דְּחֹשֶׁךְ דָּא, דִּכְתִּיב, וַיַּבְדֵּל אֱלֹהִים בֵּין הָאוֹר וּבֵין הַחֹשֶׁךְ.

61. When that Light was concealed above the Gardener, the original darkness, FROM BEFORE THE LIGHT EMERGED, came out and hit the head of the crocodile on the hole that was made there. A thread was spread between that illumination THAT REMAINED from this Light that was concealed and the dimness of this darkness, as is written: "And Elohim divided the Light from the Darkness" (Beresheet 1:4).

.62 הַאי תַּנִּין, תָּב בְּהַהוּא פְּרִישׁוּ דְּהַאי חוּטָא דְּאַפְרִישׁ, וְאַפְרִישׁ לְאִינּוּן יְאוֹרִין, גּוֹ חֲשׁוֹכָא, וְאִתְפְּרָשׁוּ נוּנִין לִזְנַיְיהוּ אִלֵּין מֵאִלֵּין, בְּהַהוּא פְּרִישׁוּ.

62. This crocodile, through the division the thread made, again divided ALSO in these rivers above the darkness. The fish separated from each other according to their kinds by that division THAT WAS MADE IN THE RIVERS.

.63 וְכַד אִתְפְּרָשׁוּ מַיִין עִלָּאִין קַדִּישִׁין. כָּל אִינּוּן יְאוֹרִין אִתְפְּרָשׁוּ, וְעָאלוּ לְגוֹ הַהוּא יְאוֹרָא שְׁכִיכָא דְּאִתְבְּרִיר מִכֻּלְּהוּ, וְנָפִיק וְעָאלִין בֵּיהּ תְּלַת זִמְנִין בְּיוֹמָא.

63. When the holy supernal waters were divided, all the rivers were divided and rose into the quiet river, which is the clearest. They go in and out of it three times daily.

.64 וְכָל אִינּוּן נוּנִין דִּמְגַדְּלָן גּוֹ אִינּוּן יְאוֹרִין, פְּרִישָׁן אִלֵּין מֵאִלֵּין, וְאִקְרוּן לֵילוֹת, וְאִלֵּין אִינּוּן רָאשִׁין לְכָל אִינּוּן נוּנִין דְּנָפְקִין לְבַר, וְאִלֵּין שַׁלְטִין עַל כֻּלְּהוּ. וְאִלֵּין אִקְרוּן בְּכוֹרֵי מִצְרַיִם, וּמֵהָכָא אִתְבַּדָּר לְבַר בּוּכְרִין, וְכֻלְּהוּ אִתְזָנוּ מִשַּׁקְיוּ דְּאִינּוּן יְאוֹרִין. וְהַאי הַתַּנִּין הַגָּדוֹל, שַׁלְטָא עַל כֻּלְּהוּ.

64. And all these fish, WHICH ARE GRADES AND SOULS that grow in these rivers, were separated one from another, and are called 'nights', BECAUSE THE GRADES OF THE LEFT ARE CALLED 'NIGHT'. The ones were chief to all the others that emerged outside, and the others INSIDE ruled over everything. These were called 'the Firstborn of Egypt', which have spread from here outside of the firstborn. All these were sustained from the watering of these rivers, and this great crocodile rules all of them.

65. וְכֹלָּא בִּפְרִישׁוּ דְּמַיִין עִלָּאִין, דִּכְתִּיב וַיְהִי מַבְדִּיל בֵּין מַיִם לָמָיִם, וְאִתְרְשִׁימוּ מַיִין קַדִּישִׁין עִלָּאִין, וְאִתְפְּרָשׁוּ לְעֵילָּא, וּמַיִין תַּתָּאִין, אִתְפְּרָשׁוּ כֻּלְּהוּ אִלֵּין מֵאִלֵּין, קַדִּישִׁין וּדְלָא קַדִּישִׁין, וע״ד אִקְרוּן מַלְאָכִין עִלָּאִין פְּרִישָׁן, בְּגִין דְּאִתְפְּרָשׁוּ אִלֵּין מֵאִלֵּין לְזִנַיְיהוּ.

65. All this came about by the division of the upper water FROM THE LOWER, as is written: "And let it divide water from water" (Beresheet 1:6). The holy upper waters were marked and separated to be above, and the lower waters were all separated from those TO BE BELOW. The holy ones WERE DIVIDED from the unholy. Therefore, the upper angels are called 'separate', because the ones were divided from the others according to their kinds.

66. וַיֹּאמֶר אֱלֹהִים תַּדְשֵׁא הָאָרֶץ דֶּשֶׁא עֵשֶׂב מַזְרִיעַ זֶרַע, רָזָא דָא, כַּד הַאי הַתַּנִּין הַגָּדוֹל, הֲוָה נָשִׁיב רוּחָא בְּהַהוּא נוּקְבָא, וּמְרַפְרְפָא לְגַבֵּי עֵילָּא, כָּל אִינּוּן עֲשָׂבִין הֲוָה מְהַפֵּךְ לוֹן לִיבִישׁוּ, עַד דְּרוּחָא אַחֲרָא נָשִׁיב בְּהַהוּא רוּחָא, וְשָׁכִיךְ לֵיהּ לְתַתָּא, וַעֲשָׂבִין צָמְחוּ כְּמִלְקַדְמִין. וְשַׁלְטִין וּמְשַׁבְּחָן וְאוֹדָן קָמֵי קוּדְשָׁא בְּרִיךְ הוּא.

66. "And Elohim said, 'Let the earth bring forth grass, herb yielding seed'" (Beresheet 1:11). THE EARTH IS THE SECRET OF MALCHUT, AND GRASSES ARE THE LIGHT THAT SPROUTS FROM SOWING OF THE TREASURED LIGHT. This is the secret: when the great crocodile would blow wind through the hole IN HIS HEAD that blew upwards, he would dry all these grasses until another wind would blow against that wind OF THE CROCODILE and would quiet him below. And the grasses grew as before, and ruled and praised and offered thanks before the Holy One, blessed be He.

67. מִסְּטַר שְׂמָאלָא, וּלְגוֹ יְאוֹרָא שְׁכִיבָא, נָפְקִין בְּעִירִין לְזִנַיְיהוּ,

וְאַזְלִין לְמִקְרַב לְגַבֵּי דְּאִינּוּן עֲשָׂבִין וְלָא יַכְלִין, וְתָבִין לְאַתְרַיְיהוּ. כָּל אִלֵּין יְאוֹרִין אַזְלִין וְשָׁאטִין, עִם הַהוּא תַּנִּינָא דְּשַׁלְטֵי בְּהוּ, וְסַחֲרִין לְאִינּוּן עֲשָׂבִין, וְלָא יַכְלִין. בַּר לְזִמְנִין, דְּרוּחָא עִלָּאָה לָא נָשִׁיב, וְאִיהוּ מְרַפְרְפָא רוּחָא בְּהַהוּא נוּקְבָּא דִּלְעֵילָּא, כְּמָה דְּאוֹקִימְנָא, כְּדֵין שָׁלִיט הַהוּא רוּחָא עַל אִינּוּן עֲשָׂבִין.

67. From the left side and from within the quiet river, emerge animals according to their species. They attempt to approach these grasses but cannot. They then return to their place. All these rivers swim with that crocodile, which dominates them, and surround these grasses but cannot BENEFIT FROM THEM, except sometimes, when the supernal wind does not blow and THE CROCODILE exhales wind through that hole IN HIS HEAD. That wind then rules over the grasses THAT IS, IT DRIES THEM.

68. וִיאוֹרָא שְׁכִיכָא תָּב לְאַתְרֵיהּ, וְסַלְקָא וְנַחְתָּא. וּבְגִין דְּמֵימוֹי שְׁכִיכִין, אָזִיל בִּשְׁכִיכוּ, וְהַאי הַתַּנִּים הַגָּדוֹל סַלְקָא לְגַבֵּי אִינּוּן יְאוֹרִין, וַעֲשָׂבִין כֻּלְּהוּ מְגַדְּלָן סַחֲרָנֵיהּ דְּהַהוּא יְאוֹרָא שְׁכִיכָא וְאִלֵּין מְגַדְּלִין בְּכָל עִיבָר, כְּדֵין סַלְקָא הַהוּא תַּנִּינָא וְאִתְרַבֵּי בֵּינַיְיהוּ, וְתָב לְכָל אִינּוּן יְאוֹרִין.

68. HE HAS ANOTHER OPPORTUNITY TO APPROACH THE GRASSES, WHEN the quiet river returns FROM MALCHUT to its place, rising and falling. Since its waters are quiet, it flows quietly. The great crocodile rises to these rivers AND IS NOT THERE IN THE QUIET RIVER. All the grasses grow around that quiet river, growing on all sides. Then that Crocodile goes up TO THE GRASSES and grows among them, AND AFTERWARDS returns to all these rivers.

69. וַיֹּאמֶר אֱלֹהִים יְהִי מְאֹרֹת בִּרְקִיעַ הַשָּׁמַיִם, דָּא אִיהוּ נָחָשׁ בָּרִיחַ. אֲמַאי בָּרִיחַ. בְּגִין דְּסָגִיר לִתְרֵין סִטְרִין, וְלָא נָפִיק לְעָלְמִין אֶלָּא חַד זִמְנָא לְיוֹבְלָא.

69. "And Elohim said, 'Let there be luminaries in the firmament of heaven'" (Beresheet 1:16). This refers to the Piercing Serpent (Heb. *bariach*). Why IS

IT CALLED *Bariach* (also: 'bolt')? This is because it locks in both sides, WHICH ARE THE TWO COLUMNS, RIGHT AND LEFT, AND DOES NOT ALLOW THE THIRD COLUMN THAT RECONCILES THEM TO EXPAND. It does not go out to HARM the world except once in a Jubilee.

70. וּבְסִפְרֵי קַדְמָאֵי, דָּא נָחָשׁ עֲקַלָּתוֹן, דְּאִיהוּ בְּעַקִּימוּ תָּדִיר, וְאַיְיתֵי לְוָוטִין עַל עָלְמָא, כַּד הַאי קָם, אִתְּבַר תּוּקְפֵּיהּ דְּהַהוּא תַּנִּינָא, וְלָא יָכִיל לְמֵיקָם, עַד דְּאָבִיד גְּשְׁמֵיהּ. בְּגִין דְּקוּדְשָׁא בְּרִיךְ הוּא כָּפִיף לֵיהּ גּוֹ יַמָּא, כַּד עָאל לְגַבֵּיהּ. וְאִיהוּ דָּרַךְ עַל תֻּקְפֵּיהּ דְּיַמָּא. וְתֻקְפֵּיהּ דְּיַמָּא דָּא, אִיהוּ תַּנִּינָא, כד"א וְדוֹרֵךְ עַל בָּמֳתֵי יָם.

70. In ancient books, THEY SAID ABOUT THE VERSE, "LET THERE BE LUMINARIES," THAT it refers to the Piercing Serpent that always goes crookedly and brought curses on the world, BECAUSE HE ENTICED EVE WITH THE TREE OF KNOWLEDGE OF GOOD AND EVIL. When this one rose, the strength of the GREAT crocodile was broken so that he could not rise, so much so that he lost his body. Because the Holy One, blessed be He, folds him into the sea when he comes to Him, treading upon the strength of the sea. The strength of the sea is the GREAT crocodile, as is written: "And He treads upon the waves of the sea" (Iyov 9:8).

71. וְכַד הַאי נָחָשׁ קָם, כְּדֵין מַה כְּתִיב, וְהָרַג אֶת הַתַּנִּין אֲשֶׁר בַּיָּם, דָּא אִיהוּ הַתַּנִּין הַגָּדוֹל. וע"ד כְּתִיב, הִנְנִי עָלֶיךָ. וְדָא נָחָשׁ, אִיהוּ מְאֹרֹת, בִּלְוָוטִין לְכֹלָּא, בְּגִין דְּאִיהוּ תַּקִּיפָא עָלֵיהּ, בְּתֻקְפֵּיהּ דְּהַהוּא נָהָר רַבְרְבָא, דְּאִקְרֵי חִדֶּקֶל, וְהָא אוֹקִימְנָא.

71. When this serpent rises it is written, "And He shall slay the crocodile that is in the sea" (Yeshayah 27:1), which is the great crocodile. Therefore, it is written: "Behold I am against you... THE GREAT CROCODILE THAT COUCHES IN THE MIDST OF HIS STREAMS" (Yechezkel 29:3). And this snake is 'luminaries (Heb. *me'orot*)' WITHOUT *VAV*, WHICH DENOTES AN EXPRESSION OF CURSE, AS IS WRITTEN: "THE CURSE (HEB. ME'ERAT) OF HASHEM IS IN THE HOUSE OF THE WICKED" (MISHLEI 3:33), for he brings curses to everyone. And He overpowers THE CROCODILE with the power of the great river, which is called Chidekel. This has already been explained.

72. הַהוּא נָחָשׁ אִיהִי בְּיַבֶּשְׁתָּא כַּד נָפְקִין דָּא בְּדָא, דָּא דִּבְיַבֶּשְׁתָּא אִתְתְּקַף תָּדִיר, בְּגִין דְּכָל אוֹרְחוֹי וְתֻקְפוֹי בְּיַבֶּשְׁתָּא אִיהוּ, וְאָכִיל אַרְעָא וְעַפְרָא תָּדִיר, כד"א וְעָפָר תֹּאכַל כָּל יְמֵי חַיֶּיךָ. דָּא גַּדִּיל בְּעַפְרָא, וְדָא גַּדִּיל בְּמַיָּא. נָחָשׁ דְּאִתְגַּדִּיל בְּמַיָּא, לָאו תַּקִּיפָא כְּהַאי דְּאִתְגַּדִּיל בְּיַבֶּשְׁתָּא, וע"ד כְּתִיב מְאֹרֹת חָסֵר.

72. That snake is on dry land. When they go to battle each other, the one on dry land always triumphs, because all his ways and his power are on dry land, WHERE MALCHUT IS WHICH CONTAINS ALL THE JUDGMENTS. And he always eats dirt and dust, as it is written: "And dust shall you eat all the days of your life" (Beresheet 3:14). The one grows in the dust and the other grows in water. The snake that grows in the water is not as strong as the one that grows on dry land. Therefore, it is written ABOUT THE SNAKE, *me'orot* with a defective spelling WITHOUT A *VAV*, BECAUSE HIS POWER IS STRONG ENOUGH TO KILL EVERYTHING.

73. וְדָא אִזְדָּמַן לְגַבֵּי הַהוּא דְּמַיָּא. ואע"ג דְּאִזְדְּמַן לְגַבֵּיהּ, לָא אָגַח לְגַבֵּיהּ, אֶלָּא קוּדְשָׁא בְּרִיךְ הוּא בִּלְחוֹדוֹי, דְּקָטִיל לֵיהּ מִגּוֹ יַמָּא, כְּמָה דְּאוֹקִימְנָא בְּגִין גַּסּוּת רוּחָא דְּבֵיהּ, כד"א אֲשֶׁר אָמַר לִי יְאֹרִי וְגוֹ'.

73. And this SNAKE comes across that CROCODILE, which is in the water. Although he meets him, he does not fight with him; the Holy One, blessed be He, alone kills him in the sea. As we explained it, because of the haughtiness in him, it is written: "My river is my own, and I have made it for myself" (Yechezkel 29:3).

4. "For Hashem will pass through...on the lintel, and on the two side posts"

A Synopsis

Rabbi Shimon tells us why God required the sign of blood to be placed outside the entrance so that He would pass over Yisrael's houses when He killed the Egyptians. He says that idol worshipping is the only thing which is punished without a person having had to commit an action of some kind. The blood placed on the three places of the lintel and side posts corresponds to the three columns. There is some discussion of the color of the columns and the color of blood, and of the two bloods of Passover and Circumcision that correspond to Mercy and Judgment. At the same time that the Egyptians were being killed, Yisrael were being healed from their circumcision. We are told that the entrance, in "And Hashem will pass over on the entrance," is the opening to draw the spirit and the body, which opening is only freed upon circumcision. Rabbi Aba says that when "pass through" is written, as in "And Hashem will pass through to smite Egypt," it always means that God passed down through the emanations of the Sfirot to perform either Judgment or Mercy.

74. וְעָבַר יְיָ' לִנְגּוֹף אֶת מִצְרַיִם וְגוֹ'. תָּנָא א"ר יוֹסֵי, הַאי קְרָא קַשְׁיָא, וְכִי וְרָאָה אֶת הַדָּם ואח"כ וּפָסַח, דְּמַשְׁמַע דְּסִימָנָא הוּא דְּעָבֵיד. וְאִי תֵּימָא בְּגִין דָּמָא דְּאִיהוּ מִצְוָה, אֲמַאי לְבַר. וַאֲמַאי בִּתְלַת דּוּכְתֵּי דְּפִתְחָא. וְהָא כְּתִיב הוּא גַּלֵּי עֲמִיקָתָא וְגוֹ'. ומ"ט בָּעָא דְּאִתְגַּלְיָא דָּמָא עַל הַמַּשְׁקוֹף וְעַל שְׁתֵּי הַמְּזוּזוֹת.

74. "For Hashem will pass through to smite Egypt..." (Shemot 12:23) We learned, as Rabbi Yosi said, that this passage is difficult. Could it be that first "He sees the blood" and then He "will pass over" (Ibid.), which means He made a sign? If you say it is because of the commandment to place the blood, then why WAS IT PLACED outside THE DOOR, and why on the lintel and two side posts? WHY DID HE NEED THIS? IS NOT EVERYTHING REVEALED BEFORE THE HOLY ONE, BLESSED BE HE? It is written: "He reveals the deep and secret things" (Daniel 2:22). And why did He have to have to reveal the blood on the lintel and two side posts?

75. אֶלָּא תָּנָא, כְּתִיב, וַיַּרְא יְיָ' וַיִּנְאָץ, וּכְתִיב, וַיַּרְא יְיָ' כִּי רַבָּה רָעַת

הָאָדָם בָּאָרֶץ. וְתָנֵינָן לָא אִתְחָזֵי אַשְׁגָּחוּתָא דִּלְעֵילָּא, אֶלָּא כַּד אִתְחָזֵי לְתַתָּא עוֹבָדָא דְּאִתְעָבֵידוּ עוֹבָדָא מִנֵּיהּ וְעַד דְּעַבְדִין עַבְדָּא לְתַתָּא לָא מַשְׁגִּיחִין לְאַבְאָשָׁא, בַּר הִרְהוּרָא דע"ז, דִּכְתִּיב הִשָּׁמְרוּ לָכֶם פֶּן יִפְתֶּה לְבַבְכֶם. וּמִדְּאִתְעָבֵיד עוֹבָדָא, אַשְׁגָּחוּתָא דִּלְעֵילָּא אִתְעַר, וּבְגִין כַּךְ, כֹּלָּא, בֵּין לְטָב וּבֵין לְבִישׁ, בְּעוֹבָדָא תַּלְיָא מִלְּתָא.

75. HE ANSWERS: But we studied that it is written: "And when Hashem saw it, He abhorred them" (Devarim 32:19), and also, "And Hashem saw that the wickedness of man was great in the earth" (Beresheet 6:5). Yet we learned that providence is not seen above unless an action below becomes manifest from it. Before an action is done below, there is no looking to punish, except for the thought of idolatry, WHICH IS PUNISHED WITHOUT AN ACTION, as is written: "Take heed to yourselves, that your heart be not deceived" (Devarim 11:16). After the action is done, providence is aroused. Therefore everything, both good and bad, depends upon action.

76. א"ר יוֹסֵי, כָּל שְׁוָקֵי מִצְרַיִם, מַלְיָין טַעֲוָון הֲווֹ, וְעוֹד דִּבְכָל בֵּיתָא וּבֵיתָא, הֲווֹ שְׁכִיחֵי זִינִין, דְּמִתְקַטְרֵי בְּחָרָשַׁיְיהוּ, בְּאִינּוּן כִּתְרִין תַּתָּאִין דִּלְתַתָּא, וּמִתְעָרִין רוּחַ מִסְאֲבָא בְּגַוַויְיהוּ.

76. Rabbi Yosi said: All the marketplaces of Egypt were full of idols. Moreover, every house had kinds OF WITCHCRAFTERS who with their witchcraft connected with the lower crowns that were below to arouse the Impure Spirit amongst them.

77. וְרָזָא דְּמִלָּה תָּנָא, כְּתִיב, וּלְקַחְתֶּם אֲגֻדַּת אֵזוֹב וּטְבַלְתֶּם בַּדָּם אֲשֶׁר בַּסַּף וְהִגַּעְתֶּם אֶל הַמַּשְׁקוֹף וְאֶל שְׁתֵּי הַמְּזוּזוֹת. אֲגוּדַּת אֵזוֹב לָמָּה. בְּגִין לְבַעֲרָא רוּחַ מִסְאֲבָא מִבֵּינַיְיהוּ, וּלְאַחֲזָאָה בְּפִתְחַיְיהוּ, בְּהָנֵי תְּלַת דּוּכְתֵּי, מְהֵימָנוּתָא שְׁלֵימָתָא. חַד הָכָא, וְחַד הָכָא, וְחַד בְּגַוַויְיהוּ בְּגִין כַּךְ, וּפָסַח יְיָ' עַל הַפֶּתַח וְלֹא יִתֵּן הַמַּשְׁחִית לָבֹא אֶל בָּתֵּיכֶם לִנְגּוֹף, מִשּׁוּם דְּחָמֵי שְׁמָא קַדִּישָׁא רָשִׁים עַל פִּתְחָא.

77. We have learnt the secret meaning of it. It is written: "And take a bunch of hyssop, and dip it in the blood that is in the basin, and touch with it the lintel and two side posts..." (Shemot 12:22). HE ASKS: Why a bunch of hyssops? HE ANSWERS: In order to destroy the Impure Spirit from among them and to indicate on their houses at these three places the Complete Faith, one on this side and one on that side – ON THE TWO SIDE POSTS THAT ALLUDE TO THE TWO COLUMNS, RIGHT AND LEFT – and one between them ON THE LINTEL THAT ALLUDES TO THE CENTRAL COLUMN. Therefore, "Hashem will pass over the door, and will not allow the Destroyer to come into your houses to smite you" (Ibid. 23), for He sees the Holy Name marked on the entrance, WHICH IS THE SECRET OF THE THREE COLUMNS.

78. **א״ר יְהוּדָה, אִי הָכִי אֲמַאי דָּמָא, דְּהָא תָּנֵינָן, חִוָּור וְסוּמָק וְחַד דְּכָלִיל בֵּינֵי גַּוְונֵי. א״ל, תְּרֵי דָּמֵי הֲווֹ, חַד דְּמִילָה, וְחַד דְּפִסְחָא. דְּמִילָה רַחֲמֵי. דְּפִסְחָא דִּינָא.**

78. Rabbi Yehuda said: If THEY ALLUDE TO THE THREE COLUMNS, why IS THIS DONE with blood? Did we not learn THAT THE COLORS OF THE THREE COLUMNS ARE white and red, and the one THAT IS BETWEEN THEM combines both colors; ITS COLOR IS GREEN LIKE THE SUN THAT COMBINES WHITE AND RED. AND WHY ARE ALL THREE COLUMNS ALLUDED TO WITH THE RED COLOR, WHICH IS BLOOD? He said to him: There were two kinds of blood, one of the Pascal sacrifice and one of circumcision AS THEY CIRCUMCISED THEMSELVES. The blood of the circumcision is Mercy, EVEN THOUGH IT IS RED, and the blood of the Pascal sacrifice is Judgment. IT THEREFORE DOES NOT DEPEND UPON COLORS IN THIS CASE.

79. **א״ר יְהוּדָה, לָאו הָכִי, אֶלָּא כְּמָה דְּאוֹלִיפְנָא, דְּאַחְזָר הַהוּא דָּמָא קוּדְשָׁא בְּרִיךְ הוּא לְרַחֲמֵי, כְּאִילּוּ הֲווֹ חִוָּור בְּגוֹ גַּוְונֵי הה״ד, וָאֶעֱבוֹר עָלַיִךְ וָאֶרְאֵךְ מִתְבּוֹסֶסֶת בְּדָמָיִךְ וָאוֹמַר לָךְ בְּדָמַיִךְ חֲיִי וְגוֹ׳. ואע״ג דַּהֲוָה סוּמָקָא, אִתְהֲדָר לְרַחֲמֵי, דִּכְתִּיב בְּדָמַיִךְ חֲיִי. ובג״כ, רָשִׁים פִּתְחָא בִּתְלַת סִטְרִין, חַד הָכָא, וְחַד הָכָא, וְחַד בֵּינַיְיהוּ.**

79. Rabbi Yehuda said: It is not so, but rather as I learned that the Holy One, blessed be He, turned that blood into Mercy as though it was the white among the colors. This is the meaning of: "And when I passed by you, and saw you weltering in your blood and I said to you, 'In your blood live'…" (Yechezkel 16:6). Even though it was red, it was transformed into Mercy, for "In your blood live." IT IS NOT DEPENDENT UPON COLORS IN THIS CASE, and one therefore marked the entrance on three sides, one here, one there and one between them FOR THEY ALLUDE TO THE THREE COLUMNS.

80. תָּאנֵי ר׳ חִזְקִיָּה, תְּרֵין דָּמֵי אִתְחָזוּ, לָקֳבֵל תְּרֵי כִּתְרִין, דְּאִתְחָזוּ לְעֵילָּא בְּהַהִיא שַׁעֲתָא. א״ר יוֹסֵי, חַד כִּתְרָא דִּכְלִילָא בִּתְרֵין סִטְרִין טְמִירִין, בְּרַחֲמֵי וְדִינָא.

80. Rabbi Chizkiyah learned that two types of blood appeared, THE BLOOD OF THE PASSOVER AND THE BLOOD OF CIRCUMCISION, which correspond to two crowns, MEANING SFIROT, that appeared above at that time – WHICH ARE THE TWO COLUMNS, CHESED AND GVURAH. Rabbi Yosi said: THEY CORRESPOND TO one crown that combines the two concealed sides, NAMELY, Mercy and Judgment.

81. אָמַר רִבִּי אַבָּא, בְּכַמָּה אַתְרִין חָס קוּדְשָׁא בְּרִיךְ הוּא עַל בְּנוֹי: עָבֵד בַּר נָשׁ בֵּיתָא, וְקוּדְשָׁא בְּרִיךְ הוּא אָמַר לֵיהּ, כְּתוֹב שְׁמִי, וְשַׁוֵּי לְפִתְחָךְ, וְאַתְּ שָׁרֵי לְגוֹ בֵּיתָא, וַאֲנָא אוֹתִיב לְבַר בְּפִתְחָךְ לְנַטְרָא לָךְ. וְהָכָא אָמַר, רְשִׁים עַל פִּתְחָא רָזָא דִּמְהֵימָנוּתָא דִּילִי, וְאַתְּ שָׁרֵי לְגוֹ בֵּיתָךְ, וַאֲנָא נָטִיר לָךְ לְבַר, דִּכְתִּיב וְאַתֶּם לֹא תֵּצְאוּ אִישׁ מִפֶּתַח בֵּיתוֹ עַד בֹּקֶר, וּכְתִיב וְרָאָה אֶת הַדָּם עַל הַמַּשְׁקוֹף וְעַל שְׁתֵּי הַמְּזוּזוֹת וּפָסַח ד׳ עַל הַפֶּתַח וְלֹא יִתֵּן הַמַּשְׁחִית לָבֹא אֶל בָּתֵּיכֶם לִנְגּוֹף.

81. Rabbi Aba said: The Holy One, blessed be He had compassion for His children on many occasions. A man made a house and the Holy One, blessed be He, said to him: 'Write My Name and place it on your door so when you sit in your house, I will sit outside by your door to guard you.' Here AT PASSOVER, He said: 'Mark on your entrance the secret of Faith in Me,' NAMELY THE THREE COLUMNS ON THE TWO SIDE POSTS AND ON THE LINTEL, AS MENTIONED. 'Sit in your house and I will guard you from outside,' as it is written: "And none of you shall go out at the door entrance of his house until the morning...and when He sees the blood on the lintel, and on the two side posts, Hashem will pass over the door, and will not allow the Destroyer to come into your house to smite you" (Shemot 12:22-23). SO WE SEE THAT THE HOLY ONE, BLESSED BE HE, GUARDED THEM FROM OUTSIDE.

82. תּוּ אָמַר רִבִּי אַבָּא, כְּגַוְונָא דִּשְׁמָא קַדִּישָׁא ה עֲבָדוּ בְּהַהוּא שַׁעֲתָא. מַה שְׁמָא קַדִּישָׁא אִתְהֲדָר בְּהַאי שַׁעֲתָא דִּינָא, אוּף הָכִי אִתְהֲדָר הַאי דָּמָא בְּהַאי שַׁעֲתָא דִּינָא, דִּכְתִּיב וְרָאָה אֶת הַדָּם עַל הַמַּשְׁקוֹף וְעַל שְׁתֵּי הַמְּזוּזוֹת, רְשִׁימָא דְּכֻלְּהוּ סוּמָקָא, לְאִתְחֲזָאָה, דְּהָא אִתְהֲדָר בְּדִינָא, לְמֶעְבַּד נוּקְמִין.

82. Rabbi Aba also said: theymade the semblance of the Holy Name *Hei* at the time, NAMELY THREE LINES – TWO ON THE SIDE POSTS AND ONE ON THE LINTEL ABOVE – WHICH RESEMBLES THE FORM OF THE LETTER *HEI*, WHICH IS MALCHUT. THEREFORE, as the Holy Name changed at that time to be of Judgment AGAINST THE EGYPTIANS, so did the blood change at that moment into Judgment, as written: "and when He sees the blood on the lintel, and on the two side posts." For everybody's mark was red, WHICH ALLUDES TO JUDGMENT, to show THAT EVEN THOUGH IT WAS MERCY FOR YISRAEL, it changed to Judgment to wreak revenge AGAINST THE EGYPTIANS

83. וְרָזָא דְּמִלָּה, כְּגַוְונָא דַּהֲוֵי לְעֵילָּא בְּהַהוּא שַׁעֲתָא, כַּד בָּעֵי לְאִתְחֲזָאָה לְתַתָּא, אִי רַחֲמֵי רַחֲמֵי, וְאִי דִּינָא דִּינָא, הֲדָא הוּא דִּכְתִּיב, וּטְבַלְתֶּם בַּדָּם אֲשֶׁר בַּסַּף וְהִגַּעְתֶּם וְגוֹ'. וּלְזִמְנָא דְּאָתֵי כְּתִיב, מִי זֶה בָּא מֵאֱדוֹם חֲמוּץ בְּגָדִים מִבָּצְרָה. דְּזַמִּין לְאַחֲזָאָה כֻּלְּהוּ דִּינָא לְמֶעְבַּד נוּקְמִין.

83. The secret of this matter is that they had to display below in the same manner it was above at the time-if it was Mercy, then Mercy, if Judgment, then Judgment. Since ABOVE THERE WAS JUDGMENT AGAINST EGYPT, it is written: "And dip it in the blood that is in the basin, and touch with it the lintel..." (Shemot 12:22), FOR BLOOD ALLUDES TO JUDGMENT. About the future time to come, it is written: "Who is this that comes from Edom, with crimsoned garments from Botzrah" (Yeshayah 63:1), for He will show Judgment to them all to wreak revenge. HIS GARMENTS WILL THEN REDDEN WITH BLOOD.

84. וְאַתֶּם לֹא תֵצְאוּ אִישׁ מִפֶּתַח בֵּיתוֹ עַד בֹּקֶר. מַאי טַעֲמָא, מִשּׁוּם דְּתָנֵינָן, אָמַר רִבִּי יִצְחָק, לָא לִיבָעֵי לֵיהּ לְאִינִשׁ לְמֵיזַל בְּשׁוּקָא, וּלְאִשְׁתַּכְּחָא בְּשׁוּקָא, בִּזְמְנָא דְּדִינָא תַּלְיָא בְּמָתָא, דְּכֵיוָן דִּרְשׁוּתָא אִתְיְיהִיב לִמְחַבְּלָא, מַאן דְּפָגַע בֵּיהּ אִתְּזַק. וְהָכָא מִשּׁוּם דְּדִינָא אִשְׁתְּכַח, לָא בַּעְיָא לְנָפְקָא לְבַר.

84. "And none of you shall go out at the door of his house until the morning." HE ASKS: What is the reason THAT THEY WERE PROHIBITED TO GO OUT OF THEIR HOUSE DOOR? HE ANSWERS: We learned that a person should not go in the market place and be in the market place at the time when Judgment hovers over the city, because once the Destroyer has been granted permission, whomever he meets comes to harm. THEREFORE, since there was Judgment FOR THE EGYPTIANS, they must not go out.

85. תַּנְיָא אָמַר רִבִּי יוֹסֵי, בְּהַהוּא מַמָּשׁ דְּאִשְׁתְּכַח דִּינָא לְמִצְרָאֵי, בְּהַהוּא מַמָּשׁ אִשְׁתְּכַח רַחֲמֵי לְיִשְׂרָאֵל, הֲדָא הוּא דִּכְתִּיב, וְרָאִיתִי אֶת הַדָּם וּפָסַחְתִּי עֲלֵיכֶם. וְכֵן תָּנָא, בְּכָל אִינּוּן כִּתְרִין קַדִּישִׁין דִּלְעֵילָּא, כְּמָה דְּאִשְׁתְּכַח דִּינָא, אִשְׁתְּכַח רַחֲמֵי, וְכֹלָּא בְּשַׁעֲתָא חֲדָא. תָּנָא רִבִּי חִזְקִיָּה, כְּתִיב, וְנָגַף יְיָ' אֶת מִצְרַיִם נָגוֹף וְרָפֹא. נָגוֹף לְמִצְרַיִם, וְרָפֹא לְיִשְׂרָאֵל. מַאי וְרָפֹא. מַאי שֶׁנִּימוֹלוּ צְרִיכִים רְפוּאָה.

85. We learned, as Rabbi Yosi said, in the same place where there was Judgment for the Egyptians, there also was Mercy for the children of Yisrael. This is the meaning of: "And when I see the blood, I will pass over you" (Shemot 12:13). So have we learned that throughout the holy crowns above, as there is Judgment in them, so is Mercy simultaneously. Rabbi Chizkiyah taught that it is written: "And Hashem will smite Egypt, He shall smite and heal" (Yeshayah 19:22), MEANING the smiting of Egypt and the healing of Yisrael. HE ASKS what is the healing for, AND ANSWERS they needed healing from their circumcision.

86. וְתָנָא, בְּאוֹתָהּ שָׁעָה שֶׁנִּגְּפוּ מִצְרָאֵי, בְּאוֹתָהּ שָׁעָה נִתְרַפְּאוּ יִשְׂרָאֵל. דְּתַנְיָא אָמַר רִבִּי יוֹסֵי, מ"ד, וּפָסַח יְיָ עַל הַפֶּתַח, מַאי עַל הַפֶּתַח. וּפָסַח יְיָ' עֲלֵיכֶם מִבָּעֵי לֵיהּ. אֲבָל עַל הַפֶּתַח, עַל הַפֶּתַח מַמָּשׁ זֶהוּ פֶּתַח הַגּוּף. וְאֵי זֶהוּ פֶּתַח הַגּוּף. הֱוֵי אוֹמֵר זוֹ מִילָה.

86. We learned that Yisrael were healed at the same moment the Egyptians were smitten. Rabbi Yosi said, we learned the verse: "Hashem will pass over the door." Why does it say "over the door," when it should have stated: 'Hashem will pass over you'? HE ANSWERS: Rather, "over the door," refers to the actual door, the opening of the body. And what is the opening of the body? Say it is the circumcision, MEANING THAT HE HEALED IT.

87. רִבִּי שִׁמְעוֹן אָמַר, בְּשַׁעֲתָא דְּאִתְפְּלַג לֵילְיָא, וְכִתְרָא קַדִּישָׁא אִתְּעַר לְגַבֵּהּ דִּכְוּרָא. וּמַאן דִּכְוּרָא. חֶסֶד עִלָּאָה, דְּמַשְׁמַע, דְּדָא בְּלָא דָא לָא סַלְקָא, וּבְגִין דָּא, דָּא מָחֵי, וְדָא מַסֵּי, וְכֹלָּא בְּשַׁעֲתָא חֲדָא.

87. Rabbi Shimon said: at midnight, the male is awakened towards the holy crown, WHICH IS MALCHUT. Who is that male? He is supreme Chesed OF ZEIR ANPIN, as is known that one does not come about without the other. EVEN THOUGH THE NIGHT IS THE ASPECT OF MALCHUT ALONE, IT WILL NEVER OCCUR THAT MALCHUT SHALL BE WITHOUT ZEIR ANPIN, HER HUSBAND. Therefore, MALCHUT smites and ZEIR ANPIN heals at the same time.

88. וּכְתִיב, וּפָסַח יְיָ' עַל הַפֶּתַח הַיָּדוּעַ. מַאי הַפֶּתַח, מִשּׁוּם דְּאִיהוּ פִּתְחָא וּמְשִׁיכָא דְּרוּחָא וְגוּפָא, וְתָא חֲזֵי, עַד לָא אִתְגְּזַר אַבְרָהָם, הֲוָה אָטִים וְסָתִים מִכָּל סִטְרוֹי. מִדְּאִתְגְּזַר אִתְפְּתַח מִכֹּלָּא, וְלָא הֲוֵי אָטִים וְסָתִים כְּקַדְמֵיתָא.

88. And it is written: "Hashem will pass over the door," NAMELY the known door, THE DOOR OF THE BODY AS MENTIONED ABOVE. What is the door, WHY IS IT CALLED DOOR? It is the opening to draw the spirit and the body, BECAUSE THEY WERE BORN FROM THERE. Come and behold: until Abraham was circumcised, he was shut off and closed from all sides, AND WAS NOT ABLE TO BEGET IN HOLINESS. As soon as he was circumcised, everything in him opened up, and he was no longer blocked and closed as before.

89. וְהַיְינוּ רָזָא דִּתְנֵינָן, וְהוּא יֹשֵׁב פֶּתַח הָאֹהֶל. מִשּׁוּם דְּאִתְגַּלְיָיא יו״ד. מַאי קָא מַיְירֵי. אֶלָּא אָמַר רִבִּי יִצְחָק דְּהוּא אַשְׁרֵי בְּגִלּוּיָא דָּא, חֶסֶד בְּצֶדֶק. וְדָא הוּא פִּתְחָא, דְּמַשְׁכְּנָא עִלָּאָה קַדִּישָׁא, מַשְׁמַע דִּכְתִּיב הָאֹהֶל, הָאֹהֶל הַיָּדוּעַ.

89. And this is the secret that we learned: "As he sat in the tent door" (Beresheet 18:1), because *Yud* was revealed. HE ASKS: Why does he say so? HE ANSWERS: But Rabbi Yitzchak says, by this revealing OF THE *YUD*, He caused Chesed to dwell in Righteousness. This is the entrance of the supernal holy Tabernacle, WHICH IS MALCHUT. This is understood from "the tent," meaning the specific tent, WHICH IS MALCHUT CALLED 'TENT'.

90. אָמַר רִבִּי אֶלְעָזָר, כַּד אִתְגַּלְיָיא הַאי יו״ד, אִתְבָּשַׂר, וְאִתְבְּרַךְ בְּפֶתַח הָאֹהֶל, דְּהִיא צֶדֶק, לְאִתְבַּסְּמָא בְּחֶסֶ״ד. הֲדָא הוּא דִּכְתִּיב, כְּחוֹם הַיּוֹם, דְּהוּא שַׁעֲתָא דְּשַׁלְטָא חֶסֶד, חוּלָקָא דְּאַבְרָהָם. ומ״ל דְּהַאי פֶּתַח הָאֹהֶל, אִתְבַּסַּם לְקָבְלֵיהּ דְּאַבְרָהָם. דִּכְתִּיב, וַיְיָ בֵּרַךְ אֶת אַבְרָהָם בַּכֹּל, דְּאִתְבָּסָם בְּחֶסֶ״ד, מִדְּאִתְגַּלְיָיא יו״ד.

90. Rabbi Elazar said: When this *Yud* was revealed, ABRAHAM was given the news and was blessed at the tent door, which is Righteousness, NAMELY MALCHUT that was sweetened with Chesed. This is the meaning of: "in the heat of the day," as DAYTIME is the time when Chesed reigns, which is the portion of Abraham, SINCE ABRAHAM IS A CHARIOT TO CHESED OF ZEIR ANPIN. How do we know that the tent door, WHICH IS MALCHUT, was mellowed with Chesed by the powers of Abraham? IT IS BECAUSE it is written: "And Hashem blessed Abraham in all things (Heb. *bakol*)" (Beresheet 24:1). *BAKOL* IS MALCHUT sweetened with Chesed BY ABRAHAM after *Yud* was revealed in him THROUGH CIRCUMCISION.

91. אָמַר רִבִּי אַבָּא, וְהוּא יוֹשֵׁב פֶּתַח הָאֹהֶל, כְּמָה דִּכְתִּיב וַיְיָ בֵּרַךְ אֶת אַבְרָהָם בַּכֹּל. דְּדָא הוּא פִּתְחָא קַדִּישָׁא, כִּתְרָא עֲשִׂירָאָה. כְּחוֹם הַיּוֹם,

כְּמָה דְּאִתְיְיהִיב לֵיהּ כִּתְרָא דְּחֶסֶד, הֲדָא הוּא דִּכְתִּיב כְּחוֹם הַיּוֹם. כְּמָה דְּיָתִיב בְּהַאי, כַּךְ יָתִיב בְּהַאי, דְּלָא סָלִיק הַאי בְּלֹא הַאי.

91. Rabbi Aba said: "As he sat in the tent door," is similar to: "And Hashem blessed Abraham in all things (Heb. *bakol*)." As THE TENT door IS MALCHUT THAT IS CALLED "*BAKOL.*" It is the tenth crown, WHICH IS MALCHUT. 'CROWN' MEANS A SFIRAH. "In the heat of the day" MEANS as the Sfirah of Chesed THAT IS CALLED 'DAY' was given to him, SO DID HE MERIT THE TENT DOOR, FOR CHESED OPENS MALCHUT CALLED 'TENT', SO IT CAN ILLUMINATE. As he sits IN CHESED, THAT IS CALLED 'DAY', so does he sit IN MALCHUT THAT IS CALLED 'THE TENT DOOR', because one does not rise without the other.

92. ד"א וְעָבַר יְיָ לִנְגּוֹף אֶת מִצְרַיִם. מַאי וְעָבַר. דְּעָבַר עַל שׁוּרֵי דִּינָא דִּכְתְרִין, דַּהֲווֹ מִתְקַשְּׁרֵי בְּכִתְרִין אַחֲרָנִין דִּלְעֵילָּא, וְשָׁרָא לְהוּ מִקִּיּוּמֵיהוֹן, וְעָבַר עַל אוֹרְחוֹי, בְּגִין לְמֶעְבַּד בְּהוּ דִּינָא, וּלְנַטְרָא לְהוּ לְיִשְׂרָאֵל, וּכְדֵין הוּא, כָּל וְעָבַר, וְעָבַרְתִּי, וַיַּעֲבֹר, דְּקוּדְשָׁא בְּרִיךְ הוּא אַעְבַּר עַל כָּל אוֹרְחוֹי, אוֹ לְדִינָא, אוֹ לְרַחֲמֵי. הָכָא וְעָבַר, בְּגִין לְמֶעְבַּד דִּינָא, הָתָם וַיַּעֲבֹר, בְּגִין לְרַחֲמָא.

92. Another explanation FOR, "For Hashem will pass through to smite Egypt." THE MEANING OF "pass through" is that He went over the line of Judgment of the crowns that were connected with other crowns above, and disconnected them from their sustenance. THUS THE HOLY ONE, BLESSED BE HE, forwent His ways, NAMELY, HE DISRUPTED THE EVOLUTION OF THE CROWNS, in order to perform Judgment BY EGYPT, and to guard Yisrael. It is so wherever it is written: "He will pass through"; "I will pass through"; "He passed through." IT INDICATES THAT the Holy One, blessed be He, forwent His ways, MEANING THE ORDER OF THE EVOLUTION OF THE SFIROT, either to perform Judgment or for Mercy. Here, "He will pass through," MEANS to perform Judgment, while, "And Hashem passed by BEFORE HIM..." (Shemot 34:6) is in order to have mercy.

5. “And it came to pass, that at midnight”

A Synopsis

Rabbi Chiya and Rabbi Yosi pause during their travelling to pray, because it is important to be punctual about the Minchah service. As they continue on, Rabbi Yosi is contemplating leadership, and says that the world gains from good leaders and suffers from bad ones, and yet if the bad leader is punished for his sin, then the people are spared. After it turns dark, the rabbis sit under a tree in some fear, until at midnight they see a doe, crying and then they hear shouting, a voice saying that their Master is going into the Garden of Eden to rejoice with the Righteous. After this event, Rabbi Yosi returns to the story of the Passover, and wonders why the slaughter of the firstborn was not done in the daytime so everyone could see it, and why all were killed rather than just those kings and ministers and warriors who cause war. They wait until daylight and then go to Rabbi Shimon for an answer. Rabbi Shimon is speaking about the philosophies of the other nations of the world, and says that their faith is as nothing, since they comprehend neither supernal mysteries nor lower wisdom. He turns to the story of Creation, and says that God created the heavens with His right hand, Chesed, and that He created the earth with His left hand, Judgment. It is “this,” Malchut, that draws them together; the Sfirah Malchut dominates at midnight in Mercy for Yisrael and in Judgment for the heathen nations. Rabbi Shimon brings up the question of how Moses could have known it was exactly midnight, in the verse, “And it came to pass, that at midnight.” He speaks of how Moses was from the highest levels, which no other man ever attained, and Moses surely knew that the night must divide in order to perform its functions; it performed its functions in the second half of the night at that time that Malchut dominates. We hear that Pharaoh, being wiser than his sorcerers, knew that Judgment would be executed against him and that his land would be destroyed. To answer Rabbi Yosi’s original question about why “every firstborn” was killed, Rabbi Shimon says this means that all the upper and lower levels were broken from their dominion. Because the Egyptians were holding Yisrael by sorcery, it took the strength and dominion of God to free them. Because of the three bonds of faith, the three Covenants of Abraham, Isaac and Jacob, God saved Yisrael. Every holiday and festival and Sabbath is in memory of the deliverance from Egypt; that is the foundation and source of the Torah and all the commandments and the faith of Yisrael. Rabbi Shimon says: Why was the judgment of Egypt not by day? Because the night opened knots and did revenge, being the secret of Malchut called ‘night’.

Rabbi Chiya and Rabbi Yosi praise Rabbi Shimon, as being the one who can open the gates of the secrets of Wisdom. Lastly Rabbi Shimon talks about watchfulness, the watchnight, and the watchman; these allude to male and female, and wherever male and female are together all praise is directed to the male.

93. וַיְהִי בַּחֲצִי הַלַּיְלָה וַיְיָ׳ הִכָּה כָּל בְּכוֹר וְגוֹ׳. ר׳ חִיָּיא ור׳ יוֹסֵי הֲווֹ אַזְלֵי מֵאוּשָׁא לְלוּד, וַהֲוָה רִבִּי חִיָּיא רָכִיב בְּחַמְרָא. אָמַר ר׳ יוֹסֵי, נֵיתִיב הָכָא וְנַצְלֵי, דְּהָא מָטָא זִמְנָא דִּצְלוֹתָא דְּמִנְחָה, וְתָנֵינָן, לְעוֹלָם יְהֵא אָדָם זָהִיר בִּצְלוֹתָא דְּמִנְחָה. אֲמַאי זָהִיר. מִשּׁוּם דְּהִיא שַׁעֲתָא דְּתַלְיָא דִּינָא וּבָעֵי ב״נ לְכַוְּונָא דַּעְתֵּיהּ, נָחַת ר׳ חִיָּיא וְצַלֵּי.

93. “And it came to pass, that at midnight Hashem smote all the firstborn...” (Shemot 12:29) Rabbi Chiya and Rabbi Yosi were traveling from Usha to Lod and Rabbi Chiya was riding on a donkey. Rabbi Yosi said: Let us rest here and pray, for the time for Minchah (‘the afternoon service’) has come. And we have learned that one should always be punctual about the Minchah service. Why DOES HE HAVE TO BE punctual? Because it is the time when Judgment is impending over the world, and one must concentrate his mind. Rabbi Chiya got down FROM THE DONKEY and prayed.

94. עַד דַּהֲווֹ אַזְלֵי, נָטָה שִׁמְשָׁא לְמֵיעַל. א״ר חִיָּיא לר׳ יוֹסֵי אֲמַאי אַתְּ שָׁתִיק. א״ר יוֹסֵי, מִסְתַּכֵּל הֲוֵינָא בְּדַעְתָּאי, דְּלֵית עָלְמָא מִתְקַיְּימָא, אֶלָּא עַל רֵישֵׁיהוֹן דְּעַמָּא. אִי רֵישֵׁי עַמָּא זַכָּאִין, טַב לְעָלְמָא, טַב לְעַמָּא. וְאִי לָא זַכָּאִין, וַוי לְעָלְמָא, וַוי לְעַמָּא.

94. While they were still traveling, the sun was setting. Rabbi Chiya said to Rabbi Yosi: Why are you silent? Rabbi Yosi said: I was contemplating that the world exists only because of the leaders of the people. If the leaders of the people are righteous, it is good for the world and good for the people. If they are not righteous, woe to the world, woe to the people.

95. א״ר חִיָּיא, וַדַּאי כַּךְ הוּא, מְנָלָן. דִּכְתִּיב, רָאִיתִי אֶת כָּל יִשְׂרָאֵל נְפוֹצִים עַל הֶהָרִים כְּצֹּאן אֲשֶׁר אֵין לָהֶן רוֹעֶה וַיֹּאמֶר יְיָ לֹא אֲדוֹנִים לָאֵלֶּה יָשׁוּבוּ אִישׁ לְבֵיתוֹ בְּשָׁלוֹם. יָשׁוּבוּ, יֵשְׁבוּ מִבָּעֵי לֵיהּ. לְבֵיתוֹ, בְּבֵיתוֹ מִבָּעֵי לֵיהּ. דְּהָא בְּאַתְרַיְיהוּ קַיְימֵי.

95. Rabbi Chiya said: It is certainly so. How do we know? Because it is written: “I saw all Yisrael scattered upon the mountains, like sheep that have no shepherd; and Hashem said, ‘These have no master; let them return therefore every man to his house in peace’” (II Divrei Hayamim 18:16). HE ASKS: It says “*Yashuvu*” (‘let them return’) when it should say ‘*Yeshvu*’ (‘let them sit’), and similarly, “to his house” should say ‘in his house’. For THE PEOPLE were in their abode, AND WHERE WERE THEY TO RETURN?

96. אֶלָּא הָכִי תָּנֵינָן, אִי רֵישָׁא דְּעַמָּא לָא זָכֵי, עַמָּא מִתָּפְסָן בְּחוֹבֵיהּ. מְנָלָן. דִּכְתִּיב, וַיֹּאמֶר דָּוִד וְגוֹ׳ הִנֵּה אָנֹכִי חָטָאתִי וְאָנֹכִי הֶעֱוֵיתִי וְאֵלֶּה הַצֹּאן מֶה עָשׂוּ, דָּוִד חָב, וְיִשְׂרָאֵל סָבְלוּ. וְאִי רֵישָׁא דְּעַמָּא מִתְפַּס בְּחוֹבֵיהּ, עַמָּא מִשְׁתֵּזְבָן. דְּהָא דִּינָא לָא שַׁרְיָא עֲלַיְיהוּ. דִּכְתִּיב, וַיֹּאמֶר יְיָ לֹא אֲדוֹנִים לָאֵלֶּה, כְּלוֹמַר, אִלּוּ לָא הֲווּ רֵישִׁין לְעַמָּא, מֵהַאי אוֹרְחָא יָשׁוּבוּ אִישׁ לְבֵיתוֹ בְּשָׁלוֹם. כֻּלְּהוּ מִשְׁתֵּזְבָן, אִי רֵישֵׁיהוֹן מִתָּפְסָן. וַאֲפִילּוּ יְהוֹשָׁפָט אִתְגְּזַר עָלֵיהּ לְאִתְעַנְשָׁא, מִשּׁוּם דְּאִתְחֲבָּר בְּאַחְאָב. אִי לָאו הַהוּא צְוָוחָא, דִּכְתִּיב, וַיִּזְעַק יְהוֹשָׁפָט.

96. HE ANSWERS: But this is what we learned. If the leader of the people is not worthy IN HIS DEEDS, the people is caught in his sin. Whence do we know – from the words: “And David spoke...Lo, I have sinned, and I have done perversely; but these sheep, what have they done?” (II Shmuel 24:17). So David sinned and Yisrael suffered. If the chief of the people is caught in his sin, then the people is spared, as Judgment no longer dwells upon them, as the passage says: “And Hashem said, ‘These have no master,’” meaning there are no leaders for the people, BECAUSE AHAB WAS SLAIN. THEREFORE, “let them return therefore every man to his house in peace” from the path, AND EVEN THOUGH JUDGMENT HAS RIDDEN ON THEM IN THIS PATH, SINCE THEIR LEADER WAS SLAIN AND CAUGHT IN HIS SIN, THEY WILL RETURN IN PEACE. They are all saved if their leader is caught. It was decreed that, because he joined with Ahab, even Yehoshafat would have been punished, were it not for his crying, as is written: “And Yehoshafat cried out” (I Melachim 22:32).

97. עַד דַּהֲווּ אַזְלֵי רָמַשׁ לֵילְיָא, אָמְרוּ, מַה נַּעְבִיד, אִי נֵיזִיל חָשַׁךְ לֵילְיָא, אִי נֵיתִיב דַּחֲלָא הוּא. סָטוּ מֵאוֹרְחָא, יָתְבוּ תְּחוֹת אִילָנָא חַד.

וְיָתְבוּ וַהֲווֹ אַמְרֵי מִלֵּי דְּאוֹרַיְיתָא, וְלָא דָּמִיכוּ.

97. While they were still traveling, it became dark. They said: What shall we do? If continue traveling, it is ALREADY dark and, if we stay IN OUR PLACE, it is frightening. They turned off from the road and sat under a tree. They rested and discussed Torah there, and did not sleep.

98. בְּפַלְגוּת לֵילְיָא, חָמוּ חַד אַיַּלְתָּא דְּעָבְרָא קָמַיְיהוּ, וַהֲוַת צַוְּחַת וּרְמִיאַת קָלִין שָׁמְעוּ, קָמוּ ר׳ חִיָּיא ור׳ יוֹסֵי וְאִזְדַּעְזָעוּ. שָׁמְעוּ חַד קָלָא דְּמַכְרְזָא וְאָמַר, מִתְעָרִין קוּמוּ. נַיְימִין אִתְּעָרוּ. עָלְמִין, אִזְדְּמָנוּ לְקַדְמֵת מָרֵיכוֹן. דְּהָא מָרֵיכוֹן מַפִּיק לג״ע, דְּאִיהוּ הֵיכָלֵיהּ, לְאִשְׁתַּעְשְׁעָא עִם צַדִּיקַיָּא, דִּכְתִּיב וּבְהֵיכָלוֹ כֻּלּוֹ אוֹמֵר כָּבוֹד.

98. At midnight they saw a doe passing before them, shouting and crying out loud. When they heard it, Rabbi Chiya and Rabbi Yosi got up and trembled. They heard a voice announcing and saying: Those who are awake rise, those who sleep awake. Worlds, prepare for Your Master. For your Master is going out to Garden of Eden, which is His palace, NAMELY MALCHUT, to delight with the Righteous, as it is written: "And in His temple everyone speaks of His glory" (Tehilim 29:9).

99. א״ר חִיָּיא, הַשְׁתָּא פַּלְגוּ דְּלֵילְיָא מַמָּשׁ. וְקָלָא דָּא, הוּא קָלָא דְּנָפַק, וְכָאִיב אַיַּלְתָּא דִּלְעֵילָּא וְתַתָּא, דִּכְתִּיב קוֹל יְיָ׳ יְחוֹלֵל אַיָּלוֹת. זַכָּאָה חוּלָקָנָא, דְּזָכֵינָא לְמִשְׁמַע דָּא.

99. Rabbi Chiya said: Now it is exactly midnight, and this voice THAT WE HEARD is the voice that emerges and causes pain to the doe above, WHICH IS MALCHUT, and below, as it is written: "The voice of Hashem makes the hinds to calve" (Ibid.). Fortunate are we to hear this.

100. וְתָא חֲזֵי רָזָא דְּמִלָּה, בְּשַׁעֲתָא דְּקוּדְשָׁא בְּרִיךְ הוּא אִתְחָזֵי עַל גִּנְתָּא, כָּל גִּנְתָּא אִתְכְּנַשׁ, וְלָא מִתְפְּרַשׁ מֵעֵדֶן. וּמֵהַאי עֵדֶן מַבּוּעֵי נָפְקִין, לְכַמָּה אוֹרְחִין וּשְׁבִילִין, וְהַאי גִּנְתָּא, אִתְקְרֵי צְרוֹרָא דְּחַיֵּי,

דְּתַמָּן מִתְעַדְּנִין צַדִּיקַיָּא, מִנְּהִירוּ דְּעָלְמָא דְּאָתֵי. וּבְהַאי שַׁעֲתָא, קוּדְשָׁא בְּרִיךְ הוּא אִתְגְּלֵי עֲלַיְיהוּ.

100. Come and behold the secret of the matter. At the time that the Holy One, blessed be He, is revealed over the Garden, the whole Garden gathers, NAMELY ALL THE RIGHTEOUS IN THE GARDEN, but does not separate from Eden, WHICH IS CHOCHMAH. Springs emerge from this Eden, NAMELY THE ILLUMINATION OF CHOCHMAH, to many ways and paths, FOR THE CONCEPTION OF THE RIGHTEOUS. This Garden is called ‘The Bundle of Life’, where the Righteous derive pleasure from the illumination of the World to Come. And at that time, the Holy One, blessed be He, reveals Himself to them.

101. יָתְבוּ ר״ח וְרִבִּי יוֹסֵי, אָמַר רִבִּי יוֹסֵי, בְּכַמָּה זִמְנִין שָׁאִילְנָא, הַאי דִּכְתִּיב, וַיְהִי בַּחֲצִי הַלַּיְלָה וַיְיָ׳ הִכָּה כָל בְּכוֹר בְּאֶרֶץ מִצְרַיִם אֲמַאי לָא הֲוָה בִּימָמָא, דְּיִתְגְּלֵי לְכָל פִּרְסוּמֵי נִיסָא, וַאֲמַאי מִיתוּ כָּל אִינּוּן חַלָּשֵׁי דְּבָתַר רֵחַיָּיא, וְאִינּוּן טַלְיָיא דִּבְנֵי עָאנָא, וְלָא מִיתוּ מַלְכֵי וּפַרְדַּשְׁכֵי, וְגוּבְרֵי מַגִּיחֵי קְרָבָא, כְּמָה דַּהֲוָה בְּסַנְחֵרִיב, דִּכְתִּיב וַיֵּצֵא מַלְאַךְ יְיָ׳ וַיַּךְ בְּמַחֲנֵה אַשּׁוּר וְגוֹ׳. וְתָנֵינָן, כֻּלְּהוּ מַלְכִין בְּנֵי מַלְכִין רוּפִינוּס וּפַרְדַּשְׁכֵי, הָתָם אִתְחָזֵי גְּבוּרְתָּא דְּחָד שְׁלִיחָא דִּילֵיהּ, יַתִּיר מֵהַאי, דַּהֲוָה יֵאוּת לְמֶהֱוֵי דִּילֵיהּ יַתִּיר.

101. Rabbi Chiya and Rabbi Yosi sat down. Rabbi Yosi said: Many a time I asked about the words: “And it came to pass, that at midnight Hashem smote all the firstborn in the land of Egypt...” Why did this not happen by day so the miracle would be visible to all? And why did all these weaklings behind the millstones and the lambs of the sheep die? And why did not only kings, princes and soldiers die, as it was by the episode of Sancheriv, of which it is written: “the Angel of Hashem went out and smote in the camp of Ashur...” (II Melachim 19:35). We learned that they were all kings, princes, ministers and officers, and the might of a single messenger of the Holy One, blessed be He, was seen there even greater THAN THIS MIRACLE THAT WAS DONE BY HIS OWN HAND. IT SEEMS THAT His miracle should have been even more GREAT.

102. אָמַר לֵיהּ יֵאוּת שָׁאַלְתְּ, וַאֲנָא לָא שְׁמַעְנָא מִידִי בְּהַאי, וְלָא

אִימָא, אֲבָל הָא זָכֵינָא לְכָל הַאי, וְאָרְחָא אִתְתְּקַן קָמָן. אֲנָא שְׁמַעְנָא דרשב״י מַדְכֵי שְׁוָקִין דִּטְבֶרְיָה, נֵיזִיל גַּבֵּיהּ. יָתְבוּ, עַד דַּהֲוָה נָהִיר יְמָמָא. כַּד סָלִיק נְהוֹרָא, קָמוּ וְאַזְלֵי. כַּד מָטוּ גַּבֵּיהּ. אַשְׁכְּחוּהוּ, דַּהֲוָה יָתִיב, וְסִפְרָא דְּאַגַּדְתָּא בִּידֵיהּ.

102. He said to him: You asked well, and I have heard nothing about this. So I have nothing to say. But since we were worthy of all this, and the way was set before us, let us go to Rabbi Shimon bar Yochai as I have heard he is cleansing the market places of the city of Tiberias. They stayed until daybreak. When it became light, they got up and went. When they reached him, they found him sitting with a book of homiletics in his hand.

103. פָּתַח וְאָמַר, כָּל הַגּוֹיִם כְּאַיִן נֶגְדּוֹ מֵאֶפֶס וָתֹהוּ נֶחְשְׁבוּ לוֹ. כֵּיוָן דְּאָמַר, כָּל הַגּוֹיִם כְּאַיִן נֶגְדּוֹ, לָמָּה כְּתִיב מֵאֶפֶס וָתֹהוּ נֶחְשְׁבוּ לוֹ. אֶלָּא אוֹלִיפְנָא, דַּעְתַּיְיהוּ דְּכָל עַמִּין דְּעָלְמָא, דִּמְהֵימָנוּתָא דִּלְהוֹן הוּא כְּאַיִן, דְּלָא אִדְבָּקוּ עִלָּאִין וְתַתָּאִין, וְשַׁוְיָין לָקָבְלַיְיהוּ מְהֵימָנוּתָא דִּשְׁטוּתָא, אֲבָל מֵאֶפֶס וָתֹהוּ נֶחְשְׁבוּ לוֹ, כְּהַאי עִלְעוֹלָא, דְּסַחֲרָא בְּרוּחָא, וּמִתְגַּלְגְּלָא בְּקַיְטָא בְּרֵיקַנְיָא, הה״ד וְכָל דַּיְירֵי אַרְעָא כְּלָא חֲשִׁיבִין.

103. He opened the discussion, saying: "All nations before Him are as nothing; and they are counted to Him less than nothing, and vanity" (Yeshayah 40:17). HE ASKS: Since it said, "All nations before Him are as nothing," why is it written also, "And they are counted to Him less than nothing, and vanity"? AND HE ANSWERS: I have learned the philosophies of all the nations of the world, whose Faith is as nothing. They conceive neither the upper LEVELS nor the lower. They place for themselves a Faith of foolishness; "and they are counted to Him less than nothing, and vanity" like chaff that turns in the wind and rolls during the summer IN THE FIELDS empty, FOR IT HAS NO CONTENTS AT ALL. This is the meaning of: "And all the inhabitants of the earth are reputed as nothing" (Daniel 4:32).

104. עוֹד פָּתַח וְאָמַר, בְּרֵאשִׁית בָּרָא אֱלֹהִים אֵת הַשָּׁמַיִם וְאֵת הָאָרֶץ, אֵת דָּא יְמִינָא דְּקוּדְשָׁא בְּרִיךְ הוּא, וְאֵת דָּא שְׂמָאלָא. אוֹלִיפְנָא, דְּסָטָא קוּדְשָׁא בְּרִיךְ הוּא יְמִינֵיהּ, וּבָרָא יַת שְׁמַיָּא, וְסָטָא שְׂמָאלָא, וּבָרָא יַת

אַרְעָא. הה״ד, אַף יָדִי יָסְדָה אֶרֶץ וִימִינִי טִפְּחָה שָׁמָיִם קוֹרֵא אֲנִי אֲלֵיהֶם יַעַמְדוּ יַחְדָּו.

104. He again opened the discussion, saying: "In the beginning Elohim created the heavens and the earth" (Beresheet 1:1). The first "*Et*" ('the') is the right hand of the Holy One, blessed be He, and that *Et* ('the') is His left hand. I learned that the Holy One, blessed be He, stretched His right hand – WHICH IS CHESED – and created the heavens, and stretched His left hand – WHICH IS JUDGMENT – and created the earth. This is the meaning of: "My hand also has laid the foundation of the earth, and My right hand has spanned the heavens: when I call to them, they stand up together" (Yeshayah 48:13).

105. מַהוּ יַעַמְדוּ יַחְדָּו. ס״ד שְׁמַיָּא וְאַרְעָא לָאו הָכִי, אֶלָּא יְמִינָא וּשְׂמָאלָא דְּאִינּוּן אֵ״ת וְאֵ״ת, וְהֵיאַךְ יַעַמְדוּ יַחְדָּו. בְּזֹאת הַהִיא, דְּשַׁלְטָא בְּפַלְגוּת לֵילְיָא, דִּכְלִילָא אֵ״ת בְּזֹאת.

105. HE ASKS: What is the meaning of THE VERSE: "They stand up together"? HE ANSWERS: If you think that these are heaven and earth THAT ARE ZEIR ANPIN AND HIS NUKVA, it is not so. THEY DO NOT STAND TOGETHER. Rather, THEY ARE right and left, SEPARATE, which are the (*et*) and the (*et*) AS MENTIONED ABOVE. THEREFORE, THE VERSE SAYS, "THEY STAND UP TOGETHER." How do they stand together? By means of "this," WHICH IS MALCHUT that rules at midnight, for then *Et* WHICH IS CHESED is combined with "this," WHICH IS MALCHUT, SO THEY STAND TOGETHER.

106. וְתָנֵינָן, כְּתִיב אֶת הַכֹּל עָשָׂה יָפֶה בְעִתּוֹ. אֶ״ת, הָא דְּאַמָרָן. הַכֹּל, כד״א, וַיְיָ׳ בֵּרַךְ אֶת אַבְרָהָם בַּכֹּל. וְתָאנָא, דְּהִיא כִּתְרָא דְּאִתְקְרֵי זֹא״ת, דִּכְלִילָא מֵאֶ״ת וְאֵ״ת. וְשָׁלְטָא בְּפַלְגוּת לֵילְיָא, בִּתְרֵין סִטְרוֹי, בְּרַחֲמֵי וְדִינָא, רַחֲמֵי לְיִשְׂרָאֵל, וְדִינָא לְעַמִּין עכו״ם.

106. We learned that it is written: "He has made every (Heb. *kol*) thing beautiful in its time" (Kohelet 3:11). *Et* MEANS CHESED OF ZEIR ANPIN as we said. "kol" is as is said, "And Hashem blessed Abraham in all (Heb. *kol*) things" (Beresheet 24:1). We learned that "kol" is the Sfirah that is called "this," NAMELY MALCHUT that includes *Et* and *Et* AS MENTIONED EARLIER, and rules at midnight in two aspects, Mercy and Judgment – Mercy for Yisrael and Judgment for the heathen nations. AND THE SCRIPTURE SAYS, "HE HAS MADE *ET KOL*," SO THAT THEY WOULD BE UNITED TOGETHER, "BEAUTIFUL IN ITS TIME," NAMELY AT MIDNIGHT.

107. פָּתַח ר׳ חִיָּיא וְאָמַר, אִי נִיחָא קָמֵיהּ דְּמֹר, דְּנֵימָא חַד מִלָּה, עַל מַה דְּאָתֵינָא כְּתִיב, וַיְהִי בַּחֲצִי הַלַּיְלָה וַיְיָ׳ הִכָּה כָל בְּכוֹר בְּאֶרֶץ מִצְרַיִם. וּמֵהַאי דְּאָמַר מֹר, אִשְׁתְּמַע דְּהַאי פְּסוּקָא בְּהַהוּא. מִלָּה אָתָא וַאֲנָן אוֹרְחָא אִתְתַּקְנָא קָמָן, לְמֵיתֵי לְמִשְׁאַל קַמָּךְ.

107. Rabbi Chiya opened the discussion, saying: If it pleases my master, I will say one thing, why I came. It is written: "And it came to pass, that at midnight Hashem smote every firstborn in the land of Egypt..." From this THING that Sir said, it is understood that this passage is ALSO explained in that manner. As for us, the way was propitious before us, to come and ask before you.

108. פָּתַח ר״ש וְאָמַר, מִי כַּיְיָ׳ אֱלֹהֵינוּ הַמַּגְבִּיהִי לָשָׁבֶת וְגוֹ׳. מִי כַּיְיָ׳ אֱלֹהֵינוּ, דְּסָלִיק וְאִתְעַטָּר לְאִתְיַשְּׁבָא בְּכִתְרָא עִלָּאָה קַדִּישָׁא, נְהִירוּ עַל כָּל בּוּצִינֵי דְּנָהֲרוּ כִּתְרִין וְעִטְרִין. הַמַּשְׁפִּילִי לִרְאוֹת, דְּנָחִית בְּכִתְרוֹי, מִכִּתְרָא לְכִתְרָא, מִנִּזְרָא לְנִזְרָא, מִנְּהִירוּ לִנְהִירוּ, מִבּוּצִינָא לְבוּצִינָא. לְאַשְׁגְּחָא בְּעִלָּאִין וְתַתָּאִין, הה״ד יְיָ׳ מִשָּׁמַיִם הִשְׁקִיף עַל בְּנֵי אָדָם וְגוֹ׳.

108. Rabbi Shimon opened the discussion, saying: "Who is like Hashem our Elohim, Who is enthroned on high...?" (Tehilim 113:5) MEANING, "Who is like Hashem our Elohim," WHO IS ZEIR ANPIN, that ascends and is crowned to settle in the holy upper crown, WHICH IS BINAH, which illumination is above all the shining lights, crowns and wreaths, FOR ALL THE MOCHIN IN THE WORLDS ARE DRAWN FROM BINAH. "and yet looks far down" (Ibid.), descending in His Sfirot from crown to crown, MEANING FROM THE RIGHT COLUMN OF BINAH TO HIS OWN RIGHT, from diadem to diadem, FROM THE LEFT COLUMN OF BINAH TO HIS OWN LEFT; from illumination to illumination, FROM THE CENTRAL COLUMN OF BINAH TO HIS OWN CENTRAL COLUMN; from luminary to luminary, FROM MALCHUT OF BINAH TO HIS OWN MALCHUT, to supervise over the upper beings IN

THE HEAVENS and the lower beings ON EARTH. This is the meaning of: "Hashem looked down from heaven upon the children of man" (Tehilim 14:2).

109. תָּא חֲזֵי, כְּתִיב, וַיְהִי בַּחֲצִי הַלַּיְלָה. כַּחֲצִי מִבָּעֵי לֵיהּ, אוֹ כַּחֲצוֹת, כְּגַוְונָא דְּאָמַר מֹשֶׁה. וְאִי כְּמָה דְּאַמְרֵי חַבְרָנָא, דְּלָא יֵימְרוּן אִצְטַגְנִינֵי פַּרְעֹה, מֹשֶׁה בַּדַּאי הוּא. הָא קוּשְׁיָא בְּאַתְרֵיהּ קַיְּימָא, בג׳ גַּוְונֵי, דַּאֲפִילוּ יִשְׂרָאֵל יֵימְרוּן הָכִי. חַד, דְּאִי הָכִי הֲוָה לֵיהּ לְמֵימָר וַיֹּאמֶר מֹשֶׁה כַּחֲצוֹת הַלַּיְלָה. אֲמַאי קָאָמַר, כֹּה אָמַר יְיָ׳ וְגוֹ׳. כְּמָה דְּלָא אִתְכְּוָון שַׁעֲתָא, דְּהָא לָא יִתְפְּסוּן בְּמֹשֶׁה, אֶלָּא בְּפַטְרוֹנָא, בְּגִין דְּאָמַר כֹּה אָמַר יְיָ׳ וְגוֹ׳. תְּרֵי, דְּהָא מֹשֶׁה אָמַר, עַד בְּכוֹר הַשִּׁפְחָה אֲשֶׁר אַחַר הָרֵחָיִם, וְלָא הֲוָה הָכִי, אֶלָּא עַד בְּכוֹר הַשְּׁבִי אֲשֶׁר בְּבֵית הַבּוֹר. עכ״פ אֲפִילוּ יִשְׂרָאֵל נַמֵי יֵימְרוּן הָכִי, דְּהָא לָא אִתְבַּרְרוּן מִלֵּי. תְּלַת דְּאִיהוּ אָמַר מִשְּׁמָא דְּפַטְרוֹנָא כַּחֲצוֹת, וּכְתִיב וַיְהִי בַּחֲצִי הַלַּיְלָה.

109. Come and behold: it is written, "And it came to pass, that at midnight..." It should have said, 'approximately midnight' or "About midnight" (Shemot 11:4), as Moses had said. And YOU MAY CONTEND, as the friends said, that this is because the astrologers of Pharaoh might say that Moses was a liar, BECAUSE IT IS IMPOSSIBLE TO DETERMINE THE EXACT MOMENT OF MIDNIGHT. So the difficult question remains in three forms, and even the children of Yisrael will agree. 1) If so, it should have said, 'And Moses said, about midnight'. Why does it say, "Thus says Hashem," if Hashem said, "At midnight"? No matter how punctual he will be, they will not blame Moses, but rather the Master, because he said, "Thus says Hashem." 2) Moses said, "even to the firstborn of the maidservant that is behind the mill" (Ibid. 5), yet it was not so, but "to the firstborn of the captive that was in the dungeon" (Shemot 12:29). Regardless, even Yisrael will agree THAT HE IS A LIAR, because these things did not occur exactly AS HE SAID. 3) He said in the name of the Master, 'About midnight' but it is written: "And it came to pass, that at midnight" AND NOT 'ABOUT MIDNIGHT', AS MOSES SAID.

110. וְעוֹד, שְׁאֵלְתָּא דִּילְכוֹן, יַתִּיר עַל מָטוּל דְּלָא יָכִיל בְּעִירָא לְמִסְבַּל. אֲמַאי הֲוָה בְּפַלְגוּת לֵילְיָא, וְלָא בִּימָמָא. וַאֲמַאי מִיתוּ כָּל אִינּוּן חַלָּשִׁין

דְּבָתַר רֵחַיָּא. אֶלָּא כֹּלָּא רָזָא עִלָּאָה הוּא, בֵּין מְחַצְּדֵי חַקְלָא, וְכֹלָּא אִתְכְּשַׁר בִּנְבִיאָה מְהֵימָנָא.

110. And also regarding your question, WHICH IS HEAVIER than a load an animal can carry. YOU ASKS: Why was the smiting of the firstborn at night and not by day? And why did the weaklings who were behind the millstone die? This is all a supernal secret among the reapers of the field, MEANING THOSE WHO MERITED THE PLANTS OF THE HIDDEN LIGHT THAT WERE SOWN IN MALCHUT THAT IS CALLED 'FIELD'. And it is all correct according to THE WORDS OF the faithful prophet.

111. זַכָּאָה חוּלָקֵיהּ דְּמֹשֶׁה, דְּעָלֵיהּ כְּתִיב יָפְיָפִיתָ מִבְּנֵי אָדָם הוּצַק חֵן בְּשִׂפְתוֹתֶיךָ עַל כֵּן בֵּרַכְךָ אֱלֹהִים לְעוֹלָם. אָהַבְתָּ צֶּדֶק וַתִּשְׂנָא רֶשַׁע עַל כֵּן מְשָׁחֲךָ אֱלֹהִים אֱלֹהֶיךָ שֶׁמֶן שָׂשׂוֹן מֵחֲבֵרֶיךָ. יָפְיָפִיתָ מִבְּנֵי אָדָם: מִשֵּׁת וַחֲנוֹךְ. הוּצַק חֵן בְּשִׂפְתוֹתֶיךָ: מִנֹּחַ וּבָנָיו. עַל כֵּן מְשָׁחֲךָ אֱלֹהִים אֱלֹהֶיךָ: מֵאַבְרָהָם וְיִצְחָק. שֶׁמֶן שָׂשׂוֹן: מִיַּעֲקֹב. מֵחֲבֵרֶיךָ: מִשְּׁאָר נְבִיאֵי. וְכִי גֶּבֶר דְּסָלִיק בְּדַרְגִּין עִלָּאִין דְּלָא סָלִיק ב״נ אַחֲרָא, לָא יָדַע מַה דְּאָמַר.

111. Praiseworthy is the portion of Moses, about whom it is written: "You are fairer than the children of men, grace is poured into your lips: therefore Elohim has blessed you forever" (Tehilim 45:3). "You love righteousness, and hate wickedness. Therefore Elohim, your Elohim, has anointed you with the oil of gladness above your fellows" (Ibid. 8). "You are fairer than the children of men," MEANS more than Seth and Enoch. "Grace is poured into you lips," more so than Noah and his sons, OF WHOM IT SAYS: "AND NOAH FOUND FAVOR" (BERESHEET 6:8). "Therefore Elohim, your Elohim, has anointed you," more than Abraham and Isaac. "With the oil of gladness" more than Jacob. "above your fellows," refers to the other prophets. Is it possible that a man who rose to the highest levels to which no other man rose did not know what he was saying?

112. אֶלָּא הָכִי תָּנֵינָן, הַאי כִּתְרָא דְּאִקְרֵי זֹא״ת, אִתְקְרֵי אִשָּׁ״ה, כד״א, לְזֹאת יִקָּרֵא אִשָּׁה. אֲמַאי. מִשּׁוּם כִּי מֵאִישׁ לֻקֳחָה זֹּאת. מַאן הוּא אִישׁ. הַהוּא דְּאִקְרֵי זֶה. וְדָא הוּא אִישׁ דְּבָר, כד״א כִּי זֶה מֹשֶׁה הָאִישׁ. הָאִישׁ

הַזֶּה. וְאִקְרֵי אִישׁ זֶה, וְזֶה אִישׁ. וְזֹאת, אִתְנְסִיבַת מִזֶּה דְּאִקְרֵי זָכָר.

112. But this is what we learned. This Sfirah that is called "*zot* ('this' fem.)" – NAMELY MALCHUT – is called 'woman', as is written: "She (Heb. *zot* fem.) shall be called woman" (Beresheet 2:23). And why IS SHE CALLED SO? BECAUSE "she (*zot*) was taken out of man" (Ibid.). Who is this man? He is the one who is called "*zeh* ('this')" and is a male man, NAMELY ZEIR ANPIN, as is written: "for as for this (Heb. *zeh* masc.) Moses, the man" (Shemot 32:23) SO 'man' is called '*zeh*', and '*zeh*' is called 'man'. And *zot* is taken from *zeh* that is called 'male'.

113. וּבְגִין דָּא, אִיהִי תָּמָר דְּכַר וְנוּקְבָּא, דְּלָא סָלִיק דָּא בְּלָא דָּא. תָּמָר: כד"א, כְּתִמְרוֹת עָשָׁן. מַה עָשָׁן, סָלִיק חִוָּור וְאוּכָם, אוּף הָכָא, כֹּלָּא כָּלִיל בָּהּ בְּפַלְגוּת לֵילְיָא, לְמֶעְבַּד נִימוּסוֹי בְּחַד שַׁעֲתָא, חִוָּור לְיִשְׂרָאֵל, וְאוּכָם לעכו"ם.

113. Therefore, she, NAMELY MALCHUT, is CALLED "a palm tree" (Heb. *tamar*), WHICH DENOTES male and female, because the palm tree does not grow one without the other, MALE WITHOUT FEMALE. SHE IS THEREFORE CALLED Tamar, as is written, "like pillars (Heb. *timrot*) of smoke" (Shir Hashirim 3:6). The same way as smoke rises with both white and black, so here too WITH MALCHUT THAT IS CALLED '*ZOT*'. Everything is included in her at midnight, so she will perform her deeds together AT ONCE, white for Yisrael, WHICH IS MERCY, and black for the heathen nations, WHICH IS JUDGMENT.

114. וְעוֹד דְּהַאי לֵילְיָא לָא אִתְפְּלַג, לָא עָבֵיד נִימוּסוֹי מ"ל. מֵאַבְרָהָם. דִּכְתִּיב וַיֵּחָלֵק עֲלֵיהֶם לַיְלָה, דְּאִתְפְּלַג לְמֶעְבַּד נִימוּסוֹי. אוּף הָכָא, מֹשֶׁה אָמַר כַּחֲצוֹת, כְּמִפְלַג. דְּמֹשֶׁה יָדַע דְּלָא יַעְבֵּיד נִימוּסוֹי, עַד דְּאִתְפְּלַג.

114. Before the night is divided in half at midnight, it does not perform its functions. Whence do we know this? From Abraham, as is written: "And he divided himself against them...night" (Beresheet 14:15), WHICH MEANS that it was divided in order to do its functions. Here too, Moses said, "About midnight," MEANING when THE NIGHT reaches the middle, for Moses knew that its functions would not be performed until it does.

115. וְהָכִי הֲוָה, דְּלָא עָבֵיד לֵילְיָא נִימוּסוֹי, עַד דְּאִתְפְּלַג, בְּפַלְגוּת בַּתְרָאָה, עָבֵד נִימוּסוֹי, הה"ד וַיְהִי בַּחֲצִי הַלַּיְלָה. מַאי בַּחֲצִי. בְּפַלְגוּת בַּתְרָאָה, בִּזְמְנָא דְּאִיהִי שַׁלְטָא, וְאִשְׁתְּכַח הַאי זֹאת, לְמֶעְבַּד נִמּוּסִין תְּדִירָא, וְכָל נִימוּסָא דְּאִתְעָבֵיד בְּלֵילְיָא, בְּפַלְגוּתָא בַּתְרָאָה אִתְעָבֵיד.

115. And so it was that the night did not perform its functions until midnight, for it performed its functions in the second half of the night. This is the meaning of: "And it came to pass, that at midnight." What is the connotation of "mid"? IT MEANS that during the second half, when MALCHUT, rules, *zot*, MALCHUT is always present to perform actions, and every action that was done at night was done in the second half.

116. וַיְיָ' הִכָּה כָל בְּכוֹר, וַיְיָ': הוּא וּבֵית דִּינוֹ, וַיְיָ': הוּא וְנִימוּסוֹי. הִכָּה כָל בְּכוֹר הִכָּה, מֹשֶׁה לֹא אָמַר אֶלָּא וּמֵת וְגוֹ', מַהוּ הִכָּה. אֶלָּא, דְּאִתְעַר כֹּה, כְּמָה דְּאַגְזִים מֹשֶׁה, דִּכְתִּיב וְהִנֵּה לֹא שָׁמַעְתָּ עַד כֹּה.

116. "And Hashem smote every firstborn." "And Hashem" IS DEFINED AS Him, ZEIR ANPIN, and His court, WHICH IS MALCHUT. "And Hashem," REFERS TO Him and His actions. "Smote every firstborn" – HE ASKS: Moses only said, "And all the firstborn…shall die" (Shemot 11:5). Why DOES IT SAY HERE "smote"? HE ANSWERS: But MALCHUT OF THE ASPECT OF JUDGMENT, WHICH IS CALLED "*KOH*", became aroused and Moses threatened him, as is written: "Behold, till now (Lit. 'to *koh*) you would not hear." THEREFORE, IT IS SAID, "HASHEM SMOTE (HEB. *HIKAH*)," WHICH IS THE NAME *KOH* THAT SLEW ALL THE FIRSTBORN OF EGYPT.

117. וְתָאנָא, פַּרְעֹה חַכִּים הֲוָה מִכָּל חֲרָשׁוֹי, וְאִסְתַּכַּל בְּהַאי זֹאת, דְּיַעֲבֵיד בֵּיהּ דִּינָא, וְזַמִּין לְחָרְבָא אַרְעֵיהּ, כְּמָה דְּאָמַר מֹשֶׁה, בְּזֹאת תֵּדַע כִּי אֲנִי יְיָ'. וּבְאִיהוּ מַה כְּתִיב, וַיִּפֶן פַּרְעֹה. מַהוּ וַיִּפֶן. דְּאַפְנֵי לִבֵּיהּ מֵהִרְהוּרָא דָּא. כד"א, וַיִּפֶן אַהֲרֹן. וַיָּבוֹא אֶל בֵּיתוֹ וְלֹא שָׁת לִבּוֹ גַּם

לְזֹאת. גַּם לְרַבּוֹת הַאי דִּזְמִינָא לְחָרְבָא אַרְעֵיהּ, וְלָא שַׁוֵּי לִבֵּיהּ לְקַבְּלֵיהּ דְּזֹא"ת.

117. We learned that Pharaoh was wiser than all his sorcerers, and observed that *zot*, NAMELY MALCHUT, would execute Judgment upon him and destroy his land, as Moses said, "In this (*zot*) you shall know that I am Hashem" (Shemot 7:17). It is written about him: "And Pharaoh turned" (Ibid. 23), "turned" MEANING that he turned his heart away from this thought, as written: "And Ahab turned" (Bemidbar 12:10). "And went to his house, neither did set his heart even to this (Heb. *zot*)" (Ibid.) THE WORD "also," WHICH IS SUPERFLUOUS, is to add that one which will destroy his land, "neither did set his heart even to this," MEANING THE WORD "ALSO" IMPLIES THAT EVEN THOUGH HE KNEW THAT THE NAME '*ZOT*', WHICH IS MALCHUT, WOULD DESTROY HIS LAND, HE DID NOT PAY ATTENTION TO IT.

118. כָּל בְּכוֹר, אֲפִילוּ דַּרְגִּין עִלָּאִין וְתַתָּאִין, אִתְּבָרוּ מִשּׁוּלְטָנֵהוֹן, כָּל אִינּוּן דְּשַׁלְטִין בְּחָכְמְתָא דִּלְהוֹן, דִּכְתִּיב, בְּאֶרֶץ מִצְרַיִם. וְכֻלְּהוּ דַּרְגִּין, עִלָּאִין וְתַתָּאִין, דְּאִתְּבָרוּ מִשּׁוּלְטָנֵהוֹן, כֻּלְּהוּ בִּפְסוּקָא אִתְחָזוּן, דִּכְתִּיב מִבְּכוֹר פַּרְעֹה הַיּוֹשֵׁב עַל כִּסְאוֹ עַד בְּכוֹר הַשִּׁפְחָה אֲשֶׁר אַחַר הָרֵחָיִם וְכֹל בְּכוֹר בְּהֵמָה, הָא כֻּלְּהוּ אִתְחָזוּן בִּפְסוּקָא.

118. IT IS WRITTEN: "all the firstborn." "FIRSTBORN" IS THE ASPECT CHOCHMAH, AND "ALL THE FIRSTBORN" DENOTES THAT even upper and lower levels were broken in power – MEANING all those levels that rule by THE POWER OF their wisdom, WHICH IS THE WISDOM OF EGYPT as is written: "ALL THE FIRSTBORN in the land of Egypt." All the upper and lower levels that were broken in power are all alluded to in the verse, "From the firstborn of Pharaoh that sits on his throne, even to the firstborn of the maidservant that is behind the mill; and all the firstborn of cattle" (Shemot 11:5). So we see that they are all alluded to in the passage.

119. סְתָמָא דְּמִלָּה, מִבְּכוֹר פַּרְעֹה הַיּוֹשֵׁב עַל כִּסְאוֹ, כִּתְרָא תַּתָּאָה דְּקוּזְמִיטָא דְּמַלְכוּתָא דִּלְעֵילָּא. עַד בְּכוֹר הַשִּׁפְחָה, כִּתְרָא שְׂמָאלָא, תַּתָּאָה מִינָהּ, דְּקוּזְמִיטָא מִבָּתַר אַרְבַּע רֵחַיִין, אַרְבַּע מַשִּׁירְיָין. מַשְׁמַע, מִשּׁוּם דִּכְתִּיב אַחַר הָרֵחָיִם, וְלֹא מִן הָרֵחָיִם. וְכֹל בְּכוֹר בְּהֵמָה, תַּתָּאִין

מִתַּתָּאִין, נוּקְבָּא מִנּוּקְבְתָא, דְּאִשְׁתְּכָחוּ בְּאַתָּנֵי בִּבְעִירֵי וַחֲמָרֵי, בְּרַבְרְבֵי בְּזוּטְרֵי, וּמְקַבְּלִין מִנְּהוֹן גּוּבְרִין וְנוּקְבִין. עַד בְּכוֹר הַשְּׁבִי אֲשֶׁר בְּבֵית הַבּוֹר, אִינּוּן דְּנָפְקִין מִשִּׁפְחָה. דִּי בְּהוֹן עַבְדִין לַאֲסִירֵי, דְּיִשְׁתַּעְבְּדוּן בְּהוֹן לְעָלְמִין, וְלָא יִפְקוּן לְחֵירוּ.

119. In brief, “From the firstborn of Pharaoh that sits on his throne,” REFERS TO the power of the lowest Sfirah OF THE KLIPOT, WHICH RECEIVE from the upper Malchut. “even to the firstborn of the maidservant,” refers to the left Sfirah, which is under the power MENTIONED EARLIER, from behind four mills, which are the four legions OF THE KLIPOT. This is understood, because it is written, “behind the millstone,” and not ‘from the millstone’. “And all the firstborn of cattle,” REFERS TO THOSE below the lower beings MENTIONED EARLIER. It is a female, of the females of donkeys, cattle and donkeys, large and small animals, WHICH ARE THE LEVELS OF IMPURITY. Males and females come out from them. “To the firstborn of the captive that was in the dungeon,” MEANS those that descend from the maidservant, for with them, SORCERY is performed on the prisoners in order to enslave them forever and ensure they never go free.

120. וּבְרוּחְצָנוּתָא דְּאִלֵּין דַּרְגִּין, סָרִיבוּ מִצְרָאֵי, דִּי בְּהוֹן עֲבָדוּ קִשְׁרָא לְיִשְׂרָאֵל, דְּלָא יִפְקוּן מִן עַבְדוּתְהוֹן לְעָלְמִין. וּבְהַאי אִתְחֲזֵי גְּבוּרְתָּא וְשֻׁלְטָנוּתָא דְּקוּדְשָׁא בְּרִיךְ הוּא, וְדִכְרָנָא דָּא לָא יִשְׁתְּצֵי מִיִּשְׂרָאֵל לְדָרֵי דָּרִין, דְּאִי לָא הֲוָה חֵילָא וּגְבוּרְתָּא דְּקוּדְשָׁא בְּרִיךְ הוּא, כָּל מַלְכֵי עַמִּין, וְכָל חָרָשֵׁי עָלְמִין, וְחַכִּימֵי עָלְמִין, לָא יִפְקוּן לְיִשְׂרָאֵל מִן עַבְדוּתָא, דְּשָׁרָא קִטְרִין דִּלְהוֹן, וְתָבַר כָּל אִינּוּן כִּתְרִין, בְּגִין לְאַפָּקָא לוֹן. עַל דָּא כְּתִיב, מִי לֹא יִרָאֲךָ מֶלֶךְ הַגּוֹיִם כִּי לְךָ יָאָתָה כִּי בְכָל חַכְמֵי הַגּוֹיִם וּבְכָל מַלְכוּתָם מֵאֵין כָּמוֹךָ.

120. Because they relied upon these levels, the Egyptians refused TO LET THE CHILDREN OF YISRAEL GO, for they formed a knot OF SORCERY against Yisrael so they would never be able to leave their bondage. The strength and dominion of the Holy One, blessed be He, is seen in this, and this memory will never cease from Yisrael for generations and generations. If not for the strength and power of the Holy One, blessed be He, none the kings of the nations and all the sorcerers of the world would be able to deliver Yisrael from bondage. For He opened their bonds and smashed all these crowns OF THE FIRSTBORN OF THE CAPTIVE MENTIONED EARLIER in order to take them out TO FREEDOM. Referring to this, it is written: "Who would not fear You, O King of the nations? For to You it is fitting. For among all the wise men of the nations, and in all their kingdom, there is none like You" (Yirmeyah 10:7).

121. בָּכָה ר"ש, אָרִים קָלֵיהּ וְאַתְנַח, אָמַר קִנְטוּרָא דְּקִיטְפָּא אִשְׁתְּכַח, חֲשַׁבְתּוּן דְּשָׁבַח קוּדְשָׁא בְּרִיךְ הוּא כַּמָּה זִמְנִין, אֲשֶׁר הוֹצֵאתִיךָ מֵאֶרֶץ מִצְרַיִם, הוֹצִיאֲךָ יְיָ' אֱלֹהֶיךָ מִמִּצְרַיִם, וַיּוֹצִיאֲךָ יְיָ' אֱלֹהֶיךָ מִשָּׁם, הוֹצֵאתִי אֶת צִבְאוֹתֵיכֶם, זָכוֹר אֶת הַיּוֹם הַזֶּה אֲשֶׁר יְצָאתֶם מִמִּצְרַיִם, וַיּוֹצִיאֲךָ בְּפָנָיו בְּכֹחוֹ הַגָּדוֹל מִמִּצְרַיִם, הוֹצִיא יְיָ' אֶתְכֶם מִזֶּה.

121. Rabbi Shimon wept, raised his voice and sighed. He said: There is an attachment formed. Have you thought HOW MUCH the Holy One, blessed be He, ATTACHED HIMSELF, AND praised HIMSELF SO many times FOR THE EXODUS FROM EGYPT? It is written: "who brought you out of the Land of Egypt" (Devarim 5:6); "Hashem your Elohim brought you forth out of Egypt" (Devarim 16:1); "Hashem your Elohim brought you out from there" (Devarim 5:15); "I brought your hosts out" (Shemot 12:17); "Remember this day, in which you came out from Egypt" (Shemot 13:3); "and brought you out, He Himself being present, with His mighty power out of Egypt" (Devarim 4:37); "Hashem brought you out from this place" (Shemot 13:3). THE EXODUS FROM EGYPT IS MENTIONED IN THE TORAH FIFTY TIMES.

122. אֶלָּא תָּאנָא, י' כִּתְרִין, אִינּוּן לְתַתָּא, כְּגַוְונָא דִּלְעֵילָּא, וְכֻלְּהוּ סְתִימִין, בִּתְלָתָא אִלֵּין דְּאַמָרָן. וּתְלַת קִשְׁרִין קָשִׁירוּ בְּהוּ, עַל ג' דַּרְגִּין אִלֵּין דִּבְהוּ עַבְדוּ, דְּיִשְׂרָאֵל לָא יִפְקוּן מִשִּׁעְבּוּדְהוֹן לְעָלְמִין.

122. HE ANSWERS: Yet we learned that there are ten crowns, MEANING SFIROT, below IN THE KLIPOT, as above IN HOLINESS. They are all blocked by the three KLIPOT we mentioned, NAMELY THE FIRSTBORN OF PHARAOH, THE FIRSTBORN OF THE MAIDSERVANT AND THE FIRSTBORN OF CATTLE. They formed three ties on these three levels, with which they caused that Yisrael would never leave their bondage.

123. זַכָּאִין אַתּוּן אַבְרָהָם יִצְחָק וְיַעֲקֹב, דִּבְזְכוּתְכוֹן שָׁרִיאוּ קִטְרִין, וְקוּדְשָׁא בְּרִיךְ הוּא דְּכַר תְּלַת קִטְרֵי מְהֵימְנוּתָא דִּלְכוֹן הה״ד וַיִּזְכֹּר אֱלֹהִים אֶת בְּרִיתוֹ אֶת אַבְרָהָם אֶת יִצְחָק וְאֶת יַעֲקֹב. אֶת אַבְרָהָם, הָא קִשְׁרָא חֲדָא, דְּאַבְרָהָם. אֶת יִצְחָק, הָא קִשְׁרָא תִּנְיָינָא, דְּיִצְחָק. וְאֶת יַעֲקֹב, הָא קִשְׁרָא תְּלִיתָאָה, שְׁלֵימָתָא דְּיַעֲקֹב.

123. Fortunate are you, Abraham, Isaac and Jacob, for the ties were untied for your sakes, and the Holy One, blessed be He, remembered your three ties of Faith. This is the meaning of: "And Elohim remembered His covenant with Abraham, with Isaac, and with Jacob" (Shemot 2:24). "With Abraham," is one tie of Abraham, "with Isaac," is the second tie of Isaac, and "with Jacob," is the third whole tie of Jacob.

124. תָּנָא, כָּל זִמְנִין וְחַגִּין וְשַׁבָּתִין, כֻּלְּהוּ דּוּכְרָנָא לְהַאי, וְעַל הַאי אִתְקַיְּימוּ כֻּלְּהוּ, דְּאִלְמָלֵא הַאי, לָא הֲוָה נְטוּרָא דִּזְמַנִּין וְחַגִּין וְשַׁבָּתִין. וּבְגִינֵי כַּךְ, לָא אִשְׁתְּצֵי דֻּכְרָנָא דְּמִצְרַיִם מִכָּל זִמְנִין וְחַגִּין וְשַׁבָּתִין. ת״ח דִּינָא דָּא, הוּא יְסוֹדָא וְשָׁרְשָׁא דְּאוֹרַיְיתָא, וְכָל פִּקּוּדוֹי, וְכָל מְהֵימְנוּתָא שְׁלֵימָתָא דְּיִשְׂרָאֵל.

124. We learned that every holiday, festival and Shabbat are all in memory of this, THE EXODUS OUT OF EGYPT. They are all based on this and were it not for this, there would be no observance of the holidays, festivals and Shabbat. Therefore, the memory of Egypt has not ceased from all holidays, festivals and Shabbatot. Come and behold: this Judgment IN THE EXODUS FROM EGYPT is the foundation and source of the Torah and all the commandments and the complete Faith of the children of Yisrael. THEREFORE, THE EXODUS OUT OF EGYPT IS MENTIONED MANY TIMES IN THE TORAH.

125. וְעוֹד אֲמַאי לָא הֲוָה בִּימָמָא דְּשָׁאִילְתּוּ. תָּנֵינָן, כְּתִיב הַיּוֹם אַתֶּם יוֹצְאִים, וּכְתִיב הוֹצִיאֲךָ יְיָ׳ אֱלֹהֶיךָ מִמִּצְרַיִם לָיְלָה. אֶלָּא תָּאנָא, עִקָּרָא דְּפוּרְקָנָא דְּיִשְׂרָאֵל, לָא הֲוָה אֶלָּא בְּלַיְלָה, דְּלֵילְיָא שָׁרָא קִטְרִין, וְעָבֵד נוּקְמִין, וְיוֹמָא אַפִּיק לוֹן בְּרֵישׁ גַּלֵּי, הֲדָא הוּא דִּכְתִּיב יָצְאוּ בְּנֵי יִשְׂרָאֵל

בְּיַד רָמָה לְעֵינֵי כָּל מִצְרָיִם. וּכְתִיב וּמִצְרַיִם מְקַבְּרִים אֵת אֲשֶׁר הִכָּה יְיָ' בָּהֶם כָּל בְּכוֹר, דָּא הוּא פִּרְסוּמֵי נִיסָא.

125. Also regarding your question why the Judgment of Egypt did not occur by day, we learned that it is written: "This day you came out" (Shemot 13:4), and, "Hashem your Elohim brought you forth out of Egypt by night" (Devarim 16:1). But we learned that the redemption of the children of Yisrael was mainly by night, WHICH IS THE SECRET OF MALCHUT CALLED 'NIGHT', for the night opened the ties and wreaked revenge, while the day brought them out with a high hand. This is the meaning of: "The children of Yisrael went out with a high hand in the sight of all Egypt. And Egypt was burying all their firstborn whom Hashem had smitten among them" (Bemidbar 33:3). This was in order to make the miracle famous.

126. אָתוּ ר' חִיָּיא ור' יוֹסֵי, אִשְׁתְּטָחוּ קָמֵיהּ, וְנָשְׁקוּ יְדוֹי. וּבָכוּ וְאָמְרוּ, גְּלִיפִין עִלָּאִין וְתַתָּאִין, זַקְפָן רֵישָׁא בְּגִינָךְ, עָבֵד קוּדְשָׁא בְּרִיךְ הוּא יְרוּשָׁלַיִם לְתַתָּא, כְּגַוְונָא דִּלְעֵילָּא. עָבֵד שׁוּרֵי קַרְתָּא קַדִּישָׁא וְתַרְעוֹי. מַאן דְּעָיֵיל, לָא עָיֵיל, עַד דְּיִפְתְּחוּן תַּרְעִין. מַאן דְּסָלִיק, לָא סָלִיק, עַד דְּיִתְתַּקְנוּן דַּרְגִּין דְּשׁוּרֵי מַאן יָכִיל לְמִפְתַּח תַּרְעִין דְּקַרְתָּא קַדִּישָׁא, וּמַאן יָכִיל לְאַתְקְנָא דַּרְגִּין דְּשׁוּרֵי, דָּא רשב"י, דְּאִיהוּ פָּתַח תַּרְעִין דְּרָזֵי דְּחָכְמְתָא, וְאִיהוּ אַתְקִין דַּרְגִּין עִלָּאִין, וּכְתִיב יֵרָאֶה כָּל זְכוּרְךָ אֶת פְּנֵי הָאָדוֹן יְיָ'. מַאן פְּנֵי הָאָדוֹן יְיָ', דָּא רשב"י, דְּמַאן דְּאִיהוּ דְּכוּרָא מִן דְּכֻרְנַיָּא, בָּעֵי לְאִתְחֲזָאָה קָמֵיהּ.

126. Rabbi Chiya and Rabbi Yosi came and prostrated before him, and kissed his hands. They wept and said: Upper and lower images raise their heads through your merit. The Holy One, blessed be He, made terrestrial Jerusalem, WHICH IS MALCHUT, in the likeness of celestial Jerusalem, WHICH IS BINAH. And He made the outer walls of the Holy City and its gates. One can not enter until the gates are opened for him. One can not ascend until the steps to the outer walls are prepared. Who can open the gates of the Holy City? And who can repair the steps to the outer walls? This is Rabbi Shimon bar Yochai, who opens the gates of the secrets of Wisdom and repairs the upper levels. And it is written: "Every one of your males shall appear before the Master Hashem" (Shemot 34:23). Who is before the Master Hashem? This is Rabbi Shimon bar Yochai. For he who is a memory (Heb. *zecher*) of the remembrances, THAT IS, HE IS THE ASPECT OF THE MALE (HEB. *ZACHAR*) OF THE SUPERNAL MOCHIN THAT ARE CALLED 'REMEMBRANCES (HEB. *ZICHRONOT*)', WHICH ARE OF THE MOCHIN OF ABA AND IMA, has to appear before Him.

127. אָמַר לוֹן, עַד הַשְׁתָּא, לָא סַיֵּימְנָא מִלָּה דִּשְׁאֶלְתָּא דִּילְכוֹן, דְּהָא תָּנֵינָן, וַיְיָ' הִכָּה כָל בְּכוֹר, כָּל בְּכוֹר סְתָם, כִּדְקָאַמְרַן. וְכֹלָּא הֲוָה כְּמָה דְּאִינּוּן דְּמִיתוּ, אִינּוּן קְטוּרֵי קִטְרִין, דַּהֲווֹ מִשְׁתַּמְּשֵׁי בְּחָרָשַׁיְיהוּ בְּאִינּוּן כִּתְרִין. מִנְהוֹן מִשְׁתַּמְּשֵׁי בְּעִלָּאֵי, וּמִנְהוֹן בְּתַתָּאֵי, וְאַף עַל גַּב דְּכֻלְּהוּ תַּתָּאִין אִינּוּן. וְכָל אַרְעָא דְּמִצְרַיִם מַלְיָא חֲרָשִׁין הֲוָה. וּכְתִיב כִּי אֵין בַּיִת אֲשֶׁר אֵין שָׁם מֵת.

127. He said to them: Even now, I have still not finished ANSWERING your questions. For we learned, "And Hashem smote all the firstborn." "all the firstborn" is general; IT DOES NOT SAY 'THE FIRSTBORN OF EGYPT', BECAUSE IT REFERS ALSO TO THE LEVELS THE EGYPTIANS WERE ATTACHED TO, WHICH ARE THE FOUR LEVELS OF THE KLIPOT, of which we spoke before. For everyone it was the same as for those that died, MEANING THAT WHATEVER WAS DONE TO THE FIRSTBORN OF EGYPT WHO DIED WAS LIKEWISE DONE TO THE LEVELS OF KLIPOT. Of those who tied the ties and used these crowns in their witchcraft, some employed the upper, and some the lower, and even though they were all lower, THEY ALSO EMPLOYED THE UPPER. And the whole land of Egypt was full of sorcery, as is written: "For there was not a house where there was not one dead" (Shemot 12:30).

128. וְאִתְעֲבֵיד דִּינָא בְּכֹלָּא, בְּשַׁעֲתָא דְּאִתְכְּנָשׁוּ כֻּלְּהוּ בְּבָתֵּיהוֹן, וְלָא הֲווֹ מִתְפַּזְּרֵי בְּמַדְבְּרָא וּבְחַקְלָא, אֶלָּא כֻּלְּהוּ אִשְׁתְּכָחוּ בְּבָתֵּיהוֹן, וְעָבֵד לֵילְיָא דִּינוֹי בְּכֹלָּא בְּהַהִיא שַׁעֲתָא. וְתָנָא הֲוָה נָהִיר לֵילְיָא כְּיוֹמָא דִּתְקוּפָה דְּתַמּוּז, וְחָמָא כָּל עַמָּא דִּינוֹי דְּקוּדְשָׁא בְּרִיךְ הוּא, הה"ד וְלַיְלָה כַּיּוֹם יָאִיר כַּחֲשֵׁכָה כָּאוֹרָה.

128. And Judgment was executed against them all. When they were all gathered in their homes, and were not scattered in the wilderness or in the field, the night, WHICH IS MALCHUT, executed its Judgments. And we learned that the night shone just like the day is the solstice of *Tamuz*, and the whole people saw the Judgments of the Holy One, blessed be He. This is the meaning of: "But the night shines like the day: the darkness and the light are both alike" (Tehilim 139:12).

129. וּבְשַׁעֲתָא דְּנָפְקוּ אִשְׁתְּכָחוּ כֻּלְּהוֹן מֵתִין בְּשׁוָקִין לְעֵינֵיהוֹן דְּכֹלָּא, בָּעְיָין לְאַקְבְּרָא לְהוּ וְלָא אַשְׁכָּחוּ, וְדָא אַקְשֵׁי לְהוּ מִכֹּלָּא. חָמוּ לְיִשְׂרָאֵל נָפְקִין לְעֵינֵיהוֹן בְּחַד גִּיסָא, וְחָמוּ לְמֵיתֵיהוֹן בְּאִידָךְ גִּיסָא. וּבְכֹלָּא הֲוָה פִּרְסוּמֵי נִיסָא, דְּלָא הֲוָה כְּהַאי מִיּוֹמָא דְּאִתְבְּרֵי עָלְמָא.

129. When YISRAEL left, they were all found dead in the marketplace before everyone's sight. They wanted to bury them but could not find them, BECAUSE THE DOGS HAD EATEN THEM. HOWEVER, NOT ALL OF THEM WERE EATEN UP. SOME OF THEM DID REMAIN, OF WHOM IT IS SAID, "AND EGYPT WAS BURYING" (BEMIDBAR 33:4). This was the most difficult thing for them, as from one side they saw Yisrael leaving and from the other side they saw their dead. It was all in order to publicize the miracle, for there was nothing like it since the day the world was created.

130. ות"ח, כְּתִיב לֵיל שִׁמּוּרִים הוּא לַיְיָ' לְהוֹצִיאָם וְגוֹ', הוּא הַלַּיְלָה הַזֶּה לַיְיָ' שִׁמּוּרִים לְכָל בְּנֵי יִשְׂרָאֵל וְגוֹ', הַאי פְּסוּקָא קַשְׁיָא כֵּיוָן דְּאָמַר לֵיל, מַהוּ שִׁמּוּרִים, וְלָא שִׁמּוּר, שִׁמּוּר מִבָּעֵי לֵיהּ. וּכְתִיב הוּא הַלַּיְלָה הַזֶּה, לֵיל קָאָמַר בְּקַדְמֵיתָא, וּבָתַר לַיְלָה.

130. Come and behold: it is written, "It is a night of (Heb. *leil*) watchfulness to Hashem for bringing them out...this is Hashem's watch night (Heb. *lailah*) for all the children of Yisrael" (Shemot 12:42). This passage is difficult. Since it says "*leil*," why does it say "watchfulness" using the plural suffix instead of the singular? MOREOVER, it is also written "*lailah*." Why does it first say "*leil*" and afterwards "*lailah*"?

131. אֶלָּא הָכִי תָּנֵינָן, כְּתִיב, כִּי יִהְיֶה נַעֲרָה בְתוּלָה. נַעַר כְּתִיב, מ"ט. מִשּׁוּם דְּכָל זְמַן דְּלָא קַבִּילַת דְּכַר, אִתְקְרֵי נַעַר, מִדְּקַבִּילַת דְּכַר, אִתְקְרֵי נַעֲרָה. אוּף הָכָא, לֵיל עַד לָא קַבִּילַת דְּכַר. ואע"ג דִּכְתִיב בֵּיהּ שִׁמּוּרִים

דְּכַר הֲוָה זַמִּין לְאִתְחַבְּרָא עִמָּהּ וּבְשַׁעֲתָא דְּאִתְחֲבָּר עִמָּהּ דְּכַר, כְּתִיב, הוּא הַלַּיְלָה הַזֶּה לַיְיָ' שִׁמּוּרִים. שִׁמּוּרִים: דְּכַר וְנוּקְבָּא. וּבְגִינֵי כַּךְ כְּתִיב הַלַּיְלָה הַזֶּה.

131. HE ANSWERS: But this is what we learned. It is written: "If there is a virgin maiden (Heb. *na'ara*)" (Devarim 22:23). It is spelled "*na'ara*" without Hei. What is the reason thereof? Because as long as she does not accept a male, she is called "*na'ara*." After she receives a male, she is considered "*na'arah*." Also, MALCHUT IS CALLED "*leil*" before she receives a male, WHICH IS ZEIR ANPIN. Even though it is written: "night of watchfulness" IN THE PLURAL, WHICH SUGGESTS THAT IT ALSO INCLUDES ZEIR ANPIN, IT IS because the male – WHICH IS ZEIR ANPIN – was going to unite with her, BUT DID NOT YET. When the male united with her, it is written: "This is Hashem's watch night (plural)," WHICH INDICATE male and female, NAMELY ZEIR ANPIN AND MALCHUT. Therefore, it is spelled "*lailah*" with Hei.

132. וּבַאֲתַר דְּאִשְׁתְּכָחוּ דְּכַר וְנוּקְבָּא, לֵית שְׁבָחָא אֶלָּא לִדְכוּרָא. וְהָכִי שַׁבָּחוּ יִשְׂרָאֵל בְּתוּשְׁבַּחְתַּיְיהוּ. לִדְכוּרָא וְלָא לְנוּקְבָּא, הה"ד, זֶה אֵלִי וְאַנְוֵהוּ. דְּלֵית שְׁבָחָא בַּאֲתָר דִּדְכוּרָא וְנוּקְבָּא אִשְׁתְּכָחוּ, אֶלָּא לִדְכוּרָא. וְעַל דָּא מְחַכָּאן יִשְׂרָאֵל, דִּכְתִּיב זֶה יְיָ' קִוִּינוּ לוֹ נָגִילָה וְנִשְׂמְחָה בִּישׁוּעָתוֹ. מִשּׁוּם דְּהָכִי זַמִּין לְמֶעְבַּד לְהוּ, דִּכְתִּיב כִּימֵי צֵאתְךָ מֵאֶרֶץ מִצְרַיִם אַרְאֶנּוּ נִפְלָאוֹת.

132. And wherever male and female are together, the praise is directed only to the male. The children of Yisrael also directed their praises to the male and not the female. This is the meaning of: "This (*zeh* masc.) is my El and I shall glorify Him" (Shemot 15:2). When both male and female are present, then the praise is directed only to the male. And this is what the children of Yisrael await, as written: "This (*zeh*) is Hashem; we have waited for Him, we will be glad and rejoice in His salvation" (Yeshayah 25:9). For He will do so for them, as is written: "As in the days of your coming out of the land of Egypt, I will show him marvelous things" (Michah 7:15).

133. וְרָזָא דָּא הָכִי הוּא, כְּגַוְונָא דְּהָכָא לֵיל וְלַיְלָה, כַּךְ זַמִּין קוּדְשָׁא

בְּרִיךְ הוּא לְמֶעְבַּד לְהוּ, דִּכְתִּיב שׁוֹמֵר מַה מִּלַּיְלָה שׁוֹמֵר מַה מִּלֵּיל. מַה לְהַלָּן שְׁמִירָה וְלֵיל, אוּף כָּאן שְׁמִירָה וְלֵיל. מַה לְהַלָּן שְׁמִירָה וְלַיְלָה, אוּף כָּאן שְׁמִירָה וְלַיְלָה.

133. Such is this secret, as is written here: "*leil*" and "*lailah.*" So will the Holy One, blessed be He, do for them in the future, as is written: "Watchman what is of the night (Heb. *lailah*), Watchman what is of the night (Heb. *leil*)" (Yeshayah 21:11). As there was watching and "*leil*" there, so here is also watching and "*leil.*" As there was watching and "*lailah*" there, so here also is watching and "*lailah.*"

134. וְלַיְלָה אִתְקְרֵי אֲגַב דְּכוּרָא, הה"ד, אָתָא בֹּקֶר וְגַם לַיְלָה. בֹּקֶר: כד"א וַיַּשְׁכֵּם אַבְרָהָם בַּבֹּקֶר. דְּהוּא מִדָּתוֹ מַמָּשׁ. וּכְתִיב יְיָ' בֹּקֶר תִּשְׁמַע קוֹלִי, בֹּקֶר מַמָּשׁ.

134. It is called "*lailah*" because of the male THAT IS INCLUDED IN HER AS MENTIONED. This is as written: "The morning comes, and also the night" (Ibid. 12), WHICH ARE ZEIR ANPIN AND MALCHUT, because morning MEANS as written: "And Abraham rose up early in the morning" (Beresheet 22:3). This is his own attribute, NAMELY CHESED OF ZEIR ANPIN, WHICH IS CALLED 'MORNING'. It is written: "My voice shall you hear in the morning, O Hashem" (Tehilim 5:4), NAMELY ALSO the morning itself, WHICH IS ZEIR ANPIN IN THE ASPECT OF CHESED.

135. יָתְבוּ ר' חִיָּיא ור' יוֹסֵי, וְאוֹלִיף לְהוּ רָזָא דְּתוֹרַת כֹּהֲנִים, וַהֲווֹ מְהַדְּרֵי בְּכָל יוֹמָא וְיַתְבֵי קָמֵיהּ. חַד יוֹמָא נָפַק ר"ש לְבַר, אָזְלוּ בַּהֲדֵיהּ, מָטוּ לְחַד חַקְלָא יָתְבוּ.

135. Rabbi Chiya and Rabbi Yosi were sitting. RABBI SHIMON was teaching them the secret of the Laws of Priests. They came back every day and sat before him. One day, Rabbi Shimon went out. They went with him until they reached a field and sat down.

6. “All things have I seen in the days of my vanity”

A Synopsis

Rabbi Shimon says that the verse, “I have seen everything in the days of my vanity. There is a righteous man who perishes in his righteousness and there is a wicked man who prolongs his life in his evil doing,” contains two themes: Solomon was alluding to wisdom, but God is patient with the wicked until they repent. A person should live among the righteous because he will receive good due to their merit, while if he lives among the wicked he will be caught in their sins. Rabbi Shimon offers another explanation of the title verse, that is that Solomon was called by seven names, the seventh of which was Kohelet, that is equivalent to them all. His names were called after Wisdom, and therefore he composed three books, Shir Hashirim, Kohelet and Mishlei, corresponding to Chesed, Judgment and Mercy. Thus he perfected wisdom. Rabbi Shimon moves to the question of breath and voice, saying that breath is made of air and water, and everything in the world is made of breath. Breath has the power to produce voice, but actual voice has the enduring power to produce speech. He says that sometimes vanity nurtures from judgment, sometimes from mercy. Then while the rabbis are sitting in the field, they see a column of smoke from incense rising and falling. Meanwhile a scent arose from the field that was more fragrant, for it was the fragrance of the Shechinah.

136. פָּתַח ר״ש וְאָמַר, תָּא חֲזֵי, כְּתִיב, אֶת הַכֹּל רָאִיתִי בִּימֵי הֶבְלִי יֵשׁ צַדִּיק אוֹבֵד בְּצִדְקוֹ וְיֵשׁ רָשָׁע מַאֲרִיךְ בְּרָעָתוֹ, שְׁלֹמֹה דַּהֲוַת חָכְמְתָא יְתֵירָא עַל כֹּלָּא, מַאי קָאָמַר בְּהַאי קְרָא. אֶלָּא, שְׁלֹמֹה רֶמֶז דְּחָכְמְתָא קָא רָמַז. דְּהָא חָזֵינָן אוֹרְחוֹי דְּקוּדְשָׁא בְּרִיךְ הוּא דְּלָאו הָכִי, דְּהָא כְּתִיב, וְלָתֵת לְאִישׁ כִּדְרָכָיו וְכִפְרִי מַעֲלָלָיו. אֶלָּא תְּרֵי עִנְיָינֵי נִינְהוּ, דְּקָא רָמַז הָכָא.

136. Rabbi Shimon opened the discussion, saying: Come and behold. It is written: “All things have I seen in the days of my vanity. There is a just man who perishes in his righteousness and there is a wicked man who prolongs his life in his wickedness” (Kohelet 7:15). What did Solomon, who possessed more wisdom then any other person, speak of in this verse? HE RESPONDS: Solomon alluded to wisdom. We see that the ways of the Holy One, blessed be He, are not so, for it is written: “To give every man according to his ways, and according to the fruit of his doings" (Yirmeyah 17:10). But he is alluding to two themes here.

137. דְּתָנֵינָן, כַּד עֵינוֹי דְּקוּדְשָׁא בְּרִיךְ הוּא בָּעָאן לְאַשְׁגָּחָא בְּעָלְמָא, וּלְעַיְינָא בֵּיהּ, כְּמָה דִּכְתִּיב כִּי יְיָ' עֵינָיו מְשׁוֹטְטוֹת בְּכָל הָאָרֶץ, וְאַשְׁכְּחָן חַיָּיבִין בְּעָלְמָא, הַהוּא צַדִּיקָא דְּאִשְׁתְּכַח בְּדָרָא, אִתְּפַס בְּחוֹבַיְיהוּ. וְחַיָּיבַיָּא מַאֲרִיךְ קוּדְשָׁא בְּרִיךְ הוּא רוּגְזֵיהּ עִמְּהוֹן עַד דִּיתוּבוּן. וְאִי לָאו, לָא יִשְׁתְּכַּח מַאן דְּיִתְבַּע רַחֲמֵי עֲלֵיהוֹן, הה"ד, יֵשׁ צַדִּיק אוֹבֵד בְּצִדְקוֹ, מִשּׁוּם דְּהַהוּא זַכָּאָה, אִסְתַּלָּק מֵעָלְמָא.

137. We have learned that the eyes of the Holy One, blessed be He, wish to watch over the world and observe it, as is written: "For the eyes of Hashem run to and fro throughout the whole earth" (II Divrei Hayamim 16:9). If there are wicked people in the world, the righteous man in that generation is snared in their sins. The Holy One, blessed be He, is longsuffering with the wicked until they repent. If they do not REPENT, then there will be no one to plead mercy for them BECAUSE THE RIGHTEOUS HAS ALREADY DIED. This is the meaning of: "There is a just man who perishes in his righteousness." It is because he is righteous that he has departed from the world, SO HE WOULD NOT PLEAD MERCY FOR THE GENERATION.

138. בְּגִינֵי כַּךְ תָּנֵינָן, לְעוֹלָם אַל יָדוּר אָדָם אֶלָּא בִּמְקוֹם שֶׁאַנְשֵׁי מַעֲשֶׂה דָּרִים בְּתוֹכוֹ. מַאי טַעֲמָא. מִשּׁוּם דְּוַוי לְהַאי דְּמָדוֹרֵיהּ בֵּין חַיָּיבַיָּא, דְּהוּא אִתְּפַס בְּחוֹבַיְיהוּ, וְאִי דִּיוֹרֵיהּ בֵּין זַכָּאִין, אוֹטִיבִין לֵיהּ בְּגִינֵיהוֹן.

138. Therefore we learned that a person should only live in a place where men of action live. For what reason? Woe unto the person who dwells among the wicked, for he is caught in their sins. And if he dwells among the righteous, he is dealt well with due to their merit.

139. דְּהָא רַב חַסְדָּא, הֲוָה דִּיוֹרֵיהּ בְּקַדְמֵיתָא בֵּינֵי קַפּוּטְקָאֵי, וַהֲוָה דְּחִיקָא לֵיהּ שַׁעֲתָא, וּמַרְעִין רַדְפִּין אֲבַתְרוֹי. נָטַל וְשַׁוֵּי מָדוֹרֵיהּ בֵּין מָארֵי תְּרִיסִין דְּצִפּוֹרִי, וְסָלִיק, וְזָכָה לְכַמָּה טָבִין, לְכַמָּה עוּתְרָא, לְכַמָּה

אוֹרַיְיתָא, וְאָמַר, כָּל הַאי זָכֵינָא, עַל דְּעָאלִית בֵּין אִינּוּן דְּקוּדְשָׁא בְּרִיךְ הוּא אַשְׁגַּח לְאוֹטָבָא לְהוּ.

139. Rabbi Chasda lived at first among the people of Cappadocia, and it was difficult for him and he was plagued with sickness. He then moved his dwelling among the protectors of Tzipori, MEANING AMONG TORAH SCHOLARS WHO ARE CALLED 'PROTECTORS'. He became great and merited much good, many riches and much Torah, and he said: I merited all this because I came among these people, whom the Holy One, blessed be He, takes care of, to do good for them.

140. ד"א, אֶת הַכֹּל רָאִיתִי בִּימֵי הֶבְלִי. וְכִי שְׁלֹמֹה, דְּדַרְגִּין עִלָּאִין דְּחָכְמְתָא הֲווֹ בֵּיהּ, עַל כָּל בְּנֵי דָּרָא דִּכְתִּיב וַיֶּחְכַּם מִכָּל הָאָדָם, דִּכְתִּיב וַיֵּשֶׁב שְׁלֹמֹה עַל כִּסֵּא יְיָ' לְמֶלֶךְ, אָמַר בִּימֵי הֶבְלִי. וּכְתִיב, הֲבֵל הֲבָלִים אָמַר קֹהֶלֶת.

140. Another explanation of the verse: "All things have I seen in the days of my vanity." Solomon had all the highest levels of wisdom, more than all the people of the generation, as it is written: "For he was wiser than all men" (I Melachim 5:11), and, "Then Solomon sat on the throne of the Hashem as king" (I Divrei Hayamim 29:23). Could he say about his life, "In the days of my vanity"? And, "'Vanity of vanities,' said Kohelet" (Kohelet 1:2)?

141. וְתָנָא, ז' שֵׁמוֹת נִקְרָא: שְׁלֹמֹה. יְדִידְיָ"ה, אָגוּר. בִּן יָקֶ"א, אִיתִיאֵ"ל, לְמוּאֵל. קֹהֶלֶת. קֹהֶלֶת כְּנֶגֶד כֻּלָּם. וְכֻלָּם נִקְרָא כְּעֵין שֶׁל מַעְלָה, קֹהֶלֶת כְּנוּפְיָא קַדִּישָׁא דְּבֵי עֲשָׂרָה, בְּגִין כַּךְ קָהָל אֵין פָּחוּת מֵעֲשָׂרָה. וְקָהָל אֲפִילּוּ מֵאָה, וְקֹהֶלֶת כְּלָלָא דְּכֹלָּא, כמד"א קְהִלַּת יַעֲקֹב.

141. We learned that Solomon was called by seven names: Solomon, Yedidyah, Agur, Bin Yake, Itiel, Lemuel, Kohelet – AND THE NAME Kohelet is equal to them all. Each of them is named in the likeness of above. Kohelet IS ALSO CALLED 'a sacred congregation of ten men'. Therefore, it is said 'Less than ten people is not considered a congregation (Heb. *kahal*).' A congregation could even be a hundred or more, BUT NOT LESS THAN

TEN. Kohelet includes everyone, ALL OF YISRAEL, as is written: "The congregation (Heb. *kehilat*) of Jacob" (Devarim 33:4).

142. וְתָאנָא, שְׁמוֹתָיו עַל שֵׁם הַחָכְמָה אִתְקְרוּן, וּבְגִין כַּךְ ג׳ סִפְרִין עָבֵד, שִׁיר הַשִּׁירִים. קֹהֶלֶת. מִשְׁלֵי. וְכֻלְּהוּ לְאַשְׁלְמָא חָכְמְתָא. שִׁיר הַשִּׁירִים לָקֳבֵל דְּחֶסֶד. קֹהֶלֶת לָקֳבֵל דְּדִינָא. מִשְׁלֵי לָקֳבֵל דְּרַחֲמֵי. בְּגִין לְאַשְׁלְמָא חָכְמְתָא, וְהוּא עָבֵד כָּל מַה דְּעָבֵד בְּגִין לְאַחֲזָאָה חָכְמְתָא, וְלָקֳבֵל דַּרְגָּא עִלָּאָה, וְהוּא אָמַר בִּימֵי הֶבְלִי הֶבֶל הֲבָלִים.

142. We learned that his names were called after Wisdom, and therefore he composed three books: Shir Hashirim, Kohelet and Mishlei. The purpose of them all is to perfect wisdom. Shir Hashirim corresponds to Chesed, Kohelet corresponds to Judgment, and Mishlei corresponds to Mercy – NAMELY, THEY CORRESPOND TO THE THREE COLUMNS, CHESED, JUDGMENT, MERCY. This is in order to perfect Wisdom. Everything that he did was for the purpose of displaying wisdom and in correspondence to the highest level. He said ABOUT HIMSELF: "In the days of my vanity," and, "Vanity of vanities" (Kohelet 1:2).

143. אֶלָּא, רָזָא דְּהֶבֶל יַקִּירָא הוּא. וְהוּא הָבַל דְּנָפִיק מִפּוּמָא, וְרָזָא דְּהֶבֶל דְּנָפִיק מִפּוּמָא, קָלָא אִתְעָבֵיד מִנֵּיהּ. וְתָאנָא, אֵין הָעוֹלָם מִתְקַיֵּים אֶלָּא בְּהֶבֶל פִּיהֶם שֶׁל תִּינוֹקוֹת שֶׁל בֵּית רַבָּן שֶׁלֹּא חָטְאוּ. שֶׁלֹּא חָטְאוּ מַמָּשׁ. וְהֶבֶל אִתְעָבֵיד בְּרוּחָא וּמַיָּא, וְכָל מַה דְּאִתְעָבֵיד בְּעָלְמָא בְּהֶבֶל אִתְעָבֵיד. וְרָזָא דְּהַאי הֶבֶל שֶׁל תִּינוֹקוֹת אִתְעָבֵיד קָלָא, וְאִתְפָּשַׁט בְּעָלְמָא, וְאִינּוּן נְטוּרֵי עָלְמָא, וּנְטוּרֵי קַרְתָּא, הה״ד אִם יְיָ׳ לֹא יִשְׁמָר עִיר וְגוֹ׳.

143. HE ANSWERS: But vanity (Heb. *hevel*) is a precious secret. It is the breath (Heb. *hevel*) that comes out of the mouth, and by means of the breath that comes out from the mouth a sound is formed. We learned that the world exists only through the breath of the mouths of the schoolchildren who have not sinned, THAT IS, who have not actually sin. IT IS NOT THAT THEY DID NOT SIN BUT IT IS NOT CONSIDERED A SIN BECAUSE OF THEIR MINOR AGE. Breath is made of air and water, and everything in the world is made of breath. The inner meaning of the breath of these children becomes a sound and spreads throughout the world. They are the guards of the world and the guards of the city. This is the meaning of: "Unless Hashem keeps the city..." (Tehilim 127:2).

144. ות"ח, הוּא הֶבֶל, הוּא קָלָא. מַה בֵּין הַאי לְהַאי. הֶבֶל קָאֵים בְּחֵילָא, לְמֵיפַק קָלָא. קָלָא מַמָּשׁ קָאֵים בְּקִיּוּמֵהּ לְאַפָּקָא מִלָּה. וְהַהוּא הֶבֶל דַּהֲוָה אַחְסַנְתֵּיהּ דַּאֲבוֹי קַרְיֵיהּ הֶבֶל, וּמִנֵּיהּ חָזָא כָּל מַה דְּחָזָא. ואע"ג דְּסִיּוּעִין סַגִּיאִין מֵעֵילָּא אַחֲרָנִין הֲווֹ לֵיהּ, וּלְאִשְׁתְּמוֹדְעָא מִלָּה, אָמַר בִּימֵי הֶבְלִי. דְּמִלָּה דָּא מִתַּמָּן אָתָא.

144. Come and behold: it is both breath and a sound. What is the difference between them? Breath has the power to produce a sound BUT actual sound has the power to produce words. Abel, who inherited from his father, is called Abel, and whatever SOLOMON saw came through him, and even though he had much support from above, from other LEVELS, he said, "In the days of my vanity," to make known that this word comes from there.

145. וְרָזָא דְּמִלָּה הַכֹּל הָבֶל אֶת הַכֹּל רָאִיתִי בִּימֵי הֶבְלִי, יֵשׁ צַדִּיק אוֹבֵד בְּצִדְקוֹ, דָּא הוּא רָזָא דְּמִלָּה, דְּגַלֵּי וּפִרְסֵם, דְּכֹלָּא תַּלְיָא בִּימֵי הֶבְלִי, כְּלוֹמַר בִּזְמְנָא דְּהַאי הֶבֶל יַנְקָא מִן דִּינָא, בְּגִין לְמֶעְבַּד דִּינָא, צַדִּיק אוֹבֵד בְּצִדְקוֹ, וּבִזְמְנָא דְּהַאי הֶבֶל יַנְקָא מֵרַחֲמֵי. רָשָׁע מַאֲרִיךְ בְּרָעָתוֹ. וְתַרְוַוייְהוּ תַּלְיָין בְּהַאי הֶבֶל, ובג"כ כְּתִיב בִּימֵי, וְלָא כְּתִיב בְּיוֹם. וְכֹלָּא תַּלְיָין בִּימֵי הֶבֶל דָּא. מַאן דְּאַעְרַע בְּדִינָא, בְּדִינָא. מַאן דְּאַעְרַע בְּרַחֲמֵי, בְּרַחֲמֵי.

145. And the secret meaning of the words: "All is vanity...," "...in the days of my vanity, I saw everything..." and, "there is a just person who perishes in his righteousness," is the secret of that which he revealed and made known, that everything depends on "the days of my vanity." This means that when *Hevel* nurtures from Judgment, in order to execute Judgment – BEFORE THE RECONCILIATION OF THE CENTRAL COLUMN – "There is a just man who perishes in his righteousness" BECAUSE OF THAT JUDGMENT. When *Hevel* nurtures from Mercy, MEANING AFTER THE RECONCILIATION OF THE CENTRAL COLUMN, then "there is a wicked man who prolongs his life in his wickedness," AS BECAUSE OF MERCY HE IS LONGSUFFERING and both THE WICKED AND THE RIGHTEOUS are dependent upon this *Hevel*. Therefore, it is written, "In the days," and not, 'in the day', for they all depend on this *Hevel*. Whoever HAPPENS TO BE at the time of Judgment is treated with Judgment, and whoever HAPPENS TO BE at the time of Mercy is treated with Mercy.

146. וְאִי תֵּימָא יֵשׁ צַדִּיק אוֹבֵד וְלָא קָאָמַר אָבוּד. הָכִי הוּא אוֹבֵד מַמָּשׁ. דְּהַהוּא דִּינָא אוֹבֵד לַצַּדִּיק מֵעָלְמָא וּמִדָּרָא. וְיֵשׁ רָשָׁע מַאֲרִיךְ בְּרָעָתוֹ, מַאֲרִיךְ מַמָּשׁ, דְּהַהוּא דִּינָא כַּד יַנְקָא מֵרַחֲמֵי, עָבִיד רַחֲמֵי לְהַהוּא רָשָׁע, וּמַאֲרִיךְ לֵיהּ.

146. It is written: "There is a just man who perishes" IN THE PRESENT CONTINUOUS TENSE. HE ASKS: Why does not it say 'perished? FOR IF IT IS DEPENDENT UPON TIME, IT SHOULD HAVE BEEN SAID IN THE PAST RATHER THAN IN THE PRESENT TENSE. HE ANSWERS: EVERY TIME IT IS AROUSED, Judgment removes the righteous man from the world and from the generation. IT IS ALWAYS THIS WAY. "There is a wicked man who prolongs his life in his wickedness, who actually prolongs his life IN HIS SIN, for when that Judgment nurtures from Mercy, it bestows mercy on that wicked man and forebears with him.

147. עַד דַּהֲווֹ יָתְבֵי חָמוּ קְטוֹרָא דַּהֲוָה סָלִיק לְעֵילָּא וְנָחִית לְתַתָּא. אָמַר אִתְעַטְּרוּתָא אִתְעַטָּר בְּטִינָּתָא דְּאַרְעָא, מִגּוֹ לְעֵילָּא. אַדְּהָכִי, סָלִיק הַהוּא חַקְלָא רֵיחָא, מִכָּל בּוּסְמִין, אָמַר נֵיתִיב הָכָא, דִּשְׁכִינְתָּא גַּבָּן אִתְקְיָים. בְּגִין כַּךְ, כְּרֵיחַ שָׂדֶה אֲשֶׁר בֵּרְכוֹ יְיָ'.

147. While they were still sitting, they saw a column of incense smoke rising up and going down. He said: this crowning, THE SMOKE is surrounded with mud of the earth from above. IT THEREFORE GOES UP AND DOWN, WHICH ALLUDES TO THE *HEVEL* MENTIONED BEFORE. In the meantime, there arose a scent from the field, WHICH WAS MORE FRAGRANT THAN ALL THE SPICES. He said: Let us sit here for the Shechinah is by us, as is written: "Like the smell of a field which Hashem has blessed" (Beresheet 27:27).

7. “And he smelled the smell of his garments”

A Synopsis

Rabbi Shimon says that when Jacob entered before his father, the scent of the Garden of Eden went in with him, and that the clothes he wore belonged to Adam. He asks what happened to the clothes of Eve, and in what clothing were Adam and Eve buried? He answers himself by saying that when they left they threw off the supernal splendor with which God had clothed them. We learn that as soon as God was clothed, as in “Who covers Himself with light as with a garment,” He created the world. The question arises of how Isaac knew about “the smell of a field that Hashem has blessed.” Rabbi Shimon explains that the field in “And Isaac went out to meditate in the field at the evening time,” was the field near the cave of the Machpelah, and that Jacob saw the Shechinah on it, and it raised supernal holy scents. The conclusion Rabbi Shimon draws is that Isaac blessed Jacob because Isaac did not attribute the scent to the clothes at all; he attributed it to Jacob himself because he saw that he was worthy and deserving of his blessing. The rabbis then talk about the tenth day of the seventh month, Yom Kippur, and the sacrifice of the lamb. We are reminded that Yisrael does an action below, and God does the action above.

148. פָּתַח וְאָמַר, וַיָּרַח אֶת רֵיחַ בְּגָדָיו וַיְבָרְכֵהוּ וַיֹּאמֶר רְאֵה רֵיחַ בְּנִי וְגוֹ', וַיָּרַח אֶת רֵיחַ בְּגָדָיו, מַשְׁמַע דְּאִינּוּן לְבוּשִׁין הֲווֹ סַלְּקִין רֵיחָא טָבָא, דְּלָא אִתְעֲדֵי מִנְּהוֹן הַהוּא רֵיחָא. הַשְׁתָּא אִית לְאִסְתַּכְּלָא, כְּתִיב, רֵיחַ בְּגָדָיו, וּכְתִיב רֵיחַ בְּנִי, וְלָא אָמַר רֵיחַ הַבְּגָדִים, אֶלָּא רֵיחַ בְּנִי. אֶלָּא תָּאנָא, כֵּיוָן שֶׁנִּכְנַס יַעֲקֹב, נִכְנַס עִמּוֹ ג"ע. וְתָאנָא, אוֹתָן הַבְּגָדִים הָיוּ שֶׁל אָדָם הָרִאשׁוֹן, דִּכְתִּיב, וַיַּעַשׂ יְיָ' אֱלֹהִים לְאָדָם וּלְאִשְׁתּוֹ כָּתְנוֹת עוֹר וַיַּלְבִּישֵׁם, וְהוֹצִיאָם מג"ע.

148. He opened the discussion, saying: “And he smelled the smell of his garments, and blessed him, and said, ‘See, the smell of my son is like the smell of a field which Hashem has blessed’” (Beresheet 27:27). “And he smelled the smell of his garments” means that the garments emitted a pleasant scent that had never left them. Now we should examine this closely; it is written: “The smell of his garments,” and, “The smell of my son.” It does not say, ‘The smell of the garments, but rather “the smell of my son.” HE ANSWERS: But we learned that when Jacob entered the Garden of Eden entered with him, and we learned that those garments belonged to Adam, as written: "For the man also and for his wife did Hashem Elohim make coats of skins, and clothed them" (Beresheet 3:21), and He took them out from the Garden of Eden.

149. וְאִי תֵּימָא, דִּכְתִּיב וַיִּתְפְּרוּ עֲלֵה תְאֵנָה דְּאִינּוּן הֲווֹ, אִי הָכִי, אֲמַאי כְּתִיב וַיַּעַשׂ ה׳ אֱלֹהִים. וּכְתִיב כָּתְנוֹת עוֹר, הָא לָא הֲווֹ אֶלָּא עֲלֵה תְאֵנָה אֶלָּא כְּתַרְגּוּמוֹ, לְבוּשִׁין דִּיקָר וַהֲווֹ סַלְּקִין רֵיחִין מִבּוּסְמָא דְּעֵדֶן.

149. You may argue that it is written: "And they sewed fig leaves together" (Ibid. 7), and from them were THE SKIN GARMENTS THAT HASHEM MADE FOR THEM. If so, then why is it written, "did Hashem Elohim make?", IF THEY SEWN THEM THEMSELVES, and: "Coats of skins," when they were but a fig leaf. But as the Aramaic translation OF "COATS OF SKINS," it is 'precious garments'. And they emitted a scent from the spices of Eden.

150. וְתַנְיָא, בְּשֵׁם מָלֵא אִתְעָבֵידוּ, דִּכְתִּיב וַיַּעַשׂ ה׳ אֱלֹהִים. מַה דְּלָא אִתְעָבֵידוּ בֵּיהּ שְׁמַיָּא וְאַרְעָא. וְלָא. וְהָא כְּתִיב, בְּיוֹם עֲשׂוֹת יְיָ׳ אֱלֹהִים אֶרֶץ וְשָׁמָיִם. לָא קַשְׁיָא הַאי כַּד אִתְעָבֵידוּ, לָא אִתְעָבֵידוּ בְּשֵׁם מָלֵא, בַּר כַּד אִתְקַיְּימוּ, בְּשֵׁם מָלֵא אִתְקַיְּימוּ.

150. And we learned that they were made with the full Name, as is written: "did Hashem Elohim make..." WHICH IS THE FULL NAME that even the heavens and earth were not made with. FOR ONLY ELOHIM IS MENTIONED IN RELATION TO THEM. HE ASKS: Is it not written: "In the day that Hashem Elohim made the earth and the heavens" (Beresheet 2:4)? HE ANSWERS: There is no difficulty here, for when they were first made they were not made with the full Name, but when they became permanent, they were maintained by the full Name. THE VERSE, "IN THE DAY THAT HASHEM ELOHIM MADE," WAS SAID FOR THE PURPOSE OF MAINTENANCE.

151. וּמַה דְּאָמְרוּ דְּאִינּוּן לְבוּשִׁין אָתוּ לְהַהוּא רָשָׁע דְּעֵשָׂו, דְּנָסִיב לוֹ מִן נִמְרוֹד הָכִי אוֹקִימְנָא, וְקַשְׁיָא מִלָּה, דְּאִי הָכִי הָא כְּתִיב לְאָדָם וּלְאִשְׁתּוֹ, לְבוּשִׁין לְאָדָם, וּלְבוּשִׁין לְחַוָּה. לְבוּשִׁין דְּחַוָּה מַה אִתְעָבֵידוּ. וְתוּ, דְּאִי הָכִי בְּמָאי אִתְקְבָרוּ, ס״ד דְּאִינּוּן שָׁבְקוּ וְרָאמוּ מִנְּהוֹן זוֹהֲרָא עִלָּאָה, דְּיָהִיב לוֹן קוּדְשָׁא בְּרִיךְ הוּא.

151. And concerning what was said, that these garments came to the wicked Esau, who took them from Nimrod, we explained this matter and it is difficult to understand. If so, why it is written: "For the man also and for his wife"? He made clothing for Adam and He made clothing for Eve, but what happened to the clothes of Eve? And if so, in what were they buried? Could you possibly conceive that they left and threw from themselves the supernal splendor that the Holy One, blessed be He, gave them.

152. אֶלָּא אִינּוּן לְבוּשִׁין דְּאִתְלְבָּשׁוּ בְּהוּ אָדָם וְאִתְּתֵיהּ, לָא אִתְלָבַשׁ בְּהוּ ב"נ אַחֲרָא, דִּבְאִינּוּן לְבוּשִׁין דָּמוּ כְּגַוְונָא דִּלְעֵילָּא וְאִי ס"ד, דְּאִינּוּן אִתְלַבָּשׁוּ מִגַּרְמַיְיהוּ בְּהוּ. תָּא חֲזֵי, כְּתִיב וַיַּלְבִּישֵׁם, דְּקוּדְשָׁא בְּרִיךְ הוּא אַלְבִּישׁ לוֹן, זַכָּאָה חוּלְקֵהוֹן.

152. No one else wore the garments with which Adam and Eve clothed themselves, because they were in likeness of above in these garments. If you think that they wore them by themselves, come and behold, it is written: "And clothed them," in that the Holy One, blessed be He, clothed them. Blessed is their portion.

153. כְּתִיב. ה' אֱלֹהַי גָּדַלְתָּ מְּאֹד הוֹד וְהָדָר לָבָשְׁתָּ. וּכְתִיב הוֹד וְהָדָר לְפָנָיו. וּכְתִיב עוֹטֶה אוֹר כַּשַּׂלְמָה וְגוֹ'. כֵּיוָן דְּאִתְלָבַּשׁ עָבֵד מַה דְּעָבֵד. מְלַמֵּד, שֶׁנִּתְעַטָּף קוּדְשָׁא בְּרִיךְ הוּא בְּאוֹר, וּבָרָא יַת שְׁמַיָּא. אֶלָּא בְּמַאי אוֹקִימְנָא הַחֲמוּדוֹת אֲשֶׁר אִתָּהּ בְּבֵית. הַחֲמוּדוֹת: בִּגְדֵי מַלְכוּת בְּמֶשִׁי וְזָהָב, וְאָרְחָא דְּעָלְמָא דְּגַנְזֵי לוֹן בְּבוּסְמִין וְרֵיחִין, לִיקָרָא דִּלְבוּשֵׁיהוֹן.

153. It is written: "O Hashem my Elohim You are very great, You are clothed with glory and majesty" (Tehilim 104:1), "Glory and majesty are before Him" (Tehilim 96:6), and: "Who covers Himself with light as with a garment..." (Tehilim 104:2). As soon as He was clothed, He accomplished His deed, THAT IS, HE CREATED THE WORLD. It teaches that the Holy One, blessed be He, clothed Himself in Light and created the heaven. THE GARMENTS OF ADAM WERE SIMILAR TO THIS CLOTHING. But how do we explain the verse: "The best clothes...which were with her in the house" (Beresheet 27:15)? HERE, the "best clothes" MEANS kingly garments of silk and gold, and it is the custom of the world to store them in spices and scents, because of the preciousness of the garments.

154. תָּא חֲזֵי וַיָּרַח אֶת רֵיחַ בְּגָדָיו, בַּתְּחִלָּה. וְכַד אַרְגִּישׁ, אָמַר רְאֵה רֵיחַ בְּנִי, דְּיָדַע דְּבֵיהּ הֲוָה תַּלְיָא מִלְּתָא, דִּבְגִינֵיהּ סָלִיק רֵיחָא. כְּרֵיחַ שָׂדֶה אֲשֶׁר בֵּרֲכוֹ יְיָ', וְכִי מְנַיִין הֲוָה יָדַע יִצְחָק רֵיחַ שָׂדֶה אֲשֶׁר בֵּרֲכוֹ יְיָ'.

154. Come and behold: first, "he smelled the smell of his garments" (Ibid. 27), BECAUSE HE THOUGHT THE SCENT CAME FROM THEM. But when he felt it, he said, "See, the smell of my son," because he knew that the scent came from him and for his sake, AND NOT FROM THE GARMENTS. "Like the smell of a field which Hashem has blessed." HE ASKS: How did Isaac know about "the smell of a field which Hashem has blessed"?

155. אֶלָּא, תְּרֵין מִלִּין אִינּוּן, וְכֹלָּא הוּא חַד. דִּכְתִּיב, וַיֵּצֵא יִצְחָק לָשׂוּחַ בַּשָּׂדֶה לִפְנוֹת עָרֶב. וְכִי לָא הֲוָה לֵיהּ בֵּיתָא, אוֹ מָקוֹם אַחֵר לְהִתְפַּלֵּל. אֶלָּא אוֹתָהּ הַשָּׂדֶה הָיָה אֲשֶׁר קָנָה אַבְרָהָם סָמוּךְ לַמְּעָרָה, דִּכְתִּיב הַשָּׂדֶה אֲשֶׁר קָנָה אַבְרָהָם מֵאֵת בְּנֵי חֵת. וּבְשַׁעֲתָא דַּהֲוָה יִצְחָק עָאל גַּבֵּיהּ, חָמָא שְׁכִינְתָּא עֲלֵיהּ, וְסָלִיק רֵיחִין עִלָּאִין קַדִּישִׁין, וּבְגִינֵי כַּךְ הֲוָה מְצַלֵּי תַּמָּן, וּקְבָעֵיהּ לִצְלוֹתֵיהּ.

155. HE ANSWERS: Rather, there are two things, which amount to the same. For it is written: "And Isaac went out to meditate in the field at the evening time" (Beresheet 24:63), AND THAT IS THE SAME ONE AS "A FIELD THAT HASHEM HAS BLESSED." Did not he have a house or another place to pray? But that field was the one that Abraham purchased near the cave OF MACHPELAH, as is written: "The field which Abraham purchased of the sons of Chet" (Beresheet 25:10). When Isaac came to the field, he saw the Shechinah over it, and it raised supernal holy scents. Therefore he prayed there, and set it AS A PLACE for prayer.

156. וְאַבְרָהָם אֲמַאי לָא הֲוָה מְצַלֵּי תַּמָּן, מִשּׁוּם דִּקְבִיעוּתָא דְּאַתְרָא אַחֲרָא הֲוָה לֵיהּ בְּקַדְמֵיתָא, וּמִלָּה אַחֲרָא רֵיחָא דְּחָמָא בְּהַר הַמּוֹרִיָּה. וְלָמָּה נִקְרָא מוֹרִיָּה. ע"ש הַמֹּר הַטּוֹב דַּהֲוָה תַּמָּן.

156. HE ASKS: Why did Abraham not pray there, IN THE FIELD OF THE

CAVE OF MACHPELAH LIKE ISAAC? HE ANSWERS: Because he had a set prayer place before. Another reason was the scent that he saw at Mount Moriyah. Why was it called Mount Moriyah? Due to the good myrrh (Heb. *mor*) that was there.

157. וְכֹלָּא הֲוָה, וג"ע דְּעָאל עִמֵּיהּ וּבַרְכֵיהּ. וּבְגִין כַּךְ לָא תָּלָה מִלָּה בִּלְבוּשִׁין, אֶלָּא בְּיַעֲקֹב מַמָּשׁ, דְּחָמָא דְּבֵיהּ הֲוָה תַּלְיָא מִלָּה וְאִתְחֲזֵי, וּזְכוּתֵיהּ סָלִיק לְאִתְבָּרְכָא, וְעָאל עִמֵּיהּ ג"ע. ובג"כ כַּד אִתְרָעַם עֵשָׂו, אֲמַר גַּם בָּרוּךְ יִהְיֶה.

157. And all was present BY JACOB SINCE IN ADDITION TO HIS OWN SCENT, the Garden of Eden also entered with him. Therefore, he blessed him. He did not attribute it to the garments, but rather to Jacob himself, for he saw that the scent originated in him, that he was worthy, and that he merited to be blessed and that the Garden of Eden entered with him. For this reason, when Esau stormed and protested, he said, "moreover, he shall be blessed" (Beresheet 27:33).

158. אָמַר רִבִּי יִצְחָק, לָא אִצְטְרִיךְ אוֹרַיְיתָא לְמִכְתַּב אֶלָּא מֵהַחֹדֶשׁ הַזֶּה לָכֶם רֹאשׁ חֳדָשִׁים. מַאי טַעֲמָא. מִשּׁוּם דְּשֵׁירוּתָא דְּסִיהֲרָא הֲוֵי, וע"ד אוֹרַיְיתָא הֲוָה אִצְטְרִיךְ לְמִכְתַּב מֵהָכָא, דְּהָא בְּקוּדְשָׁא בְּרִיךְ הוּא אִתְקָשַׁר מִלָּה.

158. Rabbi Yitzchak said: The Torah should have started with, "This month shall be to you the beginning of months" (Shemot 12:2). What is the reason? Because it is the beginning OF THE RULE of the moon. Therefore, the Torah should have STARTED with these words, for the subject is connected with the Holy One, blessed be He. THE MOON IS THE SECRET OF MALCHUT, WHICH, WHEN FULL, UNITES WITH THE HOLY ONE, BLESSED BE HE. THEREFORE, THE TORAH SHOULD HAVE STARTED AT THE BEGINNING OF THE FULLNESS OF THE MOON, WHICH IS: "THIS MONTH SHALL BE TO YOU THE BEGINNING OF MONTHS."

159. וְלָא קַשְׁיָא, דְּלָא כְּתִיב זֹאת, הַחֹדֶשׁ הַזֹּאת, דְּהָא זֶה וְזֹאת כְּחַד מִתְקַשְּׁרִין וּבַאֲתַר דְּאִית בֵּיהּ דְּכַר וְנוּקְבָא כַּחֲדָא, לֵית שְׁבָחָא אֶלָּא

לִדְכוּרָא, וְעַל דָּא רִאשׁוֹן הוּא לָכֶם לְחָדְשֵׁי הַשָּׁנָה, לְחָדְשֵׁי הַשָּׁנָה וַדַּאי. אָמַר רִבִּי יְהוּדָה, לָכֶם תְּרֵי זִמְנֵי לָמָּה. אָמַר רִבִּי יִצְחָק, מִנַּיְיהוּ, אִשְׁתְּמַע יַתִּיר, כְּמָה דִּכְתִּיב, כִּי חֵלֶק ה' עַמּוֹ. אִתְקְשָׁרוּתָא דָּא לָכֶם, וְלָא לִשְׁאַר עַמִּין.

159. It does not pose a difficulty, for it is not written: 'This (*zot* fem.)', NAMELY 'this month' BECAUSE THE NAME OF THE MOON IS '*ZOT*', and this is because *zeh* ('this' masc.) and *zot* are connected together. Wherever male and female are together, the praise is directed only to the male. THEREFORE, IT SAYS "THIS (*ZEH*) MONTH," INSTEAD OF '*ZOT*', and therefore it says, "It shall be the first month of the year to you" (Ibid.). Assuredly, it is "of the year," TO INDICATE THAT IT REFERS TO MALCHUT THAT IS CALLED 'A YEAR', ONLY IT PLACES THE PRAISE ON THE MALE. Rabbi Yehuda said: Why is "to you" said twice, AS WRITTEN, "THIS MONTH SHALL BE TO YOU...IT SHALL BE THE FIRST...TO YOU." Rabbi Yitzchak said: FROM THE DOUBLING OF "TO YOU," we understand even more THAT IT IS ONLY FOR YISRAEL AND NOT FOR THE OTHER NATIONS, as is written: "For Hashem's portion is His people" (Devarim 32:9). This connection WITH THE MONTH is to you and not to the other nations.

8. "A lamb, according to the house of their fathers"

160. דַּבְּרוּ אֶל כָּל עֲדַת יִשְׂרָאֵל לֵאמֹר בֶּעָשׂוֹר לַחֹדֶשׁ הַזֶּה וְיִקְחוּ לָהֶם אִישׁ שֶׂה וְגוֹ', בֶּעָשׂוֹר, אֲמַאי בֶּעָשׂוֹר. אָמַר רִבִּי אַבָּא, בִּזְמְנָא דְּאַנְהִיר יוֹבְלָא לְסִיהֲרָא, דִּכְתִּיב בְּיוֹבְלָא, בֶּעָשׂוֹר לַחֹדֶשׁ הַשְּׁבִיעִי הַזֶּה יוֹם הַכִּפּוּרִים הוּא.

160. "Speak to all the Congregation of Yisrael, saying, On the tenth day of this month they shall take to them every man a lamb..." (Shemot 12:3). HE ASKS: Why on the tenth of the month? Rabbi Aba said: It is the time that the Jubilee, WHICH IS BINAH, shines on the moon, WHICH IS MALCHUT. As is written in regard to the Jubilee, "On the tenth day of this seventh month shall be Yom Kippur" (Vayikra 23:27). AND YOM KIPPUR IS THE ILLUMINATION OF BINAH, FOR WE SEE THE ILLUMINATION OF BINAH IN MALCHUT IS ON THE TENTH DAY OF THE MONTH.

161. וְיִקְחוּ לָהֶם אִישׁ שֶׂה לְבֵית אָבוֹת, אֲמַאי, בְּגִין דִּבְזִמְנָא דָּא אִצְטְרִיךְ לְמֵיגַד לֵיהּ. דְּהָא תָּנֵינָן, בְּמִלְּתָא דָּא אִתְּבַר כִּתְרָא תַּתָּאָה, דְּמִתְאַחֲדִין בֵּיהּ כָּל שְׁאַר כִּתְרִין תַּתָּאִין, וְעַל דָּא פָּרִישׁ מֹשֶׁה וְאָמַר, מִשְׁכוּ וּקְחוּ לָכֶם צֹאן, כְּמָה דִּכְתִּיב, צֹאן וְעֶבֶד וְשִׁפְחָה.

161. "They shall take to them every man a lamb, according to the house of their fathers." Why? Because they had to draw it at that time, for we learned that the lower crown, to which all the other lower crowns OF THE KLIPAH are attached, is broken by this TAKING OF THE LAMB. Therefore, Moses was specific in his words, "Draw out and take you lambs" (Shemot 12:21), WHICH IS according to the verse: "Flocks, and menservants and womenservants" (Beresheet 32:6), WHICH ARE LOWER CROWNS OF THE KLIPOT, AND THE TERM FLOCK INCLUDES THEM ALL. AND THE EGYPTIANS MADE THEM INTO DEITIES.

162. אָמַר קוּדְשָׁא בְּרִיךְ הוּא, עֲבִידוּ אַתּוּן עוֹבָדָא לְתַתָּא, וַאֲנָא אִתְּבַר תֻּקְפֵיהוֹן לְעֵילָּא, וּכְמָה דְּתַעְבְּדוּן בְּנוּרָא אַתּוּן, דִּכְתִּיב כִּי אִם צְלִי אֵשׁ, אֲנָא אוּף הָכִי אַעֲבִיר אוֹתוֹ בָּאֵשׁ בִּנְהַר דִּינוּר.

8. “A lamb, according to the house of their fathers”

162. The Holy One, blessed be He, said: ‘Perform an action below BY DRAWING AND TAKEING SHEEP, and I will break their power above. As you prepare them by burning them by fire, as it is written, “but roast with fire” (Shemot 12:9) I, also, ABOVE, will pass him through fire, through *the Dinur River* (the River of Fire).”

163. אֲמַאי אִתְנְגִיד בַּעֲשָׂרָה, וְאִתְנְכִיס בְּאַרְבָּעָה עָשָׂר. אָמַר רִבִּי אַבָּא בְּדָא אִתְקַשָּׁרוּ יִשְׂרָאֵל אַרְבַּע מְאָה שְׁנִין. וְאַף עַל גַּב דְּאַרְבַּע מְאָה שְׁנִין לָא אִשְׁתַּעֲבִידוּ בְּהוּ, מִכָּל מָקוֹם, הוֹאִיל וַהֲוָה זַמִּין לְאִתְקַשְּׁרָא בְּהוּ, אִתְחַשִׁיב עָלֵיהּ כְּאִילּוּ אִשְׁתַּעֲבִידוּ בְּהוּ כָּל ת׳ שְׁנִין. בג״כ, מְעַכְּבִין לֵיהּ אַרְבַּע יוֹמִין, קְטִירָא בִּרְשׁוּתַיְיהוּ דְּיִשְׂרָאֵל, וּלְבָתַר וְשָׁחֲטוּ אוֹתוֹ כֹּל קְהַל עֲדַת יִשְׂרָאֵל בֵּין הָעַרְבָּיִם.

163. HE ASKS: Why was it drawn on the tenth day OF THE MONTH and slaughtered on the fourteenth? Rabbi Aba said: through THE LAMB, WHICH IS THE ELOHIM OF EGYPT, AS MENTIONED BEFORE, Yisrael were bound by slavery 400 years. Even though they were not enslaved 400 years, they were designated to be bound to them for 400 years. HAD NOT THE HOLY ONE, BLESSED BE HE, HASTENED THE END, it would have been as if they were enslaved all 400 years. Therefore, they detained the lamb four days, tied in the property of Yisrael, and afterwards: “and the whole assembly of the Congregation of Yisrael shall kill it towards evening” (Shemot 12:6).

164. אֲמַאי בֵּין הָעַרְבַּיִם. בְּשַׁעֲתָא דְּדִינָא תַּלְיָא, וּבְשַׁעֲתָא דְּאִתְמְסַר מִלָּה דָּא לֵיהּ, עַל יְדוֹי דְּאַבְרָהָם, דִּכְתִּיב וַיְהִי הַשֶּׁמֶשׁ בָּאָה וְתַרְדֵּמָה נָפְלָה עַל אַבְרָם וְהִנֵּה אֵימָה חֲשֵׁכָה גְדוֹלָה נוֹפֶלֶת עָלָיו. אֵימָה: כִּתְרָא חֲדָא. חֲשֵׁכָה: כִּתְרָא אַחֲרָא. גְּדוֹלָה: הַאי דְּהִיא רַבְרְבָא מִכֹּלָּא. ואע״ג דְּאוֹקִימְנָא קְרָא דָּא עַל שְׁאַר שִׁעְבּוּדַיְיהוּ דְּיִשְׂרָאֵל, וְכֹלָּא הֲוָה. כְּגַוְונָא דָּא, כִּי מָחֹה אֶמְחֶה, אַתּוּן מִתַּתָּא, וַאֲנָא מֵעֵילָּא.

164. HE ASKS: Why WAS IT SLAUGHTERED at twilight? HE ANSWERS: That is when Judgment is impending, and the time when this decree OF THE EXILE IN EGYPT was given through Abraham, as is written: “And when the sun was going down, a sleep fell upon Abram; and, lo, a horror of great darkness fell upon him" (Beresheet 15:12). "Horror" is one crown OF THE KLIPAH, "darkness" is another crown and "great" is greater than all THE CROWNS. Even though we explained this passage as referring to other kinds of bondage of Yisrael – THAT HORROR REFERS TO BABYLON, DARKNESS IS MEDIA, GREAT IS GREECE, it refers to everything. THEY ALLUDE TO THE THREE CROWNS OF THE KLIPAH AND ALSO THE EXILES. In the same way WE SPOKE OF THE LAMB, OF WHICH THE HOLY ONE, BLESSED BE HE, SAID: 'YOU PERFPRM AN ACTION BELOW AND I WILL BREAK THEIR POWER ABOVE,' SO, "I will utterly blot out" (Shemot 17:14). You ACT below and I WILL ACT above.

165. תָּנָא, לָא נָפְקוּ יִשְׂרָאֵל מִמִּצְרַיִם, עַד דְּאִתְּבָרוּ כֻּלְּהוּ שִׁלְטוֹנִין דִּלְעֵילָּא מִשּׁוּלְטָנֵיהוֹן, וְנַפְקוּ יִשְׂרָאֵל מֵרְשׁוּתְהוֹן, וְאָעלוּ לִרְשׁוּתָא קַדִּישָׁא עִלָּאָה בְּקוּדְשָׁא בְּרִיךְ הוּא, וְאִתְקָטִירוּ בֵּיהּ, הֲדָא הוּא דִּכְתִּיב, כִּי לִי בְנֵי יִשְׂרָאֵל עֲבָדִים עֲבָדַי הֵם. מַאי טַעֲמָא עֲבָדַי הֵם. אֲשֶׁר הוֹצֵאתִי אוֹתָם מֵאֶרֶץ מִצְרָיִם, דְּאַפָּקִית לְהוּ מֵרְשׁוּתָא אַחֲרָא, וְעָאַלִית לוֹן בִּרְשׁוּתִי.

165. We learned that Yisrael did not leave Egypt until the dominion of all their ministers above was broken. They left their domain, came under the authority of the Holiness above of the Holy One, blessed be He, and were bound to Him. This is the meaning of: "For to Me the children of Yisrael are servants; they are My servants" (Vayikra 25:55). What is the reason "they are My servants"? For "whom I brought forth out of the land of Egypt" (Ibid.). I took them out of another domain and brought them unto My authority.

9. Leaven and leavened dough

A Synopsis

In this discussion we read that leaven, leavened fermentation and leavened bread are all the same thing. In response to Rabbi Yehuda's query about why, if it is so important, Yisrael is only restricted from eating leaven seven days a year, Rabbi Shimon replies that this is an annual celebration of the days that they went out of bondage.

166. וְהַיְינוּ דְּאָמַר רִבִּי שִׁמְעוֹן, מַאי דִּכְתִּיב, אַךְ בַּיּוֹם הָרִאשׁוֹן תַּשְׁבִּיתוּ שְׂאוֹר מִבָּתֵּיכֶם כִּי כָּל אוֹכֵל מַחְמֶצֶת. אֲנָא הָכִי אוֹקִימְנָא, הַאי שְׂאוֹר, וְהַאי מַחְמֶצֶת, דַּרְגָּא חַד אִינּוּן, וְכֻלְּהוּ חַד. רְשׁוּ אוֹחֲרֵי, אִינּוּן שָׁלְטָנִין, דִּמְמָנָן עַל שְׁאַר עַמִּין, וְקָרֵינָן לְהוּ יֵצֶר הָרָע, רְשׁוּתָא אַחֲרָא, אֵל נֵכָר, אֱלֹהִים אֲחֵרִים. אוּף הָכִי, שְׂאוֹר, וּמַחְמֶצֶת, וְחָמֵץ, וְכֹלָּא חַד. אָמַר קוּדְשָׁא בְּרִיךְ הוּא, כָּל הָנֵי שָׁנֵי, קַיְימִתוּ בִּרְשׁוּתָא אַחֲרָא, עַבְדִּין לְעַם אַחֲרָא, מִכָּאן וּלְהָלְאָה דְּאַתּוּן בְּנֵי חוֹרִין, אַךְ בַּיּוֹם הָרִאשׁוֹן תַּשְׁבִּיתוּ שְׂאוֹר מִבָּתֵּיכֶם. כָּל מַחְמֶצֶת לֹא תֹאכֵלוּ. וְלֹא יֵרָאֶה לְךָ חָמֵץ.

166. This is what Rabbi Shimon said: It is written, "But on the first day you shall remove leaven out of your houses; for whoever eats leavened bread" (Shemot 12:15). I have explained it thus: leaven and leavened dough are one level, and are all the same. The other dominion is the ministers appointed over the other nations, whom we call Evil Inclination, another dominion, strange El, Other Elohim. Here also, leaven, leavened dough and leavened bread are all the same. The Holy One, blessed be He, said: 'All these years, you were under the authority of others and served another nation. From now on, you are free men. "But on the first day you shall remove leaven out of your houses…you shall eat nothing leavened" (Ibid. 20) and "there shall no leavened bread be seen with you" (Shemot 13:7).

167. אָמַר רִבִּי יְהוּדָה, אִי הָכִי כָּל יְמֵי שַׁתָּא נָמֵי, אֲמַאי שִׁבְעַת יוֹמִין, דִּכְתִּיב שִׁבְעַת יָמִים שְׂאוֹר לֹא יִמָּצֵא בְּבָתֵּיכֶם, שִׁבְעַת יָמִים, וְלָא יַתִּיר. א״ל, כָּל זִמְנָא דְּאִתְחַיָּיב בַּר נָשׁ לְאִתְחֲזָאָה גַּרְמֵיהּ בֶּן חוֹרִין, הָכִי אִצְטְרִיךְ, כָּל זִמְנָא דְּלָא אִתְחַיָּיב לָא אִצְטְרִיךְ.

167. Rabbi Yehuda said: If so, WE SHOULD NOT EAT LEAVEN all the days of the year. Why only seven days, as is written, "Seven days shall there be no leaven found in your houses," and not more? He said to him: At all times that a person is obliged to show himself free, it is required NOT TO EAT LEAVENED BREAD, but whenever he is not obligated then he does not need TO OBSERVE THE PROHIBITION OF LEAVENED BREAD.

168. לְמַלְכָּא דְּעָבֵד לְחַד בַּר נָשׁ רוּפִינוּס, כָּל אִינּוּן יוֹמִין דְּסָלִיק לְהַאי דַּרְגָּא, חַדֵי, וְלָבִישׁ לְבוּשֵׁי יְקָר, לְבָתַר לָא אִצְטְרִיךְ. לְשַׁתָּא אַחֲרָא נָטִיר אִינּוּן יוֹמִין דְּסָלִיק לְיָקִירוּ דָּא, וְלָבַשׁ אִינּוּן לְבוּשִׁין, וְכֵן כָּל שַׁתָּא וְשַׁתָּא כְּהַאי גַּוְונָא יִשְׂרָאֵל, כְּתִיב, שִׁבְעַת יָמִים שְׂאוֹר לֹא יִמָּצֵא, דְּאִינּוּן יוֹמֵי חֶדְוָותָא, יוֹמִין דְּסָלִיקוּ לִיקָרָא דָּא, וְנַפְקוּ מִשִּׁעְבּוּדָא אַחֲרָא. וּבְגִין כַּךְ, נַטְרִין בְּכָל שַׁתָּא וְשַׁתָּא, יוֹמִין דְּסָלִיקוּ לְהַאי יְקָר, וְנַפְקוּ מֵרְשׁוּתָא אַחֲרָא, וְעָאלוּ בִּרְשׁוּתָא קַדִּישָׁא, וְעַל דָּא כְּתִיב, שִׁבְעַת יָמִים מַצּוֹת תֹּאכֵלוּ.

168. This is comparable to a king who appointed a person to be a minister. He rejoiced and wore clothes of glory all those days that he was being elevated to this level, but afterwards he did not need it. The following year, he observed those days that he rose to this honor and wore those clothes, and he did so each and every year. Similarly with Yisrael, it is written: "Seven days shall there be no leaven found," for they are days of rejoicing, the days that they arose to this honor, and went out of another bondage. Every year, they observe those days when they rose to this honor and went out of another authority and came under holy authority. Therefore, it is written: "Seven days shall you eat unleavened bread."

10. Matzah of Judgment

A Synopsis

Rabbi Shimon talks about the time that the moon was in a decreased state, when Yisrael had not yet completed the Covenant by the uncovering of the corona. After they were uncovered, God gave them bread from a higher place, from the heavens. Then Yisrael observe those days when they entered under the wings of the Shechinah and guarded the bread, the matzot, that came from its side.

The bonds which Rabbi Shimon refers to next are those that join the upper to the lower levels, and in the observance of the sacrifice those bonds are strengthened, as when the lamb is sacrificed.

169. אָמַר רִבִּי שִׁמְעוֹן, מַצַּת כְּתִיב, כמד״א, מַרְאֹת אֱלֹהִים. וְלָמָּה אִתְקְרֵי מַצַּת. דִּינָא. דִּינָא קַדִּישָׁא. דִּינָא דְּאִתְאַחֲדָא בִּשְׁמָא קַדִּישָׁא. דִּינָא דְּלָא הֲוָה תַּקִּיפָא כָּל הַהוּא זִמְנָא בְּגַוַויְיהוּ דְּיִשְׂרָאֵל, דְּהָא קַיְימָא סִיהֲרָא בִּפְגִימוּתָא. וְעַל דְּקַיְימָא סִיהֲרָא בִּפְגִימוּתָא, לֶחֶם עֹנִי כְּתִיב.

169. Rabbi Shimon said: *Matzat* (unleavened bread) is spelled WITHOUT *VAV*, as, "visions (Heb. *mar'ot*) of Elohim" (Yechezkel 1:1) IS WITHOUT *VAV*; THEREFORE, IT ALLUDES TO JUDGMENT. Why were they called *Matzat*–for their being of Judgment, Holy Judgment, Judgment that is attached to the Holy Name, Judgment that was not strong throughout that time among Yisrael, because the moon was flawed. And since the moon was flawed, it is written: "The bread of affliction" (Devarim 16:3).

170. מ״ט קַיְימָא בִּפְגִימוּתָא. בְּגִין דְּלָא אִתְפְּרָעוּ, וְלָא אִתְגַּלְיָא הַאי אָת קַדִּישָׁא. גְּזִירִין הֲווֹ וְלָא אִתְפְּרָעוּ, אֵימָתַי אִתְפְּרָעוּ, בְּשַׁעֲתָא דִּכְתִּיב, שָׁם שָׂם לוֹ חֹק וּמִשְׁפָּט וְשָׁם נִסָּהוּ, ואע״ג דְּאוֹקִימְנָא הַאי קְרָא בְּמִלָּה אַחֲרָא, כֹּלָּא הֲוָה וְיֵאוּת.

170. HE ASKS: What is the reason THAT THE MOON, WHICH IS MALCHUT, was in a waning state? HE ANSWERS: Because they were not uncovered and the holy sign was not revealed. Yisrael were circumcised, but did not uncover the corona. When they did, it is written: "There He made for them a statute and an ordinance, and there He tested him" (Shemot 15:25). And even though we have explained this passage as referring to something else, it was all in context, and it is well.

171. וְאִי תֵּימָא דְּבִימֵי יְהוֹשֻׁעַ אִתְפְּרָעוּ. לָאו הָכִי, אֶלָּא אִינּוּן דִּכְתִּיב וְכָל הָעָם הַיִּלּוֹדִים בַּמִּדְבָּר בַּדֶּרֶךְ וְגוֹ'. בָּתַר דְּאִתְפְּרָעוּ, אָמַר קוּדְשָׁא בְּרִיךְ הוּא, בְּקַדְמֵיתָא אֲכַלְתּוּן מַצּוֹת, דְּקַיְּימָא סִיהֲרָא בִּפְגִימוּתָא, וְאִקְרֵי לֶחֶם עֹנִי, מִכָּאן וּלְהָלְאָה הַאי לֶחֶם מֵאֲתָר אַחֲרָא לֶהֱוֵי. מַאי הוּא. דִּכְתִּיב הִנְנִי מַמְטִיר לָכֶם לֶחֶם מִן הַשָּׁמָיִם. לָא מִן סִיהֲרָא כְּהַהוּא זִמְנָא, אֶלָּא מִן הַשָּׁמַיִם מַמָּשׁ, כְּמָה דִּכְתִּיב וְיִתֶּן לְךָ הָאֱלֹהִים מִטַּל הַשָּׁמַיִם.

171. If you wonder that it seems they had to be uncovered in the days of Joshua, this was not so. Only those about whom it is written: "But all the people that were born in the wilderness by the way as they came out of Egypt, them they had not circumcised" (Yehoshua 5:5). After they were uncovered, the Holy One, blessed be He, said to them: 'Before, you ate unleavened bread because the moon remained waned, and it was called "the bread of affliction." But from now on, bread will be from a different place', as written: "Behold, I will rain bread from heaven for you" (Shemot 16:4). Not from the moon, WHICH IS MALCHUT, as at that time BEFORE THEY WERE UNCOVERED, but actually from the heavens, WHICH IS ZEIR ANPIN, as is written: "Therefore Elohim give you of the dew of heaven" (Beresheet 27:28).

172. וְיִשְׂרָאֵל קַדִּישִׁין, נַטְרִין אִינּוּן יוֹמִין דְּעָאלוּ תְּחוֹת גַּדְפּוֹי דִּשְׁכִינְתָּא, וְנַטְרִין הַהוּא נַהֲמָא דְּאַתְיָא מִסִּטְרָהָא, וע"ד כְּתִיב, אֶת חַג מַצּוֹת תִּשְׁמֹר וְגוֹ', וּכְתִיב וּשְׁמַרְתֶּם אֶת הַמַּצּוֹת. מַהוּ וּשְׁמַרְתֶּם אֶת הַמַּצּוֹת. כד"א, וּשְׁמַרְתֶּם אֶת בְּרִיתִי. וְכֹלָּא בְּחַד דַּרְגָּא סַלְקָא וְאִתְאֲחָד.

172. And holy Yisrael observe the days when they came under the wings of the Shechinah and kept the bread that came from its side, NAMELY THE *MATZOT*, as is written: "And you shall observe the commandment of unleavened bread" (Shemot 12:17). What is the meaning of: "And you shall observe...the unleavened bread?" It is similar to: "And keep My covenant"

(Shemot 19:5), WHICH IS THE COVENANT OF CIRCUMCISION. And it all rises and is attached to the same level, AS MENTIONED BEFORE.

173. וְאִי תֵּימָא מֹשֶׁה הֵיךְ לָא פָּרַע לְהוּ. אֶלָּא, בְּגִין דְּלָא יִתְעַכְּבוּן יִשְׂרָאֵל תַּמָּן עַד דְּיִתְסִיאוּ, וְעַל דָּא כְּתִיב, שִׁבְעַת יָמִים תֹּאכַל עָלָיו מַצּוֹת לֶחֶם עֹנִי. מ״ט לֶחֶם עֹנִי, מִשּׁוּם כִּי בְחִפָּזוֹן יָצָאתָ וְגוֹ׳ וּכְתִיב וְלֹא יָכְלוּ לְהִתְמַהְמֵהַּ.

173. One may wonder how it could be that Moses did not uncover them BUT LET THEM REMAIN CIRCUMCISED WITHOUT BEING UNCOVERED. HE ANSWERS: In order that Yisrael would not be delayed there until they became healed, HE THEREFORE DID NOT UNCOVER THEM. Pertaining to this, it is written: "Seven days shall you eat unleavened bread with it, the bread of affliction" (Devarim 16:3). Why WAS IT "the bread of affliction"? Because, "for you came forth...in haste" (Ibid.) and SIMILARLY, it is written: "and could not delay" (Shemot 12:39). THEREFORE, THEY WERE NOT UNCOVERED, AND CIRCUMCISION WITHOUT UNCOVERING BRINGS ABOUT THE BREAD OF AFFLICTION.

174. תָּא חֲזֵי, כַּד עָאלוּ יִשְׂרָאֵל לְאַרְעָא, עָאלוּ גְּזִירִין וְאִתְפְּרָעוּ. וּמַה כְּתִיב, אֶרֶץ אֲשֶׁר לֹא בְמִסְכֵּנוּת תֹּאכַל בָּהּ לֶחֶם. מַאי בְמִסְכֵּנוּת. לֶחֶם עֹנִי. אֲמַאי אִקְרֵי לֶחֶם עֹנִי. מִשּׁוּם דְּקַיְימָא סִיהֲרָא בִּפְגִימוּתָא, וְלָא מִתְבָּרְכָא מִשִּׁמְשָׁא, וְלָא מִתְנַהֲרָא מִן שִׁמְשָׁא, כְּמָה דְּאַתְּ אָמֵר, כִּי כֹל בַּשָּׁמַיִם וּבָאָרֶץ, וְלָא אִתְנַהֲרָא מִיּוּבְלָא. מַאי טַעֲמָא. מִשּׁוּם דְּלָא אִתְפְּרָעוּ. אֲבָל הָכָא, דְּאִתְגְּזָרוּ יִשְׂרָאֵל וְאִתְפְּרָעוּ, לֹא תֶחְסַר כֹּל בָּהּ כְּתִיב, וְעַל דָּא לֹא בְמִסְכֵּנוּת תֹּאכַל בָּהּ לֶחֶם. מַאי טַעֲמָא. מִשּׁוּם דְּלָא תֶחְסַר כֹּ״ל בָּהּ, כְּמָה דְּחָסְרוּ לֵיהּ בְּמִצְרַיִם.

174. Come and behold: when Yisrael came to the Holy Land, they came circumcised and uncovered, and it is written: "A land in which you shall eat bread without scarceness" (Devarim 8:9). And what is "scarceness"? It is "the bread of affliction." And why is it called "the bread of affliction"? This is because the moon, WHICH IS MALCHUT, is waning and is not blessed from the sun, WHICH IS ZEIR ANPIN, and does not shine from the sun, as is written: "For all (Heb. *kol*) that is in heaven and on earth" (I Divrei

Hayamim 29:11), MEANING THAT *KOL* ('ALL'), WHICH IS YESOD OF ZEIR ANPIN, IS ATTACHED TO HEAVEN, WHICH IS ZEIR ANPIN, AND TO THE EARTH, WHICH IS MALCHUT, AND RECEIVES FROM THE HEAVENS AND GIVES TO THE EARTH. What is the reason that it did not shine from the Jubilee, WHICH IS BINAH? This is because they did not uncover themselves, AS MENTIONED BEFORE, but now that Yisrael were circumcised and uncovered UPON ARRIVING INTO THE HOLY LAND, it is written: "You shall not lack anything (Heb. *kol*) in it" (Devarim 8:9), NAMELY, YESOD OF ZEIR ANPIN THAT ILLUMINATES ON MALCHUT AND IS CALLED '*KOL*'. What is the reason for: "In which you will not eat bread without scarceness"? It is because "You shall not lack *kol* in it," the way they did in Egypt.

175. וּבְכָל שַׁתָּא וְשַׁתָּא דּוּכְרָנָא דְּמִצְרַיִם קָא עַבְדֵי יִשְׂרָאֵל, וְאַכְלֵי וְלָא אִשְׁתְּצֵי מִדָּרֵי דָּרִין. וּבְגִין דְּלָא אִתְפְּרָעוּ הָכָא בְּמִצְרַיִם, חַסְרוּ לֵיהּ לְהַאי כֹּל, וְקַיְּימָא סִיהֲרָא בִּפְגִימוּתָא, וְאִקְרֵי לֶחֶם עֹנִי, עֹנִי: כְּתַרְגּוּמוֹ מִסְכֵּנוּת. וּמַאי דְּאַכְלוּ לֵיהּ תַּמָּן בְּאַרְעָא, בְּגִין דּוּכְרָנָא דְּמִצְרַיִם הֲוָה, וְהַאי לְדָרֵי דָּרִין, וּלְזִמְנָא דְּאָתֵי כְּתִיב, לֹא יָבֹא עוֹד שִׁמְשֵׁךְ וִירֵחֵךְ וְגוֹ'.

175. And every year, the children of Yisrael make a memorial to Egypt and eat UNLEAVENED BREAD and have not interrupted this for generations and generations. Because they did not uncover themselves in Egypt, they lacked this "*kol,*" and the moon was waning and is called "the bread of affliction." Affliction MEANS 'poverty', as in the Aramaic translation. The reason they ate the bread of affliction in the Holy Land, EVEN THOUGH THEY HAD ALREADY UNCOVERED THEMSELVES, serves as a remembrance to Egypt. This is a custom for generations and generations. And for the future to come, it is written: "Your sun shall no more set; nor shall your moon withdraw itself" (Yeshayah 60:20), MEANING THAT THE WANING OF THE MOON, WHICH IS MALCHUT, WILL BE NO MORE.

176. תַּנָּא א"ר שִׁמְעוֹן כְּתִיב בֶּעָשׂוֹר לַחֹדֶשׁ הַזֶּה וְיִקְחוּ לָהֶם וְגוֹ', וּכְתִיב אַךְ בֶּעָשׂוֹר לַחֹדֶשׁ הַשְּׁבִיעִי הַזֶּה יוֹם הַכִּפּוּרִים הוּא, אִשְׁתְּמַע כְּמָה דְּאִתְּמַר, דִּכְתִּיב בֶּעָשׂוֹר לַחֹדֶשׁ הַזֶּה. מַאי קָא מַיְירֵי. אֶלָּא בֶּעָשׂוֹר, מִלָּה דָּא בֶּעָשׂוֹר תַּלְיָא. לַחֹדֶשׁ הַזֶּה בַּחֹדֶשׁ הַזֶּה מִבָּעֵי לֵיהּ. אֶלָּא, כַּד אָתָא נִימוּסָא לְהַאי דַּרְגָּא, כְּתִיב לַחֹדֶשׁ הַזֶּה דַּיְקָא.

176. We learned that Rabbi Shimon said: It is written, "On the tenth day of this month they shall take..." (Shemot 12:3), and, "Also on the tenth day of this seventh month there shall be Yom Kippur" (Vayikra 23:27). It is derived from what we learned, as written, "on the tenth day of this month." THE ZOHAR WONDERS AND ASKS: What does it mean by this? HE ANSWERS THAT IT ALLUDES TO THE WORDS, "on the tenth." The business OF TAKING THE LAMB comes from the tenth, WHICH IS BINAH THAT SHINES ON MALCHUT, AS MENTIONED. AND THIS IS WHY HE FIRST MENTIONS THE ANALOGY BETWEEN THE TENTH IN THIS CONTEXT AND THE TENTH OF YOM KIPPUR, WHICH IS BINAH. AND HE ASKS: It is written, "of this month," but it should say, 'In this month'. HE ANSWERS: IT IS BECAUSE when the illumination came to this level, WHICH IS MALCHUT, the prase "of this month"; "OF THE MONTH" is exact, WHICH IS MALCHUT THAT IS CALLED 'MONTH'.

177. וְיִקְחוּ לָהֶם אִישׁ שֶׂה לְבֵית אָבוֹת שֶׂה לְבָּיִת. תָּנָא תְּלַת קִשְׁרִין אִינּוּן, בְּכוֹר בְּהֵמָה, בְּכוֹר הַשְּׁבִי, בְּכוֹר הַשִּׁפְחָה. דְּכָל שְׁאַר מִתְקַשְּׁרֵי בְּהוּ בְּאִלֵּין תְּלַת גַּוְונֵי דִּלְעֵילָּא. וּבְהַאי דְּאִתְקְרֵי צֹאן, אִתְקָשַּׁר כֹּלָּא, וְכֹלָּא כָּלִיל בַּצֹּאן, אִתְקָשַּׁר צֹאן בַּצֹּאן, וְלָא יָכִיל לְאִתְפָּרְשָׁא מִקִּטְרוֹי, וּבְהַאי כֻּלְּהוּ אִתְקַשָּׁרוּ, וע"ד כְּתִיב, וְהָיָה לָכֶם לְמִשְׁמֶרֶת, קְטִירוּ לֵיהּ בְּקְטִירוּתָא, וִיְהֵא אִתְמְסָר בִּידֵיכוֹן בִּרְשׁוּתְכוֹן, עַד דְּתַנְכְּסוּ לֵיהּ, וְתַעְבְּדוּן בֵּיהּ דִּינָא, וּלְזִמְנָא דְּאָתֵי כְּתִיב מִי זֶה בָּא מֵאֱדוֹם. וּכְתִיב, כִּי זֶבַח לַיְיָ' בְּבָצְרָה. וּכְתִיב, וְהָיָה יְיָ' לְמֶלֶךְ עַל כָּל הָאָרֶץ בַּיּוֹם הַהוּא יִהְיֶה יְיָ' אֶחָד וּשְׁמוֹ אֶחָד.

177. "They shall take to them every man a lamb, according to the houses of their fathers, a lamb for a house." We learned that there are three bonds: the firstborn of cattle, the firstborn of the captive, and the firstborn of the maidservant. All the other levels OF THE KLIPAH are connected to these three aspects above. They are all bound to the one called flock, and everything is included in it. IT IS THE HIGHEST LEVEL AMONG THEM. The flock BELOW is connected to the flock ABOVE, and is unable to separate from its bond. SO WE SEE that they are all connected to this, TO THE FLOCK. This is why it is written BY IT: "and you shall keep it" (Shemot 12:6) MEANING bind it with a knot, and it would be given into your hands under your control until you slaughter it and execute Judgment upon it. In the time to come, it is written: "Who is this that comes from Edom?" (Yeshayah 63:1) and: "For Hashem has a sacrifice in Botzrah" (Yeshayah 34:6), MEANING THAT HE WILL DESTROY ALL THE OTHER SIDE FROM THE EARTH. And THEN it is written: "And Hashem shall be king over all the earth. On that day Hashem shall be one and His Name One" (Zecharyah 14:9).

11. Relating the praise of the exodus from Egypt

A Synopsis

We hear again about the commandment to remove the leaven from the bread. Then we are told that Yisrael must say the praises of the exodus from Egypt, and when relating that account they will rejoice with the Shechinah in the World to Come. When God hears that praise, His retinue gathers round and rejoices and praises Him, and then His strength and power are increased above. Just as it is important for a person to relate the miracles of God, it is important for him to relate his own sins; this is because when a person enumerates every one of his sins beforehand, he leaves no open issue for the Accuser to exploit when standing before God to seek retribution. If the person repents, all will be well, but if he does not, the Accuser will return and demand judgment. Lastly, we hear again of the commandment to eat matzah on Passover because it is a remembrance for generations and generations of the secret of the Faith.

(רעיא מהימנא)

178. וְיִשָּׂא הָעָם אֶת בְּצֵקוֹ טֶרֶם יֶחְמָץ וְגוֹ'. כ"ה פִּקּוּדָא דָּא, לְבָעֵר חָמֵץ. דְּהָא פִּקּוּדָא דָּא, אִתְמְסַר לְהוּ לְיִשְׂרָאֵל וְיִשָּׂא הָעָם אֶת בְּצֵקוֹ טֶרֶם יֶחְמָץ. וּכְתִיב שְׂאוֹר לֹא יִמָּצֵא בְּבָתֵּיכֶם, וְהָא אוּקְמוּהָ חַבְרַיָּא, וְרָזָא אוּקִימְנָא, בֵּין חָמֵץ וּמַצָּה דְּכַמָּה דוּכְתֵּי, דָּא יֵצֶר רַע, וְדָא יֵצֶר טוֹב.

Ra'aya Meheimna (the Faithful Shepherd)

178. "And the people took their dough before it was leavened" (Shemot 12:34). This (25th) commandment is to remove the leaven. For this commandment was given over to Yisrael: "And the people took up and carried their dough before it was leavened," and: "shall there be no leaven found in your houses" (Ibid. 19). The friends have already explained it, and we have explained the secret meaning of the difference between leavened and unleavened bread OF THE EXODUS FROM EGYPT in many places – that one is the Evil Inclination and the other is the Good Inclination.

179. כ"ו פִּקּוּדָא בָּתַר דָּא, לְסַפֵּר בִּשְׁבָחָא דִּיצִיאַת מִצְרַיִם, דְּאִיהוּ חִיּוּבָא עַל בַּר נָשׁ, לְאִשְׁתָּעֵי בְּהַאי שְׁבָחָא לְעָלְמִין. הָכִי אוּקִימְנָא, כָּל

בַּר נָשׁ דְּאִשְׁתָּעֵי בִּיצִיאַת מִצְרַיִם, וּבְהַהוּא סִפּוּר חַדֵּי בְּחֶדְוָה, זַמִּין אִיהוּ לְמֶחֱדֵי בִּשְׁכִינְתָּא לְעָלְמָא דְּאָתֵי דְּהוּא חֵדוּ מִכֹּלָּא, דְּהַאי אִיהוּ בַּר נָשׁ דְּחַדֵּי בְּמָרֵיהּ, וְקוּדְשָׁא בְּרִיךְ הוּא חַדֵּי בְּהַהוּא סִפּוּר.

179. The following (26th) commandment is to relate the praise of the exodus from Egypt, which is incumbent upon every person always to relate these praises. We have explained that every person who relates the exodus from Egypt and rejoices when relating that account is destined to rejoice with the Shechinah in the World to Come, which is joy from all sides. For such is a person who rejoices in his Master, and the Holy One, blessed be He, rejoices in his story.

180. בֵּיהּ שַׁעֲתָא, כָּנִישׁ קוּדְשָׁא בְּרִיךְ הוּא לְכָל פָּמַלְיָיא דִּילֵיהּ, וְאָמַר לוֹן, זִילוּ וּשְׁמָעוּ סִפּוּרָא דִּשְׁבָחָא דִּילִי, דְּקָא מִשְׁתָּעוּ בָּנַי, וְחַדָּאן בְּפוּרְקָנִי. כְּדֵין כֻּלְּהוּ מִתְכַּנְּשִׁין, וְאַתְיָין וּמִתְחַבְּרִין בַּהֲדַיְיהוּ דְּיִשְׂרָאֵל, וּשְׁמָעוּ סִפּוּרָא דִּשְׁבָחָא, דְּקָא חַדָּאן בְּחֶדְוָא דְּפוּרְקָנָא דְּמָרֵיהוֹן, כְּדֵין אַתְיָין וְאוֹדָן לֵיהּ לְקוּדְשָׁא בְּרִיךְ הוּא, עַל כָּל אִינּוּן נִסִּין וּגְבוּרָן וְאוֹדָאן לֵיהּ עַל עַמָּא קַדִּישָׁא דְּאִית לֵיהּ בְּאַרְעָא, דְּחַדָּאן בְּחֶדְוָה דְּפוּרְקָנָא דְּמָארֵיהוֹן.

180. At that time, the Holy One, blessed be He, gathers His whole retinue, and says to them: 'Go and listen to the account of My excellency that My children are relating, rejoice in My redemption.' At that time, they all gather and come and join with Yisrael to hear the story of the praise. They rejoice with the joy of the deliverance by their Master, and come to thank and praise the Holy One, blessed be He, for all these miracles and mighty deeds, and thank Him for the Holy Nation that He has on earth that rejoices in the joy of the deliverance of their Master.

181. כְּדֵין אִתּוֹסַף לֵיהּ חֵילָא וּגְבוּרְתָּא לְעֵילָּא, וְיִשְׂרָאֵל בְּהַהוּא סִפּוּרָא יַהֲבֵי חֵילָא לְמָארֵיהוֹן, כְּמַלְכָּא, דְּאִתּוֹסַף חֵילָא וּגְבוּרְתָּא, כַּד מְשַׁבְּחִין גְּבוּרְתֵּיהּ, וְאוֹדָן לֵיהּ, וְכֻלְּהוּ דַּחֲלִין מִקַּמֵּיהּ, וְאִסְתַּלַּק יְקָרֵיהּ עַל כֻּלְּהוּ. וּבְגִין כָּךְ, אִית לְשַׁבְּחָא וּלְאִשְׁתָּעֵי בְּסִפּוּר דָּא כְּמָה דְּאִתְּמַר. כְּגַוְונָא דָּא, חוֹבָה אִיהוּ עַל בַּר נָשׁ, לְאִשְׁתָּעֵי תָּדִיר קָמֵי קוּדְשָׁא בְּרִיךְ הוּא,

וּלְפַרְסוּמֵי נִיסָא בְּכָל אִינּוּן נִיסִּין דְּעָבַד.

181. Then His strength and power are increased above. By their recounting, the children of Yisrael give power to their Master, like a king whose strength and power are increased when his strength is praised and he is acknowledged. All fear him and his glory rises above all of them. Therefore, it is incumbent to praise and relate this story, as we learned. Similarly, it is the duty of every person to relate before the Holy One, blessed be He, and publicize the miracle among all these miracles that He did.

182. וְאִי תֵּימָא, אֲמַאי אִיהוּ חוֹבָתָא, וְהָא קוּדְשָׁא בְּרִיךְ הוּא יָדַע כֹּלָּא, כָּל מַה דַּהֲוָה, וְיֶהֱוֵי לְבָתַר דְּנָא, אֲמַאי פִּרְסוּמָא דָּא קָמֵיהּ, עַל מַה דְּאִיהוּ עָבַד, וְאִיהוּ יָדַע. אֶלָּא וַדַּאי אִצְטְרִיךְ בַּר נָשׁ לְפַרְסוּמֵי נִיסָא, וּלְאִשְׁתָּעֵי קָמֵיהּ בְּכָל מַה דְּאִיהוּ עָבַד, בְּגִין דְּאִינּוּן מִלִּין סַלְּקִין, וְכָל פָּמַלְיָא דִּלְעֵילָּא מִתְכַּנְּשִׁין, וְחָמָאן לוֹן, וְאוֹדָאן כֻּלְּהוּ לְקוּדְשָׁא בְּרִיךְ הוּא, וְאִסְתַּלַּק יְקָרֵיהּ עֲלַיְיהוּ עֵילָּא וְתַתָּא.

182. One may ask why it is obligatory TO RELATE THE MIRACLES; does not the Holy One, blessed be He, know everything, everything that was and will be in the future? And wherefore this publicity before Him of what He did, if He knows? HE REPLIES: BUT surely one has to make the miracle known and relate before Him all that He did, because these words ascend and all the company above gather and see them, and give thanks before the Holy One, blessed be He, and His glory rises over them above and below.

183. כְּגַוְונָא דָּא, מַאן דְּאִשְׁתָּעֵי וּמְפָרֵט חֶטְאוֹי עַל כָּל מַה דְּעָבַד, אִי תֵּימָא לְמַאי אִצְטְרִיךְ. אֶלָּא מְקַטְרְגָא קָאִים תָּדִיר קָמֵי קוּדְשָׁא בְּרִיךְ הוּא, בְּגִין לְאִשְׁתָּעֵי וּלְמִתְבַּע חוֹבֵי בְּנֵי נָשָׁא, וּלְמִתְבַּע עֲלֵיהוֹן דִּינָא. כֵּיוָן דְּאַקְדִּים בַּר נָשׁ, וּמְפָרֵיט חֶטְאוֹי, כָּל חַד וְחַד, לָא אַשְׁאִיר פִּתְחָא דְּפוּמָא לְהַהוּא מְקַטְרְגָא, וְלָא יָכִיל לְמִתְבַּע עָלֵיהּ דִּינָא. דְּהָא תָּדִיר תָּבַע דִּינָא בְּקַדְמֵיתָא, וּלְבָתַר מִשְׁתָּעֵי וּמְקַטְרֵג פְּלוֹנִי עָבֵד כַּךְ. וְעַל דָּא, אִצְטְרִיךְ לֵיהּ לְבַר נָשׁ לְאַקְדְּמָא, וּלְפָרֵט חֶטְאוֹי.

183. It is the same with he who relates and enumerates his sins, of everything that he did. If you ask why this is necessary, it is because the Accuser is constantly before the Holy One, blessed be He, in order to recount and seek retribution for the sins of people, and to demand Judgment against them. However, when the person enumerates each and every one of his sins beforehand, he does not leave any pretext to the Accuser to exploit. And the Accuser can not demand any Judgment against him, for he always demands Judgment first, and afterwards enumerates and accuses. Therefore, the person should take his own initiative before the Accuser and enumerate his own sins.

184. כֵּיוָן דִּמְקַטְרְגָא חָמֵי דָּא, לֵית לֵיהּ פִּטְרָא דְּפוּמָא עָלֵיהּ, וּכְדֵין אִתְפְּרַשׁ מִנֵּיהּ מִכֹּל וָכֹל. אִי תָּב בְּתִיוּבְתָּא יֵאוֹת, וְאִי לָאו, הָא מְקַטְרְגָא אִשְׁתְּכַח עָלֵיהּ, וְאָמַר פְּלוֹנִי דְּאָתָא לְקָמָךְ בְּתוּקְפָּא דְּאַפִּין, בָּעִיט בְּמָרֵיהּ, חוֹבוֹי כַּךְ וְכָךְ. עַל דָּא יֵאוֹת לְאִזְדַּהֲרָא בַּר נָשׁ בְּכָל הָנֵי, בְּגִין דְּיִשְׁתְּכַח עַבְדָּא מְהֵימָנָא קָמֵי קוּדְשָׁא בְּרִיךְ הוּא.

184. As soon as the Accuser sees this, he has no pretext to complain against him, and then takes leave from him entirely. If he repents, well, but if not, the Accuser rests on him and says: 'So and so who came before you AND CONFESSED unashamedly, he kicked his Master, his sins are such and such.' Therefore, it is advisable that a person be careful in all this, so that he should be considered a faithful servant before the Holy One, blessed be He.

185. כ"ז פִּקּוּדָא בָּתַר דָּא, לֶאֱכוֹל מַצָּה בְּפֶסַח, בְּגִין דְּאִיהוּ דּוּכְרָנָא לְדָרֵי דָּרִין, עַל רָזָא דִּמְהֵימְנוּתָא. וְהָא אוּקְמוּהָ, דְּיִשְׂרָאֵל נָפְקוּ בְּהַהוּא זִמְנָא מֵרָזָא דְּטַעֲוָון אַחֲרָן, וְעָאלוּ בְּרָזָא דִּמְהֵימָנוּתָא. וְהָא אוּקְמוּהָ רָזָא דְּנָא בְּכַמָּה דּוּכְתֵּי.

185. The following (27th) commandment is to eat Matzah on Pesach (Passover), because it is a remembrance for generations and generations of the secret of the Faith. It has been explained that Yisrael went out at that time from the secret of other Elohim and came into the secret of Faith. This secret has been explained in many places.

12. The Pascal sacrifice

A Synopsis

The ordinance of the Passover is to slaughter the sacrifice at twilight of the fourteenth day of Nissan as a remembrance of the Passover in Egypt. The moon becomes complete on the fifteenth day, and the sacrifice should be slaughtered at twilight of the fourteenth day because that is the time that Judgment hangs over the world. The main part of the commandment is to gain pleasure from the scent that spreads from the roasting over the fire. Only one who is circumcised can eat of it. At the time when God came to Egypt and saw the blood marked on the entrances of the houses of Yisrael, the people used hyssop to spread the blood, since hyssop removes evil spirits and any aspect of a bad odor because it arouses the supernal Redemption of Yisrael. In the time to come, God will slaughter the Evil Inclination. Because God slew all the firstborn of the Egyptians, He obligated all the firstborn of Yisrael to redeem themselves, and He guarded them against everything. Scripture says, about the sacrifice, “Neither shall you break a bone of it”, because the bones were the deities of the Other Side, and the children of Yisrael threw them out in contempt to express their contempt for the Egyptian deities.

186. וַיֹּאמֶר יְיָ׳ אֶל מֹשֶׁה וְאַהֲרֹן זֹאת חֻקַּת הַפָּסַח וְגוֹ׳. כ״ח פִּקּוּדָא דָא, לְמִשְׁחַט פֶּסַח בֵּין הָעַרְבַּיִם, בְּי״ד בְּנִיסָן, דּוּכְרָנָא דְּהַהוּא פֶּסַח דְּמִצְרַיִם. וְדָא אִיהוּ חוֹבָתָא עַל כֹּלָּא, כְּמָה דְּאַתְּ אָמֵר, וְשָׁחֲטוּ אוֹתוֹ כָּל קְהַל עֲדַת יִשְׂרָאֵל בֵּין הָעַרְבַּיִם.

186. “And Hashem said to Moses and Ahab, ‘This is the ordinance of the Passover’” (Shemot 12:43). This (28th) commandment is to slaughter the Passover at twilight of the fourteenth day of Nissan, a remembrance to the Passover in Egypt. And this is incumbent upon everyone, as it is written: “And the whole assembly of the Congregation of Yisrael shall kill it towards evening” (Ibid. 6).

187. פֶּסַח דָּא, אִצְטְרִיךְ לְמֶהֱוֵי נָטִיר, מֵעֲשָׂרָה יוֹמִין וּלְהָלְאָה, דִּכְתִּיב בֶּעָשׂוֹר לַחֹדֶשׁ הַזֶּה וְיִקְחוּ לָהֶם וְגוֹ׳. מַאי טַעֲמָא. בְּגִין דְּהָא כְּדֵין שָׁרִיאַת סִיהֲרָא לְאַנְהָרָא, מֵעֲשָׂרָה יוֹמִין וּלְהָלְאָה, עַד דְּאִשְׁתְּלִים בַּחֲמֵיסָר. וְאַרְבֵּיסָר דְּלֶיהֱוֵי נָבִיס, בְּשַׁעֲתָא דְּדִינָא תַּלְיָא עַל עָלְמָא.

187. This Pascal sacrifice has to be kept since the tenth day of the month, as is written: "On the tenth day of this month, and they shall take..." (Shemot 12:3). What is the reason? It is because that is when the moon starts to shine, from the tenth day and further until it becomes full on the fifteenth day. It should be slaughtered on the fourteenth day at the time that Judgment is impending over the world, NAMELY AT TWILIGHT.

188. רָזָא דָּא, לְאַעְבְּרָא זוּהֲמָא, מִקָּמֵי בְּרִית קַדִּישָׁא, וּלְאִתְהֲנָאָה בְּהַהוּא רֵיחָא דְּנָדִיף טְוִי נוּר. וְעַל דָּא לָא אַתְיָא אֶלָּא עַל שָׂבְעָא. וְעַל דָּא, וְכָל עָרֵל לֹא יֹאכַל בּוֹ. מַאן דְּאִית בֵּיהּ בְּרִית קַדִּישָׁא, יֵיכוּל בֵּיהּ. מַאן דְּלָא אִית בֵּיהּ בְּרִית קַדִּישָׁא, לָא יֵיכוּל בֵּיהּ. דְּהַאי מִבְּנֵי בְּרִית אִיהוּ לְתַבְרָא תּוּקְפָּא דְּחֵילָא אַחֲרָא, לְאַעְבְּרָא עָרְלָה מִקָּמֵי בְּרִית. בְּגִין כַּךְ, הַאי בִּבְנֵי בְּרִית אִיהוּ לְמֶעְבַּד, וְלָא בִּבְנֵי עָרְלָה.

188. The meaning behind this is to remove the foreskin from before the Holy Covenant and to gain pleasure from the scent that spreads from the meat roasted on fire, MEANING THE MAIN PART OF THE COMMANDMENT IS TO ENJOY ITS SCENT. Its purpose is only satiation, THEN ONE DOES NOT NEED TO EAT ANYMORE. Therefore, "no uncircumcised person shall eat of it" (Ibid. 48) but one who has the holy covenant may eat of it. This is because he of the members of the covenant breaks the power of the Other Side, and removes the foreskin from the covenant. Therefore, it must be done by members of the covenant and not by uncircumcised ones.

189. כַּד אָתָא קוּדְשָׁא בְּרִיךְ הוּא לְמִצְרַיִם, חָמָא דָּמָא דְּהַהוּא פֶּסַח, דַּהֲוָה רָשִׁים עַל פִּתְחָא, וְדָמָא דִּבְרִית, הֵיךְ הֲווֹ קַיְימִין עַל פִּתְחָא, דִּכְתִּיב, וּלְקַחְתֶּם אֲגֻדַּת אֵזוֹב וּטְבַלְתֶּם בַּדָּם אֲשֶׁר בַּסַּף וְהִגַּעְתֶּם וְגוֹ'. אֵזוֹבָא, הָא אוֹקִימְנָא דְּאִיהוּ מַעְבַּר רוּחִין בִּישִׁין, וְכָל סְטָר רוּחַ בִּישָׁא, מַעְבַּר בְּאִתְעָרוּתָא דִּילֵיהּ, בְּפוּרְקָנָא עִלָּאָה דְּיִשְׂרָאֵל.

189. When the Holy One, blessed be He, came to Egypt, He saw how the blood of the Passover that was marked on the entrance and the blood of the circumcision were on the door, as is written: "And take a bunch of hyssop, and dip it in the blood that is in the basin, and touch with it..." (Shemot 12:22). We have explained that hyssop removes evil spirits and any aspect of a bad odor when it is operative for the supernal redemption of Yisrael.

190. לְזִמְנָא דְּאָתֵי, יֵיתֵי קוּדְשָׁא בְּרִיךְ הוּא לְיֵצֶר הָרָע וְיִכּוֹס לֵיהּ. וְהַשְׁתָּא בְּפוּרְקָנָא דָּא, כְּתִיב וְשָׁחֲטוּ אוֹתוֹ כֹּל קְהַל עֲדַת יִשְׂרָאֵל וְגוֹ׳. דּוּכְרָנָא דִּזְמְנָא דְּאָתֵי, בְּהַהוּא פּוּרְקָנָא עִלָּאָה.

190. In the future to come, the Holy One, blessed be He, will come upon the Evil Inclination and slaughter it. By this redemption FROM EGYPT, it is written: "and the whole assembly of the Congregation of Yisrael shall kill it," for it is a token of remembrance for the time to come of the supernal redemption THAT IS HIGHER THAN THE ONE FROM EGYPT.

191. עַל שְׁתֵּי הַמְּזוּזוֹת וְעַל הַמַּשְׁקוֹף בְּהַאי רְשִׁימוּ דְּאָת יוֹ״ד, וּבְהַאי רְשִׁימוּ דְּאָת יוֹ״ד, לְאַחֲזָאָה רְשִׁימוּ דִּבְרִית קַדִּישָׁא, וְאִתְּבַּר עָרְלָה מִקָּמֵי דָּמָא דִּבְרִית, רָשִׁים עַל כֹּלָּא, וְאָתָא דָּמָא עַל דָּמָא. כַּד עָבַר הַהוּא מַשְׁחִית, הֲוָה חָמֵי דָּמָא, וְאִזְדְּקִיף מִבֵּיתָא, כְּמָה דְּאַתְּ אָמֵר וְלֹא יִתֵּן הַמַּשְׁחִית וְגוֹ׳.

191. "The lintel and the two side posts..." They marked the letter *Yud* ON THE DOOR POSTS. They marked the letter *Yud* ON THE LINTEL to show THROUGH THEM the mark of the holy covenant, WHICH IS THE *YUD*, and the foreskin was broken before the blood of the covenant that was marked on all. And blood came upon blood, NAMELY THE BLOOD OF THE PASCAL SACRIFICE ON THE BLOOD OF THE CIRCUMCISION. When the Destroyer passed, he would see blood and distance himself from the house, as is written: "And will not allow the Destroyer..." (Shemot 12:23)

192. אִי קוּדְשָׁא בְּרִיךְ הוּא בִּלְחוֹדוֹי קָטִיל, אַמַּאי כְּתִיב וְלֹא יִתֵּן הַמַּשְׁחִית, דְּמַשְׁמַע דְּמַשְׁחִית הֲוָה אָזִיל וְלָא קוּדְשָׁא בְּרִיךְ הוּא. אֶלָּא וַדַּאי קוּדְשָׁא בְּרִיךְ הוּא הֲוָה קָטִיל, וּמַשְׁחִית הֲוָה אָזִיל לְאַשְׁכְּחָא עִילָּה לְיִשְׂרָאֵל, כֵּיוָן דַּהֲוָה חָמֵי הַהוּא תְּבִירוּ דְּעָרְלָה, בִּתְרֵין סִטְרִין, הֲוָה עָרַק וְאִתְפְּרַשׁ מִנַּיְיהוּ.

192. HE ASKS: If the Holy One, blessed be He, Himself was killing, why is it written: "And will not allow the Destroyer," which implies that the Destroyer was doing it and not the Holy One, blessed be He. HE ANSWERS:

Assuredly the Holy One, blessed be He, alone was carrying out the killing and the Destroyer was seeking to find a pretext against Yisrael TO ACCUSE THEM. As soon as he saw the breakage of the foreskin in two aspects, BY THE BLOOD OF THE PASSOVER AND THE BLOOD OF CIRCUMCISION, he would flee and leave them.

193. וְעַל דְּקָטַל קוּדְשָׁא בְּרִיךְ הוּא כָּל אִינּוּן בּוּכְרִין דְּהַהוּא סִטְרָא, יָהִיב בּוּכְרִין דְּיִשְׂרָאֵל לְפוּרְקָנָא, דְּלָא יִשְׁכַּח עֲלַיְיהוּ סִטְרָא אַחֲרָא עִילָּה כְּלָל, וּבְכֹלָּא נָטִיר לוֹן לְיִשְׂרָאֵל קוּדְשָׁא בְּרִיךְ הוּא, כְּאַבָּא עַל בְּנִין.

193. Because the Holy One, blessed be He, slew all the firstborns of that side, He obligated the firstborn of Yisrael to redeem THEMSELVES so that the Other Side will find no pretext against them. The Holy One, blessed be He, guarded them against everything, like a father over children.

194. בְּבַיִת אֶחָד יֵאָכֵל לֹא תוֹצִיא מִן הַבַּיִת וְגוֹ', פִּקּוּדָא כ"ט דָּא, לְמֵיכַל הַאי פֶּסַח. עַל מַצּוֹת וּמְרוֹרִין, מַצּוֹת מַצַּת כְּתִיב. מַאי הַאי לָקֳבֵל הַאי, אֶלָּא לְאַחֲזָאָה גָּלוּתָא דִּשְׁכִינְתָּא עִמְּהוֹן דְּיִשְׂרָאֵל, בְּהַהוּא מְרִירוּ דִּלְהוֹן, דִּכְתִּיב וַיְמָרְרוּ אֶת חַיֵּיהֶם בַּעֲבוֹדָה קָשָׁה וְגוֹ'. וְכַד אַכְלִין לְהַאי פֶּסַח, לְאַחֲזָאָה כָּל הַאי דְּעָבְדוּ לוֹן בְּמִצְרַיִם, בְּהַהוּא גָּלוּתָא וּבְהַהוּא שִׁעְבּוּדָא.

194. "In one house shall it be eaten, you shall not take any of the meat outside, out of the house" (Shemot 12:46). This (29th) commandment is to eat the Passover with Matzot and bitter herbs. Matzot is spelled without a *Vav*. HE ASKS: What is MATZOT with regard to BITTER HERBS, THAT THE VERSE OBLIGATED TO EAT THEM TOGETHER? HE ANSWERS: It is only to show the exile of the Shechinah with Yisrael in their bitterness, as written: "And they made their lives bitter with hard bondage..." (Shemot 1:14). When the Pascal sacrifice is eaten, it shows everything that was done to them in Egypt in that exile and that bondage. THEREFORE, IT IS EATEN WITH MATZOT AND BITTER HERBS.

195. מַה כְּתִיב וְעֶצֶם לֹא תִשְׁבְּרוּ בוֹ, לְאַחֲזָאָה בֵּיהּ קְלָנָא, וּבְכָל אִינּוּן

טַעֲוָון דְּמִצְרָאֵי. דְּהָא גַּרְמִין הֲווֹ רָמָאן בְּשׁוּקָא, וְאָתוּ כַּלְבֵּי וַהֲווֹ גָּרְרֵי לוֹן מֵאֲתָר לַאֲתָר, וְדָא קַשְׁיָא לוֹן מִכֹּלָּא, דְּהָא גַּרְמֵי אִינּוּן תִּקּוּנָא דְּגוּפָא, וְדָמֵי לְגַוְונָא אַחֲרָא, וְיִשְׂרָאֵל רָמָאן לוֹן בְּשׁוּקָא אוֹרַח קְלָנָא, וע״ד כְּתִיב וְעֶצֶם לֹא תִשְׁבְּרוּ בוֹ, אַתּוּן לָא תְּשַׁבְּרוּן, אֲבָל כַּלְבֵּי הֲווֹ אַתְיָין וּמְתַבְּרִין לֵיהּ.

195. What is the meaning of: "Neither shall you break a bone of it" (Shemot 12:46)? To show contempt to it, and all the deities of Egypt because the unbroken bones were thrown out to the marketplace and dogs would come and drag them from place to place. This was the most difficult thing for them, because the bones put the body in order and resemble another side, NAMELY THEIR OTHER DEITIES. The children of Yisrael cast them out into the marketplace in contempt. Therefore, it is written: "Neither shall you break a bone of it." You must not break them, but dogs came and broke them.

196. תּוּ, מִצְרָאֵי הֲווֹ אַתְיָין לְבָתַר, וַהֲווֹ חָמָאן אִינּוּן גַּרְמֵי דַּהֲווֹ נַטְלֵי כַּלְבֵּי מֵאֲתָר לַאֲתָר, וּמַדְקָן לוֹן, וַהֲווֹ מִצְרָאֵי טָמְנֵי לוֹן גּוֹ עַפְרָא, בְּגִין כַּלְבֵּי דְּלָא יִשְׁכְּחוּן לוֹן, וְדָא אִיהוּ בְּטוּלָה דְּעַכּוּ״ם, יַתִּיר, מִסִּטְרָא דִּלְהוֹן. וּבְדָא קוּדְשָׁא בְּרִיךְ הוּא אִסְתַּלַּק בִּיקָרֵיהּ, וְאִתְכַּפְיָין כָּל חֵילִין אַחֲרָנִין, דְּהָא כְּדֵין אִתְכַּפְיָין יַתִּיר, כַּד בָּטִילוּ אִשְׁתְּכַח מִסִּטְרָא דִּלְהוֹן, וְע״ד יִשְׂרָאֵל לָא מְבַטְּלֵי לוֹן, דִּכְתִּיב וְעֶצֶם לֹא תִשְׁבְּרוּ בוֹ.

196. IT CAN also BE EXPLAINED: the Egyptians came afterwards and saw the dogs dragging these bones from place to place and breaking them. The Egyptians would bury them in the ground so that the dogs could not find them, which was the greatest obliteration of their idols on their side. The Holy One, blessed be He, was elevated in His glory by this. And all the other powers OF THE IDOLS were subdued. When the subjugation of the idols is from their own side, it is even more profound, NAMELY WHEN THEY BURIED BONES OF THEIR IDOLS IN THE EARTH. Therefore, it is not Yisrael that voided them, as written: "Neither shall you break a bone of it."

13. "Sanctify to Me all the firstborn"

A Synopsis

We are told that most people are under the domination of both the Evil Inclination and the Good Inclination. The average person should wish for two things: to be redeemed from the domination of the Evil Inclination, and to ascend to the level of Adam. Rabbi Shimon tells us how Gavriel, the Good Inclination, wrestles with man before he is born and teaches him seventy languages, and how the Evil Inclination causes him to forget the seventy languages. A man's merits and sins are always wrestling to wage war within him. Four angels descend with a man: if he has ancestral merit then they are Michael, Gavriel, Nuriel and Refael, and the Good Inclination stands above him; if he has no merit then they are the four angels of destruction – Sin, Destroyer, Anger and Fury – and the Evil Inclination stands above him to judge him in the World to Come. This is why both Gavriel and Samael judge the average person. Every person has the four elements Fire, Air, Water and Earth, but according to which of these elements is first, a different angel comes first. Next we learn of the four aspects Lion, Ox, Eagle and Adam of the right and left sides, and we are told about the characteristics of those men who are under each aspect and how they differ depending on whether they do or do not study Torah. We read that the Master Scholars of the Mishnah declared: A person should always view himself as if the whole world depends on him, because he can tip the balance. Rabbi Shimon closes by saying that every living creature is marked with the letters of the Holy Name, in order to recognize who created it.

197. קַדֶּשׁ לִי כָל בְּכוֹר פֶּטֶר רֶחֶם וְגוֹ'. פִּקּוּדָא דָּא לְקַדֵּשׁ בְּכוֹר בְּהֵמָה, וְעַם הָאָרֶץ צָרִיךְ תְּרֵין מִילִין, חַד דִּיהֵא פָּדוּי מִתְּחוֹת שֻׁלְטָנוּתָא דְּיֵצֶר הָרָע, דְּאִיהִי אֲדוֹן דִּילֵיהּ, כְּגַוְונָא דְּאָמַר יַעֲקֹב לְעֵשָׂו, יַעֲבָר נָא אֲדֹנִי לִפְנֵי עַבְדּוֹ. בְּהַאי עָלְמָא. אֲדוֹן מִצַּד חוֹבִין דִּנְפִישִׁין עַל גּוּפָא, כְּמָה דְּאוּקְמוּהָ, חַיָּיבָא, יֵצֶר הָרָע שׁוֹפְטוֹ. זַכָּאָה, יֵצֶר הַטּוֹב שׁוֹפְטוֹ. בֵּינוֹנִי זֶה וְזֶה שׁוֹפְטוֹ. בֵּינוֹנִי, הַיְינוּ אָח דְּיֵצֶר הָרָע, וְאָח דְּיֵצֶר הַטּוֹב, אָחִי יְהִי לְךָ אֲשֶׁר לָךְ.

197. "Sanctify to Me all the firstborn, whatever opens the womb..." (Shemot 13:2). This commandment is to sanctify the firstborn of the animals. A common person needs two things. He should be redeemed from under the power of the Evil Inclination, which is his master. As Jacob said to Esau, "Let my master, I pray you, pass over before his servant" (Beresheet 33:14), MEANING in this world HE IS the master because of the many sins upon the body. As we explained, the Evil Inclination judges the wicked, and the Good Inclination judges the righteous. The average man is judged by both; an average man is a brother of the Evil Inclination and a brother of the Good Inclination, AS IS WRITTEN: "My brother; keep what you have to yourself" (Ibid. 9).

198. וְכַד זַכְוָון נְפִישִׁין, רוּחָא תָּבַר תְּרֵין מִשְׁמָרוֹת, דַּחֲמוֹר נוֹעֵר, כְּלָבִים צוֹעֲקִים, וְסָלִיק לְמִשְׁמֶרֶת דְּשַׁחַר, דְּבֵיהּ אָדָם וְאִתְהַדָּר בַּר נָשׁ אֲדוֹן, הה"ד, וַיְהִי לִי שׁוֹר וַחֲמוֹר צֹאן וְעֶבֶד וְשִׁפְחָה, וְסָלִיק לְדַרְגָּא דְּאָדָם, דְּאִתְּמַר בֵּיהּ, וּרְדוּ בִּדְגַת הַיָּם וּבְעוֹף הַשָּׁמַיִם וְגוֹ', וּמוֹרַאֲכֶם וְחִתְּכֶם וְגוֹ'.

198. And when the merits are numerous, the wind breaks two of the watches OF THE NIGHT, WHICH ARE a braying donkey and barking dogs, and rises to the THIRD watch of the dawn wherein there is man, THAT IS, A WIFE CONVERSING WITH HER HUSBAND. Man again becomes master OVER ALL THE CREATURES. This is the meaning of: "And I have oxen, and donkeys, flocks, and menservants, and womenservants" (Beresheet 32:6). He ascends to the level of man, of which it says: "And have dominion over the fish in the sea, and over the birds of air..." (Beresheet 1:28) as well as: "And the fear of you and the dread of you..." (Beresheet 9:2). THIS IS THE SECOND THING THAT A COMMON PERSON SHOULD STRIVE FOR.

199. וְכַד זַכְוָון בֵּינוֹנִים, וַיֵּאָבֵק אִישׁ עִמּוֹ, זַכְוָון וְחוֹבִין מִתְחַבְּקָן לְאַגָּחָא קְרָבָא. מִסִּטְרָא דְּזַכְוָון, וַיַּרְא כִּי לֹא יָכוֹל לוֹ. מִסִּטְרָא דְּחוֹבִין, וַיִּגַּע בְּכַף יְרֵכוֹ בְּגִיד הַנָּשֶׁה. נָשֶׁה: לָשׁוֹן כִּי נַשַּׁנִי אֱלֹהִים אֶת כָּל עֲמָלִי וְאִיהוּ לְשׁוֹן נְשִׁיָּה. חַד מָדוֹרָא מֵאִינּוּן שִׁבְעָה אַרְעָאן, מַאן דְּנָחִית תַּמָּן אִתְנְשֵׁי מִנֵּיהּ אוֹרַיְיתָא.

199. When there is an average amount of merits: "And there wrestled a man with him" (Beresheet 32:25), MEANING that the merits and sins wrestle in war. From the side of the merits, IT IS WRITTEN: "And when he saw that he did not prevail against him" (Ibid. 26). From the side of the sins, IT IS

WRITTEN: "he touched the hollow of his thigh," in the sinew of the thigh (Heb. *nashe*)." "Nashe" is derived from: "For Elohim has made me forget (Heb. *nashani*) all my toil" (Beresheet 41:51). It is a term of forgetfulness, which is one compartment of the seven lands. Whoever descends there forgets his knowledge.

200. וְקֹדֶם דְּיֵיתֵי בַּר נָשׁ בְּהַאי עָלְמָא וְיִפּוֹק מֵרֶחֶם אִמֵּיהּ, וַיֵּאָבֵק אִישׁ עִמּוֹ, דָּא גַּבְרִיאֵל, בְּהַהוּא אָבָק דְּעָפָר, דְּאִתְּמַר וַיִּיצֶר יְיָ׳ אֱלֹהִים אֶת הָאָדָם עָפָר מִן הָאֲדָמָה, וְאוֹלִיף לֵיהּ שִׁבְעִים לָשׁוֹן. ובג״ד, וַיִּיצֶר: חַד יֵצֶר הַטּוֹב, דְּאוֹלִיף לֵיהּ שִׁבְעִים לָשׁוֹן. וְחַד, יֵצֶר הָרָע דְּאָבִיק עִמֵּיהּ. דְּאִתְּמַר, כִּי נָגַע בְּכַף יֶרֶךְ יַעֲקֹב בְּגִיד הַנָּשֶׁה, וְאַשְׁכַּח מִנֵּיהּ שַׁבְעִין לָשׁוֹן, דְּאוֹלִיף לֵיהּ יֵצֶר הַטּוֹב.

200. Before a person comes to this world and emerges from his mother's womb; "And there wrestled a man with him," that is Gavriel. "AND THERE WRESTLED (HEB. *VAYE'AVEK*)" MEANS in the dust (Heb. *avak*) of earth, as is written: "And Hashem Elohim formed (Heb. *vayyitzer*) man of the dust of the ground" (Beresheet 2:7). SO WE FIND THAT MAN IS EARTH AND THE DUST OF THAT EARTH IS THE EVIL INCLINATION, AND GAVRIEL IS THE GOOD INCLINATION WHO BATTLES WITH THE EVIL INCLINATION CALLED 'DUST'. He teaches him seventy languages. Therefore, "*vayyitzer*" IS SPELLED WITH TWO *YUDS*, one *YUD* corresponds to the Good Inclination, WHICH IS GAVRIEL, who taught him seventy languages, and one *YUD* corresponds to the Evil Inclination who wrestled with him, as written: "Because he touched the hollow of Jacob's thigh in the sinew of the vein" (Beresheet 32:33). And he caused him to forget the seventy languages which the Good Inclination taught him.

201. וְקֹדֶם כָּל דָּא, נַחְתִּין עִמֵּיהּ אַרְבְּעָה מַלְאָכִין, דְּאִתְּמַר בְּהוֹן כִּי מַלְאָכָיו יְצַוֶּה לָּךְ. אִי אִית לֵיהּ זְכוּת אָבוֹת, חַד מִיכָאֵל, בִּזְכוּת אַבְרָהָם. וְתִנְיָינָא גַּבְרִיאֵל, בִּזְכוּת יִצְחָק. וּתְלִיתָאָה דְּנָחִית עִמֵּיהּ נוּרִיאֵל, בִּזְכוּתָא דְּיַעֲקֹב. וּרְבִיעָאָה רְפָאֵל, בִּזְכוּתָא דְּאָדָם קַדְמָאָה. וְיֵצֶר הַטּוֹב לְעֵילָּא מִנֵּיהּ.

201. Before all this, four angels descended with him, as is written: "For He shall give His angels charge over you" (Tehilim 91:11). If he has ancestral merit, THEN one is Michael by the merit of Abraham, the second is Gavriel by the merit of Isaac, the third who descends with him is Nuriel by the merit of Jacob and the fourth is Refael by the merit of Adam. And the Good Inclination is above him.

202. וְאִי לֵית לֵיהּ זְכוּת, אָזְלֵי עִמֵּיהּ ד׳, עָוֹן, מַשְׁחִית, אַף, וְחֵימָה, וְיֵצֶר הָרָע לְעֵילָּא מִנַּיְיהוּ, לְמֵידָן לֵיהּ לְעָלְמָא דְּאָתֵי. וּבְגִין דָּא אוּקְמוּהָ, רָשָׁע, יֵצֶר הָרָע שׁוֹפְטוֹ. צַדִּיק, יֵצֶר הַטּוֹב שׁוֹפְטוֹ. בֵּינוֹנִי, זֶה וְזֶה שׁוֹפְטוֹ. וּבְגִין דָּא, אִי אִיהוּ בֵּינוֹנִי, גַּבְרִיאֵל דְּאִיהוּ יֵצֶר הַטּוֹב, וְסַמָּאֵ״ל דְּאִיהוּ יֵצֶר הָרָע, זֶה וְזֶה שׁוֹפְטוֹ.

202. If he has no merit, then four ANGELS OF DESTRUCTION accompany him: Sin, Destroyer, Anger and Fury. And the Evil Inclination is over them to judge him in the World to Come. Therefore, they explained that a wicked person is judged by the Evil Inclination, a righteous person is judged by the Good Inclination and an average man is judged by both. Therefore, if he is an average person, both Gavriel, who is the Good Inclination, and Samael, the Evil Inclination, judge him.

203. דִּלְכָל בַּר נָשׁ דְּאִית בֵּיהּ אַרְבַּע יְסוֹדִין, אַרְבַּע מַלְאָכִים נַחְתִּין עִמֵּיהּ מִימִינָא, וְאַרְבַּע מִשְּׂמָאלָא. אַרְבַּע מִימִינָא: מִיכָאֵ״ל, גַּבְרִיאֵ״ל, רְפָאֵ״ל, נוּרִיאֵ״ל. וְאַרְבַּע מִשְּׂמָאלָא: עָוֹ״ן, מַשְׁחִי״ת, אַ״ף, וְחֵמָ״ה. מִסִּטְרָא דְּגוּפָא, מְטַטְרוֹ״ן נָחִית עָלֵיהּ מִימִינָא, וְסַמָּאֵ״ל מִשְּׂמָאלָא.

203. For every person who has in him the four elements – FIRE, AIR, WATER, EARTH – four angels descend with him to his right and four to his left. The four on the right ARE Michael, Gavriel, Refael and Nuriel, while the four on the left are Sin, Destroyer, Anger and Fury. And on the side of the body, Metatron descends upon him on the right and Samael on the left.

204. וְלֵית בַּר נָשׁ דְּלֵית בֵּיהּ אַרְבַּע יְסוֹדִין, אֲבָל כְּפוּם יְסוֹדָא דְּאַקְדִּים בֵּיהּ, הָכִי מַתְחִילִין אִלֵּין אַרְבַּע. אִי מַזָּל דִּילֵיהּ אַרְיֵ״ה, אַקְדִּים מִיכָאֵ״ל, וַאֲבַתְרֵיהּ גַּבְרִיאֵ״ל וַאֲבַתְרֵיהּ נוּרִיאֵ״ל, וַאֲבַתְרֵהּ רְפָאֵ״ל. וְאִי מַזָּלֵיהּ שׁוֹר, אַקְדִּים גַּבְרִיאֵ״ל, וַאֲבַתְרֵיהּ מִיכָאֵ״ל, וַאֲבַתְרֵיהּ נוּרִיאֵ״ל,

וַאֲבַתְרֵיהּ רְפָאֵל. וְאִי מַזָּלֵיהּ נֶשֶׁר, אַקְדִּים נוּרִיאֵ״ל, וַאֲבַתְרֵיהּ מִיכָאֵ״ל, וַאֲבַתְרֵיהּ גַּבְרִיאֵ״ל, וַאֲבַתְרֵיהּ רְפָאֵ״ל. וְאִי מַזָּלֵיהּ אָדָ״ם. אַקְדִּים רְפָאֵ״ל, וַאֲבַתְרֵיהּ מִיכָאֵ״ל, וַאֲבַתְרֵיהּ גַּבְרִיאֵ״ל, וַאֲבַתְרֵיהּ נוּרִיאֵ״ל.

204. There is no person that does not have the four elements – FIRE, AIR, WATER, EARTH – but the four elements line after the preceding element. If his sign is Lion, WHICH IS CHESED, Michael comes first, followed by Gavriel, Nuriel and Refael. If his sign is Ox, WHICH IS GVURAH, Gavriel precedes followed by Michael, Nuriel and Refael. If his sign is Eagle, WHICH IS TIFERET, Nuriel precedes, then Michael, Gavriel and finally Raphael. If his sign is man, WHICH IS MALCHUT, Raphael precedes, followed by Michael, Gavriel and Nuriel.

205. וְאִינּוּן מִסִּטְרָא דִּימִינָא, מִסִּטְרָא דְּמִיכָאֵל, כֻּלְּהוּ אַנְפִּין דִּילֵיהּ, אִינּוּן רַחֲמֵי, בַּעַל גְּמִילוּת חֲסָדִים, אַנְפּוֹי חִוָּורִין, וְהַאי בַּר נָשׁ גָּמִיל חֶסֶד. חָסִיד, וְחָכָם, אִי אִשְׁתַּדַּל בְּאוֹרַיְיתָא. וְאִי לָאו, בְּהֵפֶךְ, מִסִּטְרָא דְּיֵצֶר הָרָע, גַּזְלָן, טִפֵּשׁ, לֵית בֵּיהּ חֶסֶד. דְּלָא עַם הָאָרֶץ חָסִיד.

205. All FOUR aspects – LION, OX, EAGLE, MAN – of those on the right side, which is the aspect of Michael, are of Mercy. Such men perform charitable deeds and have a pale face. Such a man is charitable, pious and wise if he is occupied with Torah. If he does not OCCUPY HIMSELF WITH TORAH, he is the opposite, coming from the side of the Evil Inclination. He is a thief, a fool and has no kindness because 'an unlearned person cannot be pious'.

206. מִסִּטְרָא דְּגַבְרִיאֵל, אַרְבַּע אַנְפִּין דִּילֵיהּ דִּינָא, מִדַּת הַדִּין עַל רַשִׁיעַיָּא, וּמִתְגָּרֶה בְּהוּ, כְּמָה דְּאוּקְמוּהָ, מוּתָּר לְהִתְגָּרוֹת בָּרְשָׁעִים בָּעוֹלָם הַזֶּה. גִּבּוֹר בְּיִצְרֵיהּ, יְרֵא חֵטְא, דַּיָּין יְהֵא, אִי יִתְעַסֵּק בְּאוֹרַיְיתָא, וְגִבּוֹר בְּתַלְמוּדֵיהּ. בְּהִפּוּכָא מִסִּטְרָא דְּיֵצֶר הָרָע, מִתְגָּרֶה בְּצַדִּיקַיָּא, דִּינָא קָשֶׁה לוֹן, גִּבּוֹר בַּעֲבֵירָה, לְמֶעְבַּד לֵיהּ, לָאו דָּחִיל חַטָּאָה הוּא, וּגְוָונִין דְּאַנְפּוֹי סוּמָקִין, עֵשָׂו שׁוֹפֵךְ דָּמִים.

206. From the side of Gavriel, WHICH IS LEFT, his four faces – OX, LION,

EAGLE, MAN – are Judgment, namely the quality of Judgment against the wicked, and he provokes them as we have explained that it is permitted to provoke the wicked in this world. He prevails against his inclination, and fears sins. He will be a magistrate if he is occupied in Torah, and excels in his study. Conversely, if he is from the side of the Evil Inclination, he provokes the righteous to punish them heavily, and he will exceed in committing transgressions. He does not fear sin, his face is reddish and he spills blood LIKE Esau.

207. מַאן דְּמַזָּלֵיהּ נֶשֶׁ״ר, לָאו רַחֲמָן סַגֵּי, וְלָאו מִדַּת הַדִּין סַגֵּי, אֶלָּא בֵּינוֹנִי, בְּיֵצֶר טוֹב בְּמִדַּת טָבִין דִּילֵיהּ, וּבֵינוֹנִי בְּיֵצֶר רָע בְּמִדּוֹת בִּישִׁין, וְלֵיהּ אַנְפִּין חִוָּורִין וְסוּמָקִין.

207. One whose sign is Eagle, WHICH IS OF THE CENTRAL COLUMN, is neither excessively compassionate nor has an excess of the quality of Judgment, but is rather intermediate in his Good Inclination and in his good traits, and intermediate in his Evil Inclination and in bad traits. His face is both pale and reddish.

208. מַאן דְּמַזָּלֵיהּ אָדָם, מִסִּטְרָא דְּטוֹב, כָּלִיל מִכָּל מִדּוֹת טוֹבוֹת, חָסִיד, וְחָכָם, וְגִבּוֹר בַּתּוֹרָה, יְרֵא חֵטְא, מְמוּלָּא בְּכָל מִדּוֹת טָבִין, וּגְוָון אַנְפּוֹי אוּכָּמִין. וּמִסִּטְרָא דְּיֵצֶר הָרָע, מְמוּלָּא מִכָּל מִדּוֹת בִּישִׁין.

208. One whose sign is man, WHICH IS MALCHUT, incorporates from the good side every good trait; he is pious, wise, mighty in the Torah, fears sin, full with many good qualities and his face will be blackish. If he is of the side of the Evil Inclination, he will be full of all kinds of bad traits.

209. וְאִי חוֹבוֹי דְּבַר נָשׁ, נְפִישִׁין שַׁלְטִין עָלֵיהּ כָּל מַשִׁרְיָין דְּיֵצֶר הָרָע, עַד דְּיִסְתַּלְּקוּ מִנֵּיהּ כֻּלְּהוּ מַשִׁרְיָין דְּיֵצֶר טוֹב, וְאַמְלִיךְ עַל אֵבָרִין דִּילֵיהּ, סָמָאֵ״ל וְכָל מַשִׁרְיָיתֵיהּ.

209. If the sins of a person are in the majority, then all the legions of the Evil Inclination have power over him until all the legions of the Good Inclination leave him. He causes Samael and all his legions to reign over his limbs.

210. וְאִי נְפִישִׁין זַכְווֹי, שַׁלְטִין מַשִׁרְיָין דְּיֵצֶר הַטּוֹב, עַד דְּיִסְתַּלְּקוּ מִנֵּיהּ כָּל מַשִׁרְיָין דְּיֵצֶר הָרָע. וְאַמְלִיךְ עַל כָּל אֵבָרִין דִּילֵיהּ, מַשִׁירְיָין דְּיֵצֶר הַטּוֹב, בְּהַהוּא זִמְנָא, שָׁלִיט עָלֵיהּ שֵׁם יְדוָ"ד.

210. If his merits are in the majority, then the legions of the Good Inclination dominate him until all the legions of the Evil Inclination leave him. He causes the legions of the Good Inclination to reign over his limbs. At that time, the name of Yud Hei Vav Hei rules over him.

211. וְאִם הוּא בֵּינוֹנִי, צְבָא הַשָּׁמַיִם עוֹמְדִים עָלָיו מִימִינוֹ וּמִשְּׂמֹאלוֹ, אִלֵּין מַיְימִינִים לִזְכוּת, וְאִלֵּין מַשְׂמְאִילִים לְחוֹבָה, וּמַאן דְּאָלִים גָּבַר. וּבְגִין דָּא אוּקְמוּהָ מָארֵי מַתְנִיתִין, לְעוֹלָם יֵרָאֶה אָדָם עַצְמוֹ כְּאִילוּ כָּל הָעוֹלָם כּוּלּוֹ תָּלוּי בּוֹ.

211. If he is average, then the hosts of heaven stand by him on his right and on his left, some urge him toward the right to merit and others urge towards the left towards sin, and whichever is stronger prevails. Therefore the sages of the Mishnah declared: A person should always view himself as if the whole world depends on him, MEANING THAT HE SHOULD CONSIDER HIMSELF AS AVERAGE PERSON AND THAT THE WHOLE WORLD IS AVERAGE. IF HE PERFORMS ONE GOOD DEED, HE TIPS THE SCALE FOR HIMSELF AND THE WHOLE WORLD TOWARDS MERIT. IF HE COMMITS ONE SIN, HE TIPS FOR THE SCALE FOR HIMSELF AND FOR THE WHOLE WORLD TOWARDS GUILT.

212. וּמִסְטְרָא דְּמִיכָאֵל, אִתְקְרֵי בְּכוֹר, דְּדַרְגֵּיהּ כֶּסֶף חִוָּורוּ, וּבְגִין דָּא, פִּדְיוֹן הַבְּכוֹר כֶּסֶף, ה' סְלָעִים, כְּחוּשְׁבָּן ה' דְּאַבְרָהָם, דְּאִי יַחְכִּים בַּתּוֹרָה יִתּוֹסַף עָלֵיהּ י', דְּאִיהוּ קֹדֶשׁ, דְּבֵיהּ צָרִיךְ לְקַדֵּשׁ בְּכוֹר בְּהֵמָה, דְּהַיְינוּ קֹדֶשׁ יִשְׂרָאֵל לַיְיָ'. וּבֵיהּ צָרִיךְ לְעַשֵּׂר וְלָדוֹת, דְּכָל וָלָד אִיהוּ מִסִּטְרָא דְּבֵן י"ה, וְאִיהוּ ו'.

212. From the side of Michael, man is called 'firstborn' whose level is white silver, WHICH ALLUDES TO CHESED. Therefore, the redemption of the firstborn son is by silver, five Selas, like the numerical value of *Hei* (= 5) of Abraham. For if he grows wise with Torah, *Yud* will be added to him, which is holy, NAMELY CHOCHMAH, with which one should make holy the firstborn of cattle; namely, "Yisrael is holy to Hashem" (Yirmeyah 2:3). He needs this to tithe newborns, for each baby is from the side of the son of *Yud-Hei*, who is *Vav*, NAMELY TIFERET.

213. דְּכָל חֵיוָן דְּאִינּוּן חֵיוַת הַקּוֹדֶשׁ, בְּאַתְוָון דִּשְׁמָא קַדִּישָׁא אִתְקְרִיאוּ, הֲדָא הוּא דִּכְתִּיב, כֹּל הַנִּקְרָא בִשְׁמִי וְלִכְבוֹדִי בְּרָאתִיו. אֲפִילוּ כָּל בִּרְיָין דְּאִתְבְּרִיאוּ בְּהוֹן, וְלֵית בְּרִיאָה דְּלָא אִתְרְשִׁים בְּהַאי שְׁמָא, בְּגִין לְאִשְׁתְּמוֹדְעָא לְמַאן דִּבְרָא לֵיהּ, וְהַאי יוֹ"ד, אִיהוּ דִּיוּקְנָא דְּרֵישָׁא דְּכָל בִּרְיָין. ה' ה': דִּיוּקְנָא דְּה' אֶצְבְּעָאָן דִּימִינָא, וְה' דִּשְׂמָאלָא. ו' דִּיוּקְנָא דְּגוּפָא.

213. All animals, which are the holy living creatures, are named after the letters of the Holy Name. This is the meaning of: "Every one that is called by My Name: for I have created him for My glory" (Yeshayah 43:7). Even all the creatures were created with THE LETTERS OF THE HOLY NAME, and there is no creature that is not marked with this name, in order to recognize who created it. This *Yud* OF THE NAME YUD HEI VAV HEI is the shape of the head of every creature. *Hei-Hei* OF THE NAME are the shapes of the five fingers of the right HAND and five of the left HAND. *Vav* is the shape of the body.

14. “For you saw no manner of form”

A Synopsis

The discussion here turns around the verse, “‘To whom then will you compare Me, that I should be equal,’ says the Holy One.” We learn that when the illumination of Malchut descends and spreads to people, then God appears to every individual according to their vision and imagination. It is prohibited to make Him out as a form or image at all. After He created the Chariot of supernal Adam, He is called by the ten Sfirot, so that men could grasp His essence by way of His attributes. However, one must not compare Him even to one of His own aspects. When His domination rises above those aspects, there is no way of comprehending His image. This is like the sea, where the waters have no shape or form, but only gain their form by way of the vessel, which is the earth. Rabbi Shimon tells us about the vessel Binah that is divided into seven streams; there is a source, a spring, a sea and seven streams which equal ten. If the vessels were broken, however, the water would return to its source and the broken vessels would remain dry. God called Himself “endless” because there is no end to the welling forth of the light from Keter, the source of His ten Sfirot – and there is no vessel by which one can give Him any form, so He cannot be known. We also learn of the vessels He made called Wisdom and Understanding. Rabbi Shimon explains that Wisdom only exists when a Wise Man fills it with his own welling forth, and the same is true for Understanding. He describes how God called Himself by the qualities of His Sfirot. While He can increase or decrease all the vessels, there is no one over Him who can increase or decrease Him. We read of the servants, the throne, and the angels that He created, and are told that the faith of the Egyptians in their god was broken when they saw that he was merely a horse under the Chariot of God. Again the importance of repentance is emphasized by Rabbi Shimon.

214. וּבְגִין דָּא אָמַר, וְאֶל מִי תְּדַמְּיוּנִי וְאֶשְׁוֶה יֹאמַר קָדוֹשׁ. לֵית בְּכָל בְּרִיָּה דְּאֶשְׁוֶה כְּוָותִי, וְאַף עַל גַּב דְּבָרָאתִי לָהּ כִּדְמוּת אַתְוָון דִּילִי, דַּאֲנָא יָכִיל לְמַחֲאָה הַהִיא צוּרָה, וּלְמֶעְבַּד לָהּ כַּמָּה זִמְנִין, וְלֵית אֱלוֹהַּ אַחֲרָא עָלַי דְּיָכִיל לְמִמְחֵי דִּיוּקְנִי׳ ובג״ד כִּי לֹא כְצוּרֵנוּ צוּרָם וְאוֹיְבֵינוּ פְּלִילִים.

214. This is the reason it says, “‘To whom then will you liken Me, that I should be his equal,' says the Holy One" (Yeshayah 40:25). There is no creature that is equal to Me, and even though I created it in the form of My letters, I can erase this form and form it AGAIN many times. There is no other deity that can erase My form.' Therefore it says, "For their rocks is not as our Rock, even our enemies being judges" (Devarim 32:31).

215. וְאִי יִקְשֶׁה ב"נ, דְּהָא כְּתִיב כִּי לֹא רְאִיתֶם כָּל תְּמוּנָה. אִיהוּ יְתָרֵץ לֵיהּ, הַאי תְּמוּנָה חָזֵינָא, דְּהָא כְּתִיב וּתְמוּנַת ה' יַבִּיט. וְלֹא בְּכָל תְּמוּנָה אַחֲרָא דְּבָרָא וְיָצַר בְּאַתווֹי, וּבְגִין דָּא אָמַר, וְאֶל מִי תְּדַמְּיוּנִי וְאֶשְׁוֶה וְאֶל מִי תְּדַמְּיוּן אֵל וּמַה דְּמוּת תַּעַרְכוּ לוֹ.

215. One may ask, is it not written: "For you saw no manner of form" (Devarim 4:15)? HOW CAN WE ATTRIBUTE TO HIM LETTERS AND NAMES? He will answer that this image that I saw is analogous to the meaning of: "And the similitude of Hashem does he behold" (Bemidbar 12:8), WHICH REFERS TO THE SFIRAH OF MALCHUT, and to no other image that He created and formed with letters. Therefore He said, "'To whom then will you like Me, that I should be his equal,' says the Holy One," and "To whom then will you liken El, or what likeness will you compare to Him" (Yeshayah 40:18).

216. וַאֲפִילּוּ הַאי תְּמוּנָה, לֵית לֵיהּ בְּאַתְרֵיהּ, אֶלָּא כַּד נָחִית לְאַמְלְכָא עַל בִּרְיָין, וְיִתְפָּשַׁט עֲלַיְיהוּ, יִתְחָזֵי לוֹן לְכָל חַד, כְּפוּם מַרְאֶה וְחֶזְיוֹן וְדִמְיוֹן דִּלְהוֹן, וְהַאי אִיהוּ וּבְיַד הַנְּבִיאִים אֲדַמֶּה.

216. Even this image, WHICH IS IN MALCHUT, does not belong in the place OF MALCHUT, but rather only when THE LIGHT OF MALCHUT descends and spreads to the creatures, TO RULE OVER THEM. Then it appears to them, to every individual, according to their vision and imagination, MEANING ONLY IN THE RECEIPIENTS THEMSELVES, BUT NOT THE ESSENCE OF MALCHUT. And this is: "and used similes by the means of the prophets" (Hoshea 12:11).

217. וּבְגִין דָּא יֵימָא אִיהוּ, אע"ג דַּאֲנָא אֲדַמֶּה לְכוּ בְּדִיוּקְנַיְיכוּ, אֶל מִי תְּדַמְּיוּנִי וְאֶשְׁוֶה, דְּהָא קֹדֶם דְּבָרָא קוּדְשָׁא בְּרִיךְ הוּא דְּיוּקְנָא בְּעָלְמָא, וְצַיֵּיר צוּרָה, הֲוָה הוּא יְחִידָאי בְּלֹא צוּרָה וְדִמְיוֹן, וּמַאן דְּאִשְׁתְּמוֹדָע

לֵיהּ, קֹדֶם בְּרִיאָה, דְּאִיהוּ לְבַר מִדְּיוֹקְנָא, אָסוּר לְמֶעְבַּד לֵיהּ צוּרָה וּדְיוֹקְנָא בְּעָלְמָא, לֹא בְּאוֹת ה', וְלֹא בְּאוֹת י' וַאֲפִילּוּ בִּשְׁמָא קַדִּישָׁא, וְלֹא בְּשׁוּם אוֹת וּנְקוּדָה בְּעָלְמָא, וְהַאי אִיהוּ כִּי לֹא רְאִיתֶם כָּל תְּמוּנָה, מִכָּל דָּבָר דְּאִית בֵּיהּ תְּמוּנָה וְדִמְיוֹן לֹא רְאִיתֶם.

217. Therefore THE HOLY ONE, BLESSED BE HE, says to them: 'Even though I am like you in your forms,' MEANING IN VISION AND LIKENESS, 'still in all: "To whom then will you liken Me, that I should be his equal." Before the Holy One, blessed be He, created an image in the world and BEFORE He formed a form, the Holy One, blessed be He, was alone in the world, without a form or likeness. For one who conceives Him before the grade of Briyah, WHICH IS BINAH when He is without any form, must not make any form or image in the world – neither with the letter *Hei* nor with the letter *Yud*, or even to call Him by the Holy Name or any letter of dot. This is why the Torah says: "For you saw no manner of form," MEANING you did not see anything with a form or likeness.

218. אֲבָל בָּתַר דְּעָבֵד הַאי דְּיוֹקְנָא דְּמֶרְכָּבָה דְּאָדָם עִלָּאָה, נָחִית תַּמָּן, וְאִתְקְרֵי בְּהַהוּא דְּיוֹקְנָא יְדוָ"ד, בְּגִין דְּיִשְׁתְּמוֹדְעוּן לֵיהּ בְּמִדּוֹת דִּילֵיהּ, בְּכָל מִדָּה וּמִדָּה, וְקָרָא: אֵל, אֱלֹהִים, שַׁדַּי, צְבָאוֹת, אדי"ד. בְּגִין דְּיִשְׁתְּמוֹדְעוּן לֵיהּ, בְּכָל מִדָּה וּמִדָּה, אֵיךְ יִתְנַהֵג עָלְמָא, בְּחֶסֶ"ד וּבְדִינָא, כְּפוּם עוֹבָדֵיהוֹן דִּבְנֵי נָשָׁא, דְּאִי לָא יִתְפָּשֵׁט נְהוֹרֵיהּ עַל כָּל בִּרְיָין, אֵיךְ יִשְׁתְּמוֹדְעוּן לֵיהּ, וְאֵיךְ יִתְקַיֵּים, מְלֹא כָל הָאָרֶץ כְּבוֹדוֹ.

218. After He made that image of the Chariot of supernal man, He descended AND WAS ATTIRED there. In him, He is named by the form of THE FOUR LETTERS Yud Hei Vav Hei, NAMELY THE TEN SFIROT – KETER, CHOCHMAH, BINAH, TIFERET AND MALCHUT–so people could grasp Him by way of His attributes, WHICH ARE THE SFIROT in each and every attribute. He was called El, Elohim, Shadai, Tzva'ot, Ehe'yeh, in order that they could recognize Him in each and every attribute, and how He rules the world with Chesed and Judgment according to the actions of the people. If His Light had not spread over all the creatures, how would they recognize Him and how would this be fulfilled: "The whole earth is full of His glory" (Yeshayah 6:3)?

219. וַוי לֵיהּ, מַאן דְּיִשְׁוֶה לֵיהּ, לְשׁוּם מִדָּה, וַאֲפִילּוּ מֵאִלֵּין מִדּוֹת דִּילֵיהּ, כָּל שֶׁכֵּן לִבְנֵי הָאָדָם, אֲשֶׁר בֶּעָפָר יְסוֹדָם, דְּכָלִים וְנִפְסָדִים. אֶלָּא דִּמְיוֹנָא דִּילֵיהּ, כְּפוּם שָׁלְטָנוּתֵיהּ עַל הַהִיא מִדָּה, וַאֲפִילּוּ עַל כָּל בִּרְיָין. וּלְעֵילָּא מֵהַהִיא מִדָּה. וְכַד אִסְתְּלִיק מִינָהּ, לֵית לֵיהּ מִדָּה, וְלֹא דִּמְיוֹן, וְלֹא צוּרָה.

219. Woe to anyone who compares Him to any attribute, even to one of His own attributes, and certainly not to humans “whose foundation is in the dust” (Iyov 4:19), who are perishable and worthless. But the likening THAT WE EMPLOY is only according to His power over that aspect, or even ACCORDING TO HIS DOMINATION over all the creatures. There is no LIKENING above that attribute, and when HIS POWER goes up from THAT ATTRIBUTE, there is no attribute, likeness or form to Him.

220. כְּגַוְונָא דְּיַמָּא, דְּלֵית בְּמַיָּא דְּיַמָּא דְּנָפְקֵי מִינֵּיהּ, תְּפִיסוּ כְּלָל וְלֹא צוּרָה, אֶלָּא דְּאִתְפַּשְּׁטוּתָא דְּמַיָּא דְּיַמָּא עַל מָאנָא, דְּאִיהוּ אַרְעָא, אִתְעֲבִיד דִּמְיוֹן, וְיָכִילְנָא לְמֶעְבַּד חוּשְׁבָּן תַּמָּן, כְּגוֹן הַמָּקוֹר דְּיַמָּא הָא חַד. נָפִיק מִינֵּיהּ מַעְיָן, כְּפוּם אִתְפַּשְּׁטוּתָא דִּילֵיהּ מֵהַהוּא מָאנָא, בְּעִגּוּלָא דְּאִיהִי י׳, הָא מָקוֹר חַד, וּמַעְיָן דְּנָפִיק מִנֵּיהּ הָא תְּרֵין.

220. This is like the sea. For the water of the sea that flow from it has no conceivable shape or form. But by the expansion of the sea water over the vessel, which is the earth, it gains a form, and we can then calculate – NAMELY the source of the sea is one. A spring emerges from it, according to its expansion in a round vessel, which is a *Yud.* SO WE HAVE TWO FORMS, the source is one, and the spring that emerges from it is second. THE SOURCE IS THE SECRET OF KETER, AND THE SPRING IS THE SECRET OF CHOCHMAH.

221. לְבָתַר עָבֵד מָאנָא רַבְרְבָא כְּגוֹן מַאן דְּעָבֵד חֲפִירָא רַבְרְבָא וְאִתְמְלֵי מִן מַיָּא, דְּנָפִיק מִן מַעְיָין. הַהִיא מָאנָא אִתְקְרֵי יָם, וְהוּא מָאנָא תְּלִיתָאָה, וְהַהוּא מָאנָא רַבְרְבָא, וְאִתְפְּלִיג לְז׳ נְחָלִין, כְּפוּם מָאנִין אֲרִיכִין, הָכִי אִתְפָּשַׁט מַיָּא מִן יַמָּא, לְשִׁבְעָה נְחָלִין וְהָא מָקוֹר,

וּמַעְיָין, וְיַמָּא, וְז׳ נְחָלִין, אִינּוּן י׳ וְאִי יִתָּבַר אוּמָנָא אִלֵּין מָאנִין דְּתַקִּין, יְהַדְּרוּן מַיָּא לְמָקוֹר, וְיִשְׁתָּאֲרוּ מָאנִין תְּבִירִין יְבֵשִׁין בְּלָא מַיָּא.

221. Afterwards He made a large vessel, similar to a large excavation, which was filled with the water that flowed from the spring. This vessel is called ‘sea’. It is the third vessel, NAMELY BINAH, and that large vessel divides into seven streams. The water spread from the sea to the seven streams as into long receptacles. And so there is a source, a spring, a sea and seven streams, which amount to ten. If the Craftsman will break these vessels that He has fashioned, the water will return to the source and the broken vessels will remain dry without water.

222. הָכִי עִלַּת הָעִלּוֹת, עָבֵיד עֶשֶׂר סְפִירוֹת, וְקָרָא לְכֶתֶר מָקוֹר, וּבֵיהּ לֵית סוֹף לִנְבִיעוּ דִּנְהוֹרֵיהּ. ובג״ד קָרָא לְגַרְמֵיהּ אֵין סוֹף, וְלֵית לֵיהּ דְּמוּת וְצוּרָה, וְתַמָּן לֵית מָאנָא לְמִתְפַּס לֵיהּ, לְמִנְדַּע בֵּיהּ יְדִיעָא כְּלָל. ובג״ד אָמְרוּ בֵּיהּ, בַּמּוּפְלָא מִמְּךָ אַל תִּדְרוֹשׁ, וּבַמְכוּסֶה מִמְּךָ אַל תַּחְקוֹר.

222. So the Cause of Causes made ten Sfirot and called Keter the source, and there is no end to the welling of its light. Therefore, He called Himself “endlessness,” and He has no likeness or image. There is no vessel there able to conceive Him or have any knowledge of Him at all. Therefore, it has been said of Him, ‘Do not seek that which is inconceivable to you nor search that which is hidden from you’.

223. לְבָתַר עָבֵד מָאנָא זְעֵירָא, וְדָא י׳, וְאִתְמַלְיָא מִנֵּיהּ, וְקָרָא לֵיהּ מַעְיָן נוֹבֵעַ חָכְמָה, וְקָרָא גַּרְמֵיהּ בָּהּ חָכָם, וּלְהַהוּא מָאנָא קָרָא לֵיהּ חָכְמָ״ה. וּלְבָתַר עָבֵד מָאנָא רַבְרְבָא, וְקָרָא לֵיהּ יָם, וְקָרָא לֵיהּ בִּינָה, וְהוּא קָרָא לְגַרְמֵיהּ מֵבִין בָּהּ.

223. Afterwards He made a small vessel that is the *Yud*. It was filled from THE SOURCE, and He called it ‘a spring welling wisdom. He called himself in it Wise, and the vessel He called Chochmah (‘Wisdom’). Then, He made a large vessel and called it ‘sea’. He called it Binah (‘Understanding’) and He called Himself an Understanding One.

224. חָכָם מֵעַצְמוֹ, וּמֵבִין מֵעַצְמוֹ, כִּי חָכְמָה אִיהִי לָא אִתְקְרִיאַת חָכְמָה מִגַּרְמָהּ, אֶלָּא בְּגִין הַהוּא חָכָם דְּאַמְלֵי לָהּ מִנְּבִיעוּ דִּילֵיהּ. וְאִיהִי לָא אִתְקְרִיאַת בִּינָה מִגַּרְמָהּ, אֶלָּא ע"ש הַהוּא מֵבִין דְּאַמְלֵי לָהּ מִנֵּיהּ. דְּאִי הֲוָה מִסְתָּלֵּק מִנָּהּ, אִשְׁתָּאֲרַת יְבֵשָׁה. הה"ד אָזְלוּ מַיִם מִנִּי יָם וְנָהָר יֶחֱרַב וְיָבֵשׁ.

224. He is wise of Himself and understands of Himself, because Chochmah is not called Chochmah of its own accord, but rather because of the Wise One who filled it with His own welling. Binah is not called so of its own accord, but rather because of the Understanding One who filled it from His own, and if He had removed Himself and risen from it, it would have remained dry. This is the meaning of: "The waters fail from the sea, and the river is parched, and dries up" (Iyov 14:11).

225. לְבָתַר וְהִכָּהוּ לְשִׁבְעָה נְחָלִים. וְעָבֵד לֵיהּ לְז' מָאנִין יַקִּירִין, וְקָרָא לוֹן: גְּדוּלָ"ה. גְּבוּרָ"ה. ת"ת. נֶצַ"ח. הוֹ"ד. יְסוֹ"ד. מַלְכוּ"ת. וְקָרָא גַּרְמֵיהּ גָּדוֹל בִּגְדוּלָ"ה וְחָסִי"ד. גִּבּוֹר, בִּגְבוּרָ"ה. מְפוֹאָר, בְּתִפְאֶרֶ"ת. מָארֵי נִצְחָן קְרָבִין, בְּנֶצַ"ח נְצָחִים. וּבְהוֹ"ד קָרָא שְׁמֵיהּ, הוֹד יוֹצְרֵנוּ. וּבִיסוֹ"ד קָרָא שְׁמֵיהּ צַדִּיק. וִיסוֹ"ד, כֹּלָּא סָמִיךְ בֵּיהּ, כָּל מָאנִין וְכָל עָלְמִין. וּבְמַלְכוּת, קָרָא שְׁמֵיהּ מֶלֶךְ. וְלוֹ הַגְּדוּלָ"ה וְהַגְּבוּרָ"ה וְהַתִּפְאֶרֶ"ת וְהַנֵּצַ"ח וְהַהוֹ"ד כִּי כֹ"ל בַּשָּׁמַיִם, דְּאִיהוּ צַדִּי"ק. וְלוֹ הַמַּמְלָכָה: דְּאִיהוּ מַלְכוּ"ת.

225. Afterwards, "and He shall smite it in seven streams" (Yeshayah 11:15), He made seven precious vessels and called them 'Greatness', NAMELY CHESED, Gvurah, Tiferet, Netzach, Hod, Yesod, and Malchut. He called Himself Great in Greatness and also Pious (Heb. *chasid*), mighty in Gvurah ('Might'), glorious in Tiferet ('Glory') and victorious in battles in Netzach Netzachim ('Victory'). In Hod ('Majesty'), He called Himself 'The Majesty of our Creator' and in Yesod, He called himself 'Righteous'. Foundation (Yesod) supports everything, all the vessels and all the worlds. And in Malchut ('Kingdom'), He called Himself 'King'. To Him is "the greatness, and the power, and the glory, and the victory, and the majesty; for all that is in heaven," NAMELY YESOD, and to Him is "the kingdom" (I Divrei Hayamim 29:11), THAT IS MALCHUT.

226. כֹּלָּא בִּרְשׁוּתֵיהּ, לְמֶחֱסַר בְּמָאנִין, וּלְאוֹסָפָא בְּהוֹן נְבִיעוּ, וּלְמֶחֱסַר כְּפוּם רְעוּתֵיהּ בְּהוֹן וְלֵית עָלֵיהּ אֱלָהָא, דְּיוֹסִיף בֵּיהּ, אוֹ יִגְרַע בֵּיהּ.

226. Everything is in His authority, whether to lessen the vessels or to increase or decrease their gushing, as is His desire with them. He does not have over Him a deity to increase or decrease in Him. THEREFORE, THIS REFERS TO THE VESSELS OF THE WORLD OF ATZILUT.

227. לְבָתַר עָבֵד מְשַׁמְּשִׁין, לְאִלֵּין מָאנִין, כֻּרְסְיָיא בְּאַרְבַּע סַמְכִין. וְשִׁית דַּרְגִּין לְכֻרְסְיָיא. הָא עֶשֶׂר. וְכֹלָּא אִיהוּ כֻּרְסְיָיא. כְּגוֹן כּוֹס דִּבְרָכָה, דְּתָקִינוּ בּוֹ עֲשָׂרָה דְּבָרִים, בְּגִין תּוֹרָה דְּאִתְיְיהִיבַת בַּעֲשָׂרָה דִּבְּרָן. בְּגִין עָלְמָא דְּאִיהוּ מַעֲשֵׂה בְּרֵאשִׁית, דְּאִתְבְּרֵי בַּעֲשָׂרָה מַאֲמָרוֹת.

227. Then He created servants to these vessels OF ATZILUT, a throne with four pillars and six steps for the throne. Altogether, they are ten. All TOGETHER IS CALLED "throne," WHICH IS THE WORLD OF BRIYAH, like the Cup of Blessing to which they ascribed ten things because of the Torah that was given in Ten Commandments and because of the world, which was the work of Creation that was created with Ten Sayings.

228. וְתָקִין לְכֻרְסְיָיא כִּתּוֹת לְשַׁמְּשָׁא לֵיהּ, דְּאִינּוּן מַלְאָכִים. אֶרְאֵלִים שְׂרָפִים. חַיּוֹת אוֹפַנִּים. חַשְׁמַלִּים. אֵלִים. אֱלֹהִים. בְּנֵי אֱלֹהִי״ם. אִישִׁי״ם. וּלְאִלֵּין עָבֵיד שַׁמָּשִׁין, סָמָאֵ״ל, וְכָל כִּתּוֹת דִּילֵיהּ, דְּאִינּוּן כַּעֲנָנִים לְמֶרְכַּב בְּהוֹן לְנַחְתָּא בְּאַרְעָא, וְאִינּוּן כְּסוּסִין לוֹן.

228. He then arranged groups to serve the throne, who are Malachim (Agels), Er'elim, Seraphim, Chayot (living creatures), Ofanim (wheels), Chashmalim, Elim, Elohim, sons of Elohim, Ishim. He made servants for these, Samael and all his groups, that are like clouds to ride on in order to descend to earth. And they are like horses FOR THE ANGELS.

229. וּמְנָלָן דַּעֲנָנִים אִקְרוּן מֶרְכָּב. הה״ד, הִנֵּה יְיָ׳ רוֹכֵב עַל עָב קַל וּבָא מִצְרַיִם. וְדָא מְמָנָא דְּמִצְרַיִם, וּמִיָּד דְּחָזוּ דֶּאֱלָהָא דִּי הוּא מְמָנָא דִּלְהוֹן, חֲזוּ לֵיהּ כְּסוּסְיָא, תְּחוֹת מֶרְכַּבְתֵּיהּ דְּקוּדְשָׁא בְּרִיךְ הוּא, מִיָּד וְנָעוּ

אֱלִילֵי מִצְרַיִם מִפָּנָיו, וּלְבַב מִצְרַיִם יִמַּס, נָעוּ מֵאֱמוּנָה דִּלְהוֹן, וְלֵב דִּלְהוֹן נָמֵס כַּדּוֹנַג, מֵהַהִיא אֱמוּנָה, וְאַמְרֵי, וְכִי עַד כְּעַן אֱמוּנָה מְמָנָא דִּילָן כְּסוּסְיָא, הֲוָה נָע לִבְהוֹן מֵאֱמוּנָה דִּלְהוֹן, וְנָמֵס כַּדּוֹנַג. וּמְנָלָן דִּימַּס לְשׁוֹן נָמֵס כַּדּוֹנַג אִיהוּ כד"א, הָיָה לִבִּי כַּדּוֹנַג נָמֵס בְּתוֹךְ מֵעָי.

229. How do we know that clouds are called 'chariots'? From the verse: "Behold Hashem rides on a swift cloud, and shall come into Egypt" (Yeshayah 19:1)? This is the appointed minister of Egypt WHO IS CALLED "A SWIFT CLOUD." As soon as they saw their deity, who is their minister, and saw him as a horse under the chariot of the Holy One, blessed be He, immediately "the idols of Egypt shall be moved at his presence, and the heart of Egypt shall melt" (Ibid.). They moved away from their Faith and their heart melted like wax from their Faith, THEY HAD IN THEIR APPOINTED MINISTER. They said: 'And now our Faith, NAMELY OUR DEITY appointed over us, has become like a horse'. Their heart was removed from their Faith and melted like wax, and we know that melting means melting like wax from the verse: "My heart is become like wax, it is melted in the midst of my bowels" (Tehilim 22:15).

230. וְכָל פֶּטֶר חֲמוֹר תִּפְדֶּה בְשֶׂה וְגוֹ'. פִּקּוּדָא דָּא לִפְדּוֹת פֶּטֶר חֲמוֹר, וְלַעֲרוֹף פֶּטֶר חֲמוֹר, אִם לֹא יִפְדֶּה לֵיהּ. הה"ד וְאִם לֹא תִפְדֶּה וַעֲרַפְתּוֹ. וְרָזָא דָּא יצה"ר, יָכוֹל לְאַחְזְרָא בִּתְיוּבְתָּא, וּלְבָתַר לְאַחְזְרָא יֵצֶר הַטּוֹב, כְּמָה דְּאוּקְמוּהָ, אִם זָכָה עֵזֶר, אִם לֹא זָכָה כְּנֶגְדּוֹ. בְּגִין דְּאִינּוּן דִּיּוּקְנָא, חַד דְּשֶׂה, וְחַד דַּחֲמוֹר, וְאִי זָכָה לְאַחְזְרָא בִּתְיוּבְתָּא, אע"ג דְּאִיהוּ חֲמוֹר עַם הָאָרֶץ, תִּפְדֶּה מִן גָּלוּתָא בְשֶׂה, דְּאִיהוּ שֶׂה פְזוּרָה יִשְׂרָאֵל. וְאִי לָא הֲדַר בִּתְיוּבְתָּא, וַעֲרַפְתּוֹ, שָׁוֵי לֵיהּ עַם קְשֵׁה קְדָל, דַּעֲתִידִין לְאִתְמְחָאָה מִן סֵפֶר חַיִּים, דְּעָלַיְיהוּ אִתְּמַר, מִי אֲשֶׁר חָטָא לִי אֶמְחֶנּוּ מִסִּפְרִי.

230. "And every firstling of an donkey you shall redeem with a lamb..." (Shemot 13:13). This commandment is to redeem the firstling of an donkey or to break the neck of the firstling of an donkey, if it is not redeemed. This is the meaning of: "And if you will not redeem it, then you shall break its neck" (Ibid.). The secret behind this is that the Evil Inclination can repent and afterwards become the Good Inclination, as was established IN THE VERSE: "I WILL MAKE HIM A HELP TO MATCH HIM" (BERESHEET 2:18).

If one merits, it is a help. If one does not merit, then it is a match against him. These images of a lamb and of an donkey – AS IS SAID ABOUT THEM, "AND EVERY FIRSTLING OF AN DONKEY YOU SHALL REDEEM WITH A LAMB" – MEAN even though he is an donkey, MEANING an ignoramus, if he has merit to repent, he will be redeemed from exile by a lamb, because he is: "Yisrael is a scattered sheep" (Yirmeyah 50:17). If he does not repent, then "break its neck," for he has made himself like a stiff-necked people who will be blotted out from the book of Life. About them, it is said, "Whoever has sinned against Me, him will I blot out of My book" (Shemot 32:33).

15. The Tefilin

A Synopsis

Rabbi Shimon expounds upon the importance and the secret of the hand Tefilin and the head Tefilin. The Tfilah, or prayer, draws holiness from above, as "All the rivers run into the sea." We are told that the four portions of the head Tefilin are Chochmah and Binah, Tiferet and Malchut, in the secret of the supernal Light that emerges from nothingness, Keter. Then Rabbi Shimon describes in detail the first portion, "sanctify," the second portion, Binah, the third portion, Sh'ma, and the fourth portion, the secret of Severe Justice. The hand Tefilin are similar, but are all in one compartment. Rabbi Shimon reminds us that a person must put on the Tefilin every day in order to be in the high image of the Above. Then Bo closes with the assertion that one day all people will know and fear God.

231. וְהָיָה לְאוֹת עַל יָדְכָה וּלְטוֹטָפוֹת בֵּין עֵינֶיךָ וְגוֹ׳ פִּקּוּדָא דָּא, פִּקּוּדָא דְּאִקְרֵי בְּגַוְונָא אַחֲרָא, דְּלָא אִקְרֵי מִצְוָה, אֶלָּא קְדוּשָׁה, וְאִלֵּין אִינּוּן תְּפִילִין. תְּפִלָּה שֶׁל יַד, וּתְפִלָּה שֶׁל רֹאשׁ. תִּקּוּנָא פְּאֵרָא שַׁפִּירוּ דִּגְוָונִין עִלָּאִין. וְע״ד אִקְרוּן טוֹטָפוֹת, כד״א, יִשְׂרָאֵל אֲשֶׁר בְּךָ אֶתְפָּאָר.

231. "And it shall be for a token upon your hand, and for frontlets between your eyes" (Shemot 13:16). This commandment is considered in a different category, since it is not considered a commandment but rather a matter of holiness. And these are the Tefilin, the hand Tefilin and the head Tefilin, for they are a manifestation of glorification and beauty of supernal visions. Therefore they are called "frontlets," as is written: "Yisrael, in whom I will be glorified" (Yeshayah 49:3).

232. וּכְתִיב כִּי נַעַר יִשְׂרָאֵל וָאֹהֲבֵהוּ, יִשְׂרָאֵל זוּטָא. שְׁמַע יִשְׂרָאֵל, יִשְׂרָאֵל סָבָא, שַׁפִּירוּ דִּגְוָונִין, עֵילָּא וְתַתָּא. יוֹסֵף סָלִיק וְאִתְעַטָּר בִּתְרֵין גַּוְונִין בְּקַדְמֵיתָא נַעַ״ר, וּבְסוֹפָא צַדִּי״ק. כַּמָּה יָאַן בֵּיהּ גַּוְונִין לְמֶחֱזֵי, וְרָזָא דָּא וַיְהִי יוֹסֵף יְפֵה תֹאַר וִיפֵה מַרְאֶה. שַׁפִּירָא בִּתְרֵין סִטְרִין, בִּתְרֵין דַּרְגִּין, בִּתְרֵין גַּוְונִין, עֵילָּא וְתַתָּא.

232. It is written: "When Yisrael was a child, then I loved him" (Hoshea 11:1). It refers to young Yisrael, MEANING ZEIR ANPIN WITH MOCHIN OF

SMALLNESS, and "Hear, O Yisrael (Heb. *Sh'ma Yisrael*)" refers to Yisrael Saba (old), WHICH IS BINAH WITH MOCHIN OF GREATNESS, which is beautiful in appearance above IN BINAH and below IN MALCHUT. HE EXPLAINS HOW ALL THE MOCHIN OF YISRAEL-SABA AND T'VUNAH COME DOWN, SAYING Joseph, WHO IS YESOD OF ZEIR ANPIN, rises up TO BINAH and is adorned there WITH TWO COLORS, WHITE AND RED, WHICH ARE IN THE TWO COLUMNS OF BINAH, BY HIS RECONCILING THE TWO COLUMNS OF BINAH, IN ACCORDANCE WITH THE MEANING OF 'THREE EMERGE FROM ONE; ONE EXISTS IN THREE'. Before HE ASCENDED TO BINAH, he is CALLED a 'lad', and in the end, AFTER HE WAS CROWNED WITH THE MOCHIN OF BINAH, he is CALLED 'righteous'. How beautiful are the sights seen in him. This is the secret of: "And Joseph was good looking and well favored" (Beresheet 39:6). HE was fair on both sides, WHICH ARE RIGHT AND LEFT; on two levels, WHICH ARE CHOCHMAH AND CHASSADIM; in two appearances, WHICH ARE WHITE AND RED; above IN BINAH and below IN MALE AND FEMALE. FOR AFTER HE MEDIATES IN BINAH, HE DESCENDS AND MEDIATES BETWEEN MALE AND FEMALE.

233. כְּתִיב וְעָשִׂיתָ הַיָּשָׁר וְהַטּוֹב. הַיָּשָׁר: דָּא תְּפִלָּה שֶׁל יַד, לְאַמְשָׁכָא לֵיהּ בִּתְפִילִין שֶׁל רֹאשׁ, לְאִתְיַחֲדָא כַּחֲדָא. וּתְפִלָּה שֶׁל יַד, אַקְדִּים לְשֶׁל רֹאשׁ. וְאִצְטְרִיךְ דְּלָא הֲוֵי פְּרוּדָא בֵּינַיְיהוּ כְּלָל.

233. It is written: "And you shall do that which is right and good" (Devarim 6:18). The "right" refers to the hand Tefilin, WHICH IS MALCHUT, TO IMPROVE HER, MEANING to bestow on her by the head Tefilin, WHICH IS ZEIR ANPIN, so that they shall become one. The hand Tefilin is DONNED before the head Tefilin, and there must be no separation at all between them.

234. מַאן דְּמִתְעַטְּרָא בִּתְפִלִּין, קָאֵים בְּרָזָא דְּגַוְונָא עִלָּאָה וְקָאֵים בְּאִינּוּן תְּרֵין רָזִין דְּקַאמְרָן כְּיוֹסֵף, דְּאִקְרֵי נַעַר, וְאִקְרֵי צַדִּיק, בְּרָזָא דְּעֶבֶד נֶאֱמָן, בְּרָזָא דְּבֵן יְחִידָאי. וְאִלֵּין אִינּוּן תְּפִלָּה שֶׁל יַד, וּתְפִלָּה שֶׁל רֹאשׁ, וְאִינּוּן כְּלָלָא חֲדָא בְּלָא פְּרוּדָא.

234. One who is crowned with Tefilin is in the same category as the above, and apprehends the two meanings we mentioned in relation to Joseph, who is called a 'lad' and also called 'Righteous', MEANING in the secret of faithful servant and the secret of only son. These are the hand Tefilin,

WHICH IS THE SECRET OF THE LAD AND FAITHFUL SERVANT, and the head Tefilin, WHICH IS THE SECRET OF THE RIGHTEOUS AND ONLY SON. They are both actually one principle, AS MENTIONED.

235. אַרְבַּע פָּרָשִׁיָּין דִּתְפִלִּין בְּד׳ בָּתִּים, בְּאִינּוּן תְּפִלִּין שֶׁל רֹאשׁ. וּכְמָה דְּאִינּוּן ד׳ פָּרָשִׁיָּין בְּאִינּוּן תְּפִלִּין שֶׁל רֹאשׁ, אוּף הָכִי כֻּלְּהוּ בִּתְפִלִּין שֶׁל יַד בְּבַיִת א׳. דְּהָא בַּתְּפִלָּה שֶׁל יַד, לֵית לָהּ מִגַּרְמָהּ כְּלוּם, אֶלָּא מַה דְּנַקְטָא מִלְעֵילָּא. וְרָזָא דָּא, כָּל הַנְּחָלִים הוֹלְכִים אֶל הַיָּם. וּמִגּוֹ דְּנַקְטָא לוֹן מִלְעֵילָּא, אִקְרֵי תְּפִלָּה, וְאִתְקַדְּשַׁת בִּקְדוּשַּׁתְהוֹן אִקְרֵי קְדוּשָׁה. וְאִקְרֵי תְּפִלָּה וּכְדֵין אִקְרֵי מַלְכוּת, מַלְכוּת שָׁמַיִם שְׁלֵימָה.

235. The four passages that are in the Tefilin are in four compartments in the head Tefilin. As there are four compartments in the head Tefilin, so are they all in one compartment in the hand Tefilin. This is because the hand Tefilin, WHICH IS MALCHUT, has nothing of its own, but what it receives from above, FROM ZEIR ANPIN. SINCE IT RECEIVES THEM AT ONCE, IT HAS ONLY ONE COMPARTMENT. BUT ZEIR ANPIN RECEIVES THEM ONE AFTER THE OTHER; THEREFORE, THEY ARE IN FOUR COMPARTMENTS. This is the secret meaning of: "All the rivers run into the sea" (Kohelet 1:7), FOR "THE RIVERS" WHICH ARE FLOWING FROM ZEIR ANPIN FLOW TO MALCHUT, WHICH IS CALLED 'SEA'. Because it receives them from above, FROM BINAH, it is called Tefilin, and is sanctified with their holiness. It is called 'Holiness' BECAUSE THE MOCHIN OF BINAH ARE CALLED 'HOLINESS', and it is called 'Tefilin', and then Malchut is called 'the Complete Kingdom of Heaven'.

236. ד׳ פָּרָשִׁיָּין, הָא אוֹקִימְנָא רָזָא דִּלְהוֹן, בְּכַמָּה דוּכְתֵּי. אֲבָל פָּרָשָׁה קַדְמָאָה, קַדֶּשׁ לִי כָל בְּכוֹר, דָּא אִיהוּ רָזָא עִלָּאָה, דְּכָלִיל כָּל ד׳ בָּתִּים, בְּרָזָא דִּנְהִירוּ עִלָּאָה, דְּנָפְקָא מֵאַיִן.

236. We have already explained the meaning of the four passages in many places. But the first passage: "Sanctify to Me all the firstborn" (Heb. *kadosh*) (Shemot 13:2), WHICH IS CHOCHMAH, is a supernal secret that incorporates all four compartments, WHICH ARE CHOCHMAH AND BINAH, TIFERET AND MALCHUT in the secret of the supernal Light, WHICH IS CHOCHMAH that emerges from nothingness, WHICH IS KETER CALLED 'NOTHINGNESS'. EACH OF THE FOUR PASSAGES – CHOCHMAH, BINAH,

TIFERET AND MALCHUT – INCLUDES THEM ALL AND EACH HAS CHOCHMAH AND BINAH, TIFERET AND MALCHUT.

237. וְכָל אִינּוּן ד׳ אִתְרְמִיזוּ הָכָא, קַדֶּשׁ: דָּא קְדוּשָּׁה עִלָּאָה. רָזָא דְּחָכְמְתָא עִלָּאָה, דְּמִתַּמָּן כֹּלָּא אִתְקַדַּשׁ, בְּרָזָא דִּגְנִיזוּ עִלָּאָה, דְּאִתְקְרֵי קַדֶּשׁ. לִי: דָּא בִּינָה, רָזָא דְּעָלְמָא עִלָּאָה, הֵיכְלָא פְּנִימָאָה. כָּ״ל: רָזָא דְּחֶסֶד, בְּכָל דּוּכְתָּא, בֵּין לְעֵילָּא בֵּין לְתַתָּא. בְּכוֹ״ר: דָּא בֶּן בְּכוֹר, דִּכְתִּיב, בְּנִי בְכוֹרִי יִשְׂרָאֵל, וְהַאי בֶּן בְּכוֹר, כָּלִיל כָּל סִטְרִין, וְכָל גַּוְונִין. וּבְגִין כַּךְ, קְרָא כָּלִיל כֻּלְּהוּ אַרְבַּע, בְּרָזָא דְּחָכְמְתָא עִלָּאָה. אֲבָל דָּא בְּאוֹרַח כְּלָל, לְמִנְדַּע דְּכֹלָּא כָּלִיל בְּהַאי, אֲבָל בְּאוֹרַח פְּרָט, כָּל חַד בִּלְחוּדוֹי, דָּא אִיהוּ פַּרְשְׁתָּא קַדְמָאָה, דְּכָלִיל כָּל שְׁאַר פָּרְשִׁיָּין.

237. All these four, CHOCHMAH AND BINAH, TIFERET AND MALCHUT, are alluded to in here, IN THE FIRST PASSAGE, "SANCTIFY" BECAUSE "sanctify" is the supernal Holiness, which is the secret of supernal Chochmah THAT IS CALLED 'HOLINESS'. From there, everything was sanctified by means of the supernal concealment that is called "sanctify." "To me" is Binah, which is the secret of the upper world, the internal chamber. "All" is uniformly the secret of Chesed, either above or below, NAMELY TIFERET OF THE ASPECT OF CHESED. "Firstborn" is the firstborn son, as is written: "Yisrael is my son, my firstborn" (Shemot 4:22), NAMELY TIFERET, and this firstborn son includes all aspects and all colors, THAT IS, IT INCLUDES MALCHUT IN IT AS WELL. Because of this, the verse includes all four – CHOCHMAH AND BINAH, TIFERET AND MALCHUT – within the secret of supernal Chochmah, WHICH IS THE FIRST PASSAGE. This is a general description to know that everything is included in it, but in details, each one in itself CORRESPONDS TO AN INDIVIDUAL SFIRAH. And the first passage includes the other passages.

238. פָּרָשָׁה תִּנְיָינָא, וְהָיָה כִּי יְבִיאֲךָ וְגוֹ׳, דָּא בִּינָה, דְּהָא בְּפַרְשְׁתָּא דָּא, אִיהִי יְצִיאַת מִצְרַיִם, דַּהֲוָה מִסִּטְרָא דְּיוֹבְלָא. וְע״ד שֵׁירוּתָא דִּילָהּ וְהָיָ״ה, דְּהָא מִלָּה דָּא אִיהִי בְּיוֹבְלָא. וּבְגִין כַּךְ שְׁמָא דִּילָהּ וְהָיָ״ה, דְּלֵית וְהָיָה אֶלָּא בַּאֲתָר דָּא, דְּאִיהוּ זַמִּין לְאִתְמַשְּׁכָא לְתַתָּא, וּלְאַנְהָרָא בּוּצִינִין, וּלְאִשְׁתַּכְּחָא בְּדַרְגָּא תַּתָּאָה, וְכֹלָּא בְּרָזָא חֲדָא. וּבְגִין דְּאִיהוּ

בְּאוֹרַח טָמִיר, לָא אִקְרֵי בְּאִתְגַּלְיָיא בִּשְׁמָא דָּא, אֶלָּא אִתְמְסַר לְחַכִּימִין לְמִנְדַּע. וְעַל דָּא אִתְרְשִׁים בִּשְׁמָא קַדִּישָׁא, בְּמִלָּה דָּא.

238. The second passage, "And it shall be when Hashem shall bring you..." (Heb. *vehayah ki yevia'cha*) (Shemot 13:11) is Binah. The exodus from Egypt is contained in this passage, which came about from the side of Jubilee WHICH IS BINAH. Therefore it begins with: "And it shall be," because this term pertains to Jubilee. Therefore its name is "And it shall be," because THE FORM OF "And it shall be (Heb. *vehayah*)," IN THE FUTURE TENSE, pertains only here IN BINAH, and WHOSE MEANING IS that it will flow down to shine on the luminaries, WHICH ARE MALE AND FEMALE, and exist in the lower level, WHICH IS MALCHUT, all pertaining to the same secret. Since it illuminates in a secret way, it is not called openly by this name, *VEHAYAH*, but is rather given over to wise to know. Therefore, BINAH is marked with the holy name in the word, *VEHAYAH* (*VAV-HEI-YUD-HEI*).

239. פָּרָשָׁה תְּלִיתָאָה, שְׁמַע, דָּא אִיהוּ רָזָא דִימִינָא, דְּאִקְרֵי חֶסֶד עִלָּאָה. דְּאִיהוּ קָא מְיַיחֵד יִחוּדָא דְּכֹלָּא לְד׳ סִטְרִין, וְקוּדְשָׁא בְּרִיךְ הוּא מְסַדֵּר בֵּיהּ, סִדּוּרָא דְּכָל עָלְמָא, וְדָא אִיהוּ דְּקָא מִתְפַּשַּׁט בְּכָל סִטְרִין, אֲפִילוּ גּוֹ תְּהוֹמֵי תַּתָּאֵי. בְּדָא קוּדְשָׁא בְּרִיךְ הוּא בָּרָא עָלְמָא, כַּד אִתְעַטָּף קוּדְשָׁא בְּרִיךְ הוּא בְּעִטוּפָא דִּזְהֲרָא, וְדָא דְּקָא מְיַיחֵד יִחוּדָא, וּבְגִין כַּךְ, שְׁמַע סָמִיךְ לִוְהָיָ״ה.

239. The third passage WHICH IS hear (Heb. *sh'ma*) (Devarim 6:4) is the secret of the right that is called supernal Chesed, MEANING DA'AT. For DA'AT unites all the four sides, THE SECRET OF THREE COLUMNS AND MALCHUT THAT RECEIVES THEM. The Holy One, blessed be He, arranges the order of the whole world through it, FOR THE WHOLE WORLD EXISTS THROUGH IT. This is what spreads in every direction and even into the lower depths, NAMELY BY MEANS OF DA'AT THAT SPREADS TO THE LOWER BEINGS. The Holy One, blessed be He, created the world with it when He wrapped Himself in a cloak of Light, and this is what affects the unison. SINCE IT IS THE CENTRAL COLUMN THAT UNITES THE TWO COLUMNS, RIGHT AND LEFT, WHICH ARE CHOCHMAH AND BINAH, therefore, "*Sh'ma*" is adjacent to "*vehayah*" BECAUSE "*VEHAYAH*" IS

BINAH, AND "*SH'MA*" IS DA'AT THAT MEDIATES BETWEEN CHOCHMAH AND BINAH.

240. יִחוּדָא דְּכָל יוֹמָא, אִיהוּ, יִחוּדָא לְמִנְדַּע וּלְשַׁוָּאָה רְעוּתָא. יִחוּדָא דָּא הָא אַמָרָן בְּכַמָּה דוּכְתֵּי, יִחוּדָא דְּכָל יוֹמָא, אִיהוּ יִחוּדָא דִּקְרָא, שְׁמַע יִשְׂרָאֵל יְיָ׳ אֱלֹהֵינוּ יְיָ׳ הָא כֻּלְּהוּ חַד, וְעַל דָּא אִקְרֵי אֶחָד. הָא תְּלַת שְׁמָהָן אִינּוּן, הֵיךְ אִינּוּן חַד, וְאַף עַל גַּב דְּקָרֵינָן אֶחָד, הֵיךְ אִינּוּן חַד.

240. The daily profession of unity is a meditation for the sake of knowledge and for paying attention. We have explained this meditation in many places. The daily meditation is the profession of unity in the verse, "Hear, O Yisrael (*Sh'ma Yisrael*), Hashem our Elohim; Hashem is One." And they are all one. Therefore He is called One. HE ASKS: There are three names here, so how are they one? We proclaim One, NAMELY "HEAR O YISRAEL, HASHEM OUR ELOHIM; HASHEM IS ONE," yet how can they be one?

241. אֶלָּא, בְּחֶזְיוֹנָא דְּרוּחַ קֻדְשָׁא אִתְיְידַע, וְאִינּוּן בְּחֵיזוּ דְּעֵינָא סְתִימָא, לְמִנְדַּע דִּתְלָתָא אִלֵּין אֶחָד. וְדָא אִיהוּ רָזָא דְּקוֹל דְּאִשְׁתְּמַע, קוֹל אִיהוּ חַד, וְאִיהוּ תְּלָתָא גַּוְונִין, אֶשָּׁא וְרוּחָא וּמַיָּא, וְכֻלְּהוּ חַד, בְּרָזָא דְּקוֹל. אוּף הָכָא: יְיָ׳ אֱלֹהֵינוּ יְיָ׳ אִינּוּן חַד. תְּלָתָא גַּוְונִין, וְאִינּוּן חַד.

241. This is made known through the vision of the Holy Spirit. They become part of the mystery of the mirror of the closed eye, to make known that the three COLUMNS ALLUDED TO IN "HASHEM OUR ELOHIM, HASHEM" are one, and this is the secret of the audible sound. Sound is one, and has three aspects – fire, air and water – which are all one in the secret of the sound. Also here, "Hashem, our Elohim; Hashem" are one. They are three aspects but are one.

242. וְדָא אִיהוּ קוֹל דְּעָבֵיד בַּר נָשׁ בְּיִחוּדָא, וּלְשַׁוָּאָה רְעוּתֵיהּ בְּיִחוּדָא דְּכֹלָּא, מֵאֵין סוֹף עַד סוֹפָא דְּכֹלָּא, בְּהַאי קוֹל דְּקָא עָבֵיד בְּהָנֵי תְּלָתָא דְּאִינּוּן חַד. וְדָא אִיהוּ יִחוּדָא דְּכָל יוֹמָא, דְּאִתְגַּלְיָא בְּרָזָא דְּרוּחַ קוּדְשָׁא.

242. And this is a sound that a person emits AS MEANS OF of professing the unity, tending to uniting all THE LEVELS – from the Endless World to the end of everything – by means of the unification affected by this sound he produces through these three COLUMNS which are one. This is the daily profession of unity that has been revealed by means of the Holy Spirit.

243. וְכַמָּה גַּוְונִין דְּיִחוּדָא אִתְּעֲרוּ, וְכֻלְּהוּ קְשׁוֹט. מַאן דְּעָבֵיד הַאי עָבֵיד. וּמַאן דְּעָבֵיד הַאי עָבֵיד. אֲבָל הַאי יִחוּדָא דְּקָא אֲנָן מִתְעָרֵי מִתַּתָּא, בְּרָזָא דְּקוֹל דְּאִיהוּ חַד דָּא הוּא בְּרִירָא דְּמִלָּה, הַאי בִּכְלָלָא, לְבָתַר פְּרָט, כִּדְקָאַמְרָן.

243. Many manners of unification were spoken of, and they are all correct. Whoever creates this UNIFICATION does WELL and one who does another UNIFICATION does WELL. But this unification that we awaken from below, by means of sound which is one, clarifies the matter. It is in general, MEANING THAT THE PASSAGE "HEAR" (HEB. *SH'MA*) INCLUDES WITHIN IT ALL THE THREE COLUMNS IN THE SECRET: "HASHEM OUR ELOHIM; HASHEM." Besides that, it is a detail, AS THE PASSAGE *SH'MA* IS ONLY ONE DETAIL, NAMELY ZEIR ANPIN, as has already been stated.

244. פָּרָשָׁה רְבִיעָאָה, הוּא רָזָא דְּדִינָא קַשְׁיָא, הִשָּׁמְרוּ לָכֶם. אִלֵּין אִינּוּן תְּפִלִּין דְּרֵישָׁא. וּתְפִלִּין דִּדְרוֹעָא, כְּגַוְונָא דָּא בְּחַד בֵּיתָא, וְהָא אִתְּעַרְנָא בְּהוּ, וְכֻלְּהוּ רָזָא חֲדָא.

244. The fourth passage is the secret of Severe Judgment, NAMELY MALCHUT, OF WHICH IT IS WRITTEN: "Take heed to yourselves" (Devarim 11:16), WHICH IS AN EXPRESSION OF JUDGMENT. These are THE FOUR PASSAGES of the head Tefilin, WHICH ARE IN FOUR COMPARTMENTS. The hand Tefilin ARE ALSO similar to these FOUR PASSAGES, BUT they are in one compartment. We have already commented that they all pertain to the same secret.

245. קִשְׁרָא דִּתְפִלִּין דְּרֵישָׁא, אִיהוּ דָּלֶ"ת, וְעַל דָּא כְּתִיב, וְרָאִיתָ אֶת אֲחוֹרָי. וְעַ"ד אִיהוּ לַאֲחוֹרָא, וְתַמָּן אִתְקַשַּׁר כֹּלָּא בְּקִשְׁרָא חֲדָא.

245. The knot of the head Tefilin is in the shape of a letter *Dalet*, and of this it is written: "And you shall see my back" (Shemot 33:23). Therefore, the knot is in the back where everything is tied into one knot.

246. וְאִיהִי, כַּד מַנְחַת אִלֵּין תְּפִלִּין דִּדְרוֹעָא לְאִתְקַשְּׁרָא, אִית קִשְׁרָא אַחֲרָא, רָזָא דִּבְרִית קַדִּישָׁא, רָזָא דָּא, כְּמָה דְּאִתְּעַר בְּכַמָּה דוּכְתֵּי, וְכֹלָּא רָזָא חֲדָא. זַכָּאִין אִינּוּן יִשְׂרָאֵל דְּיַדְעִין רָזָא דָּא, וְאִצְטְרִיךְ בַּר נָשׁ לַאֲנָחָא לוֹן כָּל יוֹמָא, לְמֶהֱוֵי בְּדִיוּקְנָא עִלָּאָה, וְעָלֵיהּ כְּתִיב, וּרְאוּ כָּל עַמֵּי הָאָרֶץ כִּי שֵׁם יְיָ' נִקְרָא עָלֶיךָ וְיָרְאוּ מִמֶּךָּ.

(ע"כ רעיא מהימנא)

246. When MALCHUT dons the hand Tefilin to connect WITH ZEIR ANPIN, there is another knot, NAMELY THE KNOT OF THE HAND TEFILIN, WHICH IS IN THE SHAPE OF A LETTER *YUD*. This is the secret of the Holy Covenant, MEANING YESOD, WITH WHICH MALCHUT CONNECTS. This secret is explained in many places, and it is all the same secret. Happy are Yisrael who know this secret. A person must don them every day to be in the celestial image. Of this it is written: "And all people of the earth shall see that you are called by the name of Hashem; and they shall be afraid of You" (Devarim 28:10).

End of Ra'aya Meheimna (the Faithful Shepherd)

Beshalach

Names of the articales

Page No.

1. "And Elisha passed to Shunem" 127
2. Three deaths 140
3. "And Elohim led the people about" 142
4. "And Hashem went before them by day" 149
5. "And he took six hundred chosen chariots" 158
6. "And when Pharaoh drew near" 161
7. "Hashem shall fight for you, and you shall hold your peace" 164
8. "Why do you cry out to Me" 170
9. "But lift up your rod" 174
10. "And He took off their chariot wheels" 176
11. "And the Angel of Elohim...moved" 195
12. "She is like the merchant ships" 198
13. "And the Angel of Elohim...moved" 201
14. "And...moved...and it came...and...stretched out" 209
15. "And Yisrael saw that great work" 222
16. "Then sang Moses" 233
17. "Yah is my strength and song" 245
18. "Hashem is a man of war" 255
19. "The chariots of Pharaoh and his host" 260
20. "Your right hand, Hashem, is glorious in power" 268
21. When Moses entered into the cloud 280
22. "And in the greatness of Your excellency You have overthrown them that rose up against You" 285
23. "The enemy said, 'I will purse, I will overtake'" 288
24. "Who is like You among the mighty, Hashem" 289
25. "You did stretch out Your right hand, the earth swallowed them" 295
26. Building the lower Temple 298
27. "And found no water" 304
28. "And He said, 'If you will diligently hearken to voice of Hashem'" 307
29. The story of the manna 314
30. The Holy One, blessed be He, avenges the honor of the righteous 340
31. A Rock and boulder 342
32. "Is Hashem among us" 347
33. "Then came Amalek" 349
34. "And they saw the Elohim of Yisrael" 366
35. "And Moses erected an altar" 371

1. "And Elisha passed to Shunem"

A Synopsis

Rabbi Shimon opens by talking about Habakkuk, but then discusses the entire story recounted in II Melachim about Elisha and the Shunamite woman who had fed him bread when he passed by, and prepared for him a "small upper chamber...with walls...a bed and table and chair and a lamp." We are told that on the day Elisha came to the Shunamite and promised her that she would bear a son it was Rosh Hashanah, when the barren women of the world were remembered. We are told that one must not be alone on the Day of Judgment because one might be noticed on his own and more subject to judgment, and the Mercies of God are always present over the whole people together. Rabbi Shimon says that when Elisha asked the woman if she would be spoken for to the king, he was offering to beseech the Supernal King on her behalf, but she did not want to separate from her people. We hear that the reason the child born to her later died was because he was from the Female side, since he was given to her and not her husband. Elisha was not told by the Holy One, blessed be He, that the boy would die, so that he would not try to save him through prayer. His servant Gehazi was not worthy of the miracle being performed through him, so the Shunamite woman insisted that Elisha come with her. When Elisha lay upon the boy to bring him back to life he reconnected him to a different high place, the place where life is found. Rabbi Shimon returns now to Habakkuk, with whom this passage began, and says that Habakkuk means 'two embraces': one from his mother and one from Elisha, one from the Female area and one from the Male. He tells us that there were various types of praises available to the prophets to cause the Spirit of Prophecy to dwell upon them, and that all prophets need pleasantness in order to draw that Spirit upon themselves. Only for Moses was this unnecessary. Rabbi Shimon ends by saying that the children of Yisrael only tasted death when they departed from Egypt, but that God healed them.

1. וַיְהִי בְּשַׁלַּח פַּרְעֹה אֶת הָעָם וְלֹא נָחָם אֱלֹהִים דֶּרֶךְ אֶרֶץ פְּלִשְׁתִּים וְגוֹ'. רִבִּי שִׁמְעוֹן פָּתַח, תְּפִלָּה לַחֲבַקּוּק הַנָּבִיא עַל שִׁגְיוֹנוֹת. הַאי קְרָא קַשְׁיָא, וְאִית לְאִסְתַּכְּלָא בֵּיהּ, מ"ש תְּפִלָּה לַחֲבַקּוּק הַנָּבִיא, יַתִּיר מִכָּל שְׁאַר נְבִיאֵי עָלְמָא, דְּלָא כְּתִיב בְּהוּ תְּפִלָּה לִישַׁעְיָה הַנָּבִיא, אוֹ לְיִרְמְיָה, אוֹ לִיחֶזְקֵאל, אוֹ לְהוֹשֵׁעַ, אוֹ לִשְׁאַר נְבִיאֵי עָלְמָא.

1. “And Elisha passed to Shunem”

1. “And it came to pass, when Pharaoh had let the people go, that Elohim led them not through the way of the land of the Philistines…” (Shemot 13:17). Rabbi Shimon opened the discussion, saying: “A prayer of the prophet Habakkuk upon errors” (Chavakuk 3:1). This passage is difficult, and should be investigated. What is the reason FOR WRITING, “A prayer of the prophet Habakkuk,” rather than any other prophet of the world, for by them, it is not written, ‘A prayer of Isaiah the Prophet’, or of Jeremiah, or Ezekiel or Hosea, or the other prophets of the world?

2. אֶלָּא הָכִי תָּנֵינָן, אֱלִישָׁע זָכָה בְּהַאי עָלְמָא מַה דְּלָא זָכָה נְבִיאָה אָחֳרָא, בַּר מִמֹּשֶׁה. תָּא חֲזֵי, מַאי כְּתִיב, וַיְהִי הַיּוֹם וַיַּעֲבוֹר אֱלִישָׁע אֶל שׁוּנֵם וְשָׁם אִשָּׁה גְּדוֹלָה. מַאי אִשָּׁה גְּדוֹלָה. אֶלָּא גְּדוֹלָה בְּעוֹבָדָהָא, דְּכָל בְּנֵי בֵּיתָא, מִשְׁתַּבְּחִין בָּהּ, וְהִיא עִקָּרָא דְּבֵיתָא, וּבְגִין דְּבַעֲלָהּ לָא הֲוָה שְׁכִיחַ בְּבֵיתָא, לְמֶהֱוֵי עִקָּרָא, לָא הֲוָה אִדְכַּר הוּא, אֶלָּא הִיא.

2. HE RESPONDS: We have learned that Elisha merited in the world what no other prophet did, except for Moses. Come and behold: it is written, “And it fell on a day and Elisha passed to Shunem, where there was a great woman” (II Melachim 4:8). What is meant by “a great woman”? It is that she was great in her actions and the entire household was proud of her. She was the mistress of the house and, since her husband was not present in the house to be the master, she was mentioned instead of him.

3. וְתוּ, וְשָׁם אִשָּׁה גְּדוֹלָה: גְּדוֹלָה עַל כָּל שְׁאַר נְשֵׁי עָלְמָא, דְּהָא שְׁאַר נְשֵׁי עָלְמָא, כַּד חָמָאן אוּשְׁפִּיזָא בְּבֵיתָא, מִצְטַעֲרָן בֵּיהּ, וְדָחֲקָן בֵּיהּ כָּל שֶׁכֵּן לְאַפָּקָא עָלֵיהּ מָמוֹנָא, וְהִיא חֲדַת בֵּיהּ בְּאוּשְׁפִּיזָא, וּלְאַפָּקָא עָלֵיהּ מָמוֹנָא, כָּל שֶׁכֵּן כֵּיוָן דְּחָמַת לֵיהּ לֶאֱלִישָׁע חַדַת בֵּיהּ לַחֲדָא. וְעַל דָּא, שְׁבָחָא דְּכַלָּא דְּאִתְּתָא הִיא, דְּהָא אוּשְׁפִּיזָא דְּבֵיתָא דְּאִתְּתָא הִיא. וּבְגִין כַּךְ וְשָׁם אִשָּׁה גְּדוֹלָה, גְּדוֹלָה עַל שְׁאַר נָשִׁין.

3. “Where there was a great woman.” Another EXPLANATION IS that she was greater than all the other women in the world because the other women were vexed and distressed when they saw a guest in the house, and they would not spend money on him. But she rejoiced with a guest, and spent money on him. When she saw Elisha she was moreover very happy with him. All the praise goes to the woman, because the guest of the house is the woman's. Therefore, it is written: "Where there was a great woman," for she was greater than all other women.

4. וַתֹּאמֶר אֶל אִישָׁהּ הִנֵּה נָא יָדַעְתִּי כִּי אִישׁ אֱלֹהִים קָדוֹשׁ הוּא, בְּמָּה יַדְעָה. אֶלָּא הָא אוּקְמוּהָ חַבְרַיָּא, דְּשׁוּשִׁיפָא חִוָּורָא זְרִיקַת לֵיהּ בְּעַרְסֵיהּ. וְלָא חָמַת בֵּיהּ קֶרִי מֵעוֹלָם, וְלָא אַעְבָּר זְבוּבָא בְּפָתוֹרֵיהּ.

4. "And she said to her husband, 'Behold now, I know that this is a holy man of Elohim'" (Ibid. 9). HE ASKS: How did she know THAT HE WAS A HOLY MAN? HE RESPONDS: THE friends explained that she would spread a white sheet on his bed and never saw an emission of semen on it. Also, a fly never passed on his table.

5. הָנֵי מִילֵי קַשְׁיָין, אִי תֵּימָא דְּלָא חָמַת בֵּיהּ קֶרִי, הָא סַגִּיאִין אִינּוּן בְּנֵי נָשָׁא הָכִי בְּעָלְמָא, מַה שְּׁנוּיָא הָכָא. וְאִי תֵּימָא דְּלָא עָבַר זְבוּבָא בְּפָתוֹרֵיהּ. אֲמַאי כְּתִיב, הִנֵּה נָא יָדַעְתִּי, וְכִי הִיא יַדְעַת, וְלָא אָחֳרָא, וְהָא כָּל אִינּוּן דְּחָמוּ לֵיהּ אָכִיל בְּפָתוֹרֵיהּ הֲווֹ יַדְעֵי.

5. HE ASKS: These words are difficult. You say that she never saw an accidental emission from him, but there are many people in the world who are so AND HAVE NO ACCIDENTAL EMISSIONS. What is the difference here? If you say that a fly never passed over his table, why is it written: "Behold now, I know"? Did only she and no one else know? Yet all those who saw him eat at his table knew, JUST LIKE HER.

6. אֶלָּא שַׁפִּיר קָאַמְרַת, אֲבָל הִנֵּה נָא יָדַעְתִּי, הִיא יַדְעָה, וְלָא אָחֳרָא, בְּגִין דְּהִיא מְתַקְּנַת עַרְסֵיהּ, בְּשַׁעֲתָא דְּשָׁכִיב בְּלֵילְיָא, וּבְשַׁעֲתָא דְּקָאֵים בְּצַפְרָא. וְהַאי דְּקַאמְרֵי דְּשׁוּשִׁיפָא חִוָּורָא זְרִיקַת לֵיהּ בְּעַרְסֵיהּ, הָכִי הֲוָה, וּבָהּ יַדְעָה, דְּאָרְחָא דְּעָלְמָא, כֵּיוָן דְּקָאֵים בַּר נָשׁ מֵעַרְסֵיהּ, סָלִיק שׁוּשִׁיפָא דְּנָאִים בָּהּ, רֵיחָא מְנוּוָלָא. וְהַאי, בְּשַׁעֲתָא דְּסַלְקַת הַהוּא שׁוּשִׁיפָא מֵעַרְסֵיהּ, הֲוָה סָלִיק רֵיחִין, כְּרֵיחִין דְּגִנְתָּא דְּעֵדֶן. אָמְרָה אִי לָאו דְּקַדִּישָׁא הוּא, וּקְדוּשָׁה דְּמָרֵיהּ עָלֵיהּ, לָא סָלִיק רֵיחָא קַדִּישָׁא הָכִי.

6. HE RESPONDS: But rather she spoke well, "Behold now, I know." Only she knew because she arranged his bed when he lay down in it at night and when he arose in the morning. It was so that she spread a white sheet in his bed, and by this did she know, for the way of the world is that when a person arises from his bed, the sheet on which he slept exudes a foul odor. But when she removed the sheet from his bed, it exuded scents like those in the Garden of Eden. She said: 'If it were not for the fact that he is holy and the Holiness of his Master is upon him, a holy scent would not arise FROM THE SHEET.'

7. בְּגִינֵי כַּךְ, בָּעֵי לְאִתְפָּרְשָׁא מִן בֵּיתָא, דְּלָא אִזְדְּהַר בַּר נָשׁ כָּל כַּךְ בְּבֵיתָא. אֲבָל אֲמְרַת, נַעֲשֶׂה נָּא עֲלִיַּית קִיר קְטַנָּה וְנָשִׂים לוֹ שָׁם מִטָּה וְשֻׁלְחָן וְכִסֵּא וּמְנוֹרָה, אַרְבַּע אִלֵּין לָמָּה. אֶלָּא בְּגִין דְּאִינּוּן תִּקּוּנָא דִּכְנֶסֶת יִשְׂרָאֵל, דְּאִתְקְרִיאַת עֲלִיַּית קִיר, וְהָכִי אִתְקְרֵיא, כְּמָה דִּכְתִּיב וַיַּסֵּב חִזְקִיָּה פָּנָיו אֶל הַקִּיר.

7. As a result, he had to separate from the house, because a person can not be so careful inside the house. But she said, "Let us make a small upper chamber, I pray you, with walls; and let us set for him there a bed and table, and a chair, and a lamp" (Ibid. 10). HE INQUIRES: Why these four? HE RESPONDS: Because they restore the Congregation of Yisrael, WHICH IS MALCHUT, that is called an 'upper chamber with walls'. And so is it called, for it is written: "Then Hezekiah turned his face towards the wall" (Yeshayah 38:2).

8. מִטָּה וְשֻׁלְחָן וְכִסֵּא וּמְנוֹרָה, לָאו אִינּוּן כְּתִיקוּן דְּשִׁמּוּשָׁא, דְּהָא כִּסֵּא קָא בָּעֵי בְּקַדְמֵיתָא, וּלְבָתַר שֻׁלְחָן, לְבָתַר מְנוֹרָה, לְבָתַר מִטָּה, אֲמַאי אַקְדִּימַת מִטָּה. בְּגִין דְּהִיא חֲבִיבָה עֲלֵיהּ יַתִּיר מִכֹּלָּא, וְאַקְדִּים בַּר נָשׁ מַה דְּחָבִיב עֲלֵיהּ.

8. "A bed, and a table, and a chair, and a lamp." HE ASKS: the order of the passage is not the order of the usage, because first a chair is needed, and afterwards a table, and afterwards a lamp, and then a bed. So why did she start with the bed? HE RESPONDS: Because she liked the bed better than everything, and a person places that which he likes first – FOR SHE

NOTICED IN THE BED A HIGHER DEGREE OF HOLINESS ABOVE EVERYTHING.

9. וַיְהִי הַיּוֹם וַיָּבוֹא שָׁמָּה. וַיְהִי הַיּוֹם, מַאן הוּא יוֹמָא דָּא. אֶלָּא כְּמָה דְּאוּקְמוּהָ. ות״ח. הַהוּא יוֹמָא, יוֹמָא טָבָא דְּרֹאשׁ הַשָּׁנָה הֲוָה, דְּאִתְפְּקָדוּ בֵּיהּ עֲקָרוֹת דְּעָלְמָא, וְאִתְפַּקְדָן בֵּיהּ בְּנֵי עָלְמָא. קָרָא לַשּׁוּנַמִּית וְאָמַר, הִנֵּה חָרַדְתְּ אֵלֵינוּ אֶת כָּל הַחֲרָדָה הַזֹּאת. בְּגִינֵי כַּךְ, אִצְטְרִיכְנָא לְעַיְּינָא יוֹמָא דָּא בְּדִינֵי דְּעָלְמָא, דְּקוּדְשָׁא בְּרִיךְ הוּא דָּאִין בְּיוֹמָא דָּא לְעָלְמָא, וּבְגִין דְּאִתְפָּרַשְׁנָא בִּלְחוֹד בַּאֲתָר דָּא, אִצְטְרִיכְנָא לְאִסְתַּכְּלָא בִּרְגִיזוּ דְּעָלְמָא.

9. "And it happened one day, that he came there" (II Melachim 4:11). HE ASKS: "And it happened one day." What day was it? HE RESPONDS: It is as we explained. Come and behold: that day was the holy day of Rosh Hashanah (the Jewish New Year), when the barren women of the world and the inhabitants of the world were remembered. He called the Shunamite and said, "Behold, you have been careful to take all this trouble for us" (Ibid. 13). Therefore, I must study the Judgments of the world today, because today the Holy One, blessed be He, Judges the world, and because I separated myself to be alone in this place, IN THE UPPER CHAMBER WITH WALLS WHICH WAS PREPARED FOR ME. I must search the sentences of the world, MEANING THAT WHOEVER SEPARATES TO BE ALONE ON THE DAY OF JUDGMENT IS SNARED FIRST, THOUGH HE MAY BE GUILTLESS.

10. וּמַה לַעֲשׂוֹת לָךְ הֲיֵשׁ לְדַבֵּר לָךְ אֶל הַמֶּלֶךְ אוֹ אֶל שַׂר הַצָּבָא. וְכִי מִלָּה דָּא לְמָה אִצְטְרִיכָא לְגַבֵּי אִתְּתָא, דְּלָא נַפְקַת וְלָא אַזְלַת וְלָא עָאלַת בְּהֵיכְלָא דְּמַלְכָּא. אֶלָּא, יוֹמָא דָּא הֲוָה גָּרִים, דְּכָל בְּנֵי עָלְמָא יַתְבִין בְּדִינָא, וּבְהַהוּא יוֹמָא אִקְרֵי קוּדְשָׁא בְּרִיךְ הוּא מֶלֶךְ. הַמֶּלֶךְ הַמִּשְׁפָּט. אָמַר לָהּ, אִי אַתְּ אִצְטְרִיךְ לָךְ לְגַבֵּי מַלְכָּא עִלָּאָה, עַל עוֹבָדִין דִּי בִּידָךְ.

10. HE ASKS: "What is to be done for you? Would you be spoken for to the king, or to the captain of the host?" (Ibid.) Is this important to a woman who never goes out or goes to the king's palace? But this day caused all the inhabitants of the world to await Judgment and on that day, the Holy One, blessed be He, shall be proclaimed as King, the King of Judgment. He said to her, 'If you need the Supernal King TO FORGIVE YOU for your actions, I WILL SPEAK AND BESEECH ON YOUR BEHALF.'

11. וַתֹּאמֶר בְּתוֹךְ עַמִּי אָנֹכִי יֹשָׁבֶת. מַאי קָאַמְרַת. אֶלָּא בְּשַׁעֲתָא דְּדִינָא תַּלְיָא בְּעָלְמָא, לָא יִתְפְּרַשׁ בַּר נָשׁ בִּלְחוּדוֹי, וְלָא יִתְרְשִׁים לְעֵילָּא, וְלָא יִשְׁתְּמוֹדְעוּן בֵּיהּ בִּלְחוּדוֹי, דְּהָא בִּזְמְנָא דְּדִינָא תַּלְיָא בְּעָלְמָא, אִינּוּן דְּאִשְׁתְּמוֹדְעוּן וּרְשִׁימִין בִּלְחוּדַיְיהוּ, אע״ג דְּזַכָּאִין אִינּוּן, אִינּוּן אִתָּפְסָן בְּקַדְמֵיתָא. וְעַל דָּא, לָא לִבָּעֵי לֵיהּ לְאִינִישׁ, לְאִתְפָּרְשָׁא מִבֵּין עַמָּא לְעָלַם, דִּבְכָל זִמְנָא רַחֲמֵי דְּקוּדְשָׁא בְּרִיךְ הוּא עַל עַמָּא כֻּלְּהוּ כְּחַד. וּבְגִינֵי כַּךְ אָמְרָה, בְּתוֹךְ עַמִּי אָנֹכִי יֹשָׁבֶת, וְלָא בְּעֵינָא לְאִתְפָּרְשָׁא מִנַּיְיהוּ, כְּמָה דְּעָבֵדְנָא עַד יוֹמָא דֵּין.

11. "And she answered, 'I dwell among my people'." HE ASKS: What does she mean? AND HE RESPONDS: At the time when Judgment prevails over the world, a person should not separate himself from the general community and be apart. Then he will not be singled out above, and will not be noticed on his own. For at the time when Judgment prevails over the world, those who were distinctly known and recorded apart are caught first, even though they may be righteous. Therefore, a person should never separate to be apart from the people, for the Mercies of the Holy One, blessed be He, are always present over the whole people together. Therefore, she said, "I dwell among my people" and I do not want to be separate from them, as I have done until this day.

12. וַיֹּאמֶר גֵּחֲזִי אֲבָל בֵּן אֵין לָהּ וְגוֹ׳. אָמַר לָהּ אֱלִישָׁע. הָא וַדַּאי שַׁעֲתָא קַיְימָא, דְּהָא יוֹמָא גָּרִים. וַיֹּאמֶר לַמּוֹעֵד הַזֶּה כָּעֵת חַיָּה אַתְּ חוֹבֶקֶת בֵּן. וַתַּהַר הָאִשָּׁה וַתֵּלֶד בֵּן לַמּוֹעֵד הַזֶּה כָּעֵת חַיָּה אֲשֶׁר דִּבֶּר אֵלֶיהָ אֱלִישָׁע. לַמּוֹעֵד וַדַּאי. לְבָתַר מִית. מַאי טַעֲמָא מִית. אֶלָּא בְּגִין דְּאִתְיְיהִב לָהּ, וְלָא לְבַעְלָהּ. וּמֵאֲתָר דְּנוּקְבָא אִתְקָשַׁר, וּמַאן דְּאִתְקָשַׁר בְּנוּקְבָא, מוֹתָא אִזְדַּמְּנַת קָמֵיהּ. מְנָא לָן דְּלָהּ אִתְיְהִיב, דִּכְתִּיב אַתְּ חוֹבֶקֶת בֵּן.

12. "And Gechazi answered, 'Verily she has no child'" (II Melachim 4:14). Elisha said to her: 'Certainly, the time is favorable for you TO REDEEM YOURSELF WITH A SON, because the day induces it', FOR ON ROSH HASHANAH, BARREN WOMEN ARE REMEMBERED. "And he said, 'About this time, in the coming year, you shall embrace a son'...And the woman conceived and bore a son in the season of which Elisha had spoken to her" (Ibid. 16-17). Assuredly, at that time and afterwards he died. HE INQUIRES: What is the reason that he died? HE RESPONDS: Because the child was given to her and not to her husband, and he was bound to the Female place. Death awaits one who is bound to the Female. Whence do we know that he was given to her? Because it is written: "And you shall embrace a son."

13. תָּא חֲזֵי, בְּאַבְרָהָם כְּתִיב שׁוֹב אָשׁוּב אֵלֶיךָ, וְלֹא אֵלֶיהָ, אֵלֶיךָ וַדַּאי, בָּךְ אִתְקָשַׁר, וְלָא בְּנוּקְבָא. מַאן דְּאָתֵי מִסִּטְרָא דְּנוּקְבָּא, מוֹתָא אַקְדִּים לְרַגְלוֹי. וַתַּעַל וַתַּשְׁכִּיבֵהוּ עַל מִטַּת אִישׁ הָאֱלֹהִים, בְּגִין דְּתַמָּן חָמַת קְדוּשָּׁה עִלָּאָה מִכֹּלָּא.

13. Come and behold: by Abraham, it is written, "I will certainly return to you at this season" (Beresheet 18:10), and not to her. He will be bound to you indeed, and not with a female, for death is premature for one who comes from the Female side. "And she went up, and laid him on the bed of the man of Elohim," because she saw there a Holiness that was higher than that of everyone.

14. וַיֹּאמֶר לָהּ הֲשָׁלוֹם לָךְ הֲשָׁלוֹם לְאִישֵׁךְ הֲשָׁלוֹם לַיָּלֶד. מִכָּאן, דְּהִיא עִקָּרָא דְּבֵיתָא, וְלֹא עוֹד אֶלָּא דְּאִיהִי אַזְלַת אֲבַתְרֵיהּ, וְלֹא בַּעְלָהּ. וַיִּגַּשׁ גֵּחֲזִי לְהָדְפָהּ הָא אוּקְמוּהָ.

14. "And say to her, 'Is it well with you, is it well with your husband, is it well with the child?" (II Melachim 4:26). From here, we know that she is the mainstay of the house, FOR HE INQUIRED FIRST ABOUT HER WELL-BEING, AND THEN HER HUSBAND'S WELL-BEING. She went behind THE PROPHET, but before her husband. "And Gechazi came near to thrust her away." This has already been explained.

15. וַיֹּאמֶר אִישׁ הָאֱלֹהִים הַרְפֵּה לָהּ. מַאי שְׁנָא הָכָא דְּאָמַר אִישׁ

הָאֱלֹהִים, וְכַד הֲוָה בְּמָתָא אֱלִישָׁע. אֶלָּא הָכָא וַדַּאי אִישׁ הָאֱלֹהִים, דְּהָכָא הוּא דּוּכְתֵּיהּ, וְלָא בְּמָתָא, וְלָא בְּשַׁעֲתָא דַּהֲווֹ בְּנֵי נְבִיאֵי קָמֵּיהּ.

15. "But the man of Elohim said, 'Let her alone'." HE INQUIRES: Why is it that here the verse calls him "the man of Elohim," yet he was referred to as "Elisha" when he was in the city? HE RESPONDS: Here he was assuredly "the man of Elohim," because here is his place, and not in the city, not at the time when the sons of the prophets were before him. THUS, THERE HE WAS NOT CALLED 'THE MAN OF ELOHIM', BUT RATHER "ELISHA."

16. וַיְיָ' הֶעְלִים מִמֶּנִּי וְגוֹ', כְּמָה דְּאַתְּ אָמֵר וַיְיָ' הִמְטִיר עַל סְדוֹם וְעַל עֲמוֹרָה, דָּא בֵּי דִּינָא דִּלְתַתָּא. וְלֹא הִגִּיד לִי, מַאי טַעֲמָא לֹא יָדַע אֱלִישָׁע. אֶלָּא אָמַר קוּדְשָׁא בְּרִיךְ הוּא, וּמָה אֲנָא קָטִיל לְהַאי, אִי אֵימָא לֵיהּ, לֹא יָמוּת, דְּהָא נְבִזְבְּזָא דִּילֵיהּ הוּא. וַדַּאי אִית לֵיהּ לְמֵימַת, דְּהָא אִתְּמַר, דִּכְתִּיב אַתְּ חוֹבֶקֶת בֵּן, וּמֵאֲתַר דְּנוּקְבָא גָּרִים מוֹתָא, וּבְגִינֵי כַּךְ לָא אָמַר לֵיהּ.

16. "And Hashem has hid it from me…" IS as written: "And Hashem rained upon S'dom and Amorah" (Beresheet 19:24), WHEREBY "AND HASHEM" MEANS HE AND HIS COURT OF JUSTICE, AND this is the court of law of below, MEANING MALCHUT. "And has not told me" (II Melachim 4:27). HE ASKS: Why did Elisha not know? HE RESPONDS: the Holy One, blessed be He, said, 'How can I kill this one? If I tell him, he will not let him die because it is his present. HE WILL PRAY FOR HIM, AND NOT PERMIT HIM TO DIE.' But he must die; as we learned, it is written: "You will embrace a son." HE WAS BOUND TO THE PLACE OF THE FEMALE, and death was caused from the Female place. Therefore, He did not tell him.

17. וַיֹּאמֶר לְגֵחֲזִי חֲגוֹר מָתְנֶיךָ וְקַח מִשְׁעַנְתִּי בְּיָדְךָ וָלֵךְ. וְהָא אוּקְמוּהָ וְאִסְתְּלַק נִיסָא מִנֵּיהּ. חַי יְיָ' וְחֵי נַפְשְׁךָ אִם אֶעֶזְבֶךָּ, אַמַּאי כֵּיוָן דְּגֵיחֲזִי הֲוָה אָזִיל. אֶלָּא הִיא יָדְעַת אָרְחוֹי דְּהַהוּא רָשָׁע דְּגֵיחֲזִי, דְּלָאו אִיהוּ כְּדַאי דְּיִשְׁתְּכַח נִיסָא עַל יְדוֹי.

17. "And he said to Gechazi, 'Gird your loins, and take my staff in your hand and go you away'." It was explained that the ability to perform the miracle had departed from him, FOR HE WAS NOT WORTHY OF IT. "As Hashem lives, and as your soul lives, I will not leave you." HE INQUIRES: Why DID SHE CONTINUE TO INSIST THAT HE SHOULD GO HIMSELF, although Gechazi was already going. HE ANSWERS: She recognized the manners of that wicked Gechazi that he is not worthy for a miracle to be performed through him.

18. וַיָּשֶׂם פִּיו עַל פִּיו וְעֵינָיו עַל עֵינָיו וְגוֹ'. אֲמַאי, אֶלָּא דְּאַשְׁגַּח אֱלִישָׁע וְיָדַע דְּאַתְרָא דָּא הוּא דְּגָרִים, דְּאִתְקְשָׁר בֵּיהּ הַשְׁתָּא. וַיָּשֶׂם פִּיו עַל פִּיו וְעֵינָיו עַל עֵינָיו, לְקַשְׁרָא לֵיהּ בְּאַתְרָא אָחֳרָא עִלָּאָה, אֲתָר דְּחַיִּין אִשְׁתְּכָחוּ בֵּיהּ.

18. "And he put his mouth upon his mouth and his eyes upon his eyes..." HE ASKS: Why DID HE DO IT THAT WAY. HE ANSWERS: Elisha observed and knew that this place OF THE FEMALE, to which he is bound now, caused him TO DIE. CONSEQUENTLY, "he put his mouth upon his mouth and his eyes upon his eyes," in order to bind him in a different, high place – MEANING IN THE PLACE OF THE MALE, the place where there is life.

19. וְלָא יָכִיל לְאַעְקְרָא לֵיהּ מֵאֲתָר דְּאִתְקַשָּׁר בֵּיהּ בְּקַדְמֵיתָא, אֶלָּא אִתְּעַר רוּחָא חֲדָא מִלְּעֵילָּא, וְאִתְקְשַׁר בְּהַאי אֲתָר, וְאָתִיב לֵיהּ נַפְשֵׁיהּ. דְּאִי לָאו הָכִי לָא הֲוָה קָאֵים לְעָלְמִין. וַיְזוֹרֵר הַנַּעַר עַד שֶׁבַע פְּעָמִים, וְלָא סָלִיק יַתִּיר, כְּמָה דְּאַתְּ אָמֵר יְמֵי שְׁנוֹתֵינוּ בָּהֶם שִׁבְעִים שָׁנָה.

19. But he was not able to uproot him from the FEMALE place, to which he was connected before until he aroused a spirit from above. He connected to the SUPERNAL place and returned to him his soul. If he had not DONE so, he would never have returned TO LIFE. "And the child sneezed seven times," and not more THAN SEVEN, WHICH CORRESPONDS TO THE SEVENTY YEARS OF HIS LIFE, as is written: "The days of our years are seventy" (Tehilim 90:10).

20. וְדָא הוּא חֲבַקּוּק נְבִיאָה, כְּמָה דְּאַתְּ אָמֵר אַתְּ חוֹקֶבֶת בֵּן. אִי הָכִי חָבוּק מִבָּעֵי לֵיהּ, אֲמַאי חֲבַקּוּק תְּרֵי. אֶלָּא, חַד דְּאִמֵּיהּ, וְחַד דֶּאֱלִישָׁע,

דְּאִתְחַבָּק עִמֵּיהּ. ד״א תְּרֵי חִבּוּקִין הֲווֹ בֵּיהּ, בֵּין לְהַאי סִטְרָא בֵּין לְהַאי סִטְרָא. חִבּוּקָא חֲדָא, הַהוּא אֲתָר דַּהֲוָה תָּלֵי בֵּיהּ בְּקַדְמֵיתָא. חִבּוּקָא אַחֲרִינָא דְּסָלִיק לֵיהּ לְדַרְגִּין עִלָּאִין יַתִּיר, ובג״כ חֲבַקּוּק תְּרֵי.

20. This is Habakkuk the prophet, as it says, "You shall embrace (Heb. *choveket*) a son." *HABAKKUK* IS DERIVED FROM 'EMBRACE'. HE ASKS: If so, he should have been called *Chavuk* ('embraced'). Why WAS HE CALLED '*Habakkuk*', which means two EMBRACES? HE RESPONDS: One EMBRACE IS of his mother and one EMBRACE IS of Elisha, who embraced him WHEN HE REVIVED HIM. Another explanation: He received two embraces, one from HIS MOTHER'S side and one from the PROPHET'S side. One embrace from the place from which he came originally – MEANING FROM THE FEMALE PLACE, AS MENTIONED – and another embrace that raised him to the higher levels, MEANING TO THE PLACE OF THE MALE, AS MENTIONED. BOTH THESE EMBRACES ARE INCLUDED IN HIS MOTHER'S EMBRACE, AND ALSO IN THE PROPHET'S EMBRACE. He was therefore called '*Habakkuk*', which means two EMBRACES.

21. תְּפִלָּה לַחֲבַקּוּק הַנָּבִיא, מַאי תְּפִלָּה. אֶלָּא דָּא הוּא אֲתָר, דַּהֲוָה קָשִׁיר בֵּיהּ בְּקַדְמֵיתָא, וְדָא הוּא תְּפִלָּה שֶׁל יָד. עַל שִׁגְיוֹנוֹת. דְּהַהוּא יוֹמָא דְּאִתְקְשַׁר בֵּיהּ, שִׁגְיוֹנוֹת דְּעָלְמָא הֲווֹ תַּלְיָין קָמֵי קוּדְשָׁא בְּרִיךְ הוּא, וּגְבוּרָה הֲוָה שָׁלִיט, וְע״ד אִתְקְשַׁר בֵּיהּ הַאי תְּפִלָּה.

21. "A prayer (Heb. *tfilah*) of the prophet Habakkuk" (Chavakuk 3:1). HE ASKS: What is the prayer THAT IS MENTIONED HERE? HE RESPONDS: This is the place to which he was originally connected FROM HIS MOTHER'S ASPECT, and this is the hand *Tfilah* ('phylactery'), MEANING THE NUKVA OF ZEIR ANPIN that is called '*Tfilah*. "Upon errors" (Ibid.) MEANS that on the day he became bound to it, the errors of the world were suspended before the Holy One, blessed be He, WHICH WAS ROSH HASHANAH, AS MENTIONED. And Gvurah, WHICH IS NUKVA, dominated. This Tfilah, WHICH IS THE NUKVA, was therefore bound to him.

22. ד״א תְּפִלָּה לַחֲבַקּוּק הַנָּבִיא, תְּפִלָּה לַחֲבַקּוּק: בְּגִין חֲבַקּוּק, דְּאִיהוּ עָבֵיד בְּגִינֵיהּ. יְיָ׳ שָׁמַעְתִּי שִׁמְעֲךָ יָרֵאתִי וְגוֹ׳, ת״ח, כַּד הֲוָה אִתְּעַר

עֲלֵיהּ רוּחָא דִּנְבוּאָה עַל אֲתָר דָּא דְּהוּא תְּפִלָּה, הֲוָה אָתֵי וַהֲוָה דָּחִיל וּמִזְדַּעְזֵעַ. מַתְלָא אַמְרֵי, מַאן דְּנָשִׁיךְ מִכַּלְבָּא, מִקָּלֵיהּ אִזְדַּעְזָע.

22. Another explanation for "A prayer of the prophet Habakkuk" is that a prayer of Habakkuk MEANS for Habakkuk, FOR THE TWO EMBRACES, which THE PROPHET gave him. "Hashem, I heard the report of You, and I was afraid" (Ibid. 2). Come and behold: when the spirit of the prophet was awakened over him – THAT IS, THE MALE WHEN HE EMBRACES, over this place, OVER THE SPIRIT OF THE FEMALE, which is *Tfilah* (lit. 'prayer'), WHICH HE HAD FROM THE EMBRACE OF HIS MOTHER – he approached with fear and trembling, LEST THE JUDGMENTS OF THE NUKVA SHOULD NOT REVISIT HIM. THEREFORE, HE SAID, "HASHEM, I HEARD THE REPORT OF YOU, AND I WAS AFRAID." This, they said, is like the proverb: 'One who is bitten by a dog trembles from his bark.'

23. יְיָ' פָּעָלְךָ בְּקֶרֶב שָׁנִים חַיֵּיהוּ, מַאן פָּעָלְךָ. אֶלָּא, עֲלֵיהּ קָאָמַר, דְּאִיהוּ פֹּעַל דִּילֵיהּ. בְּקֶרֶב שָׁנִים חַיֵּיהוּ. הָב לֵיהּ חַיִּין לְהַאי פָּעָלְךָ, בְּקֶרֶב שְׁנִין עִלָּאִין. ד"א, חַיֵּיהוּ דְּלָא יָמוּת כַּד בְּקַדְמֵיתָא.

23. "Hashem, revive Your work in the midst of the years" (Ibid.). HE ASKS: What is "Your work"? AND HE REPLIES: He said it ABOUT HIMSELF, that He is His work. "Revive Your work in the midst of the years" MEANS give him life to serve You among the supernal years, WHICH ARE THE SFIROT. Another explanation: Revive him so that he shall not die again.

24. עַל שִׁגְיוֹנוֹת, מַאי עַל שִׁגְיוֹנוֹת, עַל שְׁגִיאוֹת מִבָּעֵי לֵיהּ. כד"א שְׁגִיאוֹת מִי יָבִין. אֶלָּא שִׁגְיוֹנוֹת, כד"א שִׁגָּיוֹן לְדָוִד. זִינֵי תּוּשְׁבְּחָן הֲווֹ קַמַּיְיהוּ דִּנְבִיאֵי, לְמִישְׁרֵי עֲלַיְיהוּ רוּחַ נְבוּאָה, כד"א וּפָגַעְתָּ חֶבֶל נְבִיאִים יוֹרְדִים מֵהַבָּמָה וְלִפְנֵיהֶם נֵבֶל וְתוֹף וְגוֹ', וּכְתִיב וְעַתָּה קְחוּ לִי מְנַגֵּן וְגוֹ'. וְכָל שֶׁכֵּן חֲבַקּוּק, דְּאִצְטְרִיךְ לֵיהּ יַתִּיר מִכֻּלְּהוֹן, לְנַיְיחָא דְּרוּחָא, וּלְבַסְּמָא לְהַהוּא אֲתָר, לְאַמְשָׁכָא עֲלֵיהּ רוּחַ נְבוּאָה. וְכֵן כֻּלְּהוּ נְבִיאֵי כְּהַאי גַּוְונָא, בַּר מִמֹּשֶׁה דְּסָלִיק עַל כָּל שְׁאָר נְבִיאֵי דְּעָלְמָא, זַכָּאָה חוּלָקֵיהּ.

24. "On errors (Heb. *shigyonot*)": HE INQUIRES: What is "*shigyonot*"? It should have said '*shgiot'*, as is written: "Who can discern errors (Heb. *shgiot*)?" (Tehilim 19:13). But "*shigyonot*" is defined as is written: "*shigayon* ('musical instrument') to David" (Tehilim 7:1). THAT IS A LYRIC USED FOR PRAISE, for there were various types of praises available to the prophets to cause the Spirit of Prophecy to dwell upon them, as it is written: "That you shall meet a band of prophets coming down from the high place with a lute, and a timbrel" (I Shmuel 10:5), and: "But now bring me a minstrel" (II Melachim 3:15). Habakkuk needed pleasantness more than all of them, to sweeten that place, WHICH IS THE NUKVA, TO WHICH HE WAS PREVIOUSLY BOUND. THIS WAS IN ORDER to draw the Spirit of Prophecy upon himself. It is the same for all the other prophets except for Moses, who rose above all the prophets of the world. Happy is his portion.

25. ת״ח, כַּד נַפְקוּ יִשְׂרָאֵל מִמִּצְרַיִם, רוּחֵיהוֹן הֲוָה תָּבִיר בְּגַוַּויְיהוּ, וַהֲווֹ שַׁמְעִין אִינּוּן תּוּשְׁבְּחָן, וְלָא יַכְלִין לְמֶחֱדֵי, וּבְשַׁעֲתָא דְּכֻלְּהוּ אוּכְלְסִין וּרְתִיכִין נַפְקוּ בִּשְׁכִינְתָּא, כֻּלְּהוּ אָרִימוּ תּוּשְׁבְּחָן וְשִׁירִין קָמֵי קוּדְשָׁא בְּרִיךְ הוּא, וְאִתְּעַר קוּדְשָׁא בְּרִיךְ הוּא רוּחֵיהוֹן דְּיִשְׂרָאֵל, וַהֲווֹ שַׁמְעִין אִינּוּן תּוּשְׁבְּחָן, וְקָאֵים רוּחֵיהוֹן בְּגַוַּויְיהוּ דְּלָא פַּרְחָן.

25. Come and behold: when the Yisrael left Egypt, their spirits were broken and they heard the praises OF THE ANGELS, but they could not celebrate. When all the legions OF THE ANGELS and Chariots left with the Shechinah, they all raised THEIR VOICES in praise and song before the Holy One, blessed be He, and the Holy One, blessed be He, aroused the spirits of Yisrael. Then they heard the praises OF THE ANGELS, as their spirits remained within them and did not fly from them.

26. בַּר נָשׁ כַּד אִיהוּ שָׁבִיק פּוּלְחָנָא, כְּדֵין יָדַע תְּבִירוּ דְּגַרְמוֹי, תְּבִירוּ דְּרוּחֵיהּ. כַּךְ יִשְׂרָאֵל, כַּד נַפְקוּ מִמִּצְרַיִם, כְּדֵין טָעִימוּ טַעֲמָא דְּמוֹתָא, וְקוּדְשָׁא בְּרִיךְ הוּא אַסֵּי לוֹן, דִּכְתִּיב וַיְיָ׳ הוֹלֵךְ לִפְנֵיהֶם יוֹמָם וְגוֹ׳. וְכָל אוֹרְחִין, הֲווֹ סַלְּקִין רֵיחִין דְּאַסְוָתָא, וְעָאלִין לְגוּפַיְיהוּ וְאִתָּסְיָין, וְקַל תּוּשְׁבְּחָן דַּהֲווֹ שַׁמְעִין, הֲווֹ חַדָּאן וְנַיְיחִין בְּרוּחֵיהוֹן.

26. One knows AND FEELS his broken bones and broken spirit only after he leaves his work. Yisrael only tasted death when they departed from Egypt, but the Holy One, blessed be He, healed them, as is written: "And Hashem went before them by day..." (Shemot 13:21). All the roads exuded scents of healing which entered their bodies, and they were healed. From the sound of the praises that they heard, they rejoiced and reposed and purified their spirit.

27. וּפַרְעֹה וְכָל אִינּוּן אוּכְלוּסִין דִּילֵיהּ, הֲווֹ אַזְלֵי בַּתְרַיְיהוּ, לְאוֹזְפָא לוֹן, עַד דְּנַפְקוּ מֵאַרְעָא דְּמִצְרַיִם. וְכֵן כָּל אִינּוּן רַבְרְבִין דִּמְמָנָן עֲלַיְהוֹן, וְעַל שְׁאַר עַמִּין, אוֹזִיפוּ לָהּ לִשְׁכִינְתָּא וּלְיִשְׂרָאֵל כֻּלְּהוּ, עַד דְּשָׁארוּ בְּאֵיתָם בִּקְצֵה הַמִּדְבָּר, הה"ד, וַיְהִי בְּשַׁלַּח פַּרְעֹה אֶת הָעָם וְגוֹ'. כִּי קָרוֹב הוּא, כִּי קָרוֹב הוּא. הַהוּא אוֹמָאָה דְּאוֹמֵי אֲבִימֶלֶךְ לַאֲבָהָן, עַל הַהוּא טִיבוּ דְּעָבְדוּ פְּלִשְׁתִּים לַאֲבָהָן, דִּכְתִּיב כַּחֶסֶד אֲשֶׁר עָשִׂיתִי עִמְּךָ תַּעֲשֶׂה עִמָּדִי וְעִם הָאָרֶץ אֲשֶׁר גַּרְתָּ בָּהּ.

27. Pharaoh and all his people went after Yisrael to accompany them until they left Egypt. Likewise, all the supreme princes, who were appointed over them and the other nations, accompanied the Shechinah and all of Yisrael until they camped at Eitam, on the edge of the wilderness. This is what is written: "And it came to pass when Pharaoh had let the people go...although that was near" (Ibid. 17). "...that was near..." MEANS because that oath is near, the oath which Abimelech swore to the Patriarchs because of the good that the Philistines did for the Patriarchs, as is written: "But according to the kindness that I have done to you, you shall do to me, and to the land in which you have sojourned" (Beresheet 21:23).

2. Three deaths

A Synopsis

We hear that at the time of the first Passover, there were three revengeful deaths performed against Egypt: the one that related to the deaths of the firstborn, the one that God killed at midnight, and the one when Pharaoh saw the death in his own house. Rabbi Shimon says that Pharaoh himself killed all the ministers and advisers who counseled him to refuse to send out the children of Yisrael. Then he called Moses and Aaron and told them to leave, "and bless me also." Then he accompanied them out of the country.

28. וַיְהִי בְּשַׁלַּח פַּרְעֹה אֶת הָעָם, מַה כְּתִיב לְעֵילָּא, וַיָּקָם פַּרְעֹה לַיְלָה הוּא וְכָל עֲבָדָיו. תָּא חֲזֵי, נוּקְמָא עִלָּאָה דְּעָבֵד קוּדְשָׁא בְּרִיךְ הוּא בְּמִצְרַיִם. תְּלַת מוֹתָנֵי הֲווֹ. חַד, דְּעָבְדוּ בּוּכְרִין בְּמִצְרַיִם, דְּקָטִילוּ כָּל אִינּוּן דְּאַשְׁכָּחוּ. וְחַד, דְּקָטַל קוּדְשָׁא בְּרִיךְ הוּא בְּפַלְגוּת לֵילְיָא. וְחַד, כַּד חָמָא פַּרְעֹה מוֹתָנָא בְּבֵיתֵיהּ בִּבְנוֹי וּבְעַבְדוֹי, קָם וְזָרִיז גַּרְמֵיהּ, וְקָטִיל אֲפַרְכִין וְסַרְכִין, וְכָל דְּאַמְלִיכוּ לֵיהּ לְסָרְבָא בְּעַמָּא עַד דְּאוֹרַיְיתָא אַסְהִידַת עָלֵיהּ דְּאִיהוּ קָם בְּלֵילְיָא מַמָּשׁ. כְּמָה דְּלֵילְיָא קָטַל בּוּכְרִין וְעָבֵד נוּקְמִין, הָכִי קָם פַּרְעֹה בְּאַרְעָא דְּמִצְרַיִם, וְקָטַל וְעָבֵד נוּקְמִין בְּסַרְכוֹי, וְאָפַרְכוֹי, וַאֲמַרְכְּלוֹי, וּבְכָל אִינּוּן רַבְרְבִין הה"ד וַיָּקָם פַּרְעֹה לַיְלָה, דְּקָם לְקַטְלָא וּלְשֵׁיצָאָה.

28. "And it came to pass when Pharaoh had let the people go." It is written before: "And Pharaoh arose in the night, he and all his servants" (Shemot 12:30). Come and behold: recognize the supernal revenge that the Holy One, blessed be He, performed against Egypt. There were three deaths: one that related to the first born in Egypt, as they killed whoever was in their way; one that the Holy One, blessed be He, killed at midnight; and one when Pharaoh saw the death in his house, among his children and servants. He arose and emboldened himself and killed the ministers, the rulers, and all those who advised him to refuse TO SEND OUT the people, until the Torah bore witness against him. He arose actually at night, MEANING WITH THE JUDGMENTS OF THE NUKVA, THAT IS CALLED 'NIGHT'. As the night, WHICH IS THE NUKVA, slew the first born and took revenge, so did Pharaoh arise in the land of Egypt, slay and take revenge against his rulers, ministers, his appointees and all types of officers. This is the meaning of: "And Pharaoh arose in the night." He arose to kill and destroy.

29. אוֹרְחוֹי דְּכַלְבָּא, כַּד מַחְיָין לֵיהּ בְּאַבְנָא, אִיהוּ אָתֵי וְנָשִׁיךְ לְחַבְרֵיהּ, כָּךְ פַּרְעֹה, לְבָתַר אִיהוּ הֲוָה אָזִיל בַּשְּׁוָקֵי, וַהֲוָה מַכְרִיז וְאָמַר, קוּמוּ צְּאוּ מִתּוֹךְ עַמִּי, אַתּוּן קְטַלְתּוּן לְכָל בְּנֵי מָתָא, אַתּוּן קְטַלְתּוּן סַרְכֵי וְאָפַּרְכֵי וְכָל בְּנֵי בֵּיתִי, הה"ד וַיִּקְרָא לְמֹשֶׁה וּלְאַהֲרֹן לַיְלָה. כֵּיוָן דְּבִידְכוֹן הֲוָה כֹּלָּא, וּבֵרַכְתֶּם גַּם אוֹתִי, דְּלָא תִּקְטְלוּן לִי. לְבָתַר אִיהוּ בְּגַרְמֵיהּ אוֹזִיף לוֹן, וְאַפִּיק לוֹן מֵאַרְעָא, הה"ד וַיְהִי בְּשַׁלַּח פַּרְעֹה אֶת הָעָם וְגוֹ'.

29. The nature of a dog is that when you hit him with a stone, he goes and bites its neighbor. Pharaoh did likewise. Afterwards, he went out in the marketplaces and announced, "Rise up, and get you out from among my people" (Shemot 12:31) – you killed all the inhabitants of the city, you killed the rulers and ministers and all the members of my household. Hence, it is written: "And he called Moses and Aaron by night" (Ibid.). Since everything was caused by you, "And bless me also" (Ibid. 32), by not killing me. Afterwards, he himself accompanied them and took them out of the country. This is what is written: "And it came to pass, when Pharaoh had let the people go..."

3. "And Elohim led the people about"

A Synopsis

Rabbi Yehuda wonders why after the children of Yisrael were circumcised, had offered the Passover sacrifice and were bound to God, He still calls them "the people" and not "My people." Rabbi Shimon explains that it was because they were still attached to the mixed multitude. There follows a short story about Rabbi Yitzchak and Rabbi Yehuda turning themselves away from an evil man, wishing not to associate with him. Rabbi Yitzchak then speaks about "Fret not yourself because of evil doers." We learn that if it were not for the mixed multitudes the people of Yisrael would not have died, because the molten calf would never have been made. The Holy One, blessed be He, had wanted at that time to liberate them from death and the yoke of other nations, but that deed caused ruin to everything. The rabbis, saying that Moses instructed the people to accept the mixed multitudes, then dispute gently about how many of the multitudes were from the nation of Yisrael. Rabbi Shimon talks about the Jubilee, the fifty gates of Binah, and the fifty days that Yisrael lingered to receive the Torah. He explains why Moses took the bones of Joseph with him when they left Egypt. Serah the daughter of Asher showed Moses where the bones were hidden.

30. וַיַּסֵּב אֱלֹהִים אֶת הָעָם דֶּרֶךְ הַמִּדְבָּר יַם סוּף לְתַקְּנָא אָרְחָא לְאַתְרֵיהּ. ר׳ יְהוּדָה אָמַר, מַאי שְׁנָא כַּד הֲווֹ יִשְׂרָאֵל בְּמִצְרַיִם, דִּכְתִּיב, שַׁלַּח אֶת עַמִּי, כִּי אִם מָאֵן אַתָּה לְשַׁלֵּחַ אֶת עַמִּי, בְּנִי בְכוֹרִי יִשְׂרָאֵל, וּבְהַהוּא זִמְנָא לָא הֲווֹ גְּזִירִין, וְלָא אִתְקַשְּׁרוּ בֵּיהּ כַּדְקָא יֵאוֹת. וְהָכָא דַּהֲווֹ גְּזִירִין, וְעָבְדוּ פִּסְחָא, וְאִתְקַשְּׁרוּ בֵּיהּ, קָרֵי לוֹן אֶת הָעָם.

30. "And Elohim led the people about, through the way of the wilderness of the Sea of Reed s," NAMELY, to make way to His place IN ORDER TO EVENTUALLY SPLIT THE SEA OF REEDS. IF NOT FOR THIS, IT WOULD HAVE BEEN ENOUGH TO SIMPLY LEAD THEM THROUGH THE WILDERNESS, AND NOT BY WAY OF THE SEA OF REEDS. Rabbi Yehuda said: Why the difference? When Yisrael were in Egypt, it is written: "Let My people go" (Shemot 5:1); "if you refuse to let My people go" (Shemot 10:4); and, "Yisrael is My son, my first born" (Shemot 4:22). They were not circumcised at that time and were not bound TO THE HOLY ONE, BLESSED

BE HE, properly. But once they were circumcised, had offered the Passover sacrifice, and were bound to Him, He calls them "the people" and not "My people."

31. אֶלָּא בְּגִין הַהוּא עֵרֶב רַב, דְּאִתְדְּבָקוּ בְּהוּ, וְאִתְעָרְבוּ בַּהֲדַיְיהוּ, קָרֵי לוֹן אֶת הָעָם סְתָם. כד"א, וַיִּגּוֹף יְיָ' אֶת הָעָם עַל אֲשֶׁר עָשׂוּ אֶת הָעֵגֶל. וַיִּקָּהֵל הָעָם עַל אַהֲרֹן. וַיַּרְא הָעָם כִּי בֹשֵׁשׁ מֹשֶׁה. וְכֵן כֻּלְּהוּ.

31. HE ANSWERS: It was due to the mixed multitude that attached themselves to them and were mixed with them that He calls them "the people" AND NOT "MY PEOPLE." It is written: "And Hashem plagued the people for the calf they made" (Shemot 32:35); "the people gathered themselves together to Aaron"; and, "the people saw that Moses delayed" (Ibid. 1). DURING A PERIOD WHEN THE CHILDREN OF YISRAEL WERE IN A DECADENT STATE, HE CALLS THEM SIMPLY, "THE PEOPLE" AND NOT "MY PEOPLE."

32. ר' יִצְחָק ור' יְהוּדָה הֲווֹ אַזְלֵי מֵאוּשָׁא לְלוּד, וַהֲוָה עִמְּהוֹן יוֹסֵי טַיָּיעָא, בִּקְטִירָא דְּגַמָּלֵי עֲטוּפִירָא בְּכַתְפַּיְיהוּ. עַד דַּהֲווֹ אַזְלֵי, אַשְׁכַּח הַהוּא יוֹסֵי טַיָּיעָא אִנְתּוּ חֲדָא דִּשְׁאַר עַמִּין, דְּקָטִיר בִּירוֹקֵי חַקְלָא, אִשְׁתְּמִיט מִנַּיְיהוּ וְאַתְקִיף בָּהּ, וְאָתָא עָלָהּ. תַּוְוהוּ ר' יִצְחָק ור' יְהוּדָה, אָמְרוּ נֵיתוּב מֵאָרְחָא דָּא, דְּהָא קוּדְשָׁא בְּרִיךְ הוּא בָּעָא לְאַחְזָאָה לָן, דְּלָא נִתְחַבַּר בַּהֲדֵיהּ. תָּבוּ מֵאָרְחָא, בָּדְקוּ בַּתְרֵיהּ, וְאַשְׁכָּחוּ דִּבְרֵיהּ דְּבַת אֵל נֵכָר הֲוָה, וַאֲבוּהָ פָּסִיל זַרְעָא הֲוָה. אָמְרוּ, בְּרִיךְ רַחֲמָנָא דְּשֵׁזִיב לָן.

32. Rabbi Yitzchak and Rabbi Yehuda were traveling from Usha to Lod with camels tied TO ONE ANOTHER IN SINGLE FILE, and with loads on their shoulders. They were accompanied by Yosi the Merchant. While they were traveling, Yosi the Merchant found a woman of the other nations who was gathering among the grasses in the field. He turned away from them, and then raped her, coming in to her. Rabbi Yitzchak and Rabbi Yehuda wondered and said: Let us return from this road, for the Holy One, blessed be He, wishes to show us that we should not associate with him. They returned from that way. They investigated him and learned that he was the son of a gentile woman while his father was of unfit ancestry. They said: Blessed is the Merciful One who has saved us.

33. פָּתַח ר' יִצְחָק וְאָמַר אַל תִּתְחַר בַּמְּרֵעִים. מַאן אִינּוּן מְרֵעִים, דְּלָא כְּתִיב חַטָּאִים, אוֹ רְשָׁעִים. אֶלָּא מְרֵעִים, דְּאַבְאִישִׁין לְגַרְמַיְיהוּ, וּלְהָנֵי דְּמִתְחַבְּרָן בַּהֲדַיְיהוּ. ר' יְהוּדָה אָמַר, מְרֵעִים: אַרְחִיק גַּרְמָךְ מִמְּרֵעִים דְּלָא תֶּהֱווֹן רֵעִים וַחֲבֵרִים כַּחֲדָא, דְּלָא יַבְאִישׁוּ לָךְ עוֹבָדוֹי, וְתִתְפַּס בְּחֶטְאוֹי.

33. Rabbi Yitzchak opened the discussion, saying: "Fret not yourself because of evil doers" (Tehilim 37:1). HE ASKS: Who are these evil doers, for it is not written 'sinners' or 'wicked'? HE RESPONDS: Rather "evil doers" are those that bring evil to themselves and to those who join up with them. Rabbi Yehuda said, "FRET NOT YOURSELF BECAUSE OF evil doers," IS DEFINED as staying away from evil doers so that you do not become friends and associate with them. Also, this is so that their actions do not hurt you and you are not caught for their sins.

34. ת"ח, אִי לָא הֲווֹ אִינּוּן עֵרֶב רַב דְּאִתְחַבְּרוּ בְּהוֹן יִשְׂרָאֵל, לָא אִתְעֲבִיד הַהוּא עוֹבָדָא, וְלָא מִיתוּ מִיִּשְׂרָאֵל, כָּל אִינּוּן דְּמִיתוּ, וְלָא גָּרִים לוֹן לְיִשְׂרָאֵל כָּל מַה דְּגָרִים. ות"ח, הַהוּא עוֹבָדָא, וְהַהוּא חוֹבָה מַמָּשׁ, גָּרִים גָּלְוּתְהוֹן דְּיִשְׂרָאֵל.

34. Come and behold: if it were not for the mixed multitudes that joined with Yisrael, the deed OF THE MOLTEN CALF would not have occurred, and all those people of Yisrael would not have died. They would not have brought all that they did upon Yisrael. Come and behold: this deed and iniquity was the cause of Yisrael's exile.

35. דְּתָנֵינָן, בָּעָא קוּדְשָׁא בְּרִיךְ הוּא, דְּיִשְׁתַּכְּחוּן יִשְׂרָאֵל בְּהַהוּא שַׁעֲתָא כְּמַלְאֲכֵי עִלָּאֵי, וּלְמֶעְבַּד לוֹן חֵירִין מִכֹּלָּא, חֵירִין מִמּוֹתָא, וּלְמֶהֱוֵי חֵירִין מִן שִׁעְבּוּדָא דִּשְׁאַר עַמִּין, כמד"א, חָרוּת עַל הַלּוּחוֹת, אַל תִּקְרֵי חָרוּת, אֶלָּא חֵירוּת.

35. For we studied that the Holy One, blessed be He, desired that Yisrael be at that time, DURING THE RECEPTION OF THE TORAH, as the supernal angels. And He desired to liberate them from everything: freedom (Heb.

cherut) from death, and liberation from the yoke of other nations, as is said: "engraved (Heb. *chaurut*) on the tablets" (Shemot 32:16). Do not pronounce it "*chaurut*" WITH THE VOWEL A, but RATHER ONLY WITH THE E: '*cherut*'.

36. כֵּיוָן דְּאִתְעֲבֵיד הַהוּא עוֹבָדָא, גָּרִימוּ כֹּלָּא. גָּרִימוּ מוֹתָא, גָּרִימוּ שִׁעְבּוּד מַלְכְוָון, גָּרִימוּ דְּאִתְּבָרוּ אִינּוּן לוּחֵי קַדְמָאֵי, גָּרִימוּ דְּמִיתוּ מִיִּשְׂרָאֵל, כַּמָּה אַלְפִין מִנַּיְיהוּ. וְכָל דָּא, בְּגִין אִתְחַבְּרוּתָא דְּאִינּוּן עֵרֶב רַב, דְּאִתְחַבְּרוּ בְּהוּ.

36. As soon as that deed was done, they instigated everything. They caused the deaths of thousands among Yisrael, they caused submission to other kingdoms, and they caused the breaking of the original tablets. All this was due to the connection of the mixed multitudes who joined with them.

37. אוּף הָכָא, בְּגִינֵיהוֹן, לָא אִתְקְרוּן בְּנֵי יִשְׂרָאֵל, וְלָא יִשְׂרָאֵל, וְלָא עַמִּי, אֶלָּא הָעָם סְתָם. וְאִי תֵּימָא וַחֲמוּשִׁים עָלוּ בְּנֵי יִשְׂרָאֵל. כַּד הֲווֹ סַלְּקִין מִמִּצְרַיִם, וְלָא אִתְחַבְּרוּ בַּהֲדַיְיהוּ אִינּוּן עֵרֶב רַב, קָרֵי לוֹן בְּנֵי יִשְׂרָאֵל, כֵּיוָן דְּאִתְחַבְּרוּ בַּהֲדַיְיהוּ, דִּכְתִּיב וְגַם עֵרֶב רַב עָלָה אִתָּם, קָרֵי לוֹן הָעָם.

37. Here too, due to THE MOTLEY CROWD, they were not called 'children of Yisrael', nor 'Yisrael', nor 'My people', but merely, "the people." You may reason THAT IT IS INDEED WRITTEN: "And the children of Yisrael went up armed" (Shemot 13:18). This is because the motley crowd had not yet joined up with them when they first rose out of Egypt. Thus, He still calls them "the children of Yisrael." They are referred to as "the people" as soon as they were joined with them, as mentioned in the scripture: "And a mixed multitude went up also with them" (Shemot 12:38).

38. רִבִּי יוֹסֵי אַקְשֵׁי וְאָמַר, כְּתִיב כִּי אֲשֶׁר רְאִיתֶם אֶת מִצְרַיִם הַיּוֹם לֹא תוֹסִיפוּ לִרְאוֹתָם עוֹד עַד עוֹלָם. אִי הָכִי, כָּל יוֹמָא הֲווֹ חָמָאן לְהַהוּא עֵרֶב רַב. אָמַר רִבִּי יְהוּדָה, עֵרֶב רַב כְּתִיב, וְלֹא מִצְרַיִם, דְּהָא כַּמָּה שְׁאַר עַמִּין הֲווֹ דַּיְירֵי בְּמִצְרַיִם. וְלֹא עוֹד אֶלָּא דְּכֻלְּהוּ אִתְגְּזָרוּ, וְכֵיוָן

דְּאִתְגְּזָרוּ, לָא אִקְרוּן מִצְרָאֵי.

38. Rabbi Yosi insisted and said: It is written, "For as you have seen Egypt today you will never see them again" (Shemot 14:13). Yet every day they saw the mixed multitude, WHO WERE EGYPTIANS. Rabbi Yehuda said: It is written, "a mixed multitude" and not 'Egypt', for there were many other nations in Egypt AND FROM THEM CAME THE MOTLEY CROWD. Moreover all of them were circumcised and, since they were circumcised, they were not considered Egyptians.

39. וְעַל פּוּמָא דְּמֹשֶׁה קַבִּילוּ לוֹן. וְהַיְינוּ מַה דְּאָמַר הַכָּתוּב, לֶךְ רֵד כִּי שִׁחֵת עַמְּךָ סָרוּ מַהֵר מִן הַדֶּרֶךְ אֲשֶׁר צִוִּיתִם. צִוִּיתָם כְּתִיב. וַחֲמֻשִׁים עָלוּ בְּנֵי יִשְׂרָאֵל מֵאֶרֶץ מִצְרָיִם, חַד מֵחֲמִשָּׁה הֲווֹ. וְר׳ יוֹסֵי אוֹמֵר חֲמִשָּׁה מִיִּשְׂרָאֵל, וְחַד מִנַּיְיהוּ. רִבִּי יְהוּדָה אוֹמֵר, וַחֲמֻשִׁים: אֶחָד מֵחֲמִשִּׁים.

39. According to the instructions of Moses, they accepted them. This is what the verse said: "Go, get you down; for your people...have become corrupt: they have turned aside quickly out of the way which I commanded them" (Shemot 32:7-8). "I commanded them," is written, WHICH MEANS THAT MOSES HAD INSTRUCTED THEM TO ACCEPT THE MIXED MULTITUDES. "And the children of Yisrael went up armed (Heb. *chamushim*) out of the land of Egypt," MEANING one out of five (Heb. *chamisha*) were YISRAEL. Rabbi Yosi said: Five were of Yisrael and one FROM THE MIXED MULTITUDES. Rabbi Yehuda said: "*chamushim,*" one out of fifty (Heb. *chamishim*) WERE OF THE MIXED MULTITUDES.

40. אר״ש, בְּגִין דְּהַהוּא יוֹבְלָא סָלִיק לוֹן מִמִּצְרַיִם, בְּגִין כָּךְ וַחֲמֻשִׁים עָלוּ בְּנֵי יִשְׂרָאֵל מֵאֶרֶץ מִצְרָיִם. וְאִי לָאו, לָא סְלִיקוּ, וְעַל דָּא אִתְעַכְּבוּ חַמְשִׁין יוֹמִין לְקַבְּלָא אוֹרַיְיתָא. וּמֵהַהוּא אֲתָר נַפְקַת אוֹרַיְיתָא, וְאִתְיְהִיבַת, וְעַל דָּא וַחֲמֻשִׁים חָסֵר. דִּבְגִין דָּא עָלוּ בְּנֵי יִשְׂרָאֵל מֵאֶרֶץ מִצְרָיִם.

40. Rabbi Shimon said: the Jubilee, WHICH IS BINAH, did take them up from the land of Egypt. Therefore, it is written: "And the children of Yisrael went up armed (Heb. *chamushim*) out of the land of Egypt," WHICH

REFERS TO BINAH, CALLED 'JUBELEE (HEB. *YOVEL*), THAT CONTAINS FIFTY (HEB. *CHAMISHIM*) GATES. If not FOR JUBELEE, they would not have left. Therefore, they tarried fifty days to receive the Torah. The Torah did emerge and was given from that place OF JUBELEE. Therefore, "*chamushim*" is without a *Vav*, MEANING THAT IF IT HAD MEANT "ARMED," IT WOULD HAVE BEEN SPELLED WITH A *VAV*. BUT IT ONLY INDICATES THE NUMBER FIFTY (HEB. *CHAMISHIM*), WHICH IS THE SECRET OF JUBILEE. Due to it the children of Yisrael went up from Egypt.

41. וַיִּקַּח מֹשֶׁה אֶת עַצְמוֹת יוֹסֵף וְגוֹ׳. אֲמַאי סָלִיק גַּרְמוֹי. אֶלָּא, בְּגִין דַּהֲוָה רֵישָׁא לְנַחְתָּא לְגָלוּתָא. וְלֹא עוֹד, אֶלָּא דְּאִיהוּ סִימָנָא דִּגְאוּלָּה הֲוָה לֵיהּ וְאוֹמֵי לְהוּ לְיִשְׂרָאֵל עַל דָּא, הה״ד כִּי הַשְׁבֵּעַ הִשְׁבִּיעַ אֶת בְּנֵי יִשְׂרָאֵל, וְהָא אִתְּמַר.

41. "And Moses took the bones of Joseph..." (Shemot 13:19) HE ASKS: Why did MOSES bring up his bones? HE ANSWERS: It is because he was the first to descend into exile. And in addition, only he possessed the sign for the redemption, NAMELY, "WILL SURELY VISIT YOU" (IBID.). He bound Yisrael by oath in this. This is what is written: "He had laid an oath on the children of Yisrael" (Ibid.). And this was explained.

42. זַכָּאָה חוּלָקָא דְּמֹשֶׁה, דְּיִשְׂרָאֵל הֲווֹ עַסְקֵי לְמִשְׁאַל מָמוֹנָא מִמִּצְרָאֵי, וּמֹשֶׁה הֲוָה עָסִיק בְּאוּמָאָה דְּיוֹסֵף. וְאִית דְּאַמְרֵי אֲרוֹנָא בְּנִילוּס הֲוָה, וּבִשְׁמָא קַדִּישָׁא סָלִיק לֵיהּ, וְעוֹד אָמַר מֹשֶׁה, יוֹסֵף, הִגִּיעַ זְמַן פּוּרְקָנָא דְּיִשְׂרָאֵל, וְאָמַר עֲלֵה שׁוֹר. וְסָלִיק. וְאִית דְּאַמְרֵי, בֵּין מַלְכֵי מִצְרָאֵי הֲוָה, וּמִתַּמָּן סָלִיק. וְאִית דְּאַמְרֵי, בְּגִין דְּלָא יַעַבְדוּן לֵיהּ ע״ז, שָׁווֹ בְּנִילוּס וְסֶרַח בַּת אָשֵׁר חַוִּיאַת לֵיהּ לְמֹשֶׁה.

42. Fortunate is the part of Moses, for Yisrael were occupied with borrowing silver from Egypt and Moses was occupied with the oath of Joseph. Some said that his casket was in the Nile River, and he raised it by the Holy Name. Moses also said: 'Joseph, the time for the redemption of Yisrael has arrived.' And he said: 'Rise ox', and he rose – SINCE JOSEPH IS CALLED 'OX', AS IS WRITTEN: "HIS FIRSTLING OF HIS HERD, GRANDEUR IS HIS" (DEVARIM 33:17). Some said he was among the kings of Egypt and he ascended from there. And some said that they put him into the Nile in order that they would not make him into an idol. Serach, the daughter of Asher, WHO WAS ALIVE DURING THE HAPPENING, showed Moses HIS PLACE.

4. "And Hashem went before them by day"

A Synopsis

Rabbi Yosi says that it is necessary to be occupied with the Torah day and night, and that one must rise after midnight to study Torah because it is then that the Holy One, blessed be He, enters into the Garden of Eden to delight Himself with the righteous there. He draws a thread of kindness during the day for those who occupy themselves with Torah in the night. Rabbi Yitzchak talks about "And Hashem went before them by day," saying that the Shechinah traveled with the Patriarchs – Abraham, Isaac, Jacob and King David. They are all the Holy Chariot of above. The people traveled day and night when they left Egypt, so that they would be complete with everything, night and day together – the aspect of Zeir Anpin and the aspect of Nukva. The "pillar of cloud" was Chesed, Abraham, and the "pillar of fire" was Gvurah, Isaac, so that Yisrael was illuminated by day and by night. Again we are told of the fifty days' delay after their redemption from Egypt before they received the Torah at Mount Sinai. Then the fifty days of Jubilee, the fifty gates of Binah, dwelled upon them. Rabbi Yitzchak says that the Pharaoh's wise men and sorcerers, who saw that Yisrael were traveling by day and by night, told him that the people had fled.

43. וַיְיָ׳ הוֹלֵךְ לִפְנֵיהֶם יוֹמָם. רִבִּי יוֹסֵי פָּתַח, לַמְנַצֵּחַ עַל אַיֶּלֶת הַשַּׁחַר מִזְמוֹר לְדָוִד. כַּמָּה חֲבִיבָא אוֹרַיְיתָא קָמֵיהּ דְּקוּדְשָׁא בְּרִיךְ הוּא, דְּכָל מַאן דְּאִשְׁתָּדַּל בְּאוֹרַיְיתָא, רָחִים הוּא לְעֵילָּא, רָחִים הוּא לְתַתָּא, קוּדְשָׁא בְּרִיךְ הוּא אָצִית לֵיהּ לְמִלּוּלוֹי, לָא שָׁבִיק לֵיהּ בְּהַאי עָלְמָא וְלָא שָׁבִיק לֵיהּ בְּעָלְמָא דְּאָתֵי.

43. "And Hashem went before them by day" (Shemot 13:21). Rabbi Yosi opened the discussion, saying: "To the Chief Musician upon the hind of dawn. A psalm of David" (Tehilim 22:1). How beloved is the Torah before the Holy One, blessed be He, for anyone who is occupied with Torah is beloved above and below. The Holy One, blessed be He, hearkens to his words, He does not forsake him in this world and He does not forsake him in the World to Come.

44. וְאוֹרַיְיתָא בָּעֵי לְמִלְעֵי בָּהּ בִּימָמָא וּבְלֵילְיָא, דִּכְתִּיב, וְהָגִיתָ בּוֹ

יוֹמָם וָלַיְלָה. וּכְתִיב אִם לֹא בְרִיתִי יוֹמָם וָלַיְלָה וְגוֹ'. תִּינַח בִּימָמָא, בְּלֵילְיָא אֲמַאי. בְּגִין דְּיְהֵא שְׁכִיחַ לְגַבֵּי שְׁמָא קַדִּישָׁא שְׁלִים. כְּמָה דְּלֵית יוֹמָם בְּלָא לֵילְיָא, וְלָאו אִיהוּ שְׁלִים, אֶלָּא דָּא עִם דָּא, כַּךְ בָּעֵי אוֹרַיְיתָא, לְאִשְׁתַּכְּחָא עִמֵּיהּ דב"נ יוֹמָא וְלֵילְיָא, לְמֶהֱוֵי שְׁלֵימוּתָא לְגַבֵּי דב"נ יוֹמָם וָלַיְלָה.

44. It is necessary to be occupied with the Torah by day and night, as is written: "But you shall meditate therein day and night" (Yehoshua 1:8), and, "If my Covenant be not day and night..." (Yirmeyah 33:25). HE ASKS: It is justified by day, WHICH IS A TIME FOR WORK FOR EVERYBODY, but during the night, WHICH IS A TIME FOR REST, why IS IT NECESSARY TO BE OCCUPIED WITH TORAH? HE ANSWERS: So that a complete Holy Name will be present by him. For as there is no day without night, and it is only complete when one is with the other, so is it necessary for the Torah to be present with the person day and night. The completeness should be with the person day and night.

45. וְהָא אִתְּמַר, דְּעִקָּרָא דְּלֵילְיָא, מִפַּלְגוּתָא וְאֵילָךְ. ואע"ג דְּפַלְגוּ קַדְמֵיתָא בִּכְלָלָא דְּלֵילְיָא הוּא, אֲבָל בְּפַלְגוּת לֵילְיָא, קוּדְשָׁא בְּרִיךְ הוּא עָאל בְּגִנְתָּא דְּעֵדֶן, לְאִשְׁתַּעְשְׁעָא עִם צַדִּיקַיָּא, וּכְדֵין, בָּעֵי לֵיהּ לְבַר נָשׁ לְמֵיקָם, וּלְמִלְעֵי בְּאוֹרַיְיתָא.

45. We have learned that the main part of the night is from midnight and further. Even though the first half of the night is part of the night, the Holy One, blessed be He, enters the Garden of Eden at midnight to delight Himself with the Righteous WHO ARE THERE. Then a person should wake up and become occupied with Torah.

46. וְהָא אִתְּמַר, דְּקוּדְשָׁא בְּרִיךְ הוּא וְכָל צַדִּיקַיָּא דְּבְגִנְתָּא דְעֵדֶן, כֻּלְּהוּ צַיְיתִין לְקָלֵיהּ, הה"ד הַיּוֹשֶׁבֶת בַּגַּנִּים חֲבֵרִים מַקְשִׁיבִים לְקוֹלֵךְ הַשְׁמִיעִנִי, וְהָא אוּקְמוּהָ, הַיּוֹשֶׁבֶת בַּגַּנִּים: דָּא כְּנֶסֶת יִשְׂרָאֵל, דְּאִיהִי מְשַׁבַּחַת לֵיהּ לְקוּדְשָׁא בְּרִיךְ הוּא, בְּשִׁבְחָא דְּאוֹרַיְיתָא, בְּלֵילְיָא. זַכָּאָה חוּלָקֵיהּ, מַאן דְּאִשְׁתַּתַּף בַּהֲדָהּ, לְשַׁבְּחָא לֵיהּ לְקוּדְשָׁא בְּרִיךְ הוּא,

בִּשְׁבָחָא דְּאוֹרַיְיתָא.

46. We have learned that the Holy One, blessed be He, hearkens to the voices of all the Righteous in the Garden of Eden, as is written: "You who dwell in the gardens, the companions hearken to your voice; cause me to hear it" (Shir Hashirim 8:13). They have already explained it. "You who dwell in the gardens" is the Congregation of Yisrael, NAMELY MALCHUT, that praises the Holy One, blessed be He, with the praise of the Torah during the night. Blessed is the portion of he who joins with Her to praise the Holy One, blessed be He, with the praise of Torah.

47. וְכַד אָתֵי צַפְרָא, כ״י אַתְיָא וּמִשְׁתַּעְשְׁעָא בֵּיהּ בְּקוּדְשָׁא בְּרִיךְ הוּא, וְאוֹשִׁיט לָהּ לְגַבָּהּ שַׁרְבִיטָא דְּחֶסֶד, וְלָא עָלָּה בִּלְחוֹדָהָא, אֶלָּא עָלָּהּ, וְעַל אִינּוּן דְּמִשְׁתַּתְּפִין בַּהֲדָהּ, וְהָא אִתְּמַר דִּכְתִּיב, יוֹמָם יְצַוֶּה יְיָ׳ חַסְדּוֹ וּבַלַּיְלָה וְגוֹ׳. וְעַל דָּא אַיֶּלֶת הַשַּׁחַר אִקְרֵי.

47. When the morning arrives, the Congregation of Yisrael comes, WHICH IS MALCHUT, and delights with the Holy One, blessed be He. And He extends the scepter of kindness not only to Her, but to all those who join her. We have learned it is written: "Yet Hashem will command His steadfast love in the daytime, and in the night His song shall be with me" (Tehilim 42:9). THIS MEANS THAT THE HOLY ONE, BLESSED BE HE, DRAWS A THREAD OF KINDNESS DURING THE DAY FOR HE WHO OCCUPIES HIMSELF WITH TORAH DURING THE NIGHT. THEREFORE, MALCHUT is called 'the hind of dawn', SINCE SHE PRAISES THE HOLY ONE, BLESSED BE HE, DURING THE NIGHT WITH THE PRAISE OF TORAH.

48. ואר״ש, בְּשַׁעֲתָא דְּבָעֵי לְאִתְנַהֲרָא צַפְרָא, אִתְחֲשָׁךְ וְאִתְקַדַּר נְהוֹרָא, וְקַדְרוּתָא אִשְׁתְּכַח. כְּדֵין אִתְחַבְּרַת אִתְּתָא בְּבַעְלָהּ, דְּתָנֵינָן, אִשָּׁה מְסַפֶּרֶת עִם בַּעְלָהּ, לְמִשְׁתָּעֵי בַּהֲדֵיהּ, וְעָאלַת לְהֵיכְלֵיהּ.

48. Rabbi Shimon said: At the time when morning is to light up, the light becomes darkened and blackened and the blackness is prevalent. Then a wife unites with her husband, for we have learned that at THE THIRD WATCH, a wife converses with her husband, NAMELY, MALE AND FEMALE, to mate with him and she enters his sanctuary.

49. לְבָתַר כַּד בָּעֵי שִׁמְשָׁא לְמֵיעַל, אִתְנְהִיר וְאָתַת לֵילְיָא, וְנָטִיל לֵיהּ. כְּדֵין כָּל תַּרְעִין סְתִימִין, וְחַמְרִין נַעֲרִין, וְכַלְבִּין נַבְחִין, כַּד אִתְפְּלַג לֵילְיָא, שָׁאֲרִי מַלְכָּא לְמֵיקַם, וּמַטְרוֹנִיתָא לְזַמְּרָא, וְאָתֵי מַלְכָּא וְאַקִּישׁ לְתַרְעָא דְהֵיכְלָא, וְאָמַר פִּתְחִי לִי אֲחוֹתִי רַעְיָתִי וְגוֹ'. וּכְדֵין מִשְׁתַּעֲשַׁע בְּנִשְׁמָתְהוֹן דְּצַדִּיקַיָּא.

49. When the sun must set, the night lights up and comes and takes him. Then all the gates are closed, the donkeys bray, and the dogs bark. At midnight, the King starts to arise and the Queen, WHICH IS MALCHUT STARTS, to sing. The King, WHO IS ZEIR ANPIN, comes and knocks on the gate of the sanctuary and says, "Open for Me, My Sister, My love..." (Shir Hashirim 5:2). Then He delights with the souls of the righteous.

50. זַכָּאָה חוּלָקֵיהּ דְּהַהוּא, דְּאִתְּעַר הַהוּא זִמְנָא בְּמִלֵּי דְאוֹרַיְיתָא, בְּגִין דָּא, כָּל אִינּוּן דִּבְנֵי הֵיכְלָא דְּמַטְרוֹנִיתָא, כֻּלְּהוּ בַּעְיָין לְמֵיקַם בְּהַהוּא זִמְנָא, לְשַׁבְּחָא לְמַלְכָּא וְכֻלְּהוּ מְשַׁבְּחָן קָמֵיהּ, וּשְׁבָחָא דְּסָלִיק מֵהַאי עָלְמָא, דָּא דְּאִיהוּ רָחִיק, דָּא נִיחָא לֵיהּ לְקוּדְשָׁא בְּרִיךְ הוּא מִכֹּלָּא.

50. Blessed is the portion of he who arose at that time with words of Torah. Therefore, all the inhabitants of the sanctuary of the Queen must arise at that time to praise the King, and they all praise before Him. The praise that rises from this world, which is far FROM HIM, is more acceptable to the Holy One, blessed be He, than all the rest.

51. כַּד אִסְתְּלִיק לֵילְיָא, וְאָתֵי צַפְרָא, וְאִתְקַדַּר, כְּדֵין מַלְכָּא וּמַטְרוֹנִיתָא בְּרָזָא בְּחֶדְוָה, וְיָהִיב לָהּ מַתְּנָן, וּלְכָל בְּנֵי הֵיכְלָהּ. זַכָּאָה חוּלָקֵיהּ מַאן דְּאִיהוּ בְּמִנְיָינָא.

51. When the night is gone, the morning comes and it becomes dark. The King and the Queen are in the secret of gladness, MEANING COUPLING. And He gives presents to Her and to all those in the sanctuary. Fortunate is he who is counted among THE MEMBERS OF THE SANCTUARY.

52. וַיְיָ' הוֹלֵךְ לִפְנֵיהֶם יוֹמָם. קוּדְשָׁא בְּרִיךְ הוּא, וּבֵית דִּינֵיהּ. אָמַר רִבִּי

יִצְחָק, הַיְינוּ דְּתָנֵינָן, שְׁכִינְתָּא בַּאֲבָהָתָא נַטְלָא. הוֹלֵךְ לִפְנֵיהֶם יוֹמָם: דָּא אַבְרָהָם. בְּעַמּוּד עָנָן: דָּא יִצְחָק. לַנְחוֹתָם הַדֶּרֶךְ: דָּא יַעֲקֹב. דִּכְתִּיב בֵּיהּ וְיַעֲקֹב הָלַךְ לְדַרְכּוֹ. וְלַיְלָה בְּעַמּוּד אֵשׁ לְהָאִיר לָהֶם: דָּא דָּוִד מַלְכָּא.

52. "And Hashem went before them by day." "AND HASHEM" MEANS the Holy One, blessed be He, and His court of law, WHICH IS MALCHUT, BECAUSE THE *VAV* (='AND') OF *VAV* YUD HEI VAV HEI ('AND HASHEM') INCLUDES MALCHUT. Rabbi Yitzchak said: We learned that the Shechinah travels with the Patriarchs, BECAUSE "went before them by day," is Abraham, "in a pillar of a cloud," is Isaac, and "to lead them the way," is Jacob, of whom it is written: "And Jacob went on his way" (Beresheet 32:2). "By night in a pillar of fire, to give them light" is King David.

53. וְכֻלְּהוּ רְתִיכָא עִלָּאָה קַדִּישָׁא, לְמֵהַךְ יִשְׂרָאֵל בִּשְׁלֵימוּתָא דְּכֹלָּא, בְּגִין דְּיֶחֱזוּן אֲבָהָן פּוּרְקָנָא דִּלְהוֹן, דִּכְתִּיב וְאָנֹכִי אַעַלְךָ גַם עָלֹה, עִם הַמֶּרְכָּבָה. וּכְתִיב וַיְיָ׳ הוֹלֵךְ וְגוֹ׳, לָלֶכֶת יוֹמָם וָלָיְלָה. וְכִי אַמַּאי הֲווֹ אַזְלֵי יוֹמָם וָלַיְלָה, יְהַכוּן בִּימָמָא, וְלָא יְהַכוּן בְּלֵילְיָא, כִּבְנֵי אֱנָשָׁא דְּעַרְקִין, כֵּיוָן דְּקוּדְשָׁא בְּרִיךְ הוּא נָטִיר לוֹן, אַמַּאי אַזְלִין בִּימָמָא וּבְלֵילְיָא. אֶלָּא, לְאִשְׁתַּכְּחָא בְּהוּ שְׁלֵימוּתָא דְּכֹלָּא, דְּלֵית שְׁלִימוּ אֶלָּא יוֹם וְלַיְלָה.

53. They are all the holy Chariot of above. ABRAHAM, ISAAC AND JACOB ARE CHESED, GVURAH AND TIFERET, THE THREE LEGS OF THE THRONE, AND KING OF DAVID IS THE FOURTH LEG. In order that Yisrael should be perfect in everything and that the Patriarchs should see their redemption, as it is written: "And I will also surely bring you up" (Beresheet 46:4) with the Chariot, and: "And Hashem went...that they might go by day and by night." HE ASKS: Why did they travel day and night? Let them walk by day, and not by night like people who are fleeing. If the Holy One, blessed be He, guarded them, AND THEY DID NOT FEAR, why did they march day and night. HE ANSWERS: So they should be complete with everything, because there is no completeness unless day is with night, AS DAY IS THE ASPECT OF ZEIR ANPIN AND NIGHT IS THE ASPECT OF THE

NUKVA. AND ALL PERFECTION PREVAILS WHEN THEY ARE JOINED TOGETHER IN THE SECRET OF: "AND THERE WAS EVENING AND THERE WAS MORNING, ONE DAY" (BERESHEET 1:5).

54. א״ר אַבָּא, הָכִי אוֹקִימְנָא, וַיְיָ׳ הוֹלֵךְ לִפְנֵיהֶם יוֹמָם בְּעַמּוּד עָנָן: דָּא אַבְרָהָם. וְלַיְלָה בְּעַמּוּד אֵשׁ: דָּא יִצְחָק. וְאִי הָכִי יַעֲקֹב אָן הוּא. אֶלָּא בְּמִלָּה קַדְמָאָה אִתְּמַר, וְתַמָּן שָׁארִי, כְּמָה דִּכְתִּיב וַיְיָ׳.

54. Rabbi Aba said: We have determined, "And Hashem went before them by day in a pillar of a cloud," refers to Abraham, WHO IS CHESED, and "by night in a pillar of fire," refers to Isaac, WHO IS GVURAH. If so, we can ask: where is Jacob, WHO IS TIFERET? HE ANSWERS: In the first word he is mentioned, and there he dwells, as is written: "And Hashem," WHICH IS TIFERET AND MALCHUT, AND JACOB IS TIFERET.

55. וְלַיְלָה בְּעַמּוּד אֵשׁ, הֲוָה נָהִיר, בְּסִטְרָא דָּא וּבְדָא. בְּגִין דְּיִרְדְּפוּן מִצְרָאֵי בַּתְרֵיהוֹן, לְאִתְיַיקְרָא שְׁמָא דְּקוּדְשָׁא בְּרִיךְ הוּא, בִּרְתִּיכוֹי וּפָרָשׁוֹי. בְּגִין לְמֵיזַל יְמָמָא וְלֵילְיָא, אַסְפַּקְלַרְיָא דְּנָהֲרָא, וּדְלָא נָהֲרָא. וְתוּ, בְּגִין לְאַטְעָאָה לְמִצְרָאֵי דְּיֵימְרוּן מִקְרֶה הוּא, דִּכְתִּיב נוֹאֲלוּ שָׂרֵי צוֹעַן, וּכְתִיב מֵשִׁיב חֲכָמִים אָחוֹר, וְע״ד אַזְלֵי בִּימָמָא וּבְלֵילְיָא.

55. "And by night in a pillar of fire," in order to illuminate on this side BY DAY, WITH CHESED, and on that side BY NIGHT, WITH GVURAH. This was in order that when the Egyptians chased after them with their chariots and horsemen, THEY WOULD DROWN AND NOT EVEN ONE OF THEM WOULD SURVIVE, in order to glorify the Name of the Holy One, blessed be He. FOR THIS, HE NEEDED THE ASPECT OF GVURAH. In order to go day and night MEANS the illuminating mirror, WHICH IS ZEIR ANPIN THAT IS CALLED 'DAY', and the mirror that does not illuminate, WHICH IS MALCHUT THAT IS CALLED 'NIGHT'. It was also done in order to fool the Egyptians so they would say that it was a coincidence, AND IT WAS NOT HASHEM WHO DELIVERED THEM. THEREFORE, THEY WERE TRAVELING DAY AND NIGHT AS IF THEY WERE FLEEING, as written: "The Princes of Tzoan are become fools" (Yeshayah 19:13). "He turns wise men backwards" (Yeshayah 44:25). Therefore, they traveled day and night.

56. רִבִּי אַבָּא אָמַר, זַכָּאָה חוּלָקֵהוֹן דְּיִשְׂרָאֵל, דְּקוּדְשָׁא בְּרִיךְ הוּא אַפִּיק לוֹן מִמִּצְרַיִם, לְמֶהֱוֵי חוּלָקֵיהּ וְאַחֲסַנְתֵּיהּ. ות״ח, בְּסִטְרָא דְּיוֹבְלָא, אִשְׁתְּכַח חֵירוּ לְיִשְׂרָאֵל. וְכֵן לְזִמְנָא דְּאָתֵי, דִּכְתִּיב וְהָיָה בַּיּוֹם הַהוּא יִתָּקַע בְּשׁוֹפָר גָּדוֹל וְגוֹ׳.

56. Rabbi Aba said: Happy is the portion of Yisrael, for the Holy One, blessed be He, delivered them from Egypt in order that they should be His portion and inheritance. Come and behold: from the side of Jubilee, WHICH IS BINAH, there is freedom for Yisrael. And so in the future to come, it is written: "And it shall come to pass on that day, that a great horn shall be blown" (Yeshayah 27:13).

57. וּבְגִין הַהוּא יוֹבְלָא עִלָּאָה, אִתְעַכְּבוּ חַמְשִׁין יוֹמִין, לְקַבְּלָא אוֹרַיְיתָא, וּלְמִקְרַב לְטוּרָא דְּסִינַי. וְכֵיוָן דְּאָזְלֵי בִּימָמָא, אָזְלֵי בְּלֵילְיָא, לְמֶהֱוֵי כֹּלָּא חַד יוֹמָא, בֵּין יְמָמָא וְלֵילְיָא, וְלָא אִשְׁתְּכַח פְּרִישׁוּ.

57. Because of that Jubilee, they were delayed for fifty days AFTER THEIR REDEMPTION FROM EGYPT to receive the Torah and to approach Mount Sinai. THIS WAS BECAUSE THERE ARE FIFTY GATES IN JUBILEE, AND IN ORDER TO BETTER THEMSELVES BY THEM THEY NEEDED FIFTY DAYS. Since they traveled during the day, they ALSO traveled during the night so that it would all be one day, and there would be no separation between day and night, WHICH ARE MALE AND FEMALE.

58. וְלֹא עוֹד, אֶלָּא דְּכֻלְּהוּ בְּנַיְיחָא אַזְלִין, לִרְעוּתָא דְּנַפְשַׁיְיהוּ, בְּיוֹמָא דְּקַבִּילוּ אוֹרַיְיתָא, הֲווֹ חַמְשִׁין יוֹמִין שְׁלֵמִין, יוֹמֵי וְלֵילֵי כַּדְקָא יָאוֹת, דְּלֵית יוֹם בְּלֹא לַיְלָה, וְלֵית לַיְלָה בְּלֹא יוֹם, וְלַיְלָה וְיוֹם אִקְרֵי יוֹם אֶחָד. וְכֵיוָן דְּאָזְלוּ חַמְשִׁין יוֹמִין שְׁלֵימִין, כְּדֵין שָׁארוּ עֲלַיְיהוּ אִינּוּן נ׳ יוֹמִין דְּיוֹבְלָא, וּמִסִּטְרָא דְּיוֹבְלָא אִתְיְיהִיב לְהוּ אוֹרַיְיתָא, ובג״כ אַזְלִין יוֹמָא וְלֵילְיָא.

58. And even more, they all went at their leisure, according to their own desire, IN ORDER TO COMBINE DAY AND NIGHT, WHICH ARE MALE AND

FEMALE. On the day that they received the Torah, there were fifty complete days and nights, as it should be. There is no day without night, and there is no night without day, FOR THERE IS NO COMPLETENESS TO ZEIR ANPIN WITHOUT MALCHUT, AND THERE IS NO COMPLETENESS TO MALCHUT WITHOUT ZEIR ANPIN. Night and day are called 'one day', AS IS WRITTEN: "AND THERE WAS EVENING AND THERE WAS MORNING, ONE DAY" (BERESHEET 1:5). When they traveled fifty whole days, these fifty days of Jubilee dwelt upon them, WHICH ARE THE FIFTY GATES OF BINAH, and then the Torah was given to them through the side of Jubilee. Therefore, they traveled day and night.

59. וא״ר אַבָּא, כְּתִיב וַיְהִי כִּי זָקֵן יִצְחָק וַתִּכְהֶיןָ עֵינָיו, אֲמַאי. הָא אוּקִימְנָא, מַאן דְּרָחִים לְחַיָּיבָא, הָכִי הוּא. ות״ח, בְּיִצְחָק אִתְכְּלִיל לֵילְיָא, וְלֵילְיָא לָא בָּהִיר, וְע״ד וַתִּכְהֶיןָ עֵינָיו, וְכֹלָּא חַד.

59. Rabbi Aba said: It is written: "And it came to pass, that when Isaac was old, and his eyes were dim" (Beresheet 27:1). Why? We have explained that one who loves the wicked, HIS EYES BECOME DIM. Come and behold: in Isaac, WHO IS GVURAH, night is included, WHICH IS MALCHUT, and the night is not bright. Therefore, "his eyes were dim." It is all one, BECAUSE THE INCLUSION OF NIGHT IN ISAAC IS IN THE SAME CONTEXT AS THE LOVE OF ISAAC FOR ESAU.

60. ר׳ יִצְחָק פָּתַח וְאָמַר, וַיֻּגַּד לְמֶלֶךְ מִצְרַיִם כִּי בָרַח הָעָם, וַיֻּגַּד, מַאן קָאָמַר לֵיהּ. אֶלָּא, הָא אוּקְמוּהָ. אֲבָל חַכְמוֹי וְחַרְשׁוֹי אִתְכְּנָשׁוּ לְגַבֵּיהּ, וְאוֹדְעוּהוּ כִּי בָרַח הָעָם. וַאֲמַאי קָאמְרוּ דָּא. אֶלָּא חָמוּ בְּחָכְמְתָא דִּלְהוֹן, דַּהֲווֹ אַזְלֵי יְמָמָא וְלֵילְיָא, אָמְרוּ וַדַּאי עַרְקִין אִינּוּן. וְלֹא עוֹד אֶלָּא דְּחָמוּ דְּלָא הֲווֹ אַזְלֵי בְּאוֹרַח מֵישָׁר, כְּמָה דִּכְתִּיב וְיָשׁוּבוּ וְיַחֲנוּ לִפְנֵי פִּי הַחִירוֹת.

60. Rabbi Yitzchak opened the discussion, saying: "And it was told the king of Egypt that the people had fled" (Shemot 14:5). HE ASKS: "And it was told." Who told him? HE ANSWERS: We have explained that his wise men and sorcerers gathered about him and informed him that the people had fled. Why did they say this? Because they saw, in their wisdom, that YISRAEL were traveling day and night. They said they were fleeing and they saw that they were not traveling on the straight road, as is written: "And they turn and encamp before Pi Hachirot" (Ibid. 2). AND THEY INFORMED HIM OF THIS ALSO. THEREFORE, HE CHASED AFTER THEM.

5. "And he took six hundred chosen chariots"

A Synopsis

Rabbi Yosi says that the 600 chosen chariots corresponds to the number of the children of Yisrael, "about 600,000 men on foot." Rabbi Chiya tells us that when the Holy One, blessed be He, gives dominion to the ministers of the nations above, He gives it to their nations below, and when He brings them down from their grade above, He brings down their nations below. The minister of Egypt led the chariots of the other peoples, all of whom fell in the sea. Rabbi Chiya explains how Pharaoh harnessed the mares before the stallions, then the stallions before the mares, depending on whether he wanted them to run, or to fight. He compares this to the verse, "And Hashem went before them by day," saying that afterwards the Shechinah went behind the children of Yisrael.

61. וַיִּקַּח שֵׁשׁ מֵאוֹת וְגוֹ'. שֵׁשׁ מֵאוֹת אֲמַאי. א"ר יוֹסֵי, לָקֳבֵל מִנְיָינָא דְּיִשְׂרָאֵל, דִּכְתִּיב כְּשֵׁשׁ מֵאוֹת אֶלֶף רַגְלִי. בָּחוּר: לָקֳבֵל הַגְּבָרִים דְּאִינּוּן עִקָּרָא דְּכָל יִשְׂרָאֵל. וְכָל רֶכֶב מִצְרָיִם: שְׁאַר רְתִיכִין, דְּאִינּוּן טְפֵלִין לַאֲחוֹרֵי, לָקֳבֵל הַטַּף דִּכְתִּיב לְבַד מִטָּף. וְכֹלָּא עָבֵיד בְּעֵיטָא דְּחַרְשׁוֹי וְחַכְמוֹי. וְשָׁלִישִׁים עַל כֻּלּוֹ, כֹּלָּא בְּחָכְמְתָא, לָקֳבֵל דַּרְגִּין עִלָּאִין, תְּרֵין וְחָד. ר' יִצְחָק אָמַר, כְּתַרְגּוּמוֹ, וּמְזָרְזִין. זְרִיזִין הֲווֹ בְּכֹלָּא.

61. "And he took six hundred chosen chariots" (Ibid. 7). HE ASKS: Why 600 chariots? Rabbi Yosi said: This corresponds to the number of the children of Yisrael, as is written: "About six hundred thousand men on foot" (Shemot 12:37). The word "chosen" corresponds to the men THAT WERE IN YISRAEL, who were the principal part of all the nation of Yisrael. "And all the chariots of Egypt," were all the other chariots that were secondary and behind THE SIX HUNDRED THAT WERE MENTIONED EARLIER. They correspond to the children IN YISRAEL WHO WERE NOT INCLUDED IN THE SIX HUNDRED THOUSAND MEN ON FOOT, BUT WERE SECONDARY TO THEM, as is said: "Besides children." He did everything according to the advice of his sorcerers and wise men. "And captains over every one of them." He did everything with wisdom, for they corresponded to the celestial levels – WHICH ARE PLACED two and one OVER THEM. Rabbi Yitzchak said: This accords with the Aramaic translation: 'stimulating officers', for they were swift in everything.

62. וַיִּקַּח שֵׁשׁ מֵאוֹת רֶכֶב בָּחוּר. ר׳ חִיָּיא אָמַר, כְּתִיב יִפְקוֹד יְיָ׳ עַל צְבָא הַמָּרוֹם בַּמָּרוֹם וְעַל מַלְכֵי הָאֲדָמָה עַל הָאֲדָמָה. בִּזְמְנָא דְקוּדְשָׁא בְּרִיךְ הוּא יָהִיב שֻׁלְטָנוּתָא לְרַבְרְבֵי עַמִּין לְעֵילָּא, יָהִיב לְהוּ לְעַמָּא דִּלְהוֹן לְתַתָּא. וּבְשַׁעֲתָא דְנָחִית לוֹן מִדַּרְגֵּיהוֹן דִּלְעֵילָּא, נָחִית לוֹן לְעַמָּא לְתַתָּא, וַיִּקַּח שֵׁשׁ מֵאוֹת רֶכֶב בָּחוּר, הָא מְמָנָא דִּלְהוֹן, וְאוּקְמוּהָ, דְּדָבַר רְתִיכִין דִּשְׁאַר עַמִּין, וְכֻלְּהוּ נָפְלוּ בְּמַשְׁרִיתָא דְסִיסְרָא לְבָתַר וְהַיְינוּ בָּחוּר וְכֹל רֶכֶב מִצְרָיִם.

62. "And he took six hundred chosen chariots." Rabbi Chiya said: It is written, "That Hashem shall punish the host of the high ones on high, and the kings of the earth upon the earth" (Yeshayah 24:21). At the time that the Holy One, blessed be He, gives dominion to the ministers of the nations above, He gives it to their nations below; and when He brings them down from their grade above, He brings down their nations below. "And he took six hundred chosen chariots." It was their minister WHO TOOK THEM. We have established that he led the chariots of the other peoples, FOR THESE SIX HUNDRED CHARIOTS WERE NOT FROM EGYPT, BUT WERE ONLY FROM THE OTHER NATIONS. They all fell in the army camp of Sisra. And this is the meaning of "SIX HUNDRED CHARIOTS chosen." Afterwards, "all the chariots of Egypt," FOR ONCE IT IS WRITTEN: "AND ALL THE CHARIOTS OF EGYPT," THEN "SIX HUNDRED CHOSEN CHARIOTS" IS SUPERFLUOUS. CERTAINLY, "SIX HUNDRED CHOSEN CHARIOTS" IS ONLY FROM THE OTHER NATIONS, AND THEREFORE IT SAYS AFTERWARDS, "AND ALL THE CHARIOTS OF EGYPT."

63. כְּתִיב לְסֻסָתִי בְּרִכְבֵי פַרְעֹה דִּמִּיתִיךְ רַעְיָתִי. תָּא חֲזֵי, כְּדוּגְמַת סוּסְיָא נוּקְבָא, אִתְחָזֵי לְהוֹן לְסוּסֵיהוֹן דְּפַרְעֹה, וְאוּקְמוּהָ. אֶלָּא לְסוּסָתִי בְּרִכְבֵי פַרְעֹה, תָּא חֲזֵי, פַּרְעֹה בְּשַׁעֲתָא דַּהֲוָה רָדִיף אֲבָתְרַיְיהוּ דְּיִשְׂרָאֵל, מַה עָבֵד, נָטַל סוּסְוָון נוּקְבָן, וְכָפַת לוֹן בִּרְתִיכוֹי בְּקַדְמֵיתָא, וְסוּסִין דּוּכְרָאֵי כָּפַת לוֹן לַאֲחוֹרֵיהוֹן, וַהֲווֹ מְזַיְינִין דּוּכְרֵי לָקֳבֵל נוּקְבֵי, וְנוּקְבֵי לָא בָּעָאן, וְאוֹחֲן לְמֵיזָל. כֵּיוָן דְּקָרִיב לְגַבַּיְיהוּ דְיִשְׂרָאֵל, נָטַל נוּקְבֵי וְשַׁוֵּי לוֹן לַאֲחוֹרֵי, וְסוּסְוָון דּוּכְרִין לְקַדְמִין, לְאַבְאָשָׁא לְיִשְׂרָאֵל, וּלְאַגָּחָא בְּהוּ קְרָבָא.

5. “And he took six hundred chosen chariots”

63. It is written: “I compare you, O my love, to a mare of the chariots of Pharaoh” (Shir Hashirim 1:9). Come and behold: he appeared in the image of a mare to Pharaoh’s horses, AND THEREFORE THEY CHASED AFTER HER, INTO THE SEA. And they explained this. But, “to a mare of the chariots of Pharaoh.” Come and behold: when Pharaoh was chasing after the children of Yisrael, what did he do? He took female horses and harnessed them to the chariot up front first, and harnessed male horses behind them. The males warmed to the females, but the females were reluctant and hastened to run. When they approached Yisrael, he took the females and placed them behind and the male horses in front in order to do harm to Yisrael and to war against them, BECAUSE THE MALE HORSES WERE STRONGER THAN THE FEMALES FOR WAR.

64. כְּגַוְונָא דָּא, וַיְיָ׳ הוֹלֵךְ לִפְנֵיהֶם יוֹמָם, וּבָתַר חָזְרָה שְׁכִינְתָּא לַאֲחוֹרֵיהוֹן דְּיִשְׂרָאֵל, דִּכְתִּיב וַיִּסַּע מַלְאַךְ הָאֱלֹהִים וְגוֹ׳. בְּגִינֵי כַּךְ דִּמִּיתִיךְ רַעְיָתִי.

64. Similar to this: “And Hashem went before them by day” (Shemot 13:21). Afterwards, the Shechinah returned to the rear of Yisrael, as it is written: “And the angel of Hashem...moved and went behind them” (Shemot 14:19). Therefore, “I compare you, O my love...”

6. "And when Pharaoh drew near"

A Synopsis

Rabbi Yosi tells us that Pharaoh actually caused the children of Yisrael to come closer to the Holy One, blessed be He, because it is in times of tribulation that they remember and pray to Him. Then He becomes full of compassion for them. Speaking of Moses, Rabbi Shimon said that the shepherd of the people is really the whole people, for if he is deserving then all the people are righteous, and if he is not, the people are punished because of him. Rabbi Yehuda concludes that the merit of Jacob protected the Congregation of Yisrael.

.65 וּפַרְעֹה הִקְרִיב, וְהַאי קְרָא הָא אוּקְמוּהָ. דְּאַקְרִיב לְכָל חֵילוֹי וּרְתִיכוֹי, לְאַגָּחָא קְרָבָא. וְתוּ וּפַרְעֹה הִקְרִיב. רִבִּי יוֹסֵי אָמַר, הָא אִתְּמַר דְּקָרִיב לוֹן לִתְשׁוּבָה. וּפַרְעֹה הִקְרִיב.

65. "And when Pharaoh drew near" (Shemot 14:10). This passage has already established that he brought close his whole army and chariot riders to do battle. Rabbi Yosi said: We have learned here that he drew them closer to repentance; THEREFORE IT IS WRITTEN: "And when Pharaoh drew near," OTHERS AND NOT 'AND PHARAOH DREW NEAR' HIMSELF.

.66 כְּתִיב יְיָ' בַּצַּר פְּקָדוּךָ צָקוּן לַחַשׁ וְגוֹ'. בַּצַּר פְּקָדוּךָ: לָא פַּקְדִין יִשְׂרָאֵל לְקוּדְשָׁא בְּרִיךְ הוּא, בְּשַׁעֲתָא דְּנַיְיחָא, אֶלָּא בְּשַׁעֲתָא דְּעָקִין לְהוּ, וּכְדֵין כֻּלְּהוּ פַּקְדִין לֵיהּ. צָקוּן לַחַשׁ: וְכֻלְּהוּ צַלָּאן בִּצְלוֹתִין וּבְבָעוּתִין, וְאָרִיקוּ קָמֵיהּ צְלוֹתִין. אֵימָתַי. מוּסָרְךָ לָמוֹ, בְּשַׁעֲתָא דְּפָקִיד לוֹן קוּדְשָׁא בְּרִיךְ הוּא בִּרְצוּעוֹי. כְּדֵין קוּדְשָׁא בְּרִיךְ הוּא קָאֵים עֲלַיְיהוּ בְּרַחֲמֵי, וְנִיחָא קָמֵיהּ הַהוּא קָלָא דִּלְהוֹן, בְּגִין לְאִתְפָּרְעָא מִן שַׂנְאֵיהוֹן, וְאִתְמְלֵי עֲלַיְיהוּ בְּרַחֲמֵי.

66. It is written: "Hashem, in trouble have they sought You, they poured out a silent prayer" (Yeshayah 26:16). "In trouble have they sought You," MEANS Yisrael did not seek the Holy One, blessed be He, at times of comfort. Only when they have trouble do they all remember and seek Him. "They poured out a silent prayer." they all pray with prayers and beseeching, and pour out prayers before Him. When? "When Your chastening was upon them" (Ibid.), at the time that the Holy One, blessed be He, chastened them with His whip. The Holy One, blessed be He, stands over them with Mercy. Their voice is favorable to Him in order to take revenge from their enemies, and He becomes full of compassion for them.

67. כְּמָה דְּאוֹקִימְנָא, מְתָל לְיוֹנָה עִם הַנֵּץ וְכוּ׳, כַּךְ יִשְׂרָאֵל הֲווֹ קְרִיבִין לְיַמָּא, וַהֲווֹ חָמָאן לְיַמָּא קָמַיְיהוּ. אָזִיל וְסָעִיר וְגַלְגַּלּוֹהִי זַקְפִין לְעֵילָּא, הֲווֹ דְּחִילִין. זָקְפוּ עֵינַיְיהוּ וְחָמוּ לְפַרְעֹה וּלְמַשִׁירְיָיתֵיהּ, וְאַבְנֵי גִּירִין וּבַלִּסְטְרָאִין, כְּדֵין וַיִּירְאוּ מְאֹד. מַה עָבְדוּ, וַיִּצְעֲקוּ בְּנֵי יִשְׂרָאֵל מַאן גָּרִים הַאי דְּקָרִיבוּ יִשְׂרָאֵל לְגַבֵּי אֲבוּהוֹן דִּלְעֵילָּא, פַּרְעֹה. הֲדָא הוּא דִּכְתִּיב וּפַרְעֹה הִקְרִיב וְהָא אִתְּמַר.

67. As we have explained the parable of the dove with the hawk, so it is with Yisrael. They were approaching the sea and saw the sea before them, raging and storming. Its waves were towering above, and they feared. They raised their eyes and saw Pharaoh and his army and flying stones and arrows, and they feared greatly. What did they do? "And the children of Yisrael cried out." Who caused the children of Yisrael to come closer to their Father in heaven? Pharaoh. This is what is written: "And when Pharaoh drew near." It has already been explained.

68. וַיֹּאמֶר מֹשֶׁה אֶל הָעָם אַל תִּירָאוּ הִתְיַצְּבוּ וּרְאוּ אֶת יְשׁוּעַת יְיָ׳. אָמַר רִבִּי שִׁמְעוֹן זַכָּאָה חוּלָקֵיהוֹן דְּיִשְׂרָאֵל, דְּהָא רַעְיָא כְּמֹשֶׁה אָזִיל בְּגַוַּויְיהוּ. כְּתִיב וַיִּזְכּוֹר יְמֵי עוֹלָם מֹשֶׁה עַמּוֹ. וַיִּזְכּוֹר יְמֵי עוֹלָם: דָּא קוּדְשָׁא בְּרִיךְ הוּא. מֹשֶׁה עַמּוֹ: שָׁקִיל הֲוָה מֹשֶׁה כְּכָל יִשְׂרָאֵל. וְאוֹלִיפְנָא מֵהָא, כִּי רַעְיָא דְּעַמָּא הוּא מַמָּשׁ עַמָּא כֻּלְּהוּ, אִי אִיהוּ זָכֵי, עַמָּא כֻּלְּהוּ זָכָאן. וְאִי אִיהוּ לָא זָכֵי, עַמָּא כֻּלְּהוּ לָא זָכָאן וְאִתְעֲנָשׁוּ בְּגִינֵיהּ, וְהָא אוּקְמוּהָ.

68. "And Moses said to the people, 'Fear not, stand still and see the salvation of Hashem'" (Shemot 14:13). Rabbi Shimon said: Fortunate is the portion of Yisrael that a shepherd like Moses goes among them. It is written: "Then He remembered the days of old, Moses, and his people"

(Yeshayah 63:11). "Then He remembered the days of old" refers to the Holy One, blessed be He; "Moses, and his people," because Moses was equal to all of Yisrael. We learned from this that the shepherd of the people is really the whole people. If he merits, then all the people are righteous. If he does not merit, then all of the people have no merit and are punished because of him. This has already been explained.

69. הִתְיַצְּבוּ וּרְאוּ, לֵית לְכוּ לְאַגָּחָא קְרָבָא, דְּהָא קוּדְשָׁא בְּרִיךְ הוּא, יַגִּיחַ קְרָבָא בְּגִינֵיכוֹן, כְּמָה דְּאַתְּ אָמֵר, יְיָ׳ יִלָּחֵם לָכֶם וְאַתֶּם תַּחֲרִישׁוּן. תָּא חֲזֵי, הַהוּא לֵילְיָא, כָּנַשׁ קוּדְשָׁא בְּרִיךְ הוּא לְפָמַלְיָא דִּילֵיהּ, וְדָאִין דִּינַיְיהוּ דְּיִשְׂרָאֵל, וְאִלְמָלֵא דְּאַקְדִּימוּ אֲבָהָן עֲלַיְיהוּ דְּיִשְׂרָאֵל, לָא אִשְׁתֵּזִיבוּ מִן דִּינָא. רִבִּי יְהוּדָה אָמַר, זְכוּתָא דְּיַעֲקֹב אַגִּין עֲלַיְיהוּ דְּיִשְׂרָאֵל, הה״ד לוּלֵי יְיָ׳ שֶׁהָיָה לָנוּ יֹאמַר נָא יִשְׂרָאֵל, יִשְׂרָאֵל סָבָא.

69. "Stand still and see." You do not have to do battle because the Holy One, blessed be He, will do battle for you, as written: "Hashem shall fight for you, and you shall hold your peace" (Ibid. 14). Come and behold: that night, the Holy One, blessed be He, gathered His retinue and Judged the Judgment of Yisrael. If the Patriarchs had not hastened TO PRAY for Yisrael, they would not have been saved from the Judgment. Rabbi Yehuda said: the merit of Jacob protected the Congregation of Yisrael. This is what is written: "If not for Hashem, Who was with us, let Yisrael now say" (Tehilim 124:1), who IS Yisrael Saba, NAMELY JACOB.

7. “Hashem shall fight for you, and you shall hold your peace”

A Synopsis

Rabbi Aba says that one who observes the Sabbath is as though he observed the whole Torah, as the Sabbath is the delight of everything. One should invite the Sabbath in, like a guest. On the Sabbath secular speech is forbidden because it stimulates secular things above, and the Sabbath becomes blemished. When Pharaoh was coming to do battle with Yisrael, “Hashem shall fight for you, and you shall hold your peace”; this meant that the arousal took place from above – the children of Yisrael did not need to arouse anything from below. Rabbi Yosi wonders why if Hashem is always a connotation of Mercy, there seemed to be no mercy in the act of drowning the Egyptians. Rabbi Yehuda quotes Rabbi Shimon as saying that the Judgment had been tempered with Mercy since God had desired their honor that they be buried in the ground, and He had stretched out his hand so the earth would accept them. If Yisrael had aroused from below, Judgment would not have been executed with Mercy. Even though Hashem does Judgment, He is still compassionate for His creations.

70. יְיָ יִלָּחֵם לָכֶם וְאַתֶּם תַּחֲרִישׁוּן. רִבִּי אַבָּא פָּתַח אִם תָּשִׁיב מִשַּׁבָּת רַגְלֶךָ עֲשׂוֹת חֲפָצֶיךָ בְּיוֹם קָדְשִׁי. זַכָּאִין אִינּוּן יִשְׂרָאֵל, דְּקוּדְשָׁא בְּרִיךְ הוּא אִתְרְעֵי בְּהוֹן, לְאִתְדַּבְּקָא בְּהוּ, מִכָּל שְׁאַר עַמִּין דְּעָלְמָא, וּמִגּוֹ רְחִימוּתָא דִּלְהוֹן, קָרִיב לוֹן לְגַבֵּיהּ, וְיָהַב לוֹן אוֹרַיְיתָא, וְיָהַב לוֹן שַׁבָּת, דְּאִיהוּ קַדִּישָׁא מִכָּל שְׁאַר יוֹמִין, וְנַיְיחָא מִכֹּלָּא, וְחֶדְוָה דְּכֹלָּא, וְשָׁקִיל שַׁבָּת, לָקֳבֵל אוֹרַיְיתָא כֻּלָּא, וּמַאן דְּנָטִיר שַׁבָּת, כְּאִילּוּ נָטִיר אוֹרַיְיתָא כֻּלָּא.

70. “Hashem shall fight for you, and you shall hold your peace” (Shemot 14:14). Rabbi Aba opened the discussion, saying: “If you restrain your foot because of the Shabbat, from pursuing your business on My Holy Day” (Yeshayah 58:13). Fortunate are Yisrael that the Holy One, blessed be He, desires them and wishes to join with them more than all the nations of the world. Because of His love for them, He brought them close to Him and gave them the Torah and the Shabbat, which is holier than all the other days. And IN IT is rest from everything, and the joy of everyone. Shabbat is equal to the entire Torah, and one who observes the Shabbat is as though he observed the whole Torah.

71. וְקָרָאתָ לַשַּׁבָּת עוֹנֶג, עִנּוּגָא דְּכֹלָּא, עִנּוּגָא דְּנַפְשָׁא וְגוּפָא עִנּוּגָא דְּעִלָּאִין וְתַתָּאִין. וְקָרָאתָ לַשַּׁבָּת, מַאי וְקָרָאתָ. דְּיַזְמִין לֵיהּ. כד״א, מִקְרָאֵי קֹדֶשׁ, כְּלוֹמַר, זְמִינִין, כְּמָה דִּמְזַמִּין אוּשְׁפִּיזָא לְבֵיתֵיהּ. וְע״ד וְקָרָאתָ לַשַּׁבָּת עֹנֶג, דְּיַזְמִין לֵיהּ, כְּמָה דִּמְזַמְּנִין אוּשְׁפִּיזָא, בְּפָתוֹרָא מְתַקְּנָא, בְּבֵיתָא מְתַקְּנָא כַּדְקָא יֵאוֹת, בְּמֵיכְלָא וּבְמִשְׁתְּיָא כַּדְקָא יֵאוֹת, יַתִּיר עַל שְׁאַר יוֹמִין. וְקָרָאתָ לַשַּׁבָּת מִבְּעוֹד יוֹם. לִקְדוֹשׁ יְיָ׳ מְכוּבָּד: דָּא יוֹם כִּפּוּרִים. תְּרֵי דְּאִינּוּן חַד. וְכִבַּדְתּוֹ מֵעֲשׂוֹת דְּרָכֶיךָ, כְּמָה דְּאוּקִימְנָא.

71. "And call the Shabbat a delight" (Ibid.). NAMELY, delight of all, delight of the soul and the body, delight of those above and those below. "And call the Shabbat." HE ASKS: What does "call" mean? HE ANSWERS: ITS MEANING IS that he should invite it, as is written: "holy gatherings (lit. 'callings of holiness')" (Vayikra 23:4), which means invited FROM THE HOLINESS, as when inviting a guest to his home. And, "And call the Shabbat a delight," is that you should call and invite it as you invite a guest with a set table, with a house which is in order as it should be, with proper food and drink, more than on the other days. "And call the Shabbat," meaning beforehand, THAT YOU SHOULD ADD FROM THE WEEKDAY TO THE HOLY. "The holy day of Hashem, Honorable" (Ibid.) is Yom Kippur (Day of Atonement), and they are two that are one, BECAUSE YOM KIPPUR AND SHABBAT ARE ONE. THEREFORE, IT SAYS IMMEDIATELY FOLLOWING THEM, "And you shall honor it, not doing your own ways" in the singular, as we explained.

72. מִמְּצוֹא חֶפְצְךָ וְדַבֵּר דָּבָר, וְהָא אִתְּמַר, בְּגִין דְּהַהִיא מִלָּה סַלְּקָא, וְאִתְּעַר מִלָּה דְּחוֹל לְעֵילָא. מַאן דִּמְזַמִּין אוּשְׁפִּיזָא, בֵּיהּ בָּעֵי לְאִשְׁתַּדְּלָא, וְלָא בְּאָחֳרָא.

72. "Nor pursuing your own business, nor speaking of vain matters" (Yeshayah 58:13). And it is explained THAT YOUR SPEECH OF SHABBAT SHOULD NOT BE LIKE YOUR SPEECH OF WEEKDAY. Because that talk, SECULAR SPEECH THAT IS SPOKEN ON SHABBAT, rises and stimulates secular things above. AND THE SHABBAT BECOMES BLEMISHED. One who invites a guest should strive to please him, and not someone else.

73. תָּא חֲזֵי הַהוּא מִלָּה דְּנָפִיק מִפּוּמֵיהּ דְּבַר נָשׁ, סַלְקָא וְאִתְּעַר אִתְעָרוּתָא לְעֵילָּא, אִי לְטָב, אִי לְבִישׁ. וּמַאן דְּיָתִיב בְּעִנּוּגָא דְּשַׁבְּתָא, אָסִיר לֵיהּ לְאִתְעָרָא מִלָּה דְּחוֹל, דְּהָא פָּגִים פְּגִימוּ בְּיוֹמָא קַדִּישָׁא. מַאן דְּיָתִיב בְּהִילּוּלָא דְּמַלְכָּא, לָא יִתְחָזֵי לְמִשְׁבַּק לְמַלְכָּא, וְיִתְעַסֵּק בְּאַחֲרָא.

73. Come and behold: that word that comes from the mouth of a person rises and stimulates an awakening above, either for good or for evil. And whoever dwells in the delight of Shabbat is forbidden to stir to secular subjects, because he causes a blemish on the Holy Day. One who participates in the celebration of a king is not permitted to forsake the king and deal with someone else.

74. וּבְכָל יוֹמָא בָּעֵי לְאַחֲזָאָה עוֹבָדָא, וּלְאִתְעֲרָא אַתְעָרוּתָא מִמָּה דְּאִצְטְרִיךְ. וּבְשַׁבָּת, בְּמִלֵּי דִּשְׁמַיָּא, וּבִקְדוּשָּׁה דְּיוֹמָא בָּעֵי לְאִתְעָרָא, וְלָא בְּמִלָּה אַחֲרָא.

74. Every day, it is necessary to perform an action to aweken FROM BELOW of what must be awakened. BUT on Shabbat, it is necessary to awaken ONLY in the words of the Name and the Holiness of the day, and not in any other thing. FOR AN AWAKENING FROM BELOW IS NOT NECESSARY ON SHABBAT.

75. תָּא חֲזֵי, הָכָא כַּד אִתְקְרִיב פַּרְעֹה לְאַגָּחָא קְרָבָא בְּהוּ בְּיִשְׂרָאֵל, בְּהַהִיא זִמְנָא, לָא בָּעֵי קוּדְשָׁא בְּרִיךְ הוּא, דְּיִתְעֲרוּן יִשְׂרָאֵל אִתְעָרוּתָא לְתַתָּא כְּלָל, דְּהָא אִתְעָרוּתָא לְעֵילָּא הוּא, דְּהָא אֲבָהָן אַקְדִּימוּ וְאַתְּעֲרוּ אִתְעָרוּתָא דָּא לְעֵילָּא, וּזְכוּתָא דִּלְהוֹן קָאֵים קָמֵיהּ, וְלָא בָּעָא קוּדְשָׁא בְּרִיךְ הוּא דְּיִשְׂרָאֵל יִתְעָרוּן לְתַתָּא כְּלָל. הֲדָא הוּא דִּכְתִּיב יְיָ׳ יִלָּחֵם לָכֶם וְאַתֶּם תַּחֲרִישׁוּן. תַּחֲרִישׁוּן וַדַּאי, וְלָא תִּתְעֲרוּן מִלָּה, דְּלָא אִצְטְרִיךְ לְכוּ, וְהָכָא אִתְכְּלִיל שְׁמָא קַדִּישָׁא בְּאַתְוָון רְשִׁימָן, וְהָא אִתְעֲרוּ בֵּיהּ חַבְרַיָּיא.

75. Come and behold: when Pharaoh approached to do battle with Yisrael, the Holy One, blessed be He, did not want Yisrael to awaken from below at all, because the Patriarchs preceded and caused this awakening from above. And their merit stood before Him. The Holy One, blessed be He, did not want Yisrael to arouse from below at all. This is the meaning of, "Hashem shall fight for you, and you shall hold your peace." Assuredly, you shall hold your peace, and do not arouse what is not needed by you. THE REASON IS MENTIONED LATER, and here the Holy Name is included in imprinted letters, YUD HEI VAV HEI, WHICH INDICATE MERCY, FOR IT SAYS, "HASHEM SHALL FIGHT FOR YOU," EVEN THOUGH YUD HEI VAV HEI IS MERCY AND WAR IS JUDGMENT. The friends have already commented on this, AS IS DISCUSSED LATER ON.

76. רִבִּי יוֹסֵי וְרִבִּי יְהוּדָה הֲווֹ אַזְלֵי בְּאָרְחָא. אָמַר רִבִּי יוֹסֵי לְרִבִּי יְהוּדָה, וַדַּאי תָּנִינָא, יְיָ׳, בְּכָל אֲתָר רַחֲמֵי, וְאַף עַל גַּב דְּאַגַּח קְרָבָא, וְעָבֵיד דִּינָא, הַהוּא דִּינָא בִּרְחִימוּתָא הוּא. וְהָכָא חֲמֵינָא, דִּכְתִּיב יְיָ׳ יִלָּחֵם לָכֶם, וְלָא אִתְחָזֵי בְּהַהוּא דִּינָא רַחֲמֵי כְּלָל, דְּהָא כְּתִיב לֹא נִשְׁאַר בָּהֶם עַד אֶחָד.

76. Rabbi Yosi and Rabbi Yehuda were traveling on the road. Rabbi Yosi said to Rabbi Yehuda: Most certainly, we have learned that Hashem is always a connotation of Mercy, and even though He carrys out wars and executes Judgment, that Judgment is with Mercy. Yet here we saw that it is written: "Hashem shall fight for you," but no Mercy was visible at all in that Judgment, for it is written: "There remained not so much as one of them" (Shemot 14:28).

77. אָמַר לֵיהּ, מִלָּה דָּא שְׁמַעְנָא מֵרִבִּי שִׁמְעוֹן דְּאָמַר, דַּאֲפִילּוּ הָכָא דִּינָא בְּרַחֲמֵי הֲוָה, דְּחָפָא עָלַיְיהוּ יַמָּא וּמִיתוּ, וּלְבָתַר אַפִּיק לוֹן יַמָּא, וְקוּדְשָׁא בְּרִיךְ הוּא בָּעָא בִּיקָרֵיהוֹן, וְאִתְקְבָרוּ בְּאַרְעָא, וְלָא בָּעָאת אַרְעָא לְקַבְּלָא לוֹן, עַד דְּאוֹשִׁיט לָהּ קוּדְשָׁא בְּרִיךְ הוּא יְמִינֵיהּ, וְקַבִּילַת לוֹן, הה״ד, נָטִיתָ יְמִינְךָ תִּבְלָעֵמוֹ אָרֶץ. וּבְגִין דָּא, הַאי דִּינָא בְּרַחֲמֵי הֲוָה.

77. He said to him: This subject I heard from Rabbi Shimon, for he said that there was Judgment with Mercy even here, because the sea covered them over, they perished, and afterwards the sea ejected them. But the Holy One, blessed be He, desired their honor, that they should be buried in the ground. The earth did not want to accept them until the Holy One, blessed be He, stretched out His right hand to her, and she accepted them. This is the meaning of: "You stretched out Your right hand, the earth swallowed them" (Shemot 15:12). And because of this, this Judgment was tempered with Mercy.

78. וְעַל דָּא, לָא בָּעָא קוּדְשָׁא בְּרִיךְ הוּא דְּיִתְעָרוּן יִשְׂרָאֵל מִלָּה בְּעָלְמָא, דְּאִי יִתְעָרוּן יִשְׂרָאֵל מִלָּה, לָא יִתְעָרוּן שְׁמָא דְּרַחֲמֵי, וְלָא יִתְעֲבִיד דִּינָא בְּרַחֲמֵי, הֲדָא הוּא דִּכְתִּיב יְיָ׳ יִלָּחֵם לָכֶם וְאַתֶּם תַּחֲרִישׁוּן, דְּלָא תִּתְעֲרוּן מִידִי. דְּהָא שְׁמָא דְּרַחֲמֵי בָּעֵי לְאִתְעָרָא עֲלַיְיהוּ, לְמֶעְבַּד דִּינָא בְּרַחֲמֵי. וְעַל דָּא בָּעֵי, דְּלָא תַּעַבְדוּן פְּגִימוּ, וְתִתְעֲרוּן מִלָּה אַחֲרָא.

78. For that reason, the Holy One, blessed be He, did not want the children of Yisrael to arouse anything in the world FROM BELOW. For if the children of Yisrael had aroused something FROM BELOW, the name of Mercy would not have been aroused, and Judgment would not have been executed with Mercy. This is what is written: "Hashem shall fight for you, and you shall hold your peace." You should not arouse anything, because the name of Mercy must be aroused upon them in order to do the Judgment with Mercy. Therefore, it is necessary not to make a blemish and arouse something else; NAMELY, JUDGMENT WITHOUT MERCY. AN AWAKENING FROM BELOW WOULD CAUSE THE ACTIVATION OF ONLY JUDGMENT.

79. אָמַר לֵיהּ, וְהָא כְּתִיב, וְיָצָא יְיָ׳ וְנִלְחַם בַּגּוֹיִם הָהֵם. אִי הָכִי דָּא דִּינָא בְּרַחֲמֵי הֲוָה. אָמַר לֵיהּ, הָכִי הֲוָה וַדַּאי, דִּינָא הוּא בְּרַחֲמֵי, דְּמוֹתָא דִּלְהוֹן לָא אִשְׁתְּכַח כְּמוֹתָנָא דִּשְׁאַר בְּנֵי עָלְמָא, אֶלָּא חָס עֲלַיְיהוּ קוּדְשָׁא בְּרִיךְ הוּא, דְּלָא יְהוֹן כְּמוֹתָנָא דִּשְׁאַר בְּנֵי עָלְמָא, דְּקָטִילוּ לוֹן, אֶלָּא בְּנַחַת בְּלָא צַעֲרָא, הָא דִּינָא בְּרַחֲמֵי אִיהוּ.

79. He said to him: But it is written, "Then shall Hashem go out, and fight against those nations" (Zecharyah 14:3). Was this Judgment with Mercy?! He said to him: Certainly, the Judgment was with Mercy because their death was not like the death of the other people of the world. Rather, the Holy One, blessed be He, had Mercy on them, so that their deaths should not be like those of the other people of the world. For they were slain gently, without pain, NAMELY, "HIS FLESH WAS CONSUMED AWAY WHILE HE STANDS UPON HIS FEET" (IBID. 12). Hence, the Judgment contained Mercy.

80. וּבְכָל אֲתָר, שְׁמָא דָּא, דִּינָא בְּרַחֲמֵי אִיהוּ, בַּר אֲתָר חַד, דִּכְתִּיב יְיָ׳ כַּגִּבּוֹר יֵצֵא וְגוֹ׳. וְכִי כַּגִּבּוֹר וְלֹא גִּבּוֹר. אֶלָּא יְשַׁנֵּי לְבוּשׁוֹי, וְיִלְבַּשׁ לְבוּשִׁין אַחֲרָנִין. כְּאִישׁ מִלְחָמוֹת, יְשַׁנֵּי זִינֵיהּ.

80. This Name always refers to Judgment with Mercy, except for one place, as written: "Hashem shall go forth like a mighty man..." (Yeshayah 42:13). HE ASKS: IS HASHEM ONLY like a mighty one, but not ACTUALLY mighty? HE SAYS: rather, He will change His garments and don other garments; THAT IS, HE WILL CHANGE HIS TRAIT OF MERCY AND DON THE GARMENT OF JUDGMENT. "Like a man of war" (Ibid.), shall He change his weapons FROM MERCY TO JUDGMENT. SO WE SEE THAT IN THIS PLACE, THE MERCY WAS CHANGED TO BECOME JUDGMENT.

81. וְעִם כָּל דָּא, דִּינָא הוּא יַתִּיר, אֲבָל רַחֲמֵי בֵּיהּ, כְּמָה דִּכְתִּיב, כַּגִּבּוֹר, וְלֹא גִּבּוֹר. כְּאִישׁ מִלְחָמוֹת, וְלֹא אִישׁ מִלְחָמוֹת. דְּוַדַּאי אַף עַל גַּב דְּעָבֵיד דִּינָא, חָס עַל עוֹבָדוֹי, וְעַל דָּא, יְיָ׳ יִלָּחֵם לָכֶם וַדַּאי וְאַתֶּם תַּחֲרִישׁוּן. זַכָּאָה חוּלָקֵהוֹן דְּיִשְׂרָאֵל, דְּקוּדְשָׁא בְּרִיךְ הוּא בָּרִיר לוֹן לְחוּלָקֵיהּ וְאַחֲסָנְתֵּיהּ, דִּכְתִּיב כִּי חֵלֶק יְיָ׳ עַמּוֹ יַעֲקֹב חֶבֶל נַחֲלָתוֹ.

81. And with all this, ONLY the Judgment is HERE more THAN MERCY, yet there is some Mercy here, as it is written, "like a mighty man," and not AN ACTUAL mighty man, WHO IS COMPLETELY JUDGMENT. "Like a man of war" (Ibid.), and not literally a man of war, WHO IS COMPLETELY JUDGMENT. Even though He does Judgment, He is still compassionate for His creations. And therefore, "Hashem shall fight for you," most certainly, "and you shall hold your peace," IN ORDER THAT YOU SHALL NOT AROUSE JUDGMENT ALONE, AS MENTIONED EARLIER. Blessed is the portion of Yisrael that the Holy One, blessed be He, has selected them for His portion and His legacy, as is written: "For the portion of Hashem is His people, Jacob is the lot of His inheritance" (Devarim 32:9).

8. "Why do you cry out to me"

A Synopsis

Rabbi Yehuda speaks about Jonah crying out to Hashem out of the belly of the fish. Rabbi Elazar confirms his statement that the fish died while Jonah was still in its belly, and says that when Jonah prayed his prayer, God revived the fish and brought it out to the dry land where it vomited out Jonah. He returns to the subject of the splitting of the sea, telling us that God told the children of Yisrael to go forward and refrain from speaking, because this was not a time for prayer.

82. וַיֹּאמֶר יְיָ׳ אֶל מֹשֶׁה מַה תִּצְעַק אֵלָי. מִלָּה דָּא הוּא אוּקְמוּהָ בְּסִפְרָא דִּצְנִיעוּתָא, וְתַמָּן הוּא רָזָא דִּילֵיהּ, וַיֹּאמֶר יְיָ׳ אֶל מֹשֶׁה. ר׳ יְהוּדָה פָּתַח וְאָמַר, וַיִּתְפַּלֵּל יוֹנָה אֶל יְיָ׳ אֱלֹהָיו מִמְּעֵי הַדָּגָה, מַה כְּתִיב לְעֵילָּא, וַיְמַן יְיָ׳ דָּג גָּדוֹל. וַיְמַן: כמד״א וַיְמַן לָהֶם הַמֶּלֶךְ דְּבַר יוֹם בְּיוֹמוֹ. אֲשֶׁר מִנָּה אֶת מַאֲכַלְכֶם.

82. "And Hashem said to Moses, 'Why do you cry out to Me?'" (Shemot 14:15). This is explained in Sifra Detzni'uta ('the Hidden Book), and there is its secret. "And Hashem said to Moses…" Rabbi Yehuda opened the discussion, saying: "Then Jonah prayed to Hashem his Elohim out of the fish's belly" (Yonah 2:2). In, "Now Hashem had appointed a great fish" (Ibid. 1), "appointed" MEANS as you say, "And the king appointed them a daily provision" (Daniel 1:5), as well as, "Who has appointed your food" (Ibid. 10), WHICH IS A TERM OF GIVING A PORTION.

83. אֲבָל הַאי קְרָא הָכִי מִבָּעֵי לֵיהּ, וַיְמַן יְיָ׳ אֶת יוֹנָה לַדָּג, דְּהוּא מָנָה הוּא דִּמְשַׁדֵּר לֵיהּ. אֶלָּא וַדַּאי, הַהוּא דָּג הוּא הֲוָה מָנָה לְיוֹנָה, לְנַטְרָא לֵיהּ מִן שְׁאַר נוּנֵי יַמָּא, וְיֶהֱוֵי גָּנִיז בְּגַוֵּיהּ. וְכֵיוָן דְּאַעֲלֵיהּ בְּגַוֵּיהּ, חָמָא יוֹנָה בְּמֵעוֹי, פּוּתְיָא דַּאֲתָר דְּמֵעוֹי כְּמוֹ הֵיכְלָא רַבְרְבָא, וּתְרֵין עֵינוֹי דְּהַהוּא נוּנָא, דְּנָהֲרִין כְּשִׁמְשָׁא, וְאֶבֶן טָבָא הֲוָה בְּמֵעוֹי, דְּנָהִיר לֵיהּ, וַהֲוָה חָמֵי כָּל מַה דִּי בְּיַמָּא וּבִתְהוֹמוֹי.

83. But this passage should have said, 'And Hashem appointed Jonah for the fish', for he was the portion that HASHEM sent to THE FISH. AND HE

ANSWERS: Assuredly, this fish was a portion for Jonah, to guard him from all the other fish of the sea, and that he would be concealed in it. As soon as HASHEM brought him into the fish, Jonah saw in its belly the breadth of his entrails, WHICH WAS like a large chamber, and the two eyes of the fish were brightly illuminating, like the sun. There was a precious stone in its entrails that shown on for him, and he saw everything existing in the sea and in its depths.

84. וְאִי תֵּימָא, אִי הָכִי, מַאי דִּכְתִּיב קָרָאתִי מִצָּרָה לִי, הָא לָא אִתְחָזֵי, דְּכָל הַאי רְוָוחָא הֲוָה לֵיהּ. אֶלָּא וַדַּאי, כֵּיוָן דְּאַחְמֵי לֵיהּ הַהוּא נוּנָא, כָּל מַה דִּי בְּיַמָּא וּבִתְהוֹמוֹי, מִית, דְּלָא יָכִיל תְּלַת יוֹמִין לְמִסְבַּל. כְּדֵין עָקַת לֵיהּ לְיוֹנָה.

84. And you may question the meaning of: "I cried to Hashem out of my distress (also: 'narrow')" (Yonah 2:3)? It does not seem FROM THIS that he had very much space. HE ANSWERS: Rather, after this fish showed him all that there is in the sea and in the depths, it died. For it could not tolerate him for three days. Then it became 'narrow' for Jonah.

85. דְּאָמַר רִבִּי אֶלְעָזָר, כֵּיוָן דְּחָמָא יוֹנָה כָּל הַהוּא רְוָוחָא, הֲוָה חַדֵּי. אָמַר קוּדְשָׁא בְּרִיךְ הוּא, וּמַה תִּבְעֵי יַתִּיר, לְהָא אֲעִילְנָא לָךְ הָכָא. מָה עֲבַד, קָטַל לְהַהוּא נוּנָא וּמִית, וְכָל שְׁאַר נוּנֵי יַמָּא, הֲווֹ סַחֲרֵי סַחֲרָנֵיהּ דְּהַהוּא נוּנָא, דָּא נָשִׁיךְ לֵיהּ מֵהַאי גִּיסָא, וְדָא נָשִׁיךְ לֵיהּ מֵהַאי גִּיסָא. כְּדֵין חָמָא יוֹנָה גַּרְמוֹי בְּעָקוּ, מִיַּד וַיִּתְפַּלֵּל יוֹנָה אֶל יְיָ'.

85. Rabbi Elazar said: When Jonah saw all that spaciousness, he rejoiced. The Holy One, blessed be He, said: And what do you need more, is it for this that I brought you here? What did THE HOLY ONE, BLESSED BE HE, do? He slew that fish and it died. All the other fish circled around the fish; one bit it from one side and another bit from another side. Then Jonah saw himself in distress. Immediately, "Jonah prayed to Hashem."

86. בְּקַדְמֵיתָא דָּג, וְהַשְׁתָּא דָּגָה. כד"א, וְהַדָּגָה אֲשֶׁר בַּיְאוֹר מֵתָה. וּכְדֵין כְּתִיב, קָרָאתִי מִצָּרָה לִי. וְלָא כְּתִיב הָיִיתִי בַּצָּרָה, אוֹ יָשַׁבְתִּי

בַּצָּרָה, אֶלָּא קָרָאתִי, מֵהַהוּא עָקוּ דְּעָאקִין לִי נוּנֵי יַמָּא. מִבֶּטֶן שְׁאוֹל שִׁוַּעְתִּי, דְּהָא מִית. וְלָא כְּתִיב מִבֶּטֶן חַי, אוֹ מִבֶּטֶן דָּג, אֶלָּא דְּוַדַּאי הֲוָה מִית.

86. HE ASKS: First the verse refers to it as "*dag*" ('fish': masc.) and then it refers to it "*dagah*" ('fish': fem.). HE ANSWERS: IT IS BECAUSE IT HAD ALREADY DIED, AS IS WRITTEN: "And the fish (Heb. *dagah*) in the river died" (Shemot 7:21). Then it is written: "I cried to Hashem out of my distress," and it is not written 'I was in distress' or 'I dwelt in distress', but rather, " I cried" out of distress, as the fish of the sea distressed me. "Out of the belly of Sheol I cried" (Yonah 2:3), for it had died. It is not written: 'out of the belly of a living thing,' or 'out the belly of a fish,' but rather it was definitely dead, AND THEREFORE IT WAS CALLED *'SHEOL'*.

87. כֵּיוָן דְּצַלֵּי צְלוֹתֵיהּ, קַבִּיל לֵיהּ קוּדְשָׁא בְּרִיךְ הוּא, וְאַחְיֵיהּ לֵיהּ לְהַאי נוּנָא, וְאַפִּיק לֵיהּ לְיַבֶּשְׁתָּא לְעֵינֵיהוֹן דְּכֹלָּא. דִּכְתִּיב, וַיֹּאמֶר יְיָ' לַדָּג וַיָּקֵא אֶת יוֹנָה. וְחָמוּ כֻּלְּהוּ, עֲבִידְתָּא דְּקוּדְשָׁא בְּרִיךְ הוּא.

87. As soon as he prayed his prayer, the Holy One, blessed be He, accepted it. He revived that fish and brought it out to the dry land before the eyes of everyone, as is written: "And Hashem spoke to the fish and it vomited out Jonah" (Yonah 2:11). They all saw the work of the Holy One, blessed be He.

88. מַה כְּתִיב, וַיִּתְפַּלֵּל יוֹנָה אֶל יְיָ' אֱלֹהָיו מִמְּעֵי הַדָּגָה, לַאֲתָר דַּהֲוָה קָשִׁיר בֵּיהּ, מַשְׁמַע דִּכְתִּיב יְיָ' אֱלֹהָיו, וְלָא כְּתִיב וַיִּתְפַּלֵּל אֶל יְיָ' וְלָא יַתִּיר, אֶלָּא יְיָ' אֱלֹהָיו. אוּף הָכָא, וַיֹּאמֶר יְיָ' אֶל מֹשֶׁה מַה תִּצְעַק אֵלָי. אֵלַי דַּיְיקָא.

88. It is written, "Then Jonah prayed to Hashem his Elohim from the fish's belly," MEANING THAT HE PRAYED to the place to which he was bound, THE ASPECT OF MALCHUT. This is understood from the words: "Hashem his Elohim." It is not written: 'Then he prayed to Hashem' and nothing more, but "Hashem his Elohim," WHICH ALLUDES TO THE ASPECT TO WHICH HE WAS BOUND. Here also, "And Hashem said to Moses, 'Why do you cry to Me?'" "...to Me," NAMELY, TO MY ASPECT, WHICH IS

TIFERET, TO WHICH MOSES WAS CONNECTED. BUT RATHER IT WAS DEPENDENT UPON MAZAL AS IT IS WRITTEN THAT THE SPLITTING OF THE RED SEA IS DERIVED FROM MAZAL, THE SECRET OF THE HOLY *DIKNA* ('BEARD').

89. דַּבֵּר אֶל בְּנֵי יִשְׂרָאֵל וְיִסָּעוּ. וְיִסָּעוּ מִלְּאַסְגָּאָה מִלִּין, לָאו עִידָּנָא דִּצְלוֹתָא הַשְׁתָּא. וְיִסָּעוּ, וְכִי לְאָן אֲתָר פָּקִד לוֹן דְּיִנְטְלוּן, דְּהָא עַל יַמָּא הֲווֹ שָׁרָאן. אֶלָּא אַהְדָּר לְעֵילָּא, דִּכְתִּיב מַה תִּצְעַק אֵלָי, דְּהָא כֻּלְּהוּ בַּאֲתָר דָּא קַיְימֵי. וְע״ד וַיִּסְעוּ, יִנְטְלוּן מִן דָּא, דְּלָאו עִדָּנָא הוּא.

89. "Speak to the children of Yisrael, that they go forward" (Shemot 14:15), MEANING that they should go forward and refrain from speaking excessively, because now is not a time for prayer. HE ASKS: "That they go forward." To which place did He command them to go, seeing that they were camping by the sea? HE ANSWERS: It refers to the above, as it is written, "Why do you cry to Me?" WHICH MEANS TIFERET, AS MENTIONED EARLIER. They all stood in this place, IN TIFERET, FOR ALL THE CHILDREN OF YISRAEL WERE CONNECTED TO TIFERET. Therefore, he said, "that they go forward," that the children of Yisrael should go forth FROM TIFERET, AND COME AND CONNECT WITH MAZAL. WHICH IS *DIKNA* ('BEARD'), AS MENTIONED. For now is not the time FOR TIFERET, BUT RATHER THE MATTER DEPENDS UPON MAZAL, AS MENTIONED BEFORE.

9. “But lift up your rod”

A Synopsis

Rabbi Elazar says that the rod, whether it is called ‘the rod of Moses’ or ‘the rod of Elohim’, is for the purpose of rekindling the aspect of Gvurah. Rabbi Shimon clarifies that since water emerges from the side of Gvurah, “lift up your rod” is to dry up the water, and “stretch out your hand” is to return the water and spill it over the Egyptians.

90. וְאַתָּה הָרֵם אֶת מַטְּךָ וְגוֹ׳. הָרֵם אֶת מַטְּךָ, דִּי בֵּיהּ רָשִׁים שְׁמָא קַדִּישָׁא, אַרְכִּין יְדָךְ בְּסִטְרָא דִּשְׁמָא קַדִּישָׁא, וְכֵיוָן דְּיֶחֱמוּן מַיָּא שְׁמָא קַדִּישָׁא, יָעַרְקוּן מִנֵּיהּ. וְעַל דָּא, וּנְטֵה אֶת יָדְךָ, לְסִטְרָא חֲדָא, דְּסִטְרִין אַחֲרָנִין דְּהַהוּא מַטֶּה, אִצְטְרִיךְ לֵיהּ לְמִלִּין אַחֲרָנִין.

90. “But lift up your rod” (Shemot 14:16). Lift up your rod, upon which is etched the Holy Name, and stretch your hand to the side of the Holy Name. As soon as the waters see the Holy Name, they will flee from it. Therefore, stretch your hand to one side OF THE ROD, because the other sides of the rod will be necessary for other matters, NAMELY, TO HIT THE ROCK.

91. אָמַר רִבִּי אֶלְעָזָר, חֲמֵינָא, דִּזְמְנִין אִתְקְרֵי הַאי מַטֶּה, מַטֵּה הָאֱלֹהִים, וּלְזִמְנִין אִתְקְרֵי מַטֵּה דְּמֹשֶׁה. אָמַר ר׳ שִׁמְעוֹן בְּסִפְרָא דְּרַב הַמְנוּנָא סָבָא, שַׁפִּיר קָאָמַר, דְּכֻלְּהוּ חַד, בֵּין תֵּימָא דְּקוּדְשָׁא בְּרִיךְ הוּא, וּבֵין תֵּימָא דְּמֹשֶׁה, וְהַאי מַטֶּה, לְאַתְעֲרָא סִטְרָא דִּגְבוּרָה. וְעַל דָּא, וּנְטֵה אֶת יָדְךָ, יְדָא דִּשְׂמָאלָא, דְּאִיהוּ בְּסִטְרָא דִּגְבוּרָה.

91. Rabbi Elazar said: I see that sometimes this rod is called ‘the rod of Elohim’ and sometimes it is called ‘the rod of Moses’. Rabbi Shimon said: In the book of Rabbi Hamnuna Saba (the elder), he says that it is all one, whether it says ‘THE ROD of the Holy One, blessed be He’, or ‘THE ROD of Moses’. The purpose of this rod is to rekindle the aspect of Gvurah. Therefore, THE VERSE SAYS, “Stretch out your hand,” WHICH MEANS the left hand, which is at the side of Gvurah.

92. אָמַר רִבִּי שִׁמְעוֹן, וַוי לְאִינוּן דְּלָא חָמָאן, וְלָא מִסְתַּכְּלִין

בְּאוֹרַיְיתָא, וְאוֹרַיְיתָא קָארֵי קָמַיְיהוּ בְּכָל יוֹמָא, וְלָא מַשְׁגִּיחִין. תָּא חֲזֵי, בְּסִטְרָא דִּגְבוּרָה מִתְעָרֵי מַיָּא בְּעָלְמָא, וְנַפְקֵי מַיָּא, וְהַשְׁתָּא בָּעֵי קוּדְשָׁא בְּרִיךְ הוּא לְנַגְבָּא מַיָּא, אֲמַאי וּנְטֵה אֶת יָדְךָ, דְּאִיהוּ שְׂמָאלָא.

92. Rabbi Shimon said: Woe to those who do not see and do not look at the Torah. The Torah calls before them daily but they do not pay attention. Come and behold: water rises in the world and water emerges from the side of Gvurah. But now the Holy One, blessed be He, wanted to dry up the water. Thus, why DOES THE VERSE SAY, "And stretch out your hand," which is the left hand, NAMELY GVURAH?

93. אֶלָּא הָרֵם אֶת מַטְּךָ, לְנַגְבָּא מַיָּא. וּנְטֵה אֶת יָדְךָ, לְאָתָבָא מַיָּא, לְאַתְעֲרָא סִטְרָא דִּגְבוּרָה, וּלְאָתָבָא מַיָּא עַל מִצְרַיִם. וּבְגִין כָּךְ, תְּרֵין מִלִּין הָכָא, דִּכְתִּיב הָרֵם אֶת מַטְּךָ, וּנְטֵה אֶת יָדְךָ עַל הַיָּם וּבְקָעֵהוּ.

93. HE ANSWERS: Rather, "lift up your rod," is to dry up the water, and "stretch out your hand," is to return the water, to activate the side of Gvurah and to turn the water on Egypt. Therefore, there are two things here, for it is written: "Lift up your rod, and stretch out your hand over the sea, and divide it." ONE ELEMENT IS TO DRY OUT THE WATER, AND THE OTHER IS TO TURN THE WATER OVER EGYPT.

94. וְהָא תְּהוֹמֵי הֲווֹ. אֶלָּא קוּדְשָׁא בְּרִיךְ הוּא, עָבֵד נִיסָא גּוֹ נִיסָא, כד"א קָפְאוּ תְהוֹמוֹת בְּלֶב יָם. וַהֲוָה אַזְלִין בְּיַבֶּשְׁתָּא בְּגוֹ יַמָּא, הה"ד וַיָּבֹאוּ בְּנֵי יִשְׂרָאֵל בְּתוֹךְ הַיָּם בַּיַּבָּשָׁה.

94. HE ASKS: HOW WAS IT POSSIBLE TO DRY THE LAND IN THE MIDST OF THE SEA, for there were pits IN IT? HE ANSWERS: THE Holy One, blessed be He, performed a miracle within a miracle, as is written: "And the depths were congealed in the heart of the sea" (Shemot 15:8). They were walking on the dry ground within the sea. This is what is written: "And the children of Yisrael went into the midst of the sea on the dry ground" (Shemot 14:22).

10. "And He took off their chariot wheels"

A Synopsis

Rabbi Shimon opens with "And He took off their chariot wheels," and, "Now as I beheld the living creatures, behold one wheel upon the earth by the living creatures." He tells us that The Holy One, blessed be He establishes His dominion through the Patriarchs. Jacob is attached to the Tree of Life, which never has any death in it, so God made him the chosen among the Patriarchs. The thrust of this whole section is that when the Holy One, blessed be He wants to remove someone from power on this earth, He first removes their dominion above. We read about the legions of above with all the Chariots entwined together and under the command of the highest holy beast. They all go and swim in the great sea, where the waves are judgments. Rabbi Yitzchak tells us that when the children of Yisrael approached the Red Sea, the Holy One, blessed be He called the minister who was appointed over the sea and told him that it was time to fulfill the condition that had been made when the sea was first created, that it should split before His children when the time came. And the reason that the Egyptians were killed by the sea was that the upper sea aroused against them. The minister over Egypt had oppressed the Congregation of Yisrael with enslavement, so he was broken first, and then all the kingdoms below were broken.

95. וַיָּסַר אֶת אוֹפַן מַרְכְּבוֹתָיו. ר״ש פָּתַח, וָאֵרֶא הַחַיּוֹת וְהִנֵּה אוֹפַן אֶחָד בָּאָרֶץ אֵצֶל הַחַיּוֹת. הַאי קְרָא אוּקְמוּהָ וְאִתְּמַר, אֲבָל ת״ח, קוּדְשָׁא בְּרִיךְ הוּא בְּכוֹלָּא אִתְחָזֵי שֻׁלְטָנוּתָא דִּילֵיהּ, וְשֻׁלְטָנֵיהּ דִּי לָא תַּעְדֵּי לְעָלַם וּלְעָלְמֵי עָלְמִין.

95. "And He took off their chariot wheels" (Shemot 14:25). Rabbi Shimon opened the discussion with the verse: "Now as I beheld the living creatures, behold one wheel upon the earth by the living creatures" (Yechezkel 1:15). This passage has been explained, and we studied it. Yet come and behold: the Holy One, blessed be He, shows His dominion in every way, and His dominion will not depart forever and ever.

96. וְעָבֵיד שׁוּלְטָנוּתָא בַּאֲבָהָן, נָטַל לְאַבְרָהָם, וְקַיֵּים בֵּיהּ עָלְמָא, דִּכְתִּיב אֵלֶּה תּוֹלְדוֹת הַשָּׁמַיִם וְהָאָרֶץ בְּהִבָּרְאָם, וְאוּקְמוּהָ. נָטִיל יִצְחָק,

וְשָׁתִיל בֵּיהּ עָלְמָא, דְּאִיהוּ קַיָּים לְעָלְמִין, הה״ד וְאֶת בְּרִיתִי אָקִים אֶת יִצְחָק. נָטַל יַעֲקֹב, וְאוֹתְבֵיהּ קָמֵיהּ, וְאִשְׁתַּעֲשַׁע בַּהֲדֵיהּ, וְאִתְפָּאַר בֵּיהּ, הה״ד יִשְׂרָאֵל אֲשֶׁר בְּךָ אֶתְפָּאָר.

96. And He establishes His dominion through the Patriarchs. He took Abraham and maintained the world through him, as written: "These are the generations of the heavens and earth when they were created (Heb. *behibar'am*)" (Beresheet 2:4). And they explained it. DO NOT READ IT AS "*BEHIBAR'AM*" BUT RATHER "*BEABRAHAM*" ('IN ABRAHAM') FOR HEAVEN AND EARTH HAD BEEN MAINTAINED THROUGH HIM. He took Isaac and planted the world through him so it should exist always. This is what is written: "And My Covenant will I establish with Isaac" (Beresheet 17:21). He took Jacob and placed him before Him, and was delighted with him and glorified Himself with him. This is what is written, "Yisrael, in whom I will be glorified" (Yeshayah 49:3).

97. ות״ח, יַעֲקֹב אָחִיד בְּאִילָנָא דְּחַיֵּי, דְּלֵית בֵּיהּ מוֹתָא לְעָלְמִין, דְּכָל חַיִּין בְּהַהוּא אִילָנָא אִשְׁתָּכְלָלוּ, וְיָהַב חַיִּין לְכָל אִינּוּן דַּאֲחִידָן בֵּיהּ. ובג״כ, יַעֲקֹב לָא מִית. וְאֵימָתַי מִית, בְּשַׁעֲתָא דִּכְתִּיב וַיֶּאֱסוֹף רַגְלָיו אֶל הַמִּטָּה. הַמִּטָּה. כד״א הִנֵּה מִטָּתוֹ שֶׁלִּשְׁלֹמֹה, בְּגִין דִּבְהַאי מִטָּה כְּתִיב, רַגְלֶיהָ יוֹרְדוֹת מָוֶת, ובג״כ וַיֶּאֱסוֹף רַגְלָיו אֶל הַמִּטָּה כְּתִיב, כְּדֵין וַיִּגְוַע וַיֵּאָסֶף אֶל עַמָּיו. וְעָבֵד קוּדְשָׁא בְּרִיךְ הוּא לְיַעֲקֹב שְׁלִימוּ דַּאֲבָהָן, הה״ד יַעֲקֹב אֲשֶׁר בְּחַרְתִּיךָ.

97. Come and behold: Jacob is attached to the Tree of Life, which never has any death in it, for all the living are established and perfected in this tree that gives life to all that grasp on to it. Therefore, Jacob did not die. And when did he die? It occurred when it was written: "He gathered up his feet into the bed" (Beresheet 49:33). "The bed" is as you say, "Behold it is his litter, that of Solomon" (Shir Hashirim 2:7), WHICH IS MALCHUT. About this bed, it is written: "Her feet go down to death" (Mishlei 5:5). Therefore, it is written: "He gathered up his feet into the bed," and then, "and he expired and was gathered unto his people." BUT AS LONG AS HE HELD ON TO THE TREE OF LIFE, WHICH IS ZEIR ANPIN, HE DID NOT DIE BECAUSE DEATH IS ONLY FROM THE ASPECT OF MALCHUT, AS EXPLAINED. Then the Holy One, blessed be He, made Jacob the chosen among the Patriarchs. This is what is written: "Jacob whom I have chosen" (Yeshayah 41:8).

98. תָּ"ח, כָּל מַשִׁרְיָין דִּלְעֵילָּא, וְכָל אִינּוּן רְתִיכִין, כֻּלְּהוּ אֲחִידָן אִלֵּין בְּאִלֵּין, דַּרְגִּין בְּדַרְגִּין, אִלֵּין עִלָּאִין וְאִלֵּין תַּתָּאִין. וְחֵיוָותָא קַדִּישָׁא עָלַיְיהוּ, וְכֻלְּהוּ אוּכְלוּסִין וּמַשִׁרְיָין, כֻּלְּהוּ נַטְלִין תְּחוֹת יְדָהָא, עַל מֵימְרָהָא נַטְלִין, וְעַל מֵימְרָהָא שָׁרָאן.

98. Come and behold: see all the legions of above THAT ARE DRAWN FROM THE FOUR COMPANIES OF THE SHECHINAH, WHICH ARE THE WHEELS. All the Chariots are entwined with each other, levels with levels. The upper and the lower EVOLVE, THE ONE FROM THE OTHER, AND COMBINE, THE ONE WITH THE OTHER. And there is a holy living creature over them, WHICH IS THE NUKVA. FOR THERE ARE FOUR LIVING CREATURES, AS MENTIONED, AND THE NUKVA IS THE FOURTH. All the multitude hosts and the legions travel under her command. They travel and camp according to her instructions, FOR ALL THE CHARIOTS AND THE LIVING CREATURES AND THE WHEELS POSSESS ONLY WHAT THEY RECEIVE FROM THIS HIGHEST HOLY LIVING CREATURE.

99. וְדָא הוּא חֵיוָתָא, דְּכָל שְׁאַר חֵיוָתָא, אֲחִידָן בָּהּ וְאִשְׁתַּלְשָׁלוּ בְּגִינָהּ כַּמָּה חֵיוָן לְחֵיוָן. וְאִתְאַחֲדָן דַּרְגִּין בְּדַרְגִּין, וְכֻלְּהוּ עִלָּאִין וְתַתָּאִין אַזְלִין וְשָׁאטִין בְּיַמָּא, הה"ד זֶה הַיָּם גָּדוֹל וּרְחַב יָדַיִם שָׁם רֶמֶשׂ וְאֵין מִסְפָּר וְגוֹ'.

99. This is the living creature that all the other living creatures hold on to. And from her evolved many other living creatures upon living creatures, MEANING THAT MANY LIVING CREATURES EVOLVED ONE FROM ANOTHER, and levels combined with levels. All those of above and of below go and swim in the sea, WHICH IS THE NUKVA, FOR THOSE OF ABOVE ARE INCLUDED IN HER, THEY GIVE FORTH INFLUENCE TO HER. AND THE LOWER ARE INCLUDED IN HER AND RECEIVE FROM HER. This is what is written: "So is this great and wide sea, wherein are creeping things innumerable" (Tehilim 104:25).

100. וְכַד סָלִיק יַמָּא גַּלְגַּלּוֹי, כֻּלְּהוּ אַרְבִּין סַלְּקִין נַחְתִּין, וְזַעְפָּא

אִשְׁתְּכַח, וְרוּחָא תַּקִּיפָא אַזְלָא עֲלֵיהּ בְּתָקִיפוּ. וְנוּנֵי יַמָּא מִתְבַּדְּרִין לְכָל סְטַר, אִלֵּין לְמִזְרָח, וְאִלֵּין לְמַעֲרָב, אִלֵּין לַצָּפוֹן, וְאִלֵּין לַדָּרוֹם. וְכָל אִינּוּן בְּנֵי עָלְמָא, דְּחָמָאן רְשִׁימָא עֲלַיְיהוּ, נַטְלִין לוֹן, וּבַלְעִין לוֹן בְּקַפְטִירֵי עַפְרָא.

100. When the sea raises its waves, WHICH ARE JUDGMENTS, all the ships go up and down, MEANING THEY GO UP UNTO THE HEAVENS AND DOWN TO THE DEPTHS. It is stormy and a strong wind blows over it powerfully. And the fish of the sea are scattered to every side, these to east and these to west, these to north and these to south. THESE FISH OF THE SEA see a sign on all the people of the world BECAUSE OF THEIR SIN, and they take them and swallow them in caves in the ground.

101. וְכָל אַרְבִּין לָא נַטְלִין מֵאַתְרַיְיהוּ, וְלָא סַלְּקִין וְנַחְתִּין, בַּר מֵהַהוּא שַׁעֲתָא, דְּאָתֵי חַד דִּבְרָא בְּיַמָּא, וְיָדַע לְאַשְׁלְמָא רוּחָא דְּזַעְפָּא דְּיַמָּא, כֵּיוָן דְּסָלִיק דָּא עֲלֵיהּ דְּיַמָּא, שָׁכִיךְ מֵרוּגְזָא, וְנַיְיחָא אִשְׁתְּכַח, וּכְדֵין כֻּלְּהוּ אַרְבִּין אַזְלִין בְּאֹרַח מֵישַׁר, וְלָא סָטָאן לִימִינָא וּשְׂמָאלָא, הה״ד, שָׁם אֳנִיּוֹת יְהַלֵּכוּן לִוְיָתָן זֶה יָצַרְתָּ לְשַׂחֶק בּוֹ. זֶה דַּיְיקָא. וְכָל נוּנֵי יַמָּא מִתְכַּנְּשִׁין לְאַתְרַיְיהוּ. וְכָל אִינּוּן חֵיוָון חַדָּאן עָלָהּ, וְחֵיוָון חַקְלָא עִלָּאָה חַדָּאן, הה״ד וְכָל חַיַּת הַשָּׂדֶה יְשַׂחֲקוּ שָׁם.

101. None of the ships move from their places, or go up or down, except when the one leader of the sea arrives and knows how to settle and appease the stormy wind of the sea. As soon as he rises over the sea, it rests from its rage and becomes placid. Then all the ships continue on their straight course and do not turn right or left. This is what is written: "There go the ships: this is the Leviathan, whom you have made to play therein" (Ibid. 26). "This" is exact, WHICH IS THE SECRET OF YESOD OF ZEIR ANPIN THAT IS CALLED 'THIS' (MASC.), WHICH IS THE SECRET OF THE CENTRAL COLUMN. All the fish of the sea gather to their place and all the animals rejoice with them, and the animals of the supernal field rejoice. This is what is written: "Where all the wild beasts play" (Iyov 40:20).

102. ת״ח, כְּגַוְונָא דִּלְעֵילָּא, אִית לְתַתָּא. כְּגַוְונָא דִּלְתַתָּא, אִית בְּיַמָּא.

כְּגַוְונָא דִּלְעֵילָּא, אִית לְעֵילָּא בְּיַמָּא עִלָּאָה. כְּגַוְונָא דִּלְעֵילָּא אִית לְתַתָּא. כְּגַוְונָא דִּלְתַתָּא, אִית בְּיַמָּא תַּתָּאָה.

102. Come and behold: as it is above, IN CHESED, GVURAH AND TIFERET OF ZEIR ANPIN, so is it below, IN NETZACH, HOD AND YESOD OF ZEIR ANPIN. And what is below is also in the Lower Sea, WHICH IS MALCHUT. ANOTHER VERSION: as it is above, IN CHESED, GVURAH AND TIFERET OF ZEIR ANPIN, so it is in the supernal sea, WHICH IS BINAH, and as it is in the higher above, so it is down below, IN NETZACH, HOD AND YESOD OF ZEIR ANPIN. Whatever is down below is in the Lower Sea, WHICH IS MALCHUT.

103. גּוּפָא דְּהַהוּא יַמָּא, הָא אִתְעַרְנָא לְחַבְרָנָא, אוֹרְכָא וּפוּתְיָא, רֵישָׁא וּדְרֹעִין וְגוּפָא, כֹּלָּא כְּמָה דְּאִצְטְרִיךְ, וְכֹלָּא בִּשְׁמֵיהּ אִתְקְרֵי. וּכְגַוְונָא דָּא לְתַתָּא לְיַמָּא דִּלְתַתָּא, הָכִי נָמֵי רֵישָׁא דְּיַמָּא, וּדְרוֹעִין דְּיַמָּא, וְגוּפָא דְּיַמָּא.

103. I have already commented to the friends about the body of that SUPERNAL sea, WHICH IS BINAH. The length and breadth OF IT, the head and arms and the body are all as they should, and each is called by its name. Similarly, below in the Lower Sea, WHICH IS MALCHUT, there is also the head of the sea, the arms of the sea, and the body of the sea.

104. כְּתִיב זְבוּלוּן לְחוֹף יַמִּים יִשְׁכּוֹן. וְהָא יַמָּא חַד הֲוָה בְּעַדְבֵיהּ אֶלָּא מַאי לְחוֹף יַמִּים, וַדַּאי אוּקְמוּהָ חַבְרַיָּיא בְּרָזָא עִלָּאָה. וְיַרְכָתוֹ עַל צִידוֹן, כד״א יוֹצְאֵי יֶרֶךְ יַעֲקֹב. זְבוּלוּן שׁוֹקָא דִּימִינָא דְּגוּפָא הֲוָה, וְיַם כִּנֶּרֶת הֲוָה בְּעַדְבֵיהּ, וּמֵהָכָא אִשְׁתְּכַח חִלָּזוֹן לִתְכֶלְתָּא.

104. It is written: “Zebulun shall dwell at the shore of the seas” (Beresheet 49:13). HE ASKS: But there was only one sea in his Heritage, WHY DOES IT SAY “AT THE SHORE OF THE SEAS”? HE ANSWERS: But what does “the shore of the seas” mean, for the comrades certainly explained it in accordance with the supernal secret. “And his border shall be at Tzidon” (Ibid.), is as it is written: “That came out of the loins (also thigh) of Jacob” (Shemot 1:5), for Zebulun was the right thigh of the body, WHICH IS

NETZACH. AND THEREFORE THE TORAH VERSE SAYS, "AND HIS BORDER (ALSO: 'THIGH')." The Sea of Galilee was in his inheritance, and from here the purple fish is available for the purple dye.

105. ת״ח, כַּמָּה רְתִיכִין עַל רְתִיכִין אִשְׁתְּכָחוּ, וְגַלְגַּלּוֹי דִּרְתִיכָא רָהֲטִין בִּבְהִילוּ, וְלָא מִתְעַכְּבֵי אִינּוּן סַמְכֵי רְתִיכָא, לְנַטְלָא עֲלֵיהוֹן. וְכֵן כֻּלְּהוּ. ת״ח, רְתִיכָא דִּי מְמָנָא עַל מִצְרָאֵי, אוּקְמוּהָ, רְתִיכָא שְׁלֵימָתָא לָא אִשְׁתְּכַח, דְּהָא כְּתִיב וַיָּסַר אֵת אוֹפַן מַרְכְּבוֹתָיו, כַּמָּה רְתִיכִין הֲווֹ, דַּהֲווֹ נַטְלִין עַל חַד סָמִיךְ גַּלְגַּלָּא, דְּאִתְפְּקְדוּ עֲלַיְיהוּ, כֵּיוָן דְּאִתְעֲבָר הַאי מִשּׁוּלְטָנוּתָא דִּילֵיהּ, כֻּלְּהוּ רְתִיכִין אִתְעֲבָרוּ מִשּׁוּלְטָנֵיהוֹן, וְלָא נַטְלוּ. כְּדֵין כֻּלְּהוּ לְתַתָּא אִתְעֲבָרוּ מִשּׁוּלְטָנוּתָא, דִּכְתִּיב עַל מִצְרַיִם וְעַל פַּרְעֹה וְעַל הַבּוֹטְחִים בּוֹ.

105. Come and behold: how many chariots upon chariots there are, and the wheels of the chariot race speedily, and the supports of the chariot do not refrain from traveling on them. And it is so for all of them. Come and behold: examine the Chariot of the minister over Egypt. As was explained, there was no complete chariot to be found, as it is written: "And He took off their chariot wheels" (Shemot 14:25). There were many chariots that traveled upon the support of one wheel that was appointed over them. As soon as it was removed from its dominion, then all the Chariots were removed from their control and could not travel. Then all of those below, IN THIS WORLD, were removed from their dominion, as is written: "And Egypt even Pharaoh, and all those who trust in him" (Yirmeyah 46:25).

106. וּבְהַהוּא זִמְנָא, שֻׁלְטָנוּתָא דְּמִצְרַיִם שָׁלִיט עַל כָּל שְׁאַר עַמִּין, כֵּיוָן דְּאִתְּבַר חֵילָא דְּמִצְרַיִם, אִתְּבַר חֵילָא דִּשְׁאַר עַמִּין. מְנָלָן, דִּכְתִּיב אָז נִבְהֲלוּ אַלּוּפֵי אֱדוֹם וְגוֹ׳. וּכְתִיב שָׁמְעוּ עַמִּים יִרְגָּזוּן וְגוֹ׳. בְּגִין דְּכֻלְּהוּ הֲווֹ אֲחִידָן בְּפוּלְחָנָא דְּמִצְרַיִם, וַאֲחִידָן בְּמִצְרַיִם לְסִיּוּעָא דִּלְהוֹן. וּבְהַהוּא זִמְנָא, כֻּלְּהוּ בָּעָאן לְסִיּוּעָא דְּמִצְרַיִם, לְאִתַּתְקְפָא. וְעַל דָּא, כֵּיוָן דִּשְׁמָעוּ גְּבוּרָן דְּעָבֵד קוּדְשָׁא בְּרִיךְ הוּא בְּמִצְרַיִם, רָפוּ יְדֵיהוֹן, וְלָא יָכִילוּ לְמֵיקַם, וְאִזְדַּעֲזָעוּ כֻּלְּהוּ, וְאִתְּבָרוּ מִשּׁוּלְטָנַתְהוֹן.

10. "And He took off their chariot wheels"

106. At that time, the government of Egypt ruled over all the other nations. As soon as the power of Egypt was crushed, the power of the other nations was broken. How do we know? For it is written: "Then the chiefs of Edom shall be amazed" (Shemot 15:15). And, "The people shall hear, and be afraid" (Ibid. 14), because at that time they were all attached to the service of Egypt, they depended upon Egypt to help them, and they all requested assistance from Egypt to strengthen themselves. Therefore, when they heard of the mighty acts that the Holy One, blessed be He, performed in Egypt, they were discouraged and were unable to stand firm. And they all quaked and trembled and lost their power.

107. וַדַּאי כַּד אִתְּבַר חֵילָא דִּלְהוֹן לְעֵילָּא, אִתְּבַר חֵילָא דְּכָל אִינּוּן דַּאֲחִידָן בֵּיהּ, כֵּיוָן דְּאִתְּבַר חֵילָא דְּכֻלְּהוּ לְעֵילָּא, כָּל הָנֵי דִּלְתַתָּא אִתְּבָרוּ, בְּגִין הַאי חֵילָא דְּאִתְּבַר בְּקַדְמֵיתָא. ובג"כ וַיָּסַר אֵת אֹפַן מַרְכְּבוֹתָיו כְּתִיב. וַיְנַהֲגֵהוּ בִּכְבֵדוּת, דְּהָא כַּד דָּא אִתְּבַר, לָא הֲווֹ אַזְלִין.

107. Certainly, when their strength was broken above, the strength of all those attached to him was broken, for once the strength of all of them was broken above, all those below were broken because of that strength which was broken first. Therefore, "He took off his chariot wheels (lit. 'wheel')," NAMELY, THE STRENGTH FROM ABOVE, AS MENTIONED EARLIER. "That they drove heavily" (Shemot 14:25). Once it was broken, they could not move.

108. תָּא חֲזֵי דְּהָכִי הוּא, דְּלָא כְּתִיב וַיָּסַר אֵת אוֹפַנֵּי מַרְכְּבוֹתָיו, אוֹ אוֹפַן מֶרְכַּבְתּוֹ, אֶלָּא וַיָּסַר אֵת אוֹפַן מַרְכְּבוֹתָיו. בְּגִין הַאי חֵילָא, דְּכֻלְּהוּ הֲווֹ מִתְדַּבְּקָן בֵּיהּ.

108. Come and behold: it is so, for it is not written: 'And He took off his chariots' wheels' or 'chariot wheel', MEANING EITHER BOTH IN PLURAL, OR BOTH IN SINGULAR. But rather it is written: "And He took off his chariots' wheel." "WHEEL" IS SINGULAR, AND "HIS CHARIOTS" IS PLURAL, AND THAT IS because 'WHEEL' (HEB. *OFAN*) is the power to which all of them were attached, AS IS WRITTEN ABOVE. IT IS THEREFORE WRITTEN IN THE SINGULAR FORM.

109. וְתוּ, וַיָּסַר אֵת אוֹפַן מַרְכְּבוֹתָיו, תָּא חֲזֵי, זַכָּאָה חוּלָקֵהוֹן דְּיִשְׂרָאֵל, דְּקוּדְשָׁא בְּרִיךְ הוּא אִתְרְעֵי בְּהוּ, לְאִתְדַּבְּקָא בְּהוּ, וּלְמֶהֱוֵי לְהוּ חוּלָק, וּלְמֶהֱוֵי אִינּוּן חוּלָקֵיהּ. הֲדָא הוּא דִּכְתִּיב, וּבוֹ תִדְבָּקוּן. וּכְתִיב וְאַתֶּם הַדְּבֵקִים בַּיְיָ׳ אֱלֹהֵיכֶם, בַּיְיָ׳ מַמָּשׁ. וּכְתִיב כִּי יַעֲקֹב בָּחַר לוֹ יָהּ. וּכְתִיב כִּי חֵלֶק יְיָ׳ עַמּוֹ יַעֲקֹב חֶבֶל נַחֲלָתוֹ. דְּאַפִּיק לוֹן מִזַּרְעָא קַדִּישָׁא, לְמֶהֱוֵי חוּלָקֵיהּ, וְעַל דָּא יָהַב לוֹן אוֹרַיְיתָא קַדִּישָׁא עִלָּאָה, גְּנִיזָא תְּרֵי אַלְפִּין שְׁנִין, עַד לָא יִתְבְּרֵי עָלְמָא, וְהָא אִתְּמַר. וּבְגִין רְחִימוּתָא דִּילֵיהּ יָהֲבָא לְיִשְׂרָאֵל, לְמֵהַךְ אֲבַתְרָהּ, וּלְאִתְדַּבְּקָא בָּהּ.

109. WE CAN also EXPLAIN: "And he took off his chariots' wheel." Come and behold: happy is the portion of Yisrael that the Holy One, blessed be He, wanted to join with them and to be their portion, and that they should be His portion. This is what is written: "And hold fast to Him" (Devarim 13:5), and, "But you that did cleave to Hashem your Elohim" (Devarim 4:4), to Hashem indeed. It is also written, "For Yah, has chosen Jacob for Himself" (Tehilim 135:4), and, "For Hashem's portion is His people, Jacob is the lot of His inheritance" (Devarim 32:9), for He brought them forth from the holy seed to be His portion. THIS IS NOT SO FOR THE OTHER SIDE AND THE NATIONS OF THE WORLD, WHICH HAVE NO CONNECTION TO ZEIR ANPIN. Therefore, He gave them the Holy Torah that was concealed two hundred years before the world was created, and this has already been explained. Because of His love, He gave it to the children of Yisrael to follow and to cleave unto it.

110. תָּא חֲזֵי, כָּל מַשִׁירְיָין דִּלְעֵילָּא, וְכָל אִינּוּן רְתִיכִין, כֻּלְּהוּ אֲחִידָן אִלֵּין בְּאִלֵּין, דַּרְגִּין בְּדַרְגִּין, אִלֵּין עִלָּאִין, וְאִלֵּין תַּתָּאִין, וְהָא אוּקְמוּהָ, דִּכְתִּיב זֶה הַיָּם גָּדוֹל. וְחֵיוָתָא קַדִּישָׁא עָלֵיהּ, וְכֻלְּהוּ אוּכְלוּסִין וּמַשִׁרְיָין, כֻּלְּהוּ נַטְלִין תְּחוֹת יְדָהּ, עַל מֵימְרָהּ נַטְלִין, לְהוּ מֵימְרָהּ שָׁרָאן. בְּעִדָּנָא דְּהִיא נַטְלָא, כֻּלְּהוּ נַטְלִין, בְּגִין דְּכֻלְּהוּ אֲחִידָן בָּהּ.

110. Come and behold: All the camps of above and all the Chariots are all joined one to the other, levels by levels; those of above and those of below ARE BOUND TOGETHER. And it was explained that it is written: "So is this great and wide sea" (Tehilim 104:25). And the living creature is over them,

WHICH IS THE NUKVA THAT IS FROM THE CHEST AND HIGHER OF ZEIR ANPIN THAT RECEIVES FROM THE THREE LIVING CREATURES OF ZEIR ANPIN. AND SHE IS THE FOURTH LIVING CREATURE THAT ALL RECEIVE FROM, EVEN THE CHARIOTS OF THE OTHER SIDE, AND THE NATIONS OF THE WORLD. All the multitudes and the camps travel under her command. According to her instructions they travel, and by her word they rest. When she travels they all travel, because they are all joined to her.

111. ות"ח, בְּשַׁעֲתָא דְּבָעֵי קוּדְשָׁא בְּרִיךְ הוּא, לְאַעְבְּרָא לְאוּכְלוֹסִין דְּפַרְעֹה לְתַתָּא אַעְבַּר בְּקַדְמֵיתָא לְהַהוּא חֵילָא דִּלְהוֹן, כְּמָה דְּאוֹקִימְנָא. מַה עָבֵד. אַעְבַּר וְסָלִיק הַהוּא אֲתַר קַדִּישָׁא עִלָּאָה, דַּהֲוָה מַדְבַּר לְכָל אִינּוּן רְתִיכִין, כֵּיוָן דְּהַאי אִסְתְּלִיק, הַנְהוּ כֻּלְּהוּ מַשִּׁירְיָין לָא יָכִילוּ לְדַבְּרָא, כֵּיוָן דְּאִינּוּן לָא יָכִילוּ, הַהוּא מְמָנָא דְּמִצְרָאֵי אַעְבְּרוּ לֵיהּ מִשּׁוּלְטָנֵיהּ, וְאַעְבַּר בְּנוּרָא דְּדָלִיק, וּכְדֵין שֻׁלְטָנוּתָא דְּמִצְרָאֵי אִתְעֲדֵי. וְעַל דָּא, אָנוּסָה מִפְּנֵי יִשְׂרָאֵל. מ"ט, בְּגִין דְּחָמוּ מְמָנָא דְּמִצְרַיִם אִתּוֹקַד בְּנוּרָא.

111. Come and behold: when the Holy One, blessed be He, wanted to remove the multitudes of Pharaoh below, He first removed their power, as we explained. What did He do? He removed and detached that upper holy place that led all those Chariots OF THE MINISTER OF EGYPT ABOVE, AS EVERY CHARIOT WAS UNDER ITS COMMAND, EVEN THOSE OF THE OTHER SIDE. As soon as it left, then all the camps AND THE CHARIOTS could not travel. Since they could not, the Minister of Egypt was removed from his dominion with a flaming fire, and then the dominion of Egypt was removed. Therefore, THEY SAID, "Let us flee from the face of Yisrael." What is the reason? Because they saw the Minister of Egypt burned in fire.

112. ר' יִצְחָק אָמַר, בְּשַׁעֲתָא דְּקָרִיבוּ יִשְׂרָאֵל לְיַמָּא, קָרָא קב"ה לִמְמָנָא רַבְרְבָא דְּעַל יַמָּא, אָמַר לֵיהּ, בְּשַׁעֲתָא דַּעֲבָדִית אֲנָא עָלְמָא, מְנֵיתִי לָךְ עַל יַמָּא, וּתְנַאי אִית לִי עַל יַמָּא, דִּי יִבְזַע מֵימוֹי מִקָּמֵי בָּנַי. הַשְׁתָּא מָטָא עִדָּנָא, דְּיָעַבְרוּן בָּנַי בְּגוֹ יַמָּא. לְבָתַר מַה כְּתִיב, וַיָּשָׁב הַיָּם לִפְנוֹת בֹּקֶר לְאֵיתָנוֹ. מַאי לְאֵיתָנוֹ, לִתְנָאוֹ דַּהֲוָה לֵיהּ בְּקוּדְשָׁא בְּרִיךְ

הוּא כַּד בָּרָא עָלְמָא.

112. Rabbi Yitzchak said: When Yisrael approached the sea, the Holy One, blessed be He, called the minister who was appointed over the sea. He said to him: 'At the time that I made the world, I appointed you over the sea, and conditioned the sea so that its water should split before My children. Now the time has arrived for My children to pass in the midst of the sea.' And afterwards, it is written: "And the sea returned to its strength (Heb. *eitano*) when the morning appeared" (Shemot 14:27). What is *Eitano*? The condition (Heb. *tenao*) that it had with the Holy One, blessed be He, when He created the world, BECAUSE *EITANO* ('ITS STRENGTH') IS SPELLED WITH THE SAME LETTERS AS *TENAO* ('HIS CONDITION').

113. וַהֲווֹ יִשְׂרָאֵל שָׁרָאן עַל יַמָּא, וַהֲווֹ יִשְׂרָאֵל חָמָאן, גַּלְגַּלֵּי יַמָּא סַלְקִין וְנַחְתִּין, זָקְפוּ עֵינַיְיהוּ, וְחָמוּ לְפַרְעֹה וּלְאוּכְלוֹסִין דִּילֵיהּ, דְּחִילוּ וְצָעֲקוּ. וְהָא אִתְּמַר. הַיָּם רָאָה, מָה חָמָא יַמָּא. אֲרוֹנָא דְּיוֹסֵף קָא חָמָא, וְעָרַק מִקָּמֵיהּ. מ"ט, בְּגִין דִּכְתִּיב וַיָּנָס וַיֵּצֵא הַחוּצָה. וְעַל דָּא הַיָּם רָאָה וַיָּנוֹס, וּכְתִיב וַיָּסַר אֶת אוֹפַן מַרְכְּבוֹתָיו וְגוֹ' אָנוּסָה מִפְּנֵי יִשְׂרָאֵל. מַאי טַעֲמָא. בְּגִין דְּחָמוּ אַרְעָא דְּמִצְרַיִם, כְּאִלּוּ אִתּוֹקַד בְּנוּרָא, כְּדֵין אָמְרוּ אָנוּסָה מִפְּנֵי יִשְׂרָאֵל.

113. Yisrael were dwelling by the sea and saw the waves rising and falling. They raised their eyes and saw Pharaoh and his multitudes. They feared and cried out, as has already been explained: "The sea saw" (Tehilim 114:3). HE ASKS: What did the sea see? AND HE ANSWERS: It saw the coffin of Joseph and fled from before it. For what reason? Because it is written OF JOSEPH, "And fled, and went outside" (Beresheet 39:12). DUE TO THIS, "The sea saw it, and fled." It is written: "And He took off their chariot wheels…Let us flee from the face of Yisrael." What is the reason? It is because they saw the land of Egypt and it looked as though it was burning with fire. Then they said, "Let us flee from the face of Yisrael."

114. רִבִּי חִיָּיא וְרִבִּי יוֹסֵי, הֲווֹ אַזְלֵי בְּמַדְבְּרָא, אָמַר רִבִּי חִיָּיא לְרִבִּי יוֹסֵי, תָּא וְאֵימָא לָךְ, דְּכַד קוּדְשָׁא בְּרִיךְ הוּא בָּעֵי לְאַעְבְּרָא שׁוּלְטָנוּתָא דְּאַרְעָא, לָא עָבֵיד, עַד דְּאַעְבַּר שֻׁלְטָנוּתָא דִּלְהוֹן בִּרְקִיעָא, וְלָא אַעְבָּר

שֻׁלְטָנָא דִּלְהוֹן, עַד דְּמָנֵי אַחֲרָא בְּאַתְרֵיהּ, בְּגִין דְּלָא יִגְרַע שִׁמּוּשָׁא דִּלְהוֹן בִּרְקִיעָא, בְּגִין לְקַיְּימָא מַה דִּכְתִּיב, וּלְמַן דִּי יִצְבֵּא יִתְּנִינָּהּ. א"ר יוֹסֵי, וַדַּאי הָכִי הוּא.

114. Rabbi Chiya and Rabbi Yosi were traveling in the wilderness. Rabbi Chiya said to Rabbi Yosi: Come and I will tell you. When the Holy One, blessed be He, wishes to remove a government on the earth, He does not do it until he removes its dominion in heaven. And He does not remove the dominion in the heaven until He appoints another in its place, so that their service in heaven shall not be lacking, in order to fulfill what is written: "And gives it to whomever He will" (Daniel 4:14). Rabbi Yosi said: Certainly, it is so.

115. פָּתַח ר' יוֹסֵי וְאָמַר, יְיָ' אֲדוֹנֵינוּ מַה אַדִּיר שִׁמְךָ בְּכָל הָאָרֶץ. יְיָ' אֲדוֹנֵינוּ: כַּד בָּעֵי קוּדְשָׁא בְּרִיךְ הוּא לְתַבְרָא חֵילָא דְּעַמִּין עכו"ם, אַתְקִיף דִּינֵיהּ עָלַיְיהוּ, וְתָבַר לוֹן, וְאַעְבָּר מִקָּמֵיהּ שׁוּלְטָנוּתָא דִּלְהוֹן.

115. Rabbi Yosi opened the discussion, saying: "Hashem our Master, how majestic is Your Name on all the earth" (Tehilim 8:2). "Hashem our Master," MEANS that when the Holy One, blessed be He, wishes to break the power of the heathen nations, He strengthens His Judgment over them, breaks them, and removes their dominion from before Himself.

116. אֲשֶׁר תְּנָה הוֹדְךָ עַל הַשָּׁמָיִם, אֲשֶׁר נָתַתָּ מִבָּעֵי לֵיהּ, אוֹ תְּנָה הוֹדְךָ, מַהוּ אֲשֶׁר תְּנָה הוֹדְךָ. אֶלָּא דָּא הוּא רָזָא דְּנַהֲרָא עֲמִיקָא דְּכֹלָּא, וְדָוִד בָּעָא בָּעוּתֵיהּ, לְמִנְגַּד מִנֵּיהּ עַל הַשָּׁמַיִם, וְדָא הוּא אֲשֶׁר. כד"א, אֶהְיֶה אֲשֶׁר אֶהְיֶה.

116. "Who (Heb. *asher*) have set Your glory above the heavens" (Ibid.). HE ASKS: It should have been written 'who have set' 'or set Your glory'. Why, "Who have set Your glory"? HE ANSWERS: This is the secret of the river that is the deepest of all, WHICH IS BINAH. And David prayed his prayer to draw from it unto the heaven, WHICH IS ZEIR ANPIN. And this "*asher*," WHICH IS THE NAME OF BINAH, is as is written: "I will ever be what (Heb. *asher*) I am" (Shemot 3:14).

117. בְּשַׁעֲתָא דְּהַאי נַהֲרָא עֲמִיקְתָא דְּכֹלָּא, נָגִיד וְנָפִיק עַל הַשָּׁמַיִם, כְּדֵין כֹּלָּא בְּחִידוּ, וּמַטְרוֹנִיתָא אִתְעַטְּרַת בְּמַלְכָּא, וְכָל עָלְמִין כֻּלְּהוּ בְּחִידוּ, וְשֻׁלְטָנוּתָא דְּעַמִּין עעכו"ם, אִתְעֲבָר מִקָּמֵי מַטְרוֹנִיתָא, וּכְדֵין זַקְפִין רֵישָׁא כָּל מַאן דַּאֲחִידוּ בָּהּ.

117. At the time that this deepest river, WHICH IS BINAH, is drawn and goes out over the heaven, WHICH IS ZEIR ANPIN, then everything is joyous. And the Queen, WHO IS MALCHUT, crowns Herself with the King, WHO IS ZEIR ANPIN, and all the worlds are joyful. The domination of the heathen nations is removed before the Queen, and then all who cling to Her raise their heads.

118. אַדְּהָכִי חָמוּ חַד ב"נ, דַּהֲוָה אָתֵי, וְחַד מְטוּלָא קָמֵיהּ. א"ר חִיָּיא, נֵזִיל, דִּלְמָא הַאי בַּר נָשׁ עעכו"ם הוּא, אוֹ עַם הָאָרֶץ הוּא, וְאָסִיר לְאִשְׁתַּתְּפָא בַּהֲדֵיהּ בְּאָרְחָא. א"ר יוֹסֵי, נֵיתִיב הָכָא, וְנֶחֱמֵי, דִּלְמָא גַּבְרָא רַבָּא הוּא.

118. In the meantime, they saw a man coming with a load in front of him. Rabbi Chiya said: Let us go. Perhaps this man is a heathen or an ignoramus, and it is forbidden to join him on the road. Rabbi Yosi said: Let us sit here and watch. Perhaps he is a great man.

119. אַדְּהָכִי, אַעְבָּר קַמַּיְיהוּ, א"ל, בְּדוּקְפָּא דִּמַעְבָּרָא דְּקוֹטִיפָא דְּהַאי, חַבְרוּתָא אִבְעֵי, וַאֲנָא יָדַעְנָא אָרְחָא אַחֲרָא, וְנִסְטֵי מֵהַאי, וַאֲנָא בְּעֵינָא דְּאֵימָא לְכוּ, וְלָא אִתְחַיַּיבְנָא בְּכוּ, וְלָא אַעְבָּר עַל מַה דִּכְתִּיב וְלִפְנֵי עִוֵּר לֹא תִתֵּן מִכְשׁוֹל, וְאַתּוּן כְּסוּמִין בְּאָרְחָא דָּא, וְלָא תִּסְתַּכְּנוּ בְּנַפְשַׁיְיכוּ. א"ר יוֹסֵי, בְּרִיךְ רַחֲמָנָא דְּאוֹרִיכְנָא הָכָא, אִתְחַבְּרוּ בַּהֲדֵיהּ. אָמַר לוֹן, לָא תִּשְׁתָּעוּ מִידִי הָכָא, עַד דְּנַעֲבֹר בְּהַאי. סָטוּ בְּאָרְחָא אַחֲרָא.

119. In the meantime, he passed before them and said to them: At this crossing place, which is dangerous, I need company, FOR I AM AFRAID TO

TRAVEL ALONE. I know a different way, let us turn off from this way. And I wish to say to you, I will not sin against you and I will not transgress what is written: "Nor put a stumbling block before the blind" (Vayikra 19:14), because you are like blind people on this way and you must not endanger yourselves. Rabbi Yosi said: Blessed is the Merciful One that we waited here. They joined him. He said to them: Do not speak anything here until we pass from here. They turned to a different way.

120. בָּתַר דְּנָפְקוּ מֵהַהוּא אֲתָר, אָמַר לוֹן, בְּהַהוּא אָרְחָא אַחֲרָא, הֲווֹ אַזְלֵי זִמְנָא חֲדָא, חַד כֹּהֵן חָכָם, וְחַד כֹּהֵן עַם הָאָרֶץ בַּהֲדֵיהּ, קָם הַהוּא ע"ה בְּהַהוּא אֲתָר עָלֵיהּ וְקַטְלֵיהּ. מֵהַהוּא יוֹמָא כָּל מַאן דְּאַעְבָּר בְּהַהוּא אֲתָר, מִסְתַּכֵּן בְּנַפְשֵׁיהּ. וְהָא מִתְחַבְּרִין תַּמָּן מְשַׁדְּדֵי טוּרַיָּא, וְקַטְלִין וְקַפְּחִין לִבְנֵי נָשָׁא, וְאִינּוּן דְּיַדְעֵי לָא עַבְרֵי תַּמָּן, וּבָעֵי קוּדְשָׁא בְּרִיךְ הוּא דָּמָא דְּהַהוּא כַּהֲנָא כָּל יוֹמָא.

120. After they left that place, he said to them: On that other path, THE DANGEROUS ONE, a scholarly priest and a layman priest were once traveling. The ignoramus priest arose against him at that place and killed him. From that day AND FURTHER, anybody who passes that place endangers himself, and robbers of the hills gather there to kill and rob people. Those who are aware of this do not pass there. And the Holy One, blessed be He, demands the blood of that priest every day.

121. פָּתַח וְאָמַר, עוֹד הַיּוֹם בְּנוֹב לַעֲמוֹד וְגוֹ' הָא אוּקְמוּהָ אִינּוּן מָארֵי מְתִיבְתָּא. אֲבָל אֲנָא לָא אֲמֵינָא לְכוּ הָכִי, אֶלָּא דְּרָזָא דְּמִלָּה אוֹלִיפְנָא. עוֹד הַיּוֹם, מַאן יוֹמָא דֵּין. אֶלָּא, הָכִי כְּתִיב, וַיִּקַּח אַהֲרֹן אֶת אֱלִישֶׁבַע בַּת עֲמִינָדָב. וְרָזָא הוּא, עַל כְּנֶסֶת יִשְׂרָאֵל, דְּאַהֲרֹן הוּא שׁוֹשְׁבִינָא דִּלָיהּ, לְתַקְּנָא בֵּיתָהּ וּלְשַׁמְּשָׁא לָהּ, וּלְמֵיעַל לָהּ לְמַלְכָּא לְאִזְדַּוְּוגָא כַּחֲדָא, מִכָּאן וּלְהָלְאָה, כָּל כֹּהֵן דִּמְשַׁמֵּשׁ בְּמַקְדְּשָׁא, כְּגַוְונָא דְּאַהֲרֹן.

121. He opened the discussion with the verse: "This very day He will halt in Nov" (Yeshayah 10:32). The students of the Yeshivah have already explained this. But I do not say it this way to you, because I have learned the secret of the matter. What is "This very day"? It is written, "And Aaron took him Elisheva the daughter of Amminadab...to wife" (Shemot 6:23), and this is the secret regarding the Congregation of Yisrael, WHICH IS MALCHUT CALLED 'ELISHEVA', BECAUSE OF THE SEVEN (*SHEVA*) SFIROT SHE POSSESSES. Aaron is Her attendant who manages her house and serves Her, and brings Her to the King, WHICH IS ZEIR ANPIN, to join them together. From now onwards, every priest who serves in the Temple is MALCHUT'S ATTENDANT, like Aaron.

122. אֲחִימֶלֶךְ כַּהֲנָא רַבָּא עִלָּאָה הֲוָה, וְכָל אִינּוּן כַּהֲנֵי בַּהֲדֵיהּ, כֻּלְּהוּ הֲווֹ שׁוּשְׁבִינִין דְּמַטְרוֹנִיתָא, כֵּיוָן דְּאִתְקְטִילוּ, אִשְׁתַּאֲרַת מַטְרוֹנִיתָא בִּלְחוֹדָהָא, וְאִתְאֲבִיד שׁוֹשְׁבִינָא דִּילָהּ, וְלָא אִשְׁתְּכַח מַאן דִּמְשַׁמֵּשׁ קָמָהּ, וִיתַקֵּן בֵּיתָהּ, וִיחַדֵּי לָהּ לְאִזְדַּוְּוגָא עִם מַלְכָּא. כְּדֵין מֵהַהוּא יוֹמָא, אִתְעַבְרָא לִשְׂמָאלָא, וְקַיְּימָא עַל עָלְמָא, כָּמִין עַל כֹּלָּא, קָטִיל לְשָׁאוּל וְלִבְנוֹי, אִתְאֲבִיד מִינַיְיהוּ מַלְכוּ, מִיתוּ מִיִּשְׂרָאֵל כַּמָּה אַלְפִין וְכַמָּה רִבְוָון. וְעַד כְּעַן, הַהוּא חוֹבָה הֲוָה תָּלֵי, עַד דְּאָתָא סַנְחֵרִיב וְאַרְגִּיז כֹּלָּא.

122. Achimelech was the supernal High Priest, and all priests that were with him were all best men of the Queen, WHICH IS MALCHUT. After they were killed, the Queen remained alone, WITHOUT UNION WITH ZEIR ANPIN. Her attendant was lost, and there was no one to serve Her and manage Her house and make Her happy in order to be united with the King. So from that day, She went over to the left side, and stood lurking over the world. That sin killed Saul and his sons, and many thousands and ten thousands of Yisrael died. It was suspended, until Sancheriv came and terrified everyone.

123. וְדָא הוּא עוֹד הַיּוֹם בְּנוֹב, דָּא הוּא יוֹמָא עִלָּאָה, וּמַאן אִיהוּ. דָּא כ"י, דְּאַבְדַת שׁוֹשְׁבִינִין דִּילָהּ, הַהִיא דְּאִשְׁתְּאָרַת בְּלֹא יְמִינָא, לְאִתְדַּבְּקָא בִּשְׂמָאלָא. דְּכַהֲנָא יְמִינָא הוּא. וּבְגִין כַּךְ, עוֹד הַיּוֹם בְּנוֹב לַעֲמוֹד.

123. Thus, the meaning of, "This very day he will halt in Nov," is the supernal day. What is it? This is the Congregation of Yisrael, WHICH IS MALCHUT, who lost her attendant, so that She remained without the right to join with the left, because the priest is the right. And therefore, "this very day He will halt in Nov," TO DEMAND JUDGMENT FOR THE SLAYING OF NOV, THE CITY OF THE PRIESTS, UNTIL, THROUGH THAT SIN, THE VERSE CONCLUDES: "AND LEBANON SHALL FALL BY A MIGHTY ONE" (YESHAYAH 10:34).

124. תָּא חֲזֵי, כְּתִיב גִּבְעַת שָׁאוּל נָסָה, שָׁאוּל אֲמַאי הָכָא. אֶלָּא בְּגִין דְּהוּא קָטִיל לְכַהֲנֵי, וְגָרִים דְּרוֹעָא יְמִינָא, לְאִתְעַקְרָא מֵעָלְמָא. אוּף הָכָא, מֵהַהוּא יוֹמָא, לָא אַעְבָּר ב"נ בְּהַהוּא דוּכְתָּא, בְּגִין דְּלָא אִסְתַּכַּן בְּנַפְשֵׁיהּ. אָמַר לֵיהּ רִבִּי יוֹסֵי לְרִבִּי חִיָּיא, וְלָא אֲמָרִית לָךְ דִּלְמָא גַּבְרָא רַבָּא הוּא.

124. Come and behold: it is written: "*Giv'at* Saul is fled" (Ibid. 29). HE ASKS: Why is Saul mentioned here? AND HE ANSWERS: It is because he killed the priests IN NOV and caused that the right arm should be uprooted from the world, AS MENTIONED. BECAUSE OF HIS SIN, THE INHABITANTS OF HIS DWELLING, GIV'AT SAUL, FLED FROM THE KING OF ASHUR (ASSYRIA). From that day onward, no person passed that place, in order not to endanger himself. Rabbi Yosi said to Rabbi Chiya: Did I not say to you that he might be a great man?!

125. פָּתַח וְאָמַר, אַשְׁרֵי אָדָם מָצָא חָכְמָה. אַשְׁרֵי אָדָם, כְּגוֹן אֲנָן, דְּאַשְׁכַּחְנָא לָךְ, וְיָדַעְנָא מִינָךְ מִלָּה דְּחָכְמְתָא. וְאָדָם יָפִיק תְּבוּנָה, כְּגוֹן אֲנָן, דְּאוֹרִיכְנָא לָךְ לְאִתְחַבְּרָא בַּהֲדָךְ. וְדָא הוּא ב"נ דְּזַמִּין לֵיהּ קוּדְשָׁא בְּרִיךְ הוּא נְבִזְבְּזָא בְּאָרְחָא, אַנְפּוֹי דִּשְׁכִינְתָּא, וְעַל דָּא כְּתִיב, וְאֹרַח צַדִּיקִים כְּאוֹר נֹגַהּ. אָזְלוּ.

125. He opened the discussion, saying: "Happy is the man who finds wisdom" (Mishlei 3:13). "Happy is the man," means like us, who found you and learned from you a word of wisdom. "And the man who brings forth understanding" (Ibid.), like us who waited for you, to join with you. Such is a man for whom the Holy One, blessed be He, prepared a treasure on the road, the face of Shechinah. Referring to this, it is written: "But the path of just men is like the gleam of sunlight" (Mishlei 4:18). They walked on.

126. פָּתַח הַהוּא גַּבְרָא וְאָמַר לְדָוִד מִזְמוֹר לַיְיָ׳ הָאָרֶץ וּמְלוֹאָהּ וְגוֹ׳. לְדָוִד מִזְמוֹר בַּאֲתָר חַד, וּבַאֲתַר אַחֲרָא מִזְמוֹר לְדָוִד, מַה בֵּין הַאי לְהַאי. אֶלָּא לְדָוִד מִזְמוֹר, שִׁירָתָא דְּקָאָמַר דָּוִד, עַל כְּנֶסֶת יִשְׂרָאֵל. מִזְמוֹר לְדָוִד, שִׁירָתָא דְּקָאָמַר דָּוִד, עַל גַּרְמֵיהּ.

126. That man opened the discussion, saying: "To David a Psalm. The earth is Hashem's and the fullness thereof" (Tehilim 24:1). HE ASKS: "To David a Psalm," IS WRITTEN in one place, and in another place, IT IS WRITTEN, "A Psalm to David." What is the difference between these? HE ANSWERS: "To David a Psalm," denotes a psalm that David said about the Congregation of Yisrael, WHICH IS MALCHUT. "A psalm to David," denotes a psalm that David said about himself.

127. לַיְיָ׳ הָאָרֶץ וּמְלוֹאָהּ. לַיְיָ׳: דָּא קוּדְשָׁא בְּרִיךְ הוּא. הָאָרֶץ וּמְלוֹאָהּ: דָּא כְּנֶסֶת יִשְׂרָאֵל, וְכָל אוּכְלוֹסִין דִּילָהּ, דְּמִתְחַבְּרָן בַּהֲדָהּ, וְאִקְרוּן מְלוֹאָהּ וַדַּאי הוּא. כְּמָה דְּאַתְּ אָמֵר, מְלֹא כָל הָאָרֶץ כְּבוֹדוֹ תֵּבֵל וְיוֹשְׁבֵי בָהּ: דָּא הוּא אַרְעָא דִּלְתַתָּא, דְּאִקְרֵי תֵּבֵל, וַאֲחִידַת בְּדִינָא דִּלְעֵילָּא, הֲדָא הוּא דִּכְתִּיב וְהוּא יִשְׁפּוֹט תֵּבֵל בְּצֶדֶק, בֵּין לְחָד, בֵּין לְעַמָּא חַד, בֵּין לְכָל עָלְמָא, מֵהַאי דִּינָא הוּא אִתְּדָן.

127. "The earth is Hashem's." This is the Holy One, blessed be He, MEANING ZEIR ANPIN. "The earth...and the fullness thereof" is the Congregation of Yisrael, WHICH IS MALCHUT, and all the multitudes that join with Her. They are called "the fullness thereof," for assuredly it is so, as is written: "The whole world is full of His glory" (Yeshayah 6:3). "The world and they that dwell in it," is the earth below that is called *Tevel*' ('world'), and is held by the Judgment of above, MEANING MALCHUT. This is what is written: "And He will Judge the world in righteousness" (Tehilim 9:9). Whether an individual, a nation, or the whole world, they will be Judged according to this Judgment, MEANING FROM THE JUDGMENT OF MALCHUT THAT IS CALLED 'RIGHTEOUSNESS'.

128. תָּא חֲזֵי, פַּרְעֹה מֵהַאי דִּינָא יָנִיק, עַד דְּאִתְאֲבִידוּ הוּא וְכָל עַמֵּיהּ. כֵּיוָן דְּהַאי דִּינָא אִתְּעַר עָלֵיהּ, הַהוּא מְמָנָא דְּאִתְמָנָא עֲלַיְיהוּ

בְּשֻׁלְטָנוּתָא, אִתְעֲדֵי וְאִתְעֲבָר, כְּדֵין כֻּלְּהוּ דִּלְתַתָּא, אִתְאֲבִידוּ, דִּכְתִּיב וַיָּסַר אֶת אוֹפַן מַרְכְּבוֹתָיו. מַאי אוֹפַן מַרְכְּבוֹתָיו. מַרְכְּבוֹתָיו דְּפַרְעֹה. וּמַאן אִיהוּ הַהוּא אוֹפַן דִּלְהוֹן, הַהוּא מְמָנָא דְּשָׁלִיט עֲלַיְיהוּ. וְעַל דָּא מִיתוּ כֻּלְּהוּ בְּיַמָּא. אֲמַאי בְּיַמָּא, אֶלָּא יַמָּא עִלָּאָה אִתְּעַר עֲלַיְיהוּ, וְאִתְמְחוּ בִּידָהָא. וּבְגִין כַּךְ טֻבְּעוּ בְּיַם סוּף כְּתִיב. אָמַר רִבִּי יוֹסֵי וַדַּאי הָכִי הוּא, וְעַל דָּא כְּתִיב, טֻבְּעוּ בְּיַם סוּף. סוֹפָא דְּדַרְגִּין.

128. Come and behold: Pharaoh was nurtured by this Judgment, and so he and all his people perished. After this Judgment OF MALCHUT was aroused against them, the minister that was appointed to rule over them was removed. Then all those below perished, as it is written: "And He took off their chariots' wheels." What is "their chariots' wheels"? MEANING the chariots of Pharaoh. And who is their wheel? THE MEANING is that minister who rules over them. Therefore, they all died in the sea. And why in the sea? Rather the upper sea, WHICH IS MALCHUT, aroused against them, and they were exterminated by it. Therefore, it is written that they "drowned in the Red Sea (Heb. *suf*)." Rabbi Yosi said: Assuredly it is so. And therefore, it is written: "drowned in the Red Sea (Heb. *suf*)," WHICH MEANS the end (Heb. *sof*) of the levels, NAMELY MALCHUT – THAT THEY WERE OBLITERATED BY HER.

129. רִבִּי חִיָּיא אָמַר, וַיְנַהֲגֵהוּ בִּכְבֵדוּת. בִּכְבֵדוּת מַהוּ. אֶלָּא מִכָּאן אוֹלִיפְנָא, דִּבְהַהוּא דַּבְּרוּתָא דְּאִתְדָּבַּר בֵּיהּ בַּר נָשׁ, מְדַבְּרִין לֵיהּ. בְּפַרְעֹה כְּתִיב וַיִּכְבַּד לֵב פַּרְעֹה. בְּהַהוּא מִלָּה, דָּבַר לֵיהּ קוּדְשָׁא בְּרִיךְ הוּא, בִּכְבֵדוּת מַמָּשׁ. אָמַר לֵיהּ קוּדְשָׁא בְּרִיךְ הוּא, רָשָׁע, אַתְּ אוֹקִיר לִבָּךְ. אֲנָא אַדְבַּר לָךְ בְּהַאי, עַל דָּא וַיְנַהֲגֵהוּ בִּכְבֵדוּת.

129. Rabbi Chiya said: "that they drove heavily." What is the meaning of "heavily"? From here, we learn that a person is subsequently led on the path that he chooses to go. By Pharaoh, it is written: "And the heart of Pharaoh was hard (lit. 'heavy')" (Shemot 9:7). In this same manner, the Holy One, blessed be He, led him with actual heaviness. The Holy One, blessed be He, said to him: 'Evil one, you made your heart heavy. I will lead you in a similar way.' Therefore, "they drove heavily."

130. וַיֹּאמֶר מִצְרַיִם אָנוּסָה מִפְּנֵי יִשְׂרָאֵל וְגוֹ'. וַיֹּאמֶר מִצְרַיִם, דָּא מְמָנָא דְּאִתְמְנֵי עַל מִצְרָאֵי. אָמַר רַבִּי יוֹסֵי, הַאי מִלָּה קַשְׁיָא, כֵּיוָן דְּאַעְבְּרוּ לֵיהּ מִשּׁוּלְטָנוּתֵיהּ, הֵיךְ יָכִיל הוּא לְמִרְדַּף אֲבַתְרַיְיהוּ דְּיִשְׂרָאֵל.

130. "So that Egypt said, 'Let us flee from the face of Yisrael...'" "Egypt said," is the minister who was appointed over Egypt, NAMELY THEIR MINISTER IN THE LOFTY HEAVENS. Rabbi Yosi said: This is difficult. Since he was already removed from his dominion, how was he able to chase after Yisrael?

131. אֶלָּא וַדַּאי הָכִי הוּא. אֲבָל דָּא וַיֹּאמֶר מִצְרַיִם, מִצְרַיִם דִּלְתַתָּא. כִּי יְיָ' נִלְחָם לָהֶם בְּמִצְרָיִם, מִצְרַיִם דִּלְעֵילָּא, דְּכֵיוָן דְּאִתְּבַר חֵילֵהוֹן מִלְעֵילָּא, כְּדֵין אִתְּבַר חֵילָא וְתוּקְפָּא דִּלְהוֹן לְתַתָּא, הֲדָא הוּא דִּכְתִּיב כִּי יְיָ' נִלְחָם לָהֶם בְּמִצְרָיִם. בְּמִצְרַיִם דַּיְיקָא. דָּא הוּא תּוּקְפָּא דִּלְהוֹן דִּלְעֵילָּא. וְדָא הוּא דְּאוּקְמוּהָ מֶלֶךְ מִצְרַיִם סְתָם. הָכָא, וַיֹּאמֶר מִצְרַיִם אָנוּסָה מִפְּנֵי יִשְׂרָאֵל, דְּחָמוּ דְּהָא אִתְּבַר חֵילֵיהוֹן, וְתוּקְפָּא דִּלְהוֹן, דִּלְעֵילָּא.

131. HE ANSWERS: But certainly it is Thus. the passage, "So that Egypt said," IS NOT THEIR MINISTER BUT RATHER Egypt of below, "for Hashem fights for them against Egypt," namely Egypt of above, THEIR MINISTER. Since their power was broken above, their power and might was broken below. Hence, it is written: "For Hashem fights for them against Egypt," against Egypt specifically, which is their power above, NAMELY THEIR APPOINTED MINISTER. And as we established above, IN THE PLACE WHERE IT SAYS merely "king of Egypt," MEANING THAT PHARAOH IS NOT MENTIONED, THE REFERENCE IS TO THE MINISTER WHO IS APPOINTED OVER EGYPT. HERE ALSO, "AGAINST EGYPT," REFERS TO THE MINISTER APPOINTED OVER EGYPT. And, "So that Egypt said, 'Let us flee from the face of Yisrael,'" REFERS TO EGYPT OF BELOW, for they saw that their power and might of above were broken, NAMELY THEIR MINISTER.

132. תָּא חֲזֵי, כַּד אִתְּעָרַת הַאי כְּנֶסֶת יִשְׂרָאֵל, אִתְּעָרוּ כָּל אִינּוּן

דַּאֲחִידָן בָּהּ, וְכֻלְּהוּ אַחֲרָנִין דִּלְתַתָּא, וְיִשְׂרָאֵל לְעֵילָּא מִכֻּלְּהוּ, דְּהָא אִינּוּן נַטְלֵי לָהּ בְּגוּפָא דְּאִילָנָא, וְהָא אוּקְמוּהָ. וּבְגִינֵי כַּךְ יִשְׂרָאֵל אֲחִידָן בָּהּ, יַתִּיר מִכָּל עוֹבְדֵי כו"ם. וְכַד אִינּוּן מִתְעָרִין, אִתְּבַר תּוּקְפֵּהוֹן מֵאִינּוּן דְּשַׁלְטֵי עֲלַיְיהוּ.

132. Come and behold: When this Congregation of Yisrael becomes aroused, WHICH IS MALCHUT, all those who are affiliated with Her and all the others of below, NAMELY ALL THE NATIONS, are aroused. Yisrael are higher above all because they grasp Her by the trunk of the tree, MEANING WHEN SHE IS CONNECTED TO ZEIR ANPIN THAT IS CALLED THE 'TREE OF LIFE'. Therefore, Yisrael are more attached to it than all the nations of the world. And when they become aroused TO HARM THE CHILDREN OF YISRAEL, the power of those who dominate over them is broken, MEANING THEIR MINISTERS ABOVE.

133. תָּא חֲזֵי, הַאי מְמָנָא שֻׁלְטָנָא דְּמִצְרָאֵי, דָּחִיק לוֹן לְיִשְׂרָאֵל, בְּכַמָּה שִׁעְבּוּדִין, כְּמָה דְּאוּקְמוּהָ. לְבָתַר דְּאִתְּבַר הוּא בְּקַדְמֵיתָא, אִתְּבָּרוּ אִינּוּן מַלְכְוָותָא מִלְּתַתָּא, הה"ד כִּי יְיָ' נִלְחָם לָהֶם בְּמִצְרַיִם. נִלְחָם לָהֶם וַדַּאי.

133. Come and behold: that minister, the governor of Egypt, oppressed Yisrael with many types of enslavements, as we have established. He was broken first, and then all the kingdoms below were broken. It is written: "For Hashem fights for them against Egypt." Indeed, He fights for them.

11. "And the Angel of Elohim...moved"

A Synopsis

This passage contains an obscure but beautiful description of the energy flow on the supernal levels, the sea with its waves of judgments rising and falling, the angels which are the fish of that sea, and the four directions of the world. It ends by saying: Let those who have wings stand firm. Let those who have faces cover their faces until He departs on His journeys. Then, "And the Angel of Elohim...moved."

תּוֹסֶפְתָּא

134. וַיִּסַּע מַלְאַךְ הָאֱלֹהִים וְגוֹ׳. (מַתְנִיתִין) עַד לָא אִשְׁתְּכַח אֲוִירָא דַּכְיָא, וְלָא נְהִירִין, אֲבָנִין נְקִיבָן הֲווֹ סְתִימָאן. תְּלַת רוּחִין דִּכְלִילָן בִּתְלַת, הֲווֹ שְׁקִיעָן. וּמַיִין סְתִימָן תְּחוֹת נוּקְבֵי. בְּשַׁבְעִין וּתְרֵין אַתְוָון אִתְהַדָּרוּ לְאַתְרַיְיהוּ אִינּוּן אֲבָנִין.

Tosefta (addendum)

134. "And the Angel of Elohim...moved…" (Shemot 14:19). Mishnah: Before there was pure air and before it shone, the punctured stones were clogged. Three winds that are included in three were submerged, and water was concealed under the holes. By the 72 letters, these stones returned to their place.

135. בָּתַר שַׁבְעִין וּתְרֵין דַּרְגִּין, וְכֵן תְּלַת זִמְנִין, אִתְבְּקָעוּ וְאִתְנְקִיבוּ אֲבָנֵי, תְּחוֹת צְרוֹרָא דַּהֲוָה חָקִיק, וְאִתְכְּנָפוּ דַּרְגִּין, וְאִתְעָבִידוּ כְּנוּפְיָא חֲדָא.

135. After the 72 levels, which are three times 72 LETTERS, the stones were split and punctured under an engraved bundle. And the levels gathered together and became one group.

136. לְבָתַר אִתְפְּלָגוּ, וְאִתְעָבִידוּ תְּרֵין דַּרְגִּין, פַּלְגּוּתָא מַיָּא אַגְלִידוּ, וּפַלְגּוּתָא אִשְׁתְּקָעוּ. אִלֵּין סָלִיקוּ, וְאִלֵּין נַחְתּוּ, מֵהָכָא שָׁרָא עָלְמָא

לְאִתְפַּלְגָא.

136. Afterwards, they divided and became two levels OF WATER. Half of the water congealed and half of it sank. Part went up and part went down. From here, the world started to divide.

137. צְרוֹרָא אַחֲרָא אִית לְעֵילָּא, וְהוּא גְּלִיפָא בע״ב חֲתִימָן דְּגוּשְׁפַּנְקָא תַּקִּיפָא, וּבְהוּ שְׁקִיעַן גַּלְגַּלּוֹי דְּיַמָּא. כַּד נַטְלִין, אִתְפְּלָגוּ לְאַרְבַּע זַוְיָין. פַּלְגוּ חֲדָא סָלִיק, וּפַלְגוּ חֲדָא נָחִית, פַּלְגוּ חֲדָא לִסְטַר צָפוֹן, וּפַלְגוּ חֲדָא לִסְטַר דָּרוֹם. כַּד מִתְחַבְּרָן כַּחֲדָא, גּוּמְרִין דְּלַהֲטִין קַיְימִין, בְּלַהַט שִׁנָּנָא דְּחַרְבָּא דְּמִתְהַפְּכָא.

137. There is another bundle above that is engraved with 72 seals of the strong seal ring, and in these the waves of the sea are submerged. When they travel, they divide to four corners. One part rises, FOR IT ILLUMINATES FROM BELOW UPWARDS, THAT IS, THE NUKVA, WHICH IS THE SECRET OF WEST. One part descends, FOR IT ILLUMINATES FROM ABOVE DOWNWARDS WITH THE LIGHT OF CHASSADIM, NAMELY ZEIR ANPIN, WHICH IS THE SECRET OF EAST. One part towards the north, WHICH IS THE LEFT COLUMN, GVURAH, and one part towards the south, WHICH IS THE RIGHT COLUMN, CHESED. When they unite together, there are flaming coals in the blade of the Revolving Sword.

138. חַד קַיְימָא נָעִיץ בְּגוֹ יַמָּא, דַּרְגָּא שְׁלִיחָא דְּאַפַּרְכָא עִלָּאָה, סָלִיק בְּהַהוּא קַיָּימָא לְעֵילָּא לְעֵילָּא, אִסְתַּכָּל לְמֵרָחִיק, קְטוּרָא דְּאַרְבִּין דְּשָׁאטִין בְּיַמָּא. מַאן חָמֵי גַּלְגַּלִּין דְּסַלְקִין וְנַחְתִּין וְרוּחָא דְּנָשִׁיב בְּהוּ, וְנוּנֵי יַמָּא נַגְדִּין כָּל אִינּוּן אַרְבִּין לְכָל סִטְרֵי עָלְמָא.

138. One pillar is thrust into the sea. The level, which is a messenger of the supernal state – WHICH IS MALCHUT THAT IS FROM THE CHEST AND HIGHER – rises in this pillar higher and higher, and looks at a distance TO SEE a band of ships floating in the sea. Who observes the waves rising and falling, BECAUSE OF THE JUDGMENTS THAT THEY CONTAIN, and the wind, WHICH IS THE CENTRAL COLUMN, blows on them AND QUIETS

THEM, and the fish of the sea, WHICH ARE THE ANGELS, pull all these ships in all directions of the world. IN THIS MANNER IS CHOCHMAH REVEALED.

139. הַהוּא דַּרְגָּא, כַּד נָחִית מֵהַהוּא, קַיְימֵי אֶלֶף מִימִינֵיהּ, וְאֶלֶף מִשְּׂמָאלֵיהּ, הֲוָה תָּב וְיָתִיב בְּאַתְרֵיהּ, כְּמַלְכָּא בְּכוּרְסְיֵהּ, הַהוּא דַּרְגָּא דְּכַד שָׁאטֵי יַמָּא לְאַרְבַּע סִטְרֵי עָלְמָא, עִמֵּיהּ נַפְקַת, בֵּיהּ תֵּבַת, הוּא תָּב בְּקִיּוּמָא דְּמַלְכָּא.

139. When that level, NAMELY METATRON descended FROM ABOVE THE CHEST, a thousand stand at his right and a thousand stand at his left, MEANING THAT HE DRAWS CHOCHMAH – THAT IS ALLUDED TO IN THE NUMBER 1,000 – BOTH ON HIS RIGHT AND ON HIS LEFT. And he returns FROM THE CHEST AND LOWER, and sits in his place like a king on his throne. When the sea, WHICH IS MALCHUT, swims to the four directions of the world, that level goes out with it and returns with it, and it returns with the establishing of the king.

140. כְּדֵין כָּרוֹזִין נָפְקִין, מַאן מָארֵי דְּעַיְינִין, יִזְדַּקְפָּאן לוֹן לְעֵילָּא לְעֵילָּא. מָארֵיהוֹן דְּגַדְפִּין יְקוּמוּן בְּקִיּוּמַיְיהוּ. מָארֵי דְּאַנְפִּין, חַפְיָין לוֹן, עַד דְּנָטִיל בְּמַטְלָנוֹי. כְּדֵין וַיִּסַּע מַלְאַךְ הָאֱלֹהִים.

(עד כאן)

140. Then announcements are made. Let him, WHO IS OF THOSE who have eyes, raise them higher and higher. Let those who have wings stand firm. Let those who have faces cover their faces until He departs on His journeys. Then, "And the Angel of Elohim…moved"

(End of Tosefta)

12. "She is like the merchant ships"

A Synopsis

Rabbi Chiya opens with the verse, "She is like the merchant ships; she brings her food from afar," and "from afar she brings her food." He says that the merchant ships is the Congregation of Yisrael, and that "brings her food" means by a level that dwells on her, that is the central column. He speaks about "all the rivers flow into the sea," telling of the movement and flow through that level, Yesod, down to the sea, Malchut, and from Binah to Yesod, back and forth. Rabbi Yitzchak says that those who merit the World to Come will merit the pairing of supernal Aba and Ima, which never separate.

141. רִבִּי חִיָּיא פָּתַח, הָיְתָה כָּאֳנִיּוֹת סוֹחֵר מִמֶּרְחָק תָּבִיא לַחְמָהּ. הָיְתָה כָּאֳנִיּוֹת סוֹחֵר, דָּא כנ״י. מִמֶּרְחָק תָּבִיא לַחְמָהּ, כְּמָה דְּאַתְּ אָמֵר, הִנֵּה שֵׁם יְיָ׳ בָּא מִמֶּרְחָק. תָּבִיא לַחְמָהּ, בְּחַד דַּרְגָּא דְּשָׁארֵי עָלָהּ, וּבֵיהּ אִתְמְשָׁכוּ כָּל אִלֵּין נְחָלִין וּמַבּוּעִין דְּאַזְלִין בְּיַמָּא, כְּמָה דְּאַתְּ אָמֵר, כָּל הַנְּחָלִים הוֹלְכִים אֶל הַיָּם וְגוֹ׳.

141. Rabbi Chiya opened the discussion with the verse: "She is like the merchant ships; she brings her food from afar" (Mishlei 31:14). "She is like the merchant ships," refers to the Congregation of Yisrael, NAMELY MALCHUT. "She brings her food from afar," as is written: "Behold the Name of Hashem comes from afar" (Yeshayah 30:27). "She brings her food," meaning by one level that dwells upon her, WHICH IS THE CENTRAL COLUMN, WHICH IS THE SECRET OF YESOD OF ZEIR ANPIN. All the rivers and springs that run into the sea flow through it, as is written: "All the rivers run into the sea" (Kohelet 1:7).

142. אֶל מָקוֹם שֶׁהַנְּחָלִים הוֹלְכִים, אע״ג דְּכֻלְּהוּ נְחָלִין אִתְמַשְׁכָן בְּהַהוּא דַּרְגָּא, וְהַהוּא דַּרְגָּא נָחִית לוֹן לְהַהוּא יַמָּא, לָא תֵּימָא. דְּהָא אָרִיק לוֹן, וְהָא לָא שַׁרְיָין בֵּיהּ אַחֲרָנִין, וְלָא נַגְדִּין בֵּיהּ כְּמִלְקַדְּמִין, אַהְדָּר וְאָמַר אֶל מָקוֹם שֶׁהַנְּחָלִים הוֹלְכִים שָׁם הֵם שָׁבִים, אֶל מָקוֹם דְּהַהוּא דַּרְגָּא דְּנַחֲלִין אַזְלִין זִמְנָא חֲדָא, שָׁם הֵם שָׁבִים לָלֶכֶת, תַּמָּן

אִינּוּן תַּיְיבִין מֵהַהוּא אֲתָר עִלָּאָה, וְלָא פַּסְקִין לְעָלְמִין, וּמִתְכַּנְּשֵׁי כֻּלְּהוּ בְּהַהוּא אֲתָר. וְלָמָּה. לָלֶכֶת. לְמֵהַךְ לְהַהוּא אֲתָר דְּיַמָּא, כְּמָה דְּאִתְּמַר, מַה שְׁמֵיהּ דְּהַהוּא דַּרְגָּא. צַדִּיק אִקְרֵי.

142. "To the place that the rivers flow" (Ibid.). Although all the rivers flow through that level, WHICH IS YESOD, and that level lowers them down to the sea, WHICH IS MALCHUT, do not think that it poured those rivers INTO THE SEA, so that others do not dwell in it and do not flow through it as before. THEREFORE, it says again, "To the place that the rivers flow, thither they return" (Kohelet 1:7). THEY RETURN to the place of that level that the rivers went out from once – "Thither they return to go." There, they return from that high supernal place, NAMELY, FROM BINAH THEY RETURN AGAIN TO YESOD, FOR THE FLOW never halts from there and they all gather in that place IN YESOD. And why, "to go"? To go to that place of the sea, WHICH IS MALCHUT, as we have learned. And what is the name of that level? It is called 'Righteous', NAMELY YESOD OF ZEIR ANPIN.

143. רִבִּי יְהוּדָה אָמַר, כְּתִיב שָׁם אֳנִיּוֹת יְהַלֵּכוּן לִוְיָתָן זֶה יָצַרְתָּ לְשַׂחֶק בּוֹ. שָׁם אֳנִיּוֹת יְהַלֵּכוּן, בְּהַהוּא יַמָּא דְּאַזְלִין וְשָׁאטִין, עַד דְּאַתְיָין לְאִתְחַבְּרָא בְּהַהוּא דַּרְגָּא, כְּדֵין כְּתִיב לִוְיָתָן זֶה יָצַרְתָּ לְשַׂחֶק בּוֹ.

143. Rabbi Yehuda said: It is written: "There go the ships: there is the Leviathan, whom You have made to play therein" (Tehilim 104:26). "There go the ships" MEANS THAT in this sea traverse and go THE SHIPS until they approach to join at that level, WHICH IS YESOD. Then it is written: "There is the Leviathan, whom You have made to play therein," BECAUSE LEVIATHAN IS YESOD IN ZEIR ANPIN.

144. רִבִּי יִצְחָק אָמַר, לְעֵילָּא לְעֵילָּא יַתִּיר, אִית זִוּוּגָא אַחֲרָא, דְּשָׁארִי בַּחֲבִיבוּתָא, וְלָא מִתְפָּרַשׁ לְעָלְמִין. אָמַר רִבִּי יְהוּדָה, מַאן זָכֵי לְהַהוּא זִוּוּגָא. אָמַר לֵיהּ, מַאן דְּאִית לֵיהּ חוּלָקָא בְּעָלְמָא דְּאָתֵי. בְּעָלְמָא דְּאָתֵי דַּיְקָא.

144. Rabbi Yitzchak said: there is one union that is kept in friendship very high, and they never separate – WHICH IS THE SECRET OF THE UNION OF

SUPERNAL ABA AND IMA, WHICH ARE THE FIRST THREE SFIROT OF BINAH. Rabbi Yehuda said: Who merits that union? He said to him: One who has a share in the World to Come, WHICH IS BINAH. And it is specifically "the World to Come," FOR ONE WHO DID NOT MERIT THE WORLD TO COME, WHICH IS BINAH, WILL NOT MERIT THAT UNION.

145. אָמַר לֵיהּ, וְהָא מֵהָכָא אוֹלִיפְנָא, דִּכְתִּיב לִוְיָתָן זֶה יָצַרְתָּ לְשַׂחֶק בּוֹ, מַשְׁמַע דְּקָאָמַר זֶה, וְזֶה וְזֹאת יְדִיעָן אִינּוּן. אָמַר רִבִּי אַבָּא, תַּרְוַויְיכוּ שַׁפִּיר קָאָמְרִיתּוּ, וְהָא דְּרִבִּי יְהוּדָה שַׁפִּיר דַּיְקָא, וְכֹלָּא זַמִּין קוּדְשָׁא בְּרִיךְ הוּא לְאִתְעַנְּגָא בְּהוּ לְצַדִּיקַיָּיא, הה״ד אָז תִּתְעַנַּג עַל יְיָ׳.

145. RABBI YEHUDA said to him: Behold, from here we learned what is written: "There is the Leviathan, whom (Heb. *zeh*) You have made to play therein." So it seems, "*zeh*," is mentioned WHICH IS YESOD, and *Zeh* ('this', masc.) and *Zot* ('this', fem.) are known TO BE YESOD AND MALCHUT. SO WE SEE THAT EVEN IF HE DOES NOT MERIT BINAH, HE MERITS TO RECEIVE FROM THE SUPERNAL UNION. Rabbi Aba said: You both speak well and these words of Rabbi Yehuda are beautifully exact. And the Holy One, blessed be He, has prepared everything to delight the Righteous with them. This is what is written: "Then shall you delight yourself in Hashem" (Yeshayah 58:14).

13. "And the Angel of Elohim...moved"

A Synopsis

In this section we read of the Great Queen, Malchut, into whose hands the Holy One, blessed be He gave His authority. She is called "the way to the Tree of Life," and when she travels, her camps travel with her. We are told that she is "the Angel of Elohim" in the title verse, and she is the messenger of all, both from below to above and from above to below. Anyone who desires to speak to the Holy One, blessed be He must first notify the Queen, Malchut. The Congregation of Yisrael is also called Malchut, who are placed under her jurisdiction. Rabbi Yosi speaks about the pillar of cloud that always appears with the Shechinah. Rabbi Shimon adds that the pillar of cloud and the pillar of fire, which are Abraham and Isaac, are both present in the Shechinah. To conclude, he says that the passage, "And the Angel of Elohim, who went before the camp of the children of Yisrael, moved and went behind them," means that he moved from the side of Chesed and joined the side of Gvurah, because the time had come to become attired with Judgment.

146. אָמַר רִבִּי אַבָּא, כַּמָּה אַלְפִין, כַּמָּה רִבְבָן דְּמַשִּׁירְיָין קַדִּישִׁין, אִית לֵיהּ לְקוּדְשָׁא בְּרִיךְ הוּא, מָארֵי דְּאַנְפִּין עִלָּאִין, מָארֵי דְּעַיְינִין, מָארֵי דְּזַיְינִין, מָארֵי דִּילָלָה, מָארֵי דִּיבָבָא, מָארֵי דְּרַחֲמֵי, מָארֵי דְּדִינָא, וְעֵילָּא מִנַּיְיהוּ אַפְקַד לְמַטְרוֹנִיתָא לְשַׁמְשָׁא בְּהֵיכְלָא קָמֵיהּ.

146. Rabbi Aba said: How many thousands and how many ten thousands of holy camps does the Holy One, blessed be He, have. NAMELY, those with supernal faces, those with eyes, those with weapons, those who lament, those who sob, those who are merciful and those who judge. Above them, He appointed the Queen, WHO IS MALCHUT, to serve before Him in His sanctuary.

147. לָקֳבֵיל אִלֵּין, אִית לָהּ לְמַטְרוֹנִיתָא, מַשִּׁירְיָין מְזַיְּינִין. בְּשִׁתִּין אַנְפִּין מִשְׁתַּכְחוּ מַשִׁרְיָין מְזוּיָּינִין. וְכֻלְּהוּ חֲגִירָן חַרְבָּא, קַיְּימָאן בְּסַחֲרָנָהָא, כַּמָּה נָפְקִין, כַּמָּה עַיְילִין. בְּשִׁית גַּדְפִּין טָאסִין כָּל עָלְמָא. קַמֵּי כָּל חַד וְחַד גּוּמְרִין דְּנוּר דָּלִיק. לְבוּשׁוֹי, מִתְלָהֲטָא אֶשָּׁא. בְּגַבּוֹי,

שִׁנָּנָא דְּחַרְבָּא מִתְלַהֲטָא בְּכָל עָלְמָא, לְנַטְרָא קָמָהּ. הה"ד וְאֵת לַהַט הַחֶרֶב הַמִּתְהַפֶּכֶת לִשְׁמוֹר אֶת דֶּרֶךְ עֵץ הַחַיִּים.

147. Corresponding to them, the Queen, WHO IS MALCHUT, has armed camps OF ANGELS. These armed camps have sixty faces. They are all girded with swords encircling MALCHUT. Many are leaving and many are coming. With six wings, they fly over the whole world. Fiery coals are lit before each one so that its garments are a flaming fire, and at his back is the blade of the sword that flames in the whole world to guard before Her. This is what is written: "And the bright blade of a revolving sword to guard the way to the Tree of Life" (Beresheet 3:24).

148. מַאן דֶּרֶךְ עֵץ הַחַיִּים. דָּא הִיא מַטְרוֹנִיתָא רַבְּתָא, דְּהִיא אָרְחָא, לְהַהוּא אִילָנָא רַבְרְבָא תַּקִּיף, אִילָנָא דְּחַיֵּי. דִּכְתִּיב הִנֵּה מִטָּתוֹ שֶׁלִּשְׁלֹמֹה שִׁשִּׁים גִּבּוֹרִים סָבִיב לָהּ מִגִּבּוֹרֵי יִשְׂרָאֵל. יִשְׂרָאֵל דִּלְעֵילָּא, כֻּלָּם אֲחוּזֵי חֶרֶב.

148. HE ASKS: Who is it that is called "the way to the Tree of Life"? HE ANSWERS: This is the Great Queen, WHO IS MALCHUT, which is the path to the great strong tree, WHICH IS ZEIR ANPIN called 'the Tree of Life'. It is written: "Behold it is his litter, that of Solomon; sixty valiant men are round about it, of the mighty men of Yisrael" (Shir Hashirim 3:7), that is Yisrael of above, THAT IS ZEIR ANPIN, "all girt with swords" (Ibid.).

149. כַּד נַטְלָא מַטְרוֹנִיתָא, כֻּלְּהוּ נַטְלִין בַּהֲדָהּ, הה"ד וַיִּסַּע מַלְאַךְ הָאֱלֹהִים. וְכִי מַלְאַךְ הָאֱלֹהִים אִתְקְרֵי. א"ר אַבָּא אִין. ת"ח, הָכִי א"ר שִׁמְעוֹן, אַתְקִין קוּדְשָׁא בְּרִיךְ הוּא קָמֵיהּ, הֵיכָלָא קַדִּישָׁא, הֵיכָלָא עִלָּאָה, קַרְתָּא קַדִּישָׁא, קַרְתָּא עִלָּאָה. יְרוּשָׁלַיִם עִיר הַקֹּדֶשׁ אִקְרֵי, מַאן דְּעָאל לְמַלְכָּא, לָא עָאל, אֶלָּא מֵהַהוּא קַרְתָּא קַדִּישָׁא, נָטִיל אָרְחָא לְמַלְכָּא, דְּאָרְחָא מֵהָכָא אִתְתְּקַן.

149. When the Queen travels, they all travel with Her. This is what is written: "And the Angel of Elohim...moved" (Shemot 14:19). HE ASKS: Is then MALCHUT called "the Angel of Elohim"? Rabbi Aba said: Yes. Come and behold. Rabbi Shimon said: the Holy One, blessed be He, prepared before Him the Holy Sanctuary, the Supernal Sanctuary, the Holy City, the Supernal City. Jerusalem is called 'the Holy City'. ALL THESE ARE THE NAMES OF MALCHUT. Whoever comes to the King enters only from that Holy City, WHICH IS MALCHUT. FROM THERE begins the path to the King, because the path has been constructed from here.

150. הה״ד זֶה הַשַּׁעַר לַיְיָ׳ צַדִּיקִים יָבוֹאוּ בוֹ. כָּל שְׁלִיחוּתָא דְּבָעֵי מַלְכָּא מִבֵּי מַטְרוֹנִיתָא נָפְקָא, וְכָל שְׁלִיחוּתָא מִתַּתָּא לְמַלְכָּא, לְבֵי מַטְרוֹנִיתָא עָיֵיל בְּקַדְמֵיתָא, וּמִתַּמָּן לְמַלְכָּא. אִשְׁתְּכַח דְּמַטְרוֹנִיתָא אִיהִי שְׁלִיחָא דְּכֹלָּא, מֵעֵילָּא לְתַתָּא, וּמִתַּתָּא לְעֵילָּא. וְעַל דָּא, אִיהִי שְׁלִיחָא דְּכֹלָּא, הה״ד וַיִּסַּע מַלְאַךְ הָאֱלֹהִים הַהוֹלֵךְ לִפְנֵי מַחֲנֵה יִשְׂרָאֵל, יִשְׂרָאֵל דִּלְעֵילָּא. מַלְאַךְ הָאֱלֹהִים, הה״ד בֵּיהּ, וַיְיָ׳ הוֹלֵךְ לִפְנֵיהֶם וְגוֹ׳, וְהַאי לָלֶכֶת יוֹמָם וָלַיְלָה, כְּמָה דְּאוּקְמוּהָ.

150. Hence, it is written: "This is the gate to Hashem, into which the Righteous shall enter" (Tehilim 118:20). Every mission that the King, WHO IS ZEIR ANPIN desires, goes forth from the house of the Queen, WHO IS MALCHUT. Every mission THAT COMES from below the King, WHO IS ZEIR ANPIN, first enters before the Queen, and from there to the King. So in actuality, the Queen is the messenger of all, BOTH from below up and from above down. Therefore, she is the messenger of all. This is what is written: "And the Angel of Elohim, who went before the camp of Yisrael," meaning Yisrael of above, WHICH IS ZEIR ANPIN, and the Angel of Elohim, WHO IS MALCHUT. This is what is written about Him: "And Hashem went before them...by day and by night," and, "that they might go by day and night," as we established earlier, TO MEAN ZEIR ANPIN AND MALCHUT. SO WE SEE THAT MALCHUT WENT IN FRONT OF THE CHILDREN OF YISRAEL. THIS IS WHAT IS WRITTEN: "AND THE ANGEL OF ELOHIM, WHO WENT BEFORE THE CAMP OF THE CHILDREN OF YISRAEL, MOVED..."

151. וְכִי יְקָרָא הוּא דְּמַלְכָּא, דְּמַטְרוֹנִיתָא תֵּזִיל, וְהִיא תַּגַּח קְרָבָא, וְהִיא אַזְלַת שְׁלִיחָא. אֶלָּא, לְמַלְכָּא דְּאִזְדַּוַּוג בְּמַטְרוֹנִיתָא עִלָּאָה, חָמָא מַלְכָּא יְקִירוּ דִּילָהּ, עַל כָּל שְׁאַר מַטְרוֹנִיתָא דְּעָלְמָא, אָמַר כֻּלְּהוּ מִשְׁתַּכְּחִין לְחֵינָתָא, לָקֳבֵל הַאי מַטְרוֹנִיתָא דִּילִי. הִיא סַלְקָא עַל כֹּלָּא,

מַה אַעֲבִיד לָהּ. אֶלָּא כָּל בֵּיתָא דִּילִי יְהֵא בִּידָהָא, אַפִּיק מַלְכָּא כָּרוֹזָא, מֵהָכָא כָּל מִלִּין דְּמַלְכָּא בִּידָא דְּמַטְרוֹנִיתָא יִתְמַסְרוּן. מַה עָבֵיד. אַפְקִיד מַלְכָּא בִּידָהָא כָּל זַיְינִין דִּילֵיהּ, כָּל אִינּוּן מָארֵי מַגִּיחִין קְרָבָא, כָּל אִינּוּן אֲבָנִין יְקָרִין דְּמַלְכָּא, כָּל גִּנְזַיָּיא דְּמַלְכָּא. אָמַר, מֵהָכָא, כָּל מַאן דְּיִצְטְרִיךְ לְמַלְּלָא עִמִּי, לָא יָכִיל לְמַלְּלָא עִמִּי, עַד דְּאוֹדַע לָהּ מַטְרוֹנִיתָא.

151. HE ASKS: Is it an honor for the King, WHO IS ZEIR ANPIN, that the Queen, WHO IS MALCHUT, should go and do battle and go on a mission? HE ANSWERS: THIS IS SIMILAR to a king who married a lofty queen. The king saw her preciousness and that she exceeded all the other queens in the world. He said: 'All the others are considered concubines compared this queen of mine. She is above them all. What shall I do for her? All my house shall be in Her hands.' The king made an announcement: 'From now on, all the matters of the king will be given over to the hand of the queen.' What did He do? The king placed in Her hands all his weapons, all the men-of-war and the precious stones of the king – all the treasures of the king. He said: 'From now on, anyone who desires to speak with Me will not be able to speak to me, until he notifies the queen.

152. כַּךְ קוּדְשָׁא בְּרִיךְ הוּא, מִסְּגִיאוּת חֲבִיבוּתָא וּרְחִימוּתָא דִּילֵיהּ בכ"י, אַפְקִיד כֹּלָּא בִּרְשׁוּתָהּ, אָמַר, הָא כָּל שְׁאָרִי, לָא מִשְׁתַּכְּחֵי כְּלוּם לְגַבָּהָא. אָמַר, שִׁשִּׁים הֵמָּה מְלָכוֹת וְגוֹ', אַחַת הִיא יוֹנָתִי תַמָּתִי. מַה אַעֲבִיד לָהּ, אֶלָּא, הָא כָּל בֵּיתָא דִּילִי בִּידָהָא. אַפִּיק מַלְכָּא כָּרוֹזָא, מֵהָכָא כָּל מִלִּין דְּמַלְכָּא, בִּידָא דְּמַטְרוֹנִיתָא יִתְמַסְרוּן. אַפְקִיד בִּידָהָא כָּל זַיְינִין דִּילֵיהּ, רוּמְחִין, וְסַיְיפִין, קַשְׁתִּין, חִצִּין, וַחֲרָבִין, בַּלִּסְטְרִין. קַסְטִירָאִין, אָעִין, אֲבָנִין, כָּל אִינּוּן מָארֵי מַגִּיחֵי קְרָבָא. הה"ד, הִנֵּה מִטָּתוֹ שֶׁלִּשְׁלֹמֹה שִׁשִּׁים גִּבּוֹרִים וְגוֹ' כֻּלָּם אֲחוּזֵי חֶרֶב מְלוּמְּדֵי וְגוֹ'.

152. So the Holy One, blessed be He, in His great affection and love for the Congregation of Yisrael, WHO IS MALCHUT, placed everything in Her jurisdiction. He said: All the rest are considered as nothing compared to Her. He said: "There are sixty queens...My dove, my undefiled, is but one"

(Shir Hashirim 6:8-9). What shall I do for Her? Thus, all My house will be in Her hands. The King made an announcement. From now on all the matters of the King would be given over into the hands of the Queen. He placed in her hands all his weapons, spears, swords, bows, arrows, knives, catapult STONES, fortifications, wood, rocks and all soldiers. This is what is written, "Behold it is his litter, that of Solomon, sixty valiant men...all girt with swords, and expert in war..." (Shir Hashirim 3:8)

153. אָמַר מַלְכָּא, מִכָּאן וּלְהָלְאָה, קְרָבָא דִּילִי אִתְמְסַר בִּידָךְ, זַיְינִין דִּילִי, מָארֵי מַגִּיחֵי קְרָבָא בִּידָךְ. מִכָּאן וּלְהָלְאָה אַתְּ הֲוֵי נַטְרָא לִי, הה״ד, שׁוֹמֵר יִשְׂרָאֵל. מִכָּאן וּלְהָלְאָה, מַאן דְּאִצְטְרִיךְ לִי, לָא יָכִיל לְמַלְּלָא עִמִּי, עַד דְּאוֹדַע לְמַטְרוֹנִיתָא, הה״ד, בְּזֹאת יָבֹא אַהֲרֹן אֶל הַקֹּדֶשׁ. שְׁלִיחָא דְּמַלְכָּא בְּכֹלָּא, כְּמָה דְּאוֹקִימְנָא. אִשְׁתְּכַח דְּכֹלָּא בִּידָהָא, וְדָא הוּא יְקָרָא דְּמַטְרוֹנִיתָא. הֲדָא הוּא דִּכְתִּיב, וַיִּסַּע מַלְאַךְ הָאֱלֹהִים וְגוֹ׳, כְּמָה דְּאִתְּמַר.

153. The King said: From now on, My wars are given over into your hand. My weapons and my soldiers shall be in your hand, and from now on you will guard me. It is written, "He who keeps Yisrael" (Tehilim 121:3), WHICH IS ZEIR ANPIN CALLED 'YISRAEL'. From now on, whoever needs me will not be able to talk to me until he notifies the queen. This is what is written: "Thus (lit. 'with *Zot*') shall Aaron come into the holy place" (Vayikra 16:3). AND *ZOT* ('THIS', FEM.) IS MALCHUT, the representative of the King in everything as we have established, so we find that everything is in Her hands. This is the honor of the Queen. This is what is written: "And the Angel Elohim...moved" (Shemot 14:19), as we have learned.

154. וַיֵּלֶךְ מֵאַחֲרֵיהֶם, מ״ט מֵאַחֲרֵיהֶם. בְּגִין דְּיִשְׁתַּכְּחוּ לְקַמָּהָא מָארֵי מַגִּיחֵי קְרָבָא, מָארֵי בַּלִּסְטְרָאוֹת, מָארֵי רוֹמְחִין וְסַיְיפִין, וְאִתְגַּלְּוּן קַמָּהָא, דְּהָא הֲווֹ אַתְיָין מַשִּׁירְיָין אַחֲרָנִין, לְאַגָּחָא קְרָבָא בְּיִשְׂרָאֵל מִלְּעֵילָּא, וְע״ד וַיֵּלֶךְ מֵאַחֲרֵיהֶם.

154. "And went behind them" (Ibid.). HE ASKS: What is the reason he went behind them? HE ANSWERS: It was in order that warriors, catapultors, spearsmen and swordsmen should be positioned in front of them, so that they should be visible in front of them, because other camps were coming from above to do battle against Yisrael. Therefore, he "went behind them," IN ORDER TO GIVE ROOM FOR THE MEN OF WAR OF YISRAEL'S SIDE TO FIGHT WITH THEM.

155. וְתָאנָא, בְּהַהִיא שַׁעֲתָא, אָתָא רַבְרְבָא שֻׁלְטָנָא דִּמְמָנָא עַל מִצְרָאֵי, וְכָנַשׁ שִׁית מֵאָה רְתִיכִין מְקַטְרְגִין, וְעַל כָּל רְתִיכָא וּרְתִיכָא, שִׁית מֵאָה שָׁלְטָנִין מִמָּנָן קַטֵיגוֹרִין, הה״ד וַיִּקַּח שֵׁשׁ מֵאוֹת רֶכֶב בָּחוּר וְגוֹ׳. וְכִי שֵׁשׁ מֵאוֹת רֶכֶב בָּחוּר, לָא הֲווֹ רִכְבֵי מִצְרַיִם, מ״ט וְכֹל רֶכֶב מִצְרָיִם. אֶלָּא הָכִי תָּאנָא, הֲוָה סָמָאֵ״ל אוֹזִיף לֵיהּ, שִׁית מֵאָה רְתִיכִין מְקַטְרְגִין לְסַיְּיעָא לֵיהּ. הה״ד וַיִּקַּח שֵׁשׁ מֵאוֹת רֶכֶב בָּחוּר.

155. We learned at that time the reigning minister who was appointed over Egypt came and gathered six hundred chariots of persecutors, with six hundred appointed ruling prosecuting officers on every single chariot. This is what is written: "And he took six hundred chosen chariots..." (Shemot 14:7). HE ASKS: Were not the six hundred chosen chariots the chariots of Egypt? For what reason DOES IT SAY AFTERWARDS: "And all the chariots of Egypt"? HE ANSWERS: We learned that Samael loaned six hundred prosecuting chariots to help THE PATRON ANGEL OF EGYPT. This is what is written: "And he took six hundred chosen chariots," THAT WERE NOT OF EGYPT.

156. אֵימָתַי אַשְׁלִים קוּדְשָׁא בְּרִיךְ הוּא לְסָמָאֵ״ל. בִּקְרָבָא דְּסִיסְרָא, דְּעִקֵּר קוּדְשָׁא בְּרִיךְ הוּא לְכָל אִינּוּן רְתִיכִין, וְאִתְמְסָרוּ בִּידָא דְּמַטְרוֹנִיתָא. הה״ד, נַחַל קִישׁוֹן גְּרָפָם נַחַל קְדוּמִים וְגוֹ׳. וּלְזִמְנָא דְּאָתֵי, יִתְמְסָרוּ כֻּלְּהוּ, הה״ד, מִי זֶה בָּא מֵאֱדוֹם חֲמוּץ בְּגָדִים מִבָּצְרָה וְגוֹ׳. וְע״ד וַיֵּלֶךְ מֵאַחֲרֵיהֶם, דִּזְמִינָא שְׁכִינְתָּא בְּסוֹף יוֹמַיָּא לְאַעְקְרָא לוֹן מִן עָלְמָא.

156. When did the Holy One, blessed be He, repay Samael? It was during the wars of Sisra that the Holy One, blessed be He, uprooted all these chariots and they were given over to the hands of the Queen. This is what is written: "The waters of Kishon swept them away, that ancient brook..." (Shoftim 5:21). In the days to come, they will all be handed over, as is written: "Who is this that comes from Edom, with crimsoned garments from Batzrah..." (Yeshayah 63:1). Therefore, he "went behind them," MEANING THAT the Shechinah shall uproot them from the world in the end of the days.

157. וַיִּסַּע עַמּוּד הֶעָנָן מִפְּנֵיהֶם, מַאן עַמּוּד הֶעָנָן דָּא. רִבִּי יוֹסֵי אָמַר, דָּא הוּא עֲנָנָא דְּאִתְחָזֵי תָּדִיר עִם שְׁכִינְתָּא. וְדָא הוּא עֲנָנָא דְּעָאל מֹשֶׁה בְּגַוֵּיהּ. רִבִּי אַבָּא אָמַר, כְּתִיב וַיְיָ׳ הוֹלֵךְ לִפְנֵיהֶם יוֹמָם, אֶלָּא סִיוּעָא דְּצַדִּיק הוּא, וּפְרִישׂוּ דִּרְשִׁימוּ דִּילֵיהּ, וְע״ד אָזִיל הַאי עָנָן יוֹמָם, וּכְתִיב יוֹמָם יְצַוֶּה יְיָ׳ חַסְדּוֹ. וּמִסִּטְרָא דְּחֶסֶ״ד אָתָא עֲנָנָא דָּא, וְדָא חֶסֶד אִתְקְרֵי, וַעֲנָנָא אַחֲרָא אָזִיל בְּלֵילְיָא, וְאִתְקְרֵי עַמּוּד אֵשׁ.

157. "And the pillar of cloud went from before their face" (Shemot 14:19). HE ASKS: What is this pillar of cloud? Rabbi Yosi said: This is the cloud that always appears with the Shechinah, WHO IS THE ANGEL MICHAEL, and this is the cloud into which Moses entered. Rabbi Aba said: It is written: "And Hashem went before them by day in a pillar of cloud," SO WE SEE THAT IT IS NOT MICHAEL WHICH IS THE ASPECT OF SHECHINAH, but rather it is the support of the righteous, THAT IS, YESOD IN ZEIR ANPIN. He spreads CHASSADIM of his imprint, FOR YESOD SPREADS OUT CHASSADIM OVER THE CHOCHMAH IN MALCHUT AND THEN SHE IS ABLE TO ILLUMINATE. Therefore, this cloud goes by day, WHICH IS THE TIME WHEN CHASSADIM SHINE, as is written: "Yet Hashem commands his steadfast love (lit. 'Chesed') in the daytime" (Tehilim 42:9), because this cloud comes from the side of Chesed and is called 'Chesed'. A different cloud goes by night, and is called 'a pillar of fire', WHICH IS FROM THE SIDE OF MALCHUT.

158. רִבִּי שִׁמְעוֹן אָמַר, עָמְדוּ הֶעָנָן יוֹמָם: דָּא אַבְרָהָם. וְעַמּוּד הָאֵשׁ לַיְלָה: דָּא יִצְחָק. וְתַרְוַיְיהוּ אִשְׁתְּכָחוּ בִּשְׁכִינְתָּא, וּמַה דְּאָמַר רִבִּי אַבָּא, הָכִי הוּא וַדַּאי, דְּעַל יְדָא דְּהַאי דַּרְגָּא, אִשְׁתְּכָחוּ.

158. Rabbi Shimon said: "By day in a pillar of a cloud," refers to Abraham, who is Chesed. "By night the pillar of fire," refers to Isaac, WHO IS

GVURAH, and both of them are present in the Shechinah. Rabbi Aba said THAT IT IS THE SUPPORT OF THE RIGHTEOUS, for THEY are present IN THE SHECHINAH through that level.

159. וְהַאי וַיִּסַּע מַלְאַךְ הָאֱלֹהִים הַהוֹלֵךְ לִפְנֵי מַחֲנֵה יִשְׂרָאֵל וַיֵּלֶךְ מֵאַחֲרֵיהֶם. וַיִּסַּע: דְּנָטִיל מִסִּטְרָא דְּחֶסֶ"ד, וְאִתְדְּבַק בְּסִטְרָא דִּגְבוּרָה, בְּגִין דְּהָא מָטָא שַׁעֲתָא לְאִתְלַבְּשָׁא בְּדִינָא.

159. The passage: "And the Angel of Elohim, who went before the camp of Yisrael, moved and went behind them," MEANS that he moved from the side of Chesed and joined the side of Gvurah – BECAUSE CHESED IS FRONT AND GVURAH IS BACK – because the time had come to become attired with Judgment.

14. "And...moved...and it came...and...stretched out"

A Synopsis

Rabbi Aba tells us that at that moment the moon, Malchut, became attired on one side with the crowns of supernal Chesed, on the left side by the spears of Gvurah and on the third side by a purple garment called Tiferet. The number 72 is used repeatedly for emphasis and to draw together the various concepts. The 72 crowns in each of the three columns are combined in Malchut, and the Holy Name ascends from them, which is the secret of the Chariot. Rabbi Aba explains how the 72 letters are written and arranged. We learn that the Holy One, blessed be He is perfect because He encompasses the left side and the right side and we must never forget that Judgment is part of His concealed nature, so we must be careful not to incur it.

Rabbi Yitzchak returns to the time when Yisrael were trapped on the seashore with the enemy behind and the sea in front, and says that their prayers and cries to God awakened the collective light of above, and the sea executed the supernal laws. Rabbi Shimon adds that when the world needs Mercy the Holy One, blessed be He, takes pity and listens.

160. תָּא חֲזֵי, בְּהַהִיא שַׁעֲתָא אִשְׁתְּלִים סִיהֲרָא מִכֹּלָּא, וְיָרְתָא שַׁבְעִין וּתְרֵין שְׁמָהָן קַדִּישִׁין, בִּתְלַת סִטְרִין. חֲדָא אִתְלַבְּשָׁא בְּעִטְרוֹי דְּחֶסֶד עִלָּאָה, בְּשַׁבְעִין גְּלִיפִין דִּנְהִירוּ דְּאַבָּא עִלָּאָה, דְּאַנְהִיר לָהּ.

160. Come and behold: at that moment, the moon became full, WHICH IS MALCHUT of all THE ASPECTS, and she inherited 72 Holy Names on three sides, NAMELY THREE COLUMNS. On one side, MALCHUT was attired with the crowns of the supernal Chesed, with seventy engravings of the light of supernal Aba illuminating Her, WHICH IS THE SECRET OF "MOVED."

161. סִטְרָא תִּנְיָינָא, אִתְלַבְּשַׁת בְּרוֹמְחֵי דִּגְבוּרָ״ה, בְּשִׁתִּין פּוּלְסֵי דְּנוּרָא, וַעֲשָׂרָה דִּילָהּ דִּנְחַתוּ מִסִּטְרָא דְּאִמָּא עִלָּאָה בְּנִימוּסֵי גְּלִיפִין.

161. On the second side, MALCHUT was attired with the spears of Gvurah, MEANING THE JUDGMENTS IN HER, by sixty lashes of fire and ten lashes of Her own that descended from the side of supernal Ima in set Judgments.

AND THIS IS THE SECRET OF THE LEFT COLUMN AND THE PASSAGE: "AND IT CAME..."

162. סִטְרָא תְּלַתָאֵי, אִתְלַבְּשַׁת בִּלְבוּשֵׁי אַרְגְוָנָא, דְּלָבִישׁ מַלְכָּא עִלָּאָה קַדִּישָׁא, דְּאִקְרוּן תִּפְאֶרֶ"ת, דְּיָרִית בְּרָא קַדִּישָׁא, בְּשַׁבְעִין עִטְרִין עִלָּאִין, מִסִּטְרָא דְּאַבָּא וְאִמָּא, וְהוּא כָּלִיל לְהַאי סִטְרָא וּלְהַאי סִטְרָא.

162. On the third side, MALCHUT was attired in a purple garment that the supernal King, called 'Tiferet', wore and which the Holy Son, WHO IS TIFERET, inherited with the seventy supernal crowns from the side of Aba and Ima. He includes both sides, NAMELY THE RIGHT, WHICH IS CHESED, AND THE LEFT, WHICH IS GVURAH, WHICH IS THE SECRET OF "STRETCHED OUT."

163. וּתְרֵין עִטְרִין מִסִּטְרָא דְּאַבָּא וְאִימָּא, וְאִינּוּן שַׁבְעִין וּתְרֵין שְׁמָהָן. וְתָנֵינָן מִסִּטְרָא דְּחֶסֶ"ד שַׁבְעִין, וּתְרֵין סָהֲדִין. מִסִּטְרָא דִּגְבוּרָא שַׁבְעִין, וּתְרֵין סוֹפְרִין. מִסִּטְרָא דְּת"ת שַׁבְעִין, וּתְרֵין גַּוְונִין לְאִתְפָּאֲרָא.

163. There are two crowns from the side of Aba and Ima, which are *Ayin-Bet* (72) names. We learned that there are seventy from the side of Chesed plus two witnesses. From the side of Gvurah, there are seventy plus two scribes. From the side of Tiferet, there are seventy plus two colors for glorification.

164. וּבְהַאי אֲתָר, אִתְגְּלִיף חַד בְּחַד, וְאִסְתְּלִיק שְׁמָא קַדִּישָׁא, רָזָא דִּרְתִּיכָא, וְהָכָא אִתְגְּלִיפוּ אֲבָהָתָא, לְאִתְחַבְּרָא בְּחַד, וְהוּא שְׁמָא קַדִּישָׁא גְּלִיפָא בְּאַתְווֹי.

164. In this place, NAMELY MALCHUT, they are engraved one in the other, SO THAT THE 72 CROWNS IN EVERY COLUMN ARE COMBINED WITH EACH OTHER. And the Holy Name emerges from them, which is the secret of the Chariot, FOR THEY BECOME *AYIN-BET* (72) NAMES, EACH ONE CONSISTING OF THREE LETTERS. Here the Patriarchs are engraved, WHICH ARE CHESED, GVURAH AND TIFERET, THE THREE COLUMNS to be joined together. Thus is the Holy Name, *AYIN-BET,* engraved with its letters.

165. צֵרוּפָא דְּאַתְוָון אִלֵּין, אַתְוָון קַדְמָאֵי, רְשִׁימִין כְּסִדְרָן בְּאֹרַח מֵישָׁר, בְּגִין דְּכֻלְּהוּ אַתְוָון קַדְמָאֵי אִשְׁתְּכָחוּ בְּחֶסֶ״ד, לְמֵהַךְ בְּאֹרַח מֵישָׁר, בְּסִדּוּרָא מִתְּתַקַּן.

165. The combination of these letters are as follows. the first set of letters, NAMELY THE 72 LETTERS IN THE PASSAGE, "AND THE ANGEL...MOVED," are written in their order in a straightforward manner – BECAUSE STRAIGHT IS AN INDICATION OF CHESED – and all the original letters are in Chesed, NAMELY, IN THE RIGHT COLUMN, to follow a straightforward manner, in a proper order.

8	7	6	5	4	3	2	1
מ	מ	ע	א	ש	ל	א	ו
ד	פ	ע	ח	ר	פ	ל	י
מ	נ	מ	ר	א	נ	ה	ס
א	י	ו	י	ל	י	י	ע
ח	ה	ד	ה	ו	מ	ם	מ
ר	ם	ה	ם	י	ח	ה	ל
י	ו	ע	ו	ל	נ	ה	א
ה	י	נ	י	ך	ה	ל	ך
ם	ע	ן	ס	מ	י	ך	ה

Scanning directions

166. אַתְוָון תִּנְיָינֵי, רְשִׁימִין בְּגַלְגּוּלָא לְמַפְרֵעַ, בְּגִין דְּכֻלְּהוּ אַתְוָון תִּנְיָינֵי, מִשְׁתַּכְחוּ בִּגְבוּרָה, לְגַלָּאָה דִּינִין וְזִינִין דְּאַתְיָין מִסִּטְרָא דִּשְׂמָאלָא.

166. The second set of letters, NAMELY THE 72 LETTERS IN THE PASSAGE, "AND IT CAME," are written backwards, MEANING THEY ARE WRITTEN FROM BELOW UPWARDS, AS WRITTEN FURTHER IN THE SECOND DIAGRAM. All the second 72 letters pertain to Gvurah so as to reveal Judgments and weapons that come from the left side. AND WHEN THEY ARE

IN REVERSE ORDER, THEY ALLUDE TO JUDGMENTS.

ה	כ	ל	ה	ל	י	ל	ה	9
ק	ר	ב	ז	ה	א	ל	ז	8
ה	ל	י	ל	ה	ו	ל	א	7
ש	ך	ו	י	א	ר	א	ת	6
י	ה	ע	נ	ן	ו	ה	ח	5
י	ש	ר	א	ל	ו	י	ה	4
ו	ב	י	ן	מ	ח	נ	ה	3
ח	נ	ה	מ	צ	ר	י	ם	2
ו	י	ב	א	ב	י	ן	מ	1

Scanning directions

167. אַתְוָון תְּלִיתָאֵי, אִינּוּן אַתְוָון רְשִׁימָן, לְאַחֲזָאָה גַּוְונִין, לְאִתְעַטְּרָא בְּמַלְכָּא קַדִּישָׁא. וְכֹלָּא בֵּיהּ מִתְחַבְּרָן וּמִתְקַשְּׁרָן, וְהוּא אִתְעַטָּר בְּעִטְּרוֹי בְּאֹרַח מֵישָׁר, וְרָשִׁים לְהַאי סִטְרָא וּלְהַאי סִטְרָא, כְּמַלְכָּא דְּאִתְעַטָּר בְּכֹלָּא.

167. The third set of letters, NAMELY THE 72 LETTERS IN THE PASSAGE, "AND MOSES STRETCHED OUT," are letters that are written so as to expose the colors, WHICH ARE THE JUDGMENTS, with which to adorn the Holy King, WHICH IS THE SECRET OF THE 72 COLORS OF GLORIFICATION. They all join and are bound to Him BECAUSE HE IS THE CENTRAL COLUMN. And He glorifies in His crowns in a straight forward manner and makes an imprint on this side and the other side – NAMELY, TO THE RIGHT COLUMN AND TO THE LEFT COLUMN – AS HE ESTABLISHES THE ILLUMINATION OF BOTH OF THEM as a King who is adorned with everything.

8	7	6	5	4	3	2	1
י	ה	י	י	ה	ו	ד	ו
ב	י	ל	ם	י	ל	ו	י
ק	ם	ה	ע	ם	ך	ע	ט
ע	ל	ו	ז	ב	י	ל	מ
ו	ח	י	ה	ר	ה	ה	ש
ה	ר	ש	כ	ו	ו	י	ה
מ	ב	ם	ל	ח	ה	ם	א
י	ה	א	ה	ק	א	ו	ת
ם	ו	ת	ל	ד	ת	י	י

Scanning directions

168. הָכָא אִתְרְשִׁים שְׁמָא קַדִּישָׁא גְּלִיפָא בְּע״ב תֵּיבִין, דְּמִתְעַטְּרֵי בַּאֲבָהָתָא, רְתִיכָא קַדִּישָׁא עִלָּאָה. וְאִי תֵּימָא, הָנֵי אַתְוָון תְּלִיתָאֵי, מ״ט לָאו אִינּוּן כְּתִיבִין, מִנְּהוֹן בְּאֹרַח מֵישָׁר כְּסִדּוּרָן, וּמִנְּהוֹן לְמַפְרֵעַ, לְיַשְּׁרָא לְהַאי סִטְרָא, וּלְהַאי סִטְרָא, דְּהָא תָּנֵינָן, אַתָּה כּוֹנַנְתָּ מֵישָׁרִים, קוּדְשָׁא בְּרִיךְ הוּא עָבֵיד מֵישָׁרִים לִתְרֵי סִטְרֵי, וּכְתִיב וְהַבְּרִיחַ הַתִּיכוֹן בְּתוֹךְ הַקְּרָשִׁים וְגוֹ׳, דָּא קוּדְשָׁא בְּרִיךְ הוּא. רִבִּי יִצְחָק אָמַר, דָּא יַעֲקֹב, וְכֹלָּא חַד.

168. Here is marked the Holy Name, engraved with 72 letters. THAT IS, THREE TIMES 72 LETTERS IN EACH OF THE THREE COLUMNS COMBINE AND JOIN TOGETHER, AND THEY FORM 72 WORDS. EACH WORD CONTAINS THREE LETTERS FROM THE THREE COLUMNS that are adorned with the Patriarchs, NAMELY CHESED, GVURAH AND TIFERET, which are the supernal Holy Chariot. HE ASKS: Why is the third group of letters not written IN 2 WAYS, part of them straightforward and part of them in reverse, in order to be equal to both sides – MEANING TO THE RIGHT COLUMN AND TO THE LEFT COLUMN, SINCE IT SUSTAINS THE ILLUMINATION OF BOTH. Because we learned that, "You have established equity" (Tehilim 99:4), means that the Holy One, blessed be He, establishes equity AND SUSTAINS on both sides. It is written: "And the middle bar in the midst of the boards" (Shemot 26:28), which is the Holy One, blessed be He, NAMELY THE

CENTRAL COLUMN THAT SUSTAINS THE TWO SIDES. IF SO, IT SHOULD HAVE BEEN WRITTEN 'HALF STRAIGHT', LIKE THE RIGHT COLUMN, AND 'HALF IN REVERSE ORDER', LIKE THE LEFT COLUMN. Rabbi Yitzchak said: This is Jacob, and it is all one, BECAUSE JACOB ALSO INDICATES THE CENTRAL COLUMN.

Scanning direction ←

כהת	אכא	ללה	מהש	עלם	סיט	ילי	והו	1
הקם	הרי	מבה	יזל	ההע	לאו	אלד	הזי	2
והו	מלה	ייי	נלך	פהל	לוו	כלי	לאו	3
ושר	לכב	אום	ריי	שאה	ירת	האא	נתה	4
ייז	רהע	חעם	אני	מנד	כוק	להח	יחו	5
מיה	עשל	ערי	סאל	ילה	וול	מיכ	ההה	6
פוי	מבה	נית	ננא	עמם	החש	דני	והו	7
מחי	ענו	יהה	ומב	מצר	הרח	ייל	נמם	8
מום	היי	יבמ	ראה	חבו	איע	מנק	דמב	9

169. אֶלָּא לְמַלְכָּא דְּאִיהוּ שְׁלִים מִכֹּלָּא, דַּעְתֵּיהּ שְׁלִים מִכֹּלָּא, מָה אָרְחֵיהּ דְּהַהוּא מַלְכָּא. אַנְפּוֹי נְהִירִין כְּשִׁמְשָׁא תָּדִיר, בְּגִין דְּאִיהוּ שְׁלִים. וְכַד דָּאִין, דָּאִין לְטָב וְדָאִין לְבִישׁ. וְעַל דָּא בָּעֵי לְאִסְתַּמְּרָא מִינֵּיהּ. מַאן דְּאִיהוּ טִפְּשָׁא, חָמֵי אַנְפּוֹי דְּמַלְכָּא נְהִירִין וְחַיְיכָן, וְלָא אִסְתְּמַר מִינֵּיהּ. וּמַאן דְּאִיהוּ חַכִּימָא, אַף עַל גַּב דְּחָמֵי אַנְפּוֹי דְּמַלְכָּא נְהִירִין, אָמַר מַלְכָּא וַדַּאי שְׁלִים הוּא, שְׁלִים הוּא מִכֹּלָּא, דַּעְתֵּיהּ שְׁלִים, אֲנָא חָמֵי דִּבְהַהוּא נְהִירוּ, דִּינָא יָתִיב וְאִתְכַּסְיָא, אע"ג דְּלָא אִתְחַזְיָא, דְּאִי לָאו הָכִי, לָא יְהֵא מַלְכָּא שְׁלִים, וְעַל דָּא בָּעֵי לְאִסְתַּמְּרָא.

169. HE ANSWERS: This is similar to a king who is perfect in everything and his mind is wholesome. What is the custom of that king? His face always shines like the sun, because he is perfect. And when he judges, he judges for good and for bad. Therefore, it is necessary to be guarded from him. He who is stupid sees the shining, laughing face of the king and does not guard himself from him. But even though he sees the face of the king shining, the wise man says: the king is surely perfect and complete in everything, his mind is whole. Yet I see that in that shine there sits judgment, but it is concealed, even though it is not visible, because otherwise the king would not be perfect, it is necessary to be cautious.

170. כַּךְ קוּדְשָׁא בְּרִיךְ הוּא, שְׁלִים תָּדִיר בְּהַאי גַּוְונָא וּבְהַאי גַּוְונָא, אֲבָל לָא אִתְחַזְיָא, אֶלָּא בִּנְהִירוּ דְּאַפִּין. וּבְגִין כַּךְ, אִינּוּן טִפְּשִׁין חַיָּיבִין לָא אִסְתַּמְּרָן מִנֵּיהּ. אִינּוּן חַכִּימִין זַכָּאִין, אַמְרִין, מַלְכָּא שְׁלִים הוּא, אַף עַל גַּב דְּאַנְפּוֹי אִתְחַזְיָין נְהִירִין, דִּינָא אִתְכַּסְיָא בְּגַוֵּיהּ, בְּגִין כַּךְ בָּעֵי לְאִסְתַּמְּרָא מִנֵּיהּ.

170. So it is with the Holy One, blessed be He. He is always perfect in this manner and that manner, MEANING IN THE RIGHT SIDE AND IN THE LEFT SIDE, but He only appears with a shining face. Therefore, these wicked fools are not cautious with Him. But the righteous wise men say: the King is perfect, and even though His face appears shining, Judgment is concealed in it. Therefore, it is necessary to be cautious with Him.

171. אָמַר רִבִּי יְהוּדָה, מֵהָכָא, אֲנִי יְיָ׳ לֹא שָׁנִיתִי. לָא דָּלִיגְנָא לַאֲתָר אַחֲרָא, בִּי אִתְכְּלִיל כֹּלָּא. הָנֵי תְּרֵי גַּוְונֵי בִּי אִתְכְּלִילָן, בְּגִין כַּךְ כֹּלָּא בְּאֹרַח מֵישָׁר אִתְחַזְיָא, וְאַף עַל גַּב דְּאַתְוָון אֲחִידָן לְהַאי סִטְרָא וּלְהַאי סִטְרָא, כְּסִדְרָן כְּתִיבִין.

171. Rabbi Yehuda said: From here, WE CAN ANSWER THE QUESTION OF WHY THE 72 LETTERS OF THE CENTRAL COLUMN WERE NOT WRITTEN HALF FORWARD AND HALF IN REVERSE, FOR IT IS WRITTEN: "For I am the Hashem, I do not change" (Malachi 3:6), WHICH MEANS, 'I did not move to a different place. EVEN THOUGH THE TWO COLUMNS ARE INCLUDED IN ME, STILL IN ALL I DID NOT CHANGE MYSELF BECAUSE OF THIS TO JUMP TO THE LEFT ASPECT. RATHER, I REMAINED IN THE RIGHT ASPECT, because everything is included in Me and these two colors, WHITE

AND RED, are included in Me, NAMELY IN MY CHASSADIM. THE ILLUMINATION OF THE LEFT IS NOT VISIBLE IN ME BUT IN MALCHUT.’ THEREFORE, all THE LETTERS THAT ARE IN THE CENTRAL COLUMN appear in a straight way, even though the letters are attached to both sides, NAMELY, TO THE RIGHT AND LEFT. STILL IN ALL, they are written in their order in a straightforward way.

172. וַיִּסַּע מַלְאַךְ הָאֱלֹהִים הַהוֹלֵךְ לִפְנֵי מַחֲנֵה יִשְׂרָאֵל וַיֵּלֶךְ מֵאַחֲרֵיהֶם וַיִּסַּע עַמּוּד הֶעָנָן מִפְּנֵיהֶם וַיַּעֲמוֹד מֵאַחֲרֵיהֶם. עַד כָּאן סִטְרָא חַד, חֶסֶד לְאַבְרָהָם. אָמַר רִבִּי שִׁמְעוֹן, אֶלְעָזָר בְּרִי, תָּא חֲזֵי רָזָא דָּא. כַּד עַתִּיקָא קַדִּישָׁא אַנְהִיר לְמַלְכָּא, אַנְהִיר לֵיהּ, וְעִטְּרִין לֵיהּ, בְּכִתְרִין קַדִּישִׁין עִלָּאִין, כַּד מָטָאן לְגַבֵּיהּ מִתְעַטְּרֵי אֲבָהָתָא, בְּשַׁעֲתָה דְּמִתְעַטְּרֵי אֲבָהָתָא, כְּדֵין הוּא שְׁלִימוּ דְּכֹלָּא. כְּדֵין מַטְרוֹנִיתָא, נַטְלָא בְּמַטְלָנָהָא, בְּהַהוּא שְׁלִימוּ דַּאֲבָהָתָא. וְכַד מִתְעַטְּרָא מִכֻּלְּהוֹן, כְּדֵין אִתְבָּרְכָא, וּרְשׁוּתָא דְּכֹלָּא בִּידָהָא.

172. “And the Angel of Elohim, who went before the camp of Yisrael, moved and went behind them; and the pillar of the cloud went from before their faces, and stood behind them” (Shemot 14:19-20). Until this point is one side, Chesed to Abraham, THE RIGHT COLUMN. Rabbi Shimon said: Elazar, my son, come and behold, this secret. When Atika Kadisha shone upon the King, WHO IS ZEIR ANPIN, he illuminated on Him and crowned Him with the supernal holy crowns, WHICH ARE THE LIGHT OF CHASSADIM OF SUPERNAL ABA AND IMA, THE FIRST THREE SFIROT. When CHASSADIM reached Him, the Patriarchs, WHO WERE THE THREE COLUMNS, CHESED, GVURAH, AND TIFERET, were adorned. Then there was complete perfection. Then the Queen went on Her journeys with that perfection of the Patriarchs. And when She becomes adorned with them all, THE THREE PATRIARCHS THAT ARE THREE COLUMNS, then She is joined and has authority over everything.

173. כְּגַוְונָא דָּא שְׁמָא קַדִּישָׁא גְּלִיפָא בְּאַתְווֹי רְשִׁימִין בִּרְתִיכָא עִלָּאָה קַדִּישָׁא עִטּוּרָא דַּאֲבָהָן.

173. Similarly, the Holy Name is engraved with the letters that are imprinted on the supernal Chariot, for they are the adornment of the Patriarchs.

174. אָמַר רִבִּי יֵיסָא, אַשְׁכַּחְנָא בְּרָזָא דָא בִּתְקִיעוּתָא דְּרַב הַמְנוּנָא סָבָא, תְּלַת וּבְכֵן וּבְכֵן וּבְכֵן, לָקֳבְלֵי הָנֵי תְּלַת. וְכָךְ הוּא סִדּוּרָא. א״ר יוֹסֵי, כֹּלָּא אִתְכְּלִיל בְּהַאי שְׁמָא קַדִּישָׁא, וְאִסְתְּיִים בֵּיהּ, אִשְׁתְּכַח דִּשְׁלִימוּ דִּרְתִּיכָא קַדִּישָׁא אִית בֵּיהּ.

174. Rabbi Yisa said: We found this secret in the blowing OF THE SHOFAR of Rabbi Hamnuna Saba (the elder) three times: "thus"; "thus"; "thus." THAT IS, IN: "THUS INSTILL THE OF YOU"; "THUS SPREAD THE OF YOU"; AND "THUS GIVE GLORY." BUT IT DOES NOT ACCEPT, "THUS SHALL THE RIGHTEOUS." They correspond to these three PASSAGES: "AND THE ANGEL...MOVED"; "AND IT CAME"; "AND MOSES STRETCHED OUT." This is the order, THREE AND NO MORE. Rabbi Yosi said: Everything is included and concealed in the Holy Name, MEANING THAT ALL THREE COLUMNS OF THE NAME OF *AYIN-BET* (72) ARE INCLUDED IN MALCHUT, so we find that the perfection of the holy Chariot is IN MALCHUT. THEREFORE, THERE ARE FOUR TIMES 72: THE THREE COLUMNS, CHESED, GVURAH AND TIFERET AND MALCHUT. THEREFORE, "THUS" IS ALSO FOUR TIMES – MEANING, THAT HE MENTIONS ALSO, "THUS SHALL THE RIGHTEOUS."

175. אָמַר רִבִּי שִׁמְעוֹן, הַאי הוּא שְׁמָא קַדִּישָׁא, עִטּוּרָא דַּאֲבָהָן, דְּמִתְעַטְּרָא בִּגְלוּפַיְיהוּ, בְּחִבּוּרָא כַּחֲדָא. שְׁלִימוּ דִּרְתִּיכָא קַדִּישָׁא. וְאִתְכְּלִיל בְּאַרְבְּעִין וּתְמַנְיָא תֵּיבוּתָא, דְּאִיהוּ שְׁלִימוּ דְּכֹלָּא, וְעִקָּרָא דְּשָׁרָשִׁין.

175. Rabbi Shimon said: This is the Holy Name, the adornment of the Patriarchs, WHO ARE CHESED, GVURAH, AND TIFERET. For they become adorned in their engraving when they join together. They are the perfection of the holy Chariot, which is included in 48 words and is the perfection of everything and the mainstay of the roots.

176. תָּא חֲזֵי, גּוּפָא דְּאִילָנָא, אֲנִ״י אלֶ״ף נוּ״ן יוֹ״ד. רֵישָׁא דְּכָל עַנְפֵי

אִילָנָא, וָה״ו. וְהָא אִתְעֲרוּ חַבְרַיָּא, כְּלָלָא דַּעֲנָפִין וְנוֹפָא וְשָׁרָשָׁא, בְּאַרְבְּעִין וּתְמַנְיָא תֵּיבִין. וְהָא אִתְרְשִׁים בִּתְלַת עָלְמִין עִלָּאִין, ובג׳ עָלְמִין תַּתָּאִין.

176. Come and behold: the trunk of the tree is the name *Aleph-Nun-Yud*, THAT IS FOUND IN THE MIDDLE OF THE 72 NAMES, NAMELY, THE 37TH NAME. The top of all the branches of the tree IS THE NAME *Vav-Hei-Vav*, WHICH IS THE FIRST NAME OF THE SEVENTY TWO NAMES. The friends have already observed that the whole of the branches and the trunk and the root are found in 48 words, MEANING IN THE FIRST TWO-THIRDS OF THE SEVENTY WORDS. So it is etched in the three upper worlds – WHICH ARE CHOCHMAH, BINAH, AND DA’AT, THAT ARE INCLUDED IN THE FIRST 24 WORDS, WHICH ARE CHESED AND THE RIGHT COLUMN – and in the three lower worlds – WHICH ARE CHESED, GVURAH, AND TIFERET, THAT ARE INCLUDED IN THE SECOND 24 WORDS, WHICH ARE GVURAH AND THE LEFT COLUMN.

177. לָקֳבְלֵיהּ, קָדוֹשׁ קָדוֹשׁ קָדוֹשׁ ה׳ צְבָאוֹת. קָדוֹשׁ לְעֵילָּא. קָדוֹשׁ בְּאֶמְצָעִיתָא. קָדוֹשׁ לְתַתָּא. קָדוֹשׁ חֶסֶד. קָדוֹשׁ גְּבוּרָה. קָדוֹשׁ תִּפְאֶרֶת. וְכֻלְּהוּ בְּשַׁבְעִין וּתְרֵין אִתְגְּלִיפוּ, כְּמָה דְּאִתְּמַר. בְּרִיךְ הוּא, בְּרִיךְ שְׁמֵיהּ לְעָלַם וּלְעָלְמֵי עָלְמִין אָמֵן.

177. Corresponding TO THESE – CHESED, GVURAH, AND TIFERET IN THE THREE COLUMNS OF THE NAME *AYIN-BET* (72) – is: “Holy, holy, holy, is Hashem Tzva’ot” (Yeshayah 6:3). “Holy,” above IN CHOCHMAH, BINAH, AND DA’AT; holy in the center, IN CHESED, GVURAH, AND TIFERET; and holy below, IN NETZACH, HOD, AND YESOD. AND SO THE FIRST “Holy” is Chesed, THE SECOND “Holy” is Gvurah, and THE THIRD “Holy” is Tiferet – THAT IS, AS WAS WRITTEN BEFORE, THAT CHESED, GVURAH, AND TIFERET ARE THE SECRET OF CHOCHMAH, BINAH, DA’AT, CHESED, GVURAH, AND TIFERET, AND NETZACH, HOD AND YESOD. They are all engraved in, as explained. Blessed is He, blessed is His Name forever and ever. Amen.

178. אָמַר רִבִּי יִצְחָק, בְּשַׁעֲתָא דְּשָׁרוּ יִשְׂרָאֵל עַל יַמָּא, חָמוּ לְכַמָּה

אִכְלוּסִין, לְכַמָּה חַיָּילִין, לְכַמָּה מַשִּׁירְיָין, מֵעֵילָּא וְתַתָּא, וְכֻלְּהוּ בִּכְנוּפְיָא עֲלַיְיהוּ דְּיִשְׂרָאֵל, שָׁרִיאוּ בִּצְלוֹ מִגּוֹ עָאקוּ דִּלְהוֹן.

178. Rabbi Yitzchak said: At the time that Yisrael camped by the sea, they saw many multitudes, many soldiers, and many camps above and below. They all came and gathered against Yisrael, who started to pray from their anguish.

179. בֵּיהּ שַׁעֲתָא, חָמוּ יִשְׂרָאֵל עָאקוּ מִכָּל סִטְרִין, יַמָּא בְּגַלּוֹהִי דְּזַקְפָן קָמַיְיהוּ. בַּתְרַיְיהוּ, כָּל אִינּוּן אֻכְלוּסִין, כָּל אִינּוּן מַשִּׁירְיָין דְּמִצְרַיִם, לְעֵילָּא עֲלַיְיהוּ כַּמָּה קַטֵיגוֹרִין. שָׁרִיאוּ צַוְוחִין לְקוּדְשָׁא בְּרִיךְ הוּא.

179. At that moment, Yisrael saw trouble on all sides. The sea with its towering waves was in front of them, all these multitudes and all the camps of Egypt were behind them, and above there were many Prosecutors against them. They started to cry to the Holy One, blessed be He.

180. כְּדֵין כְּתִיב, וַיֹּאמֶר יְיָ' אֶל מֹשֶׁה מַה תִּצְעַק אֵלָי. וְתָאנָא בְּסִפְרָא דִּצְנִיעוּתָא, אֵלַי, דַּיְיקָא, בְּעַתִּיקָא תַּלְיָא כֹּלָּא. בֵּיהּ שַׁעֲתָא אִתְגַּלֵּי עַתִּיקָא קַדִּישָׁא, וְאִשְׁתְּכַח רַעֲוָא בְּכֻלְּהוּ עָלְמִין עִלָּאִין, כְּדֵין נְהִירוּ דְּכֹלָּא, אִתְנְהִיר.

180. Then it is written: "And Hashem said to Moses, 'Why do you cry to Me?'" (Shemot 14:15). We learned in the Hidden Book that "to Me" is exact, FOR IT IS THE ATTRIBUTE OF ZEIR ,ANPIN, BECAUSE it all depends upon Atika. At that moment, Atika Kadisha was revealed, goodwill was present in all the worlds above, and then the collective light shone.

181. אָמַר רִבִּי יִצְחָק, כְּדֵין, כַּד אִתְנְהִיר כֹּלָּא כַּחֲדָא, וְעָבֵד יַמָּא נִימוּסִין עִלָּאִין, וְאִתְמְסָרוּ בִּידוֹי עִלָּאִין וְתַתָּאִין. וּבְגִינֵי כַּךְ, קַשְׁיָא קָמֵי קוּדְשָׁא בְּרִיךְ הוּא כֹּלָּא, כִּקְרִיעַת יַם סוּף, וְכֹלָּא הָכִי אוּקְמוּהָ. מַאי טַעֲמָא. בְּגִין דִּקְרִיעַת יַם סוּף בְּעַתִּיקָא תַּלְיָיא.

181. Rabbi Yitzchak said: Then, when everything shone together, the sea executed the supernal laws–NAMELY, THE COMMANDMENT TO DROWN THE EGYPTIANS AND SAVE YISRAEL – because those above and those below were given over to it. Therefore, we say THAT ADMINISTERING CHILDREN, LONGEVITY AND SUSTENANCE are as difficult before the Holy One, blessed be He, as the splitting of the Red Sea. And everybody says this. What is the reason? Because splitting the sea depends on Atika, AS WRITTEN IN THE FORMER PARAGRAPH.

182. אָמַר רִבִּי שִׁמְעוֹן, חַד אַיַּילְתָּא אִית בְּאַרְעָא, וְקוּדְשָׁא בְּרִיךְ הוּא עָבֵיד סַגְיָא בְּגִינָהּ, בְּשַׁעֲתָא דְּהִיא צוֹוַחַת, קוּדְשָׁא בְּרִיךְ הוּא שָׁמַע עָאקוּ דִּילָהּ, וְקָבִּיל קָלָהּ. וְכַד אִצְטְרִיךְ עָלְמָא לְרַחֲמֵי לְמַיָּיא, הִיא יָהֲבַת קָלִין, וְקוּדְשָׁא בְּרִיךְ הוּא שָׁמַע קָלָהּ, וּכְדֵין חַיִּיס עַל עָלְמָא, הה"ד כְּאַיָּל תַּעֲרוֹג עַל אֲפִיקֵי מָיִם.

182. Rabbi Shimon said: there is one deer on earth and the Holy One, blessed be He, does much for her. When she cries, the Holy One, blessed be He, hearkens to her distress and listens to her voice. And when the world needs Mercy in relation to water, she utters voice and the Holy One, blessed be He, hearkens to her voice. Then THE HOLY ONE, BLESSED BE HE, has pity on the world, as is written: "As the heart pants after the water brooks" (Tehilim 42:2).

183. וְכַד בַּעְיָא לְאוֹלָדָא, הִיא סְתִימָא מִכָּל סִטְרִין, כְּדֵין אַתְיָיא וְשַׁוִּיאַת רֵישָׁא בֵּין בִּרְכָּהָא, וְצוֹוַחַת וְרָמַת קָלִין, וְקוּדְשָׁא בְּרִיךְ הוּא חַיִּיס עָלָהּ, וְזַמִּין לְקַבְּלָהּ חַד נָחָשׁ, וְנָשִׁיךְ בְּעַרְיָיתָא דִּילָהּ, וּפָתַח לָהּ, וְקָרַע לָהּ הַהוּא אֲתָר, וְאוֹלִידַת מִיָּד. אר"ש בְּהַאי מִלָּה,לָא תִּשְׁאַל וְלָא תְּנַסֶּה אֶת יְיָ', וְהָכִי דַּוְוקָא.

183. When she needs to give birth, she is stopped from all sides. She places her head between her knees, cries and screams, and the Holy One, blessed be He, has pity on her. He sends a snake that bites her genitals and opens her and tears that place for her, and she gives birth immediately. Rabbi Shimon said: In this matter do not question and do not test Hashem. For this exactly so.

184. וַיּוֹשַׁע יְיָ' בַּיּוֹם הַהוּא אֶת יִשְׂרָאֵל וְגוֹ', וַיַּרְא יִשְׂרָאֵל אֶת מִצְרַיִם מֵת, הַהוּא שֶׁלְטָנָא מְמָנָא דְּמִצְרָאֵי, אַחְמֵי לוֹן קוּדְשָׁא בְּרִיךְ הוּא, דְּאַעְבַּר לֵיהּ, בִּנְהַר דִּינוּר, דַּהֲוָה בִּשְׂפָתָא דְּיַמָּא רַבָּא. מֵת, מַאי טַעֲמָא מֵת. כְּמָה דְּאוּקְמוּהָ, דְּאַעְבְּרוּ לֵיהּ, מֵהַהוּא שֻׁלְטָנוּתָא דִּילֵיהּ.

184. "Thus Hashem saved Yisrael that day…and Yisrael saw Egypt dead" (Shemot 14:30). The Holy One, blessed be He, showed them the minister appointed over Egypt who He had passed through the River of fire, that was on the shore of the Upper Sea, WHICH IS MALCHUT. "Dead." What is the reason that he died, AS THERE IS NO DEATH AMONG THE ANGELS? It is, as we have established, that he was removed from his dominion, AND IT WAS CONSIDERED FOR HIM AS DEATH.

15. "And Yisrael saw that great work"

A Synopsis

Rabbi Chiya opens with "And the children of Yisrael saw that great work (lit. 'hand')." We read of the meaning of the five fingers of each hand, and the miracles that the Holy One, blessed be He does with them; it was the miracles at the Red Sea that led Yisrael and the Pharaoh to full belief in Hashem. Until then the Pharaoh had hardened his heart against Hashem. We read that the righteous are often snared in the sins of the wicked, as were the Egyptians who had not oppressed the children of Yisrael but were nonetheless slain. When Yisrael was sent into exile in Egypt, the Holy One, blessed be He gave them constant reassurance to counter their fear. At the time they were delivered from Egypt all the patriarchs gathered to see the promises that He had made to them fulfilled, for the sake of the covenants that He had made with them. Rabbi Aba says that there is a world above and a world below; from the lower world the judgments upon the lower beings are aroused. The Holy One, blessed be He performs miracles for His people in this lower world, and it was thus that the Egyptians sank into the sea.

185. וַיַּרְא יִשְׂרָאֵל אֶת הַיָּד הַגְּדוֹלָה וְגוֹ'. רִבִּי חִיָּיא אָמַר, הָכָא אִשְׁתְּלִים יְדָא, וְכֻלְּהוּ אֶצְבְּעָן, וְאִשְׁתְּלִים יְדָא, דְּאִתְכְּלִיל בֵּיהּ בִּימִינָא, דְּהָכִי תָּנֵינָן, כֹּלָּא בִּימִינָא אִתְכְּלִיל, וּבִימִינָא תַּלְיָא, הֲדָא הוּא דִּכְתִּיב, יְמִינְךָ יְיָ' נֶאְדָּרִי בַּכֹּחַ יְמִינְךָ יְיָ' תִּרְעַץ אוֹיֵב.

185. "And Yisrael saw that great work (lit. 'hand')..." (Shemot 14:31). Rabbi Chiya said: Here, WITH THE GREAT HAND was the LEFT hand completed, WHICH IS GVURAH, and all the fingers–CHESED, GVURAH, TIFERET, NETZACH, AND HOD – THAT ARE IN IT. And the LEFT hand is completed BY REASON OF it being included in the right. For we have learned that everything is included in the right and depends on the right. This is what is meant by: "Your right hand, Hashem, is glorious in power; Your right hand, Hashem, has dashed the enemy in pieces" (Shemot 15:6). EVEN THOUGH THIS PERTAINS TO GVURAH, SINCE IT DEPENDS ON THE RIGHT HAND, IT IS THEREFORE CALLED AFTER IT.

186. וְאָמַר רִבִּי יִצְחָק, לָא אַשְׁכַּחְנָא, מַאן דְּאַתְקִיף לְבֵּיהּ, לְגַבֵּיהּ

קוּדְשָׁא בְּרִיךְ הוּא, כְּפַרְעֹה. אָמַר רִבִּי יוֹסֵי, סִיחוֹן וְעוֹג הָכִי נַמִּי. אָמַר לֵיהּ, לָאו הָכִי. אִינּוּן לְגַבֵּיהּ דְּיִשְׂרָאֵל אִתְתַּקָּפוּ, אֲבָל לְגַבֵּיהּ דְּקוּדְשָׁא בְּרִיךְ הוּא, לָא, כְּמָה דְּאִתְקַף פַּרְעֹה רוּחֵיהּ לָקֳבְלֵיהּ, וַהֲוָה חָמֵי כָּל יוֹמָא גְּבוּרָאן דִּילֵיהּ, וְלָא הֲוָה תָּב.

186. And Rabbi Yitzchak said: We did not find one who hardened his heart towards the Holy One, blessed be He, like Pharaoh. Rabbi Yosi said: But Sichon and Og also HARDENED THEIR HEARTS. He said to him: It is not so. They hardened their hearts against Yisrael, but they did not harden their hearts against the Holy One, blessed be He, as Pharaoh hardened his spirit against Him, for he saw His mighty acts, yet did not repent.

187. א"ר יְהוּדָה א"ר יִצְחָק, פַּרְעֹה חַכִּים מִכָּל חֲרָשׁוֹי הֲוָה, וּבְכָל אִינּוּן כִּתְרִין, וּבְכָל אִינּוּן יְדִיעָן, אִסְתַּכַּל. וּבְכָל סִטְרָא דִּלְהוֹן, לָא חָמָא פּוּרְקָנָא דִּלְהוֹן יִשְׂרָאֵל, וְלָא הֲוָה תָּלֵי בְּחַד מִנַּיְיהוּ. וְעוֹד, דְּהָא בְּכֻלְּהוּ קְשִׁירוּ קִשְׁרָא עֲלַיְיהוּ דְּיִשְׂרָאֵל, וּפַרְעֹה לָא סָבַר דְּאִית קִשְׁרָא אַחֲרָא דִּמְהֵימְנוּתָא, דְּאִיהוּ שַׁלִּיט עַל כֹּלָּא. וְעַל דָּא הֲוָה אַתְקִיף לִבֵּיהּ.

187. Rabbi Yehuda said in the name of Rabbi Yitzchak: Pharaoh was wiser than all his sorcerers, and he gazed into all these crowns and all the knowledge OF THE OTHER SIDE. He did not see redemption for Yisrael in their entire side, and it was not dependent on any of their crowns. For in all THE SUPERNAL POWERS OF THE OTHER SIDE they found a bond against Yisrael, THAT THEY WOULD NOT BE ABLE TO EMERGE FROM UNDER THIS CONTROL. Pharaoh did not think that there was another bond of Faith that dominated all THE POWERS OF THE OTHER SIDE. Therefore, he hardened his heart.

188. רִבִּי אַבָּא אָמַר, לָא אַתְקִיף לִבָּא דְּפַרְעֹה, אֶלָּא שְׁמָא דָּא. דְּכַד הֲוָה אָמַר מֹשֶׁה, כֹּה אָמַר יְיָ', דָּא מִלָּה מַמָּשׁ, אַתְקִיף לִבֵּיהּ, הֲדָא הוּא דִּכְתִּיב, וַיְחַזֵּק יְיָ' אֶת לֵב פַּרְעֹה. דְּהָא בְּכָל חָכְמְתָא דִּילֵיהּ, לָא אִשְׁתְּכַח, דִּשְׁמָא דָּא שַׁלִּיט בְּאַרְעָא. וְעַל דָּא אָמַר, מִי יְיָ'. וּלְבָתַר אָמַר, יְיָ' הַצַּדִּיק. אָמַר רִבִּי יוֹסֵי, לְבָתַר אָמַר, חָטָאתִי לַיְיָ' הַהוּא פּוּמָא

דְּאָמַר דָּא, אָמַר דָּא.

188. Rabbi Aba said: It was not Pharaoh who strengthened his heart, but this Name, YUD HEI VAV HEI. Because when Moses said, "Thus says Hashem," the very word, NAMELY YUD HEI VAV HEI, hardened his heart, as is written: "And Hashem hardened the heart of Pharaoh" (Shemot 9:12). In all his wisdom, he did not find that this Name should dominate in the world, and therefore he said, "Who is Hashem?" (Shemot 5:2). WHEN HE THOUGHT OF REPENTING afterwards, he said, "Hashem is Righteous" (Shemot 9:27). Rabbi Yosi said: Afterwards, he said, "I have sinned against Hashem" (Shemot 10:16) with the same mouth that said, "WHO IS HASHEM?"

189. רִבִּי חִזְקִיָּה פָּתַח וְאָמַר, אַחַת הִיא עַל כֵּן אָמַרְתִּי תָּם וְרָשָׁע הוּא מְכַלֶּה. הַאי קְרָא, אוּקְמוּהָ בְּרָזָא דְּחָכְמְתָא. אַחַת הִיא, מַאי אַחַת הִיא. הָדָא הוּא דִּכְתִּיב, אַחַת הִיא יוֹנָתִי תַּמָּתִי אַחַת הִיא לְאִמָּהּ. וּבְהַאי, קוּדְשָׁא בְּרִיךְ הוּא דָּאִין דִּינוֹי לְתַתָּא, וְדָאִין דִּינוֹי לְעֵילָּא בְּכֹלָּא.

189. Rabbi Chizkiyah opened the discussion, saying: "Therefore I said, 'It is all one; He destroys the innocent and the wicked'" (Iyov 9:22). This passage was interpreted in the secret of wisdom. What is, "It is all one"? HE ANSWERS: It is written, "My dove, My undefiled is but one, she is the only one of her mother" (Shir Hashirim 6:9), SHE BEING MALCHUT. And with this does the Holy One, blessed be He, execute His Judgments below and execute His Judgments above, in everything.

190. וְכַד קוּדְשָׁא בְּרִיךְ הוּא אִתְּעַר דִּינוֹי, דָּאִין דִּינוֹי בְּהַאי כִּתְרָא, כְּדֵין כְּתִיב, תָּם וְרָשָׁע הוּא מְכַלֶּה. בְּגִין דְּאִינּוּן צַדִּיקַיָּיא, מִתְּפַסְאן בְּחוֹבֵיהוֹן דְּרַשִׁיעַיָּא, דִּכְתִּיב וַיֹּאמֶר יְיָ' לַמַּלְאָךְ הַמַּשְׁחִית בָּעָם רַב וְגוֹ', וְעַל דָּא אָמַר אִיּוֹב מִלָּה דָּא, וְלָא אַגְמָר מִלָּה, וְאוּקְמוּהָ טוֹל הַרָב, רִבִּי יֵיסָא אָמַר, אַחַת הִיא: דָּא כְּנֶסֶת יִשְׂרָאֵל בְּגָלוּתָא דְּמִצְרַיִם, דִּבְגִינָהּ קָטַל קוּדְשָׁא בְּרִיךְ הוּא בְּמִצְרָאֵי, וְעָבֵד בְּהוּ נוּקְמִין, הה"ד תָּם וְרָשָׁע הוּא מְכַלֶּה.

190. When the Holy One, blessed be He, arouses His judgments, He executes His Judgments with this crown, WHICH IS MALCHUT. Then it is written: "He destroys the innocent and the wicked," because the Righteous are snared in the sins of the wicked, as is written: "And said to the angel that destroyed the people, 'It is enough (Heb. *rav*)…" (II Shmuel 24:16) WHICH MEANS take the greatest (Heb. *rav*) among them. Therefore Job said, "HE DESTROYS THE INNOCENT AND THE WICKED," but he did not explain THAT IT MEANT THE RIGHTEOUS WHO WERE SNARED IN THE SINS OF THE WICKED. Rabbi Yisa said: "It is all one," refers to the Congregation of Yisrael in exile in Egypt and; for Her, the Holy One, blessed be He, slew the Egyptians and took vengeance among them. This is what is meant by the verse, "He destroys the innocent and the wicked," FOR THERE WERE ALSO INNOCENTS PRESENT THERE WHO DID NOT ENSLAVE YISRAEL AND WERE SLAIN TOGETHER WITH THE WICKED AMONG THEM.

191. ר׳ חִיָּיא אָמַר, אִיּוֹב לָא אַלְקֵי, אֶלָּא בִּזְמְנָא דְּנָפְקוּ יִשְׂרָאֵל מִמִּצְרַיִם. אָמַר אִיּוֹב, אִי הָכִי, כָּל אַפַּיָּיא שָׁוִין, תָּם וְרָשָׁע הוּא מְכַלֶּה, פַּרְעֹה אַתְקִיף בְּהוּ בְּיִשְׂרָאֵל, וְאָמַר מִי יְיָ׳ אֲשֶׁר אֶשְׁמַע בְּקוֹלוֹ. וַאֲנָא לָא אַתְקִיפְנָא בְּהוּ, וְלָא עֲבִידְנָא מִידִי, תָּם וְרָשָׁע הוּא מְכַלֶּה. הה״ד הַיָּרֵא אֶת דְּבַר יְיָ׳ מֵעַבְדֵי פַּרְעֹה, זֶה אִיּוֹב.

191. Rabbi Chiya said: Job was not stricken until the time that Yisrael went out of Egypt. Job said: 'If so, then all people are equal: "He destroys the innocent and the wicked." Pharaoh oppressed Yisrael and said, "Who is Hashem, that I should obey His voice" – I did not oppress them and I did nothing, but "He destroys the innocent and the wicked." "He who feared the word of Hashem among the servants of Pharaoh" (Shemot 9:20), refers to Job, BECAUSE HE WAS PRESENT AT THE TIME OF THE EXODUS FROM EGYPT.

192. ר׳ יְהוּדָה אָמַר, אִינּוּן אַבְנֵי בַּרְדָּא, דַּהֲווֹ נַחְתִּין, אִתְעַכְּבוּ עַל יְדוֹי דְּמֹשֶׁה, לְבָתַר עָבְדוּ נוּקְמִין, בְּיוֹמֵי דִּיהוֹשֻׁעַ. וּלְזִמְנָא דְּאָתֵי, זְמִינִין לַאֲחָתָא אִינּוּן דְּאִשְׁתָּאֲרוּ, עַל אֱדוֹם וּבְנוֹתֶיהָ. א״ר יוֹסֵי, הה״ד, כִּימֵי צֵאתְךָ מֵאֶרֶץ מִצְרָיִם אַרְאֶנּוּ נִפְלָאוֹת.

192. Rabbi Yehuda said: the hailstones that were falling ON THE

EGYPTIANS and were stopped by Moses wreaked vengeance later on, in the days of Joshua. And in the time to come, the rest will drop on Edom and its descendants. Rabbi Yosi said: This is what is written: "As in the days of your coming out of the land of Egypt, I will show him marvelous things" (Michah 7:15).

193. דָּבָר אַחֵר וַיַּרְא יִשְׂרָאֵל אֶת הַיָּד הַגְּדוֹלָה וְגוֹ', הַאי קְרָא לָאו רֵישֵׁיהּ סֵיפֵיהּ, וְלָאו סֵיפֵיהּ רֵישֵׁיהּ. בְּקַדְמֵיתָא וַיַּרְא יִשְׂרָאֵל, וּבָתַר וַיִּירְאוּ הָעָם אֶת יְיָ'. אֶלָּא אָמַר רִבִּי יְהוּדָה, הַהוּא סָבָא דְּנָחַת עִם בְּנוֹי בְּגָלוּתָא, וְסָבִיל עָלֵיהּ גָּלוּתָא, וְאָעִיל לִבְנוֹי בְּגָלוּתָא, הוּא מַמָּשׁ חָמָא, כָּל אִינּוּן נוּקְמִין, וְכָל גְּבוּרָאן, דְּעָבֵד קוּדְשָׁא בְּרִיךְ הוּא בְּמִצְרַיִם, הה"ד וַיַּרְא יִשְׂרָאֵל, יִשְׂרָאֵל מַמָּשׁ.

193. Another explanation of: "And Yisrael saw the great hand." the beginning of the verse is not RELATED to the ending, nor is the ending RELATED to its beginning. First, "And Yisrael saw," and afterwards, "and the people feared Hashem." IS, "AND YISRAEL SAW" THE CAUSE THAT "THE PEOPLE FEARED HASHEM"? AND BEFOREHAND, DID THEY NOT FEAR HASHEM? But Rabbi Yehuda said: That old man who went down with his children into exile and suffered the exile himself, actually saw all the vengeances and all the mighty deeds that the Holy One, blessed be He, did against Egypt. Hence, it is written: "And Yisrael saw." It was actually Yisrael, NAMELY JACOB.

194. וְאָמַר רִבִּי יְהוּדָה, סָלִיק קוּדְשָׁא בְּרִיךְ הוּא לְהַאי סָבָא, וְאָמַר לֵיהּ, קוּם חָמֵי בְּנָיךְ דְּנָפְקִין מִגּוֹ עַמָּא תַּקִּיפָא. קוּם חָמֵי גְּבוּרָן דַּעֲבָדִית, בְּגִין בְּנָיךְ בְּמִצְרַיִם.

194. Rabbi Yehuda also said: the Holy One, blessed be He, raised that old man and said to him, 'Arise, see your children who are going out from a strong nation; arise, see the mighty deeds that I did for your children in Egypt.'

195. וְהַיְינוּ דְּאָמַר רִבִּי יֵיסָא, בְּשַׁעֲתָא דְּנַטְלֵי יִשְׂרָאֵל לְנַחְתָּא בְּגָלוּתָא

דְּמִצְרַיִם, דְּחִילוּ וְאֵימְתָא תַּקִּיפָא נָפַל עֲלוֹי. אָמַר לֵיהּ קוּדְשָׁא בְּרִיךְ הוּא לְיַעֲקֹב, אֲמַאי אַתְּ דָּחִיל, אַל תִּירָא מֵרְדָה מִצְרַיְמָה. מִמַּה דִּכְתִּיב אַל תִּירָא, מַשְׁמַע דְּחִילוּ הֲוָה דָּחִיל.

195. Rabbi Yisa said: When Yisrael traveled to descend into the exile in Egypt, a strong fear and terror fell upon him. The Holy One, blessed be He, said to Jacob: 'Why do you fear?' "Fear not to go down to Egypt" (Beresheet 46:3). From the words: "fear not," we understand that he did fear.

196. אָמַר לֵיהּ כִּי לְגוֹי גָּדוֹל אֲשִׂימְךָ שָׁם. אָמַר לֵיהּ, דָּחִילְנָא דִּי יְשֵׁיצוּן בָּנַי. אָמַר לֵיהּ, אָנֹכִי אֵרֵד עִמְּךָ מִצְרַיְמָה. אָמַר לֵיהּ תּוּ דָּחִילְנָא, דְּלָא אַזְכֵּי לְאִתְקַבְּרָא בֵּינֵי אֲבָהָתַי, וְלָא אַחְמֵי פּוּרְקָנָא דִּבְנֵי, וּגְבוּרָאן דְּתַעְבִּיד לְהוּ. אָמַר לֵיהּ, וְאָנֹכִי אַעַלְךָ גַּם עָלֹה, אַעַלְךָ לְאִתְקַבְּרָא בְּקִבְרֵי אֲבָהָתָךְ. גַּם עָלֹה, לְמֶחֱמֵי פּוּרְקָנָא דִּבְרָךְ, וּגְבוּרָאן דַּאֲעָבִיד לְהוּ.

196. He said to him: "For I will there make of you a great nation" (Ibid.). He said to Him: 'I fear that they will destroy my children.' "He said to him, 'I will go down with you Egypt'." Again, he said to Him: 'I also fear that I will not merit to be buried among my fathers and I will not see the deliverance of my children, and the mighty deeds that You will do for them.' He said to him, "And I will surely bring you up again (lit. 'bringing you up')." "I will bring you up" to be buried in the tomb of your fathers, "bringing you up" to see the deliverance of your children, and the mighty deeds that I will do for them.

197. וְהַהוּא יוֹמָא דְּנָפְקוּ יִשְׂרָאֵל מִמִּצְרַיִם, סָלִיק לֵיהּ קוּדְשָׁא בְּרִיךְ הוּא לְיַעֲקֹב, וְאָמַר לֵיהּ, קוּם, חָמֵי בְּפוּרְקָנָא דִּבְרָךְ, דְּכַמָּה חֵילִין וּגְבוּרָאן עֲבָדִית לְהוּ, וְיַעֲקֹב הֲוָה תַּמָּן, וְחָמָא כֹּלָּא, הה"ד וַיַּרְא יִשְׂרָאֵל אֶת הַיָּד הַגְּדוֹלָה.

197. On the day that Yisrael went out from Egypt, the Holy One, blessed be He, raised Jacob and said to him: 'Arise and see the redemption of your children, for so many years and mighty deeds did I for them.' Jacob was there and saw everything, as it is written: "And Yisrael saw the great hand."

198. ר' יִצְחָק אָמַר, מֵהָכָא, וַיּוֹצִיאֲךָ בְּפָנָיו בְּכֹחוֹ הַגָּדוֹל מִמִּצְרַיִם. מַאי בְּפָנָיו. בְּפָנָיו דָּא יַעֲקֹב, דְּאָעִיל לְכֻלְּהוּ תַּמָּן. רִבִּי חִזְקִיָּה אָמַר, וַיּוֹצִיאֲךָ בְּפָנָיו, בְּפָנָיו: דָּא אַבְרָהָם. דִּכְתִּיב, וַיִּפֹּל אַבְרָהָם עַל פָּנָיו.

198. Rabbi Yitzchak said: From here it IS UNDERSTOOD THAT JACOB WAS PRESENT AT THE TIME OF THE REDEMPTION, FOR IT IS WRITTEN, "And brought you out, He Himself being present, with His mighty power, out of Egypt" (Devarim 4:37). What is the meaning of "being present"? It refers to Jacob, because He brought all PATRIARCHS there. Rabbi Chizkiyah said: "being present (lit. 'in his face')," refers to Abraham, as it is written, "And Abraham fell on his face" (Beresheet 17:3).

199. תָּא חֲזֵי, אַבְרָהָם אָמַר, הַלְּבֶן מֵאָה שָׁנָה יִוָּלֵד וְגוֹ', אָמַר לֵיהּ קוּדְשָׁא בְּרִיךְ הוּא, חַיֶּיךָ, אַתְּ תֶּחֱמֵי כַּמָּה אֹכְלוּסִין, וְכַמָּה חַיָּילִין דְּיִפְקוּן מִמְּךָ. בְּשַׁעֲתָא דְּנָפְקוּ יִשְׂרָאֵל מִמִּצְרַיִם, כָּל אִינּוּן שְׁבָטִין, כָּל אִינּוּן רִבְוָון, סָלִיק קוּדְשָׁא בְּרִיךְ הוּא לְאַבְרָהָם, וְחָמָא לוֹן, הה"ד וַיּוֹצִיאֲךָ בְּפָנָיו. רִבִּי אַבָּא אָמַר כֻּלְּהוּ אֲבָהָתָא אִזְדְּמָנוּ תַּמָּן בְּכָל הַהוּא פּוּרְקָנָא. הֲדָא הוּא דִּכְתִּיב וַיּוֹצִיאֲךָ בְּפָנָיו. מַאי בְּפָנָיו אִלֵּין אֲבָהָתָא.

199. Come and behold: Abraham said, "Shall a child be born to him that is a hundred years old?" (Ibid. 17). The Holy One, blessed be He, said to him: 'I swear, you will see many multitudes and many camps that have emerged from you.' By the time that Yisrael left Egypt, all the tribes and all those myriads did the Holy One, blessed be He, bring up to Abraham, who saw them. This is what is written: "And brought you out, He Himself being present." Rabbi Aba said: All the Patriarchs gathered there throughout that redemption. This is what is written: "And brought you out, He Himself being present." What is the meaning of "in his face"? these are the Patriarchs.

200. רִבִּי אֶלְעָזָר אָמַר, וַיּוֹצִיאֲךָ בְּפָנָיו: דָּא יַעֲקֹב. בְּכֹחוֹ: דָּא יִצְחָק.

הַגָּדוֹל: דָּא אַבְרָהָם. א״ר שִׁמְעוֹן, וְכֵן בְּגִינֵיהוֹן דַּאֲבָהָתָא, אִזְדָּמַן פּוּרְקָנָא תָּדִיר לְיִשְׂרָאֵל, דִּכְתִּיב וְזָכַרְתִּי אֶת בְּרִיתִי יַעֲקוֹב וְאַף אֶת בְּרִיתִי יִצְחָק וְאַף אֶת בְּרִיתִי אַבְרָהָם אֶזְכּוֹר וְהָאָרֶץ אֶזְכּוֹר. אֲבָהָתָא תִּינַח, מַהוּ וְהָאָרֶץ אֶזְכּוֹר. אֶלָּא, לְאַכְלְלָא עִמְּהוֹן דָּוִד מַלְכָּא, דְּאִיהוּ רְתִיכָא בַּאֲבָהָתָא וְאִינּוּן מִתְעָרִין פּוּרְקָנָא תָּדִיר לְיִשְׂרָאֵל.

200. Rabbi Elazar said: "And brought you out, He Himself being present." This refers to Jacob; "with His power," refers to Isaac; "mighty," refers to Abraham. Rabbi Shimon said: For the sake of the patriarchs there always occurs a redemption for Yisrael, as is written: "Then I will remember My Covenant with Jacob, and also my Covenant with Isaac, and also my Covenant with Abraham will I remember: and I will remember the land" (Vayikra 26:42). HE ASKS: THE Patriarchs are worthy of being remembered, but what is the meaning of, "And I will remember the land"? HE ANSWERS: In order to include David among them, NAMELY MALCHUT, THAT IS CALLED 'THE LAND', who is a Chariot together with the Patriarchs, WHO ARE CHESED GVURAH, AND TIFERET. And they always arouse redemption for the children of Yisrael.

201. וַיַּרְא יִשְׂרָאֵל אֶת הַיָּד הַגְּדוֹלָה אֲשֶׁר עָשָׂה יְיָ׳ בְּמִצְרַיִם. וְכִי הַשְׁתָּא עָשָׂה, וְהָא מִקַּדְמַת דְּנָא אִתְעֲבֵיד, מַאי אֶת הַיָּד הַגְּדוֹלָה אֲשֶׁר עָשָׂה יְיָ׳. אֶלָּא, יַד לָא אִקְרֵי פָּחוּת מֵחָמֵשׁ אֶצְבְּעָאן. הַגְּדוֹלָה: דִּכְלִילָן בָּהּ חָמֵשׁ אֶצְבְּעָאן אַחֲרָנִין, וְאִתְקְרוּן כְּדֵין גְּדוֹלָה. וְכָל אֶצְבְּעָא וְאֶצְבְּעָא, סָלִיק לְחוּשְׁבְּנָא רַבָּא, וקב״ה עָבֵיד בְּהוּ נִיסִּין וּגְבוּרָן, וּבְהַאי אִתְעֲקָרוּ כֻּלְּהוּ דַּרְגִּין מִשְׁלְשׁוּלֵיהוֹן.

201. "And Yisrael saw that great hand which Hashem did upon Egypt." HE ASKS: Did He do it now? It was done earlier. What is "the great hand which Hashem did"? HE ANSWERS: A hand is not so considered if there are less than five fingers. "That great," MEANS that it includes five other fingers OF THE LEFT HAND, AND THEN it is called 'great', BECAUSE THE ASPECT OF THE FIRST THREE SFIROT IS ACQUIRED BY THE RIGHT HAND BY BEING INCLUDED IN THE LEFT, and every individual finger is of great value. The Holy One, blessed be He, performs miracles and mighty deeds with them, and this way all the levels are uprooted from having continuity.

202. מִכָּאן אוֹלִיפְנָא דָּא, דִּבְחָמֵשׁ אֶצְבְּעָאן קַמָּאֵי, כְּתִיב, וַיְחַזֵּק לֵב פַּרְעֹה, כֵּיוָן דְּאִשְׁתְּלָמוּ אִינּוּן חָמֵשׁ, תּוּ לָא הֲוָה מִלָּה בִּרְשׁוּתֵיהּ דְּפַרְעֹה, כְּדֵין כְּתִיב וַיְחַזֵּק יְיָ׳ אֶת לֵב פַּרְעֹה.

202. From here we learn that with the five first fingers, NAMELY, THE FIRST FIVE PLAGUES, it is written: "And the heart of Pharaoh was hardened." As soon as these five fingers OF THE LEFT HAND were completed, there was nothing left under Pharaoh's jurisdiction TO HARDEN HIS HEART, and it is written: "And Hashem hardened the heart of Pharaoh."

203. וְעַ״ד וַיַּרְא יִשְׂרָאֵל אֶת הַיָּד הַגְּדוֹלָה וְגוֹ׳, וַיַּאֲמִינוּ בַּיְיָ׳. וְכִי עַד הַשְׁתָּא לָא הֶאֱמִינוּ בַּיְיָ׳, וְהָא כְּתִיב וַיַּאֲמֵן הָעָם וַיִּשְׁמְעוּ וְגוֹ׳. וְהָא חָמוּ כָּל אִינּוּן גְּבוּרָאן דְּעָבֵד לְהוּ קוּדְשָׁא בְּרִיךְ הוּא בְּמִצְרַיִם. אֶלָּא מַאי וַיַּאֲמִינוּ, הַהוּא מִלָּה דְּאָמַר וַיֹּאמֶר מֹשֶׁה אֶל הָעָם אַל תִּירָאוּ הִתְיַצְּבוּ וּרְאוּ וְגוֹ׳.

203. Therefore, "And Yisrael saw that great hand... and believed in Hashem." HE ASKS: Until now did they not believe in Hashem? Yet it is written: "And the people believed, and...they heard" (Shemot 4:31). And they did see all the mighty deeds that the Holy One, blessed be He, performed for them in Egypt. HE ANSWERS: But what is the meaning of: "and believed"? THEY BELIEVED what he said, "And Moses said to the people, 'Fear not, stand still, and see...'"

204. ר׳ יֵיסָא שָׁאִיל וְאָמַר, כְּתִיב וַיַּרְא יִשְׂרָאֵל אֶת מִצְרַיִם מֵת, וּכְתִיב לֹא תוֹסִיפוּ לִרְאוֹתָם עוֹד עַד עוֹלָם. א״ר יוֹסֵי, מֵתִין חָמוּ לְהוּ. אָמַר לֵיהּ, אִי כְּתִיב לֹא תוֹסִיפוּ לִרְאוֹתָם חַיִּים, הֲוָה אֲמֵינָא הָכִי. אָמַר לֵיהּ ר׳ אַבָּא יָאוּת שָׁאִילְתָּא.

204. Rabbi Yisa said: It is written, "And Yisrael saw Egypt dead," and it is written, "You will not see them again any more for ever" (Shemot 14:13).

Rabbi Yosi said: they saw them dead. He said to him: If it had been written: 'You will not see them again alive,' I would say so. Rabbi Aba said to him: You asked well.

205. אֶלָּא תָּא חֲזֵי, כְּתִיב מִן הָעוֹלָם וְעַד הָעוֹלָם, וְתָנֵינָן, עוֹלָם לְעֵילָּא, וְעוֹלָם לְתַתָּא. עוֹלָם דִּלְעֵילָּא, מִתַּמָּן הוּא שֵׁירוּתָא לְאַדְלְקָא בּוּצִינִין. עוֹלָם דִּלְתַתָּא, תַּמָּן הוּא סִיּוּמָא, וְאִתְכְּלִיל מִכֹּלָּא, וּמֵהַאי עוֹלָם דִּלְתַתָּא, מִתְעָרָן גְּבוּרָן לְתַתָּאֵי.

205. But, come and behold: it is written, "For ever and ever (lit. 'from the world and until the world')" (I Divrei Hayamim 16:36). We learned that there is a world above and there is a world below. From the world of above is the beginning of kindling the candles, WHICH IS BINAH, THE SOURCE OF ALL MOCHIN THAT ARE CALLED 'CANDLES'. The lower world is the culmination, NAMELY, MALCHUT THAT CULMINATES ALL THE SFIROT, and it is composed of them all. And from this lower world are aroused the Judgments upon the lower beings.

206. וּבְהַאי עוֹלָם, עָבֵיד קוּדְשָׁא בְּרִיךְ הוּא אָתִין לְיִשְׂרָאֵל, וְרָחִישׁ לוֹן נִיסָא. וְכַד אִתְּעַר הַאי עוֹלָם לְמֶעְבַּד נִסִּין, כֻּלְּהוּ מִצְרָאֵי אִשְׁתְּקָעוּ בְּיַמָּא, עַל יְדָא דְּהַאי עוֹלָם, וְאִתְרְחִישׁ לוֹן לְיִשְׂרָאֵל נִיסָא בְּהַאי עוֹלָם. וְע"ד כְּתִיב, לֹא תוֹסִיפוּ לִרְאוֹתָם עוֹד עַד עוֹלָם, עַד דְּיִתְּעַר הַהוּא עוֹלָם, וְיִתְמַסְרוּן בְּדִינוֹי, וְכֵיוָן דְּאִתְמְסָרוּ בֵּיהּ לְמִתְדָּן, כְּדֵין כְּתִיב וַיַּרְא יִשְׂרָאֵל אֶת מִצְרַיִם מֵת עַל שְׂפַת הַיָּם, הה"ד מִן הָעוֹלָם וְעַד הָעוֹלָם, עַד הָעוֹלָם דַּיְקָא. כְּדֵין כְּתִיב, וַיַּאֲמִינוּ בַּיְיָ' וּבְמֹשֶׁה עַבְדּוֹ.

206. The Holy One, blessed be He, performs miracles for Yisrael in this LOWER world, and marvels occur for them. When this world aroused to do miracles, all the Egyptians sank in the sea through the actions of this world, and a miracle occurred to Yisrael in this world. Therefore, it is written: "You shall not see them again any more for ever (lit. 'until the world')," MEANING until that world is aroused and they are given over to its Judgments. As soon as they were given over to it to be judged, it is written: "And Yisrael saw Egypt dead upon the sea shore." This is the meaning of the verse: "from the world and until the world" – until the world precisely, MEANING UNTIL THE WORLD OF BELOW IS AROUSED. Then it is written, "And believed in Hashem and in Moses his servant."

16. "Then sang Moses"

A Synopsis

Rabbi Yehuda opens with "Before I found you in the belly I knew you." He says that the Holy One, blessed be He sent down for the children of Yisrael a true prophet and a faithful shepherd, who was Moses. He put a great and holy spirit into him, and appointed him over all that was His. When Moses emerged into the world the Shechinah illuminated him, and the Holy One, blessed be He read over him, "Before I found you in the belly I knew you; and before you did come out of the womb I sanctified you, and I ordained you a prophet to the nations." We read various interpretations of "Then sang Moses, and the children of Yisrael." Rabbi Shimon says that it is the song of the Queen to the Holy One, blessed be He; it contains the world that has passed, and the World to Come, and the bonds of faith, and the days of King Messiah – and all the other praises of those above and below are dependent on it. Rabbi Yosi submits that "This song to Hashem" is the river that is Binah that emerges from Eden. And lastly, Rabbi Yehuda speaks about the time that "Hashem caused the sea to go back by a strong east wind all the night," saying that all the Egyptians below and the Princes above were given over into the hands of the Queen, for her to do vengeance on them.

207. אָז יָשִׁיר מֹשֶׁה. ר׳ יְהוּדָה פָּתַח, בְּטֶרֶם אֶצָּרְךָ בַבֶּטֶן יְדַעְתִּיךָ וְגוֹ׳. זַכָּאָה חוּלָקֵהוֹן דְּיִשְׂרָאֵל, דְּקוּדְשָׁא בְּרִיךְ הוּא אִתְרְעֵי בְּהוּ יַתִּיר מִכָּל שְׁאַר עַמִּין. וּמִסְּגִיאוּת רְחִימוּתָא דְּרָחִים לְהוּ, אוֹקִים עֲלַיְיהוּ נְבִיאָה דִּקְשׁוֹט, וְרַעְיָא מְהֵימָנָא. וְאִתְּעַר עָלֵיהּ רוּחָא קַדִּישָׁא, יַתִּיר מִכָּל שְׁאַר נְבִיאֵי מְהֵימְנֵי, וְאַפִּיק לֵיהּ מֵחוּלָקֵיהּ מַמָּשׁ, מִמַּה דְּאַפְרִישׁ יַעֲקֹב מִבְּנוֹי לְקוּדְשָׁא בְּרִיךְ הוּא, שִׁבְטָא דְּלֵוִי, וְכֵיוָן דַּהֲוָה לֵוִי דִּילֵיהּ, נָטַל לֵיהּ קוּדְשָׁא בְּרִיךְ הוּא, וְאַעְטַר לֵיהּ בְּכַמָּה עִטְרִין, וּמָשַׁח לֵיהּ בִּמְשַׁח רְבוּת קַדִּישָׁא דִּלְעֵילָּא, וּכְדֵין אַפִּיק מִבְּנוֹי, רוּחָא קַדִּישָׁא לְעָלְמָא, וְזָרִיז לֵיהּ בְּהֵימְנוֹיֵי קַדִּישֵׁי, מְהֵימָנוּתָא רַבָּא.

207. "Then sang Moses" (Shemot 15:1): Rabbi Yehuda opened the discussion, saying: "Before I formed you in the belly I knew you" (Yirmeyah 1:5). Blessed is the portion Yisrael that the Holy One, blessed be He, desired them more than all the other nations. And for the great love that

He had for them, He set up for them a true prophet and a faithful shepherd, and aroused over him a Holy Spirit, more than the other faithful prophets. He took him out of His own portion, MEANING from what Jacob had separated as a tithe of his sons to the Holy One, blessed be He, namely, the tribe Levi. Since Levi was His, the Holy One, blessed be He, received him and adorned him with many crowns, and anointed him with the holy anointing oil of above. And then he produced from his children a Holy Spirit into the world and girded him with his holy girdles of the great Faith, WHICH IS BINAH.

208. תָּנָא, בְּהַהִיא שַׁעֲתָא דְּמָטָא זִמְנֵיהּ דְּמֹשֶׁה נְבִיאָה מְהֵימְנָא לְאַחֲתָא לְעָלְמָא, אַפִּיק קוּדְשָׁא בְּרִיךְ הוּא רוּחָא קַדִּישָׁא מִגִּזְרָא דִּסַפִּירוּ דְּאֶבֶן טָבָא, דַּהֲוָה גָּנִיז בְּמָאתַן וְאַרְבְּעִין וּתְמַנְיָא נְהוֹרִין, וְאִתְנְהִיר עָלֵיהּ. וְאַעְטְרֵיהּ בְּשס״ה עִטְרִין, קַיְימֵי קָמֵיהּ, וְאַפְקִיד לֵיהּ בְּכָל דִּילֵיהּ. וְיָהַב לֵיהּ מֵאָה וְשַׁבְעִין וּתְלַת מַפְתְּחִין. וְאַעְטַר לֵיהּ בְּחָמֵשׁ עִטְרִין, וְכָל עִטְרָא וְעִטְרָא סָלִיק וְאַנְהִיר בְּאָלֶף עָלְמִין דְּנַהֲרִין, וּבוּצִינִין דִּגְנִיזִין בְּגִנְזַיָּיא דְּמַלְכָּא קַדִּישָׁא עִלָּאָה.

208. We learned that at that moment, the time had come for Moses, the faithful prophet, to descend to the world. The Holy One, blessed be He, withdrew a Holy Spirit from a hewn block of the precious stone, sapphire, WHICH IS MALCHUT, that was concealed within 248 lights, and shone on him. And He crowned him with 365 crowns and they stood before Him, and He appointed him over all that was His. He gave him 173 keys, and crowned him with five crowns. Every single crown ascended and illuminated in a thousand worlds that illuminate and in the candles that were concealed in the treasures of the Supernal Holy King.

209. כְּדֵין אַעְבְּרֵיהּ בְּכָל בּוּצִינִין דִּבְגִנְתָּא דְּעֵדֶן, וְאַעֲלֵיהּ בְּהֵיכָלֵיהּ, וְאַעְבְּרֵיהּ בְּכָל חַיָּילִין וְגַיָּיסִין דִּילֵיהּ. כְּדֵין אִזְדַּעְזְעוּ כֻּלְּהוּ, פָּתְחוּ וְאָמְרוּ, אִסְתַּלָּקוּ מִסַּחֲרָנֵיהּ, דְּהָא קוּדְשָׁא בְּרִיךְ הוּא אִתְּעַר רוּחָא לְשַׁלְטָאָה לְמִרְגַּז עָלְמִין. קָלָא נָפַק וְאָמַר, מַאן הוּא דֵּין, דְּכָל מַפְתְּחָן אִלֵּין בִּידוֹי. פָּתַח קָלָא אַחֲרָא וְאָמַר, קַבִּילוּ לֵיהּ בְּגַוַּויְיכוּ, דָּא הוּא דְּזַמִּין לְנַחְתָּא בֵּין בְּנֵי נָשָׁא, וּזְמִינָא אוֹרַיְיתָא, גְּנִיזָא דִּגְנִזַיָּיא,

לְאִתְמַסְּרָא בִּידוֹי, וּלְאַרְעֲשָׁא עָלְמִין דִּלְעֵילָּא וְתַתָּא עַל יְדָא דְּדֵין. בֵּיהּ שַׁעֲתָא אִתְרְגִּישׁוּ כֻּלְּהוּ, וְנַטְלִין אֲבַתְרֵיהּ, פָּתְחוּ וְאָמְרוּ, הִרְכַּבְתָּ אֱנוֹשׁ לְרֹאשֵׁנוּ בָּאנוּ בָאֵשׁ וּבַמַּיִם.

209. Then He passed him through all the lights in the Garden of Eden and brought him into His Palace, and passed him by His hosts and camps. Then they all trembled, opened and said: Remove yourselves from his vicinity, for the Holy One, blessed be He, has aroused a spirit to dominate and provoke the worlds. A voice emitted and said: Who is this with all these keys in his hands? Another voice said: Accept him among you, he is the one who will descend among the people. And the Torah, which is the most concealed of everything that is concealed, is going to be given into his hands, to shake the worlds that are above and below through him. At that moment, they all became excited and traveled after him. They opened the discussion, saying: "You have caused a man to ride over our heads; we went through fire and through water" (Tehilim 66:12).

210. כְּדֵין סַלְקָא הַהוּא רוּחָא, וְקַיְּימָא קָמֵי מַלְכָּא. **מ** פְּתִיחָא, סָלִיק וְאִתְעַטַּר בְּעִטְרוֹי, וְאַעַטְרֵיהּ בִּתְלַת מְאָה וְעֶשְׂרִין וְחָמֵשׁ עִטְרִין, וְאַפְקִיד מַפְתְּחוֹי בִּידוֹי. **ש** דַּאֲבָהָתָא, אַעַטְרוּ לֵיהּ בִּתְלַת עִטְרִין קַדִּישִׁין, וְאַפְקִידוּ כָּל מַפְתְּחָן דְּמַלְכָּא בִּידֵיהּ, וְאַפְקִידוּ לֵיהּ בְּהֵימְנוּתָא, מְהֵימְנָא דְּבֵיתָא. **ה** סַלְקָא וְאִתְעַטְּרָא בְּעִטְרוֹי, וְקַבִּילַת לֵיהּ מִן מַלְכָּא.

210. Then that spirit OF MOSES rose and stood before the King. The open *Mem* rose and put on its crowns, while He crowned THE SPIRIT with 325 crowns and deposited His keys into his hands. The *Shin* ALLUDES to the three Patriarchs, who crowned him with these holy crowns, deposited all the keys of the King in his hands, and appointed him faithfully TO BE the trustee of the house. The *Hei* rose and crowned itself with its crowns, and received him from the King.

211. כְּדֵין, נָחַת הַהוּא רוּחָא בְּאַרְבִּין דְּשָׁאטָן, בְּהַהוּא יַמָּא רַבָּא, וְקַבִּילַת לֵיהּ לְגַדְּלָא לֵיהּ לְמַלְכָּא, וְהִיא יָהֲבַת לֵיהּ מִתַּמָּן זִיוּנִין, לְאַלְקָאָה לְפַרְעֹה וּלְכָל אַרְעֵיהּ. וּבְשַׁבַּתָּא וּבְרֵישֵׁי יַרְחֵי, סַלְקַת לֵיהּ

לְמַלְכָּא, כְּדֵין אִקְרֵי שְׁמֵיהּ, בְּאִלֵּין אַתְוָון רְשִׁימִין.

211. Then that spirit OF MOSES alighted on the ships that sail in that great Sea, WHICH IS MALCHUT, AND MALCHUT accepted him in order to raise him to the King. She gave him weapons from there with which to smite Pharaoh and his whole land. And on Shabbat and the first day of the month, She elevates him to the King, WHO IS ZEIR ANPIN. Then his name is expressed in these letters that we etched, WHICH ARE *MEM*, *SHIN*, AND, *HEI* AS WRITTEN ABOVE.

212. וּבְהַהִיא שַׁעֲתָא, דְּנָפַק לְנַחְתָּא לְאַרְעָא, בְּזַרְעָא דְּלֵוִי, אִתְתָּקְנוּ אַרְבַּע מְאָה וְעֶשְׂרִין וְחָמֵשׁ בּוּצִינִין לְמַלְכָּא, וְאַרְבַּע מְאָה וְעֶשְׂרִין וְחָמֵשׁ גְּלִיפִין מְמֻנָּן, אוֹזְפוּהָ לְהַהוּא רוּחָא לְאַתְרֵיהּ, כַּד נָפַק לְעָלְמָא, אִתְנַהֲרָא ה בְּאַנְפּוֹי, וּבֵיתָא אִתְמַלְיָיא מִזִּיוְותֵיהּ. בֵּיהּ שַׁעֲתָא, קָרָא עָלֵיהּ קוּדְשָׁא בְּרִיךְ הוּא, בְּטֶרֶם אֶצָּרְךָ בַבֶּטֶן יְדַעְתִּיךָ וּבְטֶרֶם תֵּצֵא מֵרֶחֶם הִקְדַּשְׁתִּיךָ נָבִיא לַגּוֹיִם נְתַתִּיךָ.

212. At the moment that he emerged to descend to the earth to become clothed in a body in the seed of Levi, 425 candles were prepared for the King, WHO IS ZEIR ANPIN, and 425 appointed engravings escorted the spirit OF MOSES to his place. When he emerged in the world, the *Hei*, WHICH IS THE SHECHINAH, illuminated on him and the House became full with its shine. At that moment, the Holy One, blessed be He, read over him, "Before I formed you in the belly I knew you; and before you did come out of the womb I sanctified you, and I ordained you a prophet to the nations" (Yirmeyah 1:5).

213. רִבִּי יִצְחָק אָמַר, בֵּיהּ שַׁעֲתָא קָטַל קוּדְשָׁא בְּרִיךְ הוּא לְרַבְרְבָא מְמָנָא דְּמִצְרָאֵי, וְחָמוּ לֵיהּ מֹשֶׁה וּבְנֵי יִשְׂרָאֵל, כְּדֵין אָמְרוּ שִׁירָה. הה"ד, וַיַּרְא יִשְׂרָאֵל אֶת מִצְרַיִם מֵת, אָז יָשִׁיר מֹשֶׁה וּבְנֵי יִשְׂרָאֵל.

213. Rabbi Yitzchak said: At that time, the Holy One, blessed be He, slew the minister appointed over Egypt. Moses and Yisrael saw him, then recited the song. This is what is written: "And Yisrael saw Egypt dead…Then sang Moses and the children of the children of Yisrael."

214. אָז יָשִׁיר מֹשֶׁה וּבְנֵי יִשְׂרָאֵל וְגוֹ'. רִבִּי אַבָּא פָּתַח וְאָמַר, אִסְתַּכַּלְנָא בְּכָל תּוּשְׁבְּחָן דְּשַׁבְּחוּ לְקוּדְשָׁא בְּרִיךְ הוּא, וְכוּלָּם פָּתְחוּ בְּאָז. אָז אָמַר שְׁלֹמֹה. אָז יְדַבֵּר יְהוֹשֻׁעַ, אָז יָשִׁיר יִשְׂרָאֵל. מ"ט.

214. "Then sang Moses and the children of Yisrael..." Rabbi Aba opened the discussion, saying: I examined all the praises with which they praised the Holy One, blessed be He, and they all started with: "Then (Heb. *az*)": "Then spoke Solomon" (I Melachim 8:12); "Then spoke Joshua" (Yehoshua 10:12); "Then sang Moses and Yisrael." What is the reason for this?

215. אֶלָּא הָכִי תָּאנָא, כָּל נִסִּין וְכָל גְּבוּרָן דְּאִתְעֲבֵידוּ לְהוּ לְיִשְׂרָאֵל, כַּד אִתְנְהִיר נְהִירוּ דְּעַתִּיקָא קַדִּישָׁא בְּעִטְרוֹי, גְּלִיפִין רְשִׁימִין בא', בא' אַנְקִיב בַּחֲשׁוֹכֵי, וְנָהִיר לְכָל עִיבָר. וְכַד אִתְחַבָּר נְהִירוּ דְּאָלֶ"ף וּמָטֵי לְזַיִ"ן, מַאן זַיִ"ן, דָּא חֶרֶב לַיְיָ' מָלְאָה דָם. כְּדֵין עָבֵיד נִסִּין וּגְבוּרָאן, בְּגִין דְּאִתְחַבָּר א' עִם ז'. וְדָא הוּא שִׁירָתָא. שִׁירָתָא הִיא דְּכָל סִטְרִין, וְדָא הוּא אָז יָשִׁיר.

215. HE ANSWERS: This is what we learned. All the miracles and all the mighty deeds that were performed for Yisrael HAPPENED when the light of Atika Kadisha shone, WHICH IS ARICH ANPIN, with its crowns. They are engraved and imprinted by *Aleph*, SO THAT THE TOP *YUD* OF THE *ALEPH* IS THE RIGHT COLUMN AND THE LOWER LINE IS THE LEFT COLUMN, AND THE LINE BETWEEN THEM IS THE CENTRAL COLUMN THAT MEDIATES. The *Aleph* penetrates the darkness, ALLUDING TO THE CENTRAL LINE COLUMN OF THE *ALEPH* THAT PENETRATES AND DIMINISHES THE LEFT COLUMN, WHICH IS DARKNESS, INTO THE ASPECT OF SIX ENDS OF THE FIRST THREE SFIROT. THEN IT shines to every side, MEANING BOTH WITH CHOCHMAH AND IN CHASSADIM. And when the light of the *Aleph* joins and reaches the *Zayin*, that *Zayin* (lit. 'weapon') is: "The sword of Hashem is filled with blood" (Yeshayah 34:6), NAMELY, MALCHUT WHEN IT IS STRETCHED TOWARDS THE LEFT. Then it performs miracles and mighty deeds, because the *Aleph* and *Zayin* have joined. And this is a song, a song that illuminates to all sides, BOTH CHOCHMAH AND CHASSADIM. And hence "Then (Heb. *az*, Aleph-Zayin) sang."

216. יָשִׁיר, שָׁר מִבָּעֵי לֵיהּ. אֶלָּא מִלָּה דָּא תַּלְיָא, וְאַשְׁלִים לְהַהוּא

זִמְנָא, וְאַשְׁלִים לְזִמְנָא דְּאָתֵי, דִּזְמִינִין יִשְׂרָאֵל לְשַׁבְּחָא שִׁירָתָא דָּא. מֹשֶׁה וּבְנֵי יִשְׂרָאֵל, מִכָּאן אוֹלִיפְנָא, דְּצַדִּיקַיָּיא קַדְמָאֵי, אע״ג דְּאִסְתַּלָּקוּ בְּדַרְגִּין עִלָּאִין דִּלְעֵילָּא, וְאִתְקַשָּׁרוּ בְּקִשּׁוּרָא דִּצְרוֹרָא דְּחַיֵּי, זְמִינִין כֻּלְּהוּ לְאַחֲיָיא בְּגוּפָא, וּלְמֶחֱמֵי אַתְוָין וּגְבוּרָן דְּקָא עָבֵיד קוּדְשָׁא בְּרִיךְ הוּא לְיִשְׂרָאֵל. וּלְמֵימָר שִׁירָתָא דָּא, הה״ד אָז יָשִׁיר מֹשֶׁה וּבְנֵי יִשְׂרָאֵל.

216. HE ASKS: "Then sang (lit. 'will sing') MOSES." Should it have been written: "sang MOSES"? HE ANSWERS: This matter is suspended UNTIL THE TIME TO COME, for he perfected it for that time and perfected it for the future to come. For Yisrael will praise this song IN THE TIME TO COME. "Moses and the children of the children of Yisrael." From here we learned that even though the early righteous men ascended to the highest levels that are above and have been bound in the bond of life, they will all stand up to be resurrected in a body and recite this song. This is what is written: "Then will sing Moses and the children of Yisrael."

217. ר׳ שִׁמְעוֹן אָמַר מֵהָכָא, יוֹסִיף יְיָ׳ שֵׁנִית יָדוֹ לִקְנוֹת אֶת שְׁאַר עַמּוֹ. לִקְנוֹת: כד״א, יְיָ׳ קָנָנִי רֵאשִׁית דַּרְכּוֹ. אֶת שְׁאַר עַמּוֹ: אִלֵּין אִינּוּן צַדִּיקַיָּיא דִּבְהוֹן, דְּאִקְרוּן שְׁאַר, כד״א וַיִּשָּׁאֲרוּ שְׁנֵי אֲנָשִׁים בְּמַחֲנֶה. וְתָנֵינָן, לֵית עָלְמָא מִתְקַיְּימָא אֶלָּא עַל אִינּוּן דְּעַבְדֵי גַּרְמַיְיהוּ שִׁירַיִים.

217. Rabbi Shimon said: Hence, "Hashem shall again, a second time stretch forth His hand to recover the remnant of His people" (Yeshayah 11:11). "To recover" (Heb. *liknot*)" has the meaning as in: "Hashem created me (Heb. *kanani*) as the beginning of His way" (Mishlei 8:22). "The remnant of His people" refers to the Righteous among them, who are called 'remnants (Heb. *she'ar*)' as is written: "And there remained two men in the camp" (Bemidbar 11:26). We learned why they are called remnants: it is because the world exists only for the sake of those who make themselves into songs (Heb. *shirim*). THEREFORE, THE RIGHTEOUS ARE CALLED 'REMNANTS', DERIVED FROM 'SONGS'.

218. וְאִי תֵּימָא, הוֹאִיל וְאִתְקַשָּׁרוּ בִּצְרוֹרָא דְּחַיֵּי, וּמִתְעַנְּגֵי בְּעִנּוּגָא

עִלָּאָה, אֲמַאי יָחִית לוֹן קוּדְשָׁא בְּרִיךְ הוּא לְאַרְעָא. פּוּק וְאוֹלִיף מִזִּמְנָא קַדְמָאָה, דְּכָל אִינּוּן רוּחִין וְנִשְׁמָתִין, דַּהֲווֹ בְּדַרְגָּא עִלָּאָה דִּלְעֵילָּא וְקוּדְשָׁא בְּרִיךְ הוּא אָחִית לְהוּ לְאַרְעָא לְתַתָּא. כָּל שֶׁכֵּן הַשְׁתָּא, דְּבָעֵי קוּדְשָׁא בְּרִיךְ הוּא לְיַשְּׁרָא לַעֲקִימָא, כד״א כִּי אָדָם אֵין צַדִּיק בָּאָרֶץ אֲשֶׁר יַעֲשֶׂה טּוֹב וְלֹא יֶחֱטָא. וְאִי תֵּימָא, אִינּוּן דְּמִיתוּ בְּעֶטְיוֹ דְּנָחָשׁ. אֲפִילּוּ אִינּוּן יְקוּמוּן, וִיהוֹן מָארֵי דְּעֵיטָא, לְמַלְכָּא מְשִׁיחָא.

218. You may ask, since they are bundle in the bond of Life and delight in the supernal delight, why does the Holy One, blessed be He, lower them to the earth? Go and learn, even from the first time, THE TIME THEY WERE BORN AND EMERGED INTO THE WORLD, when all the spirits and souls were in the highest level above, the Holy One, blessed be He, lowered them to the earth below. All the more so now, since the Holy One, blessed be He, wants to straighten out that which is crooked BY SHOWING THEM THE MIRACLES AND MARVELS THAT HE WILL PERFORM FOR THE CHILDREN OF YISRAEL. EVEN THOUGH THEY ARE RIGHTEOUS, NEVERTHELESS, it is written: "For there is no righteous man upon the earth who does good and does not sin" (Kohelet 7:20). And you may ask: what of those who died because of the advice of the serpent, WHO DID NO SIN, WHY SHOULD THEY ARISE? HE ANSWERS: Even they will arise and will be advisers to the Messiah.

219. וְעַל דָּא תָּנֵינָן, מֹשֶׁה זַמִּין לְמֵימָר שִׁירָתָא לְזִמְנָא דְּאָתֵי. מ״ט. בְּגִין דִּכְתִּיב, כִּימֵי צֵאתְךָ מֵאֶרֶץ מִצְרַיִם אַרְאֶנּוּ נִפְלָאוֹת. אַרְאֶנּוּ, אַרְאֶךָּ מִבָּעֵי לֵיהּ. אֶלָּא אַרְאֶנּוּ מַמָּשׁ, לְמַאן דְּחָמָא בְּקַדְמֵיתָא, יֶחֱמֵי לֵיהּ תִּנְיָינוּת, וְדָא הוּא אַרְאֶנּוּ, וּכְתִיב אַרְאֶנּוּ בְּיֵשַׁע אֱלֹהִים, וְאַרְאֵהוּ בִּישׁוּעָתִי. וּכְדֵין אָז יָשִׁיר מֹשֶׁה וּבְנֵי יִשְׂרָאֵל אֶת הַשִּׁירָה הַזֹּאת לַיְיָ׳.

219. Therefore, we learned Moses will sing the song in the future to come. What is the reason? Because it is written: "As in the days of your coming out the land of Egypt, I will show him marvelous things" (Michah 7:15). HE ASKS: Should "I will show him" have been said 'I will show you'? HE ANSWERS: Rather, I will show the very one who saw originally, NAMELY MOSES, for he will see a second time, and this is the meaning of "I will show him." It is written: "I will show him the salvation of Elohim" (Tehilim

50:23), and, "show him My salvation" (Tehilim 91:16). And "Then shall sing Moses and the children of Yisrael to Hashem."

220. שִׁירָתָא דְּמַטְרוֹנִיתָא לְקוּדְשָׁא בְּרִיךְ הוּא. תָּנֵינָן, כָּל בַּר נָשׁ דְּאָמַר שִׁירָתָא דָּא בְּכָל יוֹמָא, וּמְכַוֵּון בָּהּ, זָכֵי לְמֵימְרָא לְזִמְנָא דְּאָתֵי. דְּהָא אִית בָּהּ עָלְמָא דְּעָבַר, וְאִית בָּהּ עָלְמָא דְּאָתֵי, וְאִית בָּהּ קִשְׁרֵי מְהֵימָנוּתָא, וְאִית בָּהּ יוֹמֵי דְּמַלְכָּא מְשִׁיחָא. וְתָלֵי עָלָהּ, כָּל אִינּוּן תּוּשְׁבְּחָאן אַחֲרָנִין, דְּקָאמְרֵי עִלָּאֵי וְתַתָּאֵי.

220. It is the song of the Queen, WHICH IS MALCHUT, to the Holy One, blessed be He. We learned that every person who says this song daily and has the proper intention merits to say it in the time to come. It contains the world that has passed, and it contains the World to Come, and it contains the bonds of Faith, and it contains the days of King Messiah. And all the other praises of those above and those below stir from it.

221. הַשִּׁירָה שִׁיר זֶה מִבָּעֵי לֵיהּ. אֶלָּא שִׁירָתָא, דְּקָא מְשַׁבַּחַת מַטְרוֹנִיתָא לְמַלְכָּא. וּמֹשֶׁה מִתַּתָּא לְעֵילָּא קָאָמַר, וְהָא אוּקְמוּהָ. לַיְיָ': בְּגִין דְּאַנְהִיר לָהּ מַלְכָּא אַנְפָּהָא, ר' יוֹסֵי אָמַר, דְּכָל אִינּוּן מְשָׁחִין, דַּהֲווֹ נַגְדִּין, מָשִׁיךְ מַלְכָּא קַדִּישָׁא לְקַבְּלָהּ, בְּגִינֵי כַּךְ מְשַׁבְּחָא לֵיהּ מַטְרוֹנִיתָא.

221. HE ASKS: IT IS WRITTEN, "*Hashirah*" ('this song') which IS FEMININE, but should it not have said '*shir zeh*' ('this song') IN THE MASCULINE FORM? HE ANSWERS: But this is the song with which the Queen praises the King, ZEIR ANPIN, and that Moses said from below to above, FROM MALCHUT TO ZEIR ANPIN. THEREFORE IT IS SAID *SHIRAH* (FEMININE), and it has already been explained. "To Hashem." SHE SINGS TO HASHEM because the King has welcomed Her. Rabbi Yosi said: All these ointments, MEANING THE LIGHTS that flowed, the Holy King poured to Her. Therefore, the Queen praised Him.

222. אָמַר רִבִּי יְהוּדָה, אִי הָכִי, אַמַּאי כְּתִיב מֹשֶׁה וּבְנֵי יִשְׂרָאֵל, וְהָא מַטְרוֹנִיתָא בָּעְיָא לְשַׁבְּחָא. אֶלָּא, זַכָּאָה חוּלָקֵהוֹן דְּמֹשֶׁה וְיִשְׂרָאֵל,

דְּאִינּוּן הֲווֹ יַדְעִין לְשַׁבְּחָא לְמַלְכָּא, בְּגִין מַטְרוֹנִיתָא כַּדְקָא יֵאוֹת, בְּגִין דְּכָל הַהוּא חֵילָא וּגְבוּרָה דִּילָהּ, יָרְתָא מִן מַלְכָּא.

222. Rabbi Yehuda said: If so, THAT IT IS THE SONG OF THE QUEEN TO THE KING, why is it written: "Moses and the children of Yisrael," seeing that it is for the Queen to praise? HE ANSWERS: Blessed is the portion of Moses and Yisrael that they knew how to praise the King for the Queen's sake in the proper manner, because She inherited all Her strength and might from the King.

223. ר׳ חִיָּיא פָּתַח וְאָמַר, קוּמִי רוֹנִּי בַלַּיְלָה לְרֹאשׁ אַשְׁמוּרוֹת. קוּמִי רוֹנִּי: דָּא כְּנֶסֶת יִשְׂרָאֵל. בַּלַּיְלָה: בְּגָלוּתָא. ר׳ יוֹסֵי אָמַר, בַּלַּיְלָה: בִּזְמְנָא דְּהִיא שַׁלְטָא וּמִתְעָרָא, לְרֹאשׁ אַשְׁמוּרוֹת, בְּרֹאשׁ מִבָּעֵי לֵיהּ. אֶלָּא לְרֹאשׁ, כְּמָה דִּכְתִּיב, עַל רֹאשׁ הַמִּטָּה. וְאוֹקִימְנָא, רֹאשׁ הַמִּטָּה, דָּא יְסוֹד. אוּף הָכָא לְרֹאשׁ, דָּא יְסוֹד, דְּמַטְרוֹנִיתָא מִתְבָּרְכָא בֵּיהּ. רֹאשׁ אַשְׁמוּרוֹת: דָּא הוּא רֵישָׁא, דְּנֶצַח וְהוֹד.

223. Rabbi Chiya opened the discussion, saying: "Arise, cry out in the night: in the beginning of the watches" (Eichah 2:19). "Arise, cry out," refers to the Congregation of Yisrael, WHICH IS MALCHUT; "in the night," means the Exile. Rabbi Yosi says: "In the night," refers to the time when She dominates and awakens, BECAUSE MALCHUT DOMINATES AT NIGHT. "In the beginning of the watches," should have been written, 'At the beginning'. HE ANSWERS: "In the beginning (lit. 'head')," is as it is written: "Upon the bed's head" (Beresheet 47.31). We have established that the head of the bed is Yesod. Also, here the head with which the Queen is blessed is Yesod. "Head ('beginning') of the watches" is the head of Netzach and Hod, WHICH IS YESOD.

224. ר׳ יוֹסֵי אָמַר, דָּא הוּא רֵישָׁא דְּכִתְרֵי מַלְכָּא וְסִיּוּמָא. רִבִּי אַבָּא אָמַר, לְרֹאשׁ אַשְׁמְרוֹת כְּתִיב חָסֵר, וְדָא הוּא רֵישָׁא, רֹאשׁ הַמִּטָּה. וְכֹלָּא בְּמַלְכָּא קַדִּישָׁא עִלָּאָה אִתְּמַר, וְדָא הוּא לַיְיָ׳.

224. Rabbi Yosi said: This is the beginning of all the crowns of the King and the end. FOR FROM THE ASPECT OF THE NINE SFIROT OF DIRECT

LIGHT OF ZEIR ANPIN, IT IS THE BOTTOM ONE THAT ENDS. FROM THE ASPECT OF THE NINE SFIROT OF RETURNING LIGHT OF ZEIR ANPIN THAT ILLUMINATE FROM BELOW UPWARD, YESOD IS CONSIDERED THE KETER OF RETURNING LIGHT. SINCE IT IS THE BEGINNING OF THE SFIROT OF RETURNING LIGHT, THE TORAH THEREFORE CALLS IT "THE BEGINNING OF THE WATCHES." Rabbi Aba said: "watches" is spelled without A *VAV*, WHICH ALLUDES TO MALCHUT, and this is YESOD, WHICH IS HER head, AND IS THUS CALLED "the bed's head." It is all said in reference to the Supernal Holy King, THAT IS ZEIR ANPIN, MEANING YESOD OF ZEIR ANPIN, and this is THE MEANING OF, "THIS SONG to Hashem," MEANING TO YESOD OF ZEIR ANPIN.

225. רִבִּי יֵיסָא אָמַר, הַשִּׁירָה הַזֹּאת לַיְיָ׳, דָּא הוּא נַהֲרָא דְּנָפִיק מֵעֵדֶן, דְּכָל מִשְׁחָא וּרְבוּ נָפִיק מִנֵּיהּ, לְאַדְלָקָא בּוּצִינִין. וּמַשְׁמַע לְבָתַר דִּכְתִּיב אָשִׁירָה לַיְיָ׳, דָּא הוּא מַלְכָּא קַדִּישָׁא עִלָּאָה, וְעַל דָּא לָא כְּתִיב אָשִׁירָה לוֹ.

225. Rabbi Yisa said: "This song to Hashem" is the river, WHICH IS BINAH, that emerges from Eden, WHICH IS CHOCHMAH, MEANING BINAH THAT EMERGED FROM THE HEAD OF ARICH ANPIN. For all the oil and greatness, MEANING ALL THE MOCHIN OF MALE AND FEMALE, AND BRIYAH, YETZIRAH, AND ASIYAH, emerge from it. This is understood from the following PASSAGE, which saya: "I will sing to Hashem," which refers to the Supernal Holy King, ZEIR ANPIN. Therefore it is not written, 'I will sing to Him', BECAUSE THE PREVIOUS "TO HASHEM," IN, "THIS SONG TO HASHEM," IS BINAH AND NOT ZEIR ANPIN.

226. וַיֹּאמְרוּ לֵאמֹר, לְדָרֵי דָּרִין, בְּגִין דְּלָא יִתְנְשֵׁי מִנַּיְיהוּ לְעָלְמִין. דְּכָל מַאן דְּזָכֵי לְהַאי שִׁירָתָא בְּהַאי עָלְמָא, זָכֵי לָהּ בְּעָלְמָא דְּאָתֵי, וְזָכֵי לְשַׁבְּחָא בָּהּ בְּיוֹמוֹי דְּמַלְכָּא מְשִׁיחָא, בְּחֶדְוָותָא דכ״י בְּקוּדְשָׁא בְּרִיךְ הוּא. דִּכְתִּיב לֵאמֹר, לֵאמֹר בְּהַהוּא זִמְנָא. לֵאמֹר בְּאַרְעָא קַדִּישָׁא, בְּזִמְנָא דְּשָׁרוּ יִשְׂרָאֵל בְּאַרְעָא. לֵאמֹר בְּגָלוּתָא. לֵאמֹר בְּפוּרְקָנָא דִּלְהוֹן דְּיִשְׂרָאֵל. לֵאמֹר לְעָלְמָא דְּאָתֵי.

226. "And spoke, saying," MEANING the following generations so that this will not ever be forgotten from them. Anyone who is worthy of this song in this world merits it in the World to Come, and will be worthy of praising with it in the days of King Messiah in the rejoining of the Congregation of Yisrael with the Holy One, blessed be He. It is written, "saying," meaning "saying" it at that time, "saying" it in the Holy Land in the time when Yisrael will be settled in the land, "saying" it during exile, "saying" it at the redemption of Yisrael, "saying" it in the World to Come.

227. אָשִׁירָה לַיְיָ׳ נָשִׁיר מִבָּעֵי לֵיהּ, מַאי אָשִׁירָה. אֶלָּא בְּגִין דַּהֲווֹ מְשַׁבְּחָן תּוּשַׁבְּחְתָּא דְּמַטְרוֹנִיתָא. לַיְיָ׳: דָּא מַלְכָּא קַדִּישָׁא. כִּי גָּאֹה גָּאָה: דְּסָלִיק וְאִתְעַטָּר בְּעִטְרוֹי, לְאַפָּקָא בִּרְכָּאן וְחֵילִין וּגְבוּרָאן, לְאַסָּקָא בְּכֹלָּא. כִּי גָּאֹה גָּאָה: גָּאֹה בְּהַאי עָלְמָא, גָּאָה בְּעָלְמָא דְּאָתֵי. כִּי גָּאֹה בְּהַהוּא זִמְנָא, גָּאָה, בְּגִין דְּיִתְעֲטָּר בְּעִטְרוֹי בְּחֶדְוָותָא שְׁלֵימוּתָא.

227. "I will sing to Hashem." HE ASKS: It should have said, 'We will sing'. Why DOES IT SAY, "I will sing"? HE ANSWERS: It is because they were reciting the praises of the Queen, AS MENTIONED EARLIER, AND IT IS THEREFORE WRITTEN: "I WILL SING" IN THE SINGULAR. "To Hashem," refers to the Holy King, WHO IS ZEIR ANPIN "for He has triumphed gloriously," meaning that He ascended and was crowned with His crowns to bring forth blessings and strength and mighty deeds, with all of which to be elevated. "For He has triumphed" in this world, "gloriously" in the World to Come. He triumphed gloriously at that time in order to be crowned AFTERWARDS, with His crowns in complete joy.

228. סוּס וְרוֹכְבוֹ רָמָה בַיָּם, שׁוּלְטָנוּתָא דִּלְתַתָּא, וְשׁוּלְטָנוּתָא דִּלְעֵילָּא דַּאֲחִידָן בְּהוּ, אִתְמְסָרוּ בְּהַהוּא יַמָּא רַבָּא, וְשֻׁלְטָנוּתָא רַבָּא לְמֶעְבַּד בְּהוּ נוּקְמִין. וְתָנֵינָן, לָא עָבֵיד קוּדְשָׁא בְּרִיךְ הוּא דִּינָא לְתַתָּא, עַד דְּיַעֲבֵיד בְּשׁוּלְטָנֵיהוֹן לְעֵילָּא, הה״ד, יִפְקוֹד יְיָ׳ עַל צְבָא הַמָּרוֹם בַּמָּרוֹם וְעַל מַלְכֵי הָאֲדָמָה עַל הָאֲדָמָה.

228. "The horse and his rider He cast into the sea" (Shemot 15:1), NAMELY, the dominion of below, WHICH IS THE HORSE, and the dominion of above they grasp onto, WHICH IS "HIS RIDER." Both of them were given over to that Great Sea and the great dominion, to take revenge on them. And we learned, the Holy One, blessed be He, does not execute Judgment below until He does so with their government above. This is the meaning: "Hashem will punish the host of the high ones on high, and the kings of the earth upon the earth" (Yeshayah 24:21).

229. רָמָה בַיָּם, אָמַר ר׳ יְהוּדָה, בֵּיהּ בְּלֵילְיָא, אִתְּעַר גְּבוּרָא תַּקִּיפָא, דִּכְתִּיב בֵּיהּ וַיּוֹלֶךְ יְיָ׳ אֶת הַיָּם בְּרוּחַ קָדִים עַזָּה כָּל הַלַּיְלָה. בְּהַהוּא זִמְנָא, בָּעָאת מַטְרוֹנִיתָא מִן מַלְכָּא, כָּל אִינּוּן אֻכְלוֹסִין דִּלְתַתָּא, וְכָל אִינּוּן שׁוּלְטָנִין דִּלְעֵילָּא, דְּיִתְמַסְרוּן בִּידָהָא. וְכֻלְּהוּ אִתְמְסָרוּ בִּידָהָא, לְמֶעְבַּד בְּהוּ נוּקְמִין, הה״ד סוּס וְרוֹכְבוֹ רָמָה בַיָּם. בַּיָּם סְתָם, לְעֵילָּא וְתַתָּא.

229. "He cast into the sea." Rabbi Yehuda said: That night, a mighty power was awakened, as is written: "And Hashem caused the sea to go back by a strong east wind all that night" (Shemot 14:21). At that time, the Queen requested of the King that all the multitudes OF THE EGYPTIANS below and all the Princes above be given over into Her hands. They were all given over into Her power to do vengeance with them. As it is written: "The horse and its rider He cast into the sea." Here, "Into the sea" IS WRITTEN without adjectives, ALLUDING BOTH TO THE SEA above and THE SEA below.

17. "Yah is my strength and song"

A Synopsis

Rabbi Chiya reminds us that the Holy One, blessed be He created the world and created man to dominate everything in the world; He brought him into the Garden so that he should have joy. He commanded him not to eat of one tree, but man did not obey. If Adam had observed the commandment, he could have lived forever and stayed there in the Garden forever. He knew the supernal Wisdom more than the supernal angels did, yet after he sinned the wellsprings of Wisdom became stopped for him. Adam emerged from Male and Female, says Rabbi Aba, as the Nukva was the partner of Zeir Anpin. Rabbi Yosi holds that "Yah is my strength and song" refers to those that are included one with the other and do not separate one from the other. From them the rivers flow to bless everything. Rabbi Chizkiyah then analyzes the verse, "A friend loves at all times, and a brother is born for adversity," telling us that the children of Yisrael are called brothers of the Holy One, blessed be He. From Rabbi Yisa we learn that the Holy One, blessed be He calls 'beloved' everyone who loves Him and serves Him with love. Rabbi Shimon tells Rabbi Yehuda that every person who weeps and sings to God will merit joy when Hashem returns Zion.

230. עָזִּי וְזִמְרָת יָהּ. רִבִּי חִיָּיא פָּתַח וְאָמַר, אָחוֹר וְקֶדֶם צַרְתָּנִי וַתָּשֶׁת עָלַי כַּפֶּכָה. כַּמָּה אִצְטְרִיכוּ בְּנֵי נָשָׁא לְיַקָּרָא לְקוּדְשָׁא בְּרִיךְ הוּא, בְּגִין דְּקוּדְשָׁא בְּרִיךְ הוּא כַּד בָּרָא עָלְמָא, אִסְתָּכַּל בֵּיהּ בָּאָדָם לְמֶהֱוֵי שַׁלִּיט עַל כֹּלָּא. וַהֲוָה דָּאמֵי לְעִלָּאִין וְתַתָּאִין. נָחַת לֵיהּ בִּדְמוּת יַקִּירָא, וְחָמוּ לֵיהּ בִּרְיָין, כְּדֵין אִתְכְּנָשׁוּ לְגַבֵּיהּ, וְסָגִידוּ לָקֳבְלֵיהּ, וְאֵימָתָא וְדַחֲלָא נָפְלַת עָלַיְיהוּ מִדַּחַלְתֵּיהּ, הה״ד וּמוֹרַאֲכֶם וְחִתְּכֶם יִהְיֶה עַל כָּל חַיַּת הָאָרֶץ וְעַל כָּל עוֹף הַשָּׁמָיִם.

230. "Yah is my strength and song" (Shemot 15:2). Rabbi Chiya opened the discussion, saying: "You have beset me behind and before, and You placed Your hand on me" (Tehilim 139:5). How much must a person honor the Holy One, blessed be He, because when He created the world, He saw that man would dominate everything, and he was similar to those above and those below. He lowered him to the world in a glorious form and the creatures saw him, gathered, and bowed before him. And a fear and terror fell upon them because of the fear of him. This is the meaning of: "And the fear of you and the dread of you shall be upon every beast of the earth, and upon every bird of the air" (Beresheet 9:2).

231. עַיְילֵיהּ לְגִנְתֵּיהּ דְּנָטַע, לְנַטְרֵיהּ לְמֶהֱוֵי לֵיהּ חֵדוּ עַל חִדוּ, וּלְאִשְׁתַּעְשְׁעָ בֵּיהּ. עָבֵד לֵיהּ טְרוֹצְטְבוּלִין מְחַפְיָין בְּאַבְנֵי יְקָר, וּמַלְאָכִין עִלָּאִין חַדָּאן קָמֵיהּ. לְבָתַר פָּקִיד לֵיהּ עַל אִילָנָא חַד וְלָא קָאֵים בְּפִקּוּדָא דְּמָארֵיהּ.

231. He brought him into the garden that He planted to guard it, and so that he should have joy upon joy, and delight in it. He made for him a canopy covered with precious stones, and the supernal angels used to rejoice before him. Afterwards, He commanded him not to eat of one tree, but he did not heed the commandment of his Master.

232. אַשְׁכַּחְנָא בְּסִפְרָא דַּחֲנוֹךְ, דִּלְבָתַר דְּסָלִיק לֵיהּ קוּדְשָׁא בְּרִיךְ הוּא, וְאַחְמֵי לֵיהּ כָּל גִּנְזַיָּיא דְּמַלְכָּא, עִלָּאֵי וְתַתָּאֵי, אַחְמֵי לֵיהּ אִילָנָא דְּחַיֵּי, וְאִילָנָא דְּאִתְפְּקַד עָלֵיהּ אָדָם, וְאַחְמֵי לֵיהּ דוּכְתֵּיהּ דְּאָדָם בְּגִנְתָּא דְּעֵדֶן. וְחָמָא, דְּאִלְמָלֵי נָטִיר אָדָם פִּקּוּדָא דָּא, יָכִיל לְקַיְּימָא תָּדִירָא, וּלְמֶהֱוֵי תָּדִירָא תַּמָּן. הוּא לָא נָטַר פִּקּוּדָא דְּמָארֵיהּ, נָפַק בְּדִימוֹס וְאִתְעֲנָשׁ.

232. I found in the Book of Enoch that, after the Holy One, blessed be He, elevated ENOCH and showed him all the treasures of the King, those above and those below, He showed him the Tree of Life and the tree that Adam was cautioned against. And He showed him the place of Adam in the Garden of Eden. And he saw that if Adam had observed this commandment, OF THE TREE OF KNOWLEDGE OF GOOD AND EVIL, he could have lived forever and always been there. He did not observe the commandment of his Master, so he was judged and punished.

233. רִבִּי יִצְחָק אָמַר, אָדָם דּוּ פַּרְצוּפִין אִתְבְּרֵי, וְהָא אוֹקִימְנָא, וַיִּקַּח אַחַת מִצַּלְעוֹתָיו, נְסָרוּ הַקּוּדְשָׁא בְּרִיךְ הוּא וְאִתְעֲבֵידוּ תְּרֵין, מִמִּזְרָח וּמִמַּעֲרָב, הֲדָא הוּא דִּכְתִיב, אָחוֹר וָקֶדֶם צַרְתָּנִי. אָחוֹר דָּא מַעֲרָב,

וְקֹדֶם דָּא מִזְרָח.

233. Rabbi Yitzchak said: Adam was created with two faces, and this was the way they explained it: "And He took one of his sides" (Beresheet 2:21). The Holy One, blessed be He, has sown it and it became two, from the east and from the west, ADAM FROM THE EAST AND EVE FROM THE WEST. This is what is written: "You have beset me behind and before." "Behind" is west and "before" is east.

234. ר׳ חִיָּיא אָמַר, מַה עָבֵיד קוּדְשָׁא בְּרִיךְ הוּא, תַּקִּין לְהַהוּא נוּקְבָּא וְשַׁכְלִיל שְׁפִירוּתָהּ עַל כֹּלָּא, וְעַיְילָהּ לְאָדָם, הה״ד וַיִּבֶן יְיָ׳ אֱלֹהִים אֶת הַצֵּלָע אֲשֶׁר לָקַח מִן הָאָדָם לְאִשָּׁה. תָּא חֲזֵי, מַה כְּתִיב לְעֵילָּא, וַיִּקַּח אַחַת מִצַּלְעוֹתָיו. מַאי אַחַת. כד״א אַחַת הִיא יוֹנָתִי תַּמָּתִי אַחַת הִיא לְאִמָּהּ. מִצַּלְעוֹתָיו: מִסִּטְרוֹי. כד״א, וּלְצֶלַע הַמִּשְׁכָּן.

234. Rabbi Chiya said: What did the Holy One, blessed be He, do? He prepared that female, perfected her beauty, and brought her to Adam. This is what is written: "And of the side, which Hashem Elohim has taken from the man, He made a woman" (Ibid. 22). Come and behold: it is written above: "And He took one of his sides." What is "one"? It is as in: "My dove, My undefiled is but one; she is the only one of her mother" (Shir Hashirim 6:9), WHICH IS MALCHUT. "Of his sides," MEANING from his sides, as is written: "And for the second side of the tabernacle" (Shemot 26:20), BECAUSE SHE WAS TAKEN FROM THE LEFT SIDE.

235. ר׳ יְהוּדָה אָמַר, קוּדְשָׁא בְּרִיךְ הוּא נִשְׁמְתָא עִלָּאָה יָהַב בֵּיהּ בְּאָדָם, וְכָלִיל בֵּיהּ חָכְמְתָא וְסָכְלְתָנוּ, לְמִנְדַּע כֹּלָּא. מֵאָן אֲתָר יָהַב בֵּיהּ נִשְׁמְתָא. ר׳ יִצְחָק אָמַר, מֵאֲתָר דִּשְׁאַר נִשְׁמָתִין קַדִּישִׁין קָא אַתְיָין.

235. Rabbi Yehuda said: The Holy One, blessed be He, placed a supernal soul in Adam and included in it wisdom and understanding to know everything. HE ASKS: From which place did He give him a soul? Rabbi Yitzchak said: From the place the other souls come from, NAMELY BINAH, FOR THE LIGHT OF BINAH IS CALLED 'NESHAMAH'.

236. ר׳ יְהוּדָה אָמַר, מֵהָכָא. דִּכְתִּיב תּוֹצֵא הָאָרֶץ נֶפֶשׁ חַיָּה, מַאן הָאָרֶץ. מֵהַהוּא אֲתָר דְּמַקְדְּשָׁא אִשְׁתְּכַח בֵּיהּ. נֶפֶשׁ חַיָּה, נֶפֶשׁ חַיָּה סְתָם, דָּא נַפְשָׁא דְּאָדָם קַדְמָאָה דְּכֹלָּא.

236. Rabbi Yehuda said: We understand it from here, as it is written: "Let the earth bring forth living creatures (lit. 'Nefesh')" (Beresheet 1:24). HE ASKS: From which place in the earth? HE ANSWERS: From the place where the Temple is located, BECAUSE EARTH IS MALCHUT, AND THE PLACE OF THE TEMPLE IS BINAH, THAT IS IN IT. "Living soul" (Heb. *Nefesh*) is simply written, "living soul," WITHOUT EXPLAINING WHOSE SOUL. AND HE SAYS: This is the Nefesh of Adam who was first of all.

237. ר׳ חִיָּיא אָמַר, אָדָם הֲוָה יָדַע חָכְמְתָא עִלָּאָה, יַתִּיר מִמַּלְאֲכֵי עִלָּאֵי, וַהֲוָה מִסְתַּכֵּל בְּכֹלָּא, וְיָדַע וְאִשְׁתְּמוֹדַע לְמָארֵיהּ, יַתִּיר מִכָּל שְׁאַר בְּנֵי עָלְמָא. בָּתַר דְּחָב, אַסְתִּימוּ מִנֵּיהּ מַבּוּעֵי דְּחָכְמְתָא, מַה כְּתִיב וַיְשַׁלְּחֵהוּ יְיָ׳ אֱלֹהִים מִגַּן עֵדֶן לַעֲבוֹד אֶת הָאֲדָמָה.

237. Rabbi Chiya said: Adam knew supernal Wisdom more than the supernal angels, and he gazed into everything and knew and recognized his Master more than all the inhabitants of the world. After he sinned, the wellsprings of Wisdom became stopped for him. It is written: "And Hashem Elohim sent him out of the Garden of Eden to till the ground" (Beresheet 3:23).

238. ר׳ אַבָּא אָמַר, אָדָם הָרִאשׁוֹן מִדְּכַר וְנוּקְבָּא אִשְׁתְּכַח, הה״ד וַיֹּאמֶר אֱלֹהִים נַעֲשֶׂה אָדָם בְּצַלְמֵנוּ כִּדְמוּתֵינוּ, וְעַל דָּא, דְּכַר וְנוּקְבָּא אִתְעֲבֵידוּ כַּחֲדָא, וְאִתְפְּרָשׁוּ לְבָתַר. וְאִי תֵּימָא, הָא דְּאָמַר הָאֲדָמָה אֲשֶׁר לֻקַּח מִשָּׁם. הָכִי הוּא וַדַּאי, וְדָא הִיא נוּקְבָּא, וְקוּדְשָׁא בְּרִיךְ הוּא אִשְׁתָּתַּף עִמָּהּ, וְדָא הוּא דְּכַר וְנוּקְבָּא, וְכֹלָּא הוּא מִלָּה חֲדָא.

238. Rabbi Aba said: Adam emerged from Male and Female, NAMELY ZEIR ANPIN AND NUKVA. This is what is written: "And Elohim said, 'Let us make man in our image, after our likeness'" (Beresheet 1:26). Therefore,

EVEN BY MAN male and female were made united, and were separated FROM EACH OTHER afterwards. You may question why it says, "The earth from where he was taken," AND NOT FROM THE SUPERNAL MALE AND FEMALE. HE ANSWERS: It is certainly so, THAT HE WAS TAKEN FROM THE EARTH, but this refers to the Nukva OF ZEIR ANPIN. And the Holy One, blessed be He, MEANING ZEIR ANPIN, was Her partner. These are the Male and Female THAT WE MENTIONED. And it is all one thing.

239. ר׳ יוֹסֵי אָמַר, עָזִּי וְזִמְרָת יָהּ, אִינּוּן דִּכְלִילָן דָּא בְּדָא וְלָא אִתְפָּרְשָׁאן דָּא מִן דָּא וּלְעָלְמִין אִינּוּן בַּחֲבִיבוּתָא, בִּרְעוּתָא חֲדָא, דְּמִתַּמָּן אִשְׁתְּכָחוּ מְשִׁיכָן דְּנַחֲלִין וּמַבּוּעִין לְאִסְתַּפְּקָא כֹּלָּא, וּלְבָרְכָא כֹּלָּא, לָא כְּדִיבוּ מֵימֵי מַבּוּעִין, כד״א וּכְמוֹצָא מַיִם אֲשֶׁר לֹא יְכַזְּבוּ מֵימָיו וְע״ד וַיְהִי לִי לִישׁוּעָה, דִּבְגִינֵי כַּךְ, מַלְכָּא קַדִּישָׁא מָשִׁיךְ וְאַחֲסִין לְתַתָּא, וְאִתְּעַר יְמִינָא לְמֶעְבַּד נִסִּין.

239. Rabbi Yosi said: "Yah is my strength and song," REFERS TO those that are included one with the other and do not separate one from the other. They are always in love with one desire, FOR THEY ARE ABA AND IMA THAT ARE CALLED *YUD-HEI.* From them spring the currents of the rivers and springs to supply everyone and to bless everything, and the waters of these springs do not fail. This is the meaning of: "And like a spring of water, whose waters fail not" (Yeshayah 58:11). Therefore, "He is become my salvation" (Shemot 15:2). For this reason does the Holy King draw and cause to inherit below, and the right becomes aroused to perform miracles.

240. זֶה אֵלִי וְאַנְוֵהוּ. דָּא צַדִּיק, דְּמִנֵּיהּ נָפְקִין בִּרְכָּאן בְּזִוּוּג. וְאַנְוֵהוּ: בְּהַהוּא אֲתָר דַּחֲבִיבוּתָא אִשְׁתְּכַח בֵּיהּ, וְדָא הוּא מַקְדְּשָׁא. אֱלֹהֵי אָבִי וַאֲרוֹמְמֶנְהוּ, מֹשֶׁה קָאָמַר דָּא, לְגַבֵּי אֲתָר דְּלֵוָאֵי אַתְיָין מֵהַהוּא סִטְרָא וְע״ד שְׁלֵימוּתָא דְּכֹלָּא הוּא בְּהַהוּא אֲתָר.

240. "He is my El, and I will glorify Him." This is the righteous, NAMELY YESOD, from whom emerge blessings in unity. "And I will glorify Him," in that place where there is love, which is the Temple. "Elohim of my father and I will exalt Him" (Ibid.). Moses said this to the place, from which the Levites come, NAMELY THE LEFT SIDE. Therefore, ONCE MOSES SAID

ABOUT THAT SIDE, "AND I WILL EXALT HIM" there is complete perfection in it, BECAUSE, "AND I WILL EXALT HIM," MEANS THAT HE CAUSES IT TO BE COMPRISED IN THE RIGHT SIDE, THIS BEING THE ENTIRE PERFECTION.

241. ר׳ יִצְחָק אָמַר, וַיְהִי לִי לִישׁוּעָה, דָּא מַלְכָּא קַדִּישָׁא, וְהָכִי הוּא. וּמְנָלָן. מִקְרָא אַחֲרִינָא אַשְׁכַּחְנָא לֵיהּ, דִּכְתִּיב כִּי עָזִּי וְזִמְרָת יָהּ יְיָ׳ וַיְהִי לִי לִישׁוּעָה, מִמַּשְׁמַע דְּקָאָמַר יְיָ׳ וַיְהִי לִי לִישׁוּעָה, דָּא מַלְכָּא קַדִּישָׁא.

241. Rabbi Yitzchak said: "And He is become my salvation." This is the Holy King, WHO IS ZEIR ANPIN, and so He is. How do we know this? I have found this in another passage, in which it is written: "Yah is my strength and song, and He is become my salvation." It is understood from, "Hashem...is become my salvation," that it refers to the Holy King WHO IS CALLED 'YUD HEI VAV HEI', NAMELY ZEIR ANPIN.

242. עָזִּי וְזִמְרָת יָהּ וְגוֹ׳, ר׳ חִזְקִיָּה פָּתַח וְאָמַר, בְּהַאי קְרָא דִּכְתִּיב, בְּכָל עֵת אוֹהֵב הָרֵעַ וְאָח לְצָרָה יִוָּלֵד. בְּכָל עֵת אוֹהֵב הָרֵעַ, דָּא קוּדְשָׁא בְּרִיךְ הוּא, דִּכְתִּיב בֵּיהּ רֵעֲךָ וְרֵעַ אָבִיךָ אַל תַּעֲזוֹב.

242. "Yah is my strength and my song." Rabbi Chizkiyah opened the discussion with the verse: "A friend loves at all times, and a brother is born for adversity" (Mishlei 17:17). "A friend loves at all times," refers to the Holy One, blessed be He, of whom it is written: "Do not forsake your own friend, and your father's friend" (Mishlei 27:10).

243. וְאָח לְצָרָה יִוָּלֵד, בְּשַׁעֲתָא דְּיַעִיקוּן לָךְ שַׂנְאָךְ, קב״ה מַה אָמַר, לְמַעַן אַחַי וְרֵעָי אֲדַבְּרָה נָּא שָׁלוֹם בָּךְ, דְּיִשְׂרָאֵל, אִקְרוּן אַחִים וְרֵעִים לְקוּדְשָׁא בְּרִיךְ הוּא. יִוָּלֵד מַהוּ, וְכִי הַשְׁתָּא יִוָּלֵד. אֶלָּא בְּשַׁעֲתָא דְּעַקְתָּא יִוָּלֵד בְּעָלְמָא, אָח יְהֵא לְקַבְלָךְ, לְשֵׁזְבָא לָךְ מִכָּל אִינּוּן דְּעָקִין לָךְ.

243. "And a brother is born for adversity." At the time that your enemy oppresses you, what does the Holy One, blessed be He, say? "For the sake of my brethren and my comrades, I will now say, 'Peace be within you'" (Tehilim 122:8). Yisrael are called 'brothers' and 'comrades' of the Holy One, blessed be He. What is the meaning of "is born" – is he born now, in time of trouble? HE ANSWERS: During the trouble shall be born in the world one who will be a brother to you, to save you from all those who oppress you.

244. רִבִּי יְהוּדָה אָמַר, יִוָּלֵד: דְּמַלְכָּא קַדִּישָׁא יִתְּעַר בְּהַאי עֹז, לְנַקְמָא לָךְ מֵאוּמִין, לְיַנְקָא לָךְ מֵאִימָא, בְּהַהוּא סִטְרָא, כד"א, עָזִּי וְזִמְרָת יָהּ וַיְהִי לִי לִישׁוּעָה. לְאִתְּעָרָא גְּבוּרָאן לְקָבֵל אוּמִין עכו"ם.

244. Rabbi Yehuda said: "is born" means that the Holy King will be aroused with this strength to take revenge on the nationsbecause of you, and to nurture you from Ima, WHICH IS BINAH, on this LEFT side, as is written: "Yah is my strength and song, and He is become my salvation." He will awaken powers against the idolatrous nations.

245. ר' יֵיסָא פָּתַח וְאָמַר, כַּמָּה אִית לֵיהּ לְבַר נָשׁ לְרַחֲמָא, לֵיהּ לְקוּדְשָׁא בְּרִיךְ הוּא, דְּהָא לֵית לֵיהּ פּוּלְחָנָא לְקוּדְשָׁא בְּרִיךְ הוּא, אֶלָּא רְחִימוּתָא. וְכָל מַאן דְּרָחִים לֵיהּ, וְעָבֵיד פּוּלְחָנָא בִּרְחִימוּתָא, קָארֵי לֵיהּ לְקוּדְשָׁא בְּרִיךְ הוּא רְחִימָא. אִי הָכִי, בְּמָאי אוֹקִימְנָא הָנֵי קְרָאֵי, רֵעֲךָ וְרֵעַ אָבִיךָ אַל תַּעֲזוֹב. וּכְתִיב הוֹקַר רַגְלְךָ מִבֵּית רֵעֶךָ.

245. Rabbi Yisa opened the discussion, saying: How much must a person love the Holy One, blessed be He, for there is no service before the Holy One, blessed be He, except love. The Holy One, blessed be he, calls 'beloved' everyone who loves Him and serves Him with love. HE ASKS: If so, how is it possible to reconcile these two passages: "Do not forsake your own friend, and your father's friend" (Mishlei 27:10), and, "Let your foot be seldom in your neighbor's (also: 'friend's') house" (Mishlei 25:17).

246. אֶלָּא הָא אוּקְמוּהָ חַבְרַיָּיא, הַאי קְרָא בְּעוֹלוֹת כְּתִיב. הַשְׁתָּא, רֵעֲךָ וְרֵעַ אָבִיךָ אַל תַּעֲזוֹב, לְמִפְלַח לֵיהּ, וּלְאִתְדַּבְּקָא בֵּיהּ, וּלְמֶעְבַּד פִּקּוּדוֹי. אַל תַּעֲזוֹב וַדַּאי. וְהָא דְּאִתְּמַר הוֹקַר רַגְלְךָ מִבֵּית רֵעֶךָ. כְּלוֹמַר הוֹקַר

יִצְרָךְ, דְּלָא יִרְתַּח לְקַבְלָךְ, וְלָא יִשְׁלוֹט בָּךְ, וְלָא תַּעֲבִיד הִרְהוּרָא אַחֲרָא. מִבֵּית רֵעֶךָ, מַאן בֵּית רֵעֶךָ. דָּא נִשְׁמְתָא קַדִּישָׁא, דְּאָעִיל בָּהּ רֵעֶךָ וִיהָבָהּ בְּגַוָּךְ.

246. HE ANSWERS: But the scholars have already explained that this passage, "DO NOT FORSAKE YOUR OWN FRIEND, AND YOUR FATHER'S FRIEND," is written in reference to burnt offerings, BUT IN REFERENCE TO SIN OFFERINGS AND GUILT OFFERINGS, IT IS SAID, "LET YOUR FOOT BE SELDOM IN YOUR NEIGHBOR'S HOUSE." Now WE WILL EXPLAIN: "Do not forsake your own friend, and your father's friend." DO NOT FORSAKE serving Him and cleaving unto Him and doing His commandments. "Do not forsake," indeed. And, "Let your foot be seldom in your neighbor's house" means: let your inclination be seldom there, so that it would not provoke you or dominate you, and so that no strange thought will rise "from your neighbor's house." What is "your neighbor's house"? It is the holy soul that your friend placed in you and put inside you.

247. וְעַל דָּא פּוּלְחָנָא דְּקוּדְשָׁא בְּרִיךְ הוּא, לְרַחֲמָא לֵיהּ בְּכֹלָּא, כְּמָה דִּכְתִּיב וְאָהַבְתָּ אֵת יְיָ' אֱלֹהֶיךָ. זֶה אֵלִי וְאַנְוֵהוּ, דְּכָל יִשְׂרָאֵל חָמוּ עַל יַמָּא, מַה דְּלָא חָמָא יְחֶזְקֵאל נְבִיאָה, וַאֲפִילּוּ אִינּוּן עוּבָּרֵי דִּבְמְעֵי אִמְּהוֹן, הֲווֹ חָמָאן וּמְשַׁבְּחָן לְקוּדְשָׁא בְּרִיךְ הוּא, וְכֻלְּהוּ הֲווֹ אַמְרִין זֶה אֵלִי וְאַנְוֵהוּ אֱלֹהֵי אָבִי וַאֲרוֹמְמֶנְהוּ, כד"א אֱלֹהֵי אַבְרָהָם.

247. Therefore, the service of the Holy One, blessed be He, is to love Him in everything HE MAY DO TO YOU, as is written: "And you shall love Hashem your Elohim" (Devarim 6:5). "This is my El and I will glorify Him," for all of Yisrael saw at the sea what Ezekiel the prophet did not see. Even embryos in their mothers' womb saw and praised the Holy One, blessed be He, and they all said: "This is my El and I will glorify Him, Elohim of my father and I will exalt Him." "Elohim of my father," is as is written: "Elohim of Abraham."

248. א"ר יוֹסֵי, אִי הָכִי אֲמַאי וַאֲרוֹמְמֶנְהוּ, דְּהָא אֱלֹהֵי אַבְרָהָם לְעֵילָּא הוּא. אָמַר לֵיהּ, אֲפִילּוּ הָכִי אִצְטְרִיךְ, וְכֹלָּא חַד מִלָּה, וַאֲרוֹמְמֶנְהוּ בְּכֹלָּא, לְאַכְלְלָא, מַאן דְּיָדַע לְיַחֲדָא שְׁמָא קַדִּישָׁא רַבָּא, דְּהָא הוּא

פֻּלְחָנָא עִלָּאָה דְקוּדְשָׁא בְּרִיךְ הוּא.

248. Rabbi Yosi said: If so, why does it say, "And I will exalt Him," seeing that Elohim of Abraham is above, AND THERE IS NO NEED TO EXALT HIM. IT MEANS THAT ELOHIM OF ISAAC, WHO IS THE LEFT COLUMN, NEEDS TO BE EXALTED, NOT THE RIGHT COLUMN. He said to him: Even so, it is needed TO EXALT HIM. And it all pertains to the same issue. "And I will exalt Him," on all SIDES. Also, one who knows how to proclaim the oneness of the Holy and Great Name, MUST EXALT HIM, for this is the loftiest service of the Holy One, blessed be He.

249. ר׳ יְהוּדָה הֲוָה יָתִיב קָמֵיהּ דְּר׳ שִׁמְעוֹן, וְהוּא קָארֵי, כְּתִיב קוֹל צוֹפַיִךְ נָשְׂאוּ קוֹל יַחְדָּיו יְרַנֵּנוּ. קוֹל צוֹפַיִךְ, מַאן אִינּוּן צוֹפַיִךְ. אֶלָּא אִלֵּין אִינּוּן דִּמְצַפָּאן, אֵימָתַי יְרַחֵם קוּדְשָׁא בְּרִיךְ הוּא, לְמִבְנֵי בֵּיתֵיהּ. נָשְׂאוּ קוֹל, יִשְׂאוּ קוֹל מִבָּעֵי לֵיהּ, מַאי נָשְׂאוּ קוֹל. אֶלָּא, כָּל בַּר נָשׁ דְּבָכֵי, וְאָרִים קָלֵיהּ עַל חָרְבַּן בֵּיתֵיהּ דְּקוּדְשָׁא בְּרִיךְ הוּא, זָכֵי לְמָה דִּכְתִּיב לְבָתַר יַחְדָּיו יְרַנֵּנוּ. וְזָכֵי לְמֵחֱמֵי לֵיהּ בְּיִשּׁוּבָא בְּחֶדְוָותָא.

249. Rabbi Yehuda was sitting before Rabbi Shimon and reading, it is written: "The voice of your watchmen is heard, they lift up the voice, together shall they sing" (Yeshayah 52:8). "The voice of your watchmen." Who are the watchmen? HE ANSWERS: Those who are waiting for the time when the Holy One, blessed be He, will have Mercy to build His house. "They lift up the voice." HE ASKS: It should have said, 'They will lift up the voice'; what is the meaning of, "They lift up the voice"? HE ANSWERS: Every person who weeps and raises his voice for the destruction of the House of the Holy One, blessed be He, will merit what is written afterwards, "Together shall they sing," and merit to see it restored in joy.

250. בְּשׁוּב יְיָ׳ צִיּוֹן, בְּשׁוּב יְיָ׳ אֶל צִיּוֹן מִבָּעֵי לֵיהּ, מַאי בְּשׁוּם יְיָ׳ צִיּוֹן אֶלָּא בְּשׁוּב יְיָ׳ צִיּוֹן וַדַּאי. תָּא חֲזֵי, בְּשַׁעֲתָא דְּאִתְחֲרִיב יְרוּשְׁלַם לְתַתָּא, וּכְנֶסֶת יִשְׂרָאֵל אִתְתְּרָכַת, סָלִיק מַלְכָּא קַדִּישָׁא לְצִיּוֹן, וְאַנְגִּיד לֵיהּ לְקָבְלֵיהּ, בְּגִין דִּכְנֶסֶת יִשְׂרָאֵל אִתְתְּרָכַת. וְכַד תִּתְהַדָּר כְּנֶסֶת יִשְׂרָאֵל לְאַתְרָהּ, כְּדֵין יֵתוּב מַלְכָּא קַדִּישָׁא לְצִיּוֹן לְאַתְרֵיהּ, לְאִזְדַּוְּוגָא חַד בְּחַד,

וְדָא הוּא בְּשׁוּב יְיָ׳ צִיּוֹן. וּכְדֵין זְמִינִין יִשְׂרָאֵל לְמֵימָר, זֶה אֵלִי וְאַנְוֵהוּ. וּכְתִיב, זֶה יְיָ׳ קִוִּינוּ לוֹ נָגִילָה וְנִשְׂמְחָה בִּישׁוּעָתוֹ, בִּישׁוּעָתוֹ וַדַּאי.

250. “When Hashem returns Zion” (Ibid.). HE ASKS: Should it not have said, ‘When Hashem returns to Zion’? What is the meaning of, “When Hashem returns Zion”? HE ANSWERS: “When Hashem returns Zion” is exact. Come and behold: at the time that the earthly Jerusalem was destroyed and the Congregation of Yisrael, WHICH IS MALCHUT, were exiled, the Holy King, WHO IS ZEIR ANPIN, ascended to Zion, THAT IS YESOD OF MALCHUT, and sighed before her because of the Congregation of Yisrael was exiled. When the Congregation of Yisrael return to her place, then the Holy King will return to His place, Zion, so one would unite with the other. And at is the meaning of: “When Hashem returns Zion,” AND NOT ‘TO ZION’ BECAUSE “HASHEM ZION” INDICATES THE UNION OF HASHEM WITH ZION. Then Yisrael will say: “This is my El and I will glorify Him,” and: “This is Hashem; we have waited for Him, we will be glad and rejoice in His salvation” (Yeshayah 25:9), in His salvation, assumedly NAMELY, IN THE REDEMPTION OF HASHEM WHEN HE RETURNS TO ZION.

18. "Hashem is a man of war"

A Synopsis

Rabbi Shimon says that the "Book of the Wars of Hashem" means the wars of Torah, which are peace and love rather than quarrels and destruction. Then he turns to "Seek out the Book of Hashem, and read," saying that all the powers and strengths that the Holy One, blessed be He has are dependent on that Book, that is Malchut, and emerge from there. When His powers and wars are provoked, the Judgments of the right side and the Judgments of the left side arouse mighty deeds; then "Hashem is a Man of war."

251. יְיָ׳ אִישׁ מִלְחָמָה יְיָ׳ שְׁמוֹ. רִבִּי אַבָּא פָּתַח עַל כֵּן יֵאָמַר בְּסֵפֶר מִלְחֲמוֹת יְיָ׳ אֶת וָהֵב בְּסוּפָה וְאֶת הַנְּחָלִים אַרְנוֹן. כַּמָּה אִית לָן לְאִסְתַּכְּלָא בְּפִתְגָּמֵי אוֹרַיְיתָא, כַּמָּה אִית לָן לְעַיְּינָא בְּכָל מִלָּהָא, דְּלֵית לָךְ מִלָּה בְּאוֹרַיְיתָא, דְּלָא אִתְרְמִיזָא בִּשְׁמָא קַדִּישָׁא עִלָּאָה, וְלֵית לָךְ מִלָּה בְּאוֹרַיְיתָא, דְּלֵית בָּהּ כַּמָּה רָזִין, כַּמָּה טַעֲמִין, כַּמָּה שָׁרָשִׁין, כַּמָּה עֲנָפִין.

251. "Hashem is a man of war: Hashem is His name." Rabbi Aba opened the discussion, saying: "Wherefore is said in the book of the wars of Hashem, Vahev in Sufah and the rivers of Arnon" (Bemidbar 21:14). How much must we observe on the words of Torah, how much must we concentrate on every word, for you have not one word in the Torah that does not allude to the Holy Supernal Name. And there is no word in the Torah that does not have many secrets, many senses, many sources, and many branches.

252. הָכָא אִית לְאִסְתַּכְּלָא, ע״כ יֵאָמַר בְּסֵפֶר מִלְחֲמוֹת יְיָ׳, וְכִי סֵפֶר מִלְחֲמוֹת יְיָ׳, אָן הוּא. אֶלָּא הָכִי אִתְּעָרוּ חַבְרַיָּיא, כָּל מַאן דְּאַגָּח קְרָבָא בְּאוֹרַיְיתָא, זָכֵי לְאַסְגָּאָה שְׁלָמָא בְּסוֹף מִלּוֹי. כָּל קְרָבִין דְּעָלְמָא, קְטָטָה וְחֻרְבָּנָא. וְכָל קְרָבִין דְּאוֹרַיְיתָא, שְׁלָמָא וּרְחִימוּתָא, הה״ד עַל כֵּן יֵאָמַר בְּסֵפֶר מִלְחֲמוֹת יְיָ׳ אֶת וָהֵב בְּסוּפָה, כְּלוֹמַר, אַהֲבָה בְּסוּפָה. דְּלֵית לָךְ אַהֲבָה וּשְׁלָמָא בַּר מֵהַאי.

252. Here we should observe what is written: "Wherefore is said in the book of the wars of Hashem." HE ASKS: Where is "the book of the wars of Hashem?" HE ANSWERS: This is what the friends explained. Every person who wages war in Torah merits an increase in peace at the end of his words. All the wars of the world are quarrels and destruction, and all the wars of Torah are peace and love. This is what is meant by: "Wherefore is said in the book of the wars of Hashem," NAMELY THE WARS OF TORAH. "Vahev in Sufah," meaning love (Heb. *ahavah*) at its end (Heb. *sufah*). For you have no other love and peace except this.

253. תּוּ קַשְׁיָא בְּאַתְרֵיהּ. ע"כ יֵאָמַר בְּסֵפֶר מִלְחֲמוֹת יְיָ', בְּתוֹרַת מִלְחֲמוֹת יְיָ' מִבָּעֵי לֵיהּ, מַאי בְּסֵפֶר. אֶלָּא רָזָא עִלָּאָה הוּא, אֲתָר אִית לֵיהּ לְקוּדְשָׁא בְּרִיךְ הוּא, דְּאִקְרֵי סֵפֶר כד"א, דִּרְשׁוּ מֵעַל סֵפֶר יְיָ' וְקָרָאוּ. דְּכָל חֵילִין וּגְבוּרָן דְּעָבֵיד קוּדְשָׁא בְּרִיךְ הוּא, בְּהַהוּא סֵפֶר תַּלְיָין, וּמִתַּמָּן נָפְקִין.

253. But the question remains standing, for it is written: "Wherefore is said in the book of the wars of Hashem," AND IF IT REFERS TO THE WARS IN TORAH, it should have said 'in the Torah of the wars of Hashem' What is the meaning of "in the book"? HE ANSWERS: It is a supernal secret. The Holy One, blessed be He, has a place which is called 'book', WHICH IS MALCHUT, as is written: "Seek out of the book of Hashem, and read" (Yeshayah 34:16). All the powers and strengths that the Holy One, blessed be He, has originate from that book, and from there they emerge.

254. אֶת וָהֵב בְּסוּפָה, מַאן וָהֵב. אֶלָּא כָּל אִינּוּן חֵילִין, וְכָל אִינּוּן גְּבוּרָאן דְּעָבֵיד קוּדְשָׁא בְּרִיךְ הוּא, בְּהַהוּא סֵפֶר תַּלְיָין. וְכַד אֲגַח קוּדְשָׁא בְּרִיךְ הוּא קְרָבוֹי, בְּחַד אֲתָר דְּאִיהוּ בְּסוֹפָא דְּדַרְגִּין, וְאִקְרֵי וָהֵב. כד"א לַעֲלוּקָה שְׁתֵּי בָנוֹת הַב הַב. בְּסוּפָה: בְּסוֹף דַּרְגִּין אִשְׁתְּכַח. בְּסוּפָה: יָם סוּף אִתְקְרֵי, יָם דְּאִיהוּ סוֹף לְכָל דַּרְגִּין.

254. "Vahev in Sufah." HE ASKS: What is Vahev? HE ANSWERS: All the strengths and all these mighty deeds that the Holy One, blessed be He, has come from that book, WHICH IS MALCHUT. When the Holy One, blessed be He, wages His wars, it is in one place which is the end of the levels, called

'Vahev', as is written: "The leech has two daughters, crying, 'Give, give (Heb. *hav-hav*)" (Mishlei 30:15). THEY ARE THE PLACE OF PUNISHMENTS UNDERNEATH MALCHUT. "In Sufah" means that it is at the end (Heb. *sof*) of the levels. Sufah is called the 'Red (Heb. *suf*) Sea', MALCHUT, MEANING the sea that is the end of all the levels.

255. וְאֶת הַנְּחָלִים אַרְנוֹן וְעִם נַחְלַיָּיא דְּאִשְׁתָּכְחוּ וְאַתְנְגִידוּ. לְגַבֵּיהּ, מֵהַהוּא אֲתָר עִלָּאָה, דְּאִקְרֵי אַרְנוֹן מַאי אַרְנוֹן. זִוּוּגָא עִלָּאָה דַּחֲבִיבוּתָא, דְּלָא מִתְפָּרְשָׁאן לְעָלְמִין, כְּמָה דְּאַתְּ אָמֵר וְנָהָר יוֹצֵא מֵעֵדֶן. וּבְדָא, מִשְׁתָּרְשָׁן שָׁרָשׁוֹי, וְאִתְרְבִיאוּ עֲנָפָיו, לְאוֹשָׁטָא קְרָבוֹי בְּכָל אֲתָר, לְאוֹשָׁטָא חֵילִין וּגְבוּרָאן, וּלְאִתְחֲזָאָה שׁוּלְטָנָא רַבָּא וִיַקִּירָא דְּכֹלָּא.

255. "And the wadis of Arnon" MEANS with the rivers that come and are drawn TO MALCHUT, WHICH IS THE SECRET OF "VAHEV IN SUFAH," from that highest place which is called "Arnon." What is Arnon? It is the supernal union of love that never separates, WHICH IS THE UNION OF THE SUPERNAL ABA AND IMA. As you say: "And a river went out of Eden" (Beresheet 2:10). A RIVER, WHICH IS BINAH, AND EDEN, WHICH IS CHOCHMAH, ARE COLLECTIVELY CALLED 'ABA AND IMA', BECAUSE ARNON IS COMPOSED OF THE LETTERS OF *OR-NUN* ('THE LIGHT OF FIFTY'), NAMELY THE LIGHT OF THE FIFTY GATES OF BINAH. This way its roots are rooted, and its branches OF MALCHUT grow so as to do battles in every place, perform deeds of strength and might, and show the greatest dominion and majesty.

256. ת"ח, כַּד מִתְעָרִין גְּבוּרָאן וּקְרָבִין דְּקוּדְשָׁא בְּרִיךְ הוּא, כַּמָּה גַּרְדִּינֵי טְהִירִין, מִתְעָרִין לְכָל עִיבָר, כְּדֵין שַׁנְּנָן רוּמְחִין, וְסַיְיפִין, וּמִתְעָרִין גְּבוּרָאן, וְיַמָּא אִתְרְגִישַׁת וְגַלְגַּלוֹי סַלְקִין וְנַחְתִּין, וְאַרְבִין דְּאַזְלִין וְשָׁאטָן בְּיַמָּא, לְכָל עִיבָר מִסְתַּלְקִין. שַׁנְּנָא קְרָבָא בְּאַבְנֵי בַּלִּסְטְרָאוֹת, מָארֵי דְּרוֹמְחִין וְסַיְיפִין, כְּדֵין חִצֶּיךָ שְׁנוּנִים וְקוּדְשָׁא בְּרִיךְ הוּא אִתְתָּקִיף בְּחֵילוֹי, וּלְאִתְעֲרָא קְרָבָא. וַוי לְאִינוּן דְּמַלְכָּא קַדִּישָׁא יִתְעַר עֲלַיְיהוּ קְרָבָא. כְּדֵין כְּתִיב, יְיָ' אִישׁ מִלְחָמָה.

256. Come and behold: when the powers and wars of the Holy One, blessed be He, are provoked, many Prosecutors of Judgments are stirred on every side. Then spears, WHICH ARE THE SECRET OF JUDGMENTS OF THE RIGHT SIDE, and sharp swords, WHICH ARE THE JUDGMENTS OF THE LEFT SIDE, arouse mighty deeds. The sea becomes agitated and its waves rise and fall, and the ships that tread and sail on the sea scatter to all sides. The war escalates with catapult stones, spears-men, and swordsmen. Then it is written: "Your arrows are sharp" (Tehilim 45:6). And the Holy One, blessed be He, strengthens Himself with His powers to wage war. Woe to those against whom the Holy King provokes war. It is then written: "Hashem is a man of war" (Shemot 15:3).

257. וּמֵהָכָא, וּמֵאִינּוּן אַתְוָון, וּמֵהַאי קְרָא, נָפְקִין טוּרֵי קְרָבָא לְאִינּוּן חַיָּיבַיָּא, לְאִילֵּין מָארֵי דְּבָבוּ דְּחָבוּ לְקוּדְשָׁא בְּרִיךְ הוּא. וְאַתְוָון אִתְגַּלְיָין לְאִינּוּן מָארֵי קְשׁוֹט, וְהָא אִתְפָּרְשָׁן מִלִּין וְהָא אִתְּמַר.

257. From this PASSAGE: "HASHEM IS A MAN OF WAR," from these letters and from this passage emerge lines of warriors against these wicked people and these enemies who sinned against the Holy One, blessed be He. The secret of the letters is revealed to these men of Truth. These things are explained and elucidated, and we have already learned this.

258. יְיָ' אִישׁ מִלְחָמָה יְיָ' שְׁמוֹ. כֵּיוָן דִּכְתִּיב יְיָ' אִישׁ מִלְחָמָה, לָא יְדַעְנָא דַּיְיָ' שְׁמוֹ. אֶלָּא, כְּמָה דִּכְתִּיב וַיְיָ' הִמְטִיר עַל סְדוֹם וְעַל עֲמוֹרָה גָּפְרִית וָאֵשׁ מֵאֵת יְיָ' מִן הַשָּׁמָיִם. וְכֹלָּא בְּהַאי סֵפֶר תַּלְיָין, כד"א יְגַלּוּ שָׁמַיִם עֲוֹנוֹ וְאֶרֶץ מִתְקוֹמָמָה לוֹ.

258. "Hashem is a Man of War, Hashem is His Name." HE ASKS: Since it is written, "Hashem is a man of war," do I not know that "Hashem is His Name"? HE ANSWERS: But it is written, "And Hashem rained upon Sdom and upon Amorah brimstone and fire from Hashem out of heaven" (Beresheet 11:24), IN WHICH "AND HASHEM" MEANS YUD HEI VAV HEI AND HIS COURT OF JUSTICE, WHICH IS MALCHUT. THEREFORE, IT SAYS AFTERWARDS, "FROM HASHEM." HERE TOO, "HASHEM IS A MAN OF WAR" MEANS YUD HEI VAV HEI AND, "HASHEM IS HIS NAME," MEANS MALCHUT. For all comes from that book, WHICH IS MALCHUT, as is written: "The heaven will reveal his iniquity" (Iyov 20:27), MEANING

ZEIR ANPIN, CALLED 'HEAVEN'. "And the earth shall rise up against him," MEANS MALCHUT THAT IS CALLED 'EARTH'.

19. "The chariots of Pharaoh and his host"

A Synopsis

We are told that in the time to come, the Holy One, blessed be He will wage a great and powerful war against the nations in order to honor His Name. Rabbi Yehuda narrates a dialogue between God and the angel who was appointed over the sea, wherein we learn that when He created the sea it was on condition that it would split for the children of Yisrael. Rabbi Elazar says that all the Chariots and hosts above were given into the hands of Judgment of Malchut, called the 'Great Sea' to break them in their level; when they were broken, then those below were broken and lost in the sea. He returns to the subject of the ten fingers of the hands, corresponding to the ten saying with which the Holy One, blessed be He was afterwards named. Rabbi Elazar says that all the ten plagues that He caused in Egypt were all by one hand, because the left hand was included in the right. Now Rabbi Yitzchak begins to describe the seven firmaments created by God, in each of which stars are stationed and fly; above them all is Aravot, the seventh heaven. Above Aravot is the firmament of the four holy beasts, that are comparable to all those that are below them. He talks of the seven depths and the seven sanctuaries, then of the sea that is Malchut where all the fish swim and gather and descend, illuminating downward; all the Chariots are called by their name. The dominion of the Other Side is broken by the strong power of Hashem, at the splitting of the sea.

259. תָּא חֲזֵי, בְּשַׁעֲתָא דְקוּדְשָׁא בְּרִיךְ הוּא אִתְּעַר קְרָבָא בְּעָלְמָא, עִלָּאֵי וְתַתָּאֵי אִתְעַקְּרוּ מֵאַתְרַיְיהוּ, כְּמָה דְּאוֹקִימְנָא הה"ד מַרְכְּבוֹת פַּרְעֹה וְחֵילוֹ יָרָה בַיָּם. וּלְזִמְנָא דְּאָתֵי, זַמִּין קוּדְשָׁא בְּרִיךְ הוּא לְאַגָּחָא קְרָבָא עִלָּאָה וְתַקִּיפָא בַּעֲמְמַיָּא, בְּגִין לְאוֹקְרָא שְׁמֵיהּ, הה"ד וְיָצָא יְיָ' וְנִלְחַם בַּגּוֹיִם הָהֵם כְּיוֹם הִלָּחֲמוֹ בְּיוֹם קְרָב וּכְתִיב וְהִתְגַּדִּלְתִּי וְהִתְקַדִּשְׁתִּי וְנוֹדַעְתִּי וְגוֹ'.

259. Come and behold: all the time that the Holy One, blessed be He, arouses war in the world, those above and those below, NAMELY, THE NATION BELOW AND THEIR PATRONS ABOVE, are dislodged from their places, as we have established. This is the meaning of the verse: "The chariots of Pharaoh and his host has He thrown into the sea" (Shemot 15:4).

And in the time to come, the Holy One, blessed be He, shall wage a great and powerful war against the nations in order to glorify His Name, as is written: "Then Hashem shall go forth and fight against those nations, as when He fights in the day of battle" (Zecharyah 14:3), and: "Thus will I magnify Myself and sanctify Myself; and I will make Myself known..." (Yechezkel 38:23).

.260 ר' יְהוּדָה פָּתַח וְאָמַר, רָאוּךָ מַּיִם אֱלֹהִים רָאוּךָ מַּיִם יָחִילוּ וְגוֹ', בְּשַׁעֲתָא דְּעָבְרוּ יִשְׂרָאֵל יָת יַמָּא, אָמַר קוּדְשָׁא בְּרִיךְ הוּא לְמַלְאָכָא דִּי מְמָנָא עַל יַמָּא, פְּלִיג מֵימָךְ. א"ל לָמָּה. א"ל בְּגִין דִּבְנֵי יַעַבְרוּן בְּגַוָּךְ. אָמַר לֵיהּ, פּוּרְקָנָא דְּקִיטְנָא קְשׁוֹט. מ"ש אִלֵּין מֵאִלֵּין.

260. Rabbi Yehuda opened the discussion, saying: "The waters saw You, Elohim, the waters saw You; they were afraid..." (Tehilim 77:17). At the time that Yisrael crossed the sea, the Holy One, blessed be He, said to the angel, who was appointed over the sea: 'Divide your waters.' He asked Him: 'Why?' He said to him: 'In order that My children may cross through you.' He said to Him: 'breaking the yoke of the reckoning is true', MEANING FORGIVENESS OF SINS IS TRUE, BECAUSE THE HOLY ONE, BLESSED BE HE, INDEED FORGIVES AND PARDONS SINS–'but what is the difference between the two? IF YOU FORGIVE THE CHILDREN OF YISRAEL, THEN ALSO FORGIVE THE EGYPTIANS.'

.261 א"ל עַל, תְּנַאי דָּא, עֲבָדִית לְיַמָּא כַּד בָּרָאתִי עָלְמָא. מַה עָבִיד קוּדְשָׁא בְּרִיךְ הוּא, אִתְּעַר גְּבוּרְתָּא דִּילֵיהּ, וְאִתְקָמְטוּ מַיָּא. הה"ד רָאוּךָ מַּיִם אֱלֹהִים רָאוּךָ מַּיִם יָחִילוּ. א"ל קוּדְשָׁא בְּרִיךְ הוּא, קְטוֹל כָּל אִינוּן אֻכְלוֹסִין, לְבָתַר אַרְמֵי לוֹן לְבַר. לְבָתַר חָפֵי יַמָּא עֲלַיְיהוּ, הה"ד מַרְכְּבוֹת פַּרְעֹה וְחֵילוֹ יָרָה בַיָּם.

261. THE HOLY ONE, BLESSED BE HE, said to him: It was on this condition that I made the sea when I created the world, MEANING THE CONDITION THAT IT WOULD BE SPLIT FOR THE CHILDREN OF YISRAEL. What did the Holy One, blessed be He, do? He roused His might and the waters folded. This is what is meant by: "The waters saw You, Elohim, the waters saw You: they were afraid." The Holy One, blessed be He, said TO

THE PATRON ANGEL OF THE SEA: Slay all these multitudes and afterwards cast them out. Afterwards the sea covered them, as is written: "The chariots of Pharaoh and his host has He thrown into the sea."

262. אָמַר רִבִּי אֶלְעָזָר, פּוּק חָמֵי כַּמָּה רְתִיכִין עָבֵד קוּדְשָׁא בְּרִיךְ הוּא לְעֵילָּא, כַּמָּה אֹכְלוֹסִין, כַּמָּה חַיָּילִין, וְכֻלְּהוּ קְשִׁירִין אִלֵּין בְּאִלֵּין. כֻּלְּהוּ רְתִיכִין אִלֵּין לְאִלֵּין, דַּרְגִּין עַל דַּרְגִּין, וּמִסִּטְרָא דִּשְׂמָאלָא מִתְעָרִין רְתִיכִין דְּלָא קַדִּישִׁין שַׁלִּיטִין. וְכֻלְּהוּ דַּרְגִּין יְדִיעָן לְעֵילָּא.

262. Rabbi Elazar said: Come and behold. The Holy One, blessed be He, made above many Chariots, many multitudes, and many hosts which are all tied to each other. They are all Chariots to each other, FOR EVERY LOWER IS A CHARIOT TO THAT WHICH IS ABOVE IT; there are levels upon levels. And from the left side, dominating Chariots are come that are not Holy. And they are all specific levels above.

263. וְהָא אִתְעֲרָנָא בִּבְכוֹר פַּרְעֹה, דְּהוּא דַּרְגָּא חַד, דְּקָטַל קוּדְשָׁא בְּרִיךְ הוּא וְתָבַר לֵיהּ מְשׁוּלְשְׁלֵיהּ תַּקִּיפָא, תְּחוֹת שׁוּלְטָנֵיהּ, כַּמָּה רְתִיכִין וְכַמָּה חַיָּילִין דְּקוּזְמִיטִין מִסְּטַר שְׂמָאלָא, מִנְּהוֹן אֲחִידָן בַּאֲתָר עִלָּאָה דְּשׁוּלְטָנוּתָא דִּלְהוֹן, וּמִנְהוֹן אֲחִידָן בְּמַלְכוּתָא דִּלְעֵילָּא. מִנְּהוֹן אֲחִידָן בָּתַר אַרְבַּע חֵיוָן, כְּמָה דְּאִתְּמַר.

263. We have already noted by the first born of Pharaoh, that is one level, that the Holy One, blessed be He, slew and broke loose from its strong chain. Under its domination were many Chariots and many hosts of mighty men of the left side. Some of them were attached to the highest place of their dominion, and some of them were attached to Malchut above, and some of them were attached under the four living creatures, as we already learned.

264. וְכֻלְּהוּ אִתְמְסָרוּ בִּידֵיהּ, בְּדִינָא דְּמַלְכוּתָא, דְּאִקְרֵי יַמָּא רַבָּא, לְתַבְרָא לוֹן מִדַּרְגֵּיהוֹן, וְכַד אִינּוּן אִתְּבָרוּ לְעֵילָּא, כָּל אִינּוּן דִּלְתַתָּא אִתְּבָרוּ, וְאִתְאֲבִידוּ בְּיַמָּא תַּתָּאָה. הה"ד, מַרְכְּבוֹת פַּרְעֹה וְחֵילוֹ יָרָה בַיָּם. בַּיָּם סְתָם.

264. And they were all given over into the hands of the Judgment of Malchut, that is called the 'Great Sea', to break them from their level. When these were broken above, then all these below were broken, and lost in the sea below. Hence, it is written: "The chariots of Pharaoh and his host has He thrown into the sea." "The sea," without attributes SHOWS BOTH THE SEA ABOVE FOR THEIR MINISTERS, AND ALSO THE LOWER SEA OF THE EGYPTIANS BELOW.

265. וּמִבְחַר שָׁלִישָׁיו טֻבְּעוּ בְיַם סוּף. וּמִבְחַר שָׁלִישָׁיו, הָא אִתְּמַר, וְשָׁלִישִׁם עַל כֻּלּוֹ, כֻּלְּהוּ דַּרְגִּין תְּרֵין וְחַד. אִלֵּין עַל אִלֵּין. כְּגַוְונָא עִלָּאָה הָכִי אִתְעֲבִידוּ. וְכֻלְּהוּ אִתְמְסָרוּ בִּידָהָא, לְאִתְּבְרָא מִשּׁוּלְטָנֵיהוֹן, אִלֵּין וְאִלֵּין.

265. "His chosen captains also are drowned in the Sea of Reeds." "His chosen captains" has already been explained. "And captains over every one of them" (Shemot 14:7). All the levels were as two and one FROM ABOVE, ones upon the others; they were made in the likeness of above. And all of them were given over to the hands OF MALCHUT, to break them from their domination, the ones as well as the others, THOSE ABOVE AND THOSE BELOW.

266. ת"ח, הָא אִתְּמַר דְּכֻלְּהוּ עֶשֶׂר מַחָאן דְּעָבֵד קוּדְשָׁא בְּרִיךְ הוּא בְּמִצְרַיִם, כֹּלָּא הֲוָה יְדָא חֲדָא, דִּשְׂמָאלָא אַכְלִיל בִּימִינָא. דְּעֶשֶׂר אֶצְבְּעָן כְּלִילָן דָּא בְּדָא, לָקֳבֵל עֶשֶׂר אֲמִירָן, דְּקוּדְשָׁא בְּרִיךְ הוּא אִתְקְרֵי בְּהוּ לְבָתַר. לָקֳבְלֵיהּ דְּכֹלָּא הַאי דְּיַמָּא, תַּקִּיף וְרַב וְשַׁלִּיטָא. כד"א, וְהָאַחֲרוֹן הִכְבִּיד. הה"ד מַרְכְּבוֹת פַּרְעֹה וְחֵילוֹ יָרָה בַיָּם וְגוֹ'. וּלְזִמְנָא דְּאָתֵי, זַמִּין קוּדְשָׁא בְּרִיךְ הוּא לְקַטְלָא אֻכְלוֹסִין וְקוּזְתוּרְנָטִין וְקוּנְטִירִיסִין וְקַלְטִירוּלְסִין דֶּאֱדוֹם הה"ד מִי זֶה בָּא מֵאֱדוֹם חֲמוּץ בְּגָדִים מִבָּצְרָה.

266. Come and behold: we have learned that the ten plagues that the Holy One, blessed be He, caused in Egypt were all by one hand, because the left hand was included in the right. And ten fingers were included in each other, corresponding to the ten sayings with which the Holy One, blessed be He, was afterwards named. Corresponding to them all, the one of the sea was strong and great and dominating, as is said: "And afterward (lit. 'the last one') He afflicted her more" (Yeshayah 8:23). This is what is meant by: "The chariots of Pharaoh and his host has he thrown into the sea." In the time to come, the Holy One, blessed be He, shall slay multitudes, and different officers, and leaders of Edom. This is what is said: "Who is this, who comes from Edom, with crimsoned garments from Batzrah?" (Yeshayah 63:1).

267. מַרְכְּבוֹת פַּרְעֹה וְחֵילוֹ יָרָה בַיָּם. רִבִּי יִצְחָק פָּתַח, לְקוֹל תִּתּוֹ הֲמוֹן מַיִם בַּשָּׁמַיִם וַיַּעֲלֶה נְשִׂיאִים מִקְּצֵה הָאָרֶץ בְּרָקִים לַמָּטָר עָשָׂה וַיּוֹצֵא רוּחַ מֵאוֹצְרוֹתָיו. הָא תָּנֵינָן, שִׁבְעָה רְקִיעִין עָבֵד קוּדְשָׁא בְּרִיךְ הוּא, וּבְכָל רְקִיעָא וּרְקִיעָא כֹּכָבִין קְבִיעִין, וְרַהֲטִין בְּכָל רְקִיעָא וּרְקִיעָא, וּלְעֵילָּא מִכֻּלְּהוּ עֲרָבוֹת.

267. "The chariots of Pharaoh and his host has He thrown into the sea." Rabbi Yitzchak opened the discussion, saying: "When His voice resounds with the great mass of water in the heavens, and He raises vapors from the ends of the earth; when He makes lightning flashes among the rain, and brings forth the wind out of His storehouses" (Yirmeyah 10:13). We have learned that the Holy One, blessed be He, made seven firmaments CORRESPONDING TO CHESED, GVURAH, TIFERET, NETZACH, HOD, YESOD, AND MALCHUT, and stars are stationed in every firmament, MEANING FROM THE ASPECT OF "AND RETURNED" (YECHEZKEL 1:14). Stars fly in every single firmament, MEANING LEVELS FROM THE ASPECT OF "RAN" (IBID.). And above all of them is Aravot, WHICH IS THE FIRST THREE SFIROT OF THE FIRMAMENTS.

268. וְכָל רְקִיעָא וּרְקִיעָא בְּהִלּוּכוֹ מָאתַן שְׁנִין, וְרוּמֵיהּ חֲמֵשׁ מְאָה שְׁנִין. וּבֵין רְקִיעָא וּרְקִיעָא, חֲמֵשׁ מְאָה שְׁנִין. וְהַאי עֲרָבוֹת הִלּוּכוֹ בְּאוֹרְכֵּיהּ, אֶלֶף וַחֲמֵשׁ מֵאָה שְׁנִין. וּפוּתְיֵהּ, אֶלֶף וַחֲמֵשׁ מֵאָה שְׁנִין, וּמִזִּיוָא דִּילֵיהּ, נָהֲרִין כָּל אִינּוּן רְקִיעִין.

268. And every firmament is two hundred years' walk in length and five hundred years high. Between each firmament is a distance of 500 years.

And Aravot is 1,500 years' walk in length and 1,500 years wide, and all these firmaments are illuminated from its radiance.

269. וְהָא תָּנֵינָן, לְעֵילָּא מֵעֲרָבוֹת, רָקִיעַ דְּחַיּוֹת. פַּרְסוֹת דְּחַיּוֹת קַדִּישִׁין וְרוּמְהוֹן, כְּכֻלְּהוּ. לְעֵילָּא מִנְּהוֹן קַרְסוּלַיְן דְּחַיּוֹת כְּכֻלְּהוּ. שׁוֹקֵי הַחַיּוֹת, כְּכֻלְּהוּ. אַרְכּוּבִין דְּחַיּוֹת, כְּכֻלְּהוּ. יַרְכִין דְּחַיּוֹת, כְּכֻלְּהוּ. עַגְבֵי דְּחַיּוֹת, כְּכֻלְּהוּ. וְגוּפָא דְּחַיּוֹת כְּכֻלְּהוּ. גַּדְפַּיְיהוּ, כְּכֻלְּהוּ. וְצַוָּארַיְהוּ, כְּכֻלְּהוּ. רָאשֵׁי הַחַיּוֹת, כְּכֻלְּהוּ. מַאי כְּכֻלְּהוּ. כְּקָבְלֵי כֻּלְּהוּ.

269. We have learned that above Aravot is the firmament of the living creatures, WHERE THERE ARE FOUR LIVING CREATURES: LION, OX, EAGLE AND MAN. The hoofs of the living creatures and their height resemble all of those THAT ARE UNDER THEM, BECAUSE THE UPPER ONE CONTAINS WITHIN IT ALL THAT IS BELOW IT. Above them are the ankles of living creatures, and they resemble all of those THAT ARE BELOW THEM. The shanks of the living creatures resemble all of those THAT ARE BELOW. The thighs of the living creatures resemble all of those THAT ARE BELOW. The buttocks of the living creatures resemble all of those THAT ARE BELOW, and the torsos of the living creatures resemble all of those THAT ARE BELOW. The wings resemble all of those THAT ARE BELOW. Their necks resemble all of those THAT ARE BELOW. The heads of the living creatures resemble all of those THAT ARE BELOW. HE ENUMERATES HERE TEN ASPECTS CORRESPONDING TO TEN SFIROT. HE ASKS: What is the meaning of 'resemble all of those'? AND HE ANSWERS: THEY ARE CONSIDERED comparable to all those THAT ARE BELOW THEM.

270. וְכַל שַׁיְיפָא וְשַׁיְיפָא דִּבְחַיּוֹת, לָקֳבֵל שִׁבְעָה תְּהוֹמִין, וְלָקֳבֵל שִׁבְעָה הֵיכָלִין וְלָקֳבֵל מֵאַרְעָא לִרְקִיעַ. וְלָקֳבֵל מֵרְקִיעַ לִרְקִיעַ, וְשִׁיעוּרָא דְּכֻלְּהוּ וְרוּמְהוֹן עֶשְׂרִין וַחֲמִשָּׁה אַלְפִין חוּלָקִין, מִשִּׁיעוּרָא דְּקוּדְשָׁא בְּרִיךְ הוּא, כְּמָה דְּאוֹקִימְנָא.

270. Every single limb in the living creatures corresponds to the seven depths. It corresponds to seven sanctuaries, WHICH ARE THE SECRET OF THE SEVEN MALCHUYOT, and corresponds to from the earth to the firmament, WHICH IS YESOD. It corresponds to from the firmament to the firmament, WHICH ARE CHESED, GVURAH, NETZACH, AND HOD, AS MENTIONED. Their measure and height is 25,000 parts of the measure of the Holy One, blessed be He, as we have established.

271. וְעוֹד רְקִיעָא חַד לְעֵילָּא, מִן קַרְנֵי הַחַיּוֹת, דִּכְתִּיב וּדְמוּת עַל רָאשֵׁי הַחַיָּה רָקִיעַ. מִלְּרַע כַּמָּה רְתִיכִין, בִּימִינָא וּשְׂמָאלָא.

271. There is one more firmament above the horns of the living creatures, as is written: "And over the heads of beasts there was the likeness of a firmament" (Yechezkel 1:22). Below THAT FIRMAMENT are many Chariots on the right and left.

272. מִתְּחוֹת יַמָּא שָׁרָאן כֻּלְּהוּ נוּנֵי יַמָּא, וְשָׁטָאן, אִתְכְּנָפוּ בְּזָוִיהוֹן אַרְבַּע, נַחְתִּין בְּדַרְגַּיְיהוּ, וְכֻלְּהוּ רְתִיכִין אִקְרוּן בִּשְׁמָהָן. מִתְּחוֹת אִלֵּין, אַזְלִין וְשָׁאטִין אִינּוּן זְעִירִין, דַּרְגִּין עַל דַּרְגִּין, דִּכְתִּיב זֶה הַיָּם גָּדוֹל וּרְחַב יָדַיִם שָׁם רֶמֶשׂ וְאֵין מִסְפָּר חַיּוֹת קְטַנּוֹת עִם גְּדוֹלוֹת. וְהָא אוֹקִימְנָא מִלֵּי.

272. Below the sea, WHICH IS MALCHUT, dwell all the fish of the sea. They swim and gather in their four corners – WHICH ARE CHESED, GVURAH, TIFERET AND MALCHUT – and descend in their level, MEANING THEY ILLUMINATE FROM ABOVE DOWNWARDS, and all the Chariots are called by their name. Below these go the small ones, levels upon levels, as is written: "So is this great and wide sea, wherein are creeping things innumerable, both small and great beasts" (Tehilim 104:25). We have already established these things.

273. מִסְּטָר שְׂמָאלָא תַּתָּאָה, קוּזְמִיטָא סִטְרָא אַחֲרָא וְאֲחִידָן מֵאִינּוּן דִּלְעֵילָּא, וְנַחְתּוּ לְאִתְּבְּרָא מֵחֵילָא תַּקִּיפָא קַדִּישָׁא. כְּמָה דְּאוֹקִימְנָא, מַרְכְּבֹת פַּרְעֹה וְחֵילוֹ וְגוֹ'.

273. In the lower left side there is the dominion of the Other Side. FOR, "ELOHIM HAS MADE THE ONE AS WELL AS THE OTHER" (KOHELET 7:14). AND TO EVERYTHING THAT IS IN BRIYAH, YETZIRAH, ASIYAH OF

HOLINESS, THERE IS A CORRESPONDING ONE IN THE OTHER SIDE. And they grasp onto those above, FOR THEY NURTURE FROM HOLINESS. AND NOW, AT THE SPLITTING OF THE SEA OF REEDS, they descend, broken by the strong power of Holiness, as we have established: "The chariots of Pharaoh and his host..."

20. "Your right hand, Hashem, is glorious in power"

A Synopsis

Rabbi Shimon, speaking of the doe that is Malchut, says that a person who studies Torah at midnight comes with the doe to stand before the King, and when morning comes a thread of grace is drawn over him. As he gazes at the firmament the light of understanding of the Holy Knowledge dwells upon him, and he is crowned with it. He says, "Hashem is near to all those who call upon Him, to all those who call upon Him in Truth," which means that he knows how to proclaim the unity of the Holy Name in his prayers, properly, and thus establishes a single nation in the world. Everyone who comes to pray without concentrating with his heart, desire and fear, is cast away. Rabbi Shimon talks about "The Righteous perishes," or "The righteous lost," telling us that the Righteous lost since blessings no longer dwell on him as they once did, and since the children of Yisrael, Malchut, has become distanced from him. In the time to come, his spouse will be returned to him. Man is really divided in order that he should later accept his spouse and the two should truly become one body. Rabbi Shimon compares this to "your right hand," which is divided in order to accept the left. In the time to come, in the time of Messiah, he says, "Your right hand, Hashem, has dashed (lit. 'will dash') the enemy in pieces." Then will be Armageddon and also the resurrection of the dead. Rabbi Shimon says that at that time those who will remain in the world, those who are circumcised and received the Holy Covenant, shall be blessed. Rabbi Chiya concludes that the pleasantness that sent forth light when God gave the Torah to Yisrael has been covered and concealed since the Temple was destroyed.

274. יְמִינְךָ יְיָ׳ נֶאְדָּרִי בַּכֹּחַ. אָמַר ר״ש, בְּשַׁעֲתָא דְּצַפְרָא נָהִיר, וְאַיַּלְתָּא קַיְּימָא בְּקִיּוּמָהּ, אִתְעַבְרַת בְּסִטְרָהָא, וְעָאלַת בְּמָאתָן הֵיכָלִין דְּמַלְכָּא. בַּר נָשׁ דְּאִשְׁתַּדַּל בְּפַלְגוּת לֵילְיָא בְּאוֹרַיְיתָא, בְּשַׁעֲתָא דְּאִתְּעַר רוּחָא דְּצָפוֹן, וְתִיאוּבְתָּא דְּאַיַּלְתָּא דָּא לְאִתְעָרָא בְּעָלְמָא, אָתֵי עִמָּהּ לְקַיְּימָא קֳדָם מַלְכָּא, בְּשַׁעֲתָא דְּנָהִיר צַפְרָא מַשְׁכִין עָלֵיהּ חַד חוּטָא דְּחֶסֶד.

274. "Your right hand, Hashem, is glorious in power" (Shemot 15:6). Rabbi Shimon said: At the time when the morning shines, WHICH IS THE SECRET OF THE LIGHT OF CHASSADIM OF ZEIR ANPIN, the doe, WHICH IS

MALCHUT, stands firm. She is filled from her aspect, BECAUSE THE LEFT, WHICH IS HER SIDE, IS THEN ATTIRED IN CHASSADIM AND HER LIGHT BECOMES FULL. She enters into two hundred sanctuaries of the King, WHICH IS THE SECRET OF THE RIGHT COLUMN, WHICH CONTAINS ONLY KETER AND CHOCHMAH. EACH ONE NUMBERS ONE HUNDRED; THUS, THEY ARE TWO HUNDRED. AFTER MALCHUT HAS BEEN COMPLETED AND FILLED FROM THE LEFT COLUMN, SHE IS ENTIRELY INCLUDED IN THE RIGHT, WHICH IS THE SECRET OF THE TWO HUNDRED SANCTUARIES. A person who has studied Torah at midnight – at the time that the North Wind stirs, NAMELY THE LEFT, and it is the desire of this doe to be aroused in the world TO BESTOW PLENTY – he comes with her to stand before the King. And during the time of morning light, a thread of grace is drawn over him.

275. מִסְתַּכֵּל בִּרְקִיעָא, שַׁרְיָא עָלֵיהּ נְהִירוּ דְּסָכְלְתָנוּ דְּדַעְתָּא קַדִּישָׁא, וּמִתְעַטֵּר בֵּיהּ בַּר נָשׁ, וְדָחֲלִין מִנֵּיהּ כֹּלָּא. כְּדֵין הַאי בַּר נָשׁ אִקְרֵי בְּרָא לְקוּדְשָׁא בְּרִיךְ הוּא, בַּר הֵיכָלָא דְּמַלְכָּא. עָאל בְּכָל תַּרְעוֹי, לֵית דְּיִמְחֵי בִּידֵיהּ.

275. As he gazes at the firmament, MEANING THAT HE RECEIVES FROM THE FIRMAMENT, WHICH IS YESOD OF ZEIR ANPIN, the light of understanding of the Holy Knowledge dwells upon him, and the man is crowned with it, BY ATTAINING THE FIRST THREE SFIROT. And all fear him. Then this person is called 'a son of the Holy One, blessed be He', 'a resident of the King's sanctuary', WHICH IS MALCHUT, MEANING A SON TO ZEIR ANPIN AND NUKVA. And he enters all the gates of the King and nobody can hinder him.

276. בְּשַׁעֲתָא דְּקָרֵי לְהֵיכָלָא דְּמַלְכָּא, עָלֵיהּ כְּתִיב, קָרוֹב יְיָ' לְכָל קוֹרְאָיו לְכֹל אֲשֶׁר יִקְרָאוּהוּ בֶאֱמֶת. מַאי בֶּאֱמֶת. כְּמָה דְּאוֹקִימְנָא, תִּתֵּן אֱמֶת לְיַעֲקֹב, דְּיָדַע לְיַחֲדָא שְׁמָא קַדִּישָׁא בִּצְלוֹתֵיהּ כַּדְקָא יֵאוֹת. וְדָא פּוּלְחָנָא דְּמַלְכָּא קַדִּישָׁא.

276. At the time that he is summoned to the King's sanctuary, it is written about him: "Hashem is near to all those who call upon Him, to all those who call upon Him in Truth" (Tehilim 145:18). What is "in Truth"? It is as we established in the passage: "Show Truth to Jacob" (Michah 7:20), WHICH MEANS that he knows how to proclaim the unity of the Holy Name in his prayers properly. And this is the service of the Holy King.

277. וּמַאן דְּיָדַע לְיַחֲדָא שְׁמָא קַדִּישָׁא כַּדְקָא יָאוֹת, אוֹקִים אוּמָּא יְחִידָא בְּעָלְמָא, דִּכְתִּיב וּמִי כְעַמְּךָ יִשְׂרָאֵל גּוֹי אֶחָד בָּאָרֶץ. וְעַל דָּא אוֹקִימְנָא, כָּל כֹּהֵן דְּלָא יָדַע לְיַחֲדָא שְׁמָא קַדִּישָׁא כַּדְקָא יָאוֹת, לָאו פּוּלְחָנֵיהּ פּוּלְחָנָא. דְּהָא כֹּלָּא בֵּיהּ תַּלְיָא, פּוּלְחָנָא עִלָּאָה, וּפוּלְחָנָא תַּתָּאָה. וּבָעֵי לְכַוְּונָא לִבָּא וּרְעוּתָא, בְּגִין דְּיִתְבָּרְכוּן עִלָּאֵי וְתַתָּאֵי.

277. Anyone who knows how to proclaim the unity of the Holy Name properly establishes a single nation in the world, as written: "And what one nation in the earth is like Your people, like Yisrael" (II Shmuel 7:23). Therefore, we have established that the service of any priest who does not know how to proclaim the unity of the Holy Name properly is not a proper service. This is because everything depends UPON THE PRIEST, both the service above, WHICH IS THE ESTABLISHING OF UNITY OF THE NAME, and the service below, OF SACRIFICES. And he must concentrate his heart and desire so that those above and those below are blessed.

278. כְּתִיב כִּי תָבֹאוּ לֵרָאוֹת פָּנָי. כָּל בַּר נָשׁ דְּאָתֵי לְיַחֲדָא שְׁמָא קַדִּישָׁא, וְלָא אִתְכַּוָּון בֵּיהּ בְּלִבָּא וּרְעוּתָא וּדְחִילוּ, בְּגִין דְּיִתְבָּרְכוּן בֵּיהּ עִלָּאֵי וְתַתָּאֵי, רָמָאן לֵיהּ צְלוֹתֵיהּ לְבַר, וְכֹלָּא מַכְרִיזֵי עָלֵיהּ לְבִישׁ. וְקוּדְשָׁא בְּרִיךְ הוּא קָרֵי עָלֵיהּ כִּי תָבֹאוּ לֵרָאוֹת פָּנָי.

278. It is written: "When you come to appear before Me (lit. 'see My face')" (Yeshayah 1:12), for the prayer of every person who comes to proclaim the unity of the Holy Name but does not concentrate with his heart, desire and fear in order that by it those above and those below shall be blessed, is cast away. All announce against him. And the Holy One, blessed be He, declares of him: "When you come to see My face."

279. כִּי תָבוֹאוּ לִרְאוֹת מִבָּעֵי לֵיהּ, מַאי לֵרָאוֹת פָּנָי. אֶלָּא כָּל אִינּוּן אַנְפִּין דְּמַלְכָּא, טְמִירִין בְּעָמְקָא לְבָתַר חֲשׁוֹכָא וְכָל אִינּוּן דְּיַדְעִין

לְיַחֲדָא שְׁמָא קַדִּישָׁא כַּדְקָא יָאוּת מִתְבַּקְעִין כָּל אִינּוּן כּוֹתָלֵי חֲשׁוֹכָא, וְאַנְפִּין דְּמַלְכָּא אִתְחַזְיָין, וְנָהֲרִין לְכֹלָּא. וְכַד אִינּוּן אִתְחַזְיָין וְנָהֲרִין, מִתְבָּרְכִין כֹּלָּא עִלָּאִין וְתַתָּאִין. כְּדֵין בִּרְכָּאן אִשְׁתְּכָחוּ בְּכֻלְּהוּ עָלְמִין, וּכְדֵין כְּתִיב לֵרָאוֹת פָּנָי.

279. It should have been simply, "When you come to see." Why the additional "to see My face"? HE ANSWERS: For all these faces of King, NAMELY THE ILLUMINATION OF CHOCHMAH IN THE SECRET OF THE PASSAGE: "A MAN'S WISDOM MAKES HIS FACE TO SHINE" (KOHELET 8:1), are concealed in the depth of the darkness, WHICH IS THE SECRET OF THE JUDGMENTS IN THE LEFT COLUMN. For by all those who know how to proclaim the unity of the Holy Name properly, the walls of darkness split, and the face of the King appears and shines to everyone. When they are visible and shine, then blessed are all those above and below. Then blessings are prevalent in all the world, and it is written: "to see My face."

280. מִי בִקֵּשׁ זֹאת מִיֶּדְכֶם, מַאי קָא מַיְירֵי. אֶלָּא מַאן דְּאָתֵי לְיַחֲדָא שְׁמָא קַדִּישָׁא עִלָּאָה, בָּעֵי לְיַחֲדָא מִסִּטְרָא דְּזֹאת. כְּמָה דִּכְתִיב בְּזֹאת יָבֹא אַהֲרֹן אֶל הַקֹּדֶשׁ. בְּגִין דְּיִזְדַּוְּוגֻן כַּחֲדָא, אִינּוּן תְּרֵין: צַדִּיק וְצֶדֶק, בְּזִוּוּגָא חֲדָא. בְּגִין דְּיִתְבָּרְכוּן כֹּלָּא מִנַּיְיהוּ וְאִלֵּין אִקְרוּן חֲצֵרֶךָ, כְּמָה דִּכְתִיב, אַשְׁרֵי תִּבְחַר וּתְקָרֵב יִשְׁכֹּן חֲצֵרֶךָ.

280. "Who has required this (Heb. *zot*) from your hand" (Yeshayah 1:12). HE ASKS: What does the passage mean? HE ANSWERS: Everyone who comes to establish the unity of the Holy Supernal Name must do so from this aspect of *zot,* THAT IS MALCHUT, as is written: "Thus (Heb. *zot*) shall Aaron come into the holy place" (Vayikra 16:3). This is in order that the Righteous, WHICH IS YESOD, and righteousness, WHICH IS MALCHUT, shall unite together as one pair, so that everything shall be blessed from them. And these two are called "Your courts," as is written: "Happy is the man whom You choose, and cause to approach to You, that he may dwell in Your courts" (Tehilim 65:5).

281. וְאִי אִיהוּ אָתֵי לְיַחֲדָא שְׁמָא קַדִּישָׁא, וְלָא יִתְכַּוָּון בֵּיהּ בִּרְעוּתָא דְּלִבָּא, בִּדְחִילוּ וּרְחִימוּ. קוּדְשָׁא בְּרִיךְ הוּא אָמַר, מִי בִקֵּשׁ זֹאת מִיֶּדְכֶם

רְמוֹס חֲצֵרָי. זֹאת וַדַּאי, דְּהָא לֹא אִשְׁתְּכַח בְּהוּ בִּרְכָּאן. וְלָא דֵּי דְּלָא אִשְׁתְּכָחוּ בְּהוּ בִּרְכָאן, אֶלָּא דְּשַׁרְיָא בְּהוּ דִּינָא וְאִשְׁתְּכַח דִּינָא בְּכֹלָּא.

281. And to he who is about to unite the Holy name, but does not concentrate with the heartfelt desire, with fear and love, the Holy One, blessed be He, says: "who has required this (Heb. *zot*) at your hand, to trample My courts?" (Yeshayah 1:12) *Zot* is precise, because there are no blessings IN THE RIGHTEOUS AND RIGHTEOUSNESS WHICH ARE CALLED 'MY COURTS'. And not only are there no blessings, but rather Judgment dwells in them, and we find that everything is under Judgment.

282. ת"ח, יְמִינָא דְּקוּדְשָׁא בְּרִיךְ הוּא, מִנֵּיהּ מִתְעָרִין כָּל נְהִירוּ, כָּל בִּרְכָּאן, וְכָל חִדוּ. בֵּיהּ כָּלִיל שְׂמָאלָא כְּמָה דְּאִית בְּבַר נָשׁ יְמִינָא וּשְׂמָאלָא, וּשְׂמָאלָא אִתְכְּלִיל בִּימִינָא, וִימִינָא הוּא כָּלִיל כֹּלָּא. וְכַד אִתְּעַר יְמִינָא שְׂמָאלָא אִתְּעַר עִמֵּיהּ, דְּהָא בֵּיהּ אָחִיד וְאִתְכְּלִיל.

282. Come and behold: from the right side of the Holy One, blessed be He, WHICH IS CHESED, every light is aroused, all blessings, all joy. Within it is included the left. This is just as a person has right and left sides, and the left is included in the right, and the right includes everything. And when the right stirs, the left stirs with it, for it is linked to it and is included.

283. וְת"ח, בְּשַׁעֲתָא דְּאָרִים בַּר נָשׁ יְדֵיהּ בִּצְלוֹתָא, מְכַוֵּון בְּאֶצְבְּעָן דִּילֵיהּ לְעֵילָּא. כְּמָה דִּכְתִּיב וְהָיָה כַּאֲשֶׁר יָרִים מֹשֶׁה יָדוֹ וְגָבַר יִשְׂרָאֵל. דְּהָא בִּימִינָא תַּלְיָא כֹּלָּא. וּכְתִיב וַיִּשָּׂא אַהֲרֹן אֶת יָדָו, וּכְתִיב חָסֵר. וּכְדֵין אִתְכַּוֵּון לְבָרְכָה לְעֵילָּא.

283. Come and behold: when a person raises his hands in prayer, he points his fingers upwards, as is written: "And it came pass, when Moses held up his hand, that Yisrael prevailed" (Shemot 17:11). Everything depends on the right. It is written: "And Aaron lifted up his hands (Heb. *yadav*)" (Vayikra 9:22). *YADAV* is spelled without *YUD*, WHICH MEANS ONE HAND, THE RIGHT, and then he concentrates on blessing above.

284. וְקוּדְשָׁא בְּרִיךְ הוּא לָאו הָכִי, בְּשַׁעֲתָא דְּאָרִים יְמִינָא לְעֵילָּא, וַוי

לְהוּ לְתַתָּאֵי, דְּהָא כָּל סִיַּיעְתָּא וְכָל בִּרְכָּאן אִסְתָּלִיקוּ מִנַּיְיהוּ. מְנָלָן. דִּכְתִּיב נָטִיתָ יְמִינְךָ תִּבְלָעֵמוֹ אָרֶץ. מַאי נָטִיתָ יְמִינְךָ. כְּתַרְגּוּמוֹ, אֲרִימַת יְמִינָךְ. מִיַּד תִּבְלָעֵמוֹ אָרֶץ. וְכַד יְמִינָא אִשְׁתְּכַח, שְׂמָאלָא אִשְׁתְּכַח עִמֵּיהּ, וּכְדֵין לָא שַׁלְטִין דִּינִין בְּעָלְמָא, מ״ט, בְּגִין דִּימִינָא אִשְׁתְּכַח עִמֵּיהּ. וְאִי יְמִינָא אִסְתַּלָּקַת, הָא שְׂמָאלָא אִזְדַּמְּנַת, כְּדֵין דִּינִין מִתְעָרִין בְּעָלְמָא, וְדִינָא שַׁרְיָא בְּכֹלָּא.

284. It is not so with the Holy One, blessed be He. When THE HOLY ONE, BLESSED BE HE, raises His hand above, woe to those below, because all assistance and blessing has departed from them. How do we know this? For it is written: "You did stretch out Your right hand, the earth swallowed them" (Shemot 15:12). What is "You did stretch out Your right hand"? It is like its Aramaic translation: 'You raised Your right hand' and immediately, 'the earth swallowed them'. And when the right is present, the left is also with it. And if the right departs, then the left comes, Judgments stir in the world, and Judgments prevail overall.

285. ר״ש כַּד הֲוָה מָטֵי לְהַאי קְרָא, הֲוָה בָּכֵי, דִּכְתִּיב הֵשִׁיב אָחוֹר יְמִינוֹ. וְכִי אֶפְשָׁר דְּהֵשִׁיב אָחוֹר יְמִינוֹ. אֶלָּא בְּגִין דְּאַקְדִּים שְׂמָאלָא לְנַחְתָּא בְּעָלְמָא, וִימִינָא אִשְׁתַּאֲרַת בַּאֲתָר אַחֲרָא.

285. When Rabbi Shimon reached this verse he wept, for it is written: "He has drawn back his right hand" (Eichah 2:3). Is it possible that He would draw back His right hand? AND HE ANSWERS: But because the left hastened to descent into the world first, the right remained in another place, NAMELY BEHIND.

286. אר״ש, כְּתִיב הַצַּדִּיק אָבָד. וְהָא אוֹקִימְנָא מִלֵּי, הַצַּדִּיק נֶאֱבַד לָא כְּתִיב, אֶלָּא הַצַּדִּיק אָבָד. מִכָּל אִינּוּן אַנְפֵּי מַלְכָּא, לָא אִשְׁתְּכַח דְּאָבַד, אֶלָּא צַדִּיק. אָבַד בִּתְרֵי סִטְרֵי: חַד, דְּלָא שָׁרָאן בֵּיהּ בִּרְכָּאן, כַּד בְּקַדְמֵיתָא. וְחַד, דְּאִתְרְחִיקַת מִנֵּיהּ בַּת זוּגֵיהּ דְּהִיא כ״י. אִשְׁתְּכַח, דְּצַדִּיק אָבַד יַתִּיר מִכֹּלָּא. וּלְזִמְנָא דְּאָתֵי כְּתִיב, גִּילִי מְאֹד בַּת צִיּוֹן הָרִיעִי בַּת יְרוּשָׁלַם הִנֵּה מַלְכֵּךְ יָבֹא לָךְ צַדִּיק וְנוֹשָׁע הוּא. צַדִּיק

וּמוֹשִׁיעַ לָא כְּתִיב, אֶלָּא צַדִּיק וְנוֹשָׁע הוּא. הוּא נוֹשָׁע וַדַּאי. וְהָא אִתְּמַר.

286. Rabbi Shimon said: It is written, “The righteous perishes” (Yeshayah 57:1), and we explained the words. It does not say that ‘the Righteous is lost’, but rather, “The righteous lost.” AND HE ANSWERS: From all the aspects of the King the only one who lost was the Righteous one, WHICH IS YESOD. He lost in two ways: one, since blessings no longer dwell on him as originally, and the second is that his spouse has become distanced from him, that is, the Congregation of Yisrael, NAMELY MALCHUT. Thus the Righteous one loses more than any of them, and pertaining to the time to come, it is written: “Rejoice greatly, O daughter of Zion; shout, O daughter of Jerusalem: Behold, your King comes to you, He is just, and a deliverer (lit. ‘delivered’)” (Zecharyah 9:9). It is not written, ‘Just, and a deliverer’ but rather “just, and delivered.” He is most certainly delivered, BECAUSE HIS SPOUSE HAS RETURNED TO HIM. And we have already learned this.

287. יְמִינְךָ יְיָ׳ נֶאְדָּרִי בַּכֹּחַ. מַאי נֶאְדָּרִי, נֶאְדָּר מִבָּעֵי לֵיהּ. אֶלָּא, בְּשַׁעֲתָא דִּשְׂמָאלָא אַתְיָא לְאִזְדַּוְּוגָא בִּימִינָא, כְּדֵין כְּתִיב נֶאְדָּרִי תִּרְעַץ, וּלְעוֹלָם הָכִי הוּא בְּגִין דִּשְׂמָאלָא אִשְׁתְּכַח בִּימִינָא, וְאִתְכְּלִיל בֵּיהּ.

287. “Your right hand, Hashem, is glorious (Heb. *ne’edari*) in power” (Shemot 15:6). “Why does it say “*Ne’edari*”? It should say the more common ‘*ne’edar*’. AND HE ANSWERS: When the left comes to unite with the right, then is written: “*Ne’edari*...has dashed the enemy in pieces.” It is always thus when it unites with the right, because the left is present in the right and is included in it.

288. אָמַר רִבִּי שִׁמְעוֹן, כְּמָה דְּאוֹקִימְנָא הָכִי הוּא, דְּבַר נָשׁ אִשְׁתְּכַח דְּאִתְפְּלַג. מ״ט. בְּגִין לְקַבְּלָא עִמֵּיהּ בַּת זוּגֵיהּ, דְּיִתְעֲבִידוּ חַד גּוּפָא מַמָּשׁ. כַּד יְמִינְךָ, אִשְׁתְּכַח דְּאִתְפְּלַג. מ״ט. בְּגִין לְקַבְּלָא עִמֵּיהּ שְׂמָאלָא. וְהָכִי הוּא כֹּלָּא, חַד בְּחַד. וְעַל דָּא, בְּחַד מָחֵי וּמַסֵּי, הה״ד יְמִינְךָ יְיָ׳ תִּרְעַץ אוֹיֵב.

288. Rabbi Shimon said: It is as we established, because man is really divided, MEANING THAT HE IS ONLY HALF A BODY AND HIS SECOND HALF IS A WOMAN. What is the reason? In order that afterwards he should receive his spouse and the two should truly become one body. So is "Your right hand" really divided, IT IS ONLY HALF A BODY. What is the reason? In order to receive the left. And it is all so, one with one. With one hand, He smites and cures. Therefore, it is written: "Your right hand, Hashem, has dashed the enemy in pieces."

289. תָּא חֲזֵי, שִׁירָתָא דָּא אִתְּמַר, עַל הַהוּא זִמְנָא, וְעַל זִמְנָא דְּאָתֵי, בְּיוֹמֵי דְּיִתְּעַר מַלְכָּא מְשִׁיחָא, דִּכְתִּיב, יְמִינְךָ יְיָ׳ תִּרְעַץ אוֹיֵב, רָעַצְתְּ לָא כְּתִיב, אֶלָּא תִּרְעַץ. מַה כְּתִיב בְּקַדְמֵיתָא, הֵשִׁיב אָחוֹר יְמִינוֹ, מִפְּנֵי אוֹיֵב, בְּהַהוּא זִמְנָא הִיא, תִּרְעַץ אוֹיֵב לְזִמְנָא דְּאָתֵי.

289. Come and behold: this song was sung about that time and about the time to come, when King Messiah will be aroused, as written: "Your right hand, Hashem, has dashed (lit. 'will dash') the enemy in pieces." It is not written: 'has dashed', THAT IS IN THE PAST TENSE, but "will dash," IN THE FUTURE TENSE. THUS, THIS IS ALSO FOR THE FUTURE TO COME. It is written before, REGARDING THE EXILE: "He has drawn back His right hand from before the enemy." At that time, in the time to come, it "will dash the enemy in pieces"

290. וְכֹלָּא הָכִי הוּא, תַּהֲרוֹס קָמֶיךָ, הָרַסְתָּ לָא כְּתִיב, אֶלָּא תַּהֲרוֹס. תְּשַׁלַּח חֲרוֹנְךָ יֹאכְלֵמוֹ כַּקַּשׁ, כֹּלָּא לְזִמְנָא דְּאָתֵי. יְמִינְךָ יְיָ׳ נֶאְדָּרִי בַּכֹּחַ, בְּזִמְנָא דָּא, בְּעָלְמָא דֵּין. יְמִינְךָ יְיָ׳ תִּרְעַץ אוֹיֵב, בְּזִמְנָא דְּמַלְכָּא מְשִׁיחָא. וּבְרוֹב גְּאוֹנְךָ תַּהֲרוֹס קָמֶיךָ, לְבִיאַת גּוֹג וּמָגוֹג. תְּשַׁלַּח חֲרוֹנְךָ יֹאכְלֵמוֹ כַּקַּשׁ, לִתְחִיַּית הַמֵּתִים. דִּכְתִּיב, וְרַבִּים מִיְּשֵׁנֵי אַדְמַת עָפָר יָקִיצוּ אֵלֶּה לְחַיֵּי עוֹלָם וְאֵלֶּה לַחֲרָפוֹת וּלְדִרְאוֹן עוֹלָם.

290. And it is all in this manner: "You have (lit. 'will') overthrown them that rose up against You" (Shemot 15:7). It is not written, "You have overthrown," but literally, 'You will overthrow,' and similarly, "You did (lit. 'will') send forth Your anger, which consumed them as stubble" (Ibid.). It is all in the time to come. "Your right hand, Hashem, is glorious in power" is in this time, in this world. "Your right hand, Hashem, will dash the enemy in pieces," refers to the time of King Messiah. "And in the greatness of Your excellency You have overthrown them that rose up against You," refers to the coming of Gog and Magog (Armageddon). "You will send forth Your anger, which will consume them as stubble," refers to the resurrection of the dead, as written: "And many of those who sleep in the dust of the earth shall awake, some to everlasting life, and some to shame and everlasting contempt" (Daniel 12:2).

291. בְּהַהוּא זִמְנָא, אָמַר רִבִּי שִׁמְעוֹן, זַכָּאִין אִינּוּן דְּיִשְׁתַּאֲרוּן בְּעָלְמָא, וּמַאן אִינּוּן. תָּא חֲזֵי, לָא יִשְׁתְּאַר מִבְּנֵי עָלְמָא, בַּר אִינּוּן גְּזִירִין, דְּקַבִּילוּ אָת קַיָּימָא קַדִּישָׁא, וְעָאלוּ בְּקַיָּימָא קַדִּישָׁא, בְּאִינּוּן תְּרֵין חוּלָקִין, כְּמָה דְּאוֹקִימְנָא. וְהוּא נָטִיר לֵיהּ לְהַהוּא קַיָּים, וְלָא עַיְילֵיהּ בְּאֲתָר דְּלָא אִצְטְרִיךְ, אִלֵּין אִינּוּן דְּיִשְׁתַּאֲרוּן, וְיִכָּתְבוּן לְחַיֵּי עָלְמָא.

291. Rabbi Shimon said: During that time, blessed are those who will remain in the world. And who are they? Come and behold: there will not remain any in the world except those who are circumcised, who accepted the Holy Covenant, and entered into the two parts of the Holy Covenant, NAMELY CIRCUMCISION AND MEMBRANE UNCOVERING, as we have established. And one who guards the member the Covenant, not to insert it where he should not, these are those who will remain and be inscribed for eternal life.

292. מְנָלָן. דִּכְתִּיב, וְהָיָה הַנִּשְׁאָר בְּצִיּוֹן וְהַנּוֹתָר בִּירוּשָׁלַםִ קָדוֹשׁ יֵאָמֶר לוֹ כָּל הַכָּתוּב לְחַיִּים בִּירוּשָׁלַםִ. מַשְׁמַע הַנִּשְׁאָר בְּצִיּוֹן וְהַנּוֹתָר בִּירוּשָׁלַםִ, דְּכָל מַאן דְּאִתְגְּזַר, בְּאִלֵּין תְּרֵין דַּרְגִּין עָאל. וְאִי נָטִיר לְהַהוּא קַיָּים כַּדְקָא חֲזֵי, וְיִזְדְּהַר בֵּיהּ, עָלֵיהּ כְּתִיב הַנִּשְׁאָר בְּצִיּוֹן וְהַנּוֹתָר בִּירוּשָׁלַםִ. אִלֵּין יִשְׁתַּאֲרוּן בְּהַהוּא זִמְנָא, וּבְהוּ זַמִּין קוּדְשָׁא בְּרִיךְ הוּא לְחָדְתָּא עָלְמָא, וּלְמֶחֱדֵי בְּהוּ. עַל הַהוּא זִמְנָא כְּתִיב, יְהִי כְבוֹד יְיָ׳ לְעוֹלָם יִשְׂמַח יְיָ׳ בְּמַעֲשָׂיו.

292. How do we know this? From the words: "And it shall come to pass, that he that is left in Zion, and he that remains in Jerusalem, shall be called Holy, every one in Jerusalem that is written to Life" (Yeshayah 4:3). It is understood from, "He that is left in Zion, and he that remains in Jerusalem," that everyone who is circumcised attains these two levels, ZION AND JERUSALEM. If he observes that Covenant properly and is careful and particular about it, it is written: "He that is left in Zion, and he that remains in Jerusalem." These will remain in that time. And the Holy One, blessed be He, will renew the world and rejoice with them. In reference to that time, it is written: "May the glory of Hashem endure forever, let Hashem rejoice in His works" (Tehilim 104:31).

293. ר׳ חִיָּיא הֲוָה אָזִיל לְגַבֵּי רִבִּי אֶלְעָזָר, אַשְׁכְּחֵיהּ, דַּהֲוָה יָתִיב לְגַבֵּיהּ דְּרִבִּי יוֹסֵי בר״ש בֶּן לָקוּנְיָיא חָמוּי. עַד דְּזָקִיף רֵישֵׁיהּ, חָמָא לֵיהּ לְרִבִּי חִיָּיא, אָמַר, בַּיּוֹם הַהוּא יִהְיֶה יִשְׂרָאֵל שְׁלִישִׁיָּה לְמִצְרַיִם וּלְאַשּׁוּר בְּרָכָה בְּקֶרֶב הָאָרֶץ אֲשֶׁר בֵּרֲכוֹ יְיָ׳ צְבָאוֹת לֵאמֹר בָּרוּךְ עַמִּי מִצְרַיִם וּמַעֲשֵׂה יָדַי אַשּׁוּר וְנַחֲלָתִי יִשְׂרָאֵל, וְכִי אַשּׁוּר וּמִצְרַיִם קְרִיבִין אִינּוּן לְקוּדְשָׁא בְּרִיךְ הוּא.

293. Rabbi Chiya was traveling to Rabbi Elazar. He found him sitting near Rabbi Yosi, the son of Rabbi Shimon, son of Lakunya, his father-in-law. He raised his head and saw Rabbi Chiya. He said: "In that day shall Yisrael be the third with Egypt and with Ashur (Assyria), a blessing in the midst of the land whom Hashem Tzeva'ot shall bless, saying, 'Blessed be Egypt, My people, and Ashur the work of My hands, and the children of Yisrael My inheritance" (Yeshayah 19:24-25). HE ASKS: Are then Ashur and Egypt close to the Holy One, blessed be He?

294. אֶלָּא, עַל גָּלוּתָא דְּיִסְקוּן מִמִּצְרַיִם וּמֵאַשּׁוּר אִתְּמַר, וְאִי אִתְּמַר עַל מִצְרַיִם וְעַל אַשּׁוּר, עַל אִינּוּן חֲסִידִין דִּלְהוֹן, דְּאַהַדְרוּ בְּתִיּוּבְתָּא, וְאִשְׁתַּאֲרוּן לְמִפְלַח לְיִשְׂרָאֵל וּלְמַלְכָּא מְשִׁיחָא, דִּכְתִּיב וְיִשְׁתַּחֲווּ לוֹ כָּל מְלָכִים. וּכְתִיב, וְהָיוּ מְלָכִים אוֹמְנַיִךְ וְגוֹ׳.

294. HE ANSWERS: This refers to all those members of the exiles who will go up from Egypt and Ashur. And if we say that it refers to Egypt and Ashur THEMSELVES, it refers to the pious among them who repented, and remained to serve Yisrael and King Messiah, as it is written: "And may all kings fall down before Him" (Tehilim 72:11), and, "And kings shall be your foster fathers..." (Yeshayah 49:23).

295. א"ל, מַאי דִּכְתִּיב, דְּרָכֶיהָ דַּרְכֵי נֹעַם א"ל כַּמָּה טִפְּשִׁין בְּנֵי עָלְמָא, דְּלָא יַדְעִין וְלָא מַשְׁגִּיחִין בְּמִלּוֹי דְּאוֹרַיְיתָא, דְּהָא מִלִּין דְּאוֹרַיְיתָא אִינּוּן אָרְחָא לְמִזְכֵּי בְּהַהוּא נֹעַם יְיָ' דִּכְתִּיב דְּרָכֶיהָ דַּרְכֵי נֹעַם וְכָל נְתִיבוֹתֶיהָ שָׁלוֹם. דַּרְכֵי נֹעַם וַדַּאי. מַאי נֹעַם. כְּמָה דִּכְתִּיב לַחֲזוֹת בְּנֹעַם יְיָ', וְהָא אוֹקְמוּהָ, בְּגִין דְּאוֹרַיְיתָא, וְאָרְחוֹי, מֵהַהוּא נֹעַם אַתְיָין, וְאִינּוּן אָרְחִין פְּרִישָׁן בֵּיהּ, וְעַל דָּא דְּרָכֶיהָ דַּרְכֵי נֹעַם וְכָל נְתִיבוֹתֶיהָ שָׁלוֹם.

295. He said to him: What is the meaning of, "Her ways are ways of pleasantness, and all her paths are peace" (Mishlei 3:17)? He said to him: How foolish are the people of the world, who do not know or pay attention to the words of Torah. The words of Torah are the way to merit that pleasantness of Hashem, as it is written: "Her ways are ways of pleasantness, and all her paths are peace" They are "ways of pleasantness," indeed. HE ASKS: What is "pleasantness"? AND HE ANSWERS: It is as written, "To behold the pleasantness of Hashem" (Tehilim 27:4), WHICH IS BINAH. We established that this is because the Torah and her ways are derived from that pleasantness, and these ways are explained in it. And hence, "Her ways are ways of pleasantness, and all her paths are peace."

296. א"ר חִיָּיא, תָּנֵינָן, בְּשַׁעְתָּא דְּקוּדְשָׁא בְּרִיךְ הוּא יָהַב אוֹרַיְיתָא לְיִשְׂרָאֵל, נָפַק נְהוֹרָא מֵהַהוּא נֹעַם, וְאִתְעַטַּר בֵּיהּ קוּדְשָׁא בְּרִיךְ הוּא, וּמֵהַהוּא נֹעַם אַבְהִיקוּ זִיוָון דְּכֻלְּהוּ, עָלְמִין דְּכֻלְּהוּ רְקִיעִין, דְּכֻלְּהוּ כִּתְרִין. עַל הַהִיא שַׁעְתָּא כְּתִיב, צְאֶינָה וּרְאֶינָה בְּנוֹת צִיּוֹן בַּמֶּלֶךְ שְׁלֹמֹה וְגוֹ'.

296. Rabbi Chiya said: We have learned at the time that the Holy One, blessed be He, gave the Torah to Yisrael, a light emitted from that pleasantness, WHICH IS BINAH. And the Holy One, blessed be He, WHO IS ZEIR ANPIN, crowned Himself with it, MEANING THAT HE RECEIVED THE FIRST THREE SFIROT FROM HER, CALLED 'A CROWN'. And from that pleasantness, the luster of all the worlds, of all the firmaments, and of all the crowns sparkled. About that moment, it is written: "Go forth, O daughters of Zion, and behold King Solomon…" (Shir Hashirim 3:11). KING SOLOMON

IS ZEIR ANPIN, HIS MOTHER IS BINAH, AND THE CROWN IS THE FIRST THREE SFIROT.

297. וְהַהִיא שַׁעֲתָא דְּאִתְבְּנֵי מַקְדְּשָׁא, אִתְעַטָּר קוּדְשָׁא בְּרִיךְ הוּא בְּהַהוּא עֲטָרָה, וְיָתִיב בְּכֻרְסְיָיא דִּילֵיהּ, וְאִתְעַטָּר בַּעֲטְרוֹי. וּמֵהַהוּא זִמְנָא דְּאִתְחָרַב בֵּי מַקְדְּשָׁא, לָא אִתְעַטָּר קוּדְשָׁא בְּרִיךְ הוּא בַּעֲטְרוֹי, וְהַהוּא נֹעַם אִתְטָמַּר וְאִתְגְּנִיז.

297. At the time that the Temple was built, the Holy One, blessed be He, was crowned with that crown and sat on His throne, WHICH IS MALCHUT. From the time that the Temple was destroyed, the Holy One, blessed be He, was not crowned with His crowns, and that pleasantness, WHICH IS THE LIGHT OF BINAH, was covered and concealed.

21. When Moses entered into the cloud

A Synopsis

Rabbi Elazar tells of Moses' journey into the cloud where he was met by the Angels Kemuel, and then Hadarniel and then Sandalphon, who receives prayers. Moses trembled in fright until the Holy One, blessed be He strengthened him, and Moses found his power in those realms through saying the 72 letters of the Supernal Holy Name. God taught him the Torah, but when the children of Yisrael sinned below, the Angels wished to harm Moses. God gave him His protection and His radiant light, and Moses went down with the tablets, his face shining with illumination. Rabbi Chiya says that as long as the children of Yisrael are occupied with Torah, the strength of all the heathen nations is broken.

298. א״ר אֶלְעָזָר, בְּשַׁעֲתָא דְּעָאל מֹשֶׁה בְּגוֹ עֲנָנָא, כְּמָה דִּכְתִּיב, וַיָּבֹא מֹשֶׁה בְּתוֹךְ הֶעָנָן, כְּבַר נָשׁ דַּהֲוָה אָזִיל בַּאֲתָר דְּרוּחָא. אִיעְרַע בֵּיהּ חַד מַלְאָכָא רַבְרְבָא, וְתָאנָא, קְמוּאֵ״ל שְׁמֵיהּ. וְהוּא מְמָנָא עַל תְּרֵיסָר אַלְפִין מְמָנָן שְׁלִיחָן. בָּעָא לְאִזְדַּוְּוגָא בֵּיהּ בְּמֹשֶׁה, פָּתַח מֹשֶׁה פּוּמֵיהּ, בִּתְרֵיסַר אַתְוָון גְּלִיפָן דִּשְׁמָא קַדִּישָׁא דְּאוֹלִיף לֵיהּ קוּדְשָׁא בְּרִיךְ הוּא בַּסְּנֶה, וְאִתְרְחַק מִנֵּיהּ תְּרֵיסַר אַלְפִין פַּרְסִין, וַהֲוָה אָזִל מֹשֶׁה בַּעֲנָנָא, וְעֵינוֹי מְלַהֲטָן כְּגוּמְרִין דְּאֶשָּׁא.

298. Rabbi Elazar said: When Moses entered into the cloud, it is written: "And Moses went into the midst of the cloud" (Shemot 24:18). As one who goes in the place of the spirit, a great angel met him. We learned that his name is Kemuel, and he is assigned over 12,000 appointed messengers. He wanted to join with Moses. Moses opened his mouth with the twelve engraved letters of the Holy Name that the Holy One, blessed be He, taught him at the bush, and he distanced himself twelve parasangs from Moses, who was standing in the cloud, with his eyes glowing like coals of fire.

299. עַד דְּאִיעֲרַע בֵּיהּ חַד מַלְאָכָא, רַבְרְבָא וְיַקִּירָא מִן קַדְמָאָה, וְתָאנָא הֲדַרְנִיאֵ״ל שְׁמֵיהּ, וְהוּא עִלָּאָה עַל שְׁאַר מַלְאָכִין, אֶלֶף וְשִׁתִּין רִבּוֹא פַּרְסִין, וְקָלֵיהּ אָזִיל בְּמָאתָן אֲלַף רְקִיעִין, דְּמִסְתַּחֲרָאן בְּאֶשָּׁא

חִיוָּורָא. כֵּיוָן דְּחָמָא לֵיהּ מֹשֶׁה, לָא יָכִיל לְמַלְּלָא. בָּעָא לְמִשְׁדֵי גַּרְמֵיהּ מִגּוֹ עֲנָנָא.

299. Then a certain angel who was greater and more honored than the first met him. We learned that Hadarniel is his name and he is six hundred and one thousand parasangs above the other angels, and his voice carries through two hundred thousand firmaments that revolve in a white fire. As soon as Moses saw him, he was unable to speak. He wanted to drop himself down from the midst of the cloud.

300. א"ל קוּדְשָׁא בְּרִיךְ הוּא, מֹשֶׁה, וְכִי אַנְתְּ הוּא דְּאַסְגִּית מִלִּין עִמִּי בַּסְּנֶה, דְּבָעִית לְמִנְדַּע רָזָא דִּשְׁמָא קַדִּישָׁא, וְלָא דָּחַלְתְּ. וְהַשְׁתָּא אַתְּ דָּחִיל מֵחָד מְשַׁמָּשַׁי. כֵּיוָן דִּשְׁמַע מֹשֶׁה קַלֵיהּ דְּקוּדְשָׁא בְּרִיךְ הוּא, אִתְתַּקַּף. פָּתַח פּוּמֵיהּ, בְּע"ב אַתְוָון דִּשְׁמָא עִלָּאָה, כֵּיוָן דִּשְׁמַע הֲדַרְנִי"אֵל אַתְוָון דִּשְׁמָא קַדִּישָׁא, מִפּוּמֵיהּ דְּמֹשֶׁה, אִזְדַּעְזָע. קָרִיב לְגַבֵּיהּ, א"ל, זַכָּאָה חוּלָקָךְ מֹשֶׁה, דְּאִתְגְּלֵי לָךְ, מַה דְּלָא אִתְגְּלֵי לְמַלְאֲכֵי עִלָּאֵי.

300. The Holy One, blessed be He, said to him: 'Moses, are you really the one who spoke so much with Me at the bush, who wanted to know the secret of the Holy Name, and had no fear. Yet now you are afraid of one of my attendants!' As soon as Moses heard the voice of the Holy One, blessed be He, he was strengthened and opened his mouth with the 72 letters of the Supernal Holy Name. As soon as Hadarniel heard the letters of the Holy Name from the mouth of Moses, he shuddered. He approached him and said to him: Blessed is your portion Moses, for it has been revealed to you that which has not been revealed to the highest angels.

301. וַהֲוָה אָזִיל עִמֵּיהּ, עַד דְּמָטוּ לְאֶשָּׁא תַּקִּיפָא, דְּחָד מַלְאָכָא דִּי שְׁמֵיהּ סַנְדַּלְפוֹן. וְתָאנָא, סַנְדַּלְפוֹן עִלָּאָה הוּא עַל שְׁאַר חַבְרוֹי, חֲמֵשׁ מְאָה שְׁנִין. וְהוּא קָאֵים בָּתַר פַּרְגּוֹדָא דְּמָארֵיהּ, וְקָשֵׁר לֵיהּ כִּתְרִין, מִבָּעוּתֵיהוֹן דִּצְלוֹתָא דְּיִשְׂרָאֵל. וּבְשַׁעֲתָא דְּמָטֵי הַאי כֶּתֶר לְרֵישֵׁיהּ דְּמַלְכָּא קַדִּישָׁא, הוּא מְקַבֵּל צְלוֹתֵהוֹן דְּיִשְׂרָאֵל. וְכֻלְּהוּ חַיָּילִין

וְאֻכְלוּסִין מִזְדַּעְזְעִין, וְנָהֲמִין וְאַמְרִין, בְּרִיךְ יְקָרָא דַּיְיָ' מֵאֲתַר בֵּית שְׁכִינְתֵּיהּ.

301. And he went with him until he reached the strong fire of an angel whose name is Sandalphon. We have learned that Sandalphon is 500 years higher than his other associates. He stands behind the curtain of his Master and he braids Him crowns from the requests of the prayers of Yisrael. And when this crown reaches the head of the Holy King, He receives all Yisrael's prayers. All the hosts and multitudes shudder and groan, and say: Blessed is the glory of Hashem from the dwelling place of His Shechinah.

302. א"ל הֲדַרְנִיאֵל לְמֹשֶׁה, מֹשֶׁה, לֵית אֲנָא יָכִיל לְמֵהַךְ עִמָּךְ, דְּלָא יוֹקִיד לִי אֶשָּׁא תַּקִּיפָא דְּסַנְדַּלְפוֹן. בֵּיהּ שַׁעֲתָא אִזְדַּעְזָע מֹשֶׁה, עַד דְּאַתְקִיף בֵּיהּ קוּדְשָׁא בְּרִיךְ הוּא בְּמֹשֶׁה, וְאוֹתְבֵיהּ קָמֵיהּ, וְאוֹלִיף לֵיהּ אוֹרַיְיתָא. וְחָפָא לֵיהּ לְמֹשֶׁה, בְּהַהוּא נְהוֹרָא וְזִיוָא דְּהַהוּא נֹעַם, וַהֲווֹ אַנְפּוֹי דְּמֹשֶׁה נְהִירִין בְּכָל אִינּוּן רְקִיעִין. וְכָל חֵילָא דִּשְׁמַיָּא הֲווֹ מִזְדַּעְזְעִין קָמֵיהּ, בְּשַׁעֲתָא דַּהֲוָה נָחִית בְּאוֹרַיְיתָא.

302. Hadarniel said to him: Moses, I can not go with you. I fear that the strong fire of Sandalphon will burn me. At that moment, Moses shuddered until the Holy One, blessed be He, grasped Moses, sat him before Him and taught him Torah. And He covered Moses with that Light and the radiant shine of that pleasantness, and the face of Moses illuminated throughout the firmaments. All the hosts of heaven were trembling before him at that moment that he descended with the Torah.

303. כֵּיוָן דְּחָבוּ יִשְׂרָאֵל לְתַתָּא, נָטַל קב"ה מִמֹּשֶׁה אֶלֶ"ף חוּלָקִין מֵהַהוּא זִיוָא. בֵּיהּ שַׁעֲתָא, בָּעוּ מַלְאָכִין עִלָּאִין, וְכָל אִינּוּן אֻכְלוּסִין, לְאוֹקְדָא לְמֹשֶׁה, בְּשַׁעֲתָא דא"ל קוּדְשָׁא בְּרִיךְ הוּא לֶךְ רֵד כִּי שִׁחֵת עַמְּךָ. אִזְדַּעְזָע מֹשֶׁה, וְלָא יָכִיל לְמַלְּלָא, עַד דְּאַסְגֵּי בִּצְלוֹתִין וּבָעוּתִין קָמֵי קוּדְשָׁא בְּרִיךְ הוּא.

303. As soon as Yisrael sinned below, the Holy One, blessed be He, took a thousand parts of that radiant shine from Moses. At that moment, the angels of above and all the multitudes wanted to burn Moses; NAMELY, when the Holy One, blessed be He, said to him, "Go, get you down; for your people…have become corrupt" (Shemot 32:7). Moses shuddered and could not speak until he increased and intensified supplications and prayers before the Holy One, blessed be He.

304. א"ל קוּדְשָׁא בְּרִיךְ הוּא, מֹשֶׁה, אַתְקִיף בְּכוּרְסְיָיא דִּילִי, עַד דְּגָעַר קוּדְשָׁא בְּרִיךְ הוּא בְּכָל אִינּוּן אֻכְלוּסִין, בְּכָל אִינּוּן חַיָּילִין, וְאַתְקִיף מֹשֶׁה בִּתְרֵין לוּחִין דְּאַבְנִין, וְאָחִית לוֹן לְתַתָּא. וְדָא הוּא דִּכְתִּיב, עִיר גִּבּוֹרִים עָלָה חָכָם וַיּוֹרֶד עֹז מִבְטֶחָה. וּמֵהַהוּא זִיוָא דְּאִשְׁתְּאַר בֵּיהּ, הֲווֹ מַבְהִיקִין אַנְפּוֹי דְּמֹשֶׁה. וּמַה בְּהַאי דְּאִשְׁתְּאַר בֵּיהּ לָא הֲוֵי יַכְלִין לְאִסְתַּכְּלָא בְּאַנְפּוֹי, בְּהַהוּא דְּאִסְתַּלָּק מִינֵּיהּ עאכ"ו.

304. The Holy One, blessed be He, said to him: 'Moses, grasp My throne.' Until the Holy One, blessed be He, castigated all the multitudes, all these hosts AND THEN Moses held the two stone tablets and brought them down. That is the meaning of what is written: "A wise man scales the city of the mighty, and casts down the stronghold in which it trusts" (Mishlei 21:22). From that radiant shine that remained in him, the face of Moses sparkled. And if in this remnant that remained with him they could not gaze into his face, then into what had left and gone from him most surely WOULD THEY NOT BE ABLE TO GAZE.

305. ר' חִיָּיא אָמַר, יְמִינְךָ יְיָ' נֶאְדָּרִי בַּכֹּחַ, דָּא אוֹרַיְיתָא. וע"ד, יְמִינְךָ יְיָ' תִּרְעַץ אוֹיֵב. דְּלֵית מִלָּה בְּעָלְמָא דְּיִתְבַּר חֵילֵיהוֹן דְּעַמִּין עכו"ם, בַּר בְּשַׁעֲתָא דְּיִשְׂרָאֵל מִתְעַסְּקִין בְּאוֹרַיְיתָא. דְּכָל זִמְנָא דְּיִשְׂרָאֵל מִתְעַסְּקִין בְּאוֹרַיְיתָא, יְמִינָא אִתְתְּקַף, וְאִתְּבַר חֵילָא וְתוּקְפָּא דעעכו"ם. וּבְגִינֵי כַּךְ אוֹרַיְיתָא אִקְרִית עֹז, כד"א יְיָ' עֹז לְעַמּוֹ יִתֵּן.

305. Rabbi Chiya said: "Your right hand, Hashem, is glorious in power" (Shemot 15:6), refers to the Torah, THAT GLORIFIES THE RIGHT, and therefore, "Your right hand, Hashem, has dashed the enemy in pieces." For there is nothing in the world that can break the power of the heathen peoples like Yisrael when they are occupied with Torah. As long as they are occupied with Torah, the right is strengthened, and the power and strength of the heathen are broken. Therefore, the Torah is called 'strength', as is written: "Hashem gives strength to His people" (Tehilim 29:11).

306. וּבְשַׁעֲתָא דְּיִשְׂרָאֵל לָא מִתְעַסְּקִין בְּאוֹרַיְיתָא שְׂמָאלָא אִתְתָּקַף, וְאִתְתָּקַף חֵילֵיהוֹן דעעכו"ם, וְשַׁלְטִין עֲלַייְהוּ, וְגַזְרִין עֲלַייְהוּ גְּזֵרִין, דְּלָא יַכְלִין לְמֵיקַם בְּהוּ. וְע"ד אִתְגְּלִיאוּ בְּנֵי יִשְׂרָאֵל, וְאִתְבַּדְּרוּ בֵּינֵי עַמְמַיָּא.

306. When Yisrael are not occupied with Torah, the left is strengthened and the power of the heathen nations, WHO NURTURE FROM THE LEFT, is strengthened. They rule over Yisrael and pass decrees which Yisrael can not tolerate. The children of Yisrael were exiled and dispersed among the nations for this reason.

307. דְּהָא הוּא דִּכְתִּיב עַל מָה אָבְדָה הָאָרֶץ וְגוֹ', וַיֹּאמֶר יְיָ' עַל עָזְבָם אֶת תּוֹרָתִי. דְּהָא כָּל זִמְנָא דְּיִשְׂרָאֵל יִשְׁתַּדְּלוּן בְּאוֹרַיְיתָא, אִתְּבַר חֵילָא וְתוּקְפָּא דְּכָל עע"ז, הה"ד יְמִינְךָ יְיָ' תִּרְעַץ אוֹיֵב. א"ר אֶלְעָזָר, וַדַּאי הָכִי הוּא, דְּכָל זִמְנָא דְּקָלֵיהוֹן דְּיִשְׂרָאֵל, אִשְׁתְּמַע בְּבָתֵּי כְּנֵסִיּוֹת וּבְבָתֵּי מִדְרָשׁוֹת וְכוּ', כְּמָה דְּתָנֵינָא הַקּוֹל קוֹל יַעֲקֹב, וְאִי לָאו הַיָּדַיִם יְדֵי עֵשָׂו, וְהָא אוֹקִימְנָא.

307. This is the meaning of the verse, "Why does the land perish...And Hashem says, 'Because they have forsaken My Torah'" (Yirmeyah 9:11-12). As long as Yisrael are occupied with Torah, the strength of might of all the heathens is broken. This is what is meant by: "Your right hand, Hashem, has dashed the enemy in pieces." Rabbi Elazar said: It is certainly so, AS WE LEARNED that as long as the voice of Yisrael is heard in the synagogues and study halls, "The voice is the voice of Jacob" (Beresheet 27:22). But if not, then "the hands are the hands of Esau," as we have already explained.

22. "And in the greatness of Your excellency You have overthrown them that rose up against You"

A Synopsis

Rabbi Chizkiyah opens with, "Why stand You afar off, Hashem? Why hide You Yourself in times of trouble?" He says that when the world sins the Holy One, blessed be He ascends farther away and people cry with no one to hear them; repentance is withheld from them. Rabbi Yitzchak says that the title verse of this section refers to the time that God will attire Himself with majesty over the nations that will come against Him, and destroy them. We hear that God shall resurrect the kings who were the enemies of Yisrael and provide them with a governing dominion above, and they will make war against Jerusalem; then God will take revenge on them. This will happen at the time of Messiah and Armageddon.

308. וּבְרֹב גְּאוֹנְךָ תַּהֲרוֹס קָמֶיךָ. ר׳ חִזְקִיָּה פָּתַח וְאָמַר, לָמָּה יְיָ׳ תַּעֲמוֹד בְּרָחוֹק תַּעְלִים לְעִתּוֹת בַּצָּרָה, בְּשַׁעֲתָא דְּחוֹבֵי עָלְמָא גָּרְמוּ, קוּדְשָׁא בְּרִיךְ הוּא סָלִיק לְעֵילָּא לְעֵילָּא, וּבְנֵי נָשָׁא צַוְוחִין וְנַחְתִּין דִּמְעִין, וְלֵית מַאן דְּיִשְׁגַּח עָלַיְיהוּ. מ״ט. בְּגִין דְּאִיהוּ סָלִיק לְעֵילָּא לְעֵילָּא, וּתְשׁוּבָה אִתְמְנַע מִנַּיְיהוּ, כְּדֵין כְּתִיב, וּבְרֹב גְּאוֹנְךָ תַּהֲרוֹס קָמֶיךָ.

308. "And in the greatness of Your excellency You have overthrown them that rose up against You" (Shemot 15:7). Rabbi Chizkiyah opened the discussion, saying: "Why stand You afar off, Hashem? Why hide You Yourself in times of trouble?" (Tehilim 10:1). At the time that the inequities of the world cause it, the Holy One, blessed be He, ascends higher and higher and people shed tears and cry, yet there is no one to pay attention to them. What is the reason? Because the Holy One, blessed be He, ascends higher and higher and repentance is withheld from them. Then it is written: "And in the greatness of Your excellency You have overthrown them that rose up against You."

309. ר׳ יִצְחָק אָמַר, הַאי קְרָא, בְּשַׁעֲתָא דְּאִתְלָבַּשׁ קוּדְשָׁא בְּרִיךְ הוּא גָּאוּתָא, עַל עֲמַמְיָא דְּיִתְכַּנְּשׁוּן עָלֵיהּ, כְּמָה דִּכְתִּיב, וְרוֹזְנִים נוֹסְדוּ יַחַד עַל יְיָ׳ וְעַל מְשִׁיחוֹ. וְתָאנָא זְמִינִין אִינּוּן שַׁבְעִין קַסְטוֹרִין מִכָּל עִיבָר, לְאִתְכַּנְּשָׁא בְּהַהוּא זִמְנָא בְּאוּכְלוּסִין דְּכָל עָלְמָא, וּלְמֶעְבַּד קְרָבָא עַל

22. "And in the greatness of Your excellency You have overthrown them that rose up against You"

יְרוּשָׁלַם קַרְתָּא קַדִּישָׁא, וּלְאַחֲדָא עֵיטִין עָלֵיהּ דְקוּדְשָׁא בְּרִיךְ הוּא. וּמַאי אַמְרֵי, נוֹקִים עַל פַּטְרוֹנָא בְּקַדְמֵיתָא, וּלְבָתַר עַל עַמֵּיהּ, וְעַל הֵיכָלֵיהּ.

309. Rabbi Yitzchak said: This verse refers to the time when The Holy One, blessed be He, will attire Himself with majesty over the nations that shall gather against Him, as it is written: "And the princes take counsel together, against Hashem, and against His anointed" (Tehilim 2:2). As we have learned, seventy generals of armies shall gather from every side at that time with the hosts of the entire world to wage war against Jerusalem, the Holy City, and to plan against the Holy One, blessed be He. What do they say? 'Let us rise against the protector first, and then against His people and His sanctuary'.

310. כְּדֵין זַמִּין קוּדְשָׁא בְּרִיךְ הוּא לְחַיְּיכָא עֲלַיְיהוּ. דִּכְתִּיב יוֹשֵׁב בַּשָּׁמַיִם יִשְׂחַק יְיָ' יִלְעַג לָמוֹ. בְּהַהוּא זִמְנָא יִלְבַּשׁ קוּדְשָׁא בְּרִיךְ הוּא גָּאוּתָא עֲלַיְיהוּ, וִישֵׁיצִינוּן מִן עָלְמָא, כְּמָה דִּכְתִּיב וְזֹאת תִּהְיֶה הַמַּגֵּפָה אֲשֶׁר יִגֹּף יְיָ' אֶת כָּל הָעַמִּים אֲשֶׁר צָבְאוּ עַל יְרוּשָׁלַם הָמֵק בְּשָׂרוֹ וְהוּא עוֹמֵד עַל רַגְלָיו.

310. Then the Holy One, blessed be He, will laugh at them, as is written: "He who sits in the heavens laughs: Hashem has them in derision" (Ibid. 4). At that time, the Holy One, blessed be He, will don majesty against them and will destroy them from the world, as is written: "And this shall be the plague with which Hashem will smite all the peoples that have fought against Jerusalem; their flesh shall be consumed while they stand upon their feet" (Zecharyah 14:12).

311. רִבִּי אַבָּא אָמַר מִשְּׁמֵיהּ דְּרַב יֵיסָא סָבָא, וְהָכִי אר"ש, זַמִּין קוּדְשָׁא בְּרִיךְ הוּא לְאַחֲיָיא לְכָל אִינּוּן מַלְכִּין, דְּעָקוּ לְיִשְׂרָאֵל וְלִירוּשָׁלַםִ, לְאַנְדְּרִיאָנוּס, לְלוּפִינוּס, וּנְבוּכַדְנֶצַר, וּלְסַנְחֵרִיב, וּלְכָל שְׁאַר מַלְכֵי עַמִּין, דְּחָרִיבוּ בֵּיתֵיהּ, וּלְשַׁלְטָאָה לוֹן כְּקַדְמִיתָא, וְיִתְכָּנְשׁוּן עִמְּהוֹן שְׁאַר עַמִּין, וְזַמִּין קוּדְשָׁא בְּרִיךְ הוּא לְאִתְפָּרְעָא מִנַּיְיהוּ

בְּאִתְגַּלְּיָיא, סַחֲרָנֵי יְרוּשָׁלַםִ. הה״ד, וְזֹאת תִּהְיֶה הַמַּגֵּפָה אֲשֶׁר יִגֹּף יְיָ׳ אֶת כָּל הָעַמִּים אֲשֶׁר צָבְאוּ עַל יְרוּשָׁלָםִ. אֲשֶׁר יִצְבְּאוּ לָא כְּתִיב, אֶלָּא אֲשֶׁר צָבְאוּ. כְּדֵין כְּתִיב, וּבְרֹב גְּאוֹנְךָ תַּהֲרוֹס קָמֶיךָ, וְדָא לִזְמְנָא דְּאָתָא מְשִׁיחָא, כְּתִיב, וְשִׁירָתָא דָּא שִׁירָתָא דְּעָלְמִין הִיא.

311. Rabbi Aba said, quoting Rabbi Yesa Saba (the elder), and also Rabbi Shimon said: The Holy One, blessed be He, shall resurrect those kings that distressed Yisrael and Jerusalem, NAMELY Adrianus and Lupinus, Nebuchadnezzar and Sancheriv, and all the other kings of the world that took part in the destruction of His House. Then He will provide them with a governing dominion as before, and the rest of the nations will gather with them, AND THEY WILL WAR AGAINST JERUSALEM. The Holy One, blessed be He, will take revenge on them openly around Jerusalem. This is the meaning of: "And this shall be the plague with which Hashem will smite all the peoples that have fought against Jerusalem." It is not written, 'that will fight' but rather, "that have fought" IN THE PAST TENSE, BECAUSE IT REFERS TO NEBUCHADNEZZAR, WHO HAD ALREADY FOUGHT. Then it is written: "And in the greatness of Your excellency You have overthrown them that rose up against You." This is written about the time when Messiah will come, and this song is a never-ending song.

312. וּבְרוּחַ אַפֶּיךָ נֶעֶרְמוּ מַיִם, בְּהַהוּא זִמְנָא. וּבְגִין כָּךְ אִית בְּהַהוּא זִמְנָא, וּלְזִמְנָא דְּמַלְכָּא מְשִׁיחָא, וּלְזִמְנָא דְּגוֹג וּמָגוֹג. נִצְּבוּ כְמוֹ נֵד, לִזְמְנָא דְּעָלְמָא דְּאָתֵי, דְּאִיהוּ חֶדְוָותָא דְּכָל עָלְמִין.

312. "And with the blast of Your nostrils the waters piled up" (Shemot 15:8), namely, at that time. Therefore, THIS shall happen at that time, in the time of King Messiah, and in the time of Gog and Magog (Armageddon). "The flood stood upright like a heap," refers to the World to Come, which is the joy of all the worlds.

23. “The enemy said, ‘I will purse, I will overtake’”

A Synopsis

We are told that the enemy spoken of here is the great minister appointed over Egypt. Along with all the ministers appointed over all the heathen nations he wanted to destroy the children of Yisrael, but the Holy One, blessed be He protected them when he remembered the mountains of the world, the patriarchs.

313. אָמַר אוֹיֵב אֶרְדּוֹף אַשִּׂיג אֲחַלֵּק שָׁלָל. אָמַר אוֹיֵב, דָּא הַהוּא מְמָנָא רַבְרְבָא עַל מִצְרָאֵי, בְּשַׁעֲתָא דְּאִתְיְהִיב לֵיהּ שֻׁלְטָנוּתָא עַל יִשְׂרָאֵל, חָשִׁיב דִּיְשֵׁיצִינוּן תְּחוֹת שֻׁלְטָנֵיהּ. אֶלָּא דְּדָכַר קוּדְשָׁא בְּרִיךְ הוּא טוּרֵי עָלְמָא, דַּהֲווֹ מְגִינִּין עָלַיְיהוּ. וְלָא תֵּימָא דָּא בִּלְחוֹדוֹי, אֶלָּא כָּל אִינּוּן רַבְרְבִין דִּמְמָנָן עַל כָּל עעכו״ם, וְכַד אִתְיְיהִיב לְהוּ רְשׁוּתָא וְשֻׁלְטָנוּתָא עַל יִשְׂרָאֵל, כֻּלְּהוּ בָּעָאן דִּישֵׁיצוּן יִשְׂרָאֵל תְּחוֹתַיְיהוּ.

313. “The enemy said, ‘I will purse, I will overtake, I will divide the spoil’” (Shemot 15:9). The enemy is the great minister appointed over Egypt. When he was given dominion over Yisrael, he intended to destroy them under his domination, but the Holy One, blessed be He, remembered the mountains of the world, THE PATRIARCHS, who protected them. Do not think that he alone WANTED TO DESTROY THEM, because all the ministers who were appointed over all the heathen nations desired to destroy Yisrael under them when they were granted authority and dominion over Yisrael.

314. וְעַל דָּא, אִינּוּן עַמִּין דִּתְחוֹת שׁוּלְטָנֵיהוֹן דְּאִינּוּן מְמָנָן, כֻּלְּהוּ גַּזְרִין גְּזֵרִין לְשֵׁיצָאָה לוֹן, אֶלָּא דְּקוּדְשָׁא בְּרִיךְ הוּא דְּכַר טוּרֵי עָלְמָא, וְאָגִין עָלַיְיהוּ. וְכַד חָמָא מֹשֶׁה דָּא, שָׁרָא לְשַׁבְּחָא לְקוּדְשָׁא בְּרִיךְ הוּא, וְאָמַר מִי כָמוֹכָה בָּאֵלִים יְיָ׳.

314. Therefore, these nations that are under the domination of these appointees all declare decrees to destroy Yisrael. But the Holy One, blessed be He, remembers the mountains of the world, WHICH ARE THE PATRIARCHS, and He protects them. When Moses saw this, he started to praise the Holy One, blessed be He, and said, “Who is like You among the mighty, Hashem.”

24. "Who is like You among the mighty, Hashem"

A Synopsis

Rabbi Shimon speaks of a great strong supernal tree that sustains those above and those below. The seventy branches are the seventy princes that are appointed over the seventy nations of the world; when their time of dominion arrives they want to destroy the trunk of the tree, that rules over the children of Yisrael. On the other hand, when the domination of the trunk reaches them it wants to guard them and to arrange peace among them all. It is said that this is like the Holy One, blessed be He, who guards everything and does not want to destroy the nations completely as they had wanted to do when they dominated. Rabbi Yosi turns to the verse, "I have seen all the works that are done under the sun; and behold, all is vanity and a striving after wind." In a dialogue with Rabbi Shimon we are told that a man's good deed turns into a breath that becomes an advocate before God, but that his bad deed turns into a breath that breaks his spirit. The holy breath from the good deed leads the person when his soul leaves him, and raises him to the place of glory above, and is present to bind him in the bond of life. Rabbi Shimon says that when the Temple was first built below it was based on Judgment and Anger, but in the time to come God shall perfect it in a different, higher level called 'righteousness'.

315. אָמַר ר״ש, אִילָנָא חַד רַבְרְבָא עִלָּאָה, תַּקִּיפָא, בֵּיהּ אִתְּזָנוּ עִלָּאִין וְתַתָּאִין. וְהוּא אִתְּחַם בִּתְרֵיסַר תְּחוּמִין, אִתְתָּקַּף בְּאַרְבַּע סִטְרֵי עָלְמָא, דְּאִתְחַבְּרָן בְּדוּכְתַּיְיהוּ. שַׁבְעִין עֲנָפִין סַלְּקִין בְּגַוֵּיהּ, וְאִתְּזָנוּ מִנֵּיהּ, בְּעִקַּר שָׁרְשׁוֹי יַנְיקִין אִינּוּן סַחֲרָנֵיהּ, וְאִינּוּן עֲנָפִין דְּמִשְׁתַּכְחִין בְּאִילָנָא.

315. Rabbi Shimon said: There is a great and strong, tall supernal tree, WHICH IS ZEIR ANPIN. Those above and those below are sustained through it. And it is bordered by twelve DIAGONAL border-lines, WHICH ARE THE FOUR SFIROT – CHESED, GVURAH, TIFERET, AND MALCHUT – EACH ONE CONTAINING THREE COLUMNS. It is strengthened by the four directions of the world – WHICH ARE CHESED, GVURAH, TIFERET AND MALCHUT – that are attached to their place. And seventy branches, WHICH ARE THE SEVENTY PRINCES THAT ARE APPOINTED OVER THE SEVENTY NATIONS OF THE WORLD, rise in it and are nurtured by it. From the center of its roots they nurture from around. And they are the branches that are found in the tree.

316. כַּד מָטֵי עִדָּן שֻׁלְטָנֵיהּ דְּכָל עַנְפָּא וְעַנְפָּא, כֻּלְּהוּ בָּעָאן לְשֵׁיצָאָה כֹּלָּא גּוּפָא דְּאִילָנָא, דְּאִיהוּ עִקָּרָא דְּכֻלְּהוּ עַנְפִין, הַהוּא דְּשָׁלִיט עֲלַיְיהוּ, וְיִשְׂרָאֵל אֲחִידָן בֵּיהּ. כַּד מָטָא עֲלַיְיהוּ שֻׁלְטָנוּתָא דְּהַהוּא גּוּפָא דְּאִילָנָא, חוּלָקָא דְּיִשְׂרָאֵל. בָּעֵי לְנַטְרָא לוֹן, וּלְמֵיהַב שְׁלָמָא בְּכֻלְּהוּ. וְעַל דָּא שִׁבְעִים פָּרֵי הֶחָג, לְמִיהַב שְׁלָמָא לְשַׁבְעִין עַנְפִין דִּבְגוֹ אִילָנָא.

316. When the time of dominion arrives for each branch, they all want to completely destroy the trunk of the tree, which is the mainstay of the branches, that rules over Yisrael who are joined with it. And when the domination of the trunk of the tree reaches them, which is the portion of Yisrael, it wants to guard them, and to arrange peace among them all. For this purpose, seventy oxen ARE OFFERED during Sukkot (the holiday of booths) to bring peace among the seventy branches in the tree, WHICH ARE THE SEVENTY PATRON ANGELS OF THE NATIONS OF THE WORLD.

317. וְעַל דָּא מִי כָמוֹכָה בָּאֵלִים יְיָ'. מַאי בָּאֵלִים. אִילָנָא. כד"א, כִּי יֵבוֹשׁוּ מֵאֵילִים אֲשֶׁר חֲמַדְתֶּם. דְּהוּא אִילָנָא, דַּהֲווֹ פַּלְחִין לְחַד דְּפוּסָא, דִּמְחַקְּקִין בְּגַוֵּיהּ. וְאִקְרֵי אֵלִים אִילָנָא מִי כָּמֹכָה דְּיַעֲבֵיד כְּעוֹבָדָךְ וִירַחֵם עַל כֹּלָּא. מִי כָּמֹכָה בְּכָל הַהוּא סַחֲרָנֵיהּ דְּאִילָנָא דְּאע"ג דְּאִיהוּ שַׁלְטָא, נָטִיר לְכֹלָּא, נָטִיר לְכָל שְׁאַר, וְלָא בַּעְיָא לְמֶעְבַּד עִמְּהוֹן גְּמִירָא. מִי כָּמֹכָה נֶאְדָּר בַּקֹּדֶשׁ, בְּהַהוּא חֵילָא עִלָּאָה דְּאִקְרֵי קֹדֶשׁ. נֶאְדָּר בַּקֹּדֶשׁ מַמָּשׁ, וְאִקְרֵי כֹּחַ יְיָ' נֹעַם יְיָ', וְהָא אוֹקִימְנָא מִילֵּי.

317. Pertaining to this, IT IS SAID: "Who is like You among the mighty (Heb. *Elim*), Hashem." What is the meaning of "*Elim*"? 'Tree', as is written: "For you shall be ashamed of the sacred oaks (Heb. *eilim*) on which you set your desires" (Yeshayah 1:29). For they worshipped an image that was engraved on this tree. "Who is like You," to do as You do and have Mercy upon all. "Who is like You," throughout the surrounding of the tree; even though He dominates, He guards everything, He guards all the rest and does not desire to destroy them completely, AS THEY WANTED TO DO WHEN THEY DOMINATED. "Who is like You, glorious in Holiness," MEANS THAT IT IS GLORIOUS with the supernal power, which is called 'Holiness'. Verily, it is glorious in Holiness, WHICH IS THE MOCHIN OF BINAH and is called "the strength of Hashem," and, "the pleasantness of Hashem." And we have hereby expounded on the words.

318. מִי כָמֹכָה בָּאֵלִים יְיָ׳. ר׳ יוֹסֵי פָּתַח רָאִיתִי אֶת כָּל הַמַּעֲשִׂים אֲשֶׁר נַעֲשׂוּ תַּחַת הַשָּׁמֶשׁ וְהִנֵּה הַכֹּל הֶבֶל וּרְעוּת רוּחַ. שְׁלֹמֹה מַלְכָּא, דְּאִסְתַּלָּק בְּחָכְמְתָא יְתֵירָא עַל כָּל בְּנֵי עָלְמָא, הֵיךְ אָמַר דְּכָל עוֹבָדִין הֶבֶל וּרְעוּת רוּחַ. יָכוֹל אַף מַעֲשֵׂה הַצְּדָקָה, וְהָא כְּתִיב וְהָיָה מַעֲשֵׂה הַצְּדָקָה שָׁלוֹם. אֶלָּא הָא אוּקְמוּהָ, כָּל הַמַּעֲשִׂים אֲשֶׁר נַעֲשׂוּ תַּחַת הַשָּׁמֶשׁ כְּתִיב. שָׁאנֵי מַעֲשֵׂה הַצְּדָקָה, דְּאִיהוּ לְעֵילָּא מִן שִׁמְשָׁא.

318. “Who is like You among the mighty, Hashem.” Rabbi Yosi opened the discussion with the verse: “I have seen all the works that are done under the sun; and, behold, all is vanity and a striving after wind” (Kohelet 1:14). HE ASKS: How could King Solomon, who was greater in his wisdom than all other people of the world, say that all the works are vanity and a striving after wind? Is it possible that the deed of righteousness IS ALSO VANITY AND A STRIVING AFTER WIND? Is it not written: “And the work of righteousness shall be peace” (Yeshayah 32:17)? HE ANSWERS: We have already established that it is written: “All the works that are done under the sun,” but the work of righteousness is different, for it is above the sun.

319. וְהִנֵּה הַכֹּל הֶבֶל וּרְעוּת רוּחַ, מַאי קָא מַיְירֵי. אִי תֵּימָא הַכֹּל הֶבֶל כְּמָה דְּאוֹקִימְנָא, דְּאִיהוּ בְּרָזָא דְּחָכְמְתָא, כד״א הֲבֵל הֲבָלִים אָמַר קֹהֶלֶת, וְאִינּוּן הֲבָלִים קִיּוּמָא דְּעָלְמָא דִּלְעֵילָּא וְתַתָּא. מַאי תֵּימָא בְּהַאי, דִּכְתִּיב הָכָא, הַכֹּל הֶבֶל וּרְעוּת רוּחַ.

319. “And, behold, all is vanity and a striving after wind.” HE ASKS: What is its meaning? If, “all is vanity (Heb. *hevel*),” MEANS, as we established, being in the secret of Wisdom – as is said, “‘Vanity of vanities’, says Kohelet” (Kohelet 1:2), and these vanities are the sustenance of the upper and lower world – then what can be said of this verse here: “And, behold, all is vanity and a striving after wind?”

320. אֶלָּא הָכִי אוּקְמוּהָ, וְהָכִי הוּא. ת״ח, בְּשַׁעֲתָא דְּעוֹבָדִין מִתְכַּשְּׁרָן לְתַתָּא, וּבַר נָשׁ אִשְׁתַּדַּל בְּפוּלְחָנָא דְּמַלְכָּא קַדִּישָׁא, הַהוּא מִלָּה

דְּעָבֵיד, הֲבָל אִתְעֲבֵיד מִינֵּיהּ לְעֵילָּא. וְלֵית לָךְ הֲבָל, דְּלֵית לֵיהּ קָלָא, דְּסָלִיק וְאִתְעַטָּר לְעֵילָּא, וְאִתְעֲבֵיד סַנֵּיגוֹרָא קָמֵי קוּדְשָׁא בְּרִיךְ הוּא.

320. This is the way we explained it, and this is how it is. Come and behold: when deeds in the world are good, and one strives to be occupied with the service of the Holy King, the good deed that he does turns into a breath (Heb. *hevel*) above. And each and every breath from which a voice ascends above, becomes a defense counselor before the Holy One, blessed be He.

321. וְכָל אִינּוּן עוֹבָדִין דְּאִשְׁתַּדַּל בְּהוּ בַּר נָשׁ, דְּלָאו אִינּוּן פּוּלְחָנָא דְּקוּדְשָׁא בְּרִיךְ הוּא, הַהוּא מִלָּה דְּעָבֵיד, הֲבָל יִתְעֲבִיד מִינֵּיהּ, וְאַזְלָא וְשָׁאטַת בְּעָלְמָא. וְכַד נַפְקַת נִשְׁמָתֵיהּ דְּבַר נָשׁ, הַהוּא הֲבָל מְגַלְגְּלָא לֵיהּ בְּעָלְמָא, כְּאַבְנָא בְּקוּסְפִּיתָא, כְּמָה דִּכְתִּיב, וְאֵת נֶפֶשׁ אוֹיְבֶיךָ יְקַלְּעֶנָּה בְּתוֹךְ כַּף הַקָּלַע.

321. All these works that a person is occupied with which are not in the service of the Holy One, blessed be He, become a breath, which goes and flies about the world. And when his soul departs, that breath rolls him through the world, like a stone in a sling, as is written: "And the souls of your enemies, them shall He sling out, as out of the hollow of a sling" (I Shmuel 25:29).

322. מַאי יְקַלְּעֶנָּה. הַהוּא הֲבָל דִּמְגַלְגֵּל לֵיהּ סַחֲרָנֵיהּ בְּעָלְמָא, כְּדֵין כָּל מִלִּין דְּמִתְעַבְדִין דְּלָאו אִינּוּן פּוּלְחָנָא דְּקוּדְשָׁא בְּרִיךְ הוּא, הֲבָל יִתְעֲבִיד מִנַּיְיהוּ, אִיהוּ תְּבִירָא דְּרוּחָא, דְּמִתָּבַר לְרוּחָא דְּסָלִיק וְנָחִית וּמִתְגַּלְגֵּל בְּעָלְמָא, הה״ד הֶבֶל וּרְעוּת רוּחַ.

322. He asks: What is the meaning of "shall He sling out?" And he answers: That breath rolls it around in the world. Then all the things that are done and are not in the service of the Holy One, blessed be He, turn into a breath, which is the breaking of spirit, for this breaks the spirit that goes up and down and rolls throughout the world. This is what is meant by: "vanity and a striving after wind (also: 'spirit')."

323. אֲבָל הַהִיא מִלָּה דְּאִיהִי פּוּלְחָנָא דְּמָרֵיהּ דָּא סָלִיק לְעֵילָּא מִן

שִׁמְשָׁא, וְאִתְעָבֵיד מִנֵּיהּ הֲבָל קַדִּישָׁא, וְדָא הוּא זַרְעָא דְּזָרַע בַּר נָשׁ בְּהַהוּא עָלְמָא, וּמַה שְּׁמֵיהּ. צְדָקָה. דִּכְתִּיב, זִרְעוּ לָכֶם לִצְדָקָה.

323. But that thing that is in the service of his Master ascends to a level above the sun and becomes a holy breath. This is the seed that the person sows in that world. And what is it called? righteousness, as is written: "Sow for you by righteousness" (Hoshea 10:12).

324. הַאי מְדַבָּר לֵיהּ לְבַר נָשׁ, כַּד תִּיפּוּק נִשְׁמָתֵיהּ מִינֵּיהּ, וְסַלְקָא לָהּ בְּאַתְרָא דִּכְבוֹד דִּלְעֵילָּא אִשְׁתְּכַח לְאִתְצַרְרָא בִּצְרוֹרָא דְּחַיֵּי, הה"ד וְהָלַךְ לְפָנֶיךָ צִדְקֶךָ בְּגִין לְדַבְּרָא לָךְ, לְסַלְקָא לָךְ, לַאֲתָר דְּאִקְרֵי כְּבוֹד יְיָ'. דִּכְתִּיב, כְּבוֹד יְיָ' יַאַסְפֶךָ.

324. This leads the person when his soul leaves him, raises him to the place of glory above, and is present to bind him in the bundle of life. This is what is meant by: "And your righteousness shall go before you" (Yeshayah 58:8), in order to lead you and to raise you to the place that is called 'the glory of Hashem', WHICH IS MALCHUT, as it is written: "the glory of Hashem shall be your rearguard" (Ibid.).

325. כָּל אִינּוּן נִשְׁמָתִין, דְּהַהוּא הֲבָל קַדִּישָׁא מְדַבָּר לְהוּ, הַהוּא דְּאִקְרֵי כְּבוֹד יְיָ', כָּנִישׁ לוֹן בְּגַוֵּיהּ, וְאִתְצְרִירָן בֵּיהּ. וְדָא אִקְרֵי נַיְיחָא דְּרוּחָא. אֲבָל אַחֲרָא וּרְעוּת רוּחַ אִקְרֵי. זַכָּאִין אִינּוּן צַדִּיקַיָּיא, דְּכָל עוֹבָדֵיהוֹן לְעֵילָּא מִן שִׁמְשָׁא וְזַרְעִין זַרְעָא דִּצְדָקָה, לְמִזְכֵּי לוֹן לְעָלְמָא דְּאָתֵי, וְעַל דָּא כְּתִיב וְזָרְחָה לָכֶם יִרְאֵי שְׁמִי שֶׁמֶשׁ צְדָקָה.

325. All these souls that the holy breath leads, which is called "the glory of Hashem," it gather into itself, and they are bound in it. Then there is peace of spirit. But the other BREATH THAT IS NOT THE SERVICE OF HASHEM is called "striving after wind." Blessed are the righteous, for all their actions are above the sun, NAMELY, THE SERVICE OF THE HOLY ONE, BLESSED BE HE, and they sow the seed of righteousness, so they merit in the World to Come. And about this, it is written: "But to you who fear my Name the sun of righteousness shall arise" (Malachi 3:20).

326. אָמַר רִבִּי שִׁמְעוֹן, ת"ח, בְּקַדְמֵיתָא כַּד אִתְבְּנֵי בֵּי מַקְדְּשָׁא לְתַתָּא, לָא אִתְבְּנֵי אֶלָּא בְּדִינָא וְרוּגְזָא, כְּמָה דִּכְתִּיב, כִּי עַל אַפִּי וְעַל חֲמָתִי וְגוֹ' בְּגִין דִּבַאֲתָר דְּדִינָא שַׁרְיָא. לְזִמְנָא דְּאָתֵי, זַמִּין קוּדְשָׁא בְּרִיךְ הוּא לְמִבְנֵי לֵיהּ, וּלְאַתְקְנָא לֵיהּ בְּדַרְגָּא אַחֲרָא עִלָּאָה דְּאִקְרֵי צְדָקָה, דִּכְתִּיב בִּצְדָקָה תִּכּוֹנָנִי. בְּגִין כַּךְ אִתְקַיָּים, וּשְׁמֵיהּ מַמָּשׁ צֶדֶק יִתְקְרֵי. מְנָלָן. דִּכְתִּיב וְזֶה שְׁמוֹ אֲשֶׁר יִקְרְאוֹ יְיָ' צִדְקֵנוּ.

326. Rabbi Shimon said: Come and behold. Originally, when the Temple was built below, it was only based upon Judgment and Anger, as "a provocation of My anger and of My fury..." (Yirmeyah 32:31). This is because it is in the place where Judgment dwells. In the time to come, the Holy One, blessed be He, shall build and perfect it in a different, higher level called 'righteousness', WHICH IS THE PERFECTED MALCHUT, as written: "In righteousness (Heb. *tzedakah*) shall you be established" (Yeshayah 54:14). Therefore, it will endure AND WILL NOT BE DESTROYED AGAIN. And its actual name will be called 'righteousness (Heb. *tzedek*)'. How do we know? It is written, "And this is His Name whereby He shall be called, Hashem is our righteousness (Heb. *tzedek*)" (Yirmeyah 23:6).

25. "You did stretch out Your right hand, the earth swallowed them"

A Synopsis

The rabbis have some difficulty with the fact that God stretched out His right hand seemingly to perform judgment, yet the right hand is of Chesed. The explanation is that He separated the right hand so that the left hand performed the acts of judgment. We are told that He has guided the righteous with His strength and His arm to His holy habitation. Rabbi Shimon speaks about the latter generation that Joshua circumcised, and in whom He revealed the holy imprint of the Name of God; everyone who is circumcised and in whom the holy marking has been revealed is called 'righteous'. Rabbi Shimon reminds us that there is no word or letter in the Torah that does not contain supernal secrets.

327. נָטִיתָ יְמִינְךָ תִּבְלָעֵמוֹ אָרֶץ. הָא אִתְּמַר, אֲרִימַת יְמִינְךָ. אָמַר רִבִּי יִצְחָק, הָא אִתְּעָרוּ בֵּיהּ חַבְרַיָּיא, דְּכָל אַפִּיק קוּדְשָׁא בְּרִיךְ הוּא לְמִצְרָאֵי מֵתִין מִתְּחוֹת מַיָּא, אָמַר לְאַרְעָא, כָּנִישׁ לוֹן בְּגַוָּוךְ, וְלָא בָּעָאת, עַד דְּאוֹשִׁיט קוּדְשָׁא בְּרִיךְ הוּא יְמִינָא לְקַבְּלָהּ, וְאוּמֵי לָהּ, כְּדֵין בְּלָעַתִינוּן אַרְעָא, הה"ד תִּבְלָעֵמוֹ אָרֶץ. אָמַר ר' אֶלְעָזָר, נָטִיתָ יְמִינְךָ: לְאַפְרְשָׁא לָהּ מִשְּׂמָאלָא וּכְדֵין אִתְעֲבֵיד בְּהוּ דִּינָא.

327. "You did stretch out Your right hand, the earth swallowed them" (Shemot 15:12): YET, HE WAS ASKED AGAIN, THE RIGHT ACTS WITH CHESED. AND HE ANSWERS: But we have learned THAT IT MEANS You have raised Your right hand, AND THE LEFT REMAINED ALONE AND PERFORMED ACTS OF JUDGMENT. Rabbi Yitzchak said: The friends observed that when the Holy One, blessed be He, extracted the dead Egyptians from under the water, He said to the earth: 'Gather them unto you.' It did not want to, until the Holy One, blessed be He, lifted the right hand against it and placed it under oath. Then it is written: "The earth swallowed them." Rabbi Elazar said: "You did stretch out your right hand," MEANING to separate it from the left, and Judgment was performed THROUGH THE LEFT.

328. נָחִיתָ בְחַסְדְּךָ עַם זוּ גָּאָלְתָּ, כְּמָה דִּכְתִּיב כִּי יְמִינְךָ וּזְרוֹעֲךָ וְאוֹר פָּנֶיךָ כִּי רְצִיתָם כִּי יְמִינְךָ: דָּא גְּדוֹלָה. נֵהַלְתָּ בְעָזְּךָ דָּא דִּכְתִּיב וּזְרוֹעֲךָ,

דָּא גְּבוּרָה. אֶל נְוֵה קָדְשֶׁךָ, דָּא דִּכְתִּיב, וְאוֹר פָּנֶיךָ כִּי רְצִיתָם, דָּא צַדִּיק. וְכֻלְּהוּ מִשְׁתַּכְּחֵי בִּקְרָא.

328. "You in Your mercy led forth the people whom You have redeemed" (Shemot 15:13). This is as is written: "But Your right hand, and Your arm, and the light of Your countenance, because You did favorably accept them" (Tehilim 44:4). "But Your right hand," refers to greatness, NAMELY CHESED. "You have guided them in Your strength"; what is meant by, "and your arm," which is Gvurah. "To Your holy habitation," is what is written: "and the light of Your countenance, for You did favorably accept them." It is the Righteous, WHICH IS YESOD. And they are all present in the passage, ALL THE SIX SFIROT, BECAUSE CHESED AND GVURAH INCLUDE TIFERET, AND YESOD INCLUDES NETZACH AND HOD.

329. תִּפּוֹל עֲלֵיהֶם אֵימָתָה וָפַחַד. אֵימָתָה, אֵימָה מִבָּעֵי לֵיהּ, מַאי אֵימָתָה. דְּהָא לֵית לָךְ אָת אוֹ מִלָּה חֲדָא בְּאוֹרַיְיתָא, דְּלָא אִית בָּהּ רָזִין עִלָּאִין. מַאי אֵימָתָה. אָמַר רִבִּי שִׁמְעוֹן, כְּלוֹמַר דְּחִילוּ דִּשְׁכִינְתָּא.

329. "Fear (Heb. *eimatah*) and dread shall fall upon them." HE ASKS: it is written "*eimatah,*" but the more common form, '*eimah*' should have been used. Why "*eimatah*"? There is not one word or letter in the Torah that does not contain high secrets. AND IF SO, what is the meaning of "*eiamtah* (also: 'the fear of her')?" Rabbi Shimon said: It means the terror of the Shechinah. AND IT IS LIKE THE DREAD OF *HEI* (*EIMAT-HEI*), WHICH IS THE SHECHINAH.

330. כְּהַאי גַּוְונָא, תְּבִאֵמוֹ וְתִטָּעֵמוֹ בְּהַר נַחֲלָתְךָ וְגוֹ׳, תְּבִאֵמוֹ וְתִטָּעֵמוֹ, תְּבִאֵם וְתִטָּעֵם מִבָּעֵי לֵיהּ, מַאי תְּבִאֵמוֹ. אֶלָּא רוּחָא דְּקוּדְשָׁא אָמַר, עַל אִינּוּן דָּרָא בַּתְרָאָה, דְּגָזַר יְהוֹשֻׁעַ, וְאִתְגַּלְיָיא בְּהוּ גִּלּוּיָא דִּרְשִׁימָא קַדִּישָׁא דִּשְׁמֵיהּ דְּקוּדְשָׁא בְּרִיךְ הוּא, דְּאִלֵּין אֲחִידָן בֵּיהּ בּוֹ׳, וְאִלֵּין אִתְחֲזִיאוּ לְמֵירַת אַרְעָא. כְּמָה דִּכְתִּיב וְעַמֵּךְ כֻּלָּם צַדִּיקִים לְעוֹלָם יִירְשׁוּ אָרֶץ. דְּכָל מַאן דְּאִתְגְּזַר, וְאִתְגַּלְיָיא בֵּיהּ רְשִׁימָא קַדִּישָׁא, וְנָטִיר לֵיהּ, אִקְרֵי צַדִּיק, בְּגִין, כַּךְ, לְעוֹלָם יִירְשׁוּ אָרֶץ.

330. Similarly, "You shall bring them (Heb. *tevi'emo*) in, and plant them (Heb. *tita'emo*) in the mountain of Your inheritance..." It should have said '*tevi'em*' and '*tita'em*'. Why *tevi'emo* (with *Vav*)? HE ANSWERS: The Holy Spirit is speaking about the latter generation that Joshua circumcised, and in whom He revealed the holy imprint of the Name of the Holy One, blessed be He. They were linked with the *Vav*, WHICH IS ZEIR ANPIN, and they were worthy to inherit the land, as is written: "Your people also shall be all Righteous: they shall inherit the land forever" (Yeshayah 60:21). Because everyone who is circumcised and in whom the holy marking has been revealed, and who observes it, is called 'righteous'. Therefore, "they shall inherit the land forever."

331. וְע"ד תְּבִאֵמוֹ, ו' יְתֵירָה, תְּבִיאֵמוֹ לְאִינוּן דַּאֲחִידָן בְּו'. וְתִטָּעֵמוֹ כד"א נֵצֶר מַטָּעַי מַעֲשֵׂה יָדַי לְהִתְפָּאֵר. לְאִינוּן דַּאֲחִידָן בְּו', וּלְאִינּוּן בַּתְרָאֵי, אִתְּעַר מִלָּה. וְלֵית לָךְ מִלָּה בְּאוֹרַיְיתָא, אוֹ אָת זְעֵירָא בְּאוֹרַיְיתָא, דְּלֵית בָּהּ רָזִין עִלָּאִין, וְטַעֲמִין קַדִּישִׁין, זַכָּאָה חוּלָקֵהוֹן דְּיַדְעִין בְּהוּ.

331. Therefore "*tevi'emo*" is spelled with an extra *Vav*, WHICH MEANS that You will bring those attached to the *Vav*. "And plant them," as is said, "the branch of My planting, the work of My hands, that I may be glorified" (Ibid.), those that are connected to the *Vav*, THAT IS ZEIR ANPIN. And is the allusion to those latter ones, IN THE TIMES OF JOSHUA. There is no word or small letter in the Torah that does not contain supernal secrets and holy reasons. Blessed is the portion of those who are familiar with them.

26. Building the lower Temple

A Synopsis

We hear that it is a commandment to build the lower Temple similar to the Temple of above, and that the Temple must have windows in it. One must not pray in the field because an edifice is required to bring down the Shechinah to the human beings. Isaac prayed in the field, but he was one of the Patriarchs, so he was different.

רעיא מהימנא

332. פִּקּוּדָא לְמִבְנֵי מַקְדְּשָׁא לְתַתָּא, כְּגַוְונָא דְּבֵי מַקְדְּשָׁא דִּלְעֵילָּא, כד״א, מָכוֹן לְשִׁבְתְּךָ פָּעַלְתָּ יְיָ׳. דְּאִצְטְרִיךְ לְמִבְנֵי בֵּי מַקְדְּשָׁא לְתַתָּא, וּלְצַלָּאָה בְּגַוֵּיהּ צְלוֹתָא בְּכָל יוֹמָא, לְמִפְלַח לֵיהּ לְקוּדְשָׁא בְּרִיךְ הוּא, דְּהָא צְלוֹתָא אִקְרֵי עֲבוֹדָה.

Ra'aya Meheimna (the Faithful Shepherd)

332. It is a commandment to build the lower Temple similar to the Temple of above, as is written: "In the place, Hashem, which You have made for You to dwell in" (Shemot 15:17), because it is necessary to build a Temple below, to say a prayer in it every day, and to serve the Holy One, blessed be He, because prayer is called 'service'.

333. וְהַהוּא בֵּי כְּנִשְׁתָּא, אִצְטְרִיךְ לְמִבְנֵי לֵיהּ בְּשְׁפִּירוּ סַגְיָא, וּלְאַתְקְנָא לֵיהּ בְּכָל תִּקּוּנִין, דְּהָא בֵּי כְּנִשְׁתָּא דִּלְתַתָּא, קַיְּימָא לָקֳבֵל בֵּי כְּנִשְׁתָּא דִּלְעֵילָּא.

333. It is necessary to build that particular synagogue with great beauty and to outfit it with all its necessities and improvements, because the synagogue below corresponds to the synagogue above.

334. בֵּית מְקַדֵּשׁ לְתַתָּא, אִיהוּ קָאֵים כְּגַוְונָא דְּבֵית הַמִּקְדָּשׁ דִּלְעֵילָּא, דְּקָאֵים דָּא לָקֳבֵל דָּא. וְהַהוּא בֵּי מַקְדְּשָׁא, כָּל תִּקּוּנוֹי, וְכָל פּוּלְחָנוֹי,

וְכָל אִינּוּן מָאנִין, וְשַׁמָּשִׁין, כֻּלְּהוּ אִינּוּן כְּגַוְונָא דִּלְעֵילָּא. מַשְׁכְּנָא דְּקָא עָבֵד מֹשֶׁה בְּמַדְבְּרָא, כֹּלָּא הֲוָה כְּגַוְונָא דִּלְעֵילָּא.

334. The Temple below stands similar to the Temple above, for the one corresponds to the other. All the improvements and all the services and all the vessels and the accessory instruments of that Temple are all similar to above. The Tabernacle that Moses erected in the wilderness was a similar reflection of the one above.

335. בֵּי מַקְדְּשָׁא דְּבָנָא שְׁלֹמֹה מַלְכָּא, הוּא בֵּי נַיְיחָא כְּגַוְונָא עִלָּאָה, בְּכָל אִינּוּן תִּקּוּנִין, לְמֶהֱוֵי בְּתִקּוּנָא דִּלְעֵילָּא, בֵּי נַיְיחָא וְאַחֲסַנְתָּא. הָכִי בֵּי כְּנִשְׁתָּא, אִצְטְרִיךְ בְּכָל תִּקּוּנֵי שַׁפִּירוּ, לְמֶהֱוֵי כְּגַוְונָא עִלָּאָה, לְמֶהֱוֵי בֵּית צְלוֹתָא, לְאַתְקְנָא תִּקּוּנִין בִּצְלוֹתָא, כְּמָה דְּאוּקְמוּהָ.

335. The Temple that King Solomon built is a house of rest, similar to the one above in all ITS particulars, with all its supernal perfection, completed to become the house of rest and inheritance. Similarly, a synagogue must have all the accruements of beauty like the supernal one above to be a house of prayer, in which corrections are made through prayer, as has been explained.

336. וְהַהוּא בֵּי מַקְדְּשָׁא דְּלֶיהֱוֵי בֵּיהּ חַלּוֹנוֹת, דִּכְתִּיב וְכַוִּון פְּתִיחָן. כְּגַוְונָא דִּלְעֵילָּא, וְע״ד מַשְׁגִּיחַ מִן הַחַלּוֹנוֹת מֵצִיץ מִן הַחֲרַכִּים. וְאִי תֵּימָא אֲפִילּוּ בְּחַקְלָא, בְּגִין דְּרוּחָא לֶהֱוֵי סָלִיק. לָאו הָכִי, דְּהָא אֲנָן צְרִיכִין בַּיִת וְלֵיכָּא. לְאִשְׁתַּכְּחָא בַּיִת לְתַתָּא, כְּגַוְונָא דְּבַיִת עִלָּאָה, לְנַחְתָּא דִּיּוּרָא עִלָּאָה לְדִיּוּרָא תַּתָּאָה.

336. And that Temple MUST have windows in it, as is written, "and open windows" (Daniel 6:11), similar to above. Of this it is written: "He looks in at the windows; He peers through the lattice" (Shir Hashirim 2:9). If you ask whether IT IS PERMITTED TO PRAY in the field, because a spirit can ascend there, it is not so, because we need an edifice, and there is not any. It is necessary to establish an edifice below, similar to the edifice above, WHICH IS MALCHUT, to bring down the supernal dweller, WHICH IS THE SHECHINAH, to the inhabitants of below, HUMAN BEINGS.

337. וְתוּ דְּהַהוּא צְלוֹתָא, וְהַהוּא רוּחָא, אִצְטְרִיךְ לְסַלְּקָא, וּלְנָפְקָא מִגּוֹ עָאקוּ, בְּאֹרַח מֵישָׁר, לָקֳבֵל יְרוּשְׁלֵם. וְעַל דָּא כְּתִיב, מִן הַמֵּצַר קָרָאתִי יָהּ, דְּאִצְטְרִיךְ אֲתָר דָּחִיק בְּעָאקוּ, לְשַׁדְּרָא בְּגַוֵּיהּ הַהוּא רוּחָא, דְּלָא יִסְטֵי לִימִינָא וְלִשְׂמָאלָא. וּבְחַקְלָא לָא יָכִיל קָלָא לְשַׁדְּרָא לֵיהּ הָכִי, דְּהָא כְּגַוְונָא דָּא קָלָא דְּשׁוֹפָר, אִתְדַּחְיָיא לְבַר בְּאֹרַח מֵישָׁר, מִגּוֹ אֲתָר דָּחִיק, וְאָזִיל וּבָקַע רְקִיעִין, וְסָלִיק בִּסְלִיקוּ, לְאַתְעָרָא רוּחָא לְעֵילָּא.

337. Also, that prayer and that spirit should ascend and exit from the narrow strait in a straight path towards Jerusalem. About this is written: "Out of my distress (lit. 'from the narrow strait') I called upon Yah" (Tehilim 118:5). For it is necessary to have a place that is narrow and tight to cast into it that spirit, so that it should not turn to the right or to left. But in a field the voice can not be projected to Him in this way. Similar to this is the sound of the Shofar that is projected outward in a smooth, straight way from a narrow place, and it goes and splits firmaments, and ascends upwards to stimulate the spirit of above.

338. וְאִי תֵּימָא, הָא כְּתִיב, וַיֵּצֵא יִצְחָק לָשׂוּחַ בַּשָּׂדֶה. שָׁאנֵי יִצְחָק, דְּמִלָּה אַחֲרָא הֲוָה בֵּיהּ, מַה דְּלָא הֲוָה בְּכָל עָלְמָא. וְתוּ דְּהַאי קְרָא לָאו לְהָכִי אָתָא, דְּוַדַּאי בַּשָּׂדֶה אַחֵר לָא הֲוָה מְצַלֵּי וְהָא אוֹקִימְנָא.

(ע"כ רעיא מהימנא)

338. And you may ask: is it not written, "And Isaac went out to meditate in the field?" (Beresheet 24:63). SO WE SEE THAT PRAYING TAKES PLACE EVEN IN THE FIELD. AND HE ANSWERS: Isaac was different, for he had something else that the rest of the world did not have. HE WAS ONE OF THE PATRIARCHS. And also this verse did not come for this purpose, TO PERMIT PRAYING IN THE FIELD. For certainly, in a different field he would not have been praying, as we have already explained THAT THIS FIELD WAS THE FIELD THAT ABRAHAM HAD PURCHASED.

(End of Ra'aya Meheimna)

A Synopsis

Rabbi Aba speaks of a song that is composed of 22 holy engraved letters and ten sayings, and which is imprinted on the Holy Name. Rabbi Shimon says that while the children of Yisrael were standing by the sea and singing, God appeared to them with all his Chariots and hosts; every one of them saw what the other prophets of the world did not. All of them sang the same song simultaneously and in rhythm, and the Holy Spirit was in their mouths. It is obvious that they all perceived the supernal Wisdom at that time. When the song was over the children of Yisrael did not want to leave because of their great longing to perceive God, until Moses showed them the radiant shine of the glory of the Holy One, blessed be He in the wilderness. Thus it is called "the wilderness of Shur (lit 'observe')."

339. תַּנְיָא אָמַר רִבִּי אַבָּא, זַכָּאָה חוּלָקֵהוֹן, דְּאִינּוּן דְּזַכָּאן לְמֵימָר שִׁירָתָא דָּא בְּהַאי עָלְמָא, דְּזַכָּאן לְמֵימָר לָהּ בְּעָלְמָא דְּאָתֵי. וְשִׁירָתָא דָּא, אִתְבְּנֵי בְּעֶשְׂרִין וּתְרֵין אַתְוָון קַדִּישָׁן גְּלִיפָן, וּבְעֶשֶׂר אֲמִירָן, וְכֹלָּא אִתְרְשִׁים בִּשְׁמָא קַדִּישָׁא, וְכֹלָּא שְׁלֵימוּתָא דִּשְׁמָא קַדִּישָׁא, וְהָא אִתְעַרְנָא מִלֵּי.

339. We have learned that Rabbi Aba said: Blessed is the portion of those who merit to sing this song in this world and merit to say it in the World to Come. This song is composed of 22 holy engraved letters and with ten sayings, and it is all imprinted on the Holy Name, and it is all the perfection of the Holy Name. And we have made observations about these things.

340. א״ר שִׁמְעוֹן, בְּהַהִיא שַׁעֲתָא דַּהֲווֹ קַיְימִין יִשְׂרָאֵל עַל יַמָּא, וַהֲווֹ אַמְרֵי שִׁירָתָא, אִתְגְּלֵי קוּדְשָׁא בְּרִיךְ הוּא עֲלַיְיהוּ, וְכָל רְתִיכוֹי וְחֵילוֹי, בְּגִין דְּיִנְדְּעוּן לְמַלְכֵּיהוֹן, דְּעָבֵד לוֹן כָּל אִינּוּן נִסִּין וּגְבוּרָאן, וְכָל חַד וְחַד יָדַע וְאִסְתַּכַּל, מַה דְּלָא יָדְעוּ וְאִסְתַּכָּלוּ שְׁאַר נְבִיאֵי עָלְמָא.

340. Rabbi Shimon said: At the moment that Yisrael were standing by the sea and singing songs, the Holy One, blessed be He, appeared to them with all His Chariots and hosts, in order that they should know their King who had done for them all these miracles and mighty acts. Each and every one knew and noticed what the other prophets of the world did not know or notice.

341. דְּאִי תֵּימָא דְּלָא יָדְעִין וְלָא אִדְבָּקוּ חָכְמְתָא עִלָּאָה, מִן שִׁירָתָא דָּא תֶּחֱמֵי, דְּכֻלְּהוּ בְּחָכְמְתָא אִסְתַּכָּלוּ, וְיָדְעוּ מִלִּין וְאָמְרוּ. דְּאִי לָאו הָכִי, אֵיךְ אָמְרוּ כֻּלְּהוּ מִלִּין אֲחִידָן, דְּלָא סָטוּ אִלֵּין מֵאִלֵּין, וּמַה דְּאָמַר דָּא, אָמַר דָּא, וְלָא אַקְדִּים מִלָּה דָּא, לְמִלָּה דָּא, אֶלָּא כֻּלְּהוּ בְּשִׁקּוּלָא חֲדָא, וְרוּחָא דְּקוּדְשָׁא בְּפוּמָא דְּכָל חַד וְחַד, וּמִלִּין אִתְּמָרוּ כֻּלְּהוּ כְּאִלּוּ נָפְקִין מִפּוּמָא חַד. אֶלָּא וַדַּאי כּוּלְּהוּ בְּחָכְמְתָא עִלָּאָה אִסְתַּכָּלוּ, וְיָדְעוּ מִילִּין עִלָּאִין, וְרוּחָא דְּקוּדְשָׁא בְּפוּם כָּל חַד וְחַד.

341. For if you say that they had no knowledge and did not attain supernal Wisdom, then from this song you can see that they all beheld Wisdom, and knew those things they recited. For if not, how could they all say the same words without varying one from another? Whatever this one said, the other one said, and one word was not said before the other, but rather they all said them in the same rhythm. And the Holy Spirit was in the mouth of each and every one, and the words were all enunciated as though they were emitted from one mouth. Most certainly, they all noticed and perceived the supernal Wisdom, and were familiarized with these lofty particulars, and the Holy Spirit was in the mouth of each and every one.

342. וַאֲפִילּוּ אִינּוּן דִּבְמְעֵי אִמְּהוֹן, הֲווֹ אַמְרֵי שִׁירָתָא כֻּלְּהוּ כַּחֲדָא, וַהֲווֹ חָמָאן כֻּלְּהוּ, מַה דְּלָא חָמָא יְחֶזְקֵאל נְבִיאָה. וְעַל כַּךְ הֲווֹ כֻּלְּהוּ מִסְתַּכְּלֵי, כְּאִלּוּ חָמָאן עֵינָא בְּעֵינָא. וְכַד סִיְּימוּ מִלִּין, כֻּלְּהוּ מִתְבַּסְּמָאן בְּנַפְשַׁיְיהוּ, וְתָאֳבוּן לְמֶחֱמֵי וּלְאִסְתַּכְּלָא, וְלָא הֲווֹ בָּעָאן לְנַטְלָא מִתַּמָּן, מִסְּגִיאוּת תִּיאוּבְתָּא.

342. Even those in their mothers' wombs were saying the song all as one. They all saw that which even the prophet Ezekiel did not see, and they therefore watched, as though they saw eye to eye. When they concluded the words, they all bore fragrance on their own, and yearned to conceive and perceive, and did not want to travel from there, so great was their desire.

343. בְּהַהִיא שַׁעֲתָא, אָמַר מֹשֶׁה לְקוּדְשָׁא בְּרִיךְ הוּא, בָּנַיךְ מִסְּגִיאוּת תִּיאוּבְתָּא לְאִסְתַּכְּלָא בָּךְ, לָא בָּעָאן לְנַטְלָא מִן יַמָּא. מַה עָבֵד קוּדְשָׁא

בְּרִיךְ הוּא, אַסְתִּים יְקָרֵיהּ לְבַר לְמַדְבְּרָא, וְתַמָּן אִתְגְּלֵי וְלָא אִתְגְּלֵי. אָמַר לוֹן מֹשֶׁה לְיִשְׂרָאֵל, כַּמָּה זִמְנִין אֲמֵינָא לְנַטְלָא מִתַּמָּן, וְלָא בְּעִיתּוּן, עַד דִּי אַחְזֵי לוֹן זִיוָא יְקָרָא דְקוּדְשָׁא בְּרִיךְ הוּא בְּמַדְבְּרָא, וּמִיַּד הֲווֹ תָּאֲבִין.

343. At that moment, Moses said to the Holy One, blessed be He: 'Your children, because of their great longing to perceive You, do not want to travel from the sea.' What did the Holy One, blessed be He, do? He concealed His glory out of the wilderness, and there He appeared yet did not appear. Moses said to Yisrael: 'Many times have I said that you should travel from there, but you did not want to until I showed you the splendor of the glory of the Holy One, blessed be He, in the wilderness.' They were immediately desirous.

344. וְלָא נַטְלוּ, עַד דְּאָחִיד בְּהוּ מֹשֶׁה וְאַחְמֵי לוֹן זִיוָא יְקָרָא דְּקֻבּ״ה בְּמַדְבְּרָא, כְּדֵין מִסְּגִיאוּת תִּיאוּבְתָּא וּרְעוּתָא לְאִסְתַּכְּלָא, אַנְטִיל לוֹן מֹשֶׁה, הה״ד וַיַּסַּע מֹשֶׁה אֶת יִשְׂרָאֵל מִיַּם סוּף וַיֵּצְאוּ אֶל מִדְבַּר שׁוּר. מַאי מִדְבַּר שׁוּר. מַדְבְּרָא, דַּהֲווֹ בָּעָאן לְאִסְתַּכְּלָא בֵּיהּ, זִיוָא יְקָרָא דְּמַלְכָּא קַדִּישָׁא, וְעַל דָּא אִקְרֵי מִדְבַּר שׁוּר: אִסְתַּכְּלוּתָא שָׁם.

344. But they did not travel until Moses grasped them and showed them the radiant shine of the glory of the Holy One, blessed be He, in the wilderness. Then, because of great longing and desire to perceive, Moses caused them to travel. This is what is meant by: "So Moses brought Yisrael from the Sea of Reeds, and they went out into the wilderness of Shur" (Shemot 15:22). What is the meaning of "the wilderness of Shur"? This was the desert where they wanted to perceive and gaze upon the precious splendor of the Holy King. Therefore, it is called "the wilderness of Shur (lit. 'observe')," WHICH MEANS there is gazing there.

27. “And found no water”

A Synopsis

“And they marched three days in the wilderness, and found no water”; “water” means the Torah, which had not yet been given to them. Rabbi Elazar says that is true, and that Torah is the Holy One, blessed be He. When they came to the bitter water of Marah, “Hashem showed him a tree”; the “tree” means Torah, and it means the Holy One, blessed be He. It was when they arrived at Marah that they entered fully into the Covenant with God, where “He made for them a statute and an ordinance.”

345. וַיֵּלְכוּ שְׁלשֶׁת יָמִים בַּמִּדְבָּר וְלֹא מָצְאוּ מָיִם. וְאֵין מַיִם אֶלָּא תּוֹרָה, שֶׁנֶּאֱמַר הוֹי כָּל צָמֵא לְכוּ לַמַּיִם. אָמַר רִבִּי יֵיסָא, וְכִי מַאן יָהַב לְהוּ אוֹרַיְיתָא הָכָא, וְהָא עַד כְּעַן לָא אִתְיְהִיבַת לוֹן אוֹרַיְיתָא.

345. “And they marched three days in the wilderness, and found no water” (Shemot 15:22). Water means nothing if not the Torah, as is written, “Ho, everyone that thirsts, come to the water” (Yeshayah 55:1). Rabbi Yisa said: And who gave them Torah here? For until now the Torah was not yet given to them.

346. אָמַר רִבִּי אֶלְעָזָר, אִינּוּן נָפְקוּ לְמַדְבְּרָא לְאִסְתַּכְּלָא, קוּדְשָׁא בְּרִיךְ הוּא נָטַל זִיוָא יְקָרָא דִּילֵיהּ מִתַּמָּן, וְאִינּוּן אָזְלוּ לְאִסְתַּכְּלָא בֵּיהּ, וְלָא אַשְׁכְּחוּהוּ. וְאוֹלִיפְנָא דְּקוּדְשָׁא בְּרִיךְ הוּא תּוֹרָה אִקְרֵי, וְאֵין מַיִם אֶלָּא תּוֹרָה, וְאֵין תּוֹרָה אֶלָּא קוּדְשָׁא בְּרִיךְ הוּא.

346. Rabbi Elazar said: They went out into the wilderness to gaze and perceive, but the Holy One, blessed be He, removed His precious splendor from there. They went in order to conceive Him, but did not find Him. We have learned that the Holy One, blessed be He, is called ‘Torah’. Therefore, water is Torah, and Torah is the Holy One, blessed be He.

347. אָמַר רִבִּי שִׁמְעוֹן, עַד דַּהֲווֹ אַזְלֵי בְּמַדְבְּרָא, אִתְגְּלֵי עָלַיְיהוּ רְשׁוּתָא אַחֲרָא, דִּשְׁאַר עַמִּין, הַהוּא דְּשָׁלִיט בְּמַדְבְּרָא, וְאִעֲרָעוּ בְּהוּ תַּמָּן. חָמוּ יִשְׂרָאֵל, דְּלָא הֲוָה הַהוּא זִיוָא יְקָרָא דְּמַלְכֵּיהוֹן, הֲדָא הוּא

דִּכְתִּיב, וַיָּבֹאוּ מָרָתָה וְלֹא יָכְלוּ לִשְׁתּוֹת מַיִם מִמָּרָה. מ״ט. כִּי מָרִים הֵם, לָא אִתְבְּסָם נַפְשַׁיְיהוּ כְּקַדְמִיתָא. וְלֹא עוֹד אֶלָּא דְּאָתֵי לְקַטְרְגָא עָלַיְיהוּ.

347. Rabbi Shimon said: While they were still traveling in the wilderness, a different government of the other nations, appeared to them, namely, that one which dominates the wilderness, and it met them there. Then Yisrael saw that it was not the precious splendor of their King. This is what is meant by, "And when they came to Marah, they could not drink the waters of Marah" (Shemot 15:28). Why? "For they were bitter." Their souls were not gratified, as before. And even more, he had come to accuse them.

348. מַה כְּתִיב, וְיִצְעַק אֶל יְיָ׳ וַיּוֹרֵהוּ יְיָ׳ עֵץ, וְאֵין עֵץ אֶלָּא תּוֹרָה, דִּכְתִּיב עֵץ חַיִּים הִיא לַמַּחֲזִיקִים בָּהּ. וְאֵין תּוֹרָה, אֶלָּא קוּדְשָׁא בְּרִיךְ הוּא. רִבִּי אַבָּא אָמַר, אֵין עֵץ אֶלָּא קוּדְשָׁא בְּרִיךְ הוּא, דִּכְתִּיב כִּי הָאָדָם עֵץ הַשָּׂדֶה, עֵץ הַשָּׂדֶה וַדַּאי, דָּא עֵץ שָׂדֶה דְּתַפּוּחִין קַדִּישִׁין. וְכַד אִתְגְּלֵי זִיו יְקָרָא דְּמַלְכֵּהוֹן עָלַיְיהוּ, כְּדֵין וַיַּשְׁלֵךְ אֶל הַמַּיִם וַיִּמְתְּקוּ הַמָּיִם. מַאי וַיִּמְתְּקוּ הַמָּיִם. דְּקַטֵּיגוֹרָא אִתְעָבֵיד סַנֵּיגוֹרָא.

348. It is written: "And he cried to Hashem, and Hashem showed him a tree" (Ibid. 25). A "tree" means only Torah, as is written: "She is a Tree of Life to those who lay hold on her" (Mishlei 3:18). And Torah means the Holy One, blessed be He. Rabbi Aba said: "Tree" means the Holy One, blessed be He, as is written: "For a man is the tree of the field" (Devarim 20:19). The "tree of the field," assuredly is the tree of the Field of the Holy Apples, MEANING THIS FIELD IS MALCHUT. "THE TREE OF THE FIELD" REFERS TO ZEIR ANPIN, HER HUSBAND. And when the splendor of the glory of the King appeared over them, then, "when he had cast into the waters, the waters were made sweet" (Shemot 15:25). What is the meaning of, "and the waters were made sweet"? It means that the Accuser has become an advocate.

349. אָמַר רִבִּי אַבָּא, תָּא חֲזֵי בְּקַדְמֵיתָא כַּד עָאלוּ יִשְׂרָאֵל בְּקַיָּימָא דְּקוּדְשָׁא בְּרִיךְ הוּא, לָא עָאלוּ כַּדְקָא יֵאוֹת. מַאי טַעֲמָא. בְּגִין דְּאִתְגְּזָרוּ

וְלָא אִתְפְּרָעוּ, וְלָא אִתְגַּלְיָיא רְשִׁימָא קַדִּישָׁא. כֵּיוָן דְּמָטוּ הָכָא, מַה כְּתִיב, שָׁם שָׂם לוֹ חֹק וּמִשְׁפָּט. תַּמָּן עָאלוּ יִשְׂרָאֵל בִּתְרֵין חוּלָקִין קַדִּישִׁין, בְּהַהוּא גִּלּוּיָא דְּאִתְגַּלְיָא רְשִׁימָא דִּלְהוֹן, וְאִקְרוּן חֹק וּמִשְׁפָּט. חֹק: כְּמָה דְּאַתְּ אָמַר וַתִּתֵּן טֶרֶף לְבֵיתָהּ וְחֹק לְנַעֲרוֹתֶיהָ. וּמִשְׁפָּט: כְּמָה דְּאִתְּמַר מִשְׁפַּט לֵאלֹהֵי יַעֲקֹב. וְשָׁם נִסָּהוּ, בְּהַהוּא אָת קַדִּישָׁא. כד״א, כִּי חֹק לְיִשְׂרָאֵל הוּא. בְּסִפְרָא דְּרַב יֵיבָא סָבָא, אָמַר מִלָּה עַל הַהוּא חוּטְרָא קַדִּישָׁא.

349. Rabbi Aba said: Come and behold. When Yisrael first entered into the Covenant of the Holy One, blessed be He, they did not enter properly. Why? Because they circumcised but did not uncover, thus the holy sign was not revealed. But when they arrived here, TO MARAH, it is written: “There He made for them a statue and an ordinance” (Shemot 15:25), WHICH MEANS that Yisrael entered into the two holy parts, MALCHUT AND YESOD, WHICH THEY MERITED BY THE CIRCUMCISION AND MEMBRANE UNCOVERING. In that revealing, in which their sign was uncovered and revealed, they were called ‘a statute and an ordinance’. Statute (Heb. *chok*) IS MALCHUT, as is written: “And gives food to her household, and a portion (Heb. *chok*) to her maidens” (Mishlei 31:15). IT ENCOMPASSES MALCHUT AND ALLUDES TO CIRCUMCISION. “Ordinance” as is written: “An ordinance of Elohim of Jacob” (Tehilim 81:5). THIS IS YESOD, ALLUDING TO MOCHIN THAT ARE REVEALED THROUGH THE MEMBRANE UNCOVERING THAT IS CALLED ‘ORDINANCE’. “And there He tested them,” namely with His holy sign. SINCE IT IS A STATUTE, IT CAN BE TESTED, as is written: “For this is a statute for Yisrael.” Rabbi Yiba Saba (the elder) said in his book: It refers to that holy staff, REGARDING WHICH IS SAID, “AND HASHEM SHOWED HIM A TREE.”

28. "And He said, 'If you will diligently hearken to voice of Hashem'"

A Synopsis

When they attained the Covenant, the children of Yisrael attained Malchut, Yesod, Netzach and Hod, and therefore reached the Holy King, Tiferet. We learn of the proper circumcision and uncovering and the holy anointing oil that allow the circumcised to bond with the Holy King. The text speaks of the protection for the holy mark for four things. The children of Yisrael merit welcoming the Shechinah through guarding against the impurity of menstruation. We hear of the protection of the Righteous, protection from the maidservant, protection from a heathen woman and protection from a harlot. We read that God did not want to give the children of Yisrael the Torah until they were close to Him, and He achieved this closeness by the Covenant of circumcision.

350. וַיֹּאמֶר אִם שָׁמוֹעַ תִּשְׁמַע לְקוֹל יְיָ' אֱלֹהֶיךָ. וַיֹּאמֶר, מַאי וַיֹּאמֶר. לָא כְּתִיב מַאן קָאָמַר דָּא. אֶלָּא קוּדְשָׁא בְּרִיךְ הוּא אָמַר. רִבִּי חִזְקִיָּה אָמַר, שַׁמְעִינָן אֲמִירָה סְתָם, מֵאֲמִירָה סְתָם. דִּכְתִּיב וְאֶל מֹשֶׁה אָמַר עֲלֵה אֶל יְיָ'. אָמַר, לָא כְּתִיב מַאן קָאָמַר. אוּף הָכָא וַיֹּאמֶר סְתָם, וְלָא כְּתִיב מַאן קָאָמַר.

350. "And he said, 'If you will diligently hearken to voice of Hashem your Elohim'"(Shemot 15:26) What is the meaning of, "And He said"? It does not say who said this. Rather the Holy One, blessed be He, said this. Rabbi Chizkiyah said: We derive meaning from one vague saying to another. For it is written, "And He said to Moses, 'Come up to Hashem'" (Shemot 24:1). AND THERE IT REFERS TO MALCHUT, FOR IF IT WAS THE HOLY ONE, BLESSED BE HE, IT SHOULD HAVE SAID, "COME UP TO ME." HERE ALSO, IT MEANS MALCHUT.

351. אָמַר רִבִּי יוֹסֵי, מַשְׁמַע דִּכְתִּיב, וְיִצְעַק אֶל יְיָ' וַיּוֹרֵהוּ יְיָ' עֵץ, מֵהָכָא מַשְׁמַע וַיֹּאמֶר, וּמַשְׁמַע מַאן אָמַר מִלָּה. לְקוֹל יְיָ' אֱלֹהֶיךָ, לְקוֹלִי מִבָּעֵי לֵיהּ. אֶלָּא לְהַהוּא קוֹל דְּעָאלוּ בֵּיהּ.

351. Rabbi Yosi said: It is understood from the PREVIOUS verse, "And he cried to Hashem, and Hashem showed him a tree." From this we derive THE

MEANING OF, "And He said," for it is understood who said this, NAMELY, THE HOLY ONE, BLESSED BE HE. 'To the voice of Hashem your Elohim,' or 'to my voice' should have been said. HE ANSWERS: THE meaning is this voice into which they had entered THROUGH CIRCUMCISION, WHICH IS THE VOICE OF MALCHUT. THEREFORE, IT DOES NOT SAY 'TO MY VOICE'.

352. אָמַר רִבִּי אַבָּא, בָּתַר דְּאִתְגַּלְיָא בְּהוּ רְשִׁימָא קַדִּישָׁא, עָאלוּ בִּתְרֵין חוּלָקִין קַדִּישִׁין, כְּמָה דְּאִתְּמַר, וְכֵיוָן דְּעָאלוּ בְּאִלֵּין תְּרֵין, עָאלוּ בְּאִלֵּין תְּרֵין חוּלָקִין אַחֲרָנִין, דְּכַד יִסְתַּלְּקוּן בְּאִלֵּין תְּרֵין אַחֲרָנִין, יִתְחַבְּרוּן בְּאִלֵּין, וְלָא מִמַּנְעֵי בִּרְכָּאן, וּבג"כ, בְּאִלֵּין מָטוּ בִּרְכָאן, עַד מַלְכָּא קַדִּישָׁא.

352. Rabbi Aba said: After the holy sign was revealed in them, they attained two holy parts, as we learned, WHICH ARE YESOD AND MALCHUT. THROUGH CIRCUMCISION THEY MERITED MALCHUT, AND THROUGH THE MEMBRANE UNCOVERING, YESOD. As soon as they attained these two, they also attained these other two parts, WHICH ARE NETZACH AND HOD, because when they are elevated by NETZACH AND HOD, they will join with YESOD AND MALCHUT, and the blessings THAT YESOD WILL CAUSE TO FLOW TO MALCHUT will not be withheld. Therefore, they will reach through these up to the Holy King, WHICH IS ZEIR ANPIN.

353. וּמֵאַתְרֵיהּ דִּקְרָא אִשְׁתְּמַע מִלָּה, דִּכְתִּיב, וַיֹּאמֶר אִם שָׁמוֹעַ תִּשְׁמַע. וַיֹּאמֶר: דָּא מַלְכָּא קַדִּישָׁא. וּמַאי קָאָמַר, אִם שָׁמוֹעַ תִּשְׁמַע לְקוֹל יְיָ' אֱלֹהֶיךָ, כד"א כִּי יְיָ' אֱלֹהֶיךָ אֵשׁ אוֹכְלָה הוּא, דָּא כְּנֶסֶת יִשְׂרָאֵל. וְהַיָּשָׁר בְּעֵינָיו תַּעֲשֶׂה: דָּא צַדִּיק. וְהַאֲזַנְתָּ לְמִצְוֹתָיו: דָּא נֶצַח. וְשָׁמַרְתָּ כָּל חֻקָּיו: דָּא הוֹד. כֵּיוָן דְּעָאלוּ בְּאִלֵּין, הָא מָטוּ לְמַלְכָּא קַדִּישָׁא. לְבָתַר מַה כְּתִיב, כָּל הַמַּחֲלָה אֲשֶׁר שַׂמְתִּי בְּמִצְרַיִם לֹא אָשִׂים עָלֶיךָ כִּי אֲנִי יְיָ' רוֹפְאֶךָ. כִּי אֲנִי יְיָ': דָּא מַלְכָּא קַדִּישָׁא.

353. And from the placement of the verse is the subject understood. For it is written: "And He said, 'If you will diligently hearken'." "And He said" refers to the Holy King. And what did He say? "If you hearken diligently to the voice of Hashem your Elohim"; it is as written: "For Hashem your

Elohim is a consuming fire" (Devarim 4:24), which is the Congregation of Yisrael, NAMELY MALCHUT. "And will do that which is right in His sight" refers to the righteous, WHO IS CALLED 'RIGHT'; "and give ear to His commandments," refers to Netzach; and "keep all His statutes," refers to Hod. Since they have attained these – MALCHUT, YESOD, NETZACH AND HOD – they have reached the Holy King, WHO IS TIFERET, WHOSE PLACE IS AFTER NETZACH. THEREFORE, what is written afterwards? "I will put none of these diseases upon you, which I have brought upon Egypt; for I am Hashem that heals you." "For I am Hashem," refers to the Holy One, blessed be He, WHO IS TIFERET.

354. אִשְׁתְּמַע, דְּכָל מַאן דְּנָטִיר לְהַאי רְשִׁימָא קַדִּישָׁא, מִנֵּיהּ סָלִיק עַד מַלְכָּא קַדִּישָׁא עִלָּאָה. מַאי מַשְׁמַע. מַשְׁמַע אִינּוּן תְּרֵין, דְּאִתְכְּנַשׁ בְּהוּ זַרְעָא, וּמָשַׁח רְבוּת קוּדְשָׁא, דְּשַׁדְיָין לֵיהּ בְּפוּם אָמָּה, אִתְקַשָּׁרוּ כַּחֲדָא, וּמַלְכָּא עִלָּאָה עֲלַיְיהוּ, וְאִתְקַשָּׁרוּ בֵּיהּ. וְעַל כַּךְ, מַאן דְּעָאל בְּאִלֵּין תְּרֵין, וְנָטִיר לוֹן, אִתְקָשַּׁר בִּתְרֵין אַחֲרָנִין, וְעָאל בְּהוּ, וּכְדֵין מָטֵי לְמַלְכָּא קַדִּישָׁא.

354. It is understood that whoever guards this holy sign, WHICH IS CIRCUMCISION, ascends from it unto the Supernal Holy King. HE ASKS: What is understood from these words? AND HE ANSWERS: It is understood that these two, NETZACH AND HOD, in which the seed accumulates FOR BLESSING, and the holy anointing oil that is poured over the head of the male organ, WHICH IS YESOD, combine together. And the Supernal King, TIFERET, is over them and they connect with Him. Therefore, whoever enters these two, YESOD AND MALCHUT, BY MEANS OF CIRCUMCISION AND UNCOVERING, and guards them, is connected to two others, NETZACH AND HOD, and enters them, and then reaches the Holy King, WHICH IS TIFERET.

355. אָמַר רִבִּי יִצְחָק, וַדַּאי מַאן דְּזָכֵי בְּצַדִּיק, זָכֵי בְּנֶצַח וְהוֹד, וְאִלֵּין אִינּוּן תְּלָתָא, דְּאִתְבָּרְכָא בְּהוּ כְּנֶסֶת יִשְׂרָאֵל. וּמַאן דְּזָכוּ בְּהוּ, זָכֵי בְּמַלְכָּא קַדִּישָׁא, וְעָאל בְּכֻלְּהוּ אַרְבְּעָה.

355. Rabbi Yitzchak said: Most certainly, one who merits the Righteous,

WHICH IS YESOD, merits Netzach and Hod, BECAUSE YESOD INCLUDES NETZACH AND HOD. And they are three with which the Congregation of Yisrael, WHICH IS MALCHUT, is blessed. And he who merits them merits also the Holy King, THAT IS TIFERET, and attains all four SFIROT, TIFERET, NETZACH, HOD, YESOD AND MALCHUT.

356. וְלָקֳבְלֵי אַרְבְּעָה אִלֵּין, נְטִירוּ לְהַאי רְשִׁימָא קַדִּישָׁא, מֵאַרְבַּע מִלִּין: נְטִירוּ דִּכְנֶסֶת יִשְׂרָאֵל, אִסְתַּמְּרוּתָא דְּנִדָּה. נְטִירוּ דְּצַדִּיק, אִסְתַּמְּרוּתָא דְּשִׁפְחָה. נְטִירוּ דְּנֶצַח, אִסְתַּמְּרוּתָא דְּבַת עכו"ם. נְטִירוּ דְּהוֹד, אִסְתַּמְּרוּתָא דְּזוֹנָה. וְעַל דָּא לְקוֹל יְיָ' אֱלֹהֶיךָ, דָּא כְּנֶסֶת יִשְׂרָאֵל.

356. And corresponding to these four, there is protection for the holy sign from four things: the protection of the Congregation of Yisrael, WHICH IS MALCHUT, which is protection from the impurity of menstruation; protection of the righteous, WHICH IS YESOD, that is protection from the maid servant; protection of Netzach, which is protection from a heathen woman; and protection of Hod, which is protection from a harlot. This is why "the voice of Hashem your Elohim," is the Congregation of Yisrael, WHICH IS MALCHUT, WHICH THEY ENTERED THROUGH CIRCUMCISION.

357. בַּמֶּה זָכָאן יִשְׂרָאֵל לְקַבְּלָא אַפֵּי שְׁכִינְתָּא, בְּאִסְתַּמְּרוּתָא מִן נִדָּה. וְעַל דָּא כְּתִיב, וְאֶל אִשָּׁה בְּנִדַּת טֻמְאָתָהּ לֹא תִקְרַב לְגַלּוֹת עֶרְוָתָהּ. מַאי לְגַלּוֹת עֶרְוָתָהּ דָּא כְּנֶסֶת יִשְׂרָאֵל. וּבְהַאי אֲחִידָן וּמִתְקַשְּׁרָן מִלִּין אַחֲרָנִין, דִּכְנֶסֶת יִשְׂרָאֵל אִתְקַשְּׁרַת בְּהוּ. וְהָא אוּקְמוּהָ מִלֵּי.

357. How did Yisrael merit to welcome the Shechinah? It is through guarding against the impurity of menstruation. And about this is written: "Also you shall not approach a woman in the impurity of her menstrual flow, to uncover her nakedness" (Vayikra 18:19). HE ASKS: "To uncover her nakedness" – of whom? HE ANSWERS: Of the Congregation of Yisrael, MEANING NOT TO BLEMISH HER. And in this way, other things that the Congregation of Yisrael is bound to joined and connect to. And we have already explained this matter.

358. וְהַיָּשָׁר בְּעֵינָיו תַּעֲשֶׂה: דָּא צַדִּיק. כְּמָה דִּכְתִּיב, עֵינֵי יְיָ' אֶל

צַדִּיקִים, לְאִסְתַּמְּרָא מִשִּׁפְחָה. וְהָא אוֹקִימְנָא מִלֵּי. דִּכְתִּיב וְשִׁפְחָה כִּי תִירַשׁ גְּבִירְתָּהּ, דְּגָרִים לַצַּדִּיק דְּאִתְדַּבַּק בְּשִׁפְחָה. וְהַאֲזַנְתָּ לְמִצְוֹתָיו: דָּא נֶצַח, לְאִסְתַּמְּרָא דְּלָא יֵעוּל רְשִׁימָא דָּא בְּבַת אֵל נֵכָר, וְלֹא יְשַׁקֵּר בֵּיהּ בְּנֶצַח. דִּכְתִּיב, וְגַם נֶצַח יִשְׂרָאֵל לֹא יְשַׁקֵּר. וּמַאן דְּנָטִיר הַאי, קַיֵּים מִצְוֹתָיו, דִּכְתִּיב כִּי לֹא תִשְׁתַּחֲוֶה לְאֵל אַחֵר. וְשָׁמַרְתָּ כָּל חֻקָּיו: דָּא הוֹד, לְאִסְתַּמְּרָא מִן זוֹנָה.

358. "And will do that which is right in His sight." This refers to the righteous, WHO IS YESOD, as is written: "The eyes of Hashem are toward the righteous" (Tehilim 34:16). We have discussed being wary of a maid servant in accordance with the verse: "And a handmaid that is heir to her mistress" (Mishlei 30:23), WHICH MEANS that it causes the righteous to cleave unto a handmaid. "And give ear to His commandments," refers to Netzach, for one should not insert this sign into a heathen woman, nor be false with it to Netzach. For it is written: "And also the Eternal One (lit. '*Netzach*') of Yisrael will not lie" (I Shmuel 15:29). And he who observes this, THE HOLY COVENANT, fulfills His commandments, as is written: "For you shall worship no other El" (Shemot 34:14). "And keep all His statutes." This is Hod, to beware of a harlot.

359. וְאַזְלָא הָא, כְּמָה דְּתָנֵינָן, אָמַר רִבִּי יְהוּדָה, מַאי דִּכְתִּיב חֲגוֹר חַרְבְּךָ עַל יָרֵךְ גִּבּוֹר הוֹדְךָ וַהֲדָרֶךָ. אֶלָּא, כָּל מַאן דִּמְזָרֵז גַּרְמֵיהּ, וְשַׁוֵּי דְּחִילוּ דְּחַרְבָּא שְׁנָנָא תַּקִּיפָא לָקֳבְלֵיהּ. עַל יָרֵךְ, מַאי עַל יָרֵךְ. דָּא רְשִׁימָא קַדִּישָׁא. כד"א, שִׂים נָא יָדְךָ תַּחַת יְרֵכִי.

359. This agrees with what we have learned. Rabbi Yehuda said: It is written: "Gird your sword upon your thigh, O mighty warrior: your glory and your majesty" (Tehilim 45:4). This refers to he who makes haste to place the fear of the strong sharpened sword, WHICH IS MALCHUT, before him, upon the thigh. What is "upon your thigh"? It means upon this holy sign, to guard it, as is written: "Put, I pray you, your hand under my thigh" (Beresheet 24:2).

360. ד"א חֲגוֹר חַרְבְּךָ, כְּלוֹמַר, זָרֵיז וְאַתְקִיף יִצְרְךָ בִּישָׁא, דְּאִיהוּ חַרְבְּךָ. עַל יָרֵךְ, עַל הַהוּא רְשִׁימָא קַדִּישָׁא לְנַטְרָא לֵיהּ. וְאִי נָטַר לֵיהּ, כְּדֵין

אִקְרֵי גִּבּוֹר, וְקב"ה אַלְבִּישׁ לֵיהּ בִּלְבוּשׁוֹי, וּמַאן לְבוּשׁוֹי דְּקוּדְשָׁא בְּרִיךְ הוּא. הוֹד וְנֶצַח. דִּכְתִּיב, הוֹד וְהָדָר לָבָשְׁתָּ. אוּף הָכָא הוֹדְךָ וַהֲדָרֶךָ, וּכְדֵין אִתְדַּבַּק בַּר נָשׁ בְּמַלְכָּא קַדִּישָׁא כַּדְקָא יֵאוֹת.

360. Another explanation for “Gird your sword.” It means expedite and strengthen yourself, overpower your Evil Inclination, which is your sword “upon your thigh,” upon that Holy Covenant, to guard it. If he guards it, then he is called ‘mighty’. And the Holy One, blessed be He, dresses him in His garments. What are the garments of the Holy One, blessed be He? They are Hod and Netzach, as is written: “You are clothed with glory and majesty” (Tehilim 104:1). Here also, “Your glory and your majesty.” Then the person cleaves unto the Holy King properly.

361. מִכָּאן וּלְהָלְאָה, כָּל הַמַּחֲלָה אֲשֶׁר שַׂמְתִּי בְּמִצְרַיִם לֹא אָשִׂים עָלֶיךָ כִּי אֲנִי יְיָ׳ רוֹפְאֶךָ. דָּא מַלְכָּא קַדִּישָׁא, וְעַל דָּא אַזְהַר לוֹן עַל הַהוּא מִלָּה מַמָּשׁ, דְּיָהַב וְרָשִׁים בְּהוּ, וְלָא יַתִּיר וְעַד כְּעַן לָא אִתְיְיהִיבַת לְהוּ אוֹרַיְיתָא, אֶלָּא כֵּיוָן דִּכְתִּיב, שָׁם שָׂם לוֹ חֹק וּמִשְׁפָּט, מִיַּד וַיֹּאמֶר אִם שָׁמוֹעַ תִּשְׁמַע וְגוֹ׳.

361. From here and further: “I will put none of these diseases upon you, which I have brought upon Egypt; for I am Hashem that heals you.” This is the Holy King. Therefore, He admonished them about that very thing that He gave and marked in them, WHICH IS THE COVENANT OF THE CIRCUMCISION, and no more. AND IT IS TRUE that although until now the Torah was not yet given to them, yet it is written, “there He made for them a stature and an ordinance,” WHICH ARE CIRCUMCISION AND THE UNCOVERING OF THE MEMBRANE. Forthwith, “And He said, ‘If you will diligently hearken...’” WHICH REFERS TO THE FOUR WAYS TO OBSERVE THE MEMBER OF THE HOLY COVENANT, AS EXPLAINED.

362. תָּא חֲזֵי, כַּד בָּעָא קוּדְשָׁא בְּרִיךְ הוּא לְאַזְהָרָא לְיִשְׂרָאֵל, עַל אוֹרַיְיתָא, בְּכַמָּה מִלִּין מָשִׁיךְ לְהוּ, בְּכַמָּה מְשִׁיכָן דַּחֲבִיבוּתָא, כְּבַר נָשׁ דְּמָשִׁיךְ בְּרֵיהּ לְבֵי רַב. וְת"ח, לָא בָּעָא קב"ה לְמֵיהַב לְהוּ אוֹרַיְיתָא, עַד

דְּקָרִיבוּ בַּהֲדֵיהּ. וּבַמֶּה קָרִיבוּ בַּהֲדֵיהּ, בְּגִלּוּיָא דִּרְשִׁימָא דָּא, כְּמָה דְּאִתְּמַר.

362. Come and behold: when the Holy One, blessed be He, wanted to admonish Yisrael about the Torah, with how many words and with how many persuasions of love did He draw them, like a father who draws his son to school. Come and behold: the Holy One, blessed be He, did not want to give them the Torah until they were close to Him. How did they become attracted to Him? By uncovering this sign, WHICH IS THE CIRCUMCISION, as we have learned.

363. אָמַר ר׳ יְהוּדָה, לָא קָרִיבוּ יִשְׂרָאֵל לְטוּרָא דְּסִינַי, עַד דְּעָאלוּ בְּחוּלָקָא דְּצַדִּיק, וְזָכוּ בֵּיהּ. מְנָלָן, דִּכְתִּיב בַּיּוֹם הַזֶּה בָּאוּ מִדְבָּר סִינַי, בַּיּוֹם הַזֶּה מַמָּשׁ דַּיְיקָא. וּכְתִיב וְאָמַר בַּיּוֹם הַהוּא הִנֵּה אֱלֹהֵינוּ זֶה קִוִּינוּ לוֹ וְגוֹ׳.

363. Rabbi Yehuda said: Yisrael did not come close to Mount Sinai until they entered the portion of the Righteous, NAMELY, CIRCUMCISION, and attained it. How do we know this? Because it is written: "The same (Heb. *zeh*) day they came to the wilderness of Sinai" (Shemot 19:1). The very day exactly, WHICH IS YESOD THAT IS CALLED *'ZEH'*. And it is written: "And it shall be said on that day, 'Lo, this is our Elohim; we have waited for Him...'" (Yeshayah 25:9).

29. the story of the manna

A Synopsis

Rabbi Yehuda discusses the verse, "Blessed is he who considers the poor: Hashem will deliver him in the day of evil." Rabbi Chiya wonders about "For Hashem hears the poor," asking if He listens only to the poor and no others. Rabbi Shimon says merely that it is that they are closer to the King, as there is no one in the world who has a broken heart like a needy person. We are told a story of Rabbi Yisa who brought back a poor man from the dead. The poor man's soul went to the King's throne and learned that three chairs were prepared ready for Rabbi Yosi, the son of Rabbi Ya'akov, and Rabbi Chizkiyah. We read of another incident with a poor person and Rabbi Yitzchak, and a dream about Rabbi Shimon and a poor person. Every day the dew of Atika Kadisha drips down to Zeir Anpin and is drawn to those below, and it nourishes the holy angels. The children of Yisrael ate that food in the wilderness, because it was the manna. Rabbi Shimon says that those who are occupied with the Torah day and night are still nourished from it today. When the children of Yisrael left Egypt they had unleavened bread, but now they merited a different higher bread from a high place. Scholars who are occupied with Torah are nourished from a high place. Rabbi Elazar wonders why those scholars seem weaker than other people, and Rabbi Shimon explains that the Torah scholars eat the food of the spirit and soul, and do not eat the food of the body at all; therefore their bodies are weaker. This higher food is equated to Chochmah, or Wisdom. Returning to the question of the poor, we learn that one who helps fulfill the poor person has a letter added to Tzedek, righteousness, so that it becomes Tzedekah, Charity. More precious than these is the food of the sick, and more supreme than that is the food of spirits and souls that comes from Binah that has returned to become Chochmah, and more precious than all of them is the food that comes from the Supernal Chochmah, which is what the Torah scholars eat. This is because Torah emanates from the Supernal Chochmah. Rabbi Yosi says that all believers must request their food from God on a daily basis, and pray for it, because that causes that tree that contains everyone's food to be blessed from them. Therefore one need not cook food on one day for another day; one must "hope in His steadfast love." We are reminded that "The Righteous eats to satisfy his soul." Those who do not have faith burden themselves every day over food, out of fear that perhaps they will not acquire a loaf of bread. Rabbi Elazar taught that the Righteous shall eat of that manna in the World to Come. Rabbi

Shimon says that every person who puts a desire before the Holy King must concentrate his whole will and heart on it in order to draw the blessing from the wellspring of all. A person must prepare his table on Sabbath night so that blessings from above will dwell on him; blessing is not present on an empty table. The Sabbath is the inclusion of all the other days, and from it they are blessed.

364. וַיֹּאמֶר יְיָ׳ אֶל מֹשֶׁה הִנְנִי מַמְטִיר לָכֶם לֶחֶם מִן הַשָּׁמָיִם. רִבִּי יְהוּדָה פָּתַח וְאָמַר, אַשְׁרֵי מַשְׂכִּיל אֶל דָּל בְּיוֹם רָעָה יְמַלְּטֵהוּ יְיָ׳. הַאי קְרָא אוּקִימְנָא לֵיהּ, בְּשַׁעֲתָא דְּבַר נָשׁ שָׁכִיב בְּבֵי מַרְעֵיהּ, הָא אִתְּפַס בְּאַטְרוֹנְיָא דְּמַלְכָּא, רֵישֵׁיהּ בְּקוּלְרָא, רַגְלוֹי בְּכוּפְסִירִין, כַּמָּה חֵילִין נַטְרִין לֵיהּ, מֵהַאי גִּיסָא, וּמֵהַאי גִּיסָא. שַׁיְיפוֹי כֻּלְּהוּ בְּדוֹחֲקָא, מַגִּיחִין אִלֵּין בְּאִלֵּין. מֵיכְלָא אִתְעֲדֵי מִנֵּיהּ.

364. "And Hashem said to Moses, 'Behold, I will rain bread from heaven for you'" (Shemot 26:4). Rabbi Yehuda opened the discussion, saying: "Blessed is he who considers the poor: Hashem will deliver him in the day of evil" (Tehilim 41:2). We have explained this passage. It refers to when a person is lying ill, captured by the officers of the King. His head is chained, his feat in manacles, many soldiers guard him from all sides so that he shall not escape, his limbs are in straits and fighting among themselves, and food is taken from him.

365. בְּהַהוּא זִמְנָא, פַּקְדִין עָלֵיהּ אַפּוֹטְרוֹפָּא, לְמֵילַף עָלֵיהּ זְכוּת קָמֵי מַלְכָּא, דִּכְתִּיב אִם יֵשׁ עָלָיו מַלְאָךְ מֵלִיץ אֶחָד מִנִּי אָלֶף. בְּהַהִיא שַׁעֲתָא, זַכָּאָה חוּלָקֵיהּ דְּב״נ דְּעָאל עָלֵיהּ, וְאוֹלִיף לֵיהּ אָרְחָא, לְשֵׁיזָבוּתֵיהּ מִן דִּינָא. הה״ד אַשְׁרֵי מַשְׂכִּיל אֶל דָּל.

365. At that time, they appoint for him an Interlocutor and a Defender in order to speak favorably about him to the King, as is written: "If there be an angel over him, an interpreter, one among a thousand" (Iyov 33:23). At that moment, blessed is the portion of a man who comes to him and teaches him a way to save him from Judgment. This is what is written, "Blessed is he who considers the poor."

366. וְהֵיךְ יָכִיל לְשֵׁזָבָא לֵיהּ, לְמֵילַף לֵיהּ אָרְחוֹי דְּחַיֵּי, לְאָתָבָא לְקָמֵי מָארֵיהּ, כְּדֵין אִתְעָבֵיד אַפּוֹטְרוֹפּוֹסָא עָלֵיהּ לְעֵילָּא. מַאי אַגְרֵיהּ. בְּיוֹם רָעָה יְמַלְּטֵהוּ יְיָ׳. ד״א, אַשְׁרֵי מַשְׂכִּיל אֶל דָּל, כַּמָּה תַּקִּיפָא אַגְרָא דְּמִסְכְּנָא, קָמֵי קוּדְשָׁא בְּרִיךְ הוּא.

366. HE ASKS: And how can he save the sick person? HE ANSWERS: He should teach him the way of returning and repenting before his Master. Then an Intercessor is formed for him above, AND HE IS SAVED. What is his reward? It is that "Hashem will deliver him in the day of evil." Another explanation for: "Blessed is he who considers the poor." How strong is the reward of THE ONE WHO ASSISTS the needy before the Holy One, blessed be He.

367. א״ר חִיָּיא, תָּוַוהְנָא עַל הַאי קְרָא דִּכְתִּיב, כִּי שׁוֹמֵעַ אֶל אֶבְיוֹנִים יְיָ׳, וְכִי אֶל אֶבְיוֹנִים שׁוֹמֵעַ וְלֹא לְאַחֲרָא. א״ר שִׁמְעוֹן, בְּגִין דְּאִינּוּן קְרִיבִין יַתִּיר לְמַלְכָּא, דִּכְתִּיב, לֵב נִשְׁבָּר וְנִדְכֶּה אֱלֹהִים לֹא תִבְזֶה. וְלֵית לָךְ בְּעָלְמָא, דְּאִיהוּ תָּבִיר לִבָּא כְּמִסְכְּנָא. תּוּ אָמַר רִבִּי שִׁמְעוֹן, תָּא חֲזֵי, כָּל אִינּוּן בְּנֵי עָלְמָא, אִתְחַזְיָין קָמֵי קוּדְשָׁא בְּרִיךְ הוּא, בְּגוּפָא וְנַפְשָׁא, וּמִסְכְּנָא לָא אִתְחָזֵי אֶלָּא בְּנַפְשָׁא בִּלְחוֹדוֹי, וְקוּדְשָׁא בְּרִיךְ הוּא קָרִיב לְנַפְשָׁא יַתִּיר מִגּוּפָא.

367. Rabbi Chiya said: I wondered about this passage, "For Hashem hears the poor" (Tehilim 69:34). Does He hearken only unto the poor and no others? Rabbi Shimon said: It is because they are closer to the King, as is written: "A broken and a contrite heart, O Elohim, You will not despise" (Tehilim 51:19). And there is no one in the world one who has a broken heart like a needy person. Rabbi Shimon also said: Come and behold. All the people of the world appear before the Holy One, blessed be He, in body and soul. But the poor appear before the Holy One, blessed be He, only in soul, BECAUSE HIS BODY IS BROKEN, and the Holy One, blessed be He, is closer to the soul than to the body.

368. מִסְכְּנָא חַד הֲוָה בִּשְׁבָבוּתֵיהּ דְּר׳ יֵיסָא, וְלָא הֲוָה מַאן דְּאַשְׁגַּח בֵּיהּ, וְהוּא הֲוָה אַכְסִיף, וְלָא תַּקִּיף בִּבְנֵי נָשָׁא, יוֹמָא חַד חָלַשׁ, עָאל

עָלֵיהּ רִבִּי יֵיסָא, שָׁמַע חַד קָלָא דְּאָמַר, טִילְקָא טִילְקָא, הָא נַפְשָׁא פַּרְחָא גַּבָּאי, וְלָא מָטוּ יוֹמוֹי. וַוי לִבְנֵי מָתֵיהּ דְּלָא אִשְׁתְּכַח בְּהוּ דְּיָתִיב נַפְשֵׁיהּ לְגַבֵּיהּ. קָם רִבִּי יֵיסָא, שַׁדֵּי בְּפוּמֵיהּ, מַיָּא דְּגַרְגְּרִין, אַפּוּתָא דְּקוּנְטָא אִתְבְּזַע זֵיעָא בְּאַנְפּוֹי, וְתָב רוּחֵיהּ לְגַבֵּיהּ.

368. There was a poor man who lived in the neighborhood of Rabbi Yisa. No one paid any attention to him. He himself was bashful and did not press upon other people. One day he became ill. Rabbi Yisa came in to visit him and heard a voice saying: Justice, justice – MEANING THAT HE GAVE A STATEMENT OF JUSTICE TO HEAVEN. The soul is departing from me but my time has not yet arrived. Woe to the inhabitants of the city, for there is no one among them to return his soul to him. Rabbi Yisa arose and put some fig juice and a measure of spicy wine into his mouth. A sweat broke out in his face and his spirit returned to him.

369. לְבָתַר אָתָא וְשָׁאִיל לֵיהּ, אָמַר חַיֶּיךָ רִבִּי, נַפְשָׁא נַפְקַת מִנַּאי, וּמָטוּ לָהּ קָמֵי כּוּרְסְיָיא דְּמַלְכָּא, וּבָעַת לְאִשְׁתַּאֲרָא תַּמָּן, אֶלָּא דְּבָעָא קוּדְשָׁא בְּרִיךְ הוּא לְזַכָּאָה לָךְ, וְאַכְרִיזוּ עָלָךְ, זַמִּין הוּא רִבִּי יֵיסָא, לְסַלְּקָא רוּחֵיהּ, וּלְאִתְקַשְּׁרָא בְּחַד אִדְרָא קַדִּישָׁא דִּזְמִינִין חַבְרַיָּיא לְאִתְּעָרָא בְּאַרְעָא, וְהָא אַתְקִינוּ תְּלַת כֻּרְסְיָאן, דְּקַיְימִן לָךְ וּלְחַבְרָךְ. מֵהַהוּא יוֹמָא הֲווֹ מַשְׁגִּיחִין בֵּיהּ בְּנֵי מָתֵיהּ.

369. Afterwards, he came to visit and he inquired about him. He said: I swear, Rabbi, the soul left me and reached the King's throne, and wanted to remain there. But the Holy One, blessed be He, wanted to award you, and they announced of you: Rabbi Yisa spirit will depart and he shall be bound in a particularly holy assembly, NAMELY IN THE GREAT ASSEMBLY (IDRA RABA), AND NOT IN THE SMALLER ASSEMBLY that the friends shall raise in the land. And they have prepared three chairs that are standing ready for you and your friends, RABBI YOSI, THE SON OF RABBI YA'AKOV, AND RABBI CHIZKIYAH, WHOSE SOULS DEPARTED DURING THIS ASSEMBLY. From that day onward, the inhabitants of the city watched and paid attention to him.

370. תּוּ, מִסְכְּנָא אַחֲרָא אַעְבָּר קָמֵיהּ דְּר׳ יִצְחָק, וַהֲוָה בִּידֵיהּ פְּלַג מְעָה

דְּכֶסֶף. אָמַר לֵיהּ לְרִבִּי יִצְחָק, אַשְׁלִים לִי וְלִבְנַי וְלִבְנָתַי נַפְשָׁאן. אָמַר לֵיהּ וְהֵיךְ אַשְׁלִים נַפְשַׁיְיכוּ, דְּהָא לָא אִשְׁתְּכַח גַּבָּאי בַּר פַּלְגּ מְעָה. אָמַר לֵיהּ, בְּדָא אַשְׁלִימְנָא, בִּפְלַג אַחֲרָא דְּאִית גַּבָּאי, אַפְקֵיהּ וְיָהֲבֵיהּ לֵיהּ.

370. Another incident occurred when a poor person passed before Rabbi Yitzchak with half a coin of silver in his hand. He said to Rabbi Yitzchak: Save my and my daughters' souls. He said: How can I make whole your souls, when I have only a half coin. He said: I will complete it hereby with the half coin I have in my possession. He took it out and gave it to him.

371. אַחְזִיאוּ לֵיהּ בְּחֶלְמֵיהּ, דַּהֲוָה אַעְבָּר בִּשְׂפָתָא דְּיַמָּא רַבָּא, וּבָעָאן לְמִשְׁדְּיֵיהּ בְּגַוֵּויהּ, חָמָא לְרִבִּי שִׁמְעוֹן, דַּהֲוָה אוֹשִׁיט יְדוֹי לְקַבְּלֵיהּ, וְאָתֵי הַהוּא מִסְכְּנָא וְאַפְקֵיהּ, וְיָהֲבֵיהּ בִּידוֹי דְּרִבִּי שִׁמְעוֹן, וְאִשְׁתֵּזִיב. כַּד אִתְּעַר, נָפַל בְּפוּמֵיהּ, הַאי קְרָא, אַשְׁרֵי מַשְׂכִּיל אֶל דָּל בְּיוֹם רָעָה יְמַלְּטֵהוּ יְיָ'.

371. They showed him in his dream how he was traveling along the edge of the Great Sea and they wanted to throw in him into it. He described how Rabbi Shimon stretched out his hand towards him. And that poor person came, took him out and gave him into the hands of Rabbi Shimon, and he was saved. When he awoke, his mouth uttered this passage: "Blessed is he who considers the poor: Hashem will deliver him in the day of evil."

372. וְתָא חֲזֵי, כָּל יוֹמָא וְיוֹמָא, נָטִיף טַלָּא מֵעַתִּיקָא קַדִּישָׁא לִזְעֵיר אַפִּין, וּמִתְבָּרְכָאן כָּל חֲקַל תַּפּוּחִין קַדִּישִׁין. וּמֵהַהוּא טַלָּא אַנְגִּיד לְאִינוּן דִּלְתַתָּא, וּמַלְאָכִין קַדִּישִׁין אִתְּזָנוּ מִנֵּיהּ, כָּל חַד וְחַד כְּפוּם מֵיכְלֵיהּ, הה"ד לֶחֶם אַבִּירִים אָכַל אִישׁ, וּמֵהַהוּא מְזוֹנָא אָכְלוּ יִשְׂרָאֵל בְּמַדְבְּרָא.

372. Come and behold: every day the dew of Atika Kadisha drips to Zeir Anpin, and the whole Field of Holy Apples is blessed, WHICH IS MALCHUT, and from that, dew is drawn to these below. The holy angels are nourished from it, each one according to his ability to eat. This is what is written: "Man ate the bread of angels" (Tehilim 78:25); NAMELY, THAT DEW MENTIONED EARLIER, WHICH IS THE BREAD OF ANGELS. Yisrael ate of that food in the wilderness, THE MANNA.

373. א״ר שִׁמְעוֹן, כַּמָּה בְּנֵי נָשָׁא מִתְזָנִין בְּהַאי זִמְנָא מִנֵּיהּ, וּמַאן אִינּוּן. אִלֵּין חַבְרַיָּיא דְּמִשְׁתַּדְּלֵי בְּאוֹרַיְיתָא, יוֹמֵי וְלֵילֵי. וְכִי סַלְקָא דַּעְתָּךְ מֵהַהוּא מְזוֹנָא מַמָּשׁ. לָא. אֶלָּא כְּעֵין הַהוּא מְזוֹנָא מַמָּשׁ, דְּשָׁקִיל עַל חַד תְּרֵין.

373. Rabbi Shimon said: Many people are nourished from it today. And who are they? They are the friends, who are occupied with Torah days and nights. And if it you think that it was actually the same food THAT THE CHILDREN OF YISRAEL ATE IN THE WILDERNESS, it is not, but it is very similar to that food, for it is worth double THE MANNA THAT THE CHILDREN OF YISRAEL ATE IN THE WILDERNESS.

374. תָּא חֲזֵי, יִשְׂרָאֵל כַּד עָאלוּ וְאִתְדְּבָקוּ בְּמַלְכָּא קַדִּישָׁא, בְּגִין גִּלּוּיָא דִּרְשִׁימָא קַדִּישָׁא, כְּדֵין זָכוּ לְמֵיכַל נַהֲמָא אַחֲרָא עִלָּאָה, יַתִּיר מִמַּה דַּהֲוָה בְּקַדְמֵיתָא. בְּקַדְמֵיתָא כַּד נָפְקוּ יִשְׂרָאֵל מִמִּצְרַיִם, עָאלוּ בְּנַהֲמָא, דְּאִקְרֵי מַצָּה, וְהַשְׁתָּא זָכוּ, וְעָאלוּ לְמֵיכַל נַהֲמָא אַחֲרָא עִלָּאָה יַתִּיר, מֵאֲתָר עִלָּאָה, דִּכְתִּיב הִנְנִי מַמְטִיר לָכֶם לֶחֶם מִן הַשָּׁמַיִם. מִן הַשָּׁמַיִם מַמָּשׁ. וּבְהַהוּא זִמְנָא אִשְׁתְּכַח לְהוּ לְיִשְׂרָאֵל. מֵאֲתָר דָּא. חַבְרַיָּיא דְּמִשְׁתַּדְּלֵי בְּאוֹרַיְיתָא, מֵאֲתָר אַחֲרָא עִלָּאָה יַתִּיר אִתְזָנוּ. מַאי הוּא. כְּמָה דִּכְתִּיב הַחָכְמָה תְּחַיֶּה בְעָלֶיהָ. אֲתָר עִלָּאָה יַתִּיר.

374. Come and behold: when Yisrael came and cleaved unto the Holy King, they merited then to eat a much higher bread because of the uncovering of the holy sign OF THE CIRCUMCISED ORGAN. Before, when they left Egypt, they came with bread called unleavened bread (Heb. *Matzah*), WHICH IS MALCHUT. Now they merited to eat a different, much higher bread, from a high place, as is written: "Behold I will rain bread from the heavens for you," actually from the heavens, WHICH IS ZEIR ANPIN, and it became available to Yisrael from this place at that time. The friends who are occupied with Torah are nourished from a higher place. What is it? It is as written: "Wisdom gives life to those who have it" (Kohelet 7:12), which is a place far higher THAN ZEIR ANPIN.

375. א״ל ר׳ אֶלְעָזָר, אִי הָכִי, אֲמַאי חַלְשָׁא נַפְשַׁיְיהוּ יַתִּיר מִשְּׁאָר בְּנֵי עָלְמָא, דְּהָא שְׁאַר בְּנֵי נָשָׁא, בְּחֵילָא וְתוּקְפָּא יַתִּיר אִתְחָזוּן לְאִשְׁתַּכְּחָא. אָמַר לֵיהּ יֵאוֹת שָׁאִילְתָּא.

375. Rabbi Elazar said to him: If so, why are those occupied with Torah weaker than other people, for the other people appear to be stronger than those who are occupied with Torah? He said to him: You ask well.

376. תָּא חֲזֵי, כָּל מְזוֹנֵי דִּבְנֵי עָלְמָא מִלְּעֵילָּא קָא אַתְיָין. הַהוּא מְזוֹנָא דְּאָתֵי מִן שְׁמַיָּא וְאַרְעָא, דָּא מְזוֹנָא דְּכָל עָלְמָא, וְהוּא מְזוֹנָא דְּכוֹלָּא, וְהוּא מְזוֹנָא גַּס וְעָב. וְהַהוּא מְזוֹנָא דְּאָתֵי יַתִּיר מֵעֵילָּא, הוּא מְזוֹנָא יַתִּיר דָּקִיק, קָאַתְיָא מֵאֲתָר דְּדִינָא אִשְׁתְּכַח, וְדָא הוּא מְזוֹנָא דְּאַכְלוּ יִשְׂרָאֵל כַּד נָפְקוּ מִמִּצְרַיִם. מְזוֹנָא דְּאִשְׁתְּכַח לְהוּ לְיִשְׂרָאֵל, בְּהַהוּא זִמְנָא בְּמַדְבְּרָא, מֵאֲתָר עִלָּאָה דְּאִקְרֵי שָׁמַיִם, הוּא מְזוֹנָא יַתִּיר דְּקִיקָא, דְּעָיִיל יַתִּיר לְנַפְשָׁא מִכֹּלָּא, וּמִתְפְּרַשׁ יַתִּיר מִגּוּפָא, וְאִקְרֵי לֶחֶם אַבִּירִים.

376. Come and behold: all the food of the inhabitants of the world comes from above. That food that comes from the heaven and the earth is the food of the whole world. It is the food of all, and it is coarse and thick nourishment. The food that comes from a higher source and is a finer food comes from the place where Judgment is prevalent, NAMELY MALCHUT, and this is the food that Yisrael ate when they left Egypt, NAMELY, UNLEAVENED BREAD. The food that was provided Yisrael at that time in the wilderness was from a higher place, called 'heavens', WHICH IS ZEIR ANPIN. It is a finer food that enters into the soul more THAN ANY OTHER FOOD. It is more separate from the body and is called 'the food of the angels', NAMELY MANNA.

377. מְזוֹנָא עִלָּאָה יַתִּיר מִכֹּלָּא, הוּא מְזוֹנָא דְּחַבְרַיָּיא, אִינּוּן

דְּמִשְׁתַּדְּלֵי בְּאוֹרַיְיתָא, דְּאַכְלֵי מְזוֹנָא דְּרוּחָא וְנִשְׁמְתָא, וְלָא אַכְלֵי מְזוֹנָא דְּגוּפָא כְּלָל, וְהַיְינוּ מֵאֲתַר עִלָּאָה יַקִּירָא עַל כֹּלָּא, וְאִקְרֵי חָכְמָה. בְּגִינֵי כַּךְ חָלִישׁ גּוּפָא דְּחַבְרַיָּיא, יַתִּיר מִבְּנֵי עָלְמָא, דְּהָא לָא אַכְלֵי מְזוֹנָא דְּגוּפָא כְּלָל. וְאַכְלֵי מְזוֹנָא דְּרוּחָא וְנִשְׁמְתָא, מֵאֲתָר רְחִיקָא עִלָּאָה, יַקִּירָא מִכֹּלָּא. וּבְגִינֵי כַּךְ הַהוּא מְזוֹנָא דָּקִיק מִן דְּקִיקָא, יַתִּיר מִכֹּלָּא. זַכָּאָה חוּלָקְהוֹן, הה״ד הַחָכְמָה תְּחַיֶּה בְעָלֶיהָ. זַכָּאָה חוּלָקָא דְּגוּפָא, דְּיָכִיל לְאִתְזָנָא בִּמְזוֹנָא דְּנַפְשָׁא.

377. The food that is the highest of all is the food of the friends, those who are occupied with Torah, who eat the food of the spirit and the soul and do not eat physical food at all. It is from the place that is more precious than anything, called Chochmah (Wisdom). Therefore, the bodies of the friends are weaker than the people of the world because they do not eat the food of the body at all. They eat only the food of the spirit and soul from the distant place, higher and more precious than all – WHICH IS CHOCHMAH, WHICH IS FAR AWAY, AS IS WRITTEN: "I SAID, 'I WILL BE WISE; BUT IT WAS FAR FROM ME'" (KOHELET 7:23). Therefore, that food is far more refined than all. Blessed is their portion. This is what is written: "Wisdom gives life to those who have it." Blessed is the portion of a body that can be nourished with the food of the soul.

378. א״ל ר׳ אֶלְעָזָר, וַדַּאי הָכִי הוּא. אֲבָל בְּהַאי זִמְנָא, אֵיךְ אִשְׁתַּכְּחֵי מְזוֹנֵי אִלֵּין. א״ל וַדַּאי יֵאוֹת שָׁאִילְתָּא. ת״ח, וְדָא הוּא בְּרִירוּ דְּמִלָּה, מְזוֹנָא קַדְמָאָה, הוּא מְזוֹנָא דְּכָל עָלְמָא, הַהוּא דְּאַתְיָא מִן שְׁמַיָּא וְאַרְעָא, וְהוּא מְזוֹנָא דְּגוּפָא.

378. Rabbi Elazar said to him: Certainly, it is so, but in the present time how is such food to be found? He said to him: You ask well. Come and behold: this is the clarification of the matter. The first food is the food of the whole world, that which comes from the heavens and earth. And it is the food of the body.

379. מְזוֹנָא דְּהוּא עִלָּאָה מִנֵּיהּ, הַהוּא דְּאִיהוּ דְּקִיקָא יַתִּיר, וְאָתָא מֵאֲתָר דְּדִינָא שַׁרְיָא, דְּאִקְרֵי צֶדֶק, וְדָא הוּא מְזוֹנָא דְּמִסְכְּנֵי. וְרָזָא

דְּמִלָּה, מַאן דְּאַשְׁלִים לְמִסְכְּנָא, אַשְׁלִים לֵיהּ אָת חַד, וְאִתְעֲבֵיד צְדָקָה, וְרָזָא דָּא גּוֹמֵל נַפְשׁוֹ אִישׁ חֶסֶד. גְּמִילוּת חֲסָדִים מַשְׁמַע, דְּהָא בְּדִינָא שַׁרְיָא, וְאַשְׁלִים לֵיהּ חֶסֶד, כְּדֵין הוּא רַחֲמֵי.

379. The food that is higher than it, which is finer, comes from the place where Judgment is prevalent, called righteousness (Heb. *tzedek*), WHICH IS MALCHUT. This is the food of the poor; NAMELY MATZAH, THAT IS CALLED 'THE BREAD OF AFFLICTION'. And the secret of the matter is that one who helps fulfill the poor person has a letter added to *Tzedek*, and it becomes "*tzedakah* ('charity')." This is the secret of, "The merciful man does good to his own soul" (Mishlei 11:17). Acts of kindness show that one is under Judgment but has perfected it with Chesed. Then it turns into Mercy.

380. מְזוֹנָא עִלָּאָה יַתִּיר מֵאִלֵּין, הוּא מְזוֹנָא עִלָּאָה וְיַקִּירָא, מֵאֲתָר דְּאִקְרֵי שָׁמַיִם, וְהוּא דָּקִיק מִכֻּלְּהוּ, וְהוּא מְזוֹנָא דִּבְנֵי מַרְעֵי, הה״ד יְיָ׳ יִסְעָדֶנּוּ עַל עֶרֶשׂ דְּוָי כָּל מִשְׁכָּבוֹ הָפַכְתָּ בְחָלְיוֹ. יְיָ׳, דַּיְיקָא, מ״ט. בְּגִין דְּהָנֵי בְּנֵי מַרְעֵי, לָא אִתְזְנֵי אֶלָּא בְּהַהוּא דְּקוּדְשָׁא בְּרִיךְ הוּא מַמָּשׁ.

380. A food even higher than these is a supreme nourishment, more glorious and precious, from the place called 'heaven', WHICH IS ZEIR ANPIN – NAMELY MANNA, WHICH THE CHILDREN OF YISRAEL ATE IN THE WILDERNESS. It is finer than all of them. And this is the food of the sick. This is what is meant by: "Hashem strengthens him upon the bed of sickness: whenever he is prostrate You recover him in his illness" (Tehilim 41:4). Hashem is precise, WHICH IS ZEIR ANPIN. What is the reason? Because these ill people are fed only with the actual food of the Holy One, blessed be He, WHO IS ZEIR ANPIN.

381. מְזוֹנָא עִלָּאָה קַדִּישָׁא וְיַקִּירָא דָּא הוּא מְזוֹנֵי דְּרוּחִין וְנִשְׁמָתִין, וְהוּא מְזוֹנָא דַּאֲתָר רְחִיקָא עִלָּאָה, מֵהַהוּא אֲתָר דְּאִקְרֵי נוֹעַם יְיָ׳.

381. A supreme food, holy and precious is the food of spirits and souls, and it is the food from a high and far away place – WHICH IS BINAH THAT HAS AGAIN BECOME CHOCHMAH – ABOUT WHICH IS SAID: "I SAID, 'I WILL

BE WISE; BUT IT WAS FAR FROM ME'." It is the place that is called "the pleasantness of Hashem," MEANING BINAH THAT HAS RETURNED TO CHOCHMAH.

382. וְיַקִּירָא מִכֹּלָּא הוּא, מְזוֹנָא דְּחַבְרַיָּיא דְּמִשְׁתַּדְּלֵי בְּאוֹרַיְיתָא, וְהוּא מְזוֹנָא דְּאָתֵי מֵחָכְמָה עִלָּאָה. מ״ט מֵאֲתַר דָּא. בְּגִין דְּאוֹרַיְיתָא נַפְקָא מֵחָכְמָה עִלָּאָה, וְאִינּוּן דְּמִשְׁתַּדְּלֵי בְּאוֹרַיְיתָא, עַיְילֵי בְּעִקְּרָא דְּשָׁרְשָׁהָא, וְעַל דָּא, מְזוֹנָא דִּלְהוֹן, מֵהַהוּא אֲתַר עִלָּאָה קַדִּישָׁא קָא אַתְיָא.

382. And more precious than all of them is the food that the friends who are occupied with Torah EAT. It is the food that comes from the Supernal Chochmah, WHICH IS ACTUAL CHOCHMAH. What is the reason THAT IT COMES from this place? It is because Torah emanates from the supernal Chochmah, and those who are occupied with Torah enter into the main source of the roots. Therefore, their food comes from that high, holy place.

383. אָתָא ר׳ אֶלְעָזָר, וְנָשִׁיק יְדוֹי. אָמַר, זַכָּאָה חוּלָקִי דְּקָאִימְנָא בְּמִלִּין אִלֵּין. זַכָּאָה חוּלָקְהוֹן דְּצַדִּיקַיָּיא, דְּמִשְׁתַּדְּלֵי בְּאוֹרַיְיתָא יְמָמָא וְלֵילֵי, דְּזָכֵי לוֹן בְּהַאי עָלְמָא, וּבְעָלְמָא דְּאָתֵי, דִּכְתִּיב כִּי הוּא חַיֶּיךָ וְאוֹרֶךְ יָמֶיךָ.

383. Rabbi Elazar approached and kissed the hands OF RABBI SHIMON, HIS FATHER. He said: Blessed is my portion that I understood these words. Blessed is the portion of the righteous who are occupied with Torah days and nights, for it merits them in this world and in the World to Come, as is written: "For He is your life, and the length of your days" (Devarim 30:20).

384. הִנְנִי מַמְטִיר לָכֶם לֶחֶם מִן הַשָּׁמָיִם. רִבִּי יוֹסֵי פָּתַח, פּוֹתֵחַ אֶת יָדֶךָ וּמַשְׂבִּיעַ לְכָל חַי רָצוֹן. מַה כְּתִיב לְעֵילָא, עֵינֵי כֹל אֵלֶיךָ יְשַׂבֵּרוּ. כָּל אִינּוּן בְּנֵי עָלְמָא, מְצַפָּאן וְזַקְפָּאן עַיְינִין לְקוּדְשָׁא בְּרִיךְ הוּא, בְּגִין כַּךְ, כָּל אִינּוּן בְּנֵי מְהֵימְנוּתָא בָּעָאן בְּכָל יוֹמָא וְיוֹמָא, לְשָׁאֲלָא מְזוֹנַיְיהוּ מִקּוּדְשָׁא בְּרִיךְ הוּא, וּלְצַלָּאָה צְלוֹתְהוֹן עָלֵיהּ.

384. "Behold I will rain down bread from the heavens for you." Rabbi Yosi opened the discussion with the verse: "You open your hand, and satisfy the desire of every living thing" (Tehilim 145:16). What is written above? "The eyes of all wait upon You" (Ibid. 15). All the people of the world hope and raise their eyes to the Holy One, blessed be He. Therefore, all believers must request their food from the Holy One, blessed be He, on a daily basis, and pray their prayers for it.

385. מ"ט. בְּגִין דְּכָל מַאן דִּמְצַלֵּי צְלוֹתֵיהּ לְגַבֵּי קוּדְשָׁא בְּרִיךְ הוּא עַל מְזוֹנֵיהּ, גָּרִים דְּיִתְבָּרֵךְ כָּל יוֹמָא עַל יְדוֹי, הַהוּא אִילָנָא דְּמָזוֹן דְּכֹלָּא בֵּיהּ. ואע"ג דְּאִשְׁתְּכַח עִמֵּיהּ, בָּעֵי לְמִשְׁאַל קָמֵי קוּדְשָׁא בְּרִיךְ הוּא, וּלְצַלָּאָה צְלוֹתָא עַל מְזוֹנָא כָּל יוֹמָא, בְּגִין דְּיִשְׁתַּכְּחוּ עַל יְדוֹי בִּרְכָּאן כָּל יוֹמָא וְיוֹמָא לְעֵילָּא, וְדָא הוּא בָּרוּךְ יְיָ' יוֹם יוֹם.

385. HE ASKS: What is the reason? AND HE SAYS: Because everyone who says his prayer to the Holy One, blessed be He, for his food, causes that tree that contains everyone's food to be blessed through him. Although he has food, he still must ask for it before the Holy One, blessed be He, and pray his prayer for nourishment every day, in order that through him, blessings shall be prevalent above every single day. This is the meaning of: "Blessed be Adonai day by day" (Tehilim 68:20).

386. וְעַל דָּא, לָא לִבְעֵי לֵיהּ לֶאֱינָשׁ לְבַשְּׁלָא מְזוֹנָא, מִן יוֹמָא לְיוֹמָא אַחֲרִינָא, דְּלָא לְעַכֵּב יוֹמָא לְיוֹמָא אַחֲרָא. הה"ד וְיָצָא הָעָם וְלָקְטוּ דְּבַר יוֹם בְּיוֹמוֹ. יוֹם בְּיוֹמוֹ, דַּיְיקָא. בַּר מֵעֶרֶב שַׁבָּת לְשַׁבָּת, כְּמָה דְּאוּקִימְנָא. וּכְדֵין אִשְׁתְּכַח קוּדְשָׁא בְּרִיךְ הוּא מָלֵא בִּרְכָּאן בְּכָל יוֹמָא. וּכְדֵין כְּתִיב פּוֹתֵחַ אֶת יָדֶךָ וְגוֹ'. מַאי רָצוֹן. הַהוּא רָצוֹן דְּאִשְׁתְּכַח מֵעַתִּיקָא קַדִּישָׁא, וְנָפִיק מִנֵּיהּ רָצוֹן, לְאִשְׁתַּכְּחָא מְזוֹנֵי לְכֹלָּא. וּמַאן דְּשָׁאִיל מְזוֹנֵי בְּכָל יוֹמָא וְיוֹמָא, הַהוּא אִקְרֵי בְּרָא מְהֵימְנָא, בְּרָזָא דִּבְגִינֵיהּ מִשְׁתַּכְּחָן בִּרְכָּאן לְעֵילָּא.

386. Therefore, a person should not cook food on one day for another day, in order not to leave over from one day to another. This is what is meant by:

"And the people shall go out and gather a certain portion every day" (Shemot 16:4). "Every day," is exact, except on Shabbat eve for Shabbat, as we have established. Then the Holy One, blessed be He, is full of blessings every day. Then it is written: "You open Your hand, and satisfy the desire of every living thing." What is the "desire"? That is that particular desire that comes from Atika Kadisha, WHICH IS KETER, and a desire emanates from Him that there shall be food available to all. And he who requests food every single day is called 'a faithful son', a son due to of whom blessings are prevalent above.

387. ר׳ אַבָּא פָּתַח וְאָמַר, רוֹצֶה יְיָ׳ אֶת יְרֵאָיו אֶת הַמְיַחֲלִים לְחַסְדּוֹ, כַּמָּה אִית לְהוּ לִבְנֵי נָשָׁא לְמֵהַךְ בְּאָרְחוֹי דְּמַלְכָּא קַדִּישָׁא, וּלְמֵהַךְ בְּאָרְחוֹי דְּאוֹרַיְיתָא, בְּגִין דְּיִשְׁתַּכְּחוּן בִּרְכָּאן לְכֻלְּהוּ, לְעֵלָּאֵי וּלְתַתָּאֵי.

387. Rabbi Aba opened the discussion, saying: "Hashem takes pleasure in those who fear Him, in those who hope in His steadfast love" (Tehilim 147:11). How important it is for people to go in the ways of the Holy King, and to go in the paths of the Torah, so that blessings will be prevalent for everyone, those above and those below.

388. דְּתַנְיָא, מַאי דִּכְתִּיב, יִשְׂרָאֵל אֲשֶׁר בְּךָ אֶתְפָּאָר. אֶתְפָּאָר וַדַּאי. מַאי מַשְׁמַע. דִּבְגִין יִשְׂרָאֵל לְתַתָּא, קב״ה מִתְפָּאַר לְעֵילָּא. וּמַאי פְּאֵרָא דִילֵיהּ. דְּאִתְחַבָּשׁ בִּתְפִילִין, דְּמִתְחַבְּרָא גַּוְונֵי לְאִתְפָּאֲרָא.

388. For we have learned, it is written: "Yisrael, in whom I will be glorified" (Yeshayah 49:3). Indeed, "I will be glorified." What is its meaning? It is because of Yisrael below, WHO ELEVATE MAYIN NUKVIN ('FEMALE WATERS'), that the Holy One, blessed be He, is glorified above. What is His glory-He dons Tefilin, in which colors are mixed, with which to be glorified. FOR THE FOUR PORTIONS ARE THE SECRETS OF THREE COLORS, WHITE, RED, AND GREEN, AND THEY COMBINE IN THE SECRET OF THREE COLUMNS TO ILLUMINATE IN ALL PERFECTION.

389. תָּאנָא, רוֹצֶה יְיָ׳ אֶת יְרֵאָיו, רוֹצֶה יְיָ׳ בִּירֵאָיו מִבָּעֵי לֵיהּ. מַאי רוֹצֶה יְיָ׳ אֶת יְרֵאָיו, אֶלָּא רוֹצֶה יְיָ׳ אֶת יְרֵאָיו, כְּלוֹמַר, אַפִּיק הַאי רָצוֹן,

וּמִתְרָעֵי בְּהוּ קוּדְשָׁא בְּרִיךְ הוּא, לִירֵאָיו דְּדָחֲלִין לֵיהּ. וּמַאן אִינּוּן יְרֵאָיו דְּאַפִּיק לוֹן הַאי רָצוֹן. הָדַר וְאָמַר, אֶת הַמְיַחֲלִים לְחַסְדּוֹ, אִינּוּן דִּמְצַפָּאן וּמְחַכָּאן בְּכָל יוֹמָא וְיוֹמָא, לְמִבְעֵי מְזוֹנַיְיהוּ מִן קוּדְשָׁא בְּרִיךְ הוּא, מַשְׁמַע דִּכְתִּיב אֶת הַמְיַחֲלִים לְחַסְדּוֹ.

389. We learned, "Hashem takes pleasure in (or desires) those who fear Him." HE ASKS: It should have said 'Hashem takes pleasure in those who fear Him'. What is the meaning of, "Hashem takes pleasure those who fear Him"? AND HE ANSWERS: "Hashem desires those who fear Him," means that He produced this desires and with it fulfilled the desires of those who feared Him. And who are the fearful for whom He produced this desire? He repeats and says, "Those who hope in His steadfast love," MEANING those who hope and wait every single day to request their food from the Holy One, blessed be He. This we learn from the verse, "those who hope in His steadfast love."

390. רִבִּי יֵיסָא סָבָא, לָא אַתְקִין סְעוּדָתָא בְּכָל יוֹמָא, עַד דְּבָעָא בָּעוּתֵיהּ קָמֵי קוּדְשָׁא בְּרִיךְ הוּא, עַל מְזוֹנֵי. אָמַר, לָא נַתְקִין סְעוּדָתָא, עַד דְּתִתְיְהִיב מִבֵּי מַלְכָּא. לְבָתַר דְּבָעֵי בָּעוּתֵיהּ קָמֵי קוּדְשָׁא בְּרִיךְ הוּא, הֲוָה מְחַכֶּה שַׁעֲתָא חֲדָא, אָמַר הָא עִידָן דְּתִתְיְהִיב מִבֵּי מַלְכָּא, מִכָּאן וּלְהָלְאָה אַתְקִינוּ סְעוּדָתָא. וְדָא הוּא אָרְחָא, דְּאִינּוּן דַּחֲלֵי קוּדְשָׁא בְּרִיךְ הוּא, דַּחֲלֵי חַטָּאָה.

390. Rabbi Yisa Saba (the elder) did not prepare his meal every day until he prayed his prayer before the Holy One, blessed be He, for food. He said: We will not prepare the meal until it is given from the King's house. He then prayed his prayer before the Holy One, blessed be He, waited one hour, and then would say: By now it was already given from the King's house. From now on, prepare the meal. This is the way of those who fear the Holy One, blessed be He, those who fear sin.

391. אִינּוּן חַיָּיבַיָּא דְּאַזְלִין עֲקִימִין בְּאָרְחֵי אוֹרַיְיתָא, מַה כְּתִיב בְּהוּ. הוֹי מַשְׁכִּימֵי בַבֹּקֶר שֵׁכָר יִרְדֹּפוּ. וְע"ד רוֹצֶה יְיָ' אֶת יְרֵאָיו אֶת הַמְיַחֲלִים

לְחַסְדּוֹ. לְחַסְדּוֹ דַּיְיקָא. וּבְהָא אִשְׁתְּמוֹדְעָן אִינּוּן בְּנֵי מְהֵימָנוּתָא בְּכָל יוֹמָא וְיוֹמָא, הֲדָא הוּא דִּכְתִּיב, וְיָצָא הָעָם וְלָקְטוּ דְּבַר יוֹם בְּיוֹמוֹ. יוֹם בְּיוֹמוֹ קָאָמַר, וְלֹא דְּבַר יוֹם לְיוֹם אַחֵר.

391. Of the wicked people who go crookedly in the ways of the Torah, it is written, "Woe to them that rise up early in the morning, that they may follow strong drink" (Yeshayah 5:11). And therefore, "Hashem takes pleasure in those who fear Him, in those who hope in His steadfast love." "His steadfast love," indeed. And by this those people of Faith are recognizable every single day, as is written: "And the people shall go out and gather a certain portion every day." "A certain portion every day," is said, and not a certain portion for the next day.

392. וְכָל כַּךְ לָמָּה. לְמַעַן אֲנַסֶּנּוּ הֲיֵלֵךְ בְּתוֹרָתִי אִם לֹא בְּכָאן אִשְׁתְּמוֹדְעָן אִינּוּן בְּנֵי מְהֵימָנוּתָא, דְּכָל יוֹמָא וְיוֹמָא אִינּוּן אַזְלֵי בְּאֹרַח מֵישָׁר בְּאוֹרַיְיתָא. רִבִּי יִצְחָק אָמַר מֵהָכָא, צַדִּיק אוֹכֵל לְשׂוֹבַע נַפְשׁוֹ, בָּתַר דְּשָׂבַע נַפְשֵׁיהּ מִלְּצַלֵּי וּלְמִקְרֵי בְּאוֹרַיְיתָא.

392. HE ASKS: Why to such a degree? HE SAID: IT IS, "that I may test them, whether they will follow My Torah, or no" (Shemot 16:4). By this, MEANING IN THE EATING, these people of Faith are recognizable, for every day they walk in the straight path in the Torah. Rabbi Yitzchak said: From this we understand, "the righteous eats to satisfy his soul" (Mishlei 13:25), WHICH MEANS THAT not until he has satisfied his soul with prayer and the study of Torah DOES HE EAT.

393. רִבִּי שִׁמְעוֹן אָמַר, תָּא חֲזֵי, עַד לָא יָהַב קוּדְשָׁא בְּרִיךְ הוּא אוֹרַיְיתָא לְיִשְׂרָאֵל, אַבְחִין בֵּין אִינּוּן בְּנֵי מְהֵימָנוּתָא, וּבֵין אִינּוּן חַיָּיבַיָּא דְּלָאו אִינּוּן בְּנֵי מְהֵימָנוּתָא, וְלָא קַיְימִין בְּאוֹרַיְיתָא. וּבַמֶּה אַבְחִין לוֹן. בַּמָּן. כְּמָה דְּאִתְּמַר אֲנַסֶּנּוּ. וְכָל אִינּוּן דְּאִשְׁתְּכָחוּ דְּאִינּוּן בְּנֵי מְהֵימָנוּתָא, רָשִׁים לֵיהּ קוּדְשָׁא בְּרִיךְ הוּא, בִּרְשִׁימוּ דְּכִתְרָא דְּחֶסֶ"ד, כד"א הַמְיַחֲלִים לְחַסְדּוֹ, וְע"ד לְמַעַן אֲנַסֶּנּוּ. וְכָל אִינּוּן דְּלָא מִשְׁתַּכְּחֵי בְּנֵי מְהֵימָנוּתָא, אַעְדֵּי מִנַּיְיהוּ כִּתְרָא עִלָּאָה דָּא. וּמָנָא אַכְרִיז

וְאָמַר, וּבֶטֶן רְשָׁעִים תֶּחְסָר. וְעִם כָּל דָּא לֹא הֶעְדִּיף הַמַּרְבֶּה וְהַמַּמְעִיט לֹא הֶחְסִיר.

393. Rabbi Shimon said: Come and behold. Before the Holy One, blessed be He, gave the Torah to Yisrael, He differentiated between these people of Faith and the wicked who were not faithful and did not want the Torah. How did He tell the difference between them? By the manna, as is written: "That I may test them." The Holy One, blessed be He, marked all those who were found to be faithful with the imprint of the Sfirah of Chesed. As is written: "Those who hope in his steadfast love (lit. '*Chesed'*)." And all those who are not found to be faithful, He removed from this supernal Sfirah. And the Manna announced and said: "but the belly of the wicked shall feel want" (Ibid.). And with all this, "he that gathered much had nothing over, and he that gathered little had no lack" (Shemot 16:18).

394. תָּאנָא, בְּהַהוּא שַׁעֲתָא אִשְׁתְּלִימוּ יִשְׂרָאֵל לְתַתָּא, כְּגַוְונָא דִּלְעֵילָּא, כְּמָה דְּאוּקִימְנָא, דִּכְתִּיב, וַיָּבוֹאוּ אֵילִמָה וְשָׁם שְׁתֵּים עֶשְׂרֵה עֵינוֹת מַיִם וְשִׁבְעִים תְּמָרִים וגו'. וְאִתְתָּקַּף אִילָנָא קַדִּישָׁא, בִּתְרֵיסַר תְּחוּמִין, בְּאַרְבַּע סִטְרֵי עָלְמָא. וְאִתְתָּקַּף בְּשַׁבְעִין עַנְפִּין, וְכֹלָּא כְּגַוְונָא דִּלְעֵילָּא.

394. We learned that at that time Yisrael became perfected below, similar to above, as we have established by the verse: "And they came to Elim, where were twelve springs of water, and seventy palm trees..." (Shemot 15:27). THIS MEANS THAT the holy tree, WHICH IS ZEIR ANPIN, was strengthened by twelve boundaries in the four sides of the world, CHESED AND GVURAH, TIFERET AND MALCHUT, AND THERE ARE TWELVE BOUNDARIES, WHICH ARE THE SECRET OF THE TWELVE SPRINGS OF WATER. And it was strengthened with seventy branches, WHICH ARE THE SEVENTY MINISTERS, THE SECRET OF THE SEVENTY PALM TREES. And it all resembles that which is above.

395. בְּהַהִיא שַׁעֲתָא, נָטִיף טַלָּא קַדִּישָׁא, מֵעַתִּיקָא סְתִימָאָה, וּמַלְיָא לְרֵישֵׁיהּ דִּזְעֵיר אַנְפִּין, אֲתָר דְּאִקְרֵי שָׁמַיִם. וּמֵהַהוּא טַלָּא דִּנְהוֹרָא עִלָּאָה קַדִּישָׁא, הֲוָה נָגִיד וְנָחִית מְנָא לְתַתָּא. וְכַד הֲוָה נָחִית, הֲוָה

מִתְפְּרַשׁ גְּלִידִין גְּלִידִין, וְאַקְרִישׁ לְתַתָּא. הֲדָא הוּא דִּכְתִּיב דַּק כַּכְּפוֹר עַל הָאָרֶץ.

395. At that time, the holy dew, MEANING THE ABUNDANT FLOW THAT IS CALLED 'DEW', drips from the concealed Atika, WHICH IS KETER, and fills the head of Zeir Anpin, the place that is called 'heaven'. From that dew of the supernal holy Light was the manna drawn and descended below. And when it descended, it spread like flakes of layered ice and congealed below. This is what is written: "As fine as the hoar frost on the ground" (Shemot 16:14).

396. כָּל אִינּוּן בְּנֵי מְהֵימָנוּתָא, נַפְקֵי וְלַקְטֵי, וּמְבָרְכָאן שְׁמָא קַדִּישָׁא עָלֵיהּ. וְהַהוּא מְנָא, הֲוָה סָלִיק רֵיחִין דְּכָל בּוּסְמִין דְּגִנְתָּא דְּעֵדֶן, דְּהָא בֵּיהּ אִתְמְשַׁךְ וְנָחִית לְתַתָּא. שַׁוְיֵהּ לְקַמֵּיהּ, בְּכָל טַעֲמָא דְּאִיהוּ בָּעֵי, הָכִי טָעִים לֵיהּ, וּמְבָרֵךְ לְמַלְכָּא קַדִּישָׁא עִלָּאָה.

396. All these people of Faith would go out and gather and bless the Holy Name over it. And the manna emitted fragrances of all the spices of the Garden of Eden, because they were drawn into it and descended below. And when one placed it before him, he tasted in it any taste he desired, and blessed the Supernal Holy King.

397. וּכְדֵין מִתְבָּרֵךְ בְּמֵעוֹי, וַהֲוָה מִסְתַּכֵּל וְיָדַע לְעֵילָּא, וְאִסְתָּכֵי בְּחָכְמָה עִלָּאָה, וְעַל דָּא אִקְרוּן דּוֹר דֵּעָה. וְאִלֵּין הֲווֹ בְּנֵי מְהֵימָנוּתָא, וּלְהוֹן אִתְיְהִיבַת אוֹרַיְיתָא לְאִסְתַּכְּלָא בָּהּ, וּלְמִנְדַּע אָרְחָהָא.

397. Then THE MANNA was blessed in his intestines, and he would observe closely and have knowledge of the above, to observe the supernal Chochmah. Therefore, they were called 'the Generation of Knowledge'. And these were people of Faith, and the Torah was given to them to gaze into it and to know her ways.

398. וְאִינּוּן דְּלָא אִשְׁתְּכָחוּ בְּנֵי מְהֵימָנוּתָא, מַה כְּתִיב בְּהוּ, שָׁטוּ הָעָם וְלָקְטוּ. מַאי שָׁטוּ. שְׁטוּתָא הֲווֹ נַסְבֵי לְגַרְמַיְיהוּ, בְּגִין דְּלָא הֲווֹ בְּנֵי

מְהֵימָנוּתָא. מַה כְּתִיב בְּהוּ. וְטָחֲנוּ בָרֵחַיִם אוֹ דָכוּ בַּמְּדוֹכָה וְגוֹ'. מַאן אַטְרַח לוֹן כָּל הַאי. אֶלָּא דְּאִינּוּן לָא הֲווֹ בְּנֵי מְהֵימָנוּתָא.

398. Of those who were not faithful, it is written: "And the people went about (Heb. *shatu*), and gathered it" (Bemidbar 11:8). What is "*shatu*"? They selected foolishness (Heb. *shtut*) for themselves because they were not people of Faith. It is written about them: "And ground it in mills, or beat it in mortar..." (Ibid.). Who made them toil so much? This is because they were not people of Faith.

399. כְּגַוְונָא דָא, אִינּוּן דְּלָא מְהֵימְנֵי בֵּיהּ בְּקוּדְשָׁא בְּרִיךְ הוּא, לָא בָּעָאן לְאִסְתַּכְּלָא בְּאָרְחוֹי, וְאִינּוּן בָּעָאן לְאַטְרְחָא גַּרְמַיְיהוּ כָּל יוֹמָא בָּתַר מְזוֹנָא, יְמָמָא וְלֵילֵי, דִּלְמָא לָא סָלִיק בִּידַיְיהוּ פִּתָּא דְּנַהֲמָא. מַאן גָּרִים לוֹן הַאי. בְּגִין דְּלָאו אִינּוּן בְּנֵי מְהֵימָנוּתָא.

399. Similar to this are those who do not have Faith in the Holy One, blessed be He. They do not want to pay attention to His way, and they burden themselves every day after food, days and nights, out of fear that perhaps they will not acquire a loaf of bread. What caused them to do this? It is because they are not people of Faith.

400. אוּף הָכָא, שָׁטוּ וְלָקְטוּ, שָׁטוּ בִּשְׁטוּתָא דְּגַרְמַיְיהוּ, וּבָעָאן לְאַטְרְחָא עָלֵיהּ, הֲדָא הוּא דִּכְתִּיב, וְטָחֲנוּ בָרֵחַיִם. בָּתַר כָּל טִרְחָא דָא, לָא סָלִיק בִּידַיְיהוּ, אֶלָּא דִּכְתִּיב וְהָיָה טַעְמוֹ כְּטַעַם לְשַׁד הַשָּׁמֶן. וְלָא יַתִּיר. מַאן גָּרִים לוֹן הַאי, בְּגִין דְּלָא הֲווֹ בְּנֵי מְהֵימָנוּתָא.

400. Here also, the people "went about, and gathered" in their own foolishness. And they wanted to toil over it. This is what is written: "And ground it in mills." And after all this work, they were not successful, as is written: "And the taste of it was like the taste of oil cake" (Ibid.), and no more. What caused this for them? It is because they were not people of Faith.

401. אָמַר רִבִּי יוֹסֵי, מַאי לְשַׁד הַשָּׁמֶן. אִיכָּא דְּאַמְרֵי, דְּלִישׁ בְּמִשְׁחָא,

כְּתַרְגּוּמוֹ. וְאִיכָּא דְּאַמְרֵי, מַה הַשָּׁד אִתְהֲדָר לְכַמָּה גַּוְונִין, אוּף מָנָא, אִתְהֲדָר לְכַמָּה גַּוְונִין. רִבִּי יְהוּדָה אָמַר, לְשַׁד הַשָּׁמֶן, יְנִיקָא דְּמִשְׁחָא.

401. Rabbi Yosi asked: What is "an oil (Heb. *leshad*) cake?" Some say that it was kneaded in oil, according to its Aramaic translation. And some say that as a demon (Heb. *shed*) changes to many modes, so does the manna change to many tastes, MEANING THAT THEY TASTED EVERY TASTE THEY WANTED IN IT. Rabbi Yehuda said: "An oil cake" MEANS nourishment from oil.

402. רִבִּי יִצְחָק אָמַר, אִישׁ לְפִי אָכְלוֹ לָקָטוּ. וְכִי מַאן דְּאָכִיל קִמְעָא, לָקִיט קִמְעָא, וּמַאן דְּאָכִיל יַתִּיר, לָקִיט יַתִּיר, וְהָא כְּתִיב לֹא הֶעְדִּיף הַמַּרְבֶּה וְהַמַּמְעִיט לֹא הֶחְסִיר. אֶלָּא לְפוּם אִינּוּן דְּאַכְלִין לַקְטִין. מַשְׁמַע אָכְלוֹ, מַאן דַּהֲוָה אָכִיל לֵיהּ, וּבְגִינֵי כָּךְ לָא כְּתִיב אֲכִילָתוֹ.

402. Rabbi Yitzchak said: "They gathered every man according to his eating" (Shemot 16:21). HE ASKS: Does that mean that one who ate a little gathered a little, and one who ate more gathered more? Yet is it not written: "He that gathered much had nothing over, and he that gathered little had no lack"? HE ANSWERS: Rather, they gathered according to the eaters. This is understood FROM THE WORDS "his eating," MEANING, according to the number of eaters, and therefore it is not written, 'EACH MAN ACCORDING TO what he can eat'.

403. מַאי קָא מַיְירֵי. אָחִיד בַּר נָשׁ בְּעַבְדָּא, אוֹ בְּאַמְתָא, וְאָמַר דְּהוּא דִּילֵיהּ. אָתָא חַבְרֵיהּ, וְאָמַר, הַאי עַבְדָּא דִּילִי הוּא. קְרִיבוּ לְקַמֵּיהּ דְּמֹשֶׁה לְדִינָא, אָמַר לוֹן כַּמָּה נַפְשָׁאן בְּבֵיתָךְ, וְכַמָּה נַפְשָׁאן בְּבֵיתֵיהּ דְּדֵין, אָמַר כַּךְ וְכָךְ. וְהַהוּא שַׁעֲתָא אָמַר לוֹן מֹשֶׁה, לָקָטוּ מָחָר, וְכָל חַד מְנַּיְיכוּ יֵיתֵי לְגַבָּאי. לְמָחָר, נָפְקוּ וְלָקְטוּ, וְאַתְיָין קָמֵי מֹשֶׁה, שַׁוְויָין קָמֵיהּ מְנָא, הֲוָה מָדִיד לֵיהּ. אִי הַהוּא עַבְדָּא דְּדֵין, אַשְׁכַּח הַהוּא עוֹמְרָא דְּעַבְדָּא, בְּהַאי מְנָא. דְּהָא חַד עוֹמְרָא לְכָל נֶפֶשׁ וְנֶפֶשׁ מִבֵּיתֵיהּ. מָדִיד לְדֵין, וְאִשְׁתְּכַח חַסְרָא, הַהוּא מֵיכְלָא דְּעַבְדָּא, בְּהַהוּא מָנָא

דִּילֵיהּ, וְחַד עוֹמְרָא לְכָל נֶפֶשׁ וְנֶפֶשׁ מִבֵּיתֵיהּ. אָמַר עַבְדָּא דְּדֵין הוּא, הה״ד אִישׁ לְפִי אָכְלוֹ לָקָטוּ וּכְתִיב עֹמֶר לַגֻּלְגֹּלֶת מִסְפַּר נַפְשֹׁתֵיכֶם.

403. HE ASKS: What does this, THAT EACH ONE GATHERED ACCORDING TO THE AMOUNT OF EATERS, teach us? HE ANSWERS: If someone held a servant or maid servant, and said: He is mine, and his neighbor came and said: He is mine, they would approach Moses for judgments. He would say to them: How many people are there in your house and how many people are in the other's house. They would say the number. Then Moses would say to them: Gather tomorrow, and afterwards both of you come before me. The next day they would go out and gather and then go before Moses. They would place before him a vessel, which he would measure. If that servant was the owner's, then the portion of the servant would be in that vessel, because there was one *Omer* measured for each person of his household. He would measure for the other and would find that the food portion of the servant was lacking in his vessel, and there was one *Omer* for each person in his household. THEN he would say: The servant belongs to this one. This is what is meant by: "They gathered every man according to his eating," and it: "An *Omer* for every man, according to the number of your persons."

404. אָמַר ר׳ יֵיסָא, כְּתִיב, עֶרֶב וִידַעְתֶּם כִּי יְיָ׳ הוֹצִיא אֶתְכֶם מֵאֶרֶץ מִצְרַיִם וּבֹקֶר וּרְאִיתֶם אֶת כְּבוֹד יְיָ׳. עֶרֶב וִידַעְתֶּם, בְּמַאי יִנְדְּעוּן. אֶלָּא הָכִי תָּאנָא, בְּכָל יוֹמָא וְיוֹמָא אִשְׁתְּכָחוּ נִימוּסֵי קוּדְשָׁא בְּרִיךְ הוּא, בְּצַפְרָא, אִתְּעַר חֶסֶד בְּעָלְמָא. בְּהַהוּא זִמְנָא דְּאִקְרֵי עֶרֶב, תַּלְיָא דִּינָא בְּעָלְמָא, וְהָא אוּקְמוּהָ, דִּבְגִינֵי כַּךְ, יִצְחָק תִּקֵּן תְּפִלַּת הַמִּנְחָה. וְעַל דָּא, עֶרֶב וִידַעְתֶּם, כַּד אִתְּעַר דִּינָא בְּעָלְמָא, תִּנְדְּעוּן, דִּבְהַהוּא דִּינָא אַפִּיק יְיָ׳ יַתְכוֹן מִמִּצְרַיִם. וּבֹקֶר וּרְאִיתֶם אֶת כְּבוֹד יְיָ׳ דְּהָא בְּהַהוּא זִמְנָא אִתְּעַר חֶסֶד בְּעָלְמָא וְיִתֵּן לְכוּ לְמֵיכַל.

404. Rabbi Yisa said: It is written, "At evening you shall know that Hashem has brought you out from the land of Egypt. And in the morning, you shall see the glory of Hashem" (Shemot 16:6-7). HE ASKS: "At evening you shall know." How will they know? HE ANSWERS: We have learned that every single day the laws of the Holy One, blessed be He, abide. In the morning, Chesed is roused in the world. And at the time that is called evening,

Judgment is suspended over the world. As we have established, Isaac instituted the Minchah (Afternoon Prayer,) AND ISAAC IS GVURAH. Therefore, "At evening you shall know," when Judgment is aroused over the world, you will know that with this Judgment Hashem has brought you out of Egypt. "And in the morning, you shall see the glory of Hashem," because at that time Chesed is aroused over the world, and He will give you nourishment.

405. ר׳ חִיָּיא אָמַר אִיפְּכָא, מַה כְּתִיב לְעֵילָּא, בְּשִׁבְתֵּנוּ עַל סִיר הַבָּשָׂר וְגוֹ׳. בֵּיהּ שַׁעֲתָא, אִתְּעַר עֶרֶב, דְּהַהוּא זִמְנָא דְּאִתְּעַר דִּינָא, אִתְּעַר נָמֵי חֶסֶד בְּעָלְמָא. הה״ד, וִידַעְתֶּם כִּי יְיָ׳ הוֹצִיא אֶתְכֶם מֵאֶרֶץ מִצְרָיִם. תִּנְדְּעוּן הַהוּא חֶסֶד דְּעָבֵד עִמְּכוֹן, בִּזְמְנָא דְּדִינָא וְאַפִּיק יַתְכוֹן מֵאַרְעָא דְּמִצְרַיִם. וּבֹקֶר וּרְאִיתֶם אֶת כְּבוֹד יְיָ׳, כְּבוֹד יְיָ׳ הָא יְדִיעַ. וכ״כ לָמָּה. בְּשָׁמְעוֹ יְיָ׳ אֶת תְּלֻנּוֹתֵיכֶם וְגוֹ׳.

405. Rabbi Chiya said: It is the opposite of what is written before, "When we sat by the flesh pots..." (Ibid. 3). At that moment, evening was awakened, NAMELY JUDGMENT. And at the time that Judgment was provoked, Chesed was also aroused in the world. This is what is written: "You shall know that Hashem has brought you out from the land of Egypt." You will know the Chesed that He performed by you during the time of Judgment, and that He brought you out of the land of Egypt, "and in the morning, you shall see the glory of Hashem." The glory of Hashem is already known TO BE MALCHUT. And why all this? Because "when Hashem hears your murmuring..." (Ibid. 8).

406. אָמַר ר׳ יֵיסָא, לָא שָׁנֵי קוּדְשָׁא בְּרִיךְ הוּא נִימוּסוֹי, בַּר דְּאִינּוּן חַיָּיבֵי עָלְמָא שַׁנְיָין לוֹן, וּמְהַפְּכֵי רַחֲמֵי לְדִינָא, כְּמָה דְּאִתְּמַר.

406. Rabbi Yesa said: The Holy One, blessed be He, did not change His laws SO THAT CHESED WOULD ILLUMINATE IN THE EVENING, AS RABBI CHIYA SAID. Only those wicked people of the world changed and turned Mercy into Judgment, as we learned.

407. תָּאנֵי ר׳ אֶלְעָזָר, מֵהַאי מָנָא זְמִינִין צַדִּיקַיָּיא לְמֵיכַל לְעָלְמָא

דְּאָתֵי, וְאִי תֵּימָא בְּהַאי גַּוְונָא. לָא. אֶלָּא יַתִּיר, דְּלָא הֲוָה כֵּן לְעָלְמִין. מַאי אִיהוּ. כְּמָה דְּאוֹקִימְנָא דִּכְתִּיב לַחֲזוֹת בְּנֹעַם יְיָ׳ וּלְבַקֵּר בְּהֵיכָלוֹ. וּכְתִיב עַיִן לֹא רָאָתָה אֱלֹהִים זוּלָתְךָ וְגוֹ׳.

407. Rabbi Elazar taught that the Righteous shall eat of that manna in the World to Come. And if you think that it is in that same manner THAT THE CHILDREN OF YISRAEL ATE IN THE WILDERNESS, it is not so, but rather more THAN THEY, in SUCH PERFECTION that never existed. What is it? It is as we have established, "to behold the pleasantness of Hashem, and to inquire in His temple" (Tehilim 27:4), and: "Neither has the eye seen, that an Elohim, beside You" (Yeshayah 64:3).

408. רְאוּ כִּי יְיָ׳ נָתַן לָכֶם הַשַּׁבָּת. ר׳ חִזְקִיָּה פָּתַח שִׁיר הַמַּעֲלוֹת מִמַּעֲמַקִּים קְרָאתִיךָ יְיָ׳. שִׁיר הַמַּעֲלוֹת סָתַם, וְלָא פָּרִישׁ מַאן אָמָרוּ. אֶלָּא שִׁיר הַמַּעֲלוֹת, דִּזְמִינִין כָּל בְּנֵי עָלְמָא לְמֵימַר, דְּזַמִּין הַאי שִׁיר לְמֵימְרֵיהּ לְדָרֵי עָלְמָא.

408. "See, that Hashem has given you the Shabbat" (Shemot 16:29). Rabbi Chizkiyah opened the discussion, saying: "A song of ascents, out of the depths I have cried to You, Hashem" (Tehilim 130:1). HE ASKS: "A song of ascents," is unspecified, it does not explicitly reveal who says it. HE ANSWERS: But, "A song of ascents," MEANS that all the inhabitants of the world will eventually say this, because this song will be said for eternal generations.

409. וּמַאי הוּא מִמַּעֲמַקִּים קְרָאתִיךָ. הָכִי תָּאנָא, כָּל מַאן דִּמְצַלֵּי צְלוֹתָא קָמֵי מַלְכָּא קַדִּישָׁא, בָּעֵי לְמִבְעֵי בָּעוּתֵיהּ, וּלְצַלָּאָה מֵעִמְקָא דְּלִבָּא, בְּגִין דְּיִשְׁתְּכַח לִבֵּיהּ שְׁלִים בְּקוּדְשָׁא בְּרִיךְ הוּא, וִיכַוֵּין לִבָּא וּרְעוּתָא. וּמִי אָמַר דָּוִד הָכִי, וְהָא כְּתִיב, בְּכָל לִבִּי דְּרַשְׁתִּיךָ. וְדָא קְרָא סַגִּי, מַאי בָּעֵי מִמַּעֲמַקִּים.

409. HE ASKS: What is THE MEANING OF, "Out of the depths I have cried to you"? HE ANSWERS: So have we learned. Everyone who prays his prayer before the Holy King must ask for his requests and pray from the depth of his heart, in order that his heart is completely with the Holy One, blessed be He. Thus, he should concentrate his heart and desire. THIS IS THE MEANING OF, "OUT OF THE DEPTHS I HAVE CRIED TO YOU." HE ASKS: Did David say it this way? Is it not written, "With my whole heart I have sought You" (Tehilim 119:10)? And this passage is sufficient, THAT IS, TO PRAY WITH THE WHOLE HEART. Why is, "out of the depths," necessary?

410. אֶלָּא הָכִי תָּאנָא, כָּל בַּר נָשׁ דְּבָעֵי בָּעוּתֵיהּ קָמֵי מַלְכָּא, בָּעֵי לְכַוְּונָא דַּעְתָּא וּרְעוּתָא, מֵעִיקָּרָא דְּכָל עִקָּרִין, לְאַמְשָׁכָא בִּרְכָּאן מֵעִמְקָא דְּבֵירָא, בְּגִין דְּיִנְגִּיד בִּרְכָּאן מִמַּבּוּעָא דְּכֹלָּא. וּמַאי הוּא. הַהוּא אֲתָר דְּנָפִיק מִנֵּיהּ, וְאִשְׁתְּכַח מִנֵּיהּ, הַהוּא נָהָר, דִּכְתִּיב וְנָהָר יוֹצֵא מֵעֵדֶן. וּכְתִיב נָהָר פְּלָגָיו יְשַׂמְּחוּ עִיר אֱלֹהִים. וְדָא אִקְרֵי מִמַּעֲמַקִּים. עִמְקָא דְּכֹלָּא, עִמְקָא דְּבֵירָא, דְּמַבּוּעִין נָפְקִין וְנַגְדִּין לְבָרְכָא כֹּלָּא. וְדָא הוּא שֵׁרוּתָא לְאַמְשָׁכָא בִּרְכָּאן מֵעֵילָּא לְתַתָּא.

410. HE ANSWERS: We learned, every person who makes his request before the King must concentrate his mind and desire on the source of all sources, to draw blessings from the depth of the pit, in order that blessings shall flow from the wellspring of all. And what is it? It is at that place from where that river, WHICH IS CONCEALED CHOCHMAH, emerges and comes forth, as is written: "And a river went out of Eden" (Beresheet 2:10). FOR EDEN IS CHOCHMAH, AND RIVER IS BINAH, NAMELY BINAH THAT CAME OUT OF THE TOP OF ARICH ANPIN, WHICH IS CONCEALED CHOCHMAH. And it is written: "There is a river, whose streams make glad the city of Elohim" (Tehilim 46:5), and this is called "out of the depths." The depth of all, the depth of the pit from which springs emerge and are drawn to bless all. This is the beginning of drawing blessings downward from above.

411. א"ר חִזְקִיָּה, כַּד עַתִּיקָא סְתִימָאָה דְּכָל סְתִימִין, בָּעֵי לְזִמְנָא בִּרְכָּאן לְעָלְמִין, אַשְׁרֵי כֹּלָּא, וְאַכְלִיל כֹּלָּא, בְּהַאי עֲמִיקָא עִלָּאָה, וּמֵהָכָא שָׁאִיב וְאִתְנְגִיד נָהֲרָא דְּנַחֲלִין וּמַבּוּעִין אִתְנְגִידוּ מִנֵּיהּ, וּמִתְשַׁקְיָין מִנֵּיהּ כֻּלְּהוּ. וּמַאן דִּמְצַלֵּי צְלוֹתֵיהּ, בָּעֵי לְכַוְּונָא לִבָּא

וּרְעוּתָא, לְאַמְשָׁכָא בִּרְכָּאן מֵהַהוּא עֲמִיקָא דְּכֹלָּא, בְּגִין דְּיִתְקַבַּל צְלוֹתֵיהּ, וְיִתְעֲבִיד רְעוּתֵיהּ.

411. Rabbi Chizkiyah explains HIS WORDS: When the most concealed Atik desires to bring blessings for the world, He places and includes everything in that supreme depth, WHICH IS CONCEALED CHOCHMAH OF ARICH ANPIN, OF THE ASPECT OF BINAH EMERGING OUT OF IT. And from here a river, WHICH IS BINAH, is draws and flows, and rivers and wellsprings emerge from it, WHICH ARE THE MOCHIN. And everything is watered from it. FOR ALL THE MOCHIN OF THE MALE AND THE FEMALE AND BRIYAH, YETZIRAH, AND ASIYAH ARE DRAWN FROM THERE. And whoever says his prayer must concentrate his heart and desire to draw blessings from this depth of all, in order that his prayer is accepted and his desire is carried out.

412. וַיֹּאמֶר מֹשֶׁה אֲלֵיהֶם אִישׁ אַל יוֹתֵר מִמֶּנּוּ עַד בֹּקֶר. א״ר יְהוּדָה, בְּכָל יוֹמָא וְיוֹמָא, מִתְבָּרֵךְ עָלְמָא מֵהַהוּא יוֹמָא עִלָּאָה, דְּהָא כָּל שִׁיתָּא יוֹמִין מִתְבָּרְכָאן מִיּוֹמָא שְׁבִיעָאָה. וְכָל יוֹמָא יָהִיב מֵהַהוּא בִּרְכָה דְּקַבִּיל בְּהַהוּא יוֹמָא דִּילֵיהּ.

412. "And Moses said to them, 'Let no man leave of it till morning'" (Shemot 16:19). Rabbi Yehuda said: Every single day, the world is blessed from that supernal day, for all the six days are blessed from the seventh day. And every day gives from that blessing that it receives on its own day.

413. וְע״ד מֹשֶׁה אָמַר, אִישׁ אַל יוֹתֵר מִמֶּנּוּ עַד בֹּקֶר. מ״ט. בְּגִין דְּלָא יָהִיב, וְלָא יוֹזִיף יוֹמָא דָּא לְחַבְרֵיהּ, אֶלָּא כָּל חַד וְחַד שָׁלִיט בִּלְחוֹדוֹי, בְּהַהוּא יוֹמָא דִּילֵיהּ. דְּהָא לָא שָׁלִיט יוֹמָא בְּיוֹמָא דְּחַבְרֵיהּ.

413. Therefore Moses said: "Let no man leave of it till morning." What is the reason? Because one day does not borrow or give to another. Rather, each one reigns exclusively, alone in its day, because one day can not reign in the day of its neighbor.

414. בְּגִינֵי כַּךְ, כָּל אִינּוּן חֲמִשָּׁא יוֹמִין שַׁלִּיטִין בְּיוֹמַיְיהוּ, וְאִשְׁתְּכַח

בֵּיהּ, מַה דְקַבִּילוּ, וְיוֹמָא שְׁתִיתָאָה אִשְׁתְּכַח בֵּיהּ יַתִּיר. וְאַזְלָא הָא, כְּהָא דְּאָמַר רִבִּי אֶלְעָזָר, מַאי דִּכְתִּיב יוֹם הַשִּׁשִּׁי, וְלָא אִתְּמַר הָכִי בְּכָל שְׁאַר יוֹמִין. אֶלָּא הָכִי אוּקְמוּהָ, הַשִּׁשִּׁי. דְּאִזְדַּוְּוגָא בֵּיהּ מַטְרוֹנִיתָא. לְאַתְקְנָא פָּתוֹרָא לְמַלְכָּא, ובג״כ, אִשְׁתְּכָחוּ בֵּיהּ תְּרֵין חוּלָקִין, חַד לְיוֹמֵיהּ, וְחַד לְתִקּוּנָא, בְּחֶדְוָותָא דְּמַלְכָּא בְּמַטְרוֹנִיתָא.

414. Therefore, all these five days reign on their respective days, and that which they received is available in them. The sixth day contains more, and this is according to what Rabbi Elazar said: It is written, "the sixth day," WITH THE DEFINITE ARTICLE (=*HEI*), which is not written of the other days. But this is the way they established it. "The sixth day," WITH A *HEI*, shows that the Queen is joined with it, WHO IS CALLED *HEI*, WHICH IS MALCHUT, to prepare the table for the King. Therefore, it has two parts, one from the day itself and one from establishing the joy of the King with the Queen.

415. וְהַהוּא לֵילְיָא, חֶדְוָותָא דְּמַטְרוֹנִיתָא בְּמַלְכָּא, וְזִוּוּגָא דִּלְהוֹן, וּמִתְבָּרְכָאן כָּל שִׁיתָא יוֹמִין, כָּל חַד וְחַד בִּלְחוֹדוֹי. בְּגִין כָּךְ, בָּעֵי בַּר נָשׁ לְסַדְּרָא פָּתוֹרֵיהּ בְּלֵילְיָא דְּשַׁבְּתָא, בְּגִין דְּשָׁארִי עֲלֵיהּ בִּרְכָּאן מִלְּעֵילָּא, וּבִרְכְּתָא לָא אִשְׁתְּכַח עַל פָּתוֹרָא רֵיקַנְיָא, בג״כ, ת״ח דְּיַדְעִין רָזָא דָּא, זִוּוּגָא דִּלְהוֹן מע״ש לע״ש.

415. That night is the joy of the Queen with the King and their uniting, and all the six days are blessed, each one on its own. Therefore, a person must prepare his table on Shabbat night so that blessings from above will dwell upon him, and a blessing is not present on an empty table. Therefore, scholars who know this secret mate only on Shabbat nights.

416. רְאוּ כִּי יְיָ׳ נָתַן לָכֶם הַשַּׁבָּת, מַאי שַׁבָּת. יוֹמָא דְּבֵיהּ נַיְיחִין שְׁאַר יוֹמִין, וְהוּא כְּלָלָא דְּכָל אִינּוּן שִׁיתָא אַחֲרָנִין, וּמִנֵּיהּ מִתְבָּרְכִין. רִבִּי יֵיסָא אָמַר, וְכֵן נָמֵי כְּנֶסֶת יִשְׂרָאֵל אִקְרֵי שַׁבָּת, בְּגִין דְּאִיהִי בַּת זוּגוֹ, וְדָא הִיא כַּלָּה. דִּכְתִּיב וּשְׁמַרְתֶּם אֶת הַשַּׁבָּת כִּי קֹדֶשׁ הִיא לָכֶם. לָכֶם וְלָא לִשְׁאַר עַמִּין, הה״ד בֵּינִי וּבֵין בְּנֵי יִשְׂרָאֵל. וְדָא הִיא אַחֲסָנַת

יְרוּתַת עָלְמִין לְיִשְׂרָאֵל. וְע״ד, כְּתִיב אִם תָּשִׁיב מִשַּׁבָּת רַגְלֶךָ וְגו׳ וּבְאַתְרֵיהּ אוּקִימְנָא מִלֵּי.

416. "See, that Hashem has given you the Shabbat." HE ASKS: What is Shabbat? HE ANSWERS: That is the day in which the other days rest. And it is the inclusion of all the other six days, and from it are they blessed. Rabbi Yisa said: The Congregation of Yisrael is also called 'Shabbat', for she is the spouse OF SHABBAT, and a bride, as is written: "You shall keep the Shabbat therefore, for it is holy to you" (Shemot 31:14). To you and not to the other nations. This is what is meant by: "Between Me and the children of Yisrael" (Ibid. 17). This portion is an eternal heritage of Yisrael; thus it is written: "If you restrain your foot because of Shabbat..." (Yeshayah 58:13). And we explained the matter where we discussed it.

417. כְּתִיב אַל יֵצֵא אִישׁ מִמְּקוֹמוֹ בַּיּוֹם הַשְּׁבִיעִי. מִמְּקוֹמוֹ. תָּנֵינָן, מֵהַהוּא מָקוֹם דְּאִתְחָזֵי לְמֵהַךְ. וְרָזָא דְּמִלָּה דִּכְתִּיב, בָּרוּךְ כְּבוֹד יְיָ׳ מִמְּקוֹמוֹ, וְדָא אִיהוּ מָקוֹם. וְדָא אִיהוּ רָזָא דִּכְתִּיב, כִּי הַמָּקוֹם אֲשֶׁר אַתָּה עוֹמֵד עָלָיו אַדְמַת קֹדֶשׁ הוּא. אֲתָר יְדִיעָא קָרֵינָן לֵיהּ מָקוֹם דְּאִשְׁתְּמוֹדְעָא יְקָרָא עִלָּאָה.

417. It is written: "Let no man go out of his place on the seventh day…" We learned that ITS MEANING IS from the place that is proper to go, MEANING OUT OF THE CITY. And the secret of the matter is, "Blessed be the glory of Hashem from his place" (Yechezkel 3:12), WHICH IS MALCHUT, and this is the place. This is the secret of what is written: "For the place on which you stand is holy ground" (Shemot 3:5). It is the known area that is called "place," which is known by the supernal glory, NAMELY MALCHUT.

418. וּבְגִין כַּךְ, אַזְהָרוּתָא לְבַר נָשׁ, דְּקָא מִתְעַטְּרָא בְּעִטּוּרָא קַדִּישָׁא דִּלְעֵילָּא, דְּלָא יִפּוּק מִנֵּיהּ בְּפוּמֵיהּ מִלּוּלָא דְּחוֹל, בְּגִין דְּאִי יִפּוּק מִנֵּיהּ, קָא מְחַלֵּל יוֹמָא דְּשַׁבְּתָא, בִּידוֹי בְּעוֹבַדְתָּא. בְּרַגְלוֹי, לְמֵהַךְ לְבַר מִתְּרֵין אַלְפִּין אַמִּין. כָּל אִלֵּין חִלּוּלָא דְּשַׁבְּתָא אִינּוּן.

418. Therefore, it is an admonition to the person who adorns himself with the holy crown of above ON THE SHABBAT DAY. From his mouth secular talk should not emerge, because if SECULAR TALK does emerge, he desecrates the Shabbat day. DESECRATING THE SHABBAT WITH THE HANDS is done by doing work; with his feet is by going out of the specified 2,000 cubits. All these are a desecration of the Shabbat.

419. אַל יֵצֵא אִישׁ מִמְּקוֹמוֹ, דָּא אִיהוּ אֲתָר יַקִּירָא דִּקְדוּשָּׁה, דְּהָא לְבַר מִנֵּיהּ, אֱלֹהִים אֲחֵרִים נִינְהוּ. בָּרוּךְ כְּבוֹד יְיָ׳, דָּא כָּבוֹד דִּלְעֵילָּא. מִמְּקוֹמוֹ, דָּא כָּבוֹד דִּלְתַתָּא. דָּא אִיהוּ רָזָא דַּעֲטָרָא דְּשַׁבָּת, בְּגִין כַּךְ אַל יֵצֵא אִישׁ מִמְּקוֹמוֹ. זַכָּאָה חוּלָקֵיהּ מַאן דְּזָכֵי לִיקָרָא דְּשַׁבְּתָא זַכָּאָה אִיהוּ בְּעָלְמָא דֵּין וּבְעָלְמָא דְּאָתֵי.

419. "Let no man go out of his place." This is the precious place of Holiness, because outside of it, there are other Elohim. "Blessed be the glory of Hashem." is the glory of above, NAMELY MALCHUT FROM THE CHEST AND ABOVE. "From his place," is the glory of below, NAMELY MALCHUT FROM THE CHEST AND BELOW. This is the secret of the crown of the Shabbat, WHICH IS CALLED 'PLACE'. Therefore, a person should not go out from his place, BECAUSE OUTSIDE OF IT ARE OTHER ELOHIM. Blessed is the portion of one who has merited the splendors of the Shabbat.

30. the Holy One, blessed be He, avenges the honor of the righteous

A Synopsis

This section tells of cases where the Holy One, blessed be He did not punish someone who blasphemed against Him, but punished them when they oppressed the children of Yisrael, because the Holy One, blessed be He cares more for the honor of the Righteous than for His own honor. Rabbi Chiya says that when Moses said "They are almost ready to stone me," God told him to go before the people; he asked Moses if it was with their permission that Moses stood, or with the permission of Himself.

420. וַיֹּאמֶר יְיָ' אֶל מֹשֶׁה עֲבוֹר לִפְנֵי הָעָם וְגוֹ'. רִבִּי חִיָּיא פָּתַח, חוֹנֶה מַלְאַךְ יְיָ' סָבִיב לִירֵאָיו וַיְחַלְּצֵם. זַכָּאִין אִינּוּן צַדִּיקַיָּיא, דְּקוּדְשָׁא בְּרִיךְ הוּא אִתְרְעֵי בִּיקָרֵיהוֹן, יַתִּיר עַל דִּילֵיהּ. תָּא חֲזֵי, כַּמָּה אִינּוּן בְּנֵי עָלְמָא, דִּמְחָרְפֵי וּמְגַדְּפֵי לְעֵילָּא, כְּגוֹן סַנְחֵרִיב חֵרֵף וְגִדֵּף, וְאָמַר מִי בְּכָל אֱלֹהֵי הָאֲרָצוֹת וְגוֹ'. וְקוּדְשָׁא בְּרִיךְ הוּא מָחִיל, וְלָא תָּבַע מִנֵּיהּ. כֵּיוָן דְּאוֹשִׁיט יְדֵיהּ עַל חִזְקִיָּה, מַה כְּתִיב וַיֵּצֵא מַלְאַךְ יְיָ' וַיַּךְ בְּמַחֲנֵה אַשּׁוּר וְגוֹ'.

420. "And Hashem said to Moses, 'Pass before the people...'" (Shemot 17:5). Rabbi Chiya opened the discussion, saying: "The angel of Hashem encamps round about those who fear Him, and He delivers them" (Tehilim 34:8). Blessed are the Righteous, for the Holy One, blessed be He, cares about their honor more than His own. Come and behold: how many people in the world revile and blaspheme towards above, like Sancheriv who reviled and blasphemed, saying, "Which of all Elohim of the countries…" (II Melachim, 18:35). And the Holy One, blessed be He, forgave and did not order to punish him. As soon as he stretched out his hand against Chizkiyah, it is written "that the angel of Hashem went out and smote in the camp of Ashur (Assyria)..." (II Melachim 19:35).

421. יָרָבְעָם בֶּן נְבָט הֲוָה פָּלַח לע"ז, וּמְקַטַּר לָהּ, וּמְזַבַּח לָהּ, וְקוּדְשָׁא בְּרִיךְ הוּא לָא תָּבַע מִנֵּיהּ. וְכַד אָתָא עִדּוֹ נְבִיאָה, וְאִתְנַבֵּי עָלֵיהּ, וְאוֹשִׁיט יָרָבְעָם יְדָא לְקַבְלֵיהּ, מַה כְּתִיב וַתִּיבַשׁ יָדוֹ וְגוֹ', וְלֹא יָכֹל

לַהֲשִׁיבָהּ אֵלָיו.

421. Jerobaam, the son of Nevat, worshipped idols, sacrificed to them, and offered to them, yet the Holy One, blessed be He, did not order to punish him. But when Ido the prophet came and prophesied against Him, and Jerobaam stretched out his hand against him, it is written: "And his hand...dried up, so that he could not draw it back to him" (I Melachim 13:4).

422. פַּרְעֹה חֵרֵף וְגִדֵּף, וְאָמַר מִי יְיָ׳ וְגוֹ׳. וְקוּדְשָׁא בְּרִיךְ הוּא לָא תָּבַע מִנֵּיהּ, עַד דְּסָרִיב בְּהוּ בְּיִשְׂרָאֵל, דִּכְתִּיב עוֹדְךָ מִסְתּוֹלֵל בְּעַמִּי. הִנֵּה יַד יְיָ׳ הוֹיָה בְּמִקְנְךָ וְגוֹ׳, וְכֵן בְּכָל אֲתָר, קוּדְשָׁא בְּרִיךְ הוּא תָּבַע עֶלְבּוֹנָא דְּצַדִּיקַיָּיא יַתִּיר עַל דִּילֵיהּ.

422. Pharaoh reviled and blasphemed and said: "Who is Hashem" (Shemot 5:2). Yet the Holy One, blessed be He, did not punish him until he refused to send out Yisrael, as is written: "If as yet you do exalt yourself against My people" (Shemot 9:17). "FOR IF YOU REFUSE TO LET THEM GO, behold, the hand of Hashem is upon the cattle" (Ibid. 2-3). So the Holy One, blessed be He, always avenges the honor of the righteous more than His own.

423. הָכָא מֹשֶׁה, אָמַר עוֹד מְעַט וּסְקָלוּנִי, אָמַר לֵיהּ קוּדְשָׁא בְּרִיךְ הוּא, מֹשֶׁה לָאו עִידָּן הוּא לְמִתְבַּע עֶלְבּוֹנָךְ, אֶלָּא עֲבוֹר לִפְנֵי הָעָם, וְאַחְמֵי מַאן יוֹשִׁיט יְדוֹי לְקַבְלָךְ, וְכִי בִּרְשׁוּתַיְיהוּ אַתְּ קָאֵים, אוֹ בִּרְשׁוּתִי.

423. Here Moses said: "They are almost ready to stone me" (Shemot 17:4). The Holy One, blessed be He, said to him: Now is not the time to avenge your honor, Moses. Rather, "pass before the people," and we shall see who will stretch out his hand against you. Is it with their permission that you stand or with my permission?!

31. The rock and the boulder

A Synopsis

Rabbi Chiya talks about Moses' rod that was turned into a snake, and the verse, "The way of a snake upon a rock." He says that the rock is Malchut, and the rock is God. Rock always refers to Gvurah, so that when God wants to punish, Gvurah is aroused and punishes. The flow of water in "And you shall smite the rock, and there shall come water out of it" is the flow of Gvurah from the higher to the lower levels, drawn by the Holy Name of God engraved on the rod. Rabbi Aba says there is a supernal Rock and a lower rock that emerges from it. He tells us that wherever 'water' is written it refers to the light of Chesed; it is the sign and miracle of the Holy One, blessed be He that the rock, which is judgment, should inspire the flowing forth of Chassadim. Rabbi Shimon turns to the scripture, "He is the rock, His work is perfect," saying that the rock here is Abraham, who is Chesed. The sins of Yisrael weakened the rock from what it had been originally.

424. וּמַטְּךָ אֲשֶׁר הִכִּיתָ בּוֹ אֶת הַיְאוֹר קַח בְּיָדְךָ וְהָלָכְתָּ. מ״ט. מִשּׁוּם דִּמְחַקֵּק בְּנִסִּין הֲוָה, וּשְׁמָא קַדִּישָׁא עִלָּאָה רְשִׁימָא בֵּיהּ. בְּקַדְמֵיתָא נָחָשׁ, כְּמָה דְּאִתְּמַר, דֶּרֶךְ נָחָשׁ עֲלֵי צוּר. נָחָשׁ, הָא אִתְיְדַע דְּאִתְּעַר צוּר. בְּאָן אֲתָר אִתְגְּלֵי, הָכָא אִתְגְּלֵי דִּכְתִּיב הִנְנִי עוֹמֵד לְפָנֶיךָ שָּׁם עַל הַצּוּר. וּמַאן צוּר. כד״א הַצּוּר תָּמִים פָּעֳלוֹ, וְתַמָּן יָדַע מֹשֶׁה הֵיךְ קָאֵים נָחָשׁ עֲלֵי צוּר. וְהָא אוֹקִימְנָא מִלֵּי.

424. "And your rod, with which you smote the river, take in your hand, and go" (Ibid. 5). What is the reason? Because it was engraved with miracles and the Supernal Holy Name was imprinted on it. At first, THE ROD WAS TURNED INTO a snake, WHICH IS THE SECRET OF YESOD OF ZEIR ANPIN OF SMALLNESS. As we have learned: "The way of a snake upon a rock" (Mishlei 30:19). The snake, it is known, arouses the rock, WHICH IS MALCHUT. In which area was THE HOLY ONE, BLESSED BE HE, revealed? Here He became revealed, as is written: "Behold, I will stand before you there upon the rock" (Shemot 17:6). And who is the rock? It is as written, "He is the rock, His work is perfect" (Devarim 32:4), WHICH IS MALCHUT. Moses realized there how the snake stood by the stone. And we have already explained these matters.

425. אָ"ר יְהוּדָה, אִי לִישְׁתִּיק קְרָא יֵאוֹת שָׁאִילְתָּא. אֶלָּא הָא כְּתִיב, וְהִכִּיתָ בַצּוּר וְיָצְאוּ מִמֶּנּוּ מַיִם. אָמַר לֵיהּ, וַדַּאי הָכִי הוּא, דְּלֵית לָךְ כָּל שְׁמָא וּשְׁמָא, מֵאִינּוּן שְׁמָהָן קַדִּישִׁין דְּקוּדְשָׁא בְּרִיךְ הוּא, דְּלָא עָבֵד נִסִּין וּגְבוּרָאן, וְאַפִּיק כֹּלָּא דְּאִצְטְרִיךְ לְעָלְמָא, כ"ד לְאַפָּקָא הָכָא מַיָּא.

425. Rabbi Yehuda said: If the Torah had remained silent and had not said more, it would be good. But rather, it is written, "And you shall smite the rock, and there shall come water out of it" (Shemot 17:6). IS THIS THE CUSTOM OF THE HOLY NAME? He said to him: Certainly, it is so. For there is no single Name of all the Holy Names of the Holy One, blessed be He, that does not perform miracles and mighty acts, and does not bring forth whatever is necessary for the world, especially to bring forth water here.

426. א"ל, אִי הָכִי, הָא כְּתִיב, הֵן הִכָּה צוּר וַיָּזוּבוּ מַיִם. מַאן מָחֵי לִשְׁמֵיהּ. א"ל, פַּטִּישָׁא חֲרִיפָא, בְּקִטְרוֹי יְדִיעַ, וְאַתְּ שָׁאִיל דָּא. אֶלָּא תָּא חֲזֵי, בְּכָל אֲתָר צוּר גְּבוּרָה, וְכַד בָּעֵי קוּדְשָׁא בְּרִיךְ הוּא לְמַחֲאָה, אוֹ לְאַלְקָאָה, אִתְּעַר גְּבוּרָה דָּא וְהַהוּא גְּבוּרָה מָחֵי וְלָקֵי, וְדָא הוּא דִּכְתִּיב, הֵן הִכָּה צוּר וַיָּזוּבוּ מַיִם. וְאִי לָאו דְּאִתְּעַר צוּר, וְלָקֵי בְּאֲתָר דְּאִצְטְרִיךְ, לָא נַבְיעִין מַיָּא.

426. He said to him: If so, it is written, "He smote the rock, that the waters gushed out" (Tehilim 78:20). Who strikes in His name? He said: It is recognizable from the blows that the hammer is sharp, MEANING A SHARP PERSON KNOWS HOW TO ASK, and you ask this. But come and behold: "rock" always refers to Gvurah, MEANING MALCHUT WHEN SHE IS IN THE ASPECT OF GVURAH. And when the Holy One, blessed be He, WHICH IS ZEIR ANPIN, wants to strike or punish, this Gvurah is aroused and that Gvurah smites and punishes. And this is what is written: "Behold, (he) smote the rock, that the waters gushed out," WHICH MEANS THAT THE ROCK DID SMITE. And if the rock had not been aroused to smite in the necessary place, the water would not have flowed.

427. א"ל, אִי הָכִי, הָא כְּתִיב, צוּר יְלָדְךָ תֶּשִׁי. וְתָנֵינָן מַאי תֶּשִׁי, כְּלוֹמַר חַלָּשְׁתְּ לֵיהּ. א"ל וַדַּאי הָכִי הוּא, דְּאִלְמָלֵי יִנְדְּעוּן חַיָּיבַיָּא,

דְּהַאי צוּר זְמִינָא לְאִתְעָרָא לְקַבְּלַיְיהוּ, וּלְאַלְקָאָה לוֹן, יִמָּנְעוּן מִלְּמֵיחַב קָמֵיהּ, אֶלָּא חַלְשָׁא אִיהִי בְּעֵינַיְיהוּ, הוֹאִיל וְלָא מִסְתַּכְּלֵי בָּהּ, וְלָא מִסְתַּכְּלֵי בְּאָרְחַיְיהוּ, וְעַל דָּא צוּר יְלָדְךָ תֶּשִׁי.

427. He said to him: If so, is it not written: "Of the Rock that begot you you are unmindful" (Devarim 32:18)? What is the meaning of "unmindful?" You weakened it, WHICH CAN NOT HAPPEN BY A NAME. He said to him: It is certainly so. For if the wicked had known that the rock was going to become aroused against them to punish them, they would have refrained from sinning against it. But it was weak in their sight, because they did not look at it, and it did not observe their ways TO PUNISH THEM IMMEDIATELY. And pertaining to this IT IS SAID: "Of the Rock that begot you you are unmindful."

428. ר׳ אַבָּא אָמַר, אִית צוּר, וְאִית צוּר, מִסִּטְרָא דְּצוּר עִלָּאָה, נָפַק צוּר אַחֲרָא. וּמַאי צוּר עִלָּאָה. צוּר דְּכָל צוּרִים. וּמַאי אִיהוּ, הַהוּא דְּאוֹלִידַת לְיִשְׂרָאֵל, דִּכְתִּיב צוּר יְלָדְךָ תֶּשִׁי. דְּהָא מִסִּטְרָא דְּצוּר עִלָּאָה דִּלְעֵילָּא, נָפְקָא צוּר אַחֲרָא. מִסִּטְרָא דְּאִימָא, נָפְקָא גְּבוּרָה.

428. Rabbi Aba said: There is a rock and there is a rock. From the side of the supernal rock emerges a different rock. And what is the supernal Rock? He is the Rock of every rock. And who is it? It is She who bore the children of Yisrael, ZEIR ANPIN. It is written: "Of the Rock that begot you you are unmindful," MEANING BINAH THAT GAVE BIRTH TO YISRAEL. Because from the side of the supernal Rock of above emerges another rock; from the side of Ima, WHICH IS BINAH, emerges Gvurah, WHICH IS MALCHUT.

429. וְאַזְלָא הָא כְּהָא דא״ר אֶלְעָזָר, כְּתִיב מִי יְמַלֵּל גְּבוּרוֹת יְיָ׳. מַאי גְּבוּרוֹת יְיָ׳. לְאַכְלְלָא אִימָא עִלָּאָה דְּכֹלָּא, דְּאע״ג דְּלָאו אִיהִי דִּינָא, מִסִּטְרָהָא אִשְׁתְּכַח, דְּהָא מִסִּטְרָהָא גְּבוּרָה אִשְׁתְּכַח, וּבְגִינֵי כַּךְ צוּר עִלָּאָה אִקְרֵי. וַתִּשְׁכַּח אֵל מְחוֹלְלֶךָ, דָּא נְהִירוּ דְּאַבָּא. מַאי נִיהוּ. חֶסֶד עִלָּאָה, דְּאִיהוּ נְהִירוּ דְּאַבָּא.

429. And this proceeds as Rabbi Elazar said: It is written, "Who can utter the mighty acts of Hashem?" (Tehilim 106:2). What are the mighty acts of Hashem? It is to include the supreme Ima of all, WHICH IS BINAH, that even though she HERSELF is not of Judgment, yet from her side is Judgment prevalent, because from her side there is Gvurah, WHICH IS MALCHUT THAT IS SWEETENED IN BINAH. And therefore it is called 'the supernal Rock'. "And have forgotten El that formed you" (Devarim 32:18), is the light of Aba. What is it? It is supernal Chesed, which is the light of Aba.

430. תּוּ אָמַר רִבִּי אַבָּא, מַיִם בְּכָל מָקוֹם, הָא יְדִיעָא, וְקוּדְשָׁא בְּרִיךְ הוּא בְּהַאי צוּר אִתְּעַר לְאַרְקָא מַיָּא, דְּהָא לָא אִתְחָזֵי, וְדָא הוּא אָת וְנִיסָא דְּקוּדְשָׁא בְּרִיךְ הוּא. וְעַל דָּא שַׁבַּח דָּוִד וְאָמַר, הַהֹפְכִי הַצּוּר אֲגַם מָיִם וְגוֹ'. וּמַשְׁמַע הַהֹפְכִי, דְּהָא לָאו אָרְחוֹי דְּצוּר בְּכַךְ.

430. Rabbi Aba also said: Wherever water IS WRITTEN, it is known TO ALLUDE TO THE LIGHT OF CHESED. And the Holy One, blessed be He, becomes aroused by this rock, WHICH IS JUDGMENT, to cause water to flow, WHICH IS CHESED, because it is not proper FOR IT EMERGE UNLESS IT IS FROM CHESED. And this is the sign and miracle of the Holy One, blessed be He, THAT THE ROCK, WHICH IS JUDGMENT, SHOULD INSPIRE THE FLOWING FORTH OF CHASSADIM. David praised this and said: "Who turned the rock into a pond of water..." (Tehilim 114:8). And the meaning of "turned" IS THAT HE TURNED IT FROM JUDGMENT TO CHESED, because it is not the customary way of rock TO POUR FORTH CHESED.

431. וְעַל דָּא, בְּצוּר עִלָּאָה, אַפִּיק מַיָּא מֵאֲתָר דִּלְתַתָּא. וּמַה שְׁמֵיהּ דְּהַהוּא דִּלְתַתָּא. סֶלַע. דִּכְתִּיב וְהוֹצֵאתָ לָהֶם מַיִם מִן הַסֶּלַע. וּבַמֶּה אַפִּיק הַאי סֶלַע מַיָּא. בְּחֵילָא דְּצוּר דִּלְעֵילָא.

431. And regarding this, through the supernal Rock, WHICH IS BINAH, He brought forth water from a lower place, FROM MALCHUT. And what is the name of that lower place? Boulder, as is written: "And you shall bring forth to them water out of the rock (boulder)" (Bemidbar 20:8). And this boulder brought forth water as with the power of the supernal Rock, WHICH IS BINAH.

432. ר"ש אָמַר, הַצּוּר תָּמִים פָּעֳלוֹ מַאי מַשְׁמַע הַצּוּר תָּמִים פָּעֳלוֹ.

דְּאִתְהַפַּךְ צוּר, לְמֶעְבַּד פְּעָלוֹ דְּתָמִים. וּמַאי אִיהוּ. אַבְרָהָם. דִּכְתִּיב בֵּיהּ הִתְהַלֵּךְ לְפָנַי וֶהְיֵה תָמִים. וְדָא הוּא הַהֹפְכִי הַצּוּר אֲגַם מָיִם, וּמַשְׁמַע תָּמִים פָּעֳלוֹ, וְדָא אַבְרָהָם.

432. Rabbi Shimon said, "He is the Rock, His work is perfect." What is the meaning of, "He is the Rock, His work is perfect"? IT IS that the Rock was turned and changed to do the work of the perfect one. And who is he? Abraham, WHO IS CHESED, of whom it is written: "Walk before Me, and be perfect" (Beresheet 17:1). This is the meaning of "who turned the rock into a pond of water..." – THAT IT CHANGED FROM EXECUTING JUDGMENT TO THE MINISTERING OF CHESED. This means that "His work is perfect," NAMELY CHESED. And this is Abraham, WHO IS CHESED.

433. בְּשַׁעֲתָא דָא, אִתְהֲדַר הַצּוּר, תָּמִים. בְּשַׁעֲתָא אַחֲרָא תִּנְיָינָא, כַּד בָּעָא מֹשֶׁה לְאַפָּקָא מַיָּא בְּהַאי צוּר, בְּחוֹבַיְיהוּ דְּיִשְׂרָאֵל, לָא אִתְהֲדַר תָּמִים, כְּקַדְמִיתָא. בֵּיהּ זִמְנָא, אִתְרָעַם מֹשֶׁה וְאָמַר, צוּר יְלָדְךָ תֶּשִׁי. כְּלוֹמַר, חַלָּשְׁתְּ לֵיהּ מִמַּה דַּהֲוָה בְּקַדְמֵיתָא, דִּבְגִינָךְ לָא אִשְׁתְּכַח תָּמִים הַשְׁתָּא, וְאִתְעֲבֵיד דִּינָא, מַה דְּלָא הֲוָה בְּיוֹמֵי יְלָדְךָ, כְּלוֹמַר עוּלֵימָךְ.

433. At this time, the rock reverted to being perfect. At another time, when Moses wanted to draw water from this rock, due to the sins of Yisrael, it did not return to perfection, as before. At that moment Moses raged and said: "Of the Rock that begot you you are unmindful" (Devarim 32:18). Namely, you weakened it from what it was before. For because of you it is not perfect now, and Judgment was executed; what was not so when it begot you, meaning in the days of your youth.

32. "Is Hashem among us"

A Synopsis

Rabbi Shimon explains that in the verse, "Is Hashem among us or not (Heb. ayin)?" the word 'not' refers to the most concealed Atik of all, which is called Ayin (naught). Yisrael were trying to discern between Ayin and Zeir Anpin. Because Yisrael tested God, making a separation between Atik and Zeir Anpin, they were punished. "Then came Amalek."

434. א״ר אַבָּא, מַאי דִּכְתִּיב הֲיֵשׁ יְיָ׳ בְּקִרְבֵּנוּ אִם אָיִן. וְכִי טִפְּשִׁין הֲווֹ יִשְׂרָאֵל דְּלָא יַדְעֵי מִלָּה דָּא, וְהָא חָמוּ שְׁכִינְתָּא קָמַיְיהוּ, וַעֲנָנֵי כָּבוֹד עֲלַיְיהוּ דְּסַחֲרוֹן לוֹן, וְאִינּוּן אָמְרוּ הֲיֵשׁ יְיָ׳ בְּקִרְבֵּנוּ אִם אָיִן, גּוּבְרִין דְּחָמוּ זִיו יְקָרָא דְּמַלְכֵּיהוֹן עַל יַמָּא, וְתָנֵינָן, רָאֲתָה שִׁפְחָה עַל הַיָּם מַה שֶּׁלֹּא רָאָה יְחֶזְקֵאל, אִינּוּן אִשְׁתְּכָחוּ טִפְּשִׁין, וְאָמְרוּ הֲיֵשׁ יְיָ׳ בְּקִרְבֵּנוּ אִם אָיִן.

434. Rabbi Aba said: It is written, "Is Hashem among us, or not?" (Shemot 17:7). Was Yisrael fools, who did not know this? Did they not see the Shechinah before them, and the clouds of Glory that surrounded them, that they said, "Is Hashem among us, or not?" These are people who saw the shine of the majesty of their King by the sea. And we have learned that a maidservant saw at the sea what the prophet Ezekiel never saw. It seems that they turned to be fools to say, "Is Hashem among us or not (Heb. *ayin*)?"

435. אֶלָּא הָכִי קָאָמַר ר״ש, בָּעוּ לְמִנְדַּע, בֵּין עַתִּיקָא סְתִימָאָה דְּכָל סְתִימִין, דְּאִקְרֵי אַיִן. וּבֵין זְעֵיר אַפִּין דְּאִקְרֵי יְיָ׳. וְעַל דָּא, לָא כְּתִיב הֲיֵשׁ יְיָ׳ בְּקִרְבֵּנוּ אִם לֹא, כְּמָה דִּכְתִּיב הֲיֵלֵךְ בְּתוֹרָתִי אִם לֹא. אֶלָּא הֲיֵשׁ יְיָ׳ בְּקִרְבֵּנוּ אִם אָיִן.

435. HE ANSWERS: But this is what Rabbi Shimon said. They wanted to discern between the most concealed Atik of all, WHICH IS KETER, which is called '*Ayin* ('naught')' and Zeir Anpin, which is called 'Yud Hei Vav Hei'. Therefore, it is not written, 'If Hashem is among us or no' as is written:

"Whether they will follow My Torah, or no" (Shemot 16:4), but rather, "Is Hashem among us or not (Heb. *ayin*)?"

436. אִי הָכִי אֲמַאי אִתְעַנְשׁוּ. אֶלָּא עַל דַּעֲבִידוּ פֵּרוּדָא, וַעֲבִידוּ בְּנִסְיוֹנָא, דִּכְתִּיב וְעַל נַסּוֹתָם אֶת יְיָ'. אָמְרוּ יִשְׂרָאֵל, אִי הַאי נִשְׁאַל בְּגַוְונָא חַד. וְאִי הַאי נִשְׁאַל בְּגַוְונָא אַחֲרָא. וְע"ד מִיָּד וַיָּבֹא עֲמָלֵק.

436. HE ASKS: If so, why were they punished? HE ANSWERS: Because they caused a separation BETWEEN ATIK AND ZEIR ANPIN, and they did it by testing, as is written: "Because they tempted (also: 'tested') Hashem." Said Yisrael: 'If the one is AMONG US we will ask in one form, and if that one, then we will ask in another form.' Therefore, immediately, "Then came Amalek" (Shemot 17:8).

33. "Then came Amalek"

A Synopsis

Rabbi Yosi opens with "Blessed are you that sow beside all waters, that let the feet of the ox and the donkey range freely." He says that the Holy One, blessed be He has a tree, Zeir Anpin, that contains food for all. We are reminded that Yisrael is the trunk, and that the seventy branches are the ministers of the heathen nations. When Yisrael encamped beside the water, they dominated the waters that were under the branches of that tree. The ox and donkey in the opening verse are from the left, and are brought into the discussion to emphasize that people must not give place to evil species, must remain separated from them. Rabbi Yehuda says that "Amalek was the first of the nations" because he did not fear Elohim. He is sentenced to everlasting perdition, and his name shall be utterly blotted out from the remembrance of man. Rabbi Aba now talks about "There is a sore evil which I have seen under the sun." Rabbi Shimon explains that "sore evil" is a lack of charity, wherein people cling to their money and even bear false witness in order to gain money. The Holy One, blessed be He had given Yisrael everything, yet they dealt with Him with false charges, and "Then came Amalek." The war of Amalek was a war above and a war below, ultimately a war against God. Amalek came to provoke Judgment over Mercy. During the war, when Moses held up his hands, he was fighting the battle above, while Joshua was fighting the battle below. From that time until the Redemption there will never be a greater battle. Joshua was worthy of fighting against Amalek because Moses saw that he came from the level of Metatron. Moses' hands were held up in faith, and it was this that gained them assistance from above. At the end, Moses built an altar called "Hashem is my banner"; Jacob built an altar and called it "El, the Elohim of the children of Yisrael."

437. וַיָּבֹא עֲמָלֵק וַיִּלָּחֶם עִם יִשְׂרָאֵל בִּרְפִידִים. רִבִּי יוֹסֵי פָּתַח, אַשְׁרֵיכֶם זוֹרְעֵי עַל כָּל מָיִם מְשַׁלְּחֵי רֶגֶל הַשּׁוֹר וְהַחֲמוֹר. אַשְׁרֵיכֶם זוֹרְעֵי עַל כָּל מָיִם, תַּמָּן תָּנֵינָן, כַּמָּה מַיִם וְכַמָּה מַיִם מִשְׁתַּכְּחִין. זַכָּאִין אִינּוּן יִשְׂרָאֵל, דְּלֵית זַרְעָא לְהוּ, אֶלָּא עַל הַמַּיִם, דִּכְתִּיב וַיַּחֲנוּ שָׁם עַל הַמָּיִם, אִינּוּן דַּהֲווֹ תְּחוֹת עַנְפֵי אִילָנָא דְקוּדְשָׁא בְּרִיךְ הוּא.

437. "Then came Amalek, and fought with Yisrael in Refidim" (Shemot

17:8). Rabbi Yosi opened the discussion, saying: "Blessed are you that sow beside all waters, that let the feet of the ox and the donkey range freely" (Yeshayah 32:20). "Blessed are you that sow beside all waters." There we learned that there are various types of waters, THAT THERE ARE MANY KINDS OF LIGHTS, MEANING SWEET WATERS OF HOLINESS, BITTER WATERS, AND PROUD WATERS. Happy is Yisrael who sow their seeds only beside the water, IN ORDER TO SUBDUE ALL KINDS OF WATER OF THE OTHER SIDE. As is written: "And they camped there by the water" (Shemot 15:27), MEANING over those waters that were under the branches of the tree of the Holy One, blessed be He, WHICH ARE THE TREACHEROUS WATERS, AS IS WRITTEN BEFORE US.

438. דְּתַנְיָא, אִילָנָא אִית לְקוּדְשָׁא בְּרִיךְ הוּא, וְהוּא אִילָנָא רַבְרְבָא וְתַקִּיפָא, וּבֵיהּ אִשְׁתְּכַח מְזוֹנָא לְכֹלָּא. וְהוּא אִתְּחַם בִּתְרֵיסַר תְּחוּמִין, בְּמַתְקְלָא, וְאִתְתַּקַּף בְּאַרְבַּע רוּחֵי עָלְמָא. וְע׳ עַנְפִּין אֲחִידָן בֵּיהּ וְיִשְׂרָאֵל מִשְׁתַּכְּחֵי בְּגוּפָא דְּהַהוּא אִילָנָא. וְאִינּוּן שַׁבְעִין עַנְפִּין סַחֲרָנָא דִּלְהוֹן.

438. For we have learned that the Holy One, blessed be He, WHO IS BINAH, has a tree. And this tree is big and strong, WHICH IS ZEIR ANPIN, and it contains food for all. And it is bordered with twelve borders, MEANING THREE COLUMNS TO EACH OF CHESED, GVURAH, TIFERET AND MALCHUT, WHICH ARE IN TOTAL TWELVE. And it is strengthened by the four corners of the world, THAT ARE CHESED, GVURAH, TIFERET AND MALCHUT. And seventy branches are attached to it, WHO ARE THE SEVENTY MINISTERS OF THE SEVENTY NATIONS. And Yisrael are located in the trunk of this tree, and the seventy branches are around them – AROUND YISRAEL, WHO ARE ATTACHED TO THE TRUNK OF THE TREE.

439. וְהַיְינוּ דִּכְתִּיב, וַיָּבֹאוּ אֵילִמָה וְשָׁם שְׁתֵּים עֶשְׂרֵה עֵינוֹת מַיִם וְשִׁבְעִים תְּמָרִים, וְהָא אוּקְמוּהָ, וְאִתְּמַר בְּכַמָּה אֲתָר. מַאי וַיַּחֲנוּ שָׁם עַל הַמָּיִם. אֶלָּא בְּהַהוּא זִמְנָא, שָׁלִיטוּ עַל אִינּוּן מַיָּא, דְּאִינּוּן תְּחוֹת עַנְפִּין דְּאִילָנָא, דְּאִקְרוּן הַמַּיִם הַזֵּידוֹנִים. וְע״ד אַשְׁרֵיכֶם זוֹרְעֵי עַל כָּל מָיִם.

439. This is what is meant by: "And they came to Elim, where were twelve springs of water, and seventy palm trees" (Shemot 15:27), and we have already explained and learned the meaning of this in many places. What is the meaning of, "and they encamped there by the water?" At that time, Yisrael dominated those waters that were under the branches of the tree that are called "the proud water" (Tehilim 124:5). And referring to this IS WRITTEN: "Blessed are you that sow beside all waters," NAMELY, IN ORDER TO SUBDUE ALL KINDS OF WATERS OF THE OTHER SIDE.

440. מְשַׁלְּחֵי רֶגֶל הַשּׁוֹר וְהַחֲמוֹר, אִינּוּן תְּרֵין כִּתְרֵי שְׂמָאלָא, דַּאֲחִידָן בְּהוּ עַמִּין עכו"ם, דְּאִקְרוּן שׁוֹר וַחֲמוֹר. וְהַיְינוּ דִּכְתִּיב וַיְהִי לִי שׁוֹר וַחֲמוֹר. בְּגִין דְּלָבָן חַכִּים הֲוָה בַּחֲרָשִׁין וּבְאִינּוּן כִּתְרִין תַּתָּאִין, וּבְאִינּוּן בָּעָא לְאוֹבָדָא לְיַעֲקֹב, כְּמָה דִּכְתִּיב אֲרַמִּי אוֹבֵד אָבִי, וְהָא אִתְּמַר. וּכְשֶׁיִּשְׂרָאֵל זַכָּאִין, מְשַׁלְּחֵי לְהוּ, וְלָא יַכְלֵי לְשַׁלְּטָאָה עֲלַיְיהוּ, הה"ד מְשַׁלְּחֵי רֶגֶל הַשּׁוֹר וְהַחֲמוֹר דְּלָא שַׁלְטֵי בְּהוּ.

440. "That let the feet of the ox and the donkey range freely." These are two crowns of the left that the heathen peoples joined to, which are called 'ox' and an 'ass'. This is as is written: "And I have oxen, and donkeys (lit. 'an ox and an donkey')" (Beresheet 32:6). Laban was an expert with sorcery and these lower crowns, and he wanted to destroy Jacob with THE OX AND THE DONKEY, as is written: "An Arammian wished to destroy my father" (Devarim 26:5). We have already learned that. When Yisrael is meritorious, they send them away so they can not dominate them. This is the meaning of: "That let (lit. 'send away') the feet of the ox and the donkey range freely," so that they can not dominate them.

441. א"ר אַבָּא, כַּד מִזְדַּוְּוגֵי כַּחֲדָא, לָא יַכְלֵי בְּנֵי עָלְמָא לְמֵיקָם בְּהוּ, וְעַל דָּא כְּתִיב לֹא תַחֲרוֹשׁ בְּשׁוֹר וּבַחֲמוֹר יַחְדָּיו. יַחְדָּיו דַּיְיקָא. וְתָנֵינָן, לָא יָהִיב אִינִישׁ דּוּכְתָּא לְזִינִין בִּישִׁין, דְּהָא בְּעוֹבָדָא דְּב"נ, אִתְּעַר מַה דְּלָא אִצְטְרִיךְ. וְכֹחַ מִזְדַּוְּוגֵי כַּחֲדָא, לָא יַכְלִין לְמֵיקָם בְּהוּ. מֵבִין סִטְרָא דִּלְהוֹן נָפִיק מִתְּקִיפוּתָא דִּלְהוֹן דְּאִקְרֵי כֶּלֶב, וְדָא חֲצִיפָא מִכֻּלְּהוּ, הה"ד וּלְכָל בְּנֵי יִשְׂרָאֵל לֹא יֶחֱרַץ כֶּלֶב לְשׁוֹנוֹ. אָמַר קוּדְשָׁא בְּרִיךְ הוּא, אַתּוּן אֲמַרְתּוּן, הֲיֵשׁ יְיָ' בְּקִרְבֵּנוּ אִם אָיִן, הֲרֵי אֲנִי מוֹסֵר אֶתְכֶם לַכֶּלֶב.

מִיָּד וַיָּבֹא עֲמָלֵק.

441. Rabbi Aba said: When this pair is coupled together, the world is not able to tolerate it. And referring to this is written: "You shall not plough with an ox and an donkey together" (Devarim 22:10). The word "together" IS precise. And we learned that a person should not give place to evil species. Because by the actions of a person, things are aroused that should not be. And when they paired together it was not possible to withstand them. From their side emerges a certain Klipah, called 'dog'. It is more disrespectful then all of them. This is what is meant by: "But against any of the children of Yisrael not a dog shall move its tongue" (Shemot 11:7). The Holy One, blessed be He, said: 'You said, "Is Hashem among us, or not?" Behold, I am giving you over to the dog.' Immediately, "Then came Amalek."

442. ר׳ יְהוּדָה אָמַר, רֵאשִׁית גּוֹיִם עֲמָלֵק וְאַחֲרִיתוֹ עֲדֵי אוֹבֵד. וְכִי רֵאשִׁית גּוֹיִם עֲמָלֵק, וַהֲלֹא כַּמָּה לִישָׁנִין וְעַמִּין וְאוּמִין הֲווֹ בְּעָלְמָא, עַד לָא אָתָא עֲמָלֵק.

442. Rabbi Yehuda said: "Amalek was the first of the nations, but his latter end shall be everlasting perdition" (Bemidbar 24:20). HE ASKS: Is Amalek really the first of the nations? Were there not many tongues, nations and peoples in the world before Amalek came?

443. אֶלָּא, כַּד נַפְקוּ יִשְׂרָאֵל מִמִּצְרַיִם, דְּחִילוּ וְאֵימָתָא נָפְלָה עַל כָּל עַמִּין דְּעָלְמָא מִיִּשְׂרָאֵל, הה״ד שָׁמְעוּ עַמִּים יִרְגָּזוּן חִיל אָחַז יוֹשְׁבֵי פְּלָשֶׁת. וְלָא הֲווֹ עַמָּא, דְּלָא הֲוָה דָּחִיל מִגְּבוּרָאן עִלָּאִין דְּקוּדְשָׁא בְּרִיךְ הוּא, וַעֲמָלֵק לָא הֲוָה דָּחִיל, הה״ד, וְלֹא יָרֵא אֱלֹהִים. לָא דָּחִיל לְמִקְרַב לְגַבָּךְ. וְעַל דָּא רֵאשִׁית גּוֹיִם.

443. HE ANSWERS: When Yisrael left Egypt, the fear and terror of Yisrael fell upon all the nations of the world. This is what is meant by: "The people shall hear, and be afraid: trembling shall take hold of the inhabitants of Pleshet" (Shemot 15:14). There was no nation that did not fear the superior might of the Holy One, blessed be He. But Amalek was not afraid, as is written: "And he feared not Elohim" (Devarim 25:18). He did not fear to approach You. Therefore, he is the first among the nations.

444. קַדְמָאָה דְּאָתוּ לְאַגָּחָא קְרָבָא בְּיִשְׂרָאֵל עֲמָלֵק הֲוָה. וּבְגִינֵי כַּךְ וְאַחֲרִיתוֹ עֲדֵי אוֹבֵד, דִּכְתִּיב כִּי מָחֹה אֶמְחֶה אֶת זֵכֶר עֲמָלֵק. וּכְתִיב, תִּמְחֶה אֶת זֵכֶר עֲמָלֵק, הה"ד וְאַחֲרִיתוֹ עֲדֵי אוֹבֵד. עֲדֵי אָבְדוֹ מִבָּעֵי לֵיהּ. אֶלָּא עַד דְּיֵיתֵי קוּדְשָׁא בְּרִיךְ הוּא וְיֹאבַד לֵיהּ, דִּכְתִּיב כִּי מָחֹה אֶמְחֶה וְגוֹ'. אָמַר ר' אֶלְעָזָר, ת"ח, אע"ג דְּהַצּוּר תָּמִים פָּעֳלוֹ, וְעָבֵד עִמְּהוֹן חֶסֶד לְאַפָּקָא לוֹן מַיָּא, לָא שָׁבַק דִּידֵיהּ, דְּהָא כְּתִיב וַיָּבֹא עֲמָלֵק.

444. The first who came to wage war against Yisrael was Amalek. Therefore, "his latter end shall be everlasting perdition," for it is written: "I will utterly blot out the remembrance of Amalek" (Shemot 17:14), and: "You shall blot out the remembrance of Amalek" (Devarim 25:19). It is written: "His latter end shall be everlasting perdition" (Bemidbar 24:20). HE ASKS: Should it not have been written, 'His everlasting perdition'? AND HE ANSWERS: It means until the Holy One, blessed be He, comes and destroys him, as is written: "I will utterly blot out..." Rabbi Elazar said: Come and behold. Even though "He is the Rock, His work is perfect," and He did kindness with them to bring forth water for them, He did not forsake His own, for it is written: "Then came Amalek"

445. ר' אַבָּא פָּתַח וְאָמַר, יֵשׁ רָעָה חוֹלָה רָאִיתִי תַּחַת הַשָּׁמֶשׁ. כַּמָּה בְּנֵי נָשָׁא אֲטִימִין לִבָּא, בְּגִין דְּלָא מִשְׁתַּדְּלֵי בְּאוֹרַיְיתָא. יֵשׁ רָעָה חוֹלָה, וְכִי יֵשׁ רָעָה דְּהִיא חוֹלָה, וְיֵשׁ רָעָה דְּלָאו הִיא חוֹלָה. אֶלָּא וַדַּאי יֵשׁ רָעָה חוֹלָה, דְּתָנֵינָן, מִסִּטְרָא דִּשְׂמָאלָא, נַפְקֵי כַּמָּה גַּרְדִּינֵי נִימוּסִין, דְּבַקְעָן בַּאֲוִירָא.

445. Rabbi Aba opened the discussion, saying, "There is a sore evil which I have seen under the sun" (Kohelet 5:12). There are many people who have clogged hearts, because they are not occupied with Torah. "There is a sore evil." HE ASKS: Is there then an evil which is sore and an evil that is not sore? AND HE ANSWERS: Certainly, there is a sore evil, for we learned that from the left side there emerge Accusers who split the air.

446. וְכַד בַּעְיָין לְמֵיפַק, אַזְלִין וְאִשְׁתַּאֲבִין בְּנוּקְבָא דִּתְהוֹמָא רַבָּה, לְבָתַר נָפְקִין וּמִתְחַבְּרָן כַּחֲדָא, וּבְקָעִין אֲוִירִין, וְשָׁאטִין בְּעָלְמָא, וּמִתְקָרְבִין לְגַבַּיְיהוּ דִּבְנֵי נָשָׁא, וְכָל חַד אִקְרֵי רָעָה, כד"א לֹא תְאוּנֶּה אֵלֶיךָ רָעָה. מַאי לֹא תְאוּנֶּה. בְּגִין דְּאַתְיָא בְּתַסְקוּפָא עַל בְּנֵי נָשָׁא.

446. And when they want to go out, they go and are swallowed in the hole of the great depth. And afterwards they emerge, join together, split airs and traverse through the world. And they approach people, and each one is called 'evil' as is written: "No evil will befall you" (Tehilim 91:10), which means they came with false charges against people.

447. חוֹלָה אֲמַאי הִיא חוֹלָה. כַּד שַׁרְיָא הַאי עַל בְּנֵי נָשָׁא, עָבֵיד לוֹן קַמְצָנִין מִמָּמוֹנֵיהוֹן, אַתְיָין גַּבָּאֵי צְדָקָה גַּבֵּיהּ, הִיא מָחָאת בִּידֵיהּ. א"ל לֹא תֵּיפּוּק מִדִּידָךְ. אַתְיָין מִסְכְּנֵי, הִיא מָחָאת בִּידֵיהּ. אָתֵי הוּא לְמֵיכַל מִמָּמוֹנֵיהּ, מָחָאת בִּידֵיהּ, בְּגִין לְנַטְרָא לֵיהּ לְאָחֳרָא. וּמִן יוֹמָא דְּשַׁרְיָא עָלֵיהּ דְּבַר נָשׁ, הִיא חוֹלָה, כְּהַאי שָׁכִיב מֵרַע דְּלָא אָכִיל וְלָא שָׁתֵי. וְעַל דָּא הִיא רָעָה חוֹלָה.

447. HE ASKS: "a sore EVIL" – why is it sore (lit. 'ill')? HE ANSWERS: When it dwells on people, it makes them misers with their money. When the collector of charity comes to him, it tries to prevent him from giving, and says to him: Do not take out ANYTHING of yours. When poor people come, it tries to prevent him. When he wants to eat of his money, it tries to prevent him in order to guard the money for another. And from the day that it dwells on the person, he is ill like one who is bedridden because of his illness and does not eat or drink. Therefore, it is an ill evil.

448. וּשְׁלֹמֹה מַלְכָּא צָוַוח בְּחָכְמְתָא וְאָמַר, אִישׁ אֲשֶׁר יִתֶּן לוֹ הָאֱלֹהִים עֹשֶׁר וּנְכָסִים וְכָבוֹד וְגוֹ'. הַאי קְרָא, לָאו רֵישֵׁיהּ סֵיפֵיהּ, וְלָאו סֵיפֵיהּ רֵישֵׁיהּ, כְּתִיב אִישׁ אֲשֶׁר יִתֶּן לוֹ הָאֱלֹהִים עֹשֶׁר וּנְכָסִים וְכָבוֹד וְגוֹ', מַאי וְלֹא יַשְׁלִיטֶנּוּ הָאֱלֹהִים לֶאֱכוֹל מִמֶּנּוּ. אִי הָכִי, לָאו בִּרְשׁוּתֵיהּ הוּא דְּב"נ.

448. And king Solomon cried out in his wisdom and said: “A man to whom Elohim has given riches, wealth and honor...” (Kohelet 6:2). The beginning and end of this passage are seemingly incoherent, for it is written: “A man to whom Elohim has given riches…” IF SO, what is the meaning of, “Yet Elohim does not give him power to eat of it”? If so, then it is not in the possession of the person, AND SO ELOHIM HAS NOT GIVEN HIM ANYTHING.

449. אֶלָּא, אִי כְּתִיב וְלֹא יַעַזְבֶנּוּ הָאֱלֹהִים לֶאֱכוֹל מִמֶּנּוּ, הֲוֵינָא אָמַר הָכִי. אֶלָּא וְלֹא יַשְׁלִיטֶנּוּ, דִּבְגִּין דְּהוּא הֵימְנֵיהּ לְהַהִיא רָעָה, וְאָחִיד בָּהּ. קוּדְשָׁא בְּרִיךְ הוּא לָא שַׁלְטֵיהּ עָלֵיהּ, לְאִתְבָּרְאָה תְּחוֹתֵיהּ, עַל דְּהוּא אִתְרְעֵי בָּהּ, וְאָחִיד בָּהּ.

449. HE ANSWERS: If it had been written, ‘Yet Elohim does not permit him to eat of it’, then I would say THAT HE GAVE HIM NOTHING. But it is written: “does not give him power,” because he believed in that evil and joined with it. IF SO, HE HIMSELF CAUSED THIS. The Holy One, blessed be He, did not give it dominion, THAT THE PERSON should be born under ITS DOMINATION, but rather he HIMSELF wanted it and held on to it.

450. וְכָל אָרְחוֹי כִּשְׁכִיב מֵרַע, דְּלָא אָכִיל וְלָא שָׁתֵי, וְלָא קָרִיב לְמָמוֹנֵיהּ, וְלָא אַפִּיק מִינֵּיהּ, וְנָטִיר לֵיהּ עַד דְּהוּא יִפּוּק מֵעָלְמָא, וְיֵיתֵי אַחֲרָא, וְיִטּוֹל לֵיהּ, דְּהוּא בְּעָלָיו.

450. All his ways are like one who is bedridden because of his illness. He does not eat or drink, he does not go near his money or spend any of it. And he guards it until he passes from the world and someone else comes and takes it, for he is its true owner.

451. וּשְׁלֹמֹה מַלְכָּא צָוַוח וְאָמַר, עֹשֶׁר שָׁמוּר לִבְעָלָיו לְרָעָתוֹ. מַאן בְּעָלָיו. דָּא אַחֲרָא דְּיָרִית לֵיהּ. וְלָמָּה זָכָה הַאי אַחֲרָא לְמֶהֱוֵי בְּעָלָיו דְּהַהוּא עֻתְרָא. בְּגִין דְּהַאי הַיְמִין לְהַהִיא רָעָה, וְאִתְרְעֵי בָּהּ וְאִתְדָּבַק בָּהּ. בג"כ, הַאי אַחֲרָא דְּלָא אִתְדַּבַּק בְּהַהִיא רָעָה, זָכָה לְמֶהֱוֵי בְּעָלָיו דְּהַהוּא עֻתְרָא הה"ד לְרָעָתוֹ, כְּלוֹמַר בְּגִין רָעָתוֹ דַּהֲוָה מִתְדָּבַק בָּהּ, רָוַוח לֵיהּ הַאי.

451. And King Solomon cried and said: "Riches kept for their owner to his hurt (lit. 'evil')" (Kohelet 5:12). Who is its owner? He is another one who inherited him. And why did the other merit to become the owner of those riches? It is because the first believed in this evil and desired it, and joined it. Therefore, the other who did not join this evil merited to become the owner of those riches. This is what is meant by, "to his evil," meaning because of his evil, which he joined, the other person profited.

452. ד״א יֵשׁ רָעָה חוֹלָה, הַאי מַאן דְּיָתִיב בְּחוּלָקָא טָבָא, בְּבֵית אֲבוּי, וְהוּא אָזִיל לְקַבֵּל אֲבוּי, בְּתַסְקוּפֵי מִלִּין, הָא אִתְדְּבַק בְּהַהוּא רָעָה חוֹלָה, כְּבַר נָשׁ שָׁכִיב מֵרַע דְּכָל אָרְחוֹי בְּתַסְקוּפָא, דָּא בְּעֵינָא, וְדָא לָא בְּעֵינָא, וּבְגִין הַאי עוּתְרָא אִתְדָּבַק בַּר נָשׁ בְּרָעָה חוֹלָה, וְאִתְעֲנָשׁ בְּהַאי עָלְמָא, וּבְעָלְמָא דְּאָתֵי, וְדָא הוּא עוֹשֶׁר שָׁמוּר לִבְעָלָיו לְרָעָתוֹ.

452. Another explanation for, "There is an ill evil…" It is he who dwells in a good part of his father's house, but accuses his father with false charges. He cleaves unto this ill evil like a person who is bedridden because of his illness, and all of his ways are false, saying: This I want and this I do not want. And because of these riches, this person has cleaved unto ill evil and is punished in this world and in the World to Come. This is "riches kept for their owner to his evil."

453. כַּךְ יִשְׂרָאֵל, קב״ה נָטִיל לוֹן עַל גַּדְפֵּי נִשְׁרִין, אַסְחַר לוֹן בַּעֲנָנֵי יְקָרָא, שְׁכִינְתֵּיהּ נָטִיל קָמַיְיהוּ, נָחַת לוֹן מָנָא לְמֵיכַל, אַפִּיק לוֹן מַיָּיא מְתוּקִין, וְאִינּוּן הֲווֹ אַזְלִין עִמֵּיהּ בְּתַסְקוּפִין. מִיַּד וַיָּבֹא עֲמָלֵק.

453. It is the same with Yismael. The Holy One, blessed be He, took them upon the wings of eagles and surrounded them with clouds of glory. The Shechinah went before them, brought down for them the manna to eat, brought forth for them sweet water, yet they dealt with Him with false charges. Immediately, "Then came Amalek."

454. וַיָּבֹא עֲמָלֵק, א״ר שִׁמְעוֹן, רָזָא דְּחָכְמְתָא הָכָא, מִגְּזֵרַת דִּינָא קַשְׁיָא, קָא אַתְיָא קְרָבָא דָּא. וּקְרָבָא דָּא אִשְׁתְּכַח לְעֵילָּא וְתַתָּא. וְלֵית

לָךְ מִלָּה בְּאוֹרַיְיתָא, דְּלָא אִית בָּהּ רָזִין עִלָּאִין דְּחָכְמְתָא, דְּמִתְקַשְּׁרִין בִּשְׁמָא קַדִּישָׁא. כִּבְיָכוֹל, אָמַר קב״ה, כַּד יִשְׂרָאֵל אִינּוּן זַכָּאִין לְתַתָּא, אִתְגַּבָּר חֵילָא דִּילִי עַל כֹּלָּא. וְכַד לָא אִשְׁתְּכָחוּ זַכָּאִין, כִּבְיָכוֹל, מַתִּישִׁין חֵילָא דִּלְעֵילָּא, וְאִתְגַּבַּר חֵילָא דְּדִינָא קַשְׁיָא.

454. "Then came Amalek..." Rabbi Shimon said: There is a secret of wisdom here. Because of the decree of Severe Judgment, this war came. And it took place both above and below. And there is no word in the Torah that does not contain superior secrets of Wisdom that are connected with the Holy Name. His as if the Holy One, blessed be He, said: 'When Yisrael are righteous below, My power becomes strengthened over all. But when they are not righteous, the superior power of above is weakened and the power of Severe Judgment gains strength.

455. ת״ח, בְּשַׁעֲתָא דְּחָבוּ יִשְׂרָאֵל לְתַתָּא, מַה כְּתִיב, וַיָּבֹא עֲמָלֵק וַיִּלָּחֶם עִם יִשְׂרָאֵל, אָתָא לְקַטְרְגָא דִּינָא בְּרַחֲמֵי. דְּכֹלָּא אִשְׁתְּכַח לְעֵילָּא וְתַתָּא. בִּרְפִידִים: בְּרָפוּי יָדַיִם, דְּרָפוּ יְדֵיהוֹן מֵאוֹרַיְיתָא דְּקוּדְשָׁא בְּרִיךְ הוּא, כְּמָה דְּאוֹקִימְנָא. אָמַר ר׳ יְהוּדָה, תְּרֵי זִמְנֵי אַגָּח קְרָבָא עֲמָלֵק בְּיִשְׂרָאֵל, חַד הָכָא. וְחַד דִּכְתִּיב, וַיֵּרֶד הָעֲמָלֵקִי וְהַכְּנַעֲנִי וְגוֹ׳.

455. Come and behold: When Yisrael sinned below, it is written: "Then came Amalek, and fought with Yisrael" (Shemot 17:8). He came to provoke Judgment over Mercy, WHICH IS HIS WAY OF WAR ABOVE, because everything exists above and below. "...in *refidim*," MEANS with weakened hands (Heb. *rifyon yadaim*), as they weakened their hands from the Torah of the Holy One, blessed be He, as we established. Rabbi Yehuda said: Amalek waged war twice against Yisrael, one here, and one as is written: "Then the Amaleki came down, and the Canaanite..." (Bemidbar 14:45).

456. אָמַר ר׳ שִׁמְעוֹן, לְעֵילָּא וְתַתָּא. קִטְרוּגָא דְּקוּדְשָׁא בְּרִיךְ הוּא הֲוָה, לְעֵילָּא, כְּמָה דְּאִתְּמַר. לְתַתָּא בְּקוּדְשָׁא בְּרִיךְ הוּא הֲוָה, דַּהֲווֹ נַסְבֵּי לְגַבְרֵי, וְגַזְרֵי לוֹן עָרְלָתָא דִּרְשִׁימָא קַדִּישָׁא, וְנַטְלֵי לְהוּ וְאַרְמוּ לוֹן לְעֵילָּא, וְאַמְרֵי טוֹל לָךְ מַה דְּאִתְרְעִית. ועכ״פ דְּקוּדְשָׁא בְּרִיךְ הוּא הֲוָה כֹּלָּא.

456. Rabbi Shimon said: Was THE WAR WITH AMALEK both above and below. Above was the provocation against the Holy One, blessed be He, as we learned. Below ALSO, it was all against the Holy One, blessed be He, for they took men and cut their foreskins of the holy sign, then took them and threw them upwards, and said: Take that which You desire. In any case, the entire WAR was against the Holy One, blessed be He.

457. וַיֹּאמֶר מֹשֶׁה אֶל יְהוֹשֻׁעַ בְּחַר לָנוּ אֲנָשִׁים וְצֵא הִלָּחֵם בַּעֲמָלֵק. וְכִי מַה חָמָא מֹשֶׁה, דְּסָלִיק גַּרְמֵיהּ, מֵהַאי קְרָבָא קַדְמָאָה דְּקוּדְשָׁא בְּרִיךְ הוּא פָּקִיד. אֶלָּא מֹשֶׁה זַכָּאָה חוּלָקֵיהּ, דְּאִסְתַּכַּל וְיָדַע עִקָּרָא דְּמִלָּה. אָמַר מֹשֶׁה, אֲנָא אַזְמִין גַּרְמֵי לְהַהוּא קְרָבָא דִּלְעֵילָּא, וְאַנְתְּ יְהוֹשֻׁעַ זַמִּין גַּרְמָךְ לִקְרָבָא דִּלְתַתָּא.

457. "And Moses said to Joshua, 'Choose us out men, and go out, fight with Amalek'" (Shemot 17:9). HE ASKS: What did Moses foresee that he removed himself from this very first battle of the Holy One, blessed be He? HE ANSWERS: Blessed is Moses' portion, for he noticed and saw and realized the root of the matter. Moses said: 'I will prepare myself for this battle which is above and you, Joshua, prepare yourself for the war below.'

458. וְהַיְינוּ דִּכְתִּיב, וְהָיָה כַּאֲשֶׁר יָרִים מֹשֶׁה יָדוֹ וְגָבַר יִשְׂרָאֵל: יִשְׂרָאֵל דִּלְעֵילָּא. וּבְגִין כַּךְ סָלִיק מֹשֶׁה גַּרְמֵיהּ מִקְּרָבָא דִּלְתַתָּא, בְּגִין לְאִזְדָּרְזָא בִּקְרָבָא דִּלְעֵילָּא, וְיִתְנַצַּח עַל יְדוֹי.

458. This is what is written: "And it came to pass, when Moses held up his hand, that Yisrael prevailed" (Shemot 17:11), MEANING Yisrael of above, ZEIR ANPIN. Therefore, Moses removed himself from the battle below, in order to expedite the battle above to be won through him.

459. אָמַר ר' שִׁמְעוֹן, וְכִי קַלָּה הִיא בְּעֵינֶיךָ, קְרָבָא דָּא דַּעֲמָלֵק. תָּא חֲזֵי, מִן יוֹמָא דְּאִתְבְּרֵי עָלְמָא, עַד הַהוּא זִמְנָא, וּמֵהַהוּא זִמְנָא, עַד דְּיֵיתֵי מַלְכָּא מְשִׁיחָא, וַאֲפִילּוּ בְּיוֹמוֹי דְּגוֹג וּמָגוֹג, לָא יִשְׁתְּכַּח כְּוָותֵיהּ. לָאו בְּגִין חַיָּילִין תַּקִּיפִין וְסַגִּיאִין, אֶלָּא בְּגִין דִּבְכָל סִטְרִין דְּקוּדְשָׁא בְּרִיךְ הוּא הֲוָה.

459. Rabbi Shimon said: Is this war of Amalek insignificant in your eyes?! Come and behold: from the day the world was created until that time, and from that time until King Messiah will come, and even in the days of Gog and Magog (Armageddon), there will not be anything comparable. And not because they were so mighty and numerous, but rather because it was in all the aspects of the Holy One, blessed be He.

460. וַיֹּאמֶר מֹשֶׁה אַל יְהוֹשֻׁעַ, אֲמַאי לִיהוֹשֻׁעַ, וְלָא לְאָחֳרָא, וְהָא בְּהַהוּא זִמְנָא רַבְיָא הֲוָה, דִּכְתִּיב וִיהוֹשֻׁעַ בִּן נוּן נַעַר, וְכַמָּה הֲווֹ בְּיִשְׂרָאֵל תַּקִּיפִין מִנֵּיהּ. אֶלָּא מֹשֶׁה בְּחָכְמְתָא אִסְתָּכַּל וְיָדַע. מַאי חָמָא. חָמָא לְסָמָאל דַּהֲוָה נָחִית מִסִּטְרָא דִּלְעֵילָּא, לְסַיְּיעָא לַעֲמָלֵק לְתַתָּא. אָמַר מֹשֶׁה, וַדַּאי קְרָבָא הָכָא תַּקִּיפָא אִתְחֲזֵי.

460. "And Moses said to Joshua..." HE ASKS: Why to Joshua and no one else? At that time he was only a youth, as is written: "Joshua, the son of Nun, a young man" (Shemot 33:11), and there were many among Yisrael who were stronger than he. AND HE ANSWERS: But Moses gazed with wisdom and knew. What did he see? He saw Samael descending on the side above to assist Amalek below. Moses said: 'There seems to be a difficult war here.'

461. יְהוֹשֻׁעַ בְּהַהוּא זִמְנָא בְּדַרְגָּא עִלָּאָה יַתִּיר אִשְׁתְּכַח. אִי תֵּימָא דִּבְשְׁכִינְתָּא אִשְׁתְּכַח בְּהַהוּא זִמְנָא לָאו הָכִי, דְּהָא בְּמֹשֶׁה אִתְנְסִיבַת וְאִתְאַחֲדַת, אִשְׁתְּכַח יְהוֹשֻׁעַ דְּאִתְאַחֵד לְתַתָּא מִינָּהּ. וּבַמֶּה. אָמַר ר׳ שִׁמְעוֹן, בְּהַהוּא אֲתָר, דְּאִתְקְרֵי נַעַ״ר.

461. Joshua at that time was situated in a very high level. If you think he was situated in the Shechinah at that particular time, it is not so, because She was taken and joined to Moses. So Joshua was joined below THE SHECHINAH. And where? Rabbi Shimon said: In that place that is called 'youth', WHICH IS METATRON.

462. וְהַיְינוּ דא״ר יְהוּדָה, מַאי דִּכְתִּיב עֵינֶיךָ תִּרְאֶינָה יְרוּשָׁלַם נָוֶה

שַׁאֲנָן אֹהֶל בַּל יִצְעָן בַּל יִסַּע יְתֵדוֹתָיו לָנֶצַח. יְרוּשָׁלַםִ: יְרוּשָׁלַםִ דִּלְעֵילָּא, דְּאִקְרֵי אֹהֶל בַּל יִצְעָן, דְּלָא יִשְׁתְּכַּח יַתִּיר לְמֵהַךְ בְּגָלוּתָא, וְדָא הוּא רָזָא דִּכְתִּיב, וִיהוֹשֻׁעַ בִּן נוּן נַעַר. נַעַר וַדַּאי. לֹא יָמִישׁ מִתּוֹךְ הָאֹהֶל, הַהוּא דְּאִקְרֵי אֹהֶל בַּל יִצְעָן. מְלַמֵּד דִּבְכָל יוֹמָא וְיוֹמָא, הֲוָה יָנִיק מִשְּׁכִינְתָּא, כְּמָה דְּהַהוּא נַעַר דִּלְעֵילָּא, לֹא יָמִישׁ מִתּוֹךְ הָאֹהֶל, וְיָנִיק מִנֵּיהּ תָּדִירָא. כַּךְ הַאי נַעַר דִּלְתַתָּא לֹא יָמִישׁ מִתּוֹךְ הָאֹהֶל, וְיָנִיק מִנָּהּ תָּדִירָא.

462. This is what Rabbi Yehuda said of the verse: “Your eyes shall see Jerusalem a quiet habitation, a tent that shall not be taken down; its pegs shall never be removed for ever” (Yeshayah 33:20). “Jerusalem” refers to the upper Jerusalem that is called “a tent that shall not be taken down,” MEANING that IT will no longer have to go into exile. And this is the secret of “Joshua, the son of Nun, a young man.” “A young man” indeed, BECAUSE HE CLEAVED UNTO THE SUPERNAL LAD, METATRON. “Did not depart out of the tent” (Shemot 33:11), MEANING from the one which is called “a tent that shall not be taken down,” WHICH IS THE SHECHINAH. This teaches us that each and every day, he was nurtured by the Shechinah. Just as the supernal Youth “did not depart out of the tent,” and nurtured from Her constantly, so did that youth below, WHO WAS JOSHUA, who “did not depart out of the tent,” and nurtured from it constantly.

463. בְּגִין כַּךְ, כַּד חָמָא מֹשֶׁה, לְסָמָאֵל, נָחִית לְסַיְּיעָא לַעֲמָלֵק, אָמַר מֹשֶׁה, וַדַּאי הַאי נַעַר יְקוּם לְקַבְלֵיהּ, וְיִשְׁלוֹט עָלֵיהּ, לְנַצְחָא לֵיהּ. מִיַּד וַיֹּאמֶר מֹשֶׁה אֶל יְהוֹשֻׁעַ בְּחַר לָנוּ אֲנָשִׁים וְצֵא הִלָּחֵם בַּעֲמָלֵק, דִּילָךְ הַאי קְרָבָא דִּלְתַתָּא, וַאֲנָא אִזְדָּרֵז לִקְרָבָא דִּלְעֵילָּא. בְּחַר לָנוּ אֲנָשִׁים, זַכָּאִין בְּנֵי זַכָּאִין, דְּיִתְחֲזוּן לְמֵהַךְ עִמָּךְ.

463. Therefore, when Moses saw Samael descending to assist Amalek, he said: Certainly, this youth will stand up against him and will dominate over him to overcome him. Immediately, “And Moses said to Joshua, ‘Choose us out men, and go out, fight with Amalek’” This battle below is yours, and I will hasten for the battle above. “Choose us out men,” NAMELY righteous men, the sons of righteous men, that are worthy to go with you.

464. אר"ש, בְּשַׁעֲתָא דְּנָפִיק יְהוֹשֻׁעַ נַעַר. אִתְּעַר נַעַר דִּלְעֵילָּא, וְאִתְתָּקַן בְּכַמָּה תִּיקוּנִין בְּכַמָּה זַיְינִין, דְּאַתְקִינַת לֵיהּ אִמֵּיהּ, לְקְרָבָא דָּא, לְנַקְמָא נוּקְמָא דִּבְרִית. וְהַיְינוּ דִּכְתִּיב, חֶרֶב נוֹקֶמֶת נְקַם בְּרִית, וְדָא הוּא רָזָא דִּכְתִּיב, וַיַּחֲלֹשׁ יְהוֹשֻׁעַ אֶת עֲמָלֵק וְאֶת עַמּוֹ לְפִי חָרֶב. לְפִי חֶרֶב וַדַּאי, וְלָא לְפוּם רוּמְחִין וְזַיְינִין, אֶלָּא בְּחֶרֶב וַדַּאי הִיא, הַאי דְּאִקְרֵי חֶרֶב נוֹקֶמֶת נְקַם בְּרִית.

464. Rabbi Shimon said: At the moment that Joshua, the youth, went out, the youth of above, METATRON, stirred and made many preparations with many weapons that his Mother, WHO IS THE SHECHINAH, prepared for him, for this war to avenge the vengeance of the Covenant. This is what is meant by: "A sword...that shall avenge the Covenant" (Vayikra 26:25). And this is the secret of what is meant by: "And Joshua harried Amalek and his people with the edge of the sword" (Shemot 17:13). Assuredly, "with the edge of the sword," and not with spears and weapons, but by the sword specifically, the one called "a sword...that shall avenge the Covenant."

465. וּמֹשֶׁה אִתְתָּקַן לִקְרָבָא דִּלְעֵילָּא, וִידֵי מֹשֶׁה כְּבֵדִים: כְּבֵדִים מַמָּשׁ, יַקִּירִין, קַדִּישִׁין, לָא אִסְתַּאֲבָן לְעָלְמִין. יְקִרִין דְּאִתְחָזוּן לְאַגָּחָא בְּהוּ קְרָבָא דִּלְעֵילָּא. וַיִּקְחוּ אֶבֶן וַיָּשִׂימוּ תַחְתָּיו וַיֵּשֶׁב עָלֶיהָ, בְּגִין דְּיִשְׂרָאֵל שַׁרְיָין בְּצַעֲרָא, וִיהֵא עִמְּהוֹן בְּצַעֲרֵיהוֹן.

465. Moses prepared himself for the war above. "But the hands of Moses were heavy" (Shemot 17:12), actually heavy, holy and glorified, never impure. Glorified, as they were worthy to do through them a battle that is above. "And they took a stone, and put it under him, and he sat on it" (Ibid.), THAT IS because Yisrael was in sorrow and he wanted to be together with them in their pain.

466. וְאַהֲרֹן וְחוּר תָּמְכוּ בְיָדָיו מִזֶּה אֶחָד וּמִזֶּה אֶחָד וַיְהִי יָדָיו אֱמוּנָה וְגוֹ', מַאי תָּמְכוּ בְיָדָיו. אֱמוּנָה. וְכִי עַל דְּאַהֲרֹן וְחוּר תְּמִיכוּ לִידוֹי, הֲווּ

יְדוֹי אֱמוּנָה. אֶלָּא, מֹשֶׁה כֹּלָּא בְּחָכְמְתָא עָבִיד מַה דְּעָבִיד. אַהֲרֹן וְחוּר, דָּא מִסִּטְרָא דִּילֵיהּ, וְדָא מִסִּטְרָא דִּילֵיהּ, וְיָדוֹי בְּאֶמְצָעִיתָא, וְע"ד וַיְהִי יָדָיו אֱמוּנָה, מְהֵימָנוּתָא. אַהֲרֹן בְּגִין דְּיִתְּעַר סִטְרָא דִּילֵיהּ, וְחוּר בְּגִין דְּיִתְּעַר סִטְרָא דִּילֵיהּ, וַהֲווֹ אֲחִידָן בִּידוֹי מִכָּאן וּמִכָּאן, דְּאִשְׁתַּכְחָא סִיוּעָא דִּלְעֵילָּא.

466. "And Aaron and Chur supported his hands, the one on the one side, and the other on the other side; and his hands were heavy (lit. 'faith')" (Ibid.). HE ASKS: What is the meaning of "supported his hands" ('faith')? Is it that because Aaron and Chur supported his hands, his hands were 'faith'? HE ANSWERS: Whatever Moses did, he did with wisdom. Aaron and Chur, the one was from his own side, WHICH IS THE RIGHT, and the other from his side, WHICH IS THE LEFT. And the hands of Moses were in the center, IN THE CENTRAL COLUMN. Therefore, "And his hands were Faith"; faithful were Aaron, in order to arouse from his side, WHICH IS THE RIGHT, and Chur, in order to arouse from his side, WHICH IS THE LEFT. And they held his hands from here and here, in order that assistance would be available from above.

467. וְהָיָה כַּאֲשֶׁר יָרִים מֹשֶׁה יָדוֹ וְגָבַר יִשְׂרָאֵל. כַּאֲשֶׁר יָרִים: דְּזָקִיף יְמִינָא עַל שְׂמָאלָא, וְאִתְכָּוַּון בִּפְרִישׂוּ דְּיָדוֹי. וְגָבַר יִשְׂרָאֵל: יִשְׂרָאֵל דִּלְעֵילָּא. וְכַאֲשֶׁר יָנִיחַ יָדוֹ וְגָבַר עֲמָלֵק, בְּשַׁעֲתָא דְּיִשְׂרָאֵל לְתַתָּא, מִשְׁתַּכְּכִין מִצְּלוֹתָא, לָא יַכְלִין יְדֵי מֹשֶׁה לְמֵיקַם בִּזְקִיפוּ, וְגָבַר עֲמָלֵק. מִכָּאן אוֹלִיפְנָא, אע"ג דְּכַהֲנָא פָּרִישׂ יְדוֹי, בְּקָרְבְּנָא, לְתַקְּנָא גַּרְמֵיהּ בְּכֹלָּא, יִשְׂרָאֵל בַּעְיָין לְאִשְׁתַּכְּחָא בִּצְלוֹתְהוֹן, עִמֵּיהּ.

467. "And it came to pass, when Moses held up his hand, Yisrael prevailed." "When Moses held up," MEANS that he raised the right over the left. And he was intent UPON THIS when he raised his hands. Then "Yisrael prevailed," Yisrael of above, WHICH IS ZEIR ANPIN. "And when he let down his hand, Amalek prevailed," MEANING when Yisrael below ceased to pray, the hands of Moses could not stand up and remain straight, and Amalek prevailed. From here we learn that even though the priest spreads his hands during the offering in order to perfect himself in everything, Yisrael must be present with him during his prayers.

468. תָּאנָא, בִּקְרָבָא דָּא דַּעֲמָלֵק, אִשְׁתְּכָחוּ עִלָּאִין וְתַתָּאִין, וְעַל דָּא, וַיְהִי יָדָיו אֱמוּנָה, בְּהֵימְנוּתָא כַּדְקָא חֲזֵי. וַיְהִי יָדָיו אֱמוּנָה. וַיִּהְיוּ יָדָיו מִבָּעֵי לֵיהּ. אֶלָּא, בְּגִין דְּתַלְיָא כֹּלָּא בִּימִינָא, כְּתִיב וַיְהִי. וּכְתִיב יָדָיו, בְּגִין דְּהוּא עִקָּרָא דְּכֹלָּא. וּכְתִיב, יְמִינְךָ יְיָ׳ נֶאְדָּרִי בַּכֹּחַ יְמִינְךָ יְיָ׳ תִּרְעַץ אוֹיֵב.

468. We have learned that in this war of Amalek were present both those of above, and those of below. Therefore, "And his hands were (lit. 'was') Faith," meaning proper Faith. HE ASKS: "And his hands was Faith." It should have said 'were'. HE ANSWERS: This is because everything depends upon the right hand. Therefore "was" is written, and "his hands," is written TO TEACH that the right is the most important of all. It is written: "Your right hand, Hashem, is glorious in power: Your right hand, Hashem, has dashed the enemy in pieces" (Shemot 15:6).

469. וַיֹּאמֶר יְיָ׳ אֶל מֹשֶׁה כְּתֹב זֹאת זִכָּרוֹן בַּסֵּפֶר וְגוֹ׳. תָּא חֲזֵי, מַה כְּתִיב לְעֵילָּא, וַיַּחֲלוֹשׁ יְהוֹשֻׁעַ אֶת עֲמָלֵק וְאֶת עַמּוֹ לְפִי חָרֶב. וַיַּחֲלֹשׁ, וַיַּהֲרוֹג מִבָּעֵי לֵיהּ. אֶלָּא, וַיַּחֲלֹשׁ, כְּמָה דְּאִתְּמַר, חוֹלֵשׁ עַל גּוֹיִם. יְהוֹשֻׁעַ הֲוָה חוֹלֵשׁ עֲלַיְיהוּ, וְהַהוּא חֶרֶב נוֹקֶמֶת נְקַם בְּרִית קָטִיל לוֹן, דִּכְתִּיב לְפִי חָרֶב כְּמָה דְּאִתְּמַר.

469. "And Hashem said to Moses, 'Write this for a memorial in a book...'" (Shemot 17:14). Come and behold: It is written above, "And Joshua harried Amalek and his people with the edge of the sword" HE ASKS: "harried (Heb. *yachalosh*)" should have been written, 'slew'. HE ANSWERS: But "*yachalosh*" is as we learned, "that did rule (Heb. *cholesh*) over the nations" (Yeshayah 14:12). Joshua ruled over them and, "a sword…that shall avenge the Covenant" slew them, as written, "by the edge of the sword," as we learned.

470. כְּתֹב זֹאת זִכָּרוֹן, זֹאת דַּיְקָא. וְשִׂים בְּאָזְנֵי יְהוֹשֻׁעַ, דְּהָא הוּא זָמִין לְקַטְלָא מַלְכִין אַחֲרָנִין. כִּי מָחֹה אֶמְחֶה. מָחֹה: לְעֵילָּא. אֶמְחֶה: לְתַתָּא. זֵכֶר, דּוּכְרָנָא דִּלְעֵילָּא וְתַתָּא.

470. "Write this (Heb. *zot*) for a memorial." *Zot* is precise, WHICH IS A NAME OF MALCHUT; "and rehearse it in the ears of Joshua," because he is destined to slay other kings, NAMELY 31 KINGS. "That I will utterly blot out (lit. 'I will blot a blotting')." "Blotting" refers to above; "I will blot" refers to below. "The memory," means the memory above and the memory below.

471. אָמַר רִבִּי יִצְחָק, כְּתִיב כִּי מָחֹה אֶמְחֶה, וּכְתִיב תִּמְחֶה אֶת זֵכֶר עֲמָלֵק. אֶלָּא, אָמַר קוּדְשָׁא בְּרִיךְ הוּא, אַתּוּן מָחוּן דּוּכְרָנֵיהּ לְתַתָּא, וַאֲנָא אֶמְחֶה דּוּכְרָנֵיהּ לְעֵילָּא.

471. Rabbi Yitzchak said: It is written, "I will utterly blot out" WHICH INDICATES THAT THE HOLY ONE, BLESSED BE HE, WILL BLOT OUT, and: "You shall blot out the remembrance of Amalek" (Devarim 25:19), WHICH INDICATES THAT WE ARE OBLIGATED TO ERASE REMEMBRANCE OF HIM. HE ANSWERS: But the Holy One, blessed be He, said: You will blot out the memory OF AMALEK of below, and I shall blot out the memory OF AMALEK of above.

472. אָמַר רִבִּי יוֹסֵי, עֲמָלֵק עַמִּין אַחֲרָנִין אֵייתִין עִמֵּיהּ, וְכֻלְּהוּ דְּחִילוּ לְקָרְבָא בְּהוּ בְּיִשְׂרָאֵל, בַּר אִיהוּ. וּבְגִין כַּךְ, יְהוֹשֻׁעַ הֲוָה חוֹלֵשׁ עֲלַיְיהוּ. רִבִּי יֵיסָא אָמַר, וַיַּחֲלשׁ יְהוֹשֻׁעַ, דְּתָבַר חֵילָא דִּלְהוֹן מִלְעֵילָּא.

472. Rabbi Yosi said: Other allied nations accompanied Amalek. They were all afraid to approach Yisrael, except it (Amalek). Therefore, Joshua ruled over them. Rabbi Yisa said: "And Joshua harried," for he broke their power from above.

473. וַיִּבֶן מֹשֶׁה מִזְבֵּחַ וַיִּקְרָא שְׁמוֹ יְיָ' נִסִּי. וַיִּבֶן מֹשֶׁה מִזְבֵּחַ, לָקֳבֵל הַהוּא דִּלְעֵילָּא. וַיִּקְרָא שְׁמוֹ הַהוּא מֹשֶׁה יְיָ' נִסִּי. מַאי יְיָ' נִסִּי. בְּגִין דְּאַנְקִים נְקָמְתָא דְּהַהוּא רְשִׁימָא קַדִּישָׁא דְּיִשְׂרָאֵל, וּמֵהַהוּא זִמְנָא אִתְקְרֵי, חֶרֶב נוֹקֶמֶת נְקַם בְּרִית.

473. "And Moses built an altar, and called the name of it, Hashem is my Banner" (Shemot 17:15). "And Moses built an altar," corresponding to the supernal altar. "And called the name of it," OF THAT PARTICULAR ALTAR OF ABOVE; "Hashem is my banner," because it avenged the holy sign of Yisrael. And since that time, it was commonly called "a sword...that shall avenge the Covenant." AND MOSES CALLED IT: "HASHEM IS MY BANNER."

474. רִבִּי יוֹסֵי אָמַר, וַיִּבֶן מֹשֶׁה מִזְבֵּחַ, מִזְבֵּחַ לְכַפְּרָא עֲלַיְיהוּ. וַיִּקְרָא שְׁמוֹ. שְׁמוֹ דְּמַאן. אָמַר רִבִּי חִיָּיא שְׁמֵיהּ דְּמַדְבְּחָא הַהוּא. יְיָ' נִסִּי: כד"א, וְשָׁם נִסָּהוּ. וְכֹלָּא מִלָּה חַד, עַל דְּאִתְפְּרָעוּ יִשְׂרָאֵל, וְאִתְגַּלְיָיא הַהוּא אָת קַיָּימָא, רְשִׁימָא קַדִּישָׁא. מִכָּאן אוֹלִיפְנָא, דְּכֵיוָן דְּאִתְגְּזַר בְּרֵיהּ דְּבַר נָשׁ, וְאִתְגַּלְיָיא בֵּיהּ אָת רְשִׁימָא קַדִּישָׁא קַיָּימָא. הַהוּא אִקְרֵי מִזְבֵּחַ לְכַפְּרָא עָלֵיהּ. וּמַה שְׁמֵיהּ. יְיָ' נִסִּי.

474. Rabbi Yosi said: "And Moses built an altar," NAMELY an altar to atone for YISRAEL. "And called the name of it." The name of what? Rabbi Chiya said: The name of that altar. "Hashem is my banner (Heb. *nisi*)," as is written: "And there he tested them (Heb. *nisahu*)," WHICH REFERS TO ELEVATION. It all pertains to the same issue, for Yisrael was elevated because he was uncovered, and the sign of that Covenant was revealed by them the holy sign. FROM HERE WE LEARNED that once a person's son is circumcised and the sign of the Holy Covenant is revealed by him, then that son is called 'an altar to atone upon it'. And what is its name? "Hashem is my banner."

475. כְּגַוְונָא דָּא יַעֲקֹב, בְּנָה מַדְבְּחָא, דִּכְתִּיב וַיַּצֶּב שָׁם מִזְבֵּחַ וַיִּקְרָא לוֹ אֵל אֱלֹהֵי יִשְׂרָאֵל. לְמַאן. לְהַהוּא אֲתָר דְּאִקְרֵי מִזְבֵּחַ. וּמַאן שְׁמֵיהּ. אֵל אֱלֹהֵי יִשְׂרָאֵל.

475. Similar to this, Jacob built an altar, as is written: "And he erected there an altar, and called it El, Elohim of Yisrael" (Beresheet 33:20). Whom did he call? That place which is called 'altar', NAMELY MALCHUT. And what is its name? "El Elohim of Yisrael."

34. "And they saw the Elohim of Yisrael"

A Synopsis

This section proscribes looking at the rainbow above, the Shechinah, and the rainbow below, the sign of the Covenant that is imprinted on a person. Rabbi Chiya talks about the sapphire stone in "And there was under his feet a kind of paved work of sapphire stone," saying that it means the transparent light of the sapphire, the engravings of above that flash and illuminate. The borders in the great tree illuminate the Shechinah when she joins with Zeir Anpin; all these lights and paths illuminate upon the light of the Shechinah.

476. אָמַר רִבִּי יוֹסֵי, מַאי דִּכְתִּיב, וַיִּרְאוּ אֵת אֱלֹהֵי יִשְׂרָאֵל וְגוֹ׳. וְכִי מַאן יָכִיל לְמֶחֱמֵי לֵיהּ לְקוּדְשָׁא בְּרִיךְ הוּא, וְהָא כְּתִיב כִּי לֹא יִרְאַנִי הָאָדָם וָחָי. וְהָכָא אָמַר וַיִּרְאוּ אֶלָּא דְּאִתְגַּלְיָא קֶשֶׁת עֲלַיְיהוּ בִּגְוָונִין נְהִירִין, וְהָכִי תָּנֵינָן, כָּל מַאן דְּאִסְתַּכַּל בַּקֶּשֶׁת, כְּמַאן דְּמִסְתָּכַּל בַּשְּׁכִינָה, וּלְאִסְתַּכְּלָא בִּשְׁכִינְתָּא אָסִיר.

476. Rabbi Yosi said: What is the meaning of the verse, "And they saw the Elohim of Yisrael..." (Shemot 24:10). HE ASKS: Who can possibly see the Holy One, blessed be He? Is it not written: "For no man shall see me, and live" (Shemot 33:20), yet here it says "and they saw" HE ANSWERS: Rather, the rainbow was revealed to them in illuminating colors, WHICH IS THE SHECHINAH THAT RECEIVES FROM THE THREE COLORS – WHITE, RED AND YELLOW. And so have we learned that whoever gazes upon the rainbow is as though he gazes upon the Shechinah. And it is prohibited to gaze upon the Shechinah.

477. וְעַל דָּא, אָסִיר לֵיהּ לְאִינִישׁ, לְאִסְתַּכְּלָא בְּאֶצְבְּעַיְיהוּ דְּכַהֲנֵי, בְּשַׁעֲתָא דְּפַרְסֵי יְדַיְיהוּ. אָסוּר לְאִסְתַּכְּלָא בַּקֶּשֶׁת. מַאן קֶשֶׁת. אָמַר רִבִּי אַבָּא, בַּקֶּשֶׁת סְתָם אָמַר לֵיהּ מַאי בַּקֶּשֶׁת סְתָם א״ל בַּקֶּשֶׁת דִּלְעֵילָּא, וּבַקֶּשֶׁת דִּלְתַתָּא.

477. Therefore, it is prohibited for a person to gaze upon the fingers of the priests when they stretch out their hands. It is prohibited to gaze upon the rainbow. HE ASKS: What rainbow? Rabbi Aba said: Any rainbow. He said to him: What is any rainbow? He said to him: BOTH the rainbow above AND ALSO the rainbow below.

478. בַּקֶּשֶׁת דִּלְעֵילָּא, בִּגְוָונוֹי. דְּכָל מַאן דְּיִסְתַּכַּל בִּגְוָונוֹי, כְּאִילּוּ אִסְתָּכַּל בְּאֲתָר דִּלְעֵילָּא, וְאָסִיר לְאִסְתַּכְּלָא בֵּיהּ, דְּלָא יַעֲבִיד קְלָנָא בִּשְׁכִינְתָּא. קֶשֶׁת דִּלְתַתָּא מַאי הִיא. הַהוּא אָת קַיָּימָא, דְּאִתְרְשִׁים בֵּיהּ בְּבַר נָשׁ, דְּכָל מַאן דְּיִסְתַּכַּל בֵּיהּ, עָבֵיד קְלָנָא לְעֵילָּא.

478. HE EXPLAINS HIS WORDS: Upon the rainbow above, THAT IT IS PROHIBITED TO GAZE UPON, MEANS upon its colors, WHITE, RED AND GREEN, WHICH ARE THE SECRET OF THE THREE COLUMNS THAT ILLUMINATE IN THE SHECHINAH. For anyone who gazes UPON ITS COLORS is as though he gazes upon a high, supernal place. It is prohibited to gaze at it since this is a disgraceful manner towards the Shechinah. What is the rainbow of below? It is that sign of that Covenant that is imprinted in the person, for anyone who gazes upon it conducts himself disgracefully against the above.

479. אָמַר רִבִּי יִצְחָק, אִי הָכִי וְהָכְתִּיב שִׂים נָא יָדְךָ תַּחַת יְרֵכִי, דַּהֲוָה אוֹמֵי לֵיהּ בְּהַאי אָת. א״ל, אֲנַח לְהוּ לַאֲבָהָן דְּעָלְמָא, דְּלֵית אִינּוּן כִּשְׁאַר בְּנֵי עָלְמָא. וְעוֹד, שִׂים נָא יָדְךָ תַּחַת יְרֵכִי כְּתִיב, וְלָא כְּתִיב רְאֵה תַּחַת יְרֵכִי, בג״כ אָסִיר לְאִסְתַּכְּלָא בַּקֶּשֶׁת סְתָם, כְּמָה דְּתָנֵינָן.

479. Rabbi Yitzchak said: Yet, does it not say, "Put, I pray you, your hand under my thigh" (Beresheet 24:2), that he made him swear by this sign? He said to him: Leave alone the fathers of the world, for they are not like the other people of the world. Moreover it is written, "Put, I pray you, your hand under my thigh," but not, 'Look under my thigh.' Therefore, it is prohibited to gaze upon the rainbow in general, as we learned.

480. תָּאנָא, וַיִּרְאוּ אֵת אֱלֹהֵי יִשְׂרָאֵל, דְּאִתְגַּלְיָא קֶשֶׁת עֲלַיְיהוּ, בִּגְוָונִין שַׁפִּירִין נְהִירִין, מְלַהֲטָן לְכָל עִיבָר, מַשְׁמַע דִּכְתִּיב, אֵת אֱלֹהֵי יִשְׂרָאֵל וְלָא כְּתִיב וַיִּרְאוּ אֱלֹהֵי יִשְׂרָאֵל. אָמַר רִבִּי יוֹסֵי, נְהוֹרָא דְּבוּצִינָא

דִּשְׁכִינְתָּא. וּמַאי נִיהוּ. הַהוּא דְּאִקְרֵי נַעַר, דִּמְשַׁמֵּשׁ לִשְׁכִינְתָּא, בְּמַקְדְּשָׁא. וּבְגִין כַּךְ, אֵת דַּיְיקָא.

480. We learned, "And they saw the Elohim of Yisrael" (Shemot 24:10), as the rainbow was revealed to them in beautiful colors, illuminating, flashing on all sides, WHICH IS THE SHECHINAH. This is understood from the words, "the Elohim of Yisrael," instead of, 'And they saw Elohim of Yisrael,' AS THE SHECHINAH IS CALLED "*ET* ('THE')." Rabbi Yosi said: THIS IS the light of the luminary of the Shechinah. Who is it? It is the one called 'youth', MEANING METATRON, who serves the Shechinah in the Temple. Therefore, "*Et* ('the')" is precise BECAUSE IT IS THE NAME OF THE SHECHINAH THAT INCLUDES METATRON, HER SERVANT.

481. וְתַחַת רַגְלָיו כְּמַעֲשֵׂה לִבְנַת הַסַּפִּיר, דְּאִתְרְשִׁים בֵּיהּ תְּחוֹת דּוּכְתֵּיהּ, חַד לְבֵינָתָא מֵאִינּוּן לְבֵנִין דַּהֲווֹ בָּנִין בְּמִצְרַיִם, דְּתָנֵינָן, אִתְּתָא חֲדָא אוֹלִידַת בְּמִצְרַיִם, וַהֲוָה אָתִין סַרְכֵי פַּרְעֹה, וְעָאלַת לֵיהּ בְּחַד לְבֵינָתָא, וְאָתָא פַּס יְדָא וְאָחִיד לֵיהּ, וְאִתְרְשִׁים תְּחוֹת רַגְלוֹי דִּשְׁכִינְתָּא, וְקַיְּימָא קָמֵיהּ, עַד דְּאִתּוֹקַד בֵּי מַקְדְּשָׁא דִּלְתַתָּא, דִּכְתִּיב, וְלֹא זָכַר הֲדוֹם רַגְלָיו.

481. "And there was under his feet a kind of paved work of sapphire stone" (Ibid.). A stone was marked there under His place, one of the stones that were used to build in Egypt. For we have learned that there was one woman who gave birth in Egypt. And the officers of Pharaoh came TO CAST HIM INTO THE RIVER, and she put him into THE PLACE OF a stone OF THE BUILDING. And the palm of a hand came and grasped it, and it was marked under the feet of the Shechinah. And it remained in his presence until the terrestrial Temple was burned down, as it is written, "And remembered not his footstool" (Eichah 2:1), THAT WAS THAT SAPPHIRE STONE.

482. ר' חִיָּיא אָמַר, לִבְנַת הַסַּפִּיר: נְהִירוּתָא דְּסַפִּיר, קַלְדִּיטֵי בְּקַנְדִּיטֵי גְּלִיפִין עִלָּאִין דִּלְעֵילָּא, דְּמִתְלַהֲטָא לְשַׁבְעִין וּתְרֵין עִבְרִי, הה"ד וִיסַדְתִּיךְ בַּסַּפִּירִים. וּכְעֶצֶם הַשָּׁמַיִם. מַאי עֶצֶם הַשָּׁמַיִם. א"ר אַבָּא, מָה

עֶצֶם הַשָּׁמַיִם, גְּלִיפָא בְּשַׁבְעִין וּתְרֵין עֲנָפִין, פַּרְחִין מִלַּהֲטָן בְּכָל עִיבָר. אוּף הָכָא, חֵיזוּ דְּהַהוּא עֶצֶם הַשָּׁמַיִם כְּחֵיזוּ שְׁמַיָּא מַמָּשׁ. רִבִּי יְהוּדָה אָמַר, כֹּלָּא אִתְרְשִׁים בְּהַהוּא נְהִירוּ, דְּחֵיזוּ דְּמִתְגַּלְּפָא מִסִּטְרָא דִּשְׁכִינְתָּא.

482. Rabbi Chiya said: The sapphire stone MEANS the transparent light of the sapphire, the keys of the spiced wine, the superb engravings of above that flash to 72 directions. This is what is meant by: "And lay your foundations with sapphires" (Yeshayah 54:11). "The very heaven" (Shemot 24:10). What is "the very heaven"? Rabbi Aba said: "the very heaven," WHICH IS ZEIR ANPIN, is engraved with 72 branches blossoming to every direction, MEANING THE NAME OF *AYIN-BET* (72), THAT ILLUMINATES BOTH IN CHOCHMAH AND CHASSADIM. Here also, the appearance of that very heaven was exactly like the appearance of heaven itself, WHICH IS ZEIR ANPIN. Rabbi Yehuda said: It is all imprinted with that light of the vision that is engraved from the aspect of the Shechinah.

483. אָמַר רִבִּי חִזְקִיָּה, אִי הָכִי, וְהָא שִׁתִּין אִינּוּן, בְּסַחֲרָנֵיהּ דִּשְׁכִינְתָּא, דִּכְתִּיב שִׁשִּׁים גִּבּוֹרִים סָבִיב לָהּ. א"ל הָכִי הוּא וַדַּאי. אֶלָּא אִינּוּן שִׁתִּין, אִתְנְהִירוּ בִּתְרֵיסַר תְּחוּמִין, וְלָא אַעְדִּיאוּ מִסְּחֲרָנוּתְהָא לְעָלְמִין. דְּתָנֵינָן, תְּרֵיסַר תְּחוּמִין, גְּלִיפִין עִלָּאִין, בְּמַתְקְלָא סְלִיקוּ, בְּאִילָנָא קַדִּישָׁא רַבָּא וְתַקִּיף. וְכֻלְּהוּ נְהִירִין בְּמַטְרוֹנִיתָא, כַּד אִתְחַבְּרַת בְּמַלְכָּא. וְדָא הוּא עֶצֶם הַשָּׁמַיִם, עֶצֶם הַשָּׁמַיִם מַמָּשׁ. וְכָל אִינּוּן נְהִירִין שְׁבִילִין, מְנַהֲרִין בֵּיהּ, בִּנְהִירוּ דְּמַטְרוֹנִיתָא.

483. Rabbi Chizkiyah said: Behold, there are sixty that surround the Shechinah, as is written: "sixty valiant men are round about it" (Shir Hashirim 3:7). He said to him: It is certainly so. But these sixty illuminated from the twelve boundaries THAT ARE IN ZEIR ANPIN, and were never removed from around THE SHECHINAH. For we have learned the twelve superbly engraved borders ascended balanced equally, in the great and strong tree. THEY ARE THE SECRET OF THE THREE COLUMNS THAT ILLUMINATE IN THE FOUR DIRECTIONS CHESED, GVURAH, TIFERET AND MALCHUT, WHICH ADD UP TO TWELVE. And they illuminate the Queen,

WHO IS THE SHECHINAH, when She joins with the King, WHO IS ZEIR ANPIN. "The very heaven" indeed, FOR SHE RECEIVES ALL THAT IS IN HEAVEN, WHICH IS ZEIR ANPIN. And all these lights and paths illuminate with the light of the Shechinah.

484. וְתָאנָא, נְהִירוּ דְּאִלֵּין שִׁתִּין, דְּסָחֲרָנָהָא, רְשִׁימִין בֵּיהּ בְּהַהוּא נַעַ"ר, וְקָרֵינָן לְהוּ שִׁתִּין פּוּלְסֵי דְּנוּרָא, דְּאִתְלָבַּשׁ בְּהוּ מִסְּטָר דִּשְׁכִינְתָּא, מִתְלַהֲטָן בְּדִינָא, הה"ד שִׁשִּׁים גִּבּוֹרִים סָבִיב לָהּ.

484. We have learned, the light of these sixty VALIANT MEN that surround THE SHECHINAH are imprinted in that particular youth, METATRON. We called them 'sixty lashes of fire' with which he was clothed from the aspect of the Shechinah, and they were blazing with Judgment. This is the meaning of: "sixty valiant men are round about it."

35. "And Moses erected an altar"

A Synopsis

Rabbi Yehuda concludes Beshalach by saying that there is no generation that does not contain the evil seed of Amalek. The Holy One, blessed be He wages war against them, and "The sinners (sins) will be consumed out of the earth," meaning in this world and in the World to Come. About that same time it is written: "Bless you Hashem, O my soul. Haleluyah."

485. תָּאנָא, וַיִּבֶן מֹשֶׁה מִזְבֵּחַ כְּמָה דַּאֲמֵינָא. וַיִּקְרָא שְׁמוֹ ה׳ נִסִּי. ה׳ נִסִּי מַמָּשׁ. אֲמַאי. בְּגִין דַּעֲמָלֵק נָטַל כָּל אִינּוּן דַּהֲווֹ גְּזִירִין, וְלָא אִתְפְּרָעוּ, וְגָזַר לוֹן וְשָׁדֵי לְהוּ לְעֵילָּא, וְאָמַר טוֹל מַה דְּאִתְרְעִית בֵּיהּ. בֵּיהּ שַׁעֲתָא מַה כְּתִיב. וַיֹּאמֶר כִּי יָד עַל כֵּס יָהּ מִלְחָמָה לַה׳ בַּעֲמָלֵק מִדֹּר דֹּר. מִדֹּר דֹּר חֲסֵרִין, מִדִּיּוּרִין דִּלְעֵילָּא, וּמִדִּיּוּרִין דִּלְתַתָּא.

485. We have learned: "And Moses erected an altar" (Shemot 17:15), as we have explained. "And he called the name of it, Hashem is my banner" (Or: miracle) AS THE MIRACLE IS ASCRIBED TO HASHEM, "Hashem is my banner" indeed, Why? Because Amalek took all those who were circumcised but not uncovered and cut them and threw them up, and said: 'Take what You wanted.' At that moment, it is written: "For he said, 'Because Yah has sworn by His throne that Hashem will have war with Amalek from generation (Heb. *midor*) to generation (Heb. *dor*)'" (Ibid. 16). The words '*midor*' and '*dor*' are spelt without THE *VAV* TO TEACH US THAT THOSE GENERATIONS IN WHICH THERE WERE BATTLES AGAINST AMALEK lacked inhabitants above, FOR THE NAME WAS NOT COMPLETE, NOR WAS THE THRONE COMPLETE, and THEY WERE LACKING inhabitants below, FOR THERE IS NO COMPLETENESS FOR THE LOWER BEINGS.

486. א״ר יְהוּדָה, בְּכָל דָּרָא וְדָרָא, בְּכָל דָּרִין דְּאַתְיָין לְעָלְמָא, לֵית לָךְ דָּר דְּלֵית בְּהוּ מֵהַהוּא זַרְעָא בִּישָׁא, וְקוּדְשָׁא בְּרִיךְ הוּא אֲגַח בְּהוּ קְרָבָא. וְעָלַיְיהוּ כְּתִיב יִתַּמּוּ חַטָּאִים מִן הָאָרֶץ וְגוֹ׳. מִן הָאָרֶץ: בְּעָלְמָא דֵּין, וּבְעָלְמָא דְּאָתֵי. בֵּיהּ זִמְנָא כְּתִיב, בָּרְכִי נַפְשִׁי אֶת ה׳ הַלְלוּיָהּ.

486. Rabbi Yehuda said: In every single generation and in all the subsequent generations to come into the world, there is no generation that does not contain that evil seed OF AMALEK. The Holy One, blessed be He, wages war against them. About them, it is written: "The sinners (sins) will be consumed out of the earth..." (Tehilim 104:35). "Out of the earth," MEANING in this world and in the World to Come. About that same time is written: "Bless you Hashem, O my soul. Haleluyah" (Ibid.).